About Island Press

Island Press is the only nonprofit organization in the United States whose principal purpose is the publication of books on environmental issues and natural resource management. We provide solutions-oriented information to professionals, public officials, business and community leaders, and concerned citizens who are shaping responses to environmental problems.

In 1998, Island Press celebrates its fourteenth anniversary as the leading provider of timely and practical books that take a multidisciplinary approach to critical environmental concerns. Our growing list of titles reflects our commitment to bringing the best of an expanding body of literature to the environmental community throughout North America and the world.

Support for Island Press is provided by The Jenifer Altman Foundation, The Bullitt Foundation, The Mary Flagler Cary Charitable Trust, The Nathan Cummings Foundation, The Geraldine R. Dodge Foundation, The Charles Engelhard Foundation, The Ford Foundation, The Vira I. Heinz Endowment, The W. Alton Jones Foundation, The John D. and Catherine T. MacArthur Foundation, The Andrew W. Mellon Foundation, The Charles Stewart Mott Foundation, The Curtis and Edith Munson Foundation, The National Fish and Wildlife Foundation, The National Science Foundation, The New-Land Foundation, The David and Lucile Packard Foundation, The Pew Charitable Trusts, The Surdna Foundation, The Winslow Foundation, and individual donors.

The Transit Metropolis

To Sophia, Christopher, Kristen, and Alexandria

The Transit Metropolis

A GLOBAL INQUIRY

ROBERT CERVERO

ISLAND PRESS

Washington, D.C. • Covelo, California

ISLAND PRESS is a trademark of The Center for Resource Economics.

Photographs by Robert Cervero, with the following exceptions: Photos 4.1, 4.2, 4.4, 5.3, 8.2, 11.4, 17.2, and 17.3 by Jeff Kenworthy; photo 13.4 courtesy of Transport Technologie-Consultant Karlsruhe (TTK), GmbH; photo 14.2 courtesy of the Passenger Transport Board, Adelaide; photo 17.5 courtesy of the Metropolitan Transit Authority of Harris County, Texas.

Library of Congress Cataloging-in-Publication Data
Cervero, Robert.
    The transit metropolis : a global inquiry / Robert Cervero.
        p.   cm.
    Includes bibliographical references and index.
    ISBN 1–55963–591–6
    1. Urban transportation—Planning.   2. Local transit—Planning.
    3. Land use—Planning.   4. City planning.   5. Commuting   I. Title.
    HE305.C474   1998   98–34096
    388.4—DC21   CIP

Printed on recycled, acid-free paper

Manufactured in the United States of America
10 9 8 7 6 5 4 3 2 1

Contents

Preface

Across the world, mass transit is struggling to compete with the private automobile. In many places, its market share of urban travel is rapidly eroding. Critics charge that most mass transit systems are deficit-riddled, second-class forms of mobility out of step with the times. Some contend that because of poor ridership productivity, buses and trains even worsen air quality and environmental conditions in many settings. Although the reasons for transit's decline vary, part of the explanation lies in the fact that its chief competitor—the private automobile—is often grossly underpriced. Rapid suburbanization has also hurt public transportation. Yet against this backdrop a dozen or so metropolitan areas have managed, in recent decades, to mount world-class transit services that are cost-effective and resource-conserving and provide respectable alternatives to car travel. In Singapore and Copenhagen, for example, urban development has been channeled along rail lines, producing built forms that are highly conducive to transit riding. In Ottawa and Karlsruhe, Germany, transit has been configured to efficiently deliver customers close to their destinations, absent a transfer.

What sets these places apart? Partly out of curiosity and partly because I felt this question sorely needed to be addressed, I decided to write this book. Early into the research, it became clear that what distinguished these places from others was a tight "hand in glove" fit between their transit services and settlement patterns. In particular, these places are highly *adaptive*—either their cityscapes are physically and functionally oriented to transit or transit is well tailored to serving their cityscapes. It is this harmony between transit services and urban form that makes them great transit metropolises.

Readers will find that sustainability themes pervade this book. And well they should. At no time in our history have finite resources, natural landscapes, and the social and economic well-being of our cities been more threatened than they are today. Part of the reason inescapably lies in our growing dependence on private automobile travel. As the new millennium approaches, we find ourselves on the cusp of some difficult

choices regarding how cities and regions should grow. The transit metropolis, I believe, is a promising model for building sustainable pathways to
the future. After reading this book, I hope you feel likewise.

Unfashionably, I had no sponsor for this work. No one seemed interested in paying an academic to ride trains and buses throughout the world
in a quest to tell the story of the transit metropolis. The book was pieced
together over a four-year period while I juggled this effort with other
research projects. Much of the data collection and field work were conducted by making four- or five-day side trips while in some part of the
world on other business. As patterns began to repeat themselves across
the first several case studies, it became clear that there was a book to be
written on the transit metropolis.

A work of this scope would not have been possible without the help of
many individuals and organizations. I owe a particular debt of gratitude
to several friends and colleagues whose work on related topics helped me
immensely in conceptualizing and carrying out this research. Jeff Kenworthy of Murdoch University in Australia was a source of fresh ideas on
transit's role in the city as well as some great photographs used in this
book. Carsten Gertz of Technische Universität Berlin provided helpful
comments and suggestions on the draft chapters of the Munich, Karlsruhe, and Zurich cases. Others whose ideas, suggestions, and encourage-
ment influenced this work were John Pucher, C. Kenneth Orski, Allan
Jacobs, Peter Hall, and Melvin Webber. And then there were the dozens
and dozens of people who helped during my field visits, sharing their
insights, providing background materials, and sometimes playing tour
guide, showing me firsthand why transit works so well in their communities. I particularly thank: Per-Olof Wikström, Magnus Carle, Åke Boalt,
and Stig Svallhammar of Stockholm; Ib Ferdinanansen, Faust Bovenlan-
der, Peter Andersen, Jes Møller, Hans Jørgensen, Thomas Pedersen, Ernst
Poulsen, and Jan Gehl of Copenhagen; Bruno Wildermuth, Anthony Chin,
and Pannir Ramaza of Singapore; Katsutoshi Ohta and Masaharu
Fukuyana of Tokyo; Herbert König, Dieter Wellner, Otto Goedecke, Beate
Brennauer, Ulrich Zimmer, and Hartmut Topp of Munich; Colin Leech,
Nick Tunnacliffe, John Bonsall, Ian Stacey, and Carol Christensen of
Ottawa; Carlos Ceneviva, Norberto Stavinsky, Jaime Lerner, and Jonas
Rabinovitch of Curitiba; Ernst Joos, Marcel Wildhaber, Gabby Lenggen-
hager, Paul Huber, and Ruedi Ott of Zurich; Paul Mees, David Yencken,
Victor Sposito, Evan Walker, Ross King, and Elaine Herbert of Melbourne;
Deiter Ludwig, Axel Kühn, Werner Zimmerman, Bastian Chlond, Werner
Rothengatter, and Dorothee Schäfer of Karlsruhe; Stephen Hamnett,
Thomas Wilson, Joe Mastrangelo, and Lindsay Oxlad of Adelaide; Sonia
Lizt, Jorge Aguilar, Manuel Perlo, Jose Mirabent, Hector Antunano, and
Miguel Geraldo of Mexico City; John Gartner, Rob Pringle, and Brendon
Hemily of Toronto; G. B. Arrington, Rodman Monroe, William Robertson,

and Andrew Cotugno of Portland; and Thomas Larwin, Jack Lambert, Nancy Bragado, and Bill Lieberman of San Diego.

My students at Berkeley, most notably Jodi Ketelsen, Keiro Hattori, Tom Kirk, and Alfred Round, also deserve thanks for assisting with everything from translations to literature searches. Jane Sterzinger capably prepared some of this book's maps. Cheerfully helping with some of the drawings and artwork was Chris Amado. Thanks also to Miho Rahm, Carey Pelton, Elizabeth Deakin, and Barbara Hadenfeldt for their help over the years at Berkeley's Institute of Urban and Regional Development. For aural inspirations during long journeys and wee hours at the computer, I thank Fruupp and Crimso.

I am blessed with a loving and understanding family who endured my absences while I conducted field work and holed up in my study pounding out this manuscript. Without their support, this book would have never been completed. To Sophia, Christopher, Kristen, and Alexandria, my heartfelt thanks.

Robert Cervero
Oakland, California

THE CASE FOR THE TRANSIT METROPOLIS

A transit metropolis is a region where a workable fit exists between transit services and urban form. In some cases this means compact, mixed-use development well suited to rail services, and in others it means flexible, fleetfooted bus services well suited to spread-out development. What matters is that transit and the city co-exist in harmony.

Part One of this book introduces the transit metropolis as a paradigm for sustainable regional development. Four classes of transit metropolises are identified, as are international case studies in each class. The case is made for the transit metropolis in light of the serious threats posed by increasing worldwide automobile dependence. People prize the mobility and freedom of movement conferred by the car. Because individual choice behavior—the desire to drive when and where one wants—is accompanied by increasingly high social and environmental costs, however, a change in course is more imperative now than ever. The transit metropolis, when complemented by other initiatives, such as the introduction of hefty motoring surcharges and smart technologies for transit, can help contain traffic congestion, reduce pollution, conserve energy, and promote social equity. This proposition is supported by the twelve case studies from around the world presented in this book. Part One's purpose is to build the case that alternatives to contemporary patterns of urbanization and mobility are very much needed, and that as a model for how to plan and design future cities and transit systems, the transit metropolis holds considerable promise.

Chapter 1

Transit and the Metropolis: Finding Harmony

Public transit systems are struggling to compete with the private automobile the world over. Throughout North America, in much of Europe, and even in most developing countries, the private automobile continues to gain market shares of motorized trips at the expense of public transit systems. In the United States, just 1.8 percent of all person trips were by transit in 1995, down from 2.4 percent in 1977 and 2.2 percent in 1983.[1] Despite the tens of billions of dollars invested in new rail systems and the underwriting of more than 75 percent of operating expenses, ridership figures for transit's bread-and-butter market—the work trip—remain flat. Nationwide, 4.5 percent of commutes were by transit in 1983; by 1995, this share had fallen to 3.5 percent.

The declining role of transit has been every bit as alarming in Europe, prompting some observers to warn that it is just a matter of time before cities like London and Madrid become as automobile-dominated as Los Angeles and Dallas. England and Wales saw the share of total journeys by transit fall from 33 percent in 1971 to 14 percent in 1991.[2] Since 1980, transit's market shares of trips have plummeted in Italy, Poland, Hungary, and former East Germany. Eroding market shares have likewise been reported in such megacities as Buenos Aires, Bangkok, and Manila.

Numerous factors have fueled these trends. Part of the explanation for the decline in Europe has been sharp increases in fares resulting from government deregulation of the transit sector. Public disinvestment has left the physical infrastructure of some transit systems in shambles in Italy and parts of Eastern Europe. However, transit's decline has been more an outcome of powerful spatial and economic trends that have been unfolding over the past several decades than of overt government actions (or inaction). Factors that have steadily chipped away at transit's market share worldwide include rising personal incomes and car ownership, declining real-dollar costs for motoring and parking, and the decentralization of cities and regions. Of course, these forces have partly fed off each other. Rising wealth and cheaper motoring, for instance, have prompted firms, retailers, and households to exit cities in favor of less dense environs. Spread-out development has proven to be especially troubling for mass transit. With trip origins and destinations today spread all over the map, mass transit is often no match for the private automobile and its flexible, door-to-door, no-transfer features.

Suburbanization has not crippled transit systems everywhere, however. Some cities and regions have managed to buck the trend, offering transit services that are holding their own against the automobile's ever-increasing presence, and in some cases even grabbing larger market shares of urban travel. These are places, I contend, that have been superbly adaptive, almost in a Darwinian sense. Notably, they have found a harmonious fit between mass transit services and their cityscapes. Some, like Singapore and Copenhagen, have adapted their settlement patterns so that they are more conducive to transit riding, mainly by rail transit, whether for reasons of land scarcity, open space preservation, or encouraging what are viewed as more sustainable patterns of growth and travel. This has often involved concentrating offices, homes, and shops around rail nodes in attractive, well-designed, pedestrian-friendly communities. Other places have opted for an entirely different approach, accepting their low-density, often market-driven lay of the land, and in response adapting mass transit services and technologies to better serve these spread-out environs. These are places, such as Karlsruhe in Germany and Adelaide, Australia, that have introduced flexible forms of mass transit that begin to emulate the speedy, door-to-door service features of the car. Still other places, like Ottawa, Canada, and Curitiba, Brazil, have struck a middle ground, adapting their urban landscapes so as to become more transit-supportive while at the same time adapting their transit services so as to deliver customers closer to their destinations, minimize waits, and expedite transfers. It is because these places have found a workable nexus between their mass transit services and urban settlement patterns that they either are or are on the road to becoming great transit metropolises.

What these areas have in common—adaptability—is first and fundamentally a calculated process of making change by investing, reinvesting, organizing, reorganizing, inventing, and reinventing. Adaptability is about self-survival in a world of limited resources, tightly stretched budgets, and ever-changing cultural norms, lifestyles, technologies, and personal values. In the private sector, any business that resists adapting to changing consumer wants and preferences is a short-lived business. More and more, the public sector is being held to similar standards. There is no longer the public largesse or patience to allow business as usual. Transit authorities must adapt to change, as must city and regional governments. Trends like suburbanization, advances in telecommunications, and

chained trip-making require that transit agencies refashion how they con-
figure and deliver services and that builders and planners adjust their
designs of communities and places. In the best of worlds, these efforts are
closely coordinated. This will most likely occur when and where there is
the motivation and the means to break out of traditional, entrenched
practices, which, of course, is no small feat in the public realm. Yet even
transit's most ardent defenders now concede that steadily eroding shares
of metropolitan travel are a telltale sign that fresh, new approaches are
needed. Places that appropriately adapt to changing times, finding harmony between their transit services and urban landscapes, I contend, are
places where transit stands the best chance of competing with the car well
into the next millennium.

This book tells the story of how twelve metropolitan areas across five
continents have become, or are well on their way to becoming, successful
transit metropolises. Each case study tells a story of the struggles, strides,
and successes of making transit work in the modern era. Together, the
cases offer insights and policy lessons into how more economically, socially, and environmentally sustainable transit services can be designed and
implemented.

It bears noting that a functional and sustainable transit metropolis is
not equated with a region whereby transit largely replaces the private
automobile or even captures the majority of motorized trips. Rather, the
transit metropolis represents a built form and a mobility environment
where transit is a far more respectable alternative to traveling than currently is the case in much of the industrialized world. It is an environment
where transit and the built environment harmoniously co-exist, reinforcing and enhancing each other in the process. Thus, while automobile travel might still predominate, a transit metropolis is one where enough travelers opt for transit riding, by virtue of the workable transit–land use
nexus, to place a region on a sustainable course.

It is also important to emphasize that this book focuses on the connections between transit and urbanization at the regional scale versus the
local one. While considerable attention has been given to transit-oriented
development (TOD) and the New Urbanism movement in recent years,
both by scholars and the popular press, much of this focus has been at the
neighborhood and community levels. Micro-scale designs that encourage
walking and promote community cohesion have captivated the attention
of many proponents of TODs and New Urbanism. While good quality
designs are without question absolutely essential to creating places that
are physically conducive to transit riding, they are clearly not sufficient in
and of themselves. Islands of TOD in a sea of freeway-oriented suburbs
will do little to change fundamental travel behavior or the sum quality of
regional living. The key to making TOD work is to make sure that it is well
coordinated across a metropolis. While land use planning and urban

design are local prerogatives, their impacts on travel are felt regionally. In part, this book aims to focus attention on the importance of coordinating transit-supportive development at a metropolitan scale. However, it also seeks to give balance to the equation, examining legitimate approaches to forming sustainable yet low-density transit metropolises, namely through the design of more flexible forms of mass transit.

Types of Transit Metropolises

The cases reviewed in this book illustrate cities that have successfully meshed their transit services and cityscapes in a contemporary urban context, namely one of post–World War II decentralization. There are cities— New York, London, Paris, Hong Kong, Moscow, and Toronto, for example—that certainly qualify as great transit metropolises but that are not included in this book, either because their principal transit investments date from a much earlier period (e.g., London), or their experiences are viewed as either extreme (e.g., unusually dense Hong Kong) or well chronicled (Toronto).[3] Since the book focuses on cases from free-market economies, examples from China and other communist or socialist countries, either current or former, are not included. What are presented, then, are the *best cases* of contemporary transit metropolises—ones whose co-planning and co-development of transit systems and cityscapes occurred under largely free-market conditions during the past half-century of rapid automobile growth and ascendancy.

The twelve cases examined in this book sort into four classes of transit metropolises:

- *Adaptive cities.* These are transit-oriented metropolises that have invested in rail systems to guide urban growth for purposes of achieving larger societal objectives, such as preserving open space and producing affordable housing in rail-served communities. All feature compact, mixed-use suburban communities and new towns concentrated around rail nodes. The book's case examples are Stockholm, Copenhagen, Tokyo, and Singapore.

- *Adaptive transit.* These are places that have largely accepted spread-out, low-density patterns of growth and have sought to appropriately adapt transit services and new technologies to best serve these environs. Included here are technology-based examples (e.g., dual-track systems in Karlsruhe, Germany), service innovations (e.g., track-guided buses in Adelaide, Australia), and small-vehicle, entrepreneurial services (e.g., colectivos in greater Mexico City).

- *Strong-core cities.* Two of the cases—Zurich and Melbourne—have successfully integrated transit and urban development within a more confined, central city context. They have done so by providing integrated transit services centered around mixed-traffic tram and light rail systems. In these places, trams designed into streetscapes co-exist nicely with pedestrians and bicyclists. These cities' primacies (high shares of regional jobs and retail sales in their cores) and healthy transit patronage are testaments to the success of melding together the renewal of both central city districts and traditional tramways.

- *Hybrids: adaptive cities and adaptive transit.* Three of the cases— Munich, Ottawa, and Curitiba—are best viewed as hybrids, in the sense that they have struck a workable balance between concentrating development along mainline transit corridors and adapting transit to efficiently serve their spread-out suburbs and exurbs. Greater Munich's hybrid of heavy rail trunkline services and light rail and conventional bus feeders—all coordinated through a regional transit authority—has strengthened the central city while also serving suburban growth axes. Both Ottawa and Curitiba have introduced flexible transit centered around dedicated busways, and at the same time have targeted considerable shares of regional commercial growth around key busway stations. The combination of flexible bus-based services and mixed-use development along busway corridors has given rise to unusually high per capita transit ridership rates in both cities.

The modus operandi for drawing policy lessons and insights from the cases involves identifying similarities in approach *within* the classes of transit metropolises, as well identifying differences in approaches and experiences *across* the four classes.

Diagrams are useful for conveying some of the fundamental differences in approaches to marrying transit and the urban landscape across these four classes. Schemas for thinking about the different classes of transit metropolises are provided below.

Adaptive Cities

Figure 1.1 portrays the relationship between regional transit services and urban form for adaptive cities, in both one and two dimensions. The two-dimensional bird's-eye image at the bottom of the graph is a representation of radial rail lines that connect outlying communities to a central business district (CBD). Metropolises with strong, dominant CBDs and outlying communities and subcenters connected to their CBDs via rail, like pearls on a necklace, are the archetypal adaptive cityscapes. The clustering of development at nodes along the railway, and the resulting con-

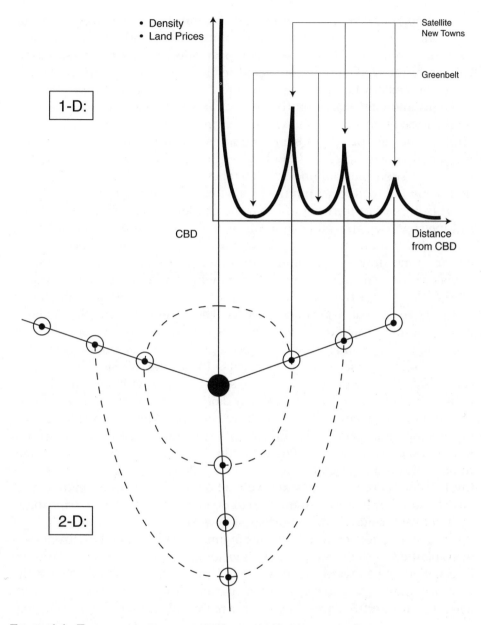

FIGURE 1.1. TRANSIT AND URBAN FORM RELATIONSHIPS IN ADAPTIVE CITIES.

finement of trips along the radial axes, are what makes the arrangement highly efficient from a mobility standpoint. The combination of a large CBD, concentrated mixed-use development around outlying stations, and long-haul radial links that invite balanced, two-way flows is the rail-oriented, adaptive city's formula to success.

As implemented in Stockholm and Copenhagen, this book's two Scandinavian cases, rail transit lines were combined with protective greenbelts to form a suburban landscape of compact satellite communities that are efficiently interlinked and connected to their regions' historical centers. Regional master planning was pivotal to creating this built form. Plotting densities and land prices on the vertical axis and distance from the CBD on the horizontal axis, as shown on the top half of Figure 1.1, conveys the kinds of density/price gradients found in master-planned, rail-oriented metropolises. Densities and land prices are the highest in the CBDs and spike near suburban rail nodes. They taper rapidly with distance from the nodes and fall to zero within the protective greenbelts themselves.

It is important to recognize that the challenges of building successful rail metropolises go well beyond physical planning and the formation of nodes of development. In particular, considerable attention goes into the design of new towns and communities themselves. In the case of Scandinavia's rail-served suburbs, town centers with public squares and outdoor marketplaces abut the train depots. Care is given to creating a milieu that is attractive to pedestrians and cyclists. The accent on livability is showcased by public amenities—park benches, newspaper kiosks, bus shelters, sidewalk cafes, open-air markets, flower stands, and arcades designed to protect pedestrians from the elements. In several of Stockholm's rail-served satellites, underground stations share space with supermarkets to allow returning commuters to do their daily shopping on the way home in the evening. Adjacent to the stations are car-free village squares lined with more shops and service establishments, including day-care centers (so moms and dads can consolidate the child-care trip with their own journey to the rail station). Despite both greater Stockholm and Copenhagen having high per capita incomes and vehicle ownership rates by global standards, public transit carries upward of 60 percent of commute trips made by employed residents of rail-oriented new towns.

The seeds for creating master-planned, rail-oriented metropolises were planted in the writings of such visionaries as Sir Ebenezer Howard in England and Edward Bellamy in the United States; both advanced the idea of building pedestrian-oriented "garden cities" more than a century ago. Howard and Bellamy saw the formation of new communities separated by green pastures and interconnected by interurban railways as means of relieving cities from oppressive overcrowding and producing socially diverse and economically sustainable suburban settlements.[4] Importantly, the rise in land values around rail nodes, as represented in the top half of Figure 1.1, would provide a means of recapturing the value added by public railway investments, allowing land price windfalls to be channeled into the finance of other supporting community facilities and services. As reviewed in Chapter 7 of this book, private railway consortia in greater Tokyo are today practicing this form of value capture, bundling

together suburban rail investments and new town development in mutually profitable ways.

Adaptive Transit

Adaptive transit represents a polar-opposite response to decentralization.
Here, spread-out, low-density development is accepted as an outcome of
rising affluence and the preferred lifestyle of many; accordingly, transit
services are adjusted and reconfigured to best serve this environment. In
keeping with this approach, Melvin Webber has called for future mass
transit to mimic the service features of its chief competitor, the private
automobile. In a piece titled "The Marriage of Autos & Transit," Webber
writes:

> If it's true that the automobile owes its tremendous suc-
> cess to its door-to-door, no-wait, no-transfer service, and if
> it's true that the structure of the modern metropolis is
> incompatible with large-vehicle transit systems . . . I sug-
> gest that the ideal suburban transit system will take its
> passengers from door-to-door with no transfers and with
> little waiting.[5]

Schematically, Figure 1.2 represents the challenges of designing mass
transit in the extreme of thinly spread development with origins and destinations distributed nearly evenly throughout a landscape. Such settings
produce almost random patterns of trip making akin to Brownian
motion—trips seemingly go from anywhere to everywhere. The ongoing
decentralization of jobs and retailing to the suburbs over the past few
decades in many parts of the world has been largely responsible for the
sharp growth in crosstown and lateral trip making. Instead of traveling
radially along well-defined corridors between suburbs and CBD, more and
more commuters want to move tangentially and are often forced onto
facilities that were never designed or oriented to serve these movements.
In the United States, the share of work trips both beginning and ending in
the suburbs increased from 39 percent in 1970 to 52 percent in 1990.[6] In
greater London, suburb-to-suburb commutes have similarly eclipsed radial journeys to the central city as the dominant commute pattern.[7]

Adaptive transit generally falls into three groups. One is technology-
based responses. An example is track-guided buses, first introduced in
Essen, Germany, and more recently applied in Adelaide, Australia. Also
called *O-Bahn*, this technology relies on buses equipped with guide rollers
that steer the vehicles along dedicated tracks to achieve high speeds and
efficiencies along mainline corridors. In the suburbs and CBD, vehicles
exit the guideway and operate as regular surface street buses, functioning

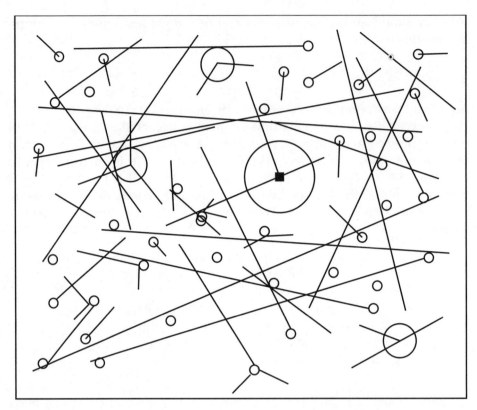

FIGURE 1.2. TRANSIT AND THE SPREAD-OUT METROPOLIS. A seemingly random pattern of movements (represented by lines) connected to a vast array of places (represented by circles).

like distributors and circulators. The marriage of mainline and feeder functions in a single vehicle helps to eliminate transfers.

A second type of adaptive transit involves service reforms aimed at dramatically reducing waits and transfers. An example is timed-transfer systems, first pioneered in the two largest cities of Alberta, Canada—Edmonton and Calgary—and since adopted by many large bus transit systems in North America, including Ottawa (Chapter 9). In Edmonton, the regional bus system was completely overhauled in the mid-1970s to mimic the area's emerging crosstown and lateral commuting pattern. All services were reorganized around some two dozen transit centers, in addition to the main downtown terminus, with routes blanketing the city in a combined crisscross and radial fashion. Today, anywhere from five to ten bus routes converge simultaneously on one of Edmonton's outlying transit centers every twenty to thirty minutes. Transit patrons scramble from one bus to another to make their connections, and almost like clockwork, buses depart three to five minutes later. Many U.S. and Canadian cities have since tried to emulate Edmonton's successes. A recent survey of eighty-eight U.S. transit operators found that 68 percent had some form of timed-transfer services; among properties with more than 350 buses, almost 90 percent used timed transfers.[8] Tidewater, Virginia's "direct transfer" network, was modeled after Edmonton's, using shopping centers as bus transfer points; among Tidewater's refinements have been the use of feeder vans that operate within cellular zones and radio-coordinated pulse scheduling (wherein buses converge and depart at regular intervals akin to a pulse beat). Seattle has combined timed-transfer networks with "fixed in/flex-out" services, involving vans that depart transit hubs at scheduled times, delivering passengers to any location within a service zone (the "flex" portion). After dropping off passengers, vans return to the hubs along a fixed route on local streets (the "fixed" portion). Other forms of flexible bus services now being tried in North America include route deviations (where bus drivers are allowed to make small detours when requested by customers paying a fare premium) and rapid bus (involving a mix of strategically located dedicated streets, interlining, checkpoints, and real-time scheduling).[9]

A third type of adaptive transit involves the use of flexibly routed paratransit services, such as shuttle vans, jitneys, and microbuses, that provide door-to-door service, or something close to it. Privately owned and operated jitneys and vans have become vital mobility options in many developing countries, filling in gaps left unserved by public transit systems and providing efficient feeder connections into rail stations. Mexico City's paratransit sector, discussed in Chapter 15, is one such example. Of particular promise for the future is the marriage of information technology and small-vehicle service to form a type of smart paratransit. Germany has experimented with automated forms of demand-responsive transit using centralized computers to link waiting customers with flexibly routed buses and vans.[10] In Winston-Salem, North Carolina, vans equipped with automated vehicle locator (AVL) transmitters and on-board terminals are today used to provide door-to-door, real-time services for elderly clients. And in Prince William County, Virginia, similar types of smart paratransit provide feeder links to commuter rail stops for the general population.

What all these forms of adaptive transit have in common is the ability to reduce and perhaps marginalize what has become the scourge of mass transit in the modern suburbs—the transfer. It is well known within the transportation field that transferring is much despised, with some studies suggesting travelers perceive transferring as taking three times longer than it actually does—it is as if one's "body clock" slows down by a factor of three when sitting idly in anticipation of a coming bus or train.[11] As much as anything, adaptive transit aims to both expedite the process and reduce the perceived burden of making connections and switching vehicles. The challenges facing transit in suburban markets is analogous to those of goods movements in the global marketplace. The emergence of

just-in-time (JIT) stock policies in manufacturing and trade has demanded that a near 0-error system of transfers be introduced.[12] With the in-
sourcing and out-sourcing of goods and raw materials from all corners of
the Earth, trans-shipment between highways, railways, seaports, and airports must today be as efficiently and tightly timed as possible if multinational companies are to remain competitive. Increasingly, urban transit
services are being held to similar standards.

A criticism of adaptive transit strategies is that by catering to low-density development, they reinforce and perhaps even perpetuate sprawl and
unsustainable patterns of growth. While there is likely a certain truth to
this, in the final analysis, this criticism is misplaced. To suggest that all
urban growth should be compact and transit-oriented is to ignore political realities and market preferences. A universal truth seems to be that as
people accumulate more wealth, they seek out roomier, more private living environs. Consumer preference surveys and buying habits, worldwide,
demonstrate a strong preference for single-family, detached living. While
such behavior might indeed press the limits of sustainability over the long
run, the preferred way to attack the problem of sprawl is to pass on true
social and economic costs to developers and consumers who build and
live in these settings—in the form of sprawl taxes, higher fuel prices, and
the like. Of course, exacting such charges can be even more elusive than
containing sprawl. As long as there is underpricing of scarce resources,
including land, and spread-out settlements as a consequence, a sensible
option for some regions will be to adapt transit to better serve this pattern.

It is important to keep in mind that what matters most about cities is
people and places, not traveling. If anything, travel is something most people want to avoid—so they can spend more time at their intended destinations rather than on the road. Our planning challenges lie with making
cities and regions healthier, safer, and more enjoyable places in which to
live, work, shop, and socialize. Accordingly, transportation planning
should be subservient to the broader goals of comprehensive land-use
planning—i.e., the planning for people and places. Thus, we should not be
creating urban environments to promote transit—this puts the transportation cart before the land-use horse. Rather, transit should be serving
land-use visions and realities, which in many cases means and will continue to mean spread-out development. In the United States, dozens of
regions have opted to build light rail transit (LRT) systems in recent years
based on the belief that rail transit, in and of itself, provides for a more
sustainable future. Unfortunately, most have allowed suburban growth—
in the form of shopping malls, campus-style office parks, and large-lot residential tract housing—to turn its back on the LRT investments. The blun-
der of letting a vision of transit rather than land use dictate investment
policy inevitably gets translated into poor ridership results. Transit investments that fail to lure motorists out of cars and into trains and buses will
do little to conserve energy, reduce pollution, or relieve congestion.

The Hybrids

Regions striking a middle ground between adapting their landscapes and their transit services can be thought of as hybrids. Their development patterns are partly transit-oriented and their transit services are partly adapted to the lay of the land. Between the extremes of a strong-centered metropolis (Figure 1.1) and a thinly spread, weak-centered region (Figure 1.2), the settlement pattern of many hybrids tends toward polycentrism, as represented in Figure 1.3. That is, orbiting the dominant center, or CBD, are secondary and tertiary centers and their surroundings. The centers, comprising multiple land uses and pedestrian-friendly design, form potential building blocks of a highly integrated regional transit network. They are normally interconnected with one another via dedicated guideways, either railways or busways. Feeding into the trunk services, often on synchronized schedules, are buses, trams, and vans that connect residents of outlying neighborhoods to the subcenters. The cases of Munich, Ottawa, and Curitiba examined in this book are representative of such hybrids.

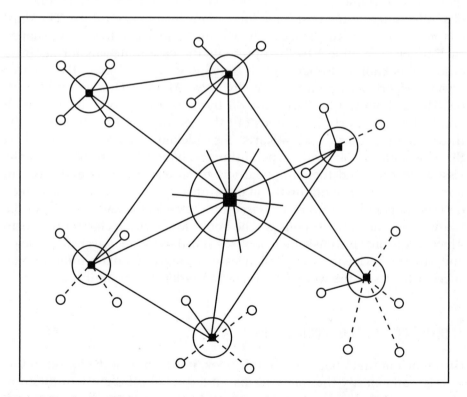

FIGURE 1.3. TRANSIT AND THE POLYCENTRIC CITY. A hierarchy or urban centers (represented by circles) interconnected by main line (represented by long lines) and feeder (represented by short lines) services.

Strong-Core Cities

An offshoot of these hybrids is a handful of places whose most noteworthy transit accomplishments have been to tie rail improvements to central
city revitalization efforts. The two cases reviewed in this book—Zurich
and Melbourne—highlight successes at using tramways both to enrich the
quality of urban living and to provide efficient forms of circulation in
built-up areas. In both instances, tramways have been used to reinforce
established development patterns (i.e., adaptive transit) while inner-city
revitalization has sought to achieve more compact, transit-supportive
built forms (i.e., adaptive cities).

Case Organization

The four classes of transit metropolises outlined above form the basis for
organizing the case materials presented in this book. Chapter 2 is a policy setter—a chapter that reviews the motivations for closely coordinating
transit and urban development, framed mostly in terms of the automobile's threat to global sustainability. Chapter 3 examines public policies
that, when introduced in combination with the model of a transit metropolis, offer some of the best hope for a more sustainable future. The third
chapter also reviews evidence on how transit and urban form have shaped
each other over time. Part Two presents the case materials for adaptive
cities—Stockholm, Copenhagen, Singapore, and Tokyo. Part Three
reviews experiences from the three hybrids—Munich, Ottawa, and Curitiba. This is followed by Part Four on the two strong-core cities—Zurich
and Melbourne. Part Five rounds out the coverage with materials on the
three adaptive transit cases—Karlsruhe, Adelaide, and Mexico City. Part
Six closes the book, with a penultimate chapter that summarizes the
lessons learned and their implications for transit systems and cities of
tomorrow. Longstanding myths about transit and the city are also taken
on (and hopefully put to rest), based on the collective evidence from the
twelve case transit metropolises. The book closes with a chapter on North
America's aspiring transit metropolises (Portland, Vancouver, San Diego,
and others), reviewing the challenges of trying to emulate international
success stories in the world's two most auto-dependent nations.

Transit Services and Technologies

Given the international scope of this book, it is helpful at the outset to sort
through and clarify the many terms—interpreted differently in different
places—used to describe transit services. I have opted for the term *transit*
to describe generically the collective forms of passenger-carrying trans-

portation services—ranging from vans and minibuses serving multiple origins and destinations (many-to-many) over nonfixed routes to modern, heavy rail trains operating point to point (one-to-one) over fixed guideways. *Transit* is the catchall used in the United States and Canada; however, almost everywhere else, *public transport* is the vernacular. And while in much of North America, *public transport* or *public transit* is associated with mass transit services provided by the public sector, almost everywhere else it means services that are available to the public at large, whether publicly or privately deployed. It is this broader, more inclusive definition of public transport that is adopted in this book.

Types or classes of transit services can be defined along a continuum according to types of vehicles, passenger-carrying capacities, and operating environments. The following sections elaborate on the forms of common-carrier transit services—i.e., those available to the general public—that are found among the case studies reviewed in this book.

Paratransit

The smallest carriers often go by the name of *paratransit*, representing the spectrum of vans, jitneys, shuttles, microbuses, and minibuses that fall between the private automobile and conventional bus in terms of capacities and service features. Often owned and operated by private companies and individuals, paratransit services tend to be flexible and highly market-responsive, connecting multiple passengers to multiple destinations within a region, sometimes door-to-door and, because of multiple occupants, at a price below a taxi (but enough to more than cover full operating costs). Driven by the profit motive, paratransit entrepreneurs aggressively seek out new and expanding markets, innovating when and where necessary. Much of their success lies in their flexibility and adaptability. Unencumbered by strict operating rules, jitney drivers will sometimes make a slight detour to deliver someone hauling groceries to his or her front door in return for an extra charge. Besides being more human-scale, jitneys and minibuses can offer service advantages over bigger buses—often, they take less time to load and unload, arrive more frequently, stop less often, and are more maneuverable in busy traffic, and, studies show, passengers tend to feel more secure since each one is closer to the driver.[13]

In many parts of the developing world, jitneys and minibuses are the mainstays of the transit network. The archetypal service consists of a constellation of loosely regulated owner-operated collective-ride vehicles that follow more or less fixed routes with some deviations as custom, traffic, and hour of day permit. Jitney drivers respond to curbside hails pretty much anywhere along a route. Every paratransit system, however—whether the 2,000 *matatus* of Nairobi, the 15,000 *carros por puesto* minibuses in Caracas, or the 40,000-plus jeepneys of Manila—differs in some way. Some load customers in the rear of vehicles and others on the side; some are governed by federations of jitney owners while others engage in daily head-to-head competition; some have comfortable padded seats and others have hard wooden benches. Manila's jeepneys (converted U.S. army jeeps that serve up to twelve riders on semifixed routes) carry about 60 percent of all peak-period trips in the region. They cost 16 percent less per seat mile than standard buses and generally provide a higher quality service (e.g., greater reliability, shorter waits) at a lower fare. Jeepney operations have historically been the last to petition for fare increases.[14]

Although banned in most wealthy countries, a handful of U.S. cities today allow private minibus and jitney operators to ply their trade as long as they meet minimum safety and insurance requirements. New York City has the largest number of privately operated van services of any American city—an estimated 3,000 to 5,000 vehicles (seating fourteen to twenty passengers) operate, both legally and illegally, on semifixed routes and variable schedules to subway stops and as connectors to Manhattan. Surveys show that more than three-quarters of New York's commuter van customers are former transit riders who value having a guaranteed seat and speedy, dependable services. Miami also has a thriving paratransit sector that caters mainly to recent immigrants from Cuba and the West Indies who find jitney-vans a more familiar and congenial form of travel than buses. Today, virtually all U.S. cities allow private shuttle vans to serve airports.

Studies consistently show that jitneys and minibuses, whether in the United States or Southeast Asia, confer substantial economic and financial benefits, both to the public sector and to private operators—namely, they are more effective at coaxing motorists out of cars than conventional transit in many settings, and do so without costly public subsidies.[15] However, as passenger volumes rise above a certain threshold (usually 4,000 or more per direction per hour), the economic advantages of paratransit begin to plummet, reflecting the limitations of smaller vehicles in carrying large line-haul loads. In both the developing and developed worlds, paratransit best operates in a supporting and supplemental, rather than substituting, role.

Bus Transit

Urban *bus transit* services come in all shapes and sizes, but in most places they are characterized by forty-five to fifty-five-passenger pneumatic-tire coaches that ply fixed routes on fixed schedules. Buses are usually diesel-propelled, though in some larger metropolises (e.g., Mexico City, Toronto), electric trolley buses powered by overhead wires also operate. Because they share road space, buses tend to be cheaper and more adaptive than rail services. However, on a per passenger kilometer basis, bus transit is generally a less efficient user of energy and emits more pollution than urban rail services. It is partly because of environmental concerns, as well as image consciousness, that some cities have sought to trade in their bus routes for urban rail services.

Bus transit is particularly important in developing countries, such as India, where some 40 percent of all urban trips are by bus. In the Third World, the private sector serves more than 75 percent of bus trips. In Karachi, Pakistan, private enterprises operating medium-size buses handle 82 percent of transit journeys.[16] Because they are highly vulnerable to traffic congestion, buses are notoriously slow in megacities such as Shanghai, China, where it is generally faster to pedal a bike for trips under 14 kilometers in length.[17] One remedy is to reward high-occupancy travel through preferential treatment, such as reserved bus lanes and traffic signal preemptions. Bangkok, Thailand, has opened some 200 kilometers of reserved, contra-flow bus lanes to expedite bus flows in a city where rush-hour speeds often fall below 10 kilometers per hour.

In most developed countries, bus transit falls largely under the domain of the public sector, though concerns over rising subsidies have prompted more and more public transit agencies to competitively tender services to private contractors. In much of the United Kingdom and Scandinavia, public bus services have been turned over to the private sector outright. For many small to medium-size metropolitan areas of the United States, Canada, and Europe, conventional coaches (operating over fixed routes on published schedules) are the predominant transit carriers; in larger areas, buses often function mainly as feeders into mainline rail corridors. Providing exclusive busways can allow buses to integrate feeder and line-haul functions in a single vehicle. In two of the cases reviewed in this book, Ottawa and Curitiba, dedicated passageways are provided for buses, enabling rubber-tire vehicles to emulate the speed advantages of conventional steel-wheel trains on line-haul segments, yet perform as regular buses on surface streets as well. Guided busways, or O-Bahns, introduced so far in Essen, Germany; Adelaide, Australia (Chapter 14); and two British cities, Leeds and Ipswich, are particularly suited to corridors (such as freeway medians) with restricted right-of-ways. Because of faster operating speeds, the theoretical maximum passenger throughputs of busways are as high as 20,000 persons per direction per hour, more than twice that of conventional surface-street buses.[18]

Trams and Light Rail Transit

Rail transit systems are mass transit's equivalents to motorized expressways, providing fast, trunkline connections between central business districts, secondary activity centers, and suburban corridors. The oldest and slowest rail services—*streetcars* in the United States and *tramways* in Europe—functioned as mainline carriers in an earlier era, but as metropolitan areas grew outward, those that remained intact were relegated to the role of central city circulators. In cities such as Zurich, Munich, and Melbourne, aging tramways have been refurbished in recent times to improve vehicle comfort, safety, and maneuverability. Trams are enjoying a renaissance in a number of European cities because their slower speeds, street-scale operations, and Old World character blend nicely with a pedestrian-oriented, car-free central city.

The modern-day version of the electric streetcar, *light rail transit* (LRT), has gained popularity as a more affordable alternative to expensive heavy rail systems, particularly in medium-size metropolitan areas of under 3 million population. Compared to tram services, LRT generally operates along exclusive or semi-exclusive right-of-ways using modern, automated train controls and technologies. The LRT vehicles tend to be roomier and more comfortable than tram cars, with more head clearance and lower floors. In the United States, where the most LRT trackage has been laid since the early 1980s, costs are often saved by building along disused railroad corridors. Medium-size U.S. cities with fairly low densities, such as Sacramento, California, have managed to build LRT for as low as US$10 million per route mile; in Sacramento's case, costs were slashed by sharing a freight railroad right-of-way, building no-frills side-platform stations, and relying predominantly on single-track services. Light rail transit is generally considered safer than heavy rail because electricity comes from an overhead wire instead of a middle third rail. There is thus no need to fence in the track, not only saving costs but also allowing LRT cars to mix with traffic on city streets.

Today there are more than 100 tramways and LRT systems worldwide (mostly in Europe and North America), with the number continually rising. Among the factors behind the growing popularity of LRT and refurbished tramways are their lower costs relative to heavy rail investments and their ability to adapt to the streetscapes of built-up areas without too much disruption. Other advantages include: they operate relatively quietly, thus are fairly environmentally benign and unobtrusive; they are electrically propelled, thus are less dependent than buses on the availability of petrochemical fuels; and they can be developed incrementally, a few miles at a time, eliminating the need for the long lead times associated with heavy rail construction.

Table 1.1 compares the physical and operating characteristics of LRT versus trams and other forms of urban rail transit. With four-car trains running as closely as three minutes apart, LRT can carry some 11,000 passengers per direction per hour; cutting the headways to ninety seconds (as found in some German cities, including Karlsruhe), maximum capacity can be doubled to more than 20,000. Advanced light rail transit (ALRT)

TABLE 1.1 COMPARISON OF CHARACTERISTICS AND OPERATING STANDARDS AMONG TYPES OF METROPOLITAN RAIL SERVICES

	Streetcars	Trams/ Light Rail	Metros/ Heavy Rail	Commuter/ Suburban Rail
Operating Environments				
Urban size (population, 1,000)	200–5,000	500–3,000	Over 4,000	Over 3000
CBD employment (jobs, 1,000)	Over 20	Over 30	Over 100	Over 40
Routes				
Tracks	At-grade/ surface	Mixed— mainly separated	Separated/ exclusive	Separated/ exclusive
Station spacing				
Suburbs	350 m	1 km	2–5 kms	3–10 kms
CBD	250 m	200–300 m	500 m to 1 km	—
CBD circulation	Surface	Surface/subway	Subway	Surface to CBD edge
Hardware				
Rolling stock (No. units per train)	1–2	2–4	Up to 8	Up to 12
Capacities (Persons per train)	125–250	260–520	800–1,600	1000–2,200
Power supply	Overhead	Overhead	3rd rail	Overhead, 3rd rail, locomotive
Operations/Performance				
Average speeds (km per hour)	10–20	30–40	30–40	45–65
Intensive peak headways (minutes)	2	3	6	2
Maximum hourly passengers (intensive headways, passengers per line per direction per hour)	7,500	11,000	22,000	48,000

Sources: R. Tolley and B. Turton, *Transport Systems, Policy and Planning: A Geographical Approach* (Essex, England: Longman Scientific & Technical, 1995); V. Vuchic, *Urban Passenger Transportation Modes, Public Transportation*, G. Gray and L. Hoel, eds. (Englewood Cliffs, NJ: Prentice Hall, 1992, pp. 79–113); B. Pushkarev and J. Zupan, *Public Transportation and Land Use Policy* (Bloomington: Indiana University Press, 1977); Parsons Brinckerhoff Quade & Douglas, Inc., R. Cervero, Howard/Stein-Hudson Associates, J. Zupan, *Commuter and Light Rail Corridors: The Land Use Connection, Transit and Urban Form* (Washington, DC: Transportation Research Board, TCRP report 16, vol. 1, 1996).

systems—such as the skytrains in Vancouver, Toronto, and London's Docklands propelled by linear induction motors—can accommodate more than 25,000 passengers per direction per hour because of their higher engineering and design standards (though automated train control in lieu of on-board drivers constrains carrying capacities). It is for this reason they are also called intermediate capacity transit systems (ICTS).

Heavy Rail and Metros

In the world's largest cities, the big-volume transit carriers are the *heavy rail* systems, also called *rapid rail transit,* and known as *metros* in Europe,

Asia, and Latin America. Metros, the term favored in this book, work best in large, dense cities. Indeed, the relationship is symbiotic. The densities found on Hong Kong's Victoria Island and New York's Manhattan Island could not be sustained without heavy rail services. And heavy rail service could not be sustained without very high densities. Presently, more than 90 percent of all peak-period trips to and from central London are by transit, mainly via the underground "tube"; for the remainder of greater London, transit serves fewer than a quarter of all peak-hour trips.[19]

Today, worldwide, there are some eighty metro systems, including twenty-seven in Europe, seventeen in Asia, seventeen in the former Soviet Union, twelve in North America, seven in Latin America, and one in Africa. Some metros have been enormously successful, including Moscow's and Tokyo's, each of which carries 2.6 billion to 2.8 billion customers a year, more than twice as many as London's or Paris's metro systems, both of which are double the size of Moscow's and Tokyo's. On a riders per track kilometer basis, the world's most intensively used metros are, in order, São Paulo, Moscow, Tokyo, St. Petersburg, Osaka, Hong Kong, and Mexico City. Most Western European, Canadian, and U.S. metros have one-third to one-quarter the passenger throughput per track kilometer of these cities, in large part because more of their residents own cars and the cost of driving is relatively low.

In contrast to light rail systems, few new metros are being built today, partly for fiscal reasons and partly because most areas that can economically justify the costly outlays already have them. Except for Southern California, no new heavy rail lines or extensions are being planned, designed, or constructed in North America. The World Bank lending for metro systems ceased completely in 1980 and has resumed again only recently. The Bank generally frowns on funding rail projects, even in megacities paralyzed by traffic congestion, viewing them as cost-ineffective means of achieving the Bank's principal missions of alleviating poverty and stimulating economic growth.[20]

The niche market of heavy rail services is high-volume, mainline corridors. Accommodating more than 50,000 passengers per hour in each direction, heavy rail services provide high-speed, high-performance connections within built-up cities as well as between outlying areas and central business districts. In city cores, heavy rail systems almost always operate below ground, thus the names *undergrounds* (in Great Britain and its former colonies) and *subways*. To justify the high costs for right-of-way acquisitions, relocations, and excavation, undergrounds require very high traffic volumes (toward the upper end of the capacity threshold). Outside the core, metro lines are normally either above ground (called elevated or aerial alignments) or at-grade within expressway medians. Most heavy rail stations are far more substantial and sited farther apart than LRT stops, usually two or more kilometers from each other, except in downtowns, where they might be three or four blocks away. Because heavy rail systems are often the most expansive metropolitan rail services and operate at the highest speeds, their impacts on accessibility, and accordingly on urban development, tend to be the greatest.[21]

Heavy rail systems are almost universally electrically propelled, usually from a third rail, and each car has its own motor. Since contact with the high-voltage third rail can be fatal, rapid rail stations usually have high platforms and at-grade tracks are fenced.

Commuter and Suburban Railways

In terms of operating speed and geographic reach, *commuter rail* or *suburban rail*, stands at the top of the rail transit hierarchy. In Germany and central Europe, where suburb-to-city rail links are widespread, these services go by the name *S-Bahn*. Today, commuter rail services can be found on five continents in over 100 cities in more than 100 countries. Japan dominates the world's commuter rail market. In 1994, Tokyo carried almost six times the number of suburban rail commuters as Bombay, the largest commuter rail market outside Japan. Metropolitan New York's suburban rail is today only 2 percent of Tokyo's. Nevertheless, metropolitan New York, along with a dozen or so other North American metropolises, is in the midst of a commuter rail renaissance. More commuter rail tracks are currently being planned, designed, and constructed in the United States and Canada than any form of rail transit. In all, twenty-one U.S. and Canadian cities either have commuter rail services or hope to have them within the next decade. This would raise the total U.S. and Canadian commuter rail trackage to some 8,000 kilometers, more than five times as long as LRT and seven times as long as heavy rail.

Commuter rail services typically link outlying towns and suburban communities to the edge of a region's central business district. They are most common in big metropolitan areas or along highly urbanized corridors and conurbations, such as the Richmond–Boston axis in the northeastern United States. Commuter rail is characterized by heavy equipment (e.g., locomotives that pull passenger coaches), widely spaced stations (e.g., 5 to 10 kilometers apart), and high maximum speeds that compete with cars on suburban freeways (although trains are slow in acceleration and deceleration). Services tend to be of a high quality, with every passenger getting a comfortable seat and ample leg room. Routes are typically 40 to 80 kilometers long and lead to a stub-end downtown terminal. Outlying depots are normally surrounded by surface parking lots that enable suburbanites and exurbanites to access stations conveniently by car. With the exception of the greater New York area (along the Metro-North corridor to Connecticut), relatively little land-use concentration or redevelopment can be found around U.S. commuter rail stations—after all, the very premise of commuter rail is to serve the low-density lifestyle preferences of well-off suburban professionals who work downtown. Serving commuter trips almost exclusively also means that ridership is highly concentrated in peak hours, more so than any other form of mass transit service.

The Case Approach

Since I have adopted the case approach for studying transit metropolises, a few words about why I have chosen this route are in order. Like any methodological approach, case studies have their pros and cons. On the plus side, cases are contextually rich. They often conjure up concrete mental images that are long retained. When well presented, cases can illuminate complex, underlying social and political dimensions that are difficult to convey any other way. And cases often resonate with politicians and the general public, something that scholarly works in the transit and urban planning fields all too often have failed to do. Research shows that cases are usually far more accessible and meaningful to those whose opinions often matter the most—elected officials. Politicians often rely on anecdotes to drive home points. Thus they are more inclined to listen to cases, in part because voters and their constituents often do. An interesting study of urban poverty in Boulder, Colorado, showed convincingly that case-wise analysis is more effective at influencing political outcomes than is variable-wise analysis based on conventional statistical techniques.[22] The research demonstrated that the effective use of cases can improve the assimilation, recall, and recognition of data among policy makers who are given priority-setting tasks. Scholars tend to think in terms of variables—e.g., studying how trends in gasoline prices and urban densities, for example, influence transit modal splits over time. Politicians and laypersons think more in terms of cases—e.g., what do experiences in several places tell us about a phenomenon?

Of course, a danger with cases is that they are unique, sometimes the result of peculiar circumstances. Thus, there is the risk that people will overgeneralize, jumping to the conclusion that experiences in one place can be tidily transplanted to another. Storytelling can also distort reality. The popular press is littered with such examples—the uncovering of a "welfare queen" as "proof" that those on public assistance are out to milk the system, the reporting of businesses shortchanging customers as a condemnation of corporate America, and so on. For these and other reasons, all cases, including the ones presented in this book, should be carefully weighed in terms of what is generalizable and relevant and what is not.

While cases are this book's principal methodological approach, it should be noted that within each case, attention is given to probing associative relationships among variables—variables such as urban densities, land-use composition, and rates of transit usage. Thus, the book's overall approach can more accurately be characterized as *variable-wise* analysis within the framework of *case-wise* comparisons. By drawing from cases across five different continents in a variety of contextual settings, I hope that underlying patterns, common themes, and useful lessons emerge on how to build and maintain successful transit metropolises for the future.

NOTES

1. Urban Mobility Corporation, The 1995 Nationwide Personal Transportation Survey, *Innovation Briefs*, vol. 8, no. 7, p. 1, 1997; A. Pisarski, *Travel Behavior Issues in the 90's* (Washington, DC: Federal Highway Administration, U.S. Department of Transportation, 1992).

2. J. Pucher and C. Lefèvre, *The Urban Transport Crisis in Europe and North America* (Basingstoke, United Kingdom: Macmillan Press, 1996).

3. New York City, for instance, evolved around subway and interurban rail lines laid a century or more ago, prior to the onslaught of the auto-expressway system. Like London and Paris, New York is a transit metropolis of a different era, and its history of transit development is well chronicled. Toronto, North America's most highly touted example of transit-oriented planning, largely represents a successful and also well-chronicled case of promoting high-rise development around stations in the 1950s. In more recent times, there has been a widening mismatch between Toronto's rail-based mainline transit services and suburbanization, resulting in declining transit modal splits and a landscape of shopping malls and tract housing outside the central city that is not terribly distinguishable from American suburbs. Chapter 3 reviews Toronto's experiences. Hong Kong represents such an extreme in terms of its urban densities (e.g., as high as 100,000 persons per square kilometer in parts of Kowloon) and geopolitics (e.g., a former island-state that now belongs to the People's Republic of China yet continues to exist as a free commercial hub) that any lessons that might be gained would be hard to apply elsewhere. And while Eastern European cities such as Moscow have among the world's highest transit ridership rates, capturing more than 85 percent of motorized trips, their extensive transit networks are largely products of a bygone era of socialist, Cold War politics.

4. P. Hall, *Cities of Tomorrow* (London: Basil Blackwell, 1988), pp. 88–108; J. Simonds, *Garden Cities 21: Creating a Livable Urban Environment* (New York: McGraw-Hill, 1994), pp. 207–212.

5. M. Webber, The Marriage of Autos & Transit: How to Make Transit Popular Again, *Access*, vol. 5, 1994, p. 31.

6. A. Pisarski, *Commuting in America II: The Second Report on Commuting Patterns and Trends* (Landsdowne, VA: Eno Transportation Foundation, 1996).

7. M. Breheny, Counter-Urbanisation and Sustainable Urban Forms, *Cities in Competition: Productive and Sustainable Cities for the 21st Century*, J.

Brotchie, M. Batty, E. Blakeley, P. Hall, and P. Newton, eds. (Sydney: Longman Australia, 1995).

8. R. Cervero, Making Transit Work in the Suburbs, *Transportation Research Record*, vol. 1451, 1994, pp. 3–11.

9. Interlining involves buses switching from one route to another when suburban terminuses are reached so as to minimize deadheading and empty back-hauling and thus increase service efficiency (route kilometers per total vehicle kilometers of service). Checkpoints are locations that serve the dual purposes of providing interchange points for passenger transfers and for monitoring schedule adherence and on-time performance. Checkpoints generally connote transfer locations for which the schedules of intersecting buses are not necessarily closely coordinated, as with timed-transfer systems.

10. Called Rufbus and first initiated in Friedrichshafen, Germany, patrons enter a three-digit code corresponding to their destination transit stop. Based on where transit vehicles are within the system, a central computer displays the scheduled arrival time of a bus or van that will take them to their destination. Patrons can either accept or reject the pickup offer. A central computer relays information on all accepted pickups to computer terminals on board assigned vehicles. Ridership rose dramatically following the introduction of Ruf-Bus services, but because of high operating costs and Germany's rising automobile ownership and usage, the system has been cut back in recent years. See: R. Behnke, *German "Smart-Bus" Systems: Potential Application in Portland, Oregon* (Washington, DC: Federal Transit Administration, U.S. Department of Transportation, 1993).

11. M. Wachs, Consumer Attitudes Toward Transit Service: An Interpretative Review. *Journal of the American Institute of Planners*, vol. 42, no. 1, 1976, pp. 96–104.

12. N. Harris, The Emerging Global City: Transport, *Cities*, vol. 11, no. 5, 1994, pp. 332–336.

13. R. Cervero, *Paratransit in America: Redefining Mass Transportation* (Westport, CT: Praeger, 1997).

14. G. Roth and G. Wynne, *Learning from Abroad: Free Enterprise Urban Transportation* (New Brunswick, NJ: Transaction Books, 1982).

15. Roth and Wynne, *op. cit.*; A. Walters, The Benefits of Minibuses, *Journal of Transport Economics and Policy*, vol. 13, 1979, pp. 320–334; I. Takyi, An Evaluation of Jitney Systems in Developing Countries, *Transportation Planning and Technology*, vol. 44, no. 1, 1990, pp. 163–177.

16. A. Armstrong-Wright, *Public Transport in Third World Cities* (London: HMSO Publications, 1993).

17. Q. Shen, Urban Transportation in Shanghai, China: Problems and Planning Implications, *International Journal of Urban and Regional Research*, vol. 21, no. 4, 1997, pp. 589–606.

18. Under ideal conditions (e.g., very light traffic, flat terrain, straight lanes, no interruptions to flow such as traffic signals), buses operating on a conven-

tional highway can move as many as 9,000 passengers per lane per direction. Sources: R. Trolley and B. Turton, *Transport Systems and Policy Planning: A Geographical Approach* (Essex, England: Longman Scientific & Technical, 1995); V. Vuchic, Urban Passenger Transportation Modes, *Public Transportation in the United States*, G. Gray and L. Hoel, eds. (Englewood Cliffs, NJ: Prentice-Hall, 1992), pp. 79–113.

19. P. Dasgupta and P. Bly, Managing Urban Travel Demand: Perspectives on Sustainability (London: Department of Transportation, United Kingdom, 1995).

20. The International Institute for Energy Conservation, *The World Bank & Transportation* (Washington, DC: The International Institute for Energy Conservation, 1996); J. Gutman and R. Scurfield, Towards a More Realistic Assessment of Urban Mass Transit, *Rail Mass Transit for Developing Countries*, Institute of Civil Engineers (London: Thomas Telford, 1990), pp. 327–338.

21. R. Knight and L. Trygg, Evidence of Land Use Impacts of Rapid Transit Systems, Transportation, vol. 6, no. 3, 1977, pp. 231–247; R. Cervero, Light Rail Transit and Urban Development, *Journal of the American Planning Association*, vol. 50, no. 2, 1984, pp. 133–147; and H. Huang, The Land-Use Impacts of Urban Rail Transit Systems, *Journal of Planning Literature*, vol. 11, no. 1, 1996, pp. 17–30.

22. R. Brunner, J. Fitch, J. Gassia, L. Kathlene, and K. Hammond, Improving Data Utilization: The Case-Wise Alternative. *Policy Sciences*, vol. 20, no. 4, 1987, pp. 365–395.

Chapter 2

Transit and the Changing World

The car culture has been blamed for a long list of local and global problems—faceless sprawl, premature deaths from accidents and air pollution, the uprooting of inner-city neighborhoods, social isolation and class segregation, depletion of fossil fuels, climate change, noise pollution, and exploitation of Third World economies (to satisfy First World consumption and energy demands). Critics charge that auto-dependent lifestyles are the main culprit behind worldwide environmental degradation and must be radically altered for the sake of sustainability. Promoting transit is just one of many options available for reversing course and deflating the automobile's expanding role in modern societies.

What's wrong with this picture? Has humankind been lulled, by some unexplained force, into a prodigious way of living and travel, seemingly oblivious to the long-term consequences? Unlikely. The spread of our cities and the growing reliance on car travel that has resulted is largely a product of rising prosperity and free choice, though, one might add, abetted considerably by government policies and inaction, such as subsidies for large-lot living and underpriced car travel, that have further promoted auto-dependent living. When people decide where to live or how to travel, they generally make rational personal choices, weighing the pros and cons of alternatives and doing what, on balance, is best for them. In America, social unrest, increased crime, and deteriorating school districts have had far more to do with the middle class leaving cities for suburbia than any innate love affair with the car. The automobile has been both figuratively and literally a vehicle—a means to an end, be it to escape central-city irritations, to cut business expenses by locating on cheaper land, or to take in bucolic scenery.

Free-market choices, however, do not alone explain transportation and land use outcomes of the past half-century. Also important have been powerful megatrends, such as telecommunication advances, economic restructuring, and the expanding roles of women in the workplace, that continue to alter and reshape how and where people live, work, shop, and travel. Together, these megatrends have worked in favor of increased automobility in nearly all corners of the globe. The long-term social and environmental consequences of rising worldwide motorization are indeed worrisome, lending credence and a certain amount of urgency to the transit metropolis as an alternative model of urbanization in the twenty-first century. Only by understanding and working with the many forces that are changing where and how people travel will it be possible to build and maintain successful and sustainable transit metropolises of the future.

This chapter examines the forces behind global motorization trends, as well as their broader social, environmental, and economic implications. It raises serious questions about the sustainability of past and present trends, providing background and hopefully some justification for why the transit metropolis, as a paradigm for regional policy making and planning, deserves serious consideration as we approach a new millennium.

Economic Restructuring: The Twin Forces of Concentration and Dispersal

The global economy is rapidly changing, and cities are feeling the shake-out. New modes of production and advancements in information technologies are fundamentally altering the landscapes of cities and regions throughout the world. Post-industrialization—the shift from goods producing and handling to information processing, as momentous as the transition from agrarian to manufacturing economies a century and a half ago—has brought about both concentration and decentralization. Some Information Age jobs are clustering in cities, some are ending up in sub-centers, and many are settling in far-flung places.

Today's global economy requires central places—such as New York, London, Tokyo, and Zurich—to serve as command and control posts for multinational corporations.[1] Financial and business services that rely on face-to-face contact and easy access to specialized skills often congregate in large CBDs. Finance and business services in the New York metropolitan area are, for example, more concentrated in Manhattan today than they were in the 1950s.[2] Where high-end businesses go, five-star hotels, upscale retailers, and major cultural draws soon follow. Thus, major urban centers in different corners of the globe are prospering under this new world order. To continue to prosper, they will need continuing improvements in public infrastructure, including mass transit systems.

Another profound change has been the trend toward flexibly specialized modes of production, such as in the high-technology sector (where highly networked small and medium-size enterprises are mutually dependent on one another's presence and proximity for innovation). "Flex spec" production favors spatial agglomeration, though not in central cities but rather in outlying clusters and corridors (e.g., California's Silicon Valley, Boston's Route 128, Stockholm's Arlanda E4 Corridor, and London's Heathrow M4 Corridor).[3] Factors such as proximity to major international airports and leading universities govern where many high-technology firms locate. Businesses that cater mostly to regional and subnational markets, such as engineering and consulting firms, often concentrate in suburban megacenters—for example, Ballston and Tysons Corner, west of Washington, D.C.; Croydon, outside London; Shinjuku, west of central Tokyo; and La Defense on Paris's west side. The clustering of restaurants, shops, and business services close to these firms has produced veritable mini-downtowns in the suburbs, what Joel Garreau has termed "edge cities."[4] Given their compactness and kaleidoscope of activities, edge cities and high-tech corridors are places where properly designed, high-quality transit services can succeed.

Of course, the countertrend to clustering and subcentering brought on by the Information Age has been dispersal. The information highway, cyberspace, and the emergence of "smart" office parks laced with fiber optic cables and satellite dishes have freed many companies to spin off their lower-tier, back-office functions to the outer suburbs and beyond. Today's workers can handle routine communications and obtain information electronically from remote, less costly locations. This is underscored by the location choices of many credit companies that have reassigned routine, low-skilled information-processing functions, such as billing and collection services, from major urban centers to such far-flung, low-cost locations as South Dakota, Jamaica, and Ireland. Similarly, most wholesaling, construction, and consumer services have located in the suburbs and exurbs to lower business expenses. During the 1980s, about three-quarters of employment growth in U.S. metropolitan areas occurred outside of central cities. Today, more than 60 percent of the nation's office stock is in the suburbs.[5]

The twin forces of concentration and dispersal brought on by economic restructuring and the Information Age have produced a variety of urban and suburban landscapes, posing significant challenges to transit as we know it. Most regions of the world today can most accurately be characterized as multicentered, or polycentric, in form, featuring a dominant central business district orbited by second, third, and even fourth tier subcenters (which in turn are flanked by loosely organized strips and sprawled development). Recent studies of growth trends in greater London, metropolitan Chicago, and the San Francisco Bay Area have documented this evolution.[6] Yet subcenters themselves vary significantly, from small to moderate-size low-intensity clusters aligned along freeway corridors to dense, nodal edge cities well suited to transit riding.[7] In some

areas, the distinction between subcenters and sprawl is beginning to blur.
A recent study of Southern California's evolving settlement pattern characterized urban form as "beyond polycentricity," noting the region's
employment density gradient has steadily flattened, with downtown Los
Angeles's share of regional jobs now at only about 5 percent, one of the
lowest anywhere.[8] Even more astonishing, the authors, Peter Gordon and
Harry Richardson of the University of Southern California's planning program, go on to note that metropolitan Los Angeles nonetheless has the
highest net population density of any American metropolitan area—with
more than 15,000 persons per square kilometer in 1990, the region was 7
percent denser than metropolitan New York, even after netting out open
space and undevelopable land.[9] How can it be? America's most spread-out
metropolis is supposedly also its densest!

Of course, accompanying job dispersal has been the steady, ongoing
exodus of households out of central cities, a trend that is centuries old but
that has accelerated since the advent of freeways. More than three-quarters of residents from the twenty-five largest U.S. metropolitan areas
today live in the suburbs. And where households go, shopping plazas, grocery stores, restaurants, and other consumer services follow. In Europe,
North America, and other parts of the developed world, once-bedroom
suburbs are being transformed into urban, mixed-use places, featuring a
mosaic of activities not too different from those historically confined to
central cities.

The scattering of activities to all corners of the modern metropolis
poses unprecedented challenges to public transportation. Dispersal
threatens to dilute transit's ridership base. Nevertheless, as reviewed in
this book, some cities have launched transit services that effectively adapt
to changing economic conditions and decentralization forces. Capitalizing on the trend toward front-office concentration, cities such as Stockholm, Zurich, Melbourne, and Munich have maintained radially focused
rail services that efficiently feed into their central cities, complemented by
surface trams that circulate within downtown. Recognizing the opportunities afforded by subcentering, other cities, including Ottawa and Curitiba, have designed interconnected networks of exclusive-lane bus services
that link together outlying depots. In both places, the process of transferring is near effortless. Still other places, Singapore and Copenhagen
among them, have created new towns that invite internal bike travel and
external rail travel.

Telecommunications and Commuting

The conventional view of communications advances is that they reduce
travel by liberating commuters from the daily strain of driving to and

from work. Others have suggested that home working and telecommuting will fail to bring about transportation and environmental benefits because people will adjust by making more and longer nonwork trips; borrowing from time-budget theory, the suggestion is that people have an innate, almost insatiable desire to travel, and they compensate for no longer having to commute by driving more often to shopping malls and taking longer weekend excursions. For the most part, research to date sides with the proposition that telecommunications substitutes for, rather than stimulates, trip making. A study of a pilot telecommuting program of 200 employees in Sacramento, California, found no increases in nonwork trips, and indeed out-of-home trips became more efficient.[10] Vehicle kilometers traveled (VKT) went down among telecommuters (to just 20 percent of the distance they normally traveled on commuting days), and on the one or two days a week they drove to their offices, they tended to make efficient chained trips (e.g., from work to a shopping center to a dry cleaners to a restaurant to home). Even greater reductions in travel were found several months into a telecommuting demonstration program in Rijswijk, the Netherlands.[11] A recent study of telework centers, which are neighborhood-based shared workplaces equipped with advanced communications facilities, in the greater Seattle-Tacoma area found VKT was cut by more than half.[12] Yet telecommunications has not proven to be the panacea that some had hoped for, in large part because most occupational roles are not suited for home working, at least not on a regular basis. Management fears of losing oversight controls over teleworkers have also thwarted past initiatives. Another concern is that home workers will feel cut off from office social life and promotion opportunities. It is for these reasons that part-time telecommuting—say, working at home one or two days a week and in the office the remaining workweek—has gained popularity.

Decentralization and Commuting

While telecommunications stands to substitute for automobile and transit trips alike, the impacts of decentralization have been one-sided—notably favoring automobile travel. The once-dominant radial commute, a legacy of the monocentric metropolis, has been replaced by a patchwork quilt of crosstown, crisscross travel. For the thirty-five largest U.S. metropolitan areas with more than a million residents, the share of workers commuting to jobs in the central city fell from 48.4 percent in 1970 to 38.3 percent in 1990.[13] Today, more than twice as many commutes occur within suburbs as between suburbs and central cities.[14] Of course, these trends do not square well with the physical configurations of most transportation networks, designed to serve radial trips. Thus, there is a mismatch between the geography of travel and the geometry of transportation facilities. Tight budgets, environmental concerns, and stiff neighborhood opposition to road building cast doubt on whether this situation will change in the foreseeable future.

Motorization

The megatrend that has the most serious global implications is the rapidly increasing rate of motorization, especially in developing countries. Of course, motorization is a sign of prosperity. A plot of cars per capita and wealth (gross national product per capita) for twenty-six world cities across five continents found a very strong positive correlation.[15] The ability of our planet to absorb astronomical increases in vehicle populations, however, both in terms of dwindling fossil fuel supplies and potential greenhouse gas emissions, is worrisome. A 1994 study by the Organization for Economic Cooperation and Development (OECD) estimated that urban travel alone will increase by 50 percent between 1990 and the year 2005.[16] Only 8 percent of the world's population owns a car. (In 1981, the fifty-nine poorest countries of the world, containing more than 60 percent of its population, together owned fewer cars than did residents of Los Angeles.[17]) If Third World countries begin to get anywhere close to the private automobile use found in the developed world, the strains placed on natural and social environments will be unprecedented. The report warned that the spread of German and U.S. auto ownership rates (520 and 750 vehicles per 1,000 inhabitants, respectively) to the citizens of Poland, Russia, India, Indonesia, and China would wreak havoc on the globe's finite resources.

All signs suggest that many countries are following a path toward America's level of vehicle ownership:

- From 1980 to 1994, per capita levels of automobile ownership rose by 1,300 percent in Korea, 225 percent in Turkey, and 175 percent in Portugal.[18]

- In the former East Germany, motor vehicle population jumped 75 percent in just three years (1989 to 1992).[19] Eastern European countries such as Poland that have been transitioning from socialist to market economies have seen vehicle ownership increase as high as 40 percent a year.

- Annual increases in vehicle registrations in China, Thailand, Hungary, and Pakistan today are four to fifteen times higher than in the United States (which itself transformed from a society of one car per household in 1969 to a society of close to two cars per household in 1995, during a time that average household size declined by 17 percent).[20] Motor vehicle fleets are growing far faster than the gross national products (GNP) of all rapidly industrializing nations.

- The fastest rates of motorization can be found in the megacities of
  Asia. One study reports that in Shanghai, China, motor vehicle population tripled from 94,400 in 1985 to 272,000 in 1994.[21] Another
  claims the vehicle fleet grew by 172 percent between 1990 and 1991
  alone.[22] Jakarta, Manila, and Bangkok have been averaging annual
  vehicle growth rates of 10 to 15 percent over the past decade.[23]

One sign of motorization pressures in many newly industrializing
economies is the fast growth in two-wheel motorcycles and motor scooters. Most Taiwanese, Malaysian, and Thai cities average more than 200
motorcycles per 1,000 inhabitants (and some have over 400), with cities in
Indonesia, Vietnam, and India following suit. For many young wage earners, motorcycles and scooters are a steppingstone to eventual car ownership—in much of Asia, just as the middle class filters through housing
stock (from rental units to eventual home ownership) as they transition
through life, they also filter through motor vehicle stocks. Smaller vehicles do not always spare the environment. Many motorcycles in Asia are
powered by two-stroke engines (largely phased out in other parts of the
world), which emit as much as ten times more hydrocarbons and smoke
per kilometer as four-stroke motorcycles and even cars.[24] According to
one estimate, the South (i.e., the Southern Hemisphere, including the
poor countries of Africa, Southeast Asia, and Latin America) is responsible for 45 percent of the annual increase in fuel emissions that are caus-
ing global warming, and much of this is attributed to rapid increases in
motorization, including two-wheelers.[25]

The Changing Nature of Travel and Its Causes

Rising incomes and car ownership, coupled with the spread of our cities,
has sharply increased motorized travel throughout much of the world.
Besides being more frequent in number, motorized trips are also occurring increasingly over longer distances and in single-occupant cars.
Despite the accelerated movement of jobs to suburbs over the past decade
or two, which one might think would put many people closer to their jobs,
average commute distances have risen in the United States—from 13.6
kilometers each way in 1983 to 18.6 kilometers in 1995, a 36.5 percent
jump.[26] A recent study of eleven large European cities similarly found that
average work trip lengths increased from 8.1 kilometers in 1980 to 9.6
kilometers in 1990, an 18.5 percent rise.[27] Longer journeys have contributed more to traffic growth in Europe than has the rising number of
trips. Qing Shen reports a similar trend in Shanghai, China, where the
average journey to work lengthened from 6.2 kilometers in 1981 to 8.1
kilometers ten years later.[28]

Clearly, decentralization has not brought people and jobs closer in many settings. Why? Research in the United States places part of the blame on exclusionary zoning that keeps apartments and affordable housing out of many areas experiencing rapid job growth since low-end housing often costs cities more in services than they produce in property tax income.[29] Others contend that the growing importance of other factors in influencing residential location, such as being in a good school district, and the trend toward two-earner households, account for rising commute distances.[30]

The decline in public transit's share of metropolitan travel has been a nearly universal trend; however, nowhere has it been more precipitous than in the United States. Despite the infusion of billions of subsidy dollars and the construction of several hundred kilometers of new rail links, annual boardings for the forty-four largest U.S. metropolitan areas fell by 534 million, or 12.2 percent, from 1990 to 1995.[31] More ridership was lost during the first half of the 1990s than during the entire decade of the 1980s. Of course, the same forces behind the automobile's growing dominance—rising incomes and decentralization—have had a hand in transit's shrinking mobility role. However, a number of additional factors—some due to deliberate public policy choices, others not—have also played a role. Among these have been changes in lifestyle and urban demography, pricing, transit service levels, and institutional arrangements.

Demographic and Lifestyle Shifts

Throughout the Western world, as baby boomers have entered their peak earning years, motor vehicle consumption has also peaked. This is reflected in the United States, where in 1990 the number of registered automobiles surpassed the number of licensed drivers. Baby boomers average more travel not only because of higher incomes and more cars, but also because they are more active—they go out more often, have more expansive social networks, and chauffeur kids. Some note that as baby boomers age and are replaced by the baby-bust generation, travel rates can be expected to dip, or at least reach their saturation levels, in coming years. This, however, will likely hold only in the developed world. In much of Africa, Asia, and Latin America, places with bottom-heavy population pyramids, each succeeding generation will continue to be much larger than the preceding one.

Also powerfully influencing travel worldwide has been the changing role of women in the workplace. Today, some three-quarters of all women in the United States are in the private labor force. The feminization of America's work force is reflected by the fact that the number of workers grew almost 250 percent faster than population during the 1980s. Since many women must balance roles as wage earners and homemakers, their

travel patterns tend to be more complex than men's. The need to chain
trips between work, child-care centers, the store to pick up groceries, and
home forces many women to drive. Their greater automobile dependence
is reflected in the fact that use of transit and carpooling has been declining faster for women than men in the United States.[32] A secondary factor
contributing to increased trip chaining has been the growth in Americans
working two jobs—estimated at 7 percent of the nation's work force in
1995 and likely growing.[33] Moonlighting increases auto dependence.

The demographic trend that might favor transit in the future is the
maturing of populations, especially in the Western world. While the elderly are generally more transit-dependent than other age groups, in car-
dominant societies such as the United States, seniors still make at least
three of four trips in a private vehicle, either as the driver or as a passenger. Winning more seniors over to transit will hinge on elevating the quality and safety of services, in addition to more effectively integrating urban
development and transit provisions.

Economic Factors

Pricing policies have also hurt transit around much of the world. In the
United States, the retail price of regular-grade gasoline, including taxes,
fell by 7 percent between 1980 and 1993 in real-dollar terms (from $1.141
to $1.113 in 1993 currency). Over the same period, fleet-averaged fuel effi-
ciency increased by 40 percent (from 24.8 to 34.6 kilometers per gallon),
a product of improved engine design, downsizing of vehicles, and better
aerodynamics.[34] As a result of both factors—declining real prices and
improved fuel economy—the real price of gasoline paid by America's
motoring public for each kilometer traveled fell by almost 50 percent. Yet
over the same period, inflation-adjusted transit fares rose by nearly the
same magnitude, 47 percent. According to John Pucher and Ira
Hirschman, whereas the cost of a transit trip averaged less than a liter of
gasoline in 1980, by a decade later it cost over 130 percent more.[35]

Differences in price trends have similarly favored motoring in much of
Europe. A study of more than 100 European cities from sixteen countries
attributed transit's eroding market shares during the early 1980s partly to
real-currency declines in automobile operating costs matched by rising
transit fares.[36] In more recent times, nowhere have the disparities been
more glaring than in the former East Germany. There, public transit fares
increased tenfold between 1990 and 1992 in the wake of national reunification and the return to a market economy. In contrast, the price of a liter
of gasoline actually fell by about 14 percent over the same two years. By
1994, the ratio of gasoline prices to transit fares was 0.7:1 in eastern Germany. According to John Pucher, these changing price differentials, along
with the extremely important social status and symbol of freedom

attached to owning a car, have been behind transit's steadily declining share of urban travel in the former East Germany, from 60 percent in 1977 to 35 percent in 1991.[37]

In the United States, free parking—which motorists enjoy 99 percent of the time they make a trip—has long been a strong inducement to drive.[38] Donald Shoup has calculated that free parking is usually worth more than if motorists received free gasoline for their daily work trips. Zoning standards that inflate parking supplies, as a hedge against cars possibly spilling over into neighborhood streets, have only magnified the problem. A study of hundreds of parking facilities across ten U.S. cities found that peak parking demand absorbed, on average, only 56 percent of capacity.[39] Since parking lots are such big space consumers, their overdesign only adds insult to injury for transit riders and pedestrians, who end up having to trek longer distances, such as between a bus stop on the perimeter of a parking lot and a shopping mall entrance.

Comparatively cheap gasoline and free parking probably have a bigger impact on mode choice than we think. When people decide whether to drive or take a bus, they compare costs mainly in terms of conspicuous, out-of-the-pocket payments, such as bus fares, parking, and bridge tolls. Many overlook the sunk, fixed costs of owning a car and having to periodically pay for insurance and upkeep when making marginal choices on how to travel. It is when cash has to be regularly pulled out of the pocket, such as for transit fares, that travelers take strong notice of prices. Many Americans accept the $20,000 to $40,000 they pay for owning a car as a "subscription fee," a payment necessary to have full access to societal offerings.

The economic incentives to drive go well beyond cheap gasoline and free parking. Total subsidies to U.S. motorists have been placed at between $300 billion and more than $2,400 billion annually.[40] American motorists pay only 60 percent of the costs of road construction, maintenance, administration, and law enforcement through taxes and user charges—resulting in an annual subsidy to motorists of some $35 billion in 1993 currency.[41] America's direct motoring subsidies contrast sharply with European experiences, where the ratio of roadway taxes to expenditures range from 1.3 in Switzerland to 5.1 in the Netherlands.[42] Overall, fuel taxes per liter in Europe are five to ten times higher than in the United States, resulting in fuel prices that are two to four times heftier, mainly due to the tax differential. Differences in sales tax rates on new car purchases and gasoline are even greater in Europe—three to eighteen times higher than in the United States—with Denmark laying claim to the highest markup. It is no coincidence that both the Netherlands and Denmark, the two European countries that tax the car the heaviest, also channel the largest shares of their transportation budgets to mass transit services and bicycling.

   Far larger and more worrisome are the indirect subsidies to motoring, such as the underpricing of scarce resources such as clean air, land (including space consumed by free parking), and fossil fuels. Studies show that indirect subsidies from free parking alone are at least twice as high as direct motoring subsidies (i.e., undertaxed fees for road construction, maintenance, and traffic law enforcement). Totaling the unpaid hidden costs of accidents, pollution, social disruption, global climate change, and other externalities puts subsidies for motoring in the United States in the neighborhood of $2,000 for every man, woman, and child, or about 5 percent of the gross domestic product (GDP).[43] Studies of hidden subsidies to motorists in Europe similarly place the monetary figure at about 5 percent of the continent's total GDP.[44] While (as discussed later in this chapter) subsidies for transit riding in the United States are probably comparable to those for motoring on a per passenger kilometer basis, motoring subsidies are so huge in the aggregate (again, as much as $2,400 billion annually) that they probably swamp the impacts of some $15 billion in annual subsidies to U.S. transit riders.

   Cross-country comparisons illuminate some of the basic economic forces at play that affect travel demand. Figure 2.1 shows that among the most affluent countries of the world and on a per capita basis, fewer roads and cars, matched by higher gasoline prices, are associated with substantially less vehicle kilometers traveled—specifically in comparison to the United States, the world's most prodigious consumer of fossil fuels and

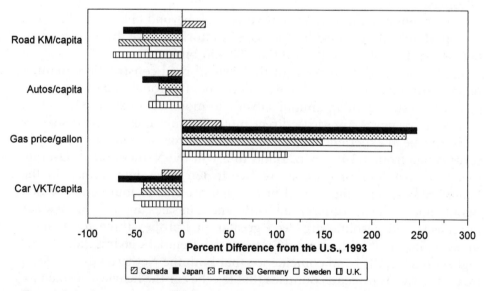

FIGURE 2.1. COMPARISON OF TRANSPORTATION SUPPLY, PRICE, AND TRAVEL DATA FOR SIX AFFLUENT COUNTRIES, RELATIVE TO THE UNITED STATES.

emitter of greenhouse gases.[45] Part of the explanation for these differences is America's generally lower population densities. Overall, however, Sweden is 25 percent less densely populated than the United States (although its cities tend to be much more densely populated); yet the typical Swede still logs only half as many VKT per capita as the average American. Clearly, America's comparatively high levels of automobility and cheap gasoline prices are matched by comparatively high levels of resource consumption.

Changing Transit Service Levels and Financial Support

Deteriorating service levels have undermined transit in many cities. Declining ridership often triggers service cuts, which in turn drive even more customers away, forcing even further service cuts—the all too familiar vicious cycle of decline that has crippled transit the world over. Only through an infusion of government subsidies has it been possible to sustain transit service levels in most wealthy countries. Nevertheless, shifting political priorities, tight budgets, and government's retrenchment from the public transit arena have in many cases cut into subsidy transfers. In the United States, federal operating assistance for transit fell by 50 percent in real-dollar terms from 1985 to 1995; the losses were partly made up by higher fares and increased local assistance, but also by reduced service levels.[46]

Critics point out, with some justification, that aid to transit in the United States has produced relatively little payoff—nationwide transit ridership has remained fairly stagnant over the past three decades, at about 7 to 8 billion passenger trips (ignoring transfers) annually, while its market share of motorized trips has fallen from about 5 percent to under 3 percent. By comparison, highway travel has more than quadrupled since 1970. Studies show that a large share of government subsidies to transit get consumed by higher labor costs and fewer kilometers of service per worker.[47] Where transit agencies enjoy a protected monopoly status and face little competition from other common-carrier services, operating subsidies have led more to lax management practices and overly generous worker compensation packages than they have to increased ridership. Competitive contracting of public transit services has been used in many countries to contain rising costs.

Capital support for transit has generally increased faster than operating assistance in North America and Europe over the past decade. Most money, however, has gone toward modernization of aging equipment as opposed to system expansion. America's older subway and commuter rail systems, such as those in New York, Philadelphia, and Boston, have been substantially upgraded through station modernization and the rehabilitation of tracks, tunnels, and signaling systems. The New York metropolitan area alone, which accounts for about a third of all transit trips made in the United States, spent about $15 billion on rehabilitation during the 1980s. Still, capital support for transit continues to lag way behind the roadway sector (which itself is, in many instances, in need of significant rehabilitation). For the United States as a whole, for example, $74 billion went into highway programs in 1994, seven times as much money as went into transit (though highway backers are quick to note that transit got a lot more capital assistance on a per passenger kilometer basis than did highways). In Eastern and Central Europe, between 1989 and 1994 nearly 60 percent of all funds from three sources—the European Bank for Reconstruction and Development, the European Investment Bank, and the International Bank for Reconstruction and Development—went to the road sector, versus 5 percent for transit. Approximately 60 percent of the World Bank's urban transport lending goes to roads, compared to 17 percent for transit.[48] Even fiscal conservatives have chimed in about favoritism in government programs. Paul Weyrich and William Lind of the Free Congress Foundation in Washington, D.C., remark:

> The current division of market share between the automobile and mass transit is no way the product of a free market. On the contrary, it reflects massive and sustained government intervention on behalf of automobiles. . . . Massive government intervention has so skewed the market toward the automobile that many consumers do not have the option of a high-quality transit system.[49]

Government assistance to transit is often defended on the basis that countervailing subsidies are necessary to offset the historical underpricing of auto motoring and subsidized highway projects. Finding ways to channel more of the assistance into service enhancements as opposed to supporting higher wages and less work continues to be a challenge for many transit properties. Economists often call for directing subsidies at users, in the form of vouchers for the poor, instead of providers (i.e., transit agencies), while at the same time deregulating the market so that operators compete for voucher income, as ways to remove the perverse impacts of subsidies and inject greater competition into the urban transportation sector.

Institutional Factors

Some institutional factors have probably hurt transit services, and some have likely abetted them. In many areas with multiple transit providers and oversight authorities, services coordination is hampered by the balkanization of decision making. In Bangkok, Thailand, for instance, more than thirty government agencies are responsible for the city's transportation policy, management, and operations. Until the recession hit in early 1997, three different rail transit projects, each sponsored by a different federal ministry, were proceeding along toward implementation in hopes of relieving Bangkok of its worsening traffic nightmares. Where private operators dominate the local transit scene, coordination can be all the more difficult. In Rio de Janeiro, more than sixty private bus companies currently service the city. Fragmentation not only produces inefficiencies and duplication, but also leads to uncoordinated services and quite often fare structures that penalize those who must transfer across transit systems.

Efforts to expand the role of the private sector in delivering transit services has probably, on balance, been a positive institutional trend. With the onset of federal subsidy cuts under the Reagan administration, many U.S. transit properties began competitively contracting out services in the 1980s to the lowest bidder that could meet minimal service standards. Studies show private operators of fixed-route bus services brought cost savings of between 22 and 54 percent (mainly from hiring nonunionized, lower-waged employees), along with higher labor productivity (more vehicle kilometers per driver).[50] Great Britain's sweeping privatization program, introduced under the Thatcher administration in the mid-1980s, similarly cut transit operating costs. While fares have generally risen throughout Great Britain, so have service levels and patronage in most markets. Deregulation led to the introduction of private minibus services in many outlying areas.[51] Many rural and exurban residents, however, have seen services totally withdrawn. Privatization of urban and interurban bus services has also occurred in much of Norway, Sweden, and Denmark. In the Netherlands, Germany, and other parts of Europe, privatization has been fostered mainly by governments selling off railway assets, other than tracks, and competitively tendering with the private franchisers to operate on the tracks at agreed-upon minimum service levels.

Problems of an Automobile-Dependent World

Transit's eroding mobility role, matched by rising levels of automobile travel, have heightened concerns over whether these trends are sustainable over the long run. By "sustainable" is meant the stewardship of natural and humanmade resources so that the quality of living and the health of our cities, countrysides, and open spaces do not deteriorate from one generation to another. While the word *sustainability* is often associated with natural ecologies and habitats, increasingly the notion is being extended to other spheres as well—economic health and well-being, preservation of the historical significance of cities, and improvements in overall social conditions. Coming up with good criteria for monitoring progress toward achieving sustainability in the transportation sector has proven elusive. Some analysts call for tracking per capita trends in vehicle hours and vehicle kilometers traveled, numbers of motorized trips, and single-occupant vehicular travel since increases in tailpipe emissions, energy usage, and land consumption are strongly correlated with these measures.[52] Of course, the impact of transportation on livability is also an important dimension of sustainability. There is a growing, unsettling feeling among many urbanites that quality of life is slipping, and indeed something has gone seriously awry in how we plan, design, and manage our cities and surrounding environs. John Whitelegg, who directs an environmental epidemiology research unit in the United Kingdom, believes that child health is the ultimate gauge of sustainability—only when we build cities and transportation systems that lower the risks of asthma and respiratory illnesses, that allow kids to play with little fear of passing cars, and that reduce the vast distances that impede social interactions, he argues, will humankind be on a sustainable course.[53]

This section reviews recent evidence on the consequences of changing mobility trends and their broader implications for sustainability, including worsening traffic congestion, deteriorating air quality, and costly sprawl. Of course, most of these impacts are interconnected, suggesting that a systems approach is needed if they are to be effectively dealt with. The section also reviews recent studies that have attempted to attach dollar figures to the net social costs of motorization and considers, finally, whether there are net benefits to the car culture.

Traffic Congestion

Traffic congestion is pandemic in many cities of the world. Sitting in traffic wastes time and energy, dumps extra pollutants into the air, causes stress, cuts into worker productivity, and prompts drivers to be more reckless than they otherwise would, increasing accidents. Of course, traffic congestion is not necessarily all bad—it is a sign that a community has a healthy, growing economy and has refrained from overinvesting in roads. In theory, the economically efficient level of congestion is where the costs of delays and accidents experienced by motorists are balanced by the costs of added capacity over the full service life of a project. The fact that prices (e.g., land costs, value of time among motorists, etc.) vary so much across corridors makes setting "optimal congestion" levels impractical. The net social costs of traffic congestion are high in most industrialized countries, estimated at between 2 and 3 percent of GDP.[54]

The traditional response to traffic congestion has been to widen existing roads and build new ones. This often provides only ephemeral relief since added capacity attracts new growth and lures motorists from other, more crowded corridors. A recent panel study of California metropolitan areas found new road capacity induced travel: between 1973 and 1990, every 10 percent increase in highway lane-kilometers led to a 9 percent increase in vehicle kilometers traveled (VKT) within a four-year period, controlling for the influences of other factors.[55] Usually it is just a matter of time before newly improved roads fill up again. It is now widely accepted that "you can't pave your way out of traffic congestion." Nor does it seem many places would be able to even if they could. Community opposition, environmental regulations, and funding shortages have conspired to make new road construction virtually impossible in many urban corridors. Among the thirty-nine largest U.S. metropolitan areas, the number of lane-kilometers of expressways and major arterials increased just 13 percent during the 1980s compared to a 32 percent increase in VKT. This translated into an increase in average travel delay of 57 percent.[56]

Slowdowns in road building, combined with rapid motorization, have proven to be a recipe for traffic tie-ups the world over. In continental Europe, densities on the main highway network increased 45 percent from 1980 to 1995.[57] Conditions have deteriorated the most in Eastern Europe's capital cities. Warsaw's peak-period speeds fell from 30 kilometers per hour in 1988 to 14 to 20 kilometers per hour in 1994.[58]

Of course, the worst traffic snarls are found in the world's megacities. Decades of haphazard growth and little or no planning, combined with rapid motorization, have finally caught up with the developing world. Few Third World cities devote more than 10 percent of their land area to roads; in contrast, roads take up 20 to 25 percent of total area in most European cities and more than 35 percent of all space in U.S. cities. Not only are roads relatively few and narrow, their designs are rarely coordinated in any functional or hierarchical sense. Main arteries sometimes abruptly dead-end, and narrow neighborhood streets do double duty as major distributors. Also, many thoroughfares in Third World cities are poorly maintained and pocked with potholes. During bad weather, traffic can slow to a standstill. The spillover of food vendors and pedestrians onto streets, the siting of markets at critical intersections, and poor enforcement of traffic laws only make matters worse.

Congestion, be it on roads or on a golf course, is generally a sign that prices are too low. When traffic volumes approach about 95 percent of capacity, it takes only a few more cars entering the stream for the system to break down, forcing all traffic to a stop-and-go crawl. These few additional motorists absorb only the time delays they themselves incur, not the collective costs of additional time delays inflicted on others upstream. These are deadweight losses in the sense that some motorists would pay for less delay and others would forgo travel if they were charged for their contribution to congestion; however, there is no mechanism for these transactions to take place. Traffic congestion is a classic case of the "tragedy of the commons"—the shared, underpriced public resource, road space, is overconsumed since no one pays marginal social costs, to the detriment of the community as a whole.[59] While traffic tie-ups affect all vehicles, buses are particularly susceptible since they are less nimble and slower to accelerate and decelerate. Thus bus riders usually end up absorbing a larger share of costs from congestion than the average motorist.

Government tax policies, it is worth noting, have had a direct hand in rising motorization and traffic congestion. In 1991, the Thai government reduced import duties on small cars from about 300 percent to 20 to 30 percent to spur competition between local and foreign automobile manufacturers. One year later, Bangkok's ownership rates ballooned to 200 cars per 1,000 residents, higher than in Singapore and Hong Kong and only slightly less than Tokyo's rate. Today, Bangkok is one of the highest car-owning, car-using, and energy-consuming cities in the developing world. It is also one of the most congested. Traffic currently crawls at below 8 kilometers per hour during much of the day, and along several major thoroughfares at just 3.7 kilometers per hour, slower than a brisk walk. One recent study put the average delay for motorized trips of more than 5 kilometers at two hours.[60] Because of traffic paralysis, Bangkok is losing its competitive edge in attracting investment, both domestically and from abroad. Shipment delays due to traffic jams have driven up the cost of local goods. One of Bangkok's fastest-growing housing rental markets today is said to be downtown apartments, leased by suburbanites seeking to avoid daily commutes.[61]

Similar stories can be told of South America. Lima's vehicle population soared when the Peruvian government relaxed import restrictions in the early 1990s. From 1992 to 1995, the number of commuter vans jumped from 6,000 to 47,000. In Bogotá, Colombia, the lowering of import tariffs contributed to a 12 percent annual increase in vehicle registration, yet the road system has remained virtually unchanged over the past two decades. A crosstown trip in Bogotá can today take up to three hours during rush hour.[62] Brazil's anti-inflation plan has allowed many lower-income households to buy a vehicle for the first time, triggering a meteoric rise in car ownership, on the order of 12 to 15 percent annually in São Paulo and Brasília. São Paulo's last comprehensive city plan was drawn up in 1968. It called for 100 kilometers of new metro lines and 135 kilometers of new freeways by the time the region's population surpassed 10 million. Since the plan, not a single freeway has been built and only 43 kilometers of rail lines have been added. São Paulo's traffic engineering department estimates that on a typical day, traffic jams extend 85 kilometers in length across the city, which over an entire year costs residents some US$10 billion in time delays.[63]

Transit advocates tout buses and trains as a solution to traffic woes. The American Public Transit Association (APTA) maintains that a fully loaded 14-meter bus can replace a lane of cars moving at 40 kilometers per hour over six 100-meter city blocks.[64] By their calculations, a fully loaded, six-car heavy rail train can substitute for nearly 100 city blocks of moving cars. Of course, coaxing motorists over to transit is no small feat. One study of bus-only cities in the United States and Europe estimated that it is generally twice as fast to travel by car as by bus.[65] Even in larger rail-based cities in Japan and Europe, the study found point-to-point travel times by car to be 3 to 23 percent shorter than by transit. The central premise of this book is that transit will only become time-competitive with the car by improving the match between how services are configured and cities are designed. Reduced time delays, especially for transit users, would be an important benefit. Of course, the aim is not to eliminate congestion fully, for to do so would, over time, lull people back to their old motoring habits. Rather, the hope would be to reduce traffic congestion to more socially acceptable and manageable levels.

Air Pollution

In most developed countries, air pollution is largely a product of an auto-dependent society. Motor vehicles produce numerous air pollutants, including carbon monoxide, particulate matter, nitrogen oxides, hydrocarbons, sulfur oxides, carbon dioxide, and methane. In the United States, between 30 and 40 percent of humanmade hydrocarbon and nitrogen oxide emissions, two of the chief precursors to the formation of ground-level photochemical smog, and about two-thirds of carbon monoxide emissions come from the tailpipes of cars and trucks. In Europe, the shares attributable to motor vehicles are even higher.[66] Today, smog is a serious problem in more than 100 U.S. cities, with the worst conditions in California and the industrial areas of the Northeast.[67] At extreme levels, smog can impair visibility, damage crops, dirty buildings, and, most troubling, threaten human health. Smog has been linked to asthma attacks, eye irritations, and upper and lower respiratory problems.[68] There is growing concern that the most serious long-term health threat might come from very fine particulate matter (of ten or fewer microns). Tiny particulates can more easily bypass the body's natural filtration system, posing long-term risks to the respiratory system by lodging deeply in the lungs. Recent research suggests that non-tailpipe particulate pollution (e.g., attrition dust from brake pads and tires) may be a more serious health threat than previously thought.[69]

The damage attributable to auto-related air pollution in the United States has been placed at approximately $10 billion annually according to one estimate and just over two cents per vehicle mile traveled according to another (both in 1990 currency).[70] Despite much cleaner automobiles (1996 model cars emitted 90 percent less pollution than the typical 1970 model) and trip reduction mandates, air quality in many urban areas of the United States has improved little and in some places has worsened. This is partly because mitigation measures have been swamped by the growth in vehicle population, number of trips, and miles driven, especially in slow-moving traffic.

Air pollution from cars, trucks, and scooters is especially troubling in large cities of the developing world, where emissions and leaded fuel are often not regulated and vehicle fleets tend to be fairly old. Bangkok reputedly has the highest concentrations of volatile hydrocarbons and particulates in the world, a result of too many inefficient, poorly maintained vehicles and two-stroke motorcycles idling in traffic jams for hours.[71] A study of Bangkok police officers regularly exposed to road traffic found they had blood lead levels significantly above World Health Organization (WHO) standards.[72] With so many cars and trucks belching smoke, gas masks have become standard uniform equipment among Bangkok's traffic patrol officers.

The potential value of transit in reducing air pollution has long been a source of contention. Obviously, fully loaded buses and trains emit less pollutants per passenger kilometer than do automobiles with one or two occupants. The American Public Transit Association (APTA) claims that, on a per-passenger-kilometer basis (using national averages for vehicle occupancy), riding transit in lieu of driving for a typical work trip will reduce emissions as follows: hydrocarbons and carbon monoxide by 99 percent, and nitrogen oxides by 60 percent if the trip is by electric rail transit; and hydrocarbons by 90 percent, carbon monoxide by 75 percent, and nitrogen oxides by 12 percent if travel is by diesel bus.[73] From 1965 to 1995, APTA contends that transit riding has kept some 1.6 million tons of hydrocarbons and 10 million tons of carbon monoxide from ever entering urban air basins. Others counter that these estimates are skewed by oversampling peak-period services, and that half-empty diesel buses running during slack hours and the construction emissions from building lightly used rail systems have hurt air quality in some cities.[74] There can be little disputing that significant air quality benefits will accrue only if transit wins over large numbers of former motorists. Significant shares of passengers on many new light rail systems in the United States have been drawn from buses and carpools, thus negating some of the hoped-for air quality benefits. Transit's best hope for materially improving air quality in the future, I believe, is to better align itself with urban settlement patterns. Only then can enough trips be diverted from cars and trucks to yield substantial air quality benefits.

Greenhouse Gases and Climate Change

If there is one truly global issue raised by rapid motorization, it is the risk of increased greenhouse gas emissions changing climates and meteoro-

logical conditions throughout the world. There is a growing scientific consensus that humanmade greenhouse gases—including carbon dioxide,
chlorofluorocarbons, and methane—are building up in the Earth's atmosphere, and that global temperatures are rising as a result.[75] Climate
changes can alter levels of precipitation, ocean currents, and seasonal
weather patterns, leading to crop damage, rising sea levels, and possibly
even the extinction of plant and animal species. In the United States,
Western Europe, and the rest of the developed world, automobiles and
trucks are the two largest sources of carbon dioxide emissions, responsible for 22 percent of the total.[76] The United States, with just 4.6 percent of
the world's population, produces nearly one-quarter of all energy-related
carbon dioxide emissions. However, it is the rapidly developing and
motorizing countries of the Southern Hemisphere that pose the greatest
threat to global climate change. Walter Hook and Michael Replogle estimate that the South is responsible for 45 percent of the annual increases
in greenhouse gas emissions.[77]

   Climate change took center stage among environmental concerns discussed by world leaders at the 1992 Earth Summit in Rio de Janeiro and
the 1996 World Habitat Conference in Istanbul. More than 160 countries
are now parties to the U.N. Framework Convention on Climate Change. A
hefty carbon tax is viewed widely as an important first step toward significantly reducing greenhouse gas emissions. One recent study estimated
that fuel prices would have to increase by 7 percent per year in real terms
over a twenty-year period in order to cut worldwide greenhouse gas emissions in half.[78] Among the other called-for strategies is a reduction in the
use of coal for electrical power generation, such as for urban rail services.
Peter Newman warns that this is not unilaterally the best course of action
for reducing carbon dioxide emissions. He argues that rail transit allows
for compact, mixed-use development that substantially lowers travel—
according to his calculations, by as much as 84 percent in Asia's wealthiest cities, Hong Kong, Tokyo, and Singapore, each of which is compact
and well served by rail transit.[79] The workable nexus of transit and urban
form, Newman contends, more than offsets the greenhouse gas impacts of
coal-generated electricity used to propel metro trains. Conditions would
be much worse if megacity travelers relied as much on gasoline-fueled
transportation as Americans.

Energy Consumption

As countries modernize and industrialize, increased consumerism and
motorization sharply increase the demand for energy. Finite supplies of
fossil fuels, however, pose serious threats to sustained economic growth
and even world peace. Because of the heavy reliance of major world powers on imported oil, especially from the Middle East, major interruptions
in supplies can not only throw the global economy into a tailspin but, as

experiences have shown, can also spark political tensions and military confrontations.

From 1973 to 1990, global transportation energy use grew by an average of 2.4 percent per year; by 1990, the transportation sector accounted for at least one-quarter of primary energy use.[80] Transportation consumes considerably higher shares of energy supplies in rapidly developing countries. In the United States, the transportation sector accounts for about three-quarters of petroleum used, and about two-thirds of this amount is burned in motor vehicles. Though just 4.6 percent of the world's population, Americans consume more than 25 percent of all petroleum sold at the pump each year. The per capita rate of fuel consumption in the United States is 87 percent higher than in the United Kingdom, 155 percent higher than in Japan, 460 percent higher than in Mexico, 56 *times* that of Nigeria, and 280 *times* more than Nepal's (though 57 percent less than Qatar's).[81] One study estimated that each U.S. urbanite consumes, on average, ten times as much gasoline as his or her Japanese counterpart and more than twenty times as much as European city-dwellers.[82] Such differences drive up the costs of U.S. goods and products in international markets, undermining the country's international competitiveness.

Current trends suggest that transport energy use may well double over the next twenty to thirty years.[83] Although new automobiles are far more fuel-efficient than ever before, as in the case of air quality, these gains are being offset by ever-increasing traffic volumes and lengthening trips. In wealthy countries, gasoline consumption rates have risen in recent years as motor vehicles have increased in weight, a result of improvements in safety, comfort, and in-car amenities. Heavier vehicles also reflect changing taste preferences, such as for minivans and sports utility vehicles (despite the trend toward declining household sizes). In the United States, big-vehicle preferences have been buttressed by cheap fuel and motoring prices.

Transit metropolises can help conserve energy in several ways. Compact, transit-oriented development shortens trips, thus encouraging non-motorized travel. And conversion of low-occupancy auto trips to mass transit cuts down on per capita fuel consumption.[84] In 1995, the average commute by private automobiles in the United States consumed 6,500 BTUs per passenger kilometer, compared to 5,940 BTUs per passenger kilometer if the trip was by bus transit and 5,440 if the trip was by rail transit.[85] Transit's energy advantages are even higher elsewhere. In German cities, bus transit is estimated to be four times more energy-efficient than the car, and tram and metro services 2.5 times more efficient.[86] In addition to moving more people with less energy, rail transit can be propelled by electricity generated from renewable, nonpetroleum sources, such as wind and hydro-power. Some critics charge, however, that when the energy expenditures for constructing rail systems are counted, rail investments can be net energy losers. One study estimated that, because of the high energy outlays in building the transbay tube, San Francisco's Bay Area Rapid Transit (BART) system uses 3.6 percent more energy annually than would an exclusive busway along the Bay Bridge.[87] Clearly, unless trains attract large numbers of former motorists, the energy conservation benefits of new metros will remain questionable. Targeting new growth around rail stations will be essential if new rail investments are to yield meaningful environmental benefits and energy savings.

Other Environmental Concerns

Other environmental concerns associated with automobile dependence include noise pollution, premature loss of farmland, wetlands, and open space (from auto-induced sprawl), soil pollution and contamination, water pollution from drilling and processing of petroleum as well as from drainage of automobile fluids and road salts, and the scarring of natural landscapes from scrapping vehicles and tires. To this list might be added visual intrusion and community severance. Of course, transit investments are guilty of many of the same sins, but environmental damage would be far less if busways and railways were favored over six-lane freeways.

Noise from roaring engines, screeching tires, and blaring horns is stressful. Using real estate sales data, one study put the noise damage from cars and trucks on residential properties for the United States as a whole at about $9 billion annually (in 1989 dollars).[88] Residents of the world's megacities experience the worst noise pollution. Roadside monitors in Bangkok regularly record daily ambient noise levels of 75 to 80 decibels, considerably above the 65-decibel maximum considered safe for humans.[89] While buses and trains are certainly noisier than the typical car or truck, the substitution of public transport trips for private motoring can substantially reduce ambient noise levels. On the other hand, compact development can expose many residents to high noise levels. Japanese cities tend to be noisier than their U.S. and European counterparts, with 30 percent of Japan's urban population regularly exposed to noise levels above 65 decibels.[90] However, many well-planned, rail-oriented communities in Japan are far less noisy than central Tokyo or Osaka. Experiences in the privately built, rail-served new towns of outer Tokyo suggest careful attention to design can mitigate noise impacts and other potential problems associated with urban agglomeration (see Chapter 7).

Another serious threat posed by rapid motorization is the loss of arable land. Cars and freeways are notorious land consumers, pushing the envelope of urban development outward and in the process threatening productive farmland, natural habitats, wetlands, and open space. Not only does a typical fast-moving four-seat sedan take up the amount of road space occupied by forty bus passengers or twelve cyclists, but each car requires up to 25 square meters (including aisles and driveways) to park in an urban setting. A well-patronized light rail line can substitute for highways and parking that require fifty times as much space.[91] Because of automobile dependence, U.S. cities average twice as much road space and parking per capita as their Western Europe counterparts. The impacts of space consumption go well beyond consuming pastureland and open expanses. The spreading out of urban activities lengthens journeys and deters walking and cycling, increasing tailpipe emissions and energy consumption in the process. In many U.S. cities, where up to 30 percent of the land is occupied by parking, the high proportion of bitumen surfaces to natural vegetation reduces oxygen production and increases stormwater pollution.

Traffic Accidents

Worldwide, there are more than 2,500 fatalities and 50,000 injuries each day from traffic accidents.[92] The economic losses amount to an estimated 2 to 4 percent of the GDPs of most wealthy countries.[93] Research suggests that traffic fatalities decline with lower motor vehicle use. In a recent international comparison, Jeff Kenworthy and his research associates found that, relative to the U.S. sample, fatality rates were 18 percent lower in Australian cities, 40 percent lower in European cities, and 55 percent lower in the three wealthy Asian cities (Hong Kong, Tokyo, and Singapore).[94]

In the developing world, traffic accidents are reaching epidemic proportions. According to the World Health Organization (WHO), three-quarters of all traffic accidents occur in the Southern Hemisphere, even though there are many more motorized vehicles north of the equator.[95] In 1990, traffic accidents ranked ninth among causes of death and disability worldwide. By 2020, WHO expects the road-traffic toll to jump to third place worldwide (second place in developing countries). Part of the problem is the poor enforcement of traffic laws in developing countries, but the more serious problem is pedestrians, cyclists, carts, and scooters competing against cars, trucks, and buses for limited road space. In New Delhi, three-quarters of people killed on the road are pedestrians, cyclists, and motorcyclists.[96] Shanghai averages ten times as many traffic fatalities per capita as Tokyo, partly because of the high exposure of pedestrians and cyclists to fast-moving traffic, but also because of delays, caused by traffic congestion, in providing first aid to accident victims.[97]

Unlike the other negative impacts of car dependence reviewed so far, most economists do not view traffic accidents as an externality—although fatalities and injuries certainly cost society, these costs are largely borne by those who willfully choose to travel. People weigh the risk of traffic accidents when they opt to drive or pedal a bike, and the very act of travel suggests that they generally consider net benefits to offset whatever risks. In wealthy countries, most citizens indemnify themselves against the risk of traffic accidents through insurance payments, thus absorbing costs and, should they require it, receiving compensation. Of course, in the developing world, where insurance is often a luxury, the losses, pain, and suffering experienced by victims and their families, who often are among society's poorest, can be catastrophic.

Social Inequities

Among the most troubling concerns about a car-dependent society are the social injustices that result from physically and socially isolating signifi-cant segments of society. Those who are too poor, disabled, young, or old to own or drive a car are effectively shut out of many of society's offerings. For the elderly and physically disabled, isolation can mean loneliness, depression, and inattention to health-care needs. For many working moms, isolation all too often means thousands of extra hours spent escorting kids and family members to and from out-of-the-way places. And for far too many of the inner-city poor, isolation means an inability to reach or even find out about job opportunities, what has been called the "spatial mismatch" problem. This view holds that, in America, inner-city joblessness and intergenerational poverty are rooted in the physical sepa-ration of the urban poor, and in particular young black males, from expanding job opportunities in the suburbs. A study of commuting in Philadelphia, Chicago, and Los Angeles found that unequal accessibility to jobs explained nearly half of the difference in employment rates between black and white teenagers.[98]

In her classic account of city life, *The Death and Life of Great American Cities*, Jane Jacobs underscores how essential diversity and day-to-day human contact are toward maintaining social cohesion, a sense of well-being, and attachment to a community.[99] The car culture, it seems, has brought with it an unraveling of long-held community bonds. The *Chica-go Tribune* in the summer of 1996 ran a series called "Nation of Strangers," warning that the "hypermobility" of the suburban era—working, sleeping, playing, and schooling at locations reached only by long automobile rides—has broken down community identity, created sterile environ-ments, and impoverished the nation's collective spirit.[100] Cloistered, class-segregated growth, made possible by the automobile, has been blamed for widening racial divisions in America. Anthony Downs warns that Ameri-cans will eventually suffer the social costs of continuing to isolate signifi-cant segments of society in impoverished inner-city areas, in the form of increasing crime, drug abuse, births out of wedlock, fatherless house-holds, and gang warfare.[101] Douglas Massey and Nancy Denton equate the systematic segregation of African Americans that has resulted from white flight and urban sprawl to *American Apartheid,* the title of their 1993 book, concluding that isolated ghetto conditions stimulate the very kinds of antisocial behavior that middle-class America deplores.[102]

Concerns about automobile-led sprawl, and its role in creating a permanent underclass of city-dwellers, are voiced mainly in the United States. Concentrated inner-city poverty is less of a problem in Western Europe and virtually nonexistent in Japan. In contrast to the Western world, many poor households in developing countries have been displaced to the periphery of metropolitan areas. Living on the outskirts, away from central city jobs, often imposes significant financial hardships. In large cities with poor public transit connections, low-income households spend as much as a quarter of their earnings on transportation, and those living on the fringe can spend more than three to four hours a day getting to and from work.[103] Many pay multiple fares transferring from one private transit carrier to another.

Transit is often looked upon to help narrow the mobility gaps created by auto-dependent landscapes. In Philadelphia, Los Angeles, Milwaukee, and other U.S. cities, reverse-commute buses and vanpools connect inner-city residents to suburban job sites, usually at deeply discounted fares. There is some evidence that these services have made a difference. Milwaukee's Job-Ride reverse-commute van service, for instance, has been credited with placing more than 3,000 inner-city residents in permanent jobs and reducing welfare rolls.[104] In much of Latin America, jitneys provide vital mobility links between shanty-towns on the periphery and in-city job opportunities.

An equally important role for transit is to function as a catalyst to central-city redevelopment as well as culturally diverse suburban growth. As discussed later in this book, rail stations have become focal points for rebuilding what once were declining central districts in Singapore, Melbourne, Munich, and other cities. In Scandinavia, rail lines built in advance of demand have been used to guide spillover growth into planned communities that are richly diverse in terms of residents' ages, backgrounds, and incomes. In the United States, efforts are now under way to transform once-decaying inner-city neighborhoods in Oakland and San Diego, California, into socially diverse and economically viable "transit villages." The Federal Transit Administration has launched the Livable Communities Initiative to fund transit-supportive projects, such as adult-training centers sited near rail stops, as a means of leveraging central-city redevelopment. These movements share a "back to the future" sentiment—an underlying belief that communities of tomorrow should be built more like the streetcar suburbs of yesteryear. A century or so ago, many Americans lived in communities huddled around rail stops. The compactness and defined edges of these rail-served communities gave them distinct identities and instilled a strong sense of place among their inhabitants. When people took transit, they encountered others from all walks of life each and every day. Whether on the trolley or en route to or from the depot, they met, talked, and got to know each other. While the contemporary transit village movement remains modest in scope, a growing number of developers and architects are betting that more and more

Americans would gladly trade in an auto-dependent suburban lifestyle for a chance to live in a safe, well-designed traditional community oriented to transit.

The Bottom Line: Social Costs of an Auto-Dependent World

Putting a price tag on the cumulative social costs of automobility is fraught with methodological difficulties. Regardless, a plethora of recent studies have sought to tally up these costs. All of the studies net out the amount road users pay in the form of fuel taxes, tolls, and user fees to get at estimates of hidden subsidies to motoring. As discussed earlier, most investigations have focused on the world's most auto-dependent country, the United States. All take great pains to achieve a full accounting of costs, measuring everything from the external costs of air pollution and greenhouse gas emissions to the costs associated with maintaining a military presence in the Middle East to secure oil imports. Expressed in 1990 currency, research by the World Resources Institute, the Natural Resources Defense Council, the Transportation Policy Institute, and the U.S. Transportation Systems Center have independently put the unborne hidden subsidies for motoring at between $370 billion and $780 billion annually.[105] In what is perhaps the most complete and rigorous evaluation conducted to date, Mark DeLucchi of the University of California at Davis placed the hidden subsidies to U.S. motorists as high as slightly more than $1,000 billion each year.[106] DeLucchi's work incorporated the latest scientific evidence on the health and natural resource impacts of air pollution and greenhouse gas emissions and, unlike earlier studies, included the cost of bundled goods (e.g., free retail parking raises the price of goods since landowners pass their expenses for building and maintaining parking lots on to tenants, who in turn pass them on to customers).

Of course, cars and trucks alone are not solely responsible for these cumulative costs. Buses and trains also pollute, burn fuel, and disrupt communities. In fact, on a distance-unit basis, subsidies to U.S. motorists are probably somewhat comparable to, if not less than, what transit riders receive. Depending on which cost study one uses, hidden subsidies to U.S. motorists are between 11 and 23 cents per passenger kilometer, whereas the annual capital and operating subsidies to transit are about 23 cents per passenger kilometer (almost identical to the high-end subsidy estimate for motorists).[107] In the aggregate, however, the hidden costs of bus and train travel pale in comparison to those attributable to cars and trucks, and, of course, if bus and rail travel were replaced by private automobile trips, the net social bill would be considerably higher.

Outside the United States, studies on the full social costs of highway travel are few. Estimates have been derived, however, for individual cities. One study calculated the cost of automobile travel in West Berlin at about US$0.40 per passenger kilometer, expressed in 1988 currency. Public transit was estimated to cost the city about US$0.23 per passenger kilometer. The study concluded that West Berlin should refrain from improving roads in the future and instead expand and upgrade its transit services.

What about Benefits?

So far, this discussion has been silent about the benefits of the car culture. This is partly because very little is known, at least in a quantitative sense. There is simply no credible way to get at the full social benefits of auto-mobility. Many analysts maintain that unborne costs are more than offset by the benefits conferred by private motor vehicles, including higher economic productivity and freedom to live and travel as one chooses. Even Mark DeLucchi, who has assigned higher social costs to automobile travel than anyone, writes: "motor-vehicle use provides enormous social benefits and, in our view, probably greatly exceeds the social cost."[108] While for some this is no doubt true, for many who are too poor to own a car, the social costs of an auto-oriented world could very well exceed purported benefits. This is an area where disparities likely abound.

Throughout much of the world, people aspire to the American way of living—owning single-family homes and cars and residing in places that are free from signs of poverty. In his book *New Visions for Metropolitan America,* Anthony Downs warns that "this vision is now so strongly entrenched that it has become almost political suicide for elected officials to challenge any of these elements."[109] The very fact that residents of pluralistic, free, democratic societies like the United States continue to elect politicians who perpetuate past practices of road building and auto-oriented development suggests that, on balance, most feel the benefits outweigh the costs.

Of course, it is the values and aspirations of Americans, Europeans, and others to live in low-density settings and to separate home from work that has given rise to sprawl, pollution, and traffic congestion, not the car per se. This does not mean, however, that people prefer to live far from their jobs and drive a lot. Many do because in auto-reliant, suburban environs they can find affordable housing, decent schools, and clean, safe neighborhoods. An important challenge in creating successful transit-oriented environments, then, is to plan, design, and build compact yet attractive communities that are well served by alternative modes such as transit and that are also affordable, have good schools, are safe to be in, and, in short, are like traditional suburbs in most other ways.

The apparent lifestyle preferences of many middle-income people to live in low-density settings and drive their cars at will have prompted some transportation analysts to argue in favor of "sustainable automobility" as a preferred policy direction for the future.[110] This view holds that most problems of the car culture can be fixed by developing more clean-fueled vehicles. After all, scientific advances and technological breakthroughs have solved many societal problems in the past, and there is no reason to believe, some argue, that the same will not hold in the future. In reality, however, the environmental benefits of innovations such as pre-heated catalytic converters and reformulated gasoline are being swamped by geometric growth in vehicle populations and motorized travel, especially in developing countries. And while we might be able to re-engineer the car to spew nontoxic emissions and run on renewable energy resources, and perhaps even bypass traffic snarls using on-board navigational aids, there is no technology that will redress the social injustices inherent in a sprawling, autocentric landscape—be it isolation of the poor from job opportunities or the immobility imposed on those too disabled to drive.

Even if we were to accept that the benefits of an auto-dependent world exceed costs, it is unclear whether this will hold over the long run. Many are skeptical, pointing out that known reserves of economically retrievable fossil fuels will support current levels of travel demand for only another thirty years or so. The reality is that we do not know the long-term consequences of extending current travel habits well into the future. By continuing along a path of increasing automobile dependence, we are taking risks whose outcomes will be borne by future generations. These are risks that growing numbers of people would prefer not to take.

NOTES

1. M. Castells, *The Informational City: Information Technology, Economic Restructuring and the Urban-Regional Process* (Oxford, England: Basil Blackwell, 1991); P. Hall, The Rise and Fall of Great Cities: Economic Forces and Population Responses, *The Rise and Fall of Great Cities: Aspects of Urbanization in the Western World*, R. Lawton, ed. (London: Belhaven Press, 1989), pp. 20–31; S. Sassen, *Cities in a World Economy* (Pine Forge: Sage, 1994).

2. R. Harris, The Geography of Employment and Residence in New York Since 1950, *Dual City: Restructuring New York*, J. H. Mollenkoph and M. Castells, eds. (New York: Russell Sage Foundation, 1991).

3. The trademarks of flexibly specialized ("flex spec") industries, or what has been called post-Fordist modes of production, are strong interfirm linkages, extensive subcontracting, reliance on specialized skills, and relatively clean manufacturing. Only through small-scale, horizontally integrated modes of production—akin to craft industries of a century ago—are firms in the high-technology arena nimble and adaptive enough to introduce new product lines and innovations that respond to rapidly changing consumer preferences.

4. J. Garreau, *Edge City: Life on the New Frontier* (New York: Doubleday, 1991).

5. N. Pierce, *Citistates: How Urban America Can Prosper in a Competitive World* (Washington, DC: Seven Locks Press, 1993).

6. M. Breheny, Counter-Urbanization and Sustainable Urban Forms, *Cities in Competition: Productive and Sustainable Cities for the 21st Century*, J.

Brotchie, M. Batty, E. Blakely, P. Hall, and P. Newton, eds. (Sydney: Longman Australia, 1995); J. MacDonald and P. Prather, Suburban Employment Centers: The Case of Chicago, *Urban Studies,* vol. 31, 1994, pp. 201–218; R. Cervero and K. L. Wu, Polycentrism, Commuting, and Residential Location in the San Francisco Bay Area, *Environment and Planning A,* vol. 29, 1997, pp. 865–886.

7. G. Pivo, The Net of Beads: Suburban Office Development in Six Metropolitan Areas, *Journal of the American Planning Association,* vol. 56, no. 4, 1990, pp. 457–469.

8. P. Gordon and H. Richardson, Beyond Polycentricity: The Dispersed Metropolis, Los Angeles, 1970–1990, *Journal of the American Planning Association,* vol. 62, no. 3, 1996, pp. 161–173.

9. P. Gordon and H. Richardson, Where's the Sprawl? *Journal of the American Planning Association,* vol. 63, no. 1, 1997, pp. 275–278; also see the accompanying letter to the editor: N. Levine, Credit Distributed, New Points Raised, *Journal of the American Planning Association,* vol. 63, no. 1, 1997, pp. 279–282.

10. P. Mohktarian, Defining Telecommuting, *Transportation Research Record,* vol. 1305, 1991, pp. 273–281.

11. Travers Morgan, Ltd., *Travel Demand Management Programs: Review of International Experiences* (Auckland: Auckland Regional Council, 1995).

12. B. Koenig, D. Henderson, and P. Mokhtarian, Travel and Emission Impacts of Telecommuting for the State of California Telecommuting Pilot Project, *Transportation Research C,* vol. 4, no. 1, 1996, pp. 13–32; D. Henderson and P. Mokhtarian, Impacts of Center-Based Telecommuting on Travel and Emissions: Analysis of the Puget Sound Demonstration Project, *Transportation Research D,* vol. 1, no. 1, 1996, pp. 29–45.

13. R. Dunphy, *Moving Beyond Gridlock: Traffic and Development* (Washington, DC: The Urban Land Institute, 1997).

14. Bureau of Transportation Statistics, U.S. Department of Transportation, *Transportation Statistics: Annual Report 1994* (Washington, DC: Bureau of Transportation Statistics, 1995).

15. H. Dimitriou, *Transport Planning for Third World Cities* (London: Routledge, 1990).

16. Organization for Economic Cooperation and Development (OECD), *Road Transport Research: Outlook 2000* (Paris: Organization for Economic Cooperation and Development, 1997).

17. J. Adams, *Transport Planning: Vision and Practice* (London: Routledge and Kegan Paul, 1981).

18. OECD, *Road Transport.*

19. J. Pucher and C. Lefèvre, *The Urban Transport Crisis in Europe and North America* (Basingstoke, England: Macmillan Press, 1996).

20. International Institute for Energy Conservation, *The World Bank and Transportation* (Washington, DC: The International Institute for Energy Conservation, 1996); Federal Highway Administration, *Our Nation's Travel: 1995,*

NPTS, Early Results Report (Washington, DC: Federal Highway Administration, Office of Highway Information Management, U.S. Department of Transportation, 1997).

21. Q. Shen, Urban Transportation in Shanghai, China: Problems and Planning Implications, *International Journal of Urban and Regional Research*, vol. 21, no. 4, 1997, pp. 589–606.

22. W. Hook and M. Replogle, Motorization and Non-motorized Transport in Asia: Transport System Evolution in China, Japan and Indonesia, *Land Use Policy*, vol. 13, no. 1, 1996, pp. 69–84.

23. H. Kubota, Traffic Congestion: A Tale of Three Cities, Impressions of Bangkok, Jakarta, and Manila, *The Wheel Extended*, no. 96, 1996.

24. P. Midgeley, *Urban Transport in Asia: An Operational Agenda for the 1990s*, Technical Department Series, World Bank Technical Paper number 224 (Washington, DC: The World Bank, 1993).

25. M. Replogle and W. Hook, Improving Access for the Poor in Urban Areas, *Race, Poverty & the Environment*, vol. 6, no. 1, 1993, pp. 48–50.

26. Federal Highway Administration, *Our Nation's Travel: 1995 NPTS Early Results Report* (Washington, DC: Federal Highway Administration, U.S. Department of Transportation, 1997).

27. P. Newman, J. Kenworthy, and F. Laube, The Global City and Sustainability: Perspectives from Australian Cities and a Survey of 37 Global Cities (Paper presented at the Fifth International Workshop on Technological Change and Urban Form, sponsored by the Commonwealth Scientific Industrial Research Organization, Melbourne, Australia, held in Jakarta, Indonesia, June 18–20, 1997).

28. Shen, *op. cit.*, 1997.

29. R. Cervero, Jobs-Housing Balancing and Regional Mobility, *Journal of the American Planning Association*, vol. 55, no. 2, 1989, pp. 136–150; R. Cervero, Jobs-Housing Balance Revisited: Trends and Impacts in the San Francisco Bay Area, *Journal of the American Planning Association*, vol. 62, no. 4, 1996, pp. 492–511; Cervero and Wu, *op. cit.*, 1997.

30. G. Giuliano, The Weakening Transportation–Land Use Connection, *Access*, vol. 6, 1995, pp. 3–11; A. Downs, *Stuck in Traffic: Coping with Peak-Hour Traffic Congestion* (Washington, DC: The Brookings Institution, 1992).

31. Wendell Cox Consultancy, *Urban Transport Fact Book* (Belleville, IL: Wendell Cox Consultancy, 1997). These figures were compiled from records obtained from the American Public Transit Association and are available from the following web site URL: www.publicpurpose.com/ut-met95.htm.

32. R. Dunphy, *op. cit.*, 1997.

33. *Ibid.*

34. Bureau of Transportation Statistics, *op. cit.*

35. J. Pucher and I. Hirschman, Urban Public Transport in the United States: Recent Development and Policy Perspective, *Public Transport International*, vol. 3, 1993, pp. 12–25.

36. F. Webster and P. Bly, Changing Patterns of Urban Travel and Implications

for Land Use and Transport Strategies. *Transportation Research Record,* vol. 1125, 1987, pp. 21–28.

37. J. Pucher and C. Lefèvre, *op. cit.*

38. D. Shoup, The High Cost of Free Parking, *Access,* no. 10, 1997, pp. 2–9.

39. R. Willson, Suburban Parking Requirements: A Tacit Policy for Automobile Use and Sprawl, *Journal of the American Planning Association,* vol. 61, no. 1, 1995, pp. 29–42.

40. These studies are reviewed later in this chapter, in the section "The Bottom Line: Social Costs of an Auto-Dependent World."

41. OECD, *Road Transport.*

42. Pucher and Lefèvre, *op. cit.*

43. J. MacKenzie, R. Dower, and D. Chen, *The Going Rate: What It Really Costs to Drive* (Washington, DC: World Resources Institute, 1992); OECD, *Road Transport;* Natural Resources Defense Council, *Uncovering Hidden Costs of Transportation* (Washington, DC: Natural Resources Defense Council, 1993).

44. V. Himanen, P. Nijkamp, and J. Padjen, Environmental Quality and Transport Policy in Europe, *Transportation Research,* vol. 26A, no. 2, 1992, pp. 147–157.

45. All of these countries could be considered affluent and are certainly among the richest in the world. Comparing incomes is problematic depending on how GDP per capita is indexed. Based on international exchange rates, the GDP per capita in 1995 among these seven countries was, in descending order and in 1995 U.S. dollars: Japan ($40,726); Germany ($29,542); France ($26,445); United States ($26,438); Sweden ($26,096); Canada ($18,915); United Kingdom ($18,777). When indexed according to purchasing power parities, probably the stronger indicator of the relative well-being of residents in these countries, the GDP per capita figures for 1995 are: United States ($26,439); Japan ($21,795); Canada ($21,031); Germany ($20,491); France ($19,939); Sweden ($18,673); and United Kingdom ($17,757). Even these parity measures are problematic, however, since they fail to account for the implied value of goods and services provided in countries with stronger social services traditions, such as Sweden. Source of data: OECD, *National Accounts, Main Aggregates, Volume 1* (Paris: OECD, 1997). Data are also available at the URL: www.oecd.org.std.gdpperca.htm.

46. American Public Transit Association, *The Transit Fact Book, 1996–97* (Washington, DC: American Public Transit Association, 1997).

47. J. Sale and B. Green, Operating Costs and Performance of American Public Transit Systems, *Journal of the American Planning Association,* vol. 4, no. 2, 1978, pp. 22–27; R. Cervero, The Anatomy of Transit Operating Deficits, *Urban Law and Policy,* vol. 6, no. 3, 1985, pp. 281–298; D. Pickrell, Federal Operating Assistance for Urban Mass Transit: Assessing a Decade of Experience, *Transportation Research Record,* vol. 1078, 1985, pp. 1–10.

48. International Institute for Energy Conservation, *op. cit.*

49. P. Weyrich and W. Lind, *Conservatives and Mass Transit: Is It Time for a New Look?* (Washington, DC: The Free Congress Foundation, 1997), pp. 11–12.

50. R. Teal, Transit Service Contracting: Experiences and Issues, *Transportation Research Record*, vol. 1036, 1985, pp. 28–36; J. Perry and T. Babitsky, Comparative Performance in Urban Bus Transit: Assessing Privatization Strategies, *Public Administration Review*, vol. 46, 1986, pp. 45–59.

51. J. Gomez-Ibañez and J. Meyer, Privatizing and Deregulating Local Public Services: Lessons from Britain's Buses, *Journal of the American Planning Association*, vol. 56, no. 1, 1990, pp. 9–21.

52. R. Ewing, Measuring Transportation Performance, *Transportation Quarterly*, vol. 49, no. 1, 1995, pp. 91–104.

53. J. Whitelegg, *Transport for a Sustainable Future: The Case for Europe* (London: Belhaven Press, 1993).

54. OECD, *Road Transport;* F. Varella, The Car Trap: Auto Dreams Collide with Reality, *World Press Review*, vol. 43, no. 12, 1996, pp. 6–8; R. Rowand, You Sit, and You Wait, and You Boil, *Automotive News*, December 1989, p. 25.

55. M. Hansen, Do New Highways Generate Traffic? Access, vol. 7, no. 2, 1995, pp. 16–22.

56. Federal Highway Administration, *Our Nation's Highways* (Washington, DC: Federal Highway Administration, U.S. Department of Transportation, 1995).

57. M. Dasgupta and P. Bly, Managing Urban Travel Demand: Perspectives on Sustainability (London: Department of Transportation, United Kingdom, 1995).

58. Pucher and Lefèvre, *op. cit.*

59. Garrett Hardin coined the phrase "tragedy of the commons" to draw a historical parallel between traffic congestion and the overgrazing of community-owned pasture land by privately owned cattle during medieval times. Overconsumption caused the destruction of the commons areas, forcing the abandonment of entire communities. See: G. Hardin, The Tragedy of the Commons, *Science*, vol. 162, 1968, pp. 1243–1248.

60. J. Sussman and R. Bonsignore., Urban Congestion in Bangkok: A Framework for Immediate Action and for a Strategic Plan, working paper (Cambridge: MIT, Strategic Planning for Metropolitan Bangkok, 1993).

61. Y. Tanaboriboon, Bangkok's Traffic Crisis: Can "Demand Management" Cool It? *The Wheel Extended*, no. 98, 1997, pp. 2–3.

62. Varella, *op. cit.*

63. S. Lehman, Think LA is Bad? In Brazil, Gridlock Can Span 100 Miles, *Los Angeles Times*, vol. 110, no. 316, October 12, 1997, Section A, p. 1.

64. This calculation assumes 70 people, including standees, per bus, an average of 1.2 passengers per car, an average car length of 5.4 meters, and one car length per 16 kilometers per hour of speed. Calculations for heavy rail trains assume an average of 180 riders per rail car and six car trains. Source: American Public Transit Association, *op. cit.*

65. J. Kenworthy, F. Laube, P. Newman, and P. Barter, *Indicators of Transport Efficiency in 37 Global Cities*, a report for the World Bank (Perth: Institute for Science and Technology Policy, Murdoch University, 1997).

66. In Western European cities, road traffic is responsible for 40 to 65 percent

of nitrogen oxides, 50 percent of hydrocarbons, and 90 percent of carbon monoxide emissions. These shares have steadily increased with time. Sources: OECD, *Road Transport;* J. Whitelegg, *op. cit.;* C. Holman, *Air Pollution and Health* (London: Friends of the Earth, 1989).

67. Nitrogen oxide and hydrocarbons combine in the presence of sunlight to form ground-level ozone, or photochemical smog. Temperature inversions can help trigger the formation of smog.

68. Carbon monoxide, which forms from incomplete combustion, slows the absorption of oxygen into the bloodstream. High levels of exposure can cause death. Nitrogen oxides increase the susceptibility of people's lungs to allergies as well as viral and bacterial infections. Sulfur oxides can irritate lungs, triggering attacks of asthma, bronchitis, and emphysema. By irritating mucous membranes, hydrocarbons can reduce people's resistance to viral infections. Lead, still widely prevalent in the motor vehicle fuels in developing countries, impairs many parts of the body, including the circulatory, reproductive, nervous, and kidney systems. At high levels of intake, lead can cause mental retardation in young children.

69. B. Williams, Latex Allergen in Respirable Particulate Air Pollution. *Journal of Allergy and Clinical Immunology,* vol. 95, 1995, pp. 88–95.

70. See, respectively, MacKenzie, Dower, and Chen, *op. cit.;* K. Small and C. Kamzimi, On the Costs of Air Pollution from Motor Vehicles, *Journal of Transport Economics and Policy,* vol. 29, no. 1, 1994, pp. 12–24.

71. J. Shibata, Traffic Management in Rapidly Growing Asian Metropolises: Escape from Vicious Circle of Car-Oriented Societies, *The Wheel Extended,* no. 98, pp. 17–21; C. Poboon, *Anatomy of a Traffic Disaster: Towards Sustainable Solutions to Bangkok's Transport Problems* (Ph.D. dissertation, Murdoch University, Institute for Science and Technology Policy, 1997); J. Kenworthy, P. Newman, P. Barter, and C. Poboon, Is Increasing Automobile Dependence Inevitable in Booming Economies? Asian Cities in an International Context, *IATSS Research,* vol. 19, no. 2, 1995, pp. 58–67.

72. Midgeley, *op. cit.*

73. American Public Transit Association, *op. cit.*

74. J. Kain, Choosing the Wrong Technology: Or How to Spend Billions and Reduce Transit Use, *Journal of Advanced Transportation,* vol. 21, no. 3, 1988, pp. 197–213

75. Intergovernmental Panel on Climate Change (IPCC), *Climate Change 1995: Impacts, Adaptations, and Migration of Climate Change: Scientific-Technical Analyses* (Cambridge, England: Cambridge University Press, 1996).

76. OECD, *Road Transport;* Whitelegg, *op. cit.;* World Resources Institute, *World Resources 1996–97: The Urban Environment* (New York: Oxford University Press, 1996).

77. W. Hook and M. Replogle, *op. cit.*

78. European Council for Ministers of Transport and the Organization for Economic Cooperation and Development, *Urban Travel and Sustainable Devel-*

opment (Paris: European Council for Ministers of Transport and the Organization for Economic Cooperation and Development, 1995).

79. P. Newman, Reducing Automobile Dependence, *Environment and Urbanization*, vol. 8, no. 1, 1996, pp. 67–92.

80. Intergovernmental Panel on Climate Change, *op. cit.;* International Institute for Energy Conservation, *op. cit.*

81. Bureau of Transportation Statistics, *op. cit.*

82. P. Newman and J. Kenworthy, *Cities and Automobile Dependence: An International Sourcebook* (Brookfield, VT: Gower, 1989).

83. Intergovernmental Panel on Climate Change, *op. cit.*

84. One study found higher per capita energy consumption in London, which is served by an extensive rail transit network, than in smaller British cities without rail systems. However, this was found to be a product of more frequent and longer average trips in London than in the comparison cities. Another study of travel and energy consumption in metropolitan Chicago found outer suburbanites consumed more energy per capita than residents of mature, denser, inner suburbs, both because they average longer trips and were automobile-dependent. Sources, respectively: D. Banister, *Transport Planning* (London: E & FN Spon, 1994); P. Prevedousros and J. Schofer, Trip Characteristics and Travel Patterns of Suburban Residents, *Transportation Research Record*, vol. 1328, 1991, pp. 49–57.

85. Short for "British thermal unit," a BTU is a standardized measure of energy-use intensity. Source: American Public Transit Association, *op. cit.* Also see: D. Gordon, *Steering a New Course: Transportation, Energy, and the Environment* (Washington, DC: Island Press, 1991).

86. Whitelegg, *op. cit.*

87. C. Lave, Rail Rapid Transit and Energy: The Adverse Effects, *Transportation Research Record*, vol. 648, 1977, pp. 14–30.

88. B. Hokanson, Measures of Noise Damage Cost Attributable to Motor Vehicle Travel, Technical Report 133 (Iowa City: Institute of Urban and Regional Research, University of Iowa, 1989).

89. Safe hearing levels are defined in terms of dBA, a decibel measure of hearing level as subjectively experienced by humans. Decibels are measured on a logarithmic scale, meaning a ten-point differential represents a significantly higher noise impact. Source of Bangkok data: Midgeley, *op. cit.*

90. Data source: OECD, *Road Transport*, Annex I.

91. P. Newman and J. Kenworthy, *An Urbanising World: United Nations Global Report on Human Settlements*, D. Satterthwaite, ed. (Oxford, England: United Nations Centre for Human Settlements, Oxford University Press, 1996).

92. The World Health Organization places the number of people dying in motor vehicle accidents worldwide at near 1 million annually. Source: World Health Organization. *The World Health Report: Bridging the Gaps* (Geneva: World Health Organization, 1995).

93. OECD, *Road Transport*.

94. Source: Kenworthy, Laube, Newman, and Barter, *op. cit.* The following cities were included in the study's sample: United States—Houston, Phoenix, Detroit, Denver, Los Angeles, San Francisco, Boston, Washington, D.C., Chicago, New York, Portland, Sacramento, and San Diego; Australia—Perth, Brisbane, Melbourne, Adelaide, Sydney, and Canberra; Canada—metropolitan Toronto; Europe—Hamburg, Frankfurt, Zurich, Stockholm, Brussels, Paris, London, Munich, Copenhagen, Vienna, and Amsterdam; Asia—Singapore, Tokyo, and Hong Kong.

95. World Health Organization, *op. cit.*

96. J. Seymour, A New Epidemic of Accidents, *World Press Review*, vol. 43, no. 12, 1996, pp. 8–9.

97. Midgeley, *op. cit.*

98. K. Ihlandfeldt and D. Sjoquist, The Impact of Job Decentralization on the Economic Welfare of Central City Blacks, *Journal of Urban Economics*, vol. 26, 1989, pp. 110–130; J. Kain, The Spatial Mismatch Hypothesis: Three Decades Later, *Housing Policy Debate*, vol. 3, 1993, pp. 371–460.

99. J. Jacobs, *The Death and Life of Great American Cities* (New York: Vintage Books, 1961).

100. Cited in N. Peirce, Keynote Address at the 39th Annual North Carolina Planning Conference and Robert and Helen Siler Lecture, *Carolina Planning*, vol. 21, no. 2, 1996, pp. 2–7.

101. A. Downs, *New Visions for Metropolitan America* (Washington, DC: The Brookings Institution and Lincoln Institute of Land Policy, 1994).

102. D. Massey and N. Denton, *American Apartheid: Segregation and the Making of the Underclass* (Cambridge: Harvard University Press, 1993).

103 The World Bank, *Urban Transport: A World Bank Policy Study* (Washington, DC: The World Bank, 1996).

104. Weyrich and Lind, *op. cit.*

105. These studies include some combination of the following costs: uncovered outlays for roadway construction, maintenance, services, and parking; externalities (air pollution, noise pollution, emission of greenhouse gases); costs associated with strategic petroleum reserves and maintaining a foreign military presence to secure oil imports; oil spill damage to the environment; losses from vibration to homes and business; vehicle and tire scrappage; premature loss of agriculture land, wetlands, watershed regions, aquifer discharge areas, parklands, scenic areas, and historical sites; blight and aesthetic losses; water pollution from road salt use; runoff damage and drainage costs associated with impervious roadway and parking surfaces; and pollution and accidents related to highway construction, maintenance, and servicing. Sources: MacKenzie, Dower, and Chen, *op. cit.;* Natural Resources Defense Council, *op. cit.;* D. Lee, *Full Cost of Pricing Highways* (Cambridge, MA: John A. Volpe National Transportation Systems Center, 1995); T. Litman, *Transportation Cost Analysis: Techniques, Estimates, and Implications* (Victoria, British Columbia: Transportation Policy Institute, 1995).

106. DeLucchi's study quantified total social cost of motor-vehicle use, including

costs both borne and not borne by motorists. Three of DeLucchi's categories that can be assumed to represent unborne costs are: bundled private-sector goods (e.g., free parking at shopping malls); monetary externalities (e.g., travel time delay imposed on others); and nonmonetary externalities (e.g., air pollution). Two categories that can be assumed to represent costs borne directly by motorists are: personal nonmonetary costs of using motor vehicles (e.g., time spent traveling) and private-sector motor-vehicle goods and services (e.g., cost of purchasing a car). A sixth category—public infrastructure and services—can be assumed to include both borne and unborne costs, although DeLucchi does not break down cost estimates into these subgroups. Perhaps the most conservative estimate to date of the share of highway capital, maintenance, and administration costs not recovered from users is from Douglass Lee. He estimated the figure to be about $55 billion for the United States as a whole for 1991, expressed in 1990 currency. Applying Lee's figure to the other categories of unborne costs from DeLucchi's study produced the range of $452 billion to $1,018 billion. Sources: M. DeLucchi, Total Cost of Motor-Vehicle Use, *Access*, vol. 8, 1996, pp. 7–13; J. Murphy and M. DeLucchi, A Review of the Literature on the Social Cost of Motor Vehicle Use in the United States, *Journal of Transportation and Statistics*, vol. 1, no. 1, 1998, pp. 16–42; and Lee, *op. cit.*

107. Estimates were calculated for the 1992 calendar year as follows, with all monetary figures expressed in 1990 currency. In 1992, $4.3 billion in capital subsidy grants were funneled to U.S. public transit operators from state, federal, and local sources; this was slightly below grant totals for other years during the 1990s. Operating assistance from all sources was $10.1 billion. Thus, the direct financial subsidies to transit totaled $14.4 billion in 1992. Dividing this by the 64,616 million passenger kilometers traveled on transit that year yields a subsidy of $0.223 per passenger kilometer. Dividing DeLucchi's high-end estimate of total hidden subsidies to highway transportation of $1,018 billion by the 4,442 billion passenger kilometers traveled on America's roads during 1992 yields a per passenger kilometer subsidy of $0.229, virtually identical to the average for transit users. If lower estimates of the hidden subsidies to motorists are used, such as those derived by such environmental advocacy groups as the Natural Resources Defense Council, then the per passenger kilometer subsidies for auto motoring are actually less than those for transit riders. Setting the aggregate hidden subsidies to motorists at $500 billion annually, for instance, produces a per passenger kilometer subsidy of $0.113. Source of data on transit subsidies: American Public Transit Association, *op. cit.* Source of data on passenger kilometers traveled: Bureau of Transportation Statistics, *op. cit.*

108. DeLucchi, *op. cit.*, p. 8.

109. Downs, *op. cit.*, p. 7.

110. D. Hensher, Selective but Important Challenges Facing the Transport Sector, *Designing Transport & Urban Forms for the Australia of the 21st Century*, J. Richmond, ed. (Sydney: Institute of Transport Studies, University of New South Wales, 1996).

Chapter 3

Public Policies and the Sustainable Transit Metropolis

Historically, traffic congestion, air pollution, and other dis-benefits of auto motoring reviewed in the previous chapter have been tackled through initiatives that work on either the *demand side* or the *supply side* of the problem. Demand-side measures seek either to reduce traffic volumes (e.g., travel bans) or to shift them over time (e.g., flex-time programs), space (e.g., land-use management), or mode (e.g., ride-share promotion). Thus, creating compact, mixed-use neighborhoods that are conducive to transit riding is a demand-side response—the aim is align, or shift, trips over space so as to support desirable levels of bus or rail transit services. In contrast, supply-side initiatives aim to provide facilities and services that adequately accommodate peoples' wishes to travel. New roads, systems enhancements (such as synchronized signals), and transit investments are the standard supply-side responses to traffic congestion. However, as other considerations, such as air quality, weigh into decisions about how scarce resources are allocated, road expansion is no longer a preferred choice in many instances. Fiscal constraints and community concerns over the disruptive impacts of urban highways have tempered new road construction. Transit improvements are just one of many potential supply-side alternatives to highway expansion. Among supply-side options, this chapter focuses mainly on the role of intelligent technology. Transit technologies, which were reviewed in Chapter 1, are discussed only briefly.

It is noted that transit metropolises, as defined in this book, embody both demand-side and supply-side elements—compact built forms work to produce demand levels that are sufficient to support intensive rail services, and flexible technologies work to adapt the supply of transit services to support the travel needs of spread-out areas. And, of course, demand-side and supply-side responses do not work in isolation or independently of each other. Quite to the contrary, urban environments continually shape and reshape how transit services are organized and delivered, and transit services themselves continually alter and reshape the very communities they serve.

As a segue to the twelve case study chapters that follow, this chapter reviews demand-side and supply-side strategies that are consonant with the broader objectives of the sustainable transit metropolis. The intent is not to be exhaustive but rather to review experiences with complementary programs, such as road pricing and traffic calming, that can work in concert with the transit metropolis in promoting alternative travel options and built forms. In light of this book's emphasis on harmonizing transit and urban development, what we know about the often delicate interrelationships of transit investments, land-use patterns, and travel behavior, and how the interrelationships might be strengthened, is also explored. The chapter concludes by reviewing lessons on the impacts of transit investments on urban form, drawn mainly from several decades of experiences in metropolitan Toronto and San Francisco.

Demand-Side Approaches

This section reviews four demand-side approaches that are felt to be particularly complementary to the formation of a transit metropolis: (1) transportation demand management; (2) restraints on automotive use; (3) regulation of automobile performance; and (4) pricing.

Transportation Demand Management

Empty automobile seats, parking lots, and roadway stretches are among the most wasted of societal resources. In the United States, shopping centers are typically designed to serve parking demand at the twentieth-busiest hour of the year (during the week before Christmas), which leaves spaces vacant more than 99 percent of the time they are open, and leaves at least half of the spaces vacant 40 or more percent of the time.[1] In contrast to transportation systems management (TSM) which seeks low-cost ways (such as improved signalization) to expedite traffic flows, transportation demand management (TDM) aims to make more efficient use of transportation resources already in place by shifting demand (e.g., into carpools or outside the peak), or eliminating trips altogether (e.g., telecommuting). The TDM approach embraces the adage "You can't pave your way out of traffic congestion."

In the United States, where TDM has been most aggressively pursued, the primary motivation behind ride-share promotion, parking management, and other demand-shifting tactics has been government strictures mandating improvements in air quality. In regions (e.g., Southern California and metropolitan Denver) where clean air standards are often violated, many TDM requirements fall squarely on employers. In 1991, Southern California enacted Regulation XV, requiring large employers to introduce measures aimed at substantially reducing single-occupant automobile trips made by their workers. Companies were given a fair amount of latitude as to which specific measures they introduced, and compliance was measured not in terms of achieving specific trip reduction targets but rather in terms of making a good-faith effort. Most employers opted for low-cost initiatives, such as providing carpoolers with preferential parking and free lunches. Within the first two years, single-occupant commuting fell only slightly, and public transit ridership remained unchanged.[2] Studies showed that Regulation XV affected fewer than 10 percent of motorized trips in the region since it focused only on large employers (with more than 100 workers) and journeys to work (a shrinking share of the travel pie). Because of mounting political pressure, high implementation costs (about $200 per employee per year), and growing resentment of unfunded federal mandates, Regulation XV was repealed in 1995. The region has instead turned to market-based strategies, such as giving companies the option of paying for the removal of old, precatalytic converter vehicles from the streets in lieu of potentially more costly and less effective programs, such as company-sponsored vanpools. Overall, America's foray into trip reduction requirements such as Regulation XV have fallen far short of expectations because such programs have no "teeth." Any public policy whose compliance is gauged in terms of inputs (i.e., effort) instead of outcomes (i.e., performance) is wrongheaded and destined to please few. The programs that most effectively modify travel behavior pass on clear and unmistakable price signals, such as by underwriting carpools and vanpools, charging for parking, and providing free or heavily subsidized transit passes (thus partly offsetting the parking subsidies).

In the United States and Canada, there is a growing consensus that parking management is the one TDM strategy with high payoff potential that is also politically palatable. The minimum parking requirements of zoning ordinances inflate supplies and seriously distort the markets for both transportation and land. Donald Shoup, who has studied the perverse effects of U.S. parking policies in greater depth than anyone, cites experiences in Oakland, California, where the introduction of a requirement in 1961 that there be one parking space per apartment immediately resulted in an 18 percent increase in cost per dwelling unit, a 30 percent drop in housing density, and a 33 percent decrease in land values on a per gross square meter basis.[3] Free parking, enjoyed 99 percent of the time Americans make an automobile trip, dissuades many travelers from even considering transit options. Studies show that charging for parking can make a big difference. The introduction of parking charges in seven U.S. and Canadian cities over the past fifteen years led to an average reduction of 19 cars driven to work per 100 employees.[4] In California, legislation now requires large employers who subsidize employee parking to offer their employees a cash equivalent to the cost of renting a parking space. Employees can take either the space or the cash, thus eliminating a built-in bias that favors driving.

Restraints on Automobile Use

In certain situations, restraints on the use of automobiles can be just as effective at inducing modal shifts as improvements in transit services themselves. One form of constraint on car use that has elements of TDM and that enhances the livability of neighborhood streets is traffic calming. The central premise of traffic calming is that local streets belong to their residents. The street is viewed as an extension of the livable space of one's own home and yard—a place to walk, chat, and play. Vital to creating a safe and livable neighborhood street is reducing the speeds of automobiles. Motorists travel faster when roads are wide, straight, and have long sight lines. So far, Europeans have made the greatest strides in taming traffic by designing skinny, curvilinear residential streets (called *woonerven* by the Dutch), implanting street trees and furniture that force cars to a crawl, necking down intersections, installing speed tables (like speed bumps, but wider), and using bumpy road surfaces (such as brick). Special signs designate the boundaries of sheltered neighborhoods, alerting motorists that they are entering a protected residential area where pedestrians can walk and children can play anywhere in the street. The idea is to slow, not ban, traffic. The overall effect is to instill a sense of tranquility and intimacy rarely found on ordinary city streets.

Because *woonerven* usually divert traffic to the next street over, some cities have begun introducing area-wide calming schemes. Berlin's area-wide traffic-calming measures have been credited with removing traffic out of residential neighborhoods and onto commercial streets and reducing citywide accidents involving pedestrians by 43 percent.[5] The French city of Bordeaux has sought to control speeds on all residential streets through landscaping and redesign, effectively achieving citywide calming. To date, traffic calming has yet to find its way into the design of many residential streets outside Europe. In the United States, Montgomery County, Maryland, has gone the furthest in calming traffic, installed more than a thousand speed humps, about a hundred intersection chokers, and a few dozen mini-roundabouts along residential streets over the past three years. As a county with more Ph.D.s and neighborhood associations per capita than any in the United States, Montgomery County had no choice but to turn to traffic calming to appease angry residents and neighborhood groups upset about the build-up of through traffic on local streets. Requests for new traffic-calming projects from neighborhood residents are pouring in faster than ever.

Many cities around the world have banned automobile traffic altogether in their cores. Restrictions vary in scope and intensity, from temporary traffic prohibitions in shopping districts to permanent automobile bans in historical city centers, such as in Munich, Germany, and Bologna, Italy. Today, virtually all European cities have imposed some degree of control over the entry of cars into their historical centers. In the United States, the cities of Minneapolis, Boston, Portland, and Denver have similarly banned traffic from portions of downtown. When combined with high-quality urban design, turning downtown streets over to shoppers and pedestrians has generally proven effective at increasing downtown retail sales and commercial property values.

In developing countries, restraints on automobile usage tend to be more heavy-handed. Depending on their license plate numbers, cars are banned from operating on particular days of the week in Athens, Mexico City, and Manila. Some areas have introduced episodic controls aimed at reducing car use during times when meteorological conditions are most conducive to smog formation. São Paulo recently introduced a July-to-September pollution-control program that requires motorists to leave cars at home one day a week. The program has removed some 600,000 cars a day from city streets and cut daily emissions of carbon monoxide by an estimated 550 tons. In Santiago, Chile, pollution alerts during summer months force as many as 60 percent of the city's 350,000 motor vehicles to stay off roads. And in Bangkok and Jakarta, severe traffic congestion has spawned such actions as the banning of trucks and heavy vehicles from central-city streets during the busiest hours of the day.

Regulation of Automobile Performance

Regulations targeted at improving the performance of automobiles have generally been far more successful, politically speaking, than those that seek to modify travel behavior. Initiatives such as America's CAFE (corporate average fuel efficiency) standards have garnered support because they focus on the ills of automobile usage (e.g., excessive fuel consumption), not on the automobile *per se*. Moreover, the burden to comply falls on large corporations, not individuals (or more accurately, not on voters).

The United States has made more headway in legislating the design of fuel-efficient, low-emission cars than any nation. The CAFE standards prompted Detroit's big three automobile manufacturers to re-engineer the car so as to markedly improve fuel economy—for example, by replacing heavy steel components with lighter polymer composites, improving aerodynamics, and upgrading transmissions. Through stringent emission standards, the Clean Air Act has brought about large reductions in the amount of lead, carbon monoxide, and smog-producing pollutants spewed out of tailpipes. Equipped with advanced-design catalytic converters and running on reformulated gasoline, new cars today emit 90 percent less pollutants than the typical 1970 model. (This has been at a slight loss of fuel efficiency and at the expense of more carbon dioxide emitted into the air, however.) Today, with the stepped-up use of oxygenated fuels and the retiring of older vehicles, carbon monoxide is no longer a serious outdoor air pollution problem in most American cities.[6] Fewer inroads have been made in eliminating the serious health threats posed by fine air-borne particles. Since diesel engines are a significant source of particulate emissions, introducing alternative propulsion systems and restricting truck traffic would help, although so far there has been little movement on these fronts.

While technological progress in redesigning the car has been impressive, from a global standpoint, the reality remains that each step forward is being outpaced by the rapid growth in automobile populations. Even though the air basins of Los Angeles and Denver might be cleaner today than a decade ago, the world's finite resource base and capacity to absorb greenhouse gases without adverse climate change continue to be pushed toward the limit. As the most populous countries of Africa and Asia, which have one-hundredth as many passenger cars per person as the world's wealthiest nations, begin to mimic car ownership patterns elsewhere, far more will be needed than just redesigning cars to achieve global sustainability.

Setting the Right Prices

Economists often argue that proper pricing—such as congestion fees, carbon taxes, and parking surcharges—would eliminate the need for heavy-handed controls over car use and public interventions into private land markets. With substantially higher motoring fees, people would, in time, move closer to jobs and transit stops to economize on travel. Employers would locate as close as possible to labor pools to lower their workers' travel expenses (and thus their salaries as well). Retailers would be warmly welcomed into residential neighborhoods by those wanting to reduce the cost of driving to shops.

True social-cost pricing of metropolitan travel has proven to be a theoretical ideal that so far has eluded real-world implementation. The primary obstacle is that except for professors of transportation economics and a cadre of vocal environmentalists, few people are in favor of considerably higher charges for peak-period travel. Middle-class motorists often complain they already pay too much in gasoline taxes and registration fees to drive their cars, and that to pay more during congested periods would add insult to injury. In the United States, few politicians are willing to champion the cause of congestion pricing in fear of reprisal from their constituents. Indeed, some have been voted out of office in recent times for raising motoring fees. Critics also argue that charging more to drive is elitist policy, pricing the poor off of roads so that the wealthy can move about unencumbered. It is for all these reasons that peak-period road pricing remains a pipe dream in the minds of many. So far, the only places with even cursory forms of area-wide congestion pricing are the city-state of Singapore, which, as discussed in Chapter 6, is governed by all-powerful centralized planning, and the politically progressive cities of Trondheim, Bergen, and Oslo in the sparsely populated, culturally homogeneous country of Norway. Elsewhere there has simply been no political will to advance this cause. Even Hong Kong, one of the most crowded spots on Earth, abandoned the idea of congestion pricing in the wake of a political backlash following a successful 1984 field test of automated vehicle identification systems that showed the idea was technologically feasible.

It is precisely because of barriers to social-cost pricing of the automobile that consideration must be given to the co-orchestration of transportation and urban development as a "second best" alternative. If first-best pricing is politically unfeasible, then encouraging transit-supportive densities and land-use compositions that would otherwise be achieved through proper pricing is among the next best things.

Supply-Side Approaches

Several supply-side approaches to global transportation problems are available that could complement demand-side strategies. These are reviewed below.

Advanced Technologies

Considerable hope rests today with the use of advanced technologies and information systems to relieve transportation problems the world over. Besides mitigating the automobile's negative by-products (e.g., tailpipe emissions), technologies are being used to guide motorists around congestion hot spots and even eliminate the need to physically traverse space (e.g., telecommunications). While technologies embody many features of demand-side programs, because they can involve multimillion-dollar capital outlays and are often used in lieu of roadway expansion, they are treated as supply-side approaches in this section.

In recent years, considerable progress has been made in designing advanced systems that optimize traffic flows, control vehicle positions on passageways, relay real-time information to travelers, and automatically collect tolls from passing motorists. Billions of dollars have been spent worldwide on making roadways and cars smarter, under the guise of the Intelligent Transportation System (in the United States) and PROMETHEUS/DRIVE (in Europe). These initiatives seek to ratchet up the efficiency of automobile movements many orders of magnitude as we enter into a new millennium, relying on the kind of technology and intelligence gathering once reserved for tactical warfare. If all goes according to plan, on-board guidance systems will one day give directions, using digital voice messages, on how to navigate city streets most efficiently. Computerized control and guidance devices embedded underneath heavily trafficked corridors will allow specially equipped cars and trucks with ultra-acceleration and -braking capabilities to race along almost bumper to bumper. Smart cards mounted on dashboards will enable motorists to whiz by toll gantries that automatically debit charges depending on time of day and degree of traffic congestion. Message boards will prominently inform motorists of upstream traffic conditions and suggest alternative, congestion-free routes.

Impressive progress in implementing advanced technologies is continually being made. Oakland County, Michigan, just north of Detroit, has introduced a "Fast-Trac" system of inductive loop sensors, TV monitors, autoscope cameras, and roadside beacons to detect vehicles and monitor traffic flows. Data are transmitted to a central computer that automatically adjusts traffic signals throughout the county's street network to optimize traffic flows and minimize delays. In Great Britain, some 120,000 motorists currently subscribe to Traffic*master*, a nationwide traveler information system being installed by a private firm. Infrared cameras located every four miles automatically record the license plates of passing vehicles and transmit the data via radio to a centralized data center in Milton Keynes. Upon matching license plates across different camera locations, a megacomputer calculates the average speed of traffic for each six-kilometer segment and relays the information in encrypted form to small receivers and visual displays mounted on the dashboards of subscribers' cars. Licensing agreements have been signed to set up Traffic*master* programs in Germany, France, and the Netherlands.

While the goals of making cars more comfortable and safer are laudable, the inevitable consequences of making them speedier and far smarter than mass transit options is cause for concern. New-age technologies could very well spell a future of even greater automobile reliance and an even more spread-out cityscape. And while intelligent systems may lessen traffic congestion, air pollution, and energy consumption, nothing can be done to the car or road system to reduce the social segregation and inequalities in accessing places that are inherent in a car-dependent culture. While smart technologies can yield important societal benefits, they are not panaceas in and of themselves.

The one area in which all sides agree that advanced technologies can make positive differences is in the ability to introduce more efficient pricing. Along the 16-kilometer stretch of State Route 91 in Orange County, one of California's busiest freeway sections, automated toll collection has enabled the introduction of variable time-of-day pricing. Four new privately financed toll lanes (two in each direction) have been built next to the original eight-lane freeway, which remains toll-free. Drivers using the express lanes pay between $.50 during periods of lowest demand and $2.75 during the height of the morning and afternoon peak period. Vehicles with three or more passengers travel free. Motorists approaching the 91 express lanes see an easy-to-read sign that displays the current toll. They have more than a kilometer to decide whether to switch to an express lane or stay on the freeway. Called high occupancy toll (HOT) lanes, these express lanes have been credited with shortening the peak period, encouraging the formation of carpools, and generating much-needed revenues for improving transit services.[7] In contrast to area-wide congestion pricing, HOT lanes have won acceptance because they are seen as offering choice (people can still travel in the free lanes) and value for the money in the form of tangible time savings. It is for this reason that proponents refer to the tariff scheme as "value pricing" rather than "congestion pricing." Furthermore, if there is elitism, it is mainly among those who assume that people of lower incomes do not want the option of paying for swift travel. As a customer of Orange County's 91 express lanes put it, "Anyone who calls the variable toll express lanes 'Lexus Lanes' isn't a working mom worried about being charged $5 every time she's late picking up her child at day care."[8]

Another promising direction for new technologies lies in revolutionizing how vehicles are propelled. Hybrid electric propulsion can boost energy efficiency by an estimated 30 to 50 percent by electronically recovering braking energy, temporarily storing it, and then reusing it for hill climbing and acceleration.[9] Some visionaries see a future of ultralight hybrid vehicles that combine the advantages of regenerative electronic braking with on-board fuel cells. Hydro-powered fuel cells would act as mini–power stations, generating electricity as hydrogen reacts with oxygen in the air. Fuel cells, however, face problems—they are heavy, involve complex engineering, and pose risks in the usage of hydrogen (as demonstrated by the *Hindenburg* disaster). Most observers agree that until the pump prices of petrochemical fuels rise dramatically or far stricter fuel-economy standards are imposed, alternative fuels and propulsion systems will be hard-pressed to penetrate today's marketplace.

Telecommunications

Another supply-side alternative to the eight-lane motorway is the information superhighway. Video-conferencing, tele-shopping, and working at home can eliminate the need to traverse space physically. Today, however, there are far fewer telecommuters than enthusiasts predicted there would be a decade ago. Only a small minority of jobs, mainly involving routine clerical and information-processing tasks, allow people to regularly work at home. In California, just 1 to 1.5 percent of the work force telecommutes on a given day.[10] The prospects for part-time telecommuting—say, one or two days a week—are brighter. Perhaps more promising will be the impacts of cyberspace on shopping behavior. Instead of haggling with dealers at a local auto row, more and more prospective car buyers are surfing the Internet to find the best deals, sometimes through a broker who lives thousands of kilometers away. Purchases of gifts, household items, and clothing through the web sites of major retailers and cable TV outlets are also on the rise. On-line auction systems have gained popularity for selling everything from jewelry to secondhand cars.

The information revolution promises not only to change how and the amount we travel, but also the very landscapes across which information, people, and goods flow. The growth in information-processing businesses, remote offices, contract workers, self-employed entrepreneurs, and cottage industries has spread more and more workplaces to the suburbs, exurbs, and beyond. With computers, multimedia devices, satellite communications, and the World Wide Web increasingly within reach of the average consumer, new types of communities are already beginning to take form. Some, like the village of Montgomery, 90 kilometers north of Toronto, are laced with fiber optic cable for high-speed data transmission and feature neighborhood tele-work centers, equipped with video-conferencing, high-capacity voice-data links, Internet connections, and wireless transmission devices. Such in-neighborhood centers allow telecommuters to walk or bike to their "remote" job sites a few days a week. Oberlin, Kansas, and Steamboat Springs, Colorado, have built telecommunication posts in their town centers. Where tele-work centers open, so do local coffee shops and corner cafes, which often become the watering holes where home-based workers socialize and "network." Today's cyberkids, reared on the Internet and interactive media, are apt to be even more receptive to the idea of working at home and telecommuting when they reach adulthood. By providing focal points for rural and exurban living, remote telecommunities could form the building blocks of successful intermetropolitan transit networks of the future.

Nonmotorized Transportation

Not to be overlooked as potentially important supply-side responses, especially within a transit metropolis, are bicycle facilities and provisions. As discussed in the Copenhagen case study (see Chapter 5), bicycles can function valuably as feeders into fixed-route transit lines. In the Netherlands, more than 30 percent of all out-of-home trips and about one-quarter of journeys to train stations are by bicycle. Part of the reason for the Netherlands' unusually high bicycle usage is its flat terrain. Also important, however, are the resources devoted to nonmotorized transportation. The Netherlands spends 10 percent of its surface transportation budget on bicycle facilities, compared to countries like the United States where a very small fraction of 1 percent of all public sector spending on transportation goes to nonmotorized modes. The Dutch city of Delft created a citywide network of segregated bike paths situated 400 to 600 meters apart along a rectangular grid. An even finer-grain mesh of bike paths was installed for in-neighborhood travel. As a result, bicycle speeds have risen sharply and accidents have fallen. Today, 43 percent of all trips by Delft residents are by bicycle and 26 percent by foot, owing in large part to the city's bike-friendly landscape.

Built Environments and the Demand for Transit

Given the central premise of this book—that sustainable transit metropolises of tomorrow will embody an intimate "fit" between their transit services and built forms—it is important to review what we know about the transit–land use nexus. This section examines evidence of the impacts of land-use patterns on travel demand in general and transit usage in particular. It is followed by a section that explores relationships in the other direction—that is, how transit investments and services shape land-use patterns and urban form.

The kinds of urban landscapes that are most conducive to transit riding are those that, as one would expect, are fairly compact, made up of a variety of land uses, and attractive to pedestrians (since all transit trips require some degree of foot travel). I call these the three dimensions, or 3-Ds, of transit-supportive cities and suburbs: density, diversity, and design. Indeed, foremost behind the success of some of the cities (e.g., Stockholm and Munich) profiled in this book, is the very fact that their built environments make riding trains and buses more convenient and generally more pleasant than driving a car.

Transit and the Compact City

It is widely agreed that higher urban densities will do more than any single change to our cityscapes in attracting people to trains and buses. A cumulative body of empirical studies over the past half-century convincingly show this to be the case. Statistical comparisons between cities and across corridors within cities suggest that every 10 percent increase in population and employment densities yields anywhere between a 5 and 8 percent increase in transit ridership, controlling for other factors (such as the lower incomes, restricted parking, and better transit services generally associated with more compact settings).[11] Studies also consistently show that transit demand rises most sharply when going from very low to modest densities—say, from 4 dwelling units per net residential acre to 10 to 15 units per acre—that is, from settings with quarter-acre spacious home sites to ones with mixes of small-lot detached units and duplexes/triplexes.[12] In the case of New York City, for example, a 1984 study showed neighborhoods with 5 dwelling units per acre averaged 0.2 daily transit trips per resident, while otherwise comparable neighborhoods (mainly in terms of incomes) with 15 units per acre averaged 0.7 daily trips per capita.[13] While very dense New York neighborhoods of 100 units per acre generated more transit trips—on average, one per resident per day—the increase was not proportional to the rise in density. The lesson: high-rise, Hong Kong–like densities are not necessary to support decent-quality transit services.

Cross-national comparisons run the risk of oversimplification. Still, they provide insights into basic relationships, such as how urban densities influence transit usage. In a 1988 study, John Pucher found Western European cities to be about 50 percent denser than their American counterparts, which along with substantially higher automobile taxation policies, he argued, was mainly responsible for transit ridership rates that were two to three times higher.[14] Data on thirty-seven global cities (including eight of the twelve cities used as cases in this book) recently compiled for the World Bank reveal a strong correlation between urban densities, auto and road supplies, and transit usage. All are "wealthy" cities by global standards.[15] Using U.S. cities as the benchmark, Figure 3.1 shows that other cities (ignoring Australia for the moment) average substantially higher densities, matched by, on a per capita basis, less road space, fewer

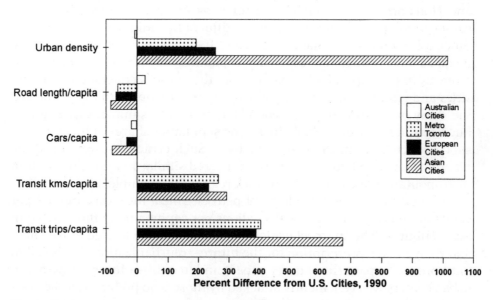

FIGURE 3.1. CROSS-CITY COMPARISONS OF URBAN DENSITIES, AUTOMOBILE AND ROADWAY SUPPLIES, AND TRANSIT USAGE.

cars, and noticeably more transit services and patronage. While high densities, restricted automobility, and high transit ridership appear to be closely linked, the relationship is not one-to-one. Australian cities are less dense than their American counterparts and have more road capacity per capita, yet still average 44 percent more transit trips per capita, mainly due to substantially higher quality transit services (see the Melbourne and Adelaide cases in this book). The biggest differentials are between U.S. cities and the three "wealthy" Asian cities of Hong Kong, Singapore, and Tokyo, which together average 13 percent the car use and eight times the transit use of U.S. cities. Lower per capita incomes explain a relatively small part of these differentials—the per capita gross domestic products of these three Asian cities were only 12 to 26 percent less than those of the thirteen U.S. cities in the sample. More relevant are land constraints, which force efficient use of space throughout urbanized Asia. While U.S. cities have far fewer land constraints, this does not preclude compact patterns of development. As discussed in Chapter 17, Portland, Oregon, has opted to artificially constrain land supplies by drawing an urban growth boundary around the metropolis, in part to support a rapidly expanding regional rail network.

Perhaps no single cross-national study has done more to "stir the pot" about the role of densities in altering travel behavior and inducing transit riding than the 1989 book *Cities and Automobile Dependence*, by Peter Newman and Jeff Kenworthy of Murdoch University in Perth, Australia.[16] Using international comparisons of U.S., European, Asian, and Australian cities, the authors found that sprawling American cities such as Phoenix and Houston average four to five times as much fuel consumption per capita as comparable size and equally affluent Scandinavian cities such as Stockholm and Copenhagen. Since differences in petroleum prices, incomes, and vehicle fuel efficiency explained only about half of the differences in per capita fuel consumption, the authors concluded that densities and land-use patterns explained the rest. Critics ruthlessly attacked the study on methodological grounds, noting, for example, that automobile fleets in many European cities consist of larger shares of fuel-efficient subcompacts than in the United States.[17] Such criticisms overlooked the fact that Newman and Kenworthy uncovered similar relationships within metropolitan areas. For the New York region, for example, Manhattanites were found to average 90 gallons of petrochemical fuel consumption per capita annually, compared to 454 gallons per capita among those living in outer suburbs. The sharpest criticisms, however, were leveled at Newman and Kenworthy's prescription for the future—reurbanization. Their call to halt spread-out patterns of development and to redirect future growth into urban centers was vehemently attacked by those who prefer to let the marketplace dictate how cities grow. Two American commentators, Peter Gordon and Harry Richardson, warned of a veiled attempt to bring about the

"Beijingization" of America's cities (a reference to China-style "command and control" planning).[18] Automobile-led decentralization, Gordon, Richardson, and others[19] argued, was a positive outcome of market forces, allowing residents and companies to co-locate so as to minimize commuting times and distances. That transit ridership has plummeted, open space has dwindled, and Americans have segregated themselves by race and class as a consequence didn't matter, evidently; what did matter was the freedom to choose where to live and how to travel. Subsequent studies have produced often conflicting findings on whether travel times and distances are falling or rising, and whether spread-out growth is, on balance, socially desirable or not.[20] These mixed signals have inevitably confused public policy-making, certainly in the United States.

A 1995 conference on sprawl convened by the Brookings Institution in Washington, D.C., underscored how contentious the debate over auto-oriented growth has become. The president of the National Trust for Historic Preservation, Richard Moe, kicked off the conference with this appeal: "We need clear-headed, far-sighted planning and better development models to replace the random collision of economic forces that has turned much of our landscape into 'God's own junkyard.'" Sociologist Roger Ulrich presented research findings that suggested sprawl is responsible for increasing the stress level of millions of Americans, creating "a serious national health problem." Peter Linneman, director of the Wharton School of Real Estate at the University of Pennsylvania, followed with these words: "So much elitist nonsense has been said that I don't know where to begin. Seeing a 7-11 is not as stressful as wondering if your kids will get shot in a city. Cities are romantic for two types—the wealthy and the tourists. For most it is hell—and today, most people want to get the hell out."[21]

Notwithstanding such controversy, more and more institutions worldwide seem committed to containing urban development. In the 1990 *Green Paper on the Urban Environment*, the European Commission called for future urban growth to be contained within established urban borders. The UK government endorsed "urban containment" in its 1994 *UK Strategy for Sustainable Development* and in a first-ever joint policy of the Department of Transport and the Department of the Environment, PPG13, which called for higher urban densities in general and exceptionally high densities around transit nodes. In the United States, the state of New Jersey recently embraced the "compact city" in its statewide growth management plan; there, studies show that to accommodate 520,000 new residents projected over the next twenty years, the state would save US$1.3 billion in infrastructure construction and US$400 million in annual operating and maintenance costs relative to a "sprawl" scenario extrapolated from past development trends.[22] Since the early 1980s, Florida, Minnesota, Vermont, Oregon, and Maryland have passed growth management laws that attempt to hem in urban sprawl through such initiatives as creating urban growth boundaries, enacting concurrency rules (to pace the rate of land development and infrastructure improvements), and tying state aid to controlling sprawl. In California, even the Bank of America, the state's mightiest financial institution and financier of much of California's postwar expansion, has gone on record as condemning urban sprawl as a threat to future prosperity.[23] In New South Wales, the state's recently released policy, *Cities for the 21st Century*, calls for fundamental changes in Sydney's urban structure from a U.S.-style auto-reliant form to a more neighborhood-focused, walking-friendly, and transit-supportive one.

Public opinion polls and consumer purchasing behavior indicate that, almost universally, people dislike living in higher-density settings. It is not density *per se* that people dislike (at least at modest levels), however, but what often accompanies density—congestion, noise, graffiti, street crimes, overcrowded schools, and so on. The challenge is to create more attractive compact places, partly through high-quality design but also through community rebuilding that focuses on solving deeply rooted social problems as well. If higher densities are to gain acceptance in affluent countries, they will clearly need to be matched by more amenities, open spaces, and quality design. Only recently have designers begun to recognize that actual and perceived densities can vary widely. Studies show effective ways of making higher-density projects seem less dense: extensive landscaping; adding parks, civic spaces, and small consumer services in neighborhoods; varying building heights, materials, and textures to break the visual monotony of structures; detailing rooflines; adding rear-lot, in-law units; and designing mid-rise buildings on podiums with tuck-under, below-grade parking.[24] Many compact European cities—such as Delft in the Netherlands, the Swedish city of Roskilde, and the Italian cities of Bologna and Florence—show that the middle class can be drawn to restored in-city neighborhoods when treated to such niceties as public courtyards, refurbished shopping arcades, museums, open-air markets, and outdoor cafes. Indeed, many of the transit-friendly cities reviewed in this book, such as Curitiba and Zurich, support high levels of transit services in part because compact living is readily accepted in return for high-quality neighborhood amenities.

Land-Use Diversity

It is increasingly recognized that the mixing of land uses can also encourage transit riding. A fine-grained mix of housing, shops, offices, and civic places allows those who take transit to easily connect multiple destinations by foot once they alight the train or bus. My own research of fifty-nine large-scale suburban office developments across the United States found that every 20 percent increase in the share of floor space that is devoted to retail and commercial activities was associated with a 4.5 percent increase in the share of trips by vanpool or transit.[25] Suburban workers felt less compelled to drive their cars to work as long as they could conveniently reach restaurants and shops by foot during the midday. Studies also show that having retail shops near residences can encourage transit commuting. A recent analysis of work trips across eleven large U.S. metropolitan areas showed that having stores between a transit stop and one's residence increased the share of work trips via transit by several percentage points.[26] Conveniently sited retail outlets meant transit riders could do their shopping en route home in the evening, thus linking work and shop trips in a single tour.

In the developed world, the common practice of separating land uses is a legacy of Euclidean zoning principles that, when first introduced some eighty years ago, sought to protect residences from nuisances such as smokestacks and foul odors. In today's world of predominantly clean, nonpolluting businesses and service industries, there is little logic to segregating urban activities. Two U.S. cities, San Diego, California, and Fort Collins, Colorado, have recently replaced traditional zoning with performance-based land development guidance systems wherein any use is allowed on a piece of property as long as it is compatible with neighboring uses. The Houston, Texas, system of restrictive covenants, used in lieu of zoning, has actually produced more land-use combinations in many suburban settings than found in traditionally zoned suburbs of other U.S. cities.

Mixed land uses are important beyond inducing people to ride transit or walk. Importantly, they promote resource efficiency. One example is shared parking. When offices and theaters are side by side, for example, parking spaces used by office workers from 8:00 A.M. to 5:00 P.M., Mondays through Fridays, can be used by movie-goers during evenings and on weekends. Shared parking can shrink the scale of suburban activity centers by as much as 25 percent, which can mean a 25 percent more pedestrian-friendly environment. Also, less road capacity is needed in mixed-use settings. At an executive park with only office space, for instance, most tenants will arrive in the morning and leave in the evening. This means sizing the road infrastructure to handle peak loads. If the same amount of floor space is instead split among offices, shops, and residences, trips could be more evenly balanced throughout the day and week, reducing the amount of peak road capacity needed. Efficiencies can also be enjoyed by transit operators. As shown in Stockholm and Curitiba, mixed land uses can translate into balanced, bidirectional traffic flows. This means buses and trains will be more fully utilized along a route. When residences, shops, and workplaces are poles apart and disconnected, the spectacle of near-empty back-hauling transit vehicles is all too common.

Many of the cases reviewed in this book—such as Copenhagen, Zurich, Munich, and Tokyo, for example—also highlight how important mixed-use environments are to the livability of a city. Having shops, restaurants, newsstands, coffeehouses, and open-air markets near neighborhoods and work centers adds variety and vitality to an area. One only has to go to a campus-style suburban office park in the evening or on a weekend to see how devoid of life these places can be. A mixed-use community, on the other hand, draws people all hours of the day and week. Because of continuous activity and the casual surveillance of many eyes, mixed-use environments feel safer. It is for such reasons that sociologist Jane Jacobs's recipe for a healthy city is "an intricate and close-grained diversity of uses that give each other constant mutual support, both economically and socially."[27]

Urban Design

One can find many examples of compact, mixed-use cities with active street life—Bangkok, Jakarta, and São Paulo come to mind—that are hardly paragons of sustainable development. What is often missing is good-quality urban design. In recent years, a small but influential group of architects, mostly from America, has elevated urban design toward the top of the list of what makes cities functional and livable. The movement that has grabbed the most attention, the "New Urbanism," seeks to transform suburbia into pedestrian-friendly and transit-supportive communities.[28] While embracing compact and mixed-use development, New Urbanists also dwell on the fine details of what makes communities enjoyable—such as gridiron street patterns well suited to walking, prominent civic spaces that draw people together, tree-lined "skinny streets" with curbside parking and back-lot alleys, commercial cores within walking distance of most residents, generous amounts of open space, and pleasant vistas. A central premise of the New Urbanism is that designing communities like those of yesteryear will reduce automobile dependence by making them more pleasant places in which to walk and cycle. New Urbanism designs are not just motivated by transportation objectives, however. At least as important is the desire to build cities and suburbs that are culturally more diverse and instill a sense of community—an attachment to place and a milieu where people come into daily face-to-face contact rather being confined to their cars and homes. Critics charge that such humanist design principles smack of social engineering and physical determinism; of course, one could level similar charges, in America at least, against the federally subsidized interstate highways and home mortgages that nurtured the automobile industry and suburban sprawl in the post–World War II era.

Evidence of the impact of urban design, in and of itself, on travel behavior is scant, in large part because design treatments must accompany compact, mixed-use development for their benefits to be meaningfully felt. The best insights come from matched-pair studies that compare travel among residents of traditional communities that are pedestrian-friendly and transit-supportive in their designs versus the travel habits of those living in auto-oriented suburbs. A recent study compared commuting among two classes of San Francisco Bay Area neighborhoods that were similar in all respects—comparable incomes, geographic locations, highway and transit services, and topographies—except their built environments.[29] "Transit communities" consisted of traditional, neighborhoods that were built prior to World War II, had grid-pattern streets, and evolved around a streetcar line. In contrast, "auto communities" comprised 1960s-style suburban tract developments with curvilinear street patterns and no prior rail services. Whereas 22 percent of residents from transit communities traveled to work by train or bus, transit captured only 3 percent of work trips made by residents of auto communities. Transit communities generated about 70 percent more transit trips and 120 percent more pedestrian-bicycle trips per capita than nearby auto-oriented communities.

A matched-pair study of two European cities—the master-planned British new town, Milton Keynes, and the more traditional Dutch community, Almere—produced comparable findings.[30] While Almere occupies a similar land area, is slated for a similar target population (250,000), and has a similar average household income as Milton Keynes, its physical design is much different. Almere features a fine-grained gridded street pattern, plentiful ped-ways and bike paths, a car-free town center, and an intermingling of co-dependent land uses (e.g., shops, homes, and jobs). Milton Keynes is an unabashedly auto-oriented city laid out on a super-grid of four-lane thoroughfares that tidily separate homes, offices, and shops into different quadrants. In 1991, two-thirds of all out-of-home trips in Milton Keynes were by car, compared to just 42 percent in Almere. Average trip distances in Almere were 25 percent shorter.

Will Land-Use Strategies Work?

Critics oppose land-use initiatives as means of managing travel demand on the grounds that accessibility levels in developed countries are already so high, settlement patterns are so well established, and preferences for low-density living are so firmly ingrained that attempting to shape travel through physical planning is doomed to fail.[31] Despite the encouraging evidence reviewed in this chapter, critics often point to other studies that paint a different picture. One study employing large-scale urban simulation models to examine the effects of raising urban population densities by 2 percent per annum in four world cities (Bilbao, Dortmund, Leeds, and Tokyo) estimated that modal splits, trip length, and carbon-dioxide emissions would be only marginally affected, in the range of 2 to 8 percent.[32]

Certainly land-use initiatives, in and of themselves, are not cure-alls. When combined with other demand-management strategies, such as constraints on parking, they can exert far stronger and more enduring influences. This was the finding from a study of how land-use patterns and transportation demand management (TDM) strategies have worked together in reducing drive-alone commuting to large employment sites in Southern California after the enactment of the Regulation XV trip reduction mandate.[33] Workplaces with on-site convenience stores and ambitious TDM programs promoting ride-sharing, transit riding, and parking management realized 8 to 16 percent greater reductions in drive-alone commuting than did campus-style office parks and other single-use employment sites. Research in New South Wales concluded that TDM policies coupled with jobs-housing balance and mixed-use development will have a greater effect on reducing greenhouse gas emissions than urban consolidation policies that might have to wait a half-century or so for significant payoff.[34]

Of course, financial incentives, such as density bonuses and reduced parking requirements for building near rail stops, would also help leverage transit-supportive development. Feebates might make a lot of sense in some areas—using the income from fees charged to inefficient, auto-oriented development to provide rebates as a reward to efficient, transit-supportive projects. Another novel idea is for banks to grant those living near transit nodes an "efficient location" mortgage for home purchases.[35] If living near rail nodes lowers transportation costs (mainly in the form of a family having to own only one car), then these savings might be subtracted from principal, interest, taxes, and insurance expenses when qualifying applicants for home loans. This acknowledges that reduced transportation outlays free up more money for housing consumption. A recent study found that residents of highly accessible, transit-served neighborhoods in metropolitan Chicago spent about $3,400 less on transportation per year than residents with comparable incomes living in auto-dependent neighborhoods.[36] Under a joint public-private initiative, efficient-location mortgage programs are currently being pilot-tested in Chicago, San Francisco, and Washington, D.C. This concept has been taken to the extreme in Bremen, Germany. There, a new complex of 200 apartments and homes, Bremen-Hollerland, accepts only tenants and homeowners who renounce car ownership.[37] Germany has also advanced the concept of car sharing, wherein neighborhoods pool resources to purchase jointly owned automobiles that are used by members only on an as-needed basis. Called *Stattauto* (German for "car alternative"), the program has so far attracted more than 8,000 members who have collectively reduced the number of cars they own by 75 percent.[38] Car sharing is today spreading rapidly throughout Europe, comprising some 45,000 members who currently share around 2,500 vehicles in 600-plus cities across Germany, Switzerland, Austria, Denmark, the Netherlands, Norway, Sweden, and Great Britain.

Several of the case studies reviewed in this book, such as Singapore, Stockholm, and Curitiba, provide compelling evidence that efficient land-use planning, if carefully integrated with transit services, can yield significant transportation and environmental dividends. It is perhaps no surprise that, given the prevalence of free parking and subsidized auto travel, the transportation payoffs of land-use management in the United States have been less than impressive. America's suboptimal transportation–land use outcomes partly reflect suboptimal pricing. Surely if motoring and vehicle ownership costs were as high in the United States as in Europe and most of Asia, cities would become more compact and activities would be more integrated. Facing substantially higher motoring fees, more and more Americans would be inclined to move closer to their jobs and transit stops in order to economize on travel. Land-use strategies can work if given a fair chance. Indeed, much of the story behind successful transit metropolises has to do with the intelligent linkage of complementary policies, such as controls on parking and motoring surcharges, with the co-development of land use and transit services.

Transit's Impacts on Land Uses and Urban Form

Just as built environments shape transit demand, transit investments shape built environments. Many of the cases reviewed in this book underscore this point—such as Stockholm and Tokyo, where rail lines were built in advance of new communities, and Curitiba and Ottawa, where busways have channeled urbanization along targeted growth axes. This section complements the previous one by investigating the evidence on how transit investments and services shape cities and regions. The lessons outlined are amplified throughout this book's twelve case studies.

Historical case studies provide some of the richest insights into how transit has shaped the structure and character of cities and regions, with most lessons drawn from the United States. Classic works by Sam Bass Warner, Jay Vance, and Robert Fogelson trace how the extensions of electric streetcar lines to suburbia in the early 1900s led to massive decentralization in Boston, the San Francisco Bay Area, and Southern California.[39] Streetcar suburbs not only defined the radial spines of large East Coast and West Coast metropolises, but also allowed for the physical separation of home from work and of social classes.[40]

Urban location theory provides clues as to how transit investments can and should affect urban form. Transit's influences result chiefly from improving regional accessibility for areas served. In theory, new rail lines and bus services should provide locational advantages relative to other sites. It is people's desires for locational advantages in order to minimize travel—and real estate developers' awareness of those desires—that largely give rise to urban form. Barring zoning restrictions or other restraints (e.g., a lackluster regional economy), the competition for locational advantages will drive up land values. As offices and upscale businesses outbid other activities for choice sites near rail nodes, a dynamic set of events is set into motion. Those who sell their products and wares to offices and businesses (or their employees)—photocopy shops, computer software outlets, delis, etc.—try to locate as close to their potential clients as possible. Thus ancillary businesses begin commingling among these high-end activities. Perhaps a half-kilometer out from the rail station, but within a five-minute walk, apartments and duplexes might follow, catering to households that want to live close enough to the rail stop to economize on commuting and perhaps save on the cost of owning a second car. Some might be attracted by the urbanity and amenities offered by a compact, mixed-use, transit-served milieu. The desirability of the station area can be enhanced all the more through urban design—by providing internal bike paths, opening up civic gathering areas, and abundantly landscaping the neighborhood with trees, shrubbery, and playgrounds. And, of course, where residents locate, so will convenience shops, grocery stores, movie theaters, and other activities that cater to them. Eventually, then, a compact, mixed-use community will emerge—a community that features many of the same activities normally scattered throughout suburbia, one whose high-quality environment is reflected by land and rent premiums. Transit is the magnet, the glue, that attracts this efficient cluster of diverse urban activities to a well-defined and internally walkable district.

Of course, this is all theory, and what occurs in practice often departs substantially from textbook economics. Actual experiences suggest that a number of prerequisites—some within and some outside the sphere of policy influence—must often accompany transit investments if compact, mixed-use development is to follow. Transit can be a powerful shaper of cities and regions, though rarely on its own. It needs help from the public sector, and sometimes a stroke of good fortune, to capitalize upon the gift it provides—regional accessibility. Many of the cases highlighted in this book convincingly drive home this point. However, some of the best empirical and statistical evidence comes not from this book's case studies but rather from a series of in-depth investigations carried out over the past three decades, mainly from recent-generation rail investments in Canada and the United States. It is largely because Canada and the United States have been relative latecomers in the development of metropolitan rail systems, at least by European standards, and are wealthy enough countries to have supported comprehensive research investigations, that this is the case.

Several dozen studies have investigated the land-use and urban-form impacts of new-generation rail systems built since the early 1950s in Toronto, Montreal, San Francisco, Atlanta, Washington, D.C., Philadelphia, and other cities, generally reaching similar conclusions: rail investments can induce meaningful changes in urban landscapes, though only when the public sector is committed to closely working with the private sector to bring this about.[41] This section concentrates on just two case experiences—Toronto and the San Francisco Bay Area—to underscore this point. Toronto and the Bay Area make interesting case comparisons because they represent fundamentally different approaches to public-sector involvement at the regional level. They also provide insights into how other factors, such as the fortuitous co-timing of a transit investment with a period of buoyant regional growth, can make a big imprint on urban form.

Toronto: Leveraging Transit Investments Through Pro-active Planning

Toronto, Canada, is often heralded as the best North American example of rail transit's city-shaping abilities. The urban-form impacts of the initial 24.3-kilometer subway system, opened over the 1954 to 1966 period, were immediate and dramatic. Before-and-after aerial photos show station areas dotted by high-rise towers that replaced what a few years earlier were one-to-two-story aging commercial buildings. A frequently cited statistic is that during the subway's first decade of operations, about one-half of high-rise apartments and 90 percent of office construction in the city of Toronto occurred within a five-minute walk of a train station.[42] The subway not only triggered the development of vacant or underused areas (some within a few kilometers of the city center), but it also spurred the recycling of decaying in-town commercial buildings and blighted parcels. One study claimed that the subway brought about a US$12 billion appreciation in citywide land values during its first decade of service.[43]

When Toronto's 7.4-kilometer Yonge Street subway line opened in 1954, extending from the heart of downtown northward to a traditional, though stagnant, commercial center, Eglington, it replaced an aging streetcar line that was heavily patronized and badly in need of upgrading. The system, which since the beginning has been planned, managed, and operated by the Toronto Transit Commission (TTC), grew in stages to the east and west of downtown over the 1954 to 1966 period. Only a few extensions have since been added. One was the opening of a fully automated advanced light rail transit (ALRT) line, called SkyTrain, eastward to the regional town center, Scarborough. Today, the TTC system, shown in

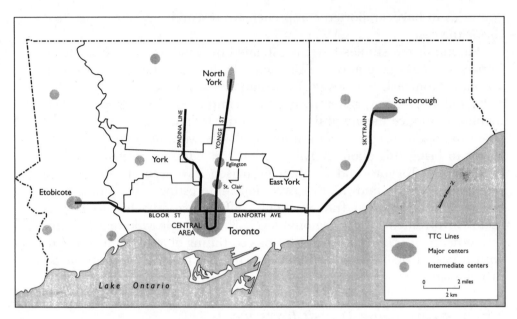

MAP 3.1. METROPOLITAN TORONTO AND ITS TTC HEAVY RAIL SERVICES, 1995.

Map 3.1, stretches some 57 kilometers in length, served by sixty stations. The outer boundary of Map 3.1 represents what historically has been called metropolitan Toronto—the 630-square-kilometer area that is home to some 2.39 million residents (that encompasses the cities of Toronto, Etobicoke, North York, Scarborough, York, and East York). Feeding into mainline rail stations are among the richest mixes of surface transit connections found anywhere, comprising trolley buses, diesel buses, historic trams, and modern mixed-traffic light rail vehicles. Key to service integration has been the close coordination of schedules across modes and a free transfer policy. At some stations, trams and trolley buses penetrate directly into enclosed areas, enabling transferring patrons to step directly onto subway concourses without passing through turnstiles, what locals call "free body" transfers.

One of the greatest accomplishments of the TTC system has been in strengthening the central business district (CBD)—partly a consequence of the radially oriented subway system, but mainly a result of strategic regional land-use planning. (Downtown Toronto's inventory of office space tripled from 1.87 million square meters in 1960 to 5.76 million square meters in 1985). A strong CBD has in turn spawned high ridership levels—about 65 percent of all trips entering the CBD and historically well over 200 transit trips per capita per year, higher than in any U.S. metropolitan area, including greater New York. Indeed, radial rail connections and CBD dominance have been co-dependent. Today, an estimated 45 percent of regional office employment is downtown (officially called the Central Area), the largest share in North America.[44] As everywhere else, however, this share has been steadily eroding. Toronto's decades-old subway system has been unable to stem the tide of job decentralization. Continuing expansion of the provincially operated regional commuter rail system, GO Transit, has helped spur growth beyond the traditional metropolitan boundaries. Of course, were it not for the TTC system, far more jobs would have migrated out of downtown Toronto, probably shrinking the CBD's share of regional jobs closer to the 10 to 20 percent of market shares found in most U.S. metropolises.

While many jobs exiting the CBD have ended up in auto-oriented, suburban offices, a considerable share—much larger than found in U.S. rail cities—have ended up in rail-served subcenters. This is largely a product of metropolitan Toronto's strong tradition of regional governance. Up until 1998, the Metropolitan Corporation, or Metro for short, was responsible for coordinating the planning and the delivery of government services across the six municipalities shown in Map 3.1. On January 1, 1998, Metro was abolished and its six former municipalities were combined to form the newly expanded city of Toronto. This consolidation has essentially streamlined planning and decision making by replacing seven separate council bodies (the six municipalities plus Metro) with a single, enlarged city council. The boundaries, and jurisdiction over transportation and land-use issues, of the city of Toronto today correspond to the former Metro boundaries shown in Map 3.1.

Created in 1953 just prior to the opening of the Youge Street subway, Metro's chief responsibility was to orchestrate regional growth, in particular the co-development of TTC services and land-uses, a role now performed by the planning office of the newly expanded city of Toronto. In 1980, Metro's plan endorsed a hierarchical pattern of regional subcentering. Downtown Toronto was to be complemented by two transit-served regional subcenters, Scarborough and North York (later expanded to three, including Etobicoke), and four tertiary centers. With financial backing from the Ontario government, Scarborough was designated as the region's flagship of contemporary transit-oriented design.[45] A mix of office, retail, institutional, and residential activities have concentrated around the Scarborough Town Centre and the SkyTrain station since 1980. Over time, however, local planners seem resigned to the fact that the presence of a mega–shopping mall enveloped by a sea of asphalt parking, just north of the rail station, preestablished Scarborough's character as a largely auto-oriented place. Rail transit and pro-active planning have proven incapable of undoing this. More successful has been the region's other subcenter, North York, which today features a more human-scale, less auto-oriented shopping center integrated into the subway station and an impressive array of surrounding high-rise offices and apartment towers, all flanking a central open civic space. Today, some 35 percent of workers heading to central North York and 22 percent of those going to the Scarborough Town Centre take transit, respectable shares by any standard.[46]

Why has Toronto been so successful in making the transit–land use nexus work? The short answer is pro-active and strategic planning, though in reality other factors have contributed importantly as well. The ingredients to Toronto's success can be divided into exogenous and endogenous factors—respectively, those that have been outside versus inside the sphere of public policy influence.

Exogenous Factors

Two fortuitous events worked in Toronto's favor. One was good timing. The subway system was built and opened during a period of rapid growth. Between 1951 and 1971, metropolitan Toronto was one of the fastest-growing regions in North America, adding an average of 45,000 new residents each year.[47] Thus, rail transit was in an unusually good position to channel where this growth occurred.

The second favorable circumstance was the backgrounds of the very people who were arriving. Many were immigrants from Europe who took up Canadian citizenship following World War II, an echo of the wave of foreign immigrants who had come to America's shores decades earlier. Many came from places with excellent transit services and brought a heritage of transit-oriented city living with them. They supported mass transit at the fare box and the ballot box. Moreover, most immigrants were provided public housing, which was consciously located away from downtown but close to suburban rail stations. This benefited the new residents by keeping their housing and travel expenses low and, of course, aided TTC by guaranteeing plentiful transit customers.

Endogenous Factors

While good fortune played a role in Toronto's successes, more important have been the effects of deliberate, carefully reasoned public policies—some introduced at the federal level, though mainly regionally initiated. Four key factors are summarized below.

Tax laws. Toronto's high proportion of residents living in apartments and multifamily housing is partly a product of federal tax laws. In Canada, there is less of an incentive to own a single-family home than in the United States because mortgage interest payments and property taxes are nondeductible from income taxes. Partly as a consequence, metropolitan Toronto's population density is three times higher than that of the ten largest U.S. metropolitan areas.[48]

Absence of a federal freeway program. In contrast to the United States, Canada has no federal ministry in charge of promoting or building highways, be they transnational, intercity, or intrametropolitan. There is no equivalent to America's Federal Highway Administration, the builder of the world's largest public-works project, the U.S. interstate highway system. (While sold to Congress during the Eisenhower administration mainly as a carrier of interstate commerce and militia in the event of war, the vast majority of vehicle kilometers logged on America's interstate highways are on the 4 percent of total linear kilometers that are within metropolitan areas; America's interstate system has functioned more as a conduit for suburban living than as a passageway for hauling goods, commerce, or battalions.) The absence of a federal road builder meant there was no post–World War II freeway construction program during metropolitan Toronto's fast-growing 1950s and 1960s.

Freeway revolts and the power of personalities. While Canada's federal government has refrained from building freeways, this has not held back provincial governments from assuming this role. One of the first organized grassroots freeway revolts anywhere was in reaction to an Ontario-sponsored inner-city freeway proposal. Little did backers know that two of the most respected and influential urban sociologists of the time, Jane Jacobs and Hans Blumenfeld, lived in their own backyard. In the early 1970s, when construction of the proposed Spadina Expressway was moving forward, Jane Jacobs was a recent transplant from New York City, drawn by Toronto's vibrance and strong tradition of in-city living. Hans Blumenfeld, who had spent considerable time in Europe, was a firm supporter of the TTC and arch-enemy of the car culture. Jacobs and Blumenfeld took on leadership roles in organizing opposition to the planned expressway, passionately arguing that Toronto was poised to commit the sins of many American cities by uprooting established neighborhoods collaring the CBD so that suburbanites could more swiftly drive their cars. The fact that some of Toronto's nicest and priciest residential neighborhoods ring the CBD only added fuel to the controversy. The freeway opposition eventually won, prompting Metro Toronto to add a new subway, the Spadina line, in its place. As a result of the anti-freeway movement and federal abstinence from road building, greater Toronto and, indeed, all Canadian urbanized areas today have far fewer lane kilometers of freeway per capita than their U.S. counterparts.

Pro-active, coordinated land-use planning and management. Early on, Toronto's metropolitan government took a pro-active stance in coordinating the development of regional rail services and land-use patterns. While zoning has always been controlled by municipalities, the metro government had, at least in theory, veto powers over local land-use decisions that were inconsistent with the official regional plan. Rarely were override authorities exercised, in large part because of the historically strong level of local commitment to strengthening regional rail transit services. The overriding principle of integrated rail and urban development has always been to promote, and indeed reward, compact growth using the powers vested in local governments. In Toronto, parcels near rail stops are treated as an invaluable resource, not to be idly wasted as parking spots for cars or left solely to the dictates of speculative real-estate interests. The following four steps have been taken to maximize the development potential around TTC stations.[49]

- Density bonuses. Early on, the city of Toronto upzoned land around most stations as inducement to high-rise development, allowing plot ratios (building area divided by land area) as high as 15:1. The highest bonuses were granted to parcels within 250 meters of a station portal, allowing densities to taper, like a wedding-cake pattern, with distance from stations. Performance zoning was also introduced, granting even higher bonuses for commercial structures that included upper-level housing.

- Park-and-ride constraints. The predominant land use around many suburban rail stations in America is parking lots. Not in Toronto. Instead, mid- and high-rise housing and commercial centers huddle around most stops. Toronto has restricted parking mainly to terminal stations—the stations that serve a potentially large catchment of suburban and exurban residents commuting to the city. As a result, Toronto averages far higher shares of walk-and-ride, bus-and-ride, and bike-and-ride customers at its suburban stations than found in U.S. rail cities.[50] Parking supplies are also capped for projects near rail stops. Around the North York station, parking is limited to one space per three workers.

- Transferable development rights. Toronto was one of the first cities to aggressively use transferable development rights, or TDR, to intensify development around stations. With TDR, landowners away from stations can sell their development rights to those planning high-rise projects near stations. In addition to targeting growth around rail stops, TDR provides the side benefit of promoting historical preservation by allowing owners of heritage buildings to sell the air rights to others.

- Supplemental land acquisitions. Compared to the United States, Canadian constitutional law permits local governments to be entrepreneurial in leveraging large-scale public-works projects. Canadian cities are granted considerable latitude in exercising their police powers to seize private properties, with due compensation, when doing so is in the broader public interest. During the mid-1950s, the city of Toronto obtained twenty-two city blocks over and beyond what was necessary to build the Yonge Street subway line. Some parcels were sold to selected developers for large-scale commercial projects (which attracted high-quality development since land had already been assembled). Most publicly acquired properties, however, were leased according to terms that were at least as favorable to public interests as private ones. By controlling much of the land around stations, the city could target activities with the highest potential to generate ridership to station areas, while also recapturing much of the value added by the subway investment—both through lease revenues and property tax income. In contrast, U.S. transit agencies and local governments are constitutionally prohibited from acquiring supplemental land, except in unusual cases where odd-shaped remnant parcels are left after project construction.[51]

Postscript

The story of Toronto is largely the story of successes of a quarter-century and more ago. Since the mid-1970s, regional development patterns have mimicked those of many American metropolises. The emergence of American-style suburbs outside compact, transit-oriented Toronto has produced what longtime Toronto transit planner Juri Pill describes as "Vienna surrounded by Phoenix."[52] Three-quarters of regional population growth from 1991 to 1996 occurred in urbanizing areas surrounding the boundaries of former Metro Toronto shown in Map 3.1. Suburban sprawl has translated into a declining share of regional trips by transit, down from more than 200 annual transit trips per capita in 1980 to about 135 today, comparable to the bus-only Ottawa region. While one in four trips in the newly expanded city of Toronto is by transit, in the surrounding suburbs the shares are 7 to 11 percent. Interestingly, Toronto's declining transit market share has sparked a spirited debate among Australian planners, who have long held Toronto as a role model of sustainable growth, as to whether Sydney, Melbourne, and Perth should continue to invest in rail transit.[53]

Perhaps most worrisome has been the unraveling of Toronto's regional system of governance, the very foundation upon which past successes at integrating transit and urban development were built. Greater Toronto has grown well beyond the boundaries of the former Metro, now the city of Toronto. In 1988, Metro Toronto's clout was undercut by the formation of a provincial entity, the Office of Greater Toronto Area (OGTA), that coordinates activities across six regions—making Metro (now the city of Toronto) one of many actors in a vastly expanding region whose power base continues to gravitate outward.[54] Shifting OGTA priorities, combined with hard economic times, have halted several planned TTC rail extensions in recent years.[55]

Notwithstanding these and other problems, Toronto remains one of the most desirable places in the world to live and do business. Despite rapid suburbanization, Toronto still has one of the most viable, liveliest downtowns of any North American city. A recent campaign to build housing in the central core for downtown workers has been hugely successful.[56] Planners also hold high hopes for the city's Main Streets program—an all-out effort to jump-start private reinvestment in traditional tram-served commercial corridors. Main streets are being revitalized by upgrading the physical armatures of active commercial streets, promoting vertical land-use mixing and upper-level loft space, and providing tax incentives for refurbishing older commercial buildings.

The San Francisco Bay Area: BART System

In contrast to metropolitan Toronto, growth in the San Francisco Bay Area following the 1973 initiation of regional rail services—the Bay Area Rapid Transit (BART) system—has been shaped almost exclusively by free-market forces. The absence of a regional planning counterpart to Toronto's Metro has left station-area development decisions largely in the hands of private real-estate interests and the whims of municipal zoning. Thus, BART's impacts on land use and urban form provide an interesting contrast to TTC's.

When BART was conceived in the early 1950s, planners hoped the system would channel growth along radial corridors, leading to a star-shaped multicentered metropolitan form—in the words of the 1956 *Regional Rapid Transit* plan, "something between the tightly nucleated clusters which form the typical metropolitan areas of the East Coast and vast low-density sprawl of the West Coast's Los Angeles."[57] Proponents felt that BART would help differentiate the Bay Area from Los Angeles, its freeway-oriented sibling to the south, and help catapult San Francisco into the role of, again in the words of the 1956 plan, "the Manhattan of the West."

I recently led a study that focused on the impact of BART on land use and urban form from 1973 to 1993—that is, during its first twenty years of existence. Map 3.2 shows the alignment of the 116-kilometer, 34-station BART system as it existed after twenty years of operations. The key findings of the "BART @ 20" study are summarized below.[58]

Strengthening the Core

The one impact of BART that most closely parallels Toronto's experiences has been the preservation of the CBD as the region's primary employment hub (i.e., retaining its primacy). During BART's first twenty years, some 2.6 million square meters of office floorspace was added within a half-kilometer of downtown BART stations. This represented more than three-

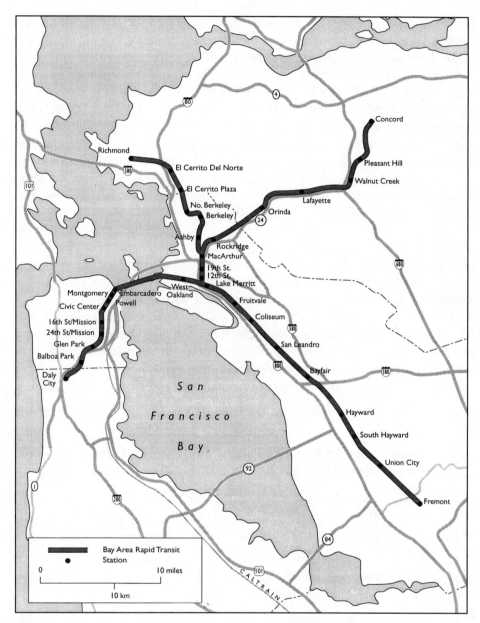

MAP 3.2. SAN FRANCISCO BAY AREA RAPID TRANSIT (BART) SYSTEM, 1995.

quarters of all office additions within a half-kilometer radius of all BART stations over the 1973 to 1993 period. The use of tax increment financing (wherein all proceeds from the tax base are returned to the station areas to pay for other public improvements, such as landscaping and civic plazas) was instrumental in spurring downtown office development. BART's role in maintaining downtown San Francisco's primacy is hinted at by comparing employment trends with California's other megame- tropolis, greater Los Angeles, which had no urban rail system in 1990. From 1980 to 1990, the share of regional jobs in San Francisco's CBD fell from 17.4 percent to 16.3 percent, a 1.1 percentage point drop. Over the same period, downtown Los Angeles's share of Southern California jobs fell from 7.6 percent to 5.7 percent, a 1.9 percentage point decline. However, since Los Angeles's percentage base was much lower, the relative loss of regional employment in downtown Los Angeles has been far more substantial. The absence of a regional radially designed rail system, like BART, likely had something to do with this.

Decentralization

Outside downtown San Francisco, BART has generally been a stronger force toward decentralization than concentration. Other than a handful of stations in the East Bay where development was aggressively sought, lit- tle new clustering has occurred along BART's suburban alignments. For the most part, suburban development has turned its back on BART, opt- ing for freeway-served corridors instead. This is revealed by Table 3.1, which compares population and employment growth rates between 1970 and 1990 for subareas, or superdistricts,[59] that contain BART stations

TABLE 3.1. COMPARISON OF 1970–1990 POPULATION AND EMPLOYMENT GROWTH IN BART-SERVED AND NON-BART SUPERDISTRICTS, BY THREE COUNTIES AND TOTAL SERVICE DISTRICT

County	Population		Employment		% Change, 1970 to 1990	
Superdistrict	1970	1990	1970	1990	Population	Employment
San Francisco						
BART (2)	387,180	402,538	357,761	442,370	4.0	23.6
Non-BART (2)	327,729	321,421	94,436	113,037	−1.3	19.7
Alameda						
BART (3)	990,497	1,143,347	393,755	532,872	15.4	35.3
Non-BART (1)	77,637	135,835	19,908	71,674	75.0	260.7
Contra Costa						
BART (4)	410,288	547,470	120,406	236,174	33.4	96.1
Non-BART (2)	146,301	256,259	27,817	77,390	75.2	178.2
Three-County Total						
BART (9)	1,787,965	2,093,355	871,922	1,211,416	17.1	38.9
Non-BART (25)	551,667	713,515	142,161	262,101	29.3	84.4

Note: Values in brackets represent the number of superdistricts in each group.

versus those that do not. The table presents results for the three BART-served counties—San Francisco, Alameda, and Contra Costa—as well as the BART service district as a whole. Over the 1970 to 1990 period, population grew 29.3 percent in the twenty-five Bay Area superdistricts not served by BART compared to 17.1 percent in the nine BART-served superdistricts. Relative employment gains in non-BART superdistricts were even greater than population gains. The largest differentials were between the outer East Bay districts without BART and the inner East Bay districts with BART services. BART's modest role in guiding suburban growth is even more strongly underscored by floor-space statistics. Of the 5.6 million square meters of office inventory added to Alameda and Contra Costa Counties from 1975 to 1992, 37 percent was within a half-mile of freeway interchanges compared to 17 percent within a half-mile of BART stations. Parcels near freeway interchanges, not BART stations, were the preferred choice of new businesses locating in the East Bay suburbs.

Some Subcentering Successes

In a few instances where pro-active municipal planning occurred, growth has clustered around suburban BART stations, comparable to Toronto's experiences. The two notable success stories are Walnut Creek and Pleasant Hill. Walnut Creek, on the Concord line some 35 kilometers east of downtown San Francisco, has emerged as one of the Bay Area's premier edge cities. Some half a million square meters of modern, class-A office space have been added within a 1-kilometer ring of the Walnut Creek station since BART's opening, more than any nondowntown station. The underwriting of land assemblage costs and the targeting of supportive infrastructure improvements (e.g., new sidewalks and better road access to a nearby freeway) helped to jump-start private office investments. While these office additions would have occurred in the East Bay suburbs without BART, they likely would have been in the form of executive parks and stand-alone structures accessible only by car.

The Pleasant Hill BART station area is one of the best examples of suburban transit-oriented development in the United States. Between 1988 and 1995, more than 2,000 housing units and 200,000 square meters of prime office and commercial space were built within a half-kilometer of the Pleasant Hill station (located one station out from Walnut Creek). Prior to BART the area was characterized by a declining stock of housing and and transitional, low-end commercial establishments. Although average densities of recently built apartments are about 40 dwelling units per net residential acre, very high by suburban U.S. standards, the projects nonetheless cater to a fairly upscale market, with most featuring on-site swimming pools, spas, and recreational facilities. An estimated one-half of employed residents living near the Pleasant

Hill station work in downtown San Francisco or Oakland, compared to a citywide average of just 10 percent. Many consciously located near BART to economize on commuting—surveys show that 46 percent take BART to work, compared to 16 percent of Pleasant Hill's employed residents who live away from the station. The strong demand for station-area living has also produced a monthly apartment rent premium of about 15 percent.

Pleasant Hill's success in attracting housing and office development can be credited to local officials borrowing a chapter from cities like Toronto in leveraging the benefits provided by rail transit. In the early 1980s, a specific plan was crafted that served as a blueprint for attracting compact, mixed-use growth around the station. No other Bay Area suburban community committed itself to transit-oriented development like Pleasant Hill. In fact, many (e.g., Orinda and Lafayette) downzoned land around stations and openly welcomed park-and-ride lots in hopes of retaining their sprawling suburban character. Also vital to Pleasant Hill's turnaround was the good fortune of there being a pro-active local redevelopment authority whose staff aggressively sought to implement the specific plan—by assembling irregular parcels into developable tracts, seeking out private co-ventures, and using tax increment and special assessment financing to install some $30 million in complementary infrastructure improvements, including the undergrounding of utility lines. And then there was the important role of a local elected official—Pleasant Hill's version of Jane Jacobs—who became the project's political champion, working tirelessly to shepherd the idea of a transit village through a minefield of local public hearings and environmental reviews. Today, efforts are under way to add a massive entertainment complex next to the Pleasant Hill station on what is currently BART surface parking. This initiative builds upon Toronto's experiences—using publicly owned land, in Pleasant Hill's case, a parking lot, to lure transit-supportive development and the tax proceeds it generates. Unable to acquire extra land to leverage private development and recapture value, as Toronto did, BART officials are turning to one of their greatest assets—surface parking adjacent to stations—in a roundabout effort to produce similar results.

Inner-City Redevelopment

BART's experiences with spurring the redevelopment of declining central-city districts has been uneven. Its successes and failures reveal the depth of public commitment that is often required and the sober realities of how hard it is to entice private capital into risky settings. Downtown Oakland has largely been a success, mainly due to the siting of institutional and public-sector office development, 180,000 square meters in all, around parcels surrounding its central BART station. Private investors are now beginning to follow suit, drawn by Oakland's attractive rents, pro-development policies, and good transportation services. The city has leveraged much of the station-area development through a combination of assistance with land assemblage, tax increment financing of public infrastructure, securing federal urban renewal grants, providing government-backed loans, and equity participation (including majority ownership of a downtown convention hotel).

Elsewhere, however, little redevelopment has occurred following the opening of an in-city BART station. One of the greatest disappointments has been with inactivity around the Richmond station. When BART arrived, city officials had high hopes it would trigger a building boom because of the area's good access and large inventory of vacant land, but little new growth has occurred around the Richmond station over the past quarter-century, despite gallant efforts by the city's redevelopment authority to coax new investment through various incentive programs. A sagging local economy, urban blight, and lingering crime problems have hampered redevelopment. In Richmond and elsewhere, the mere presence of BART proved incapable of turning around depressed neighborhoods or overcoming the negative images of these places.

Drawing Lessons from Toronto, San Francisco, and Elsewhere

Experiences in metropolitan Toronto, San Francisco, and other North American locations impart important lessons about the likely impacts of transit investments on urban form. While not reviewed in this chapter, studies of light rail and busway investments generally reinforce those findings. Cumulative lessons, summarized in the list below, are further amplified in comprehensive literature reviews by Robert Knight and Lisa Trygg, Eric Kelly, Herman Huang, myself, and others.[60]

- *Transit redistributes rather than creates growth.* Transit influences the distribution, not the amount, of development within a region. It channels where already committed growth occurs, often shifting it from one radial corridor (i.e., a highway-oriented one) to another radial corridor (i.e., a rail-served one).

- *A prerequisite is a healthy regional economy.* If transit is to have much impact, there needs to be growth to channel. Regardless of how much pro-active planning occurs or public-sector money is spent, transit will exert negligible land-use impacts in areas with weak regional economies. The meager land-use changes following light rail investments in U.S. Rust Belt cities such as Buffalo are a case in point.

- *Land-use impacts are greatest when transit investments occur just prior to an upswing in regional growth.* Experiences tell us that the timing of transit investments matters an awful lot. Noted urban sociologist Homer Hoyt observed more than a half century ago that urban form is largely a product of the dominant transportation technology during a city's prevailing period of growth.[61] This tenet is certainly borne out by the experiences of metropolitan Toronto and San Francisco. As illustrated in Figure 3.2, the growth of cities usually follows an attenuated S-shaped curve. Toronto timed its opening of the TTC subway perfectly. In the case of BART, new rail services were generally "too little, too late" to exert a big influence on urban form. With most of the region's freeway system and settlement pattern already in place, BART's incremental additions to regional accessibility were too small to substantially sway development decisions. The lesson: the biggest potential payoffs from proactive planning around transit stations in coming years will be in the fastest growing areas—in general, the Jakartas, Bangkoks, and Shanghais of the world, cities that are now implementing or seriously contemplating major new regional transit investments.

• *Radial rail systems can strengthen downtown cores.* Experiences in Toronto and San Francisco, as well as in other North American cities such as Washington, D.C., and Baltimore, underscore this

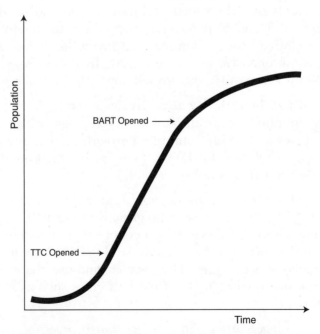

FIGURE 3.2. REGIONAL GROWTH AND THE TIMING OF TRANSIT INVESTMENTS.

point. While regional shares of jobs and retailing that are down-town often still fall in the wake of new rail investments, they would have fallen a lot further were it not for CBD-focused transit services.

- *Regional transit investments generally reinforce decentralization trends.* By improving accessibility to different corners of a region, extensive rail and busway networks, like highways, generally encourage suburbanization, to some degree. While growth might be funneled in a particular direction as a result of new transit services, more often than not this direction will be outward.

- *Pro-active planning is necessary if decentralized growth is to take the form of subcenters.* Whether decentralized growth takes a multicen-tered form rests largely with the degree of public commitment to strategic station-area planning, carried out on a regional scale. Experiences in Toronto, and to a lesser extent in the Bay Area, show that an aggressive stand to leverage the benefits of rail services can lead to a more concentrated form of decentralized growth. As illus-trated in Figure 3.3, under the right conditions and given enough

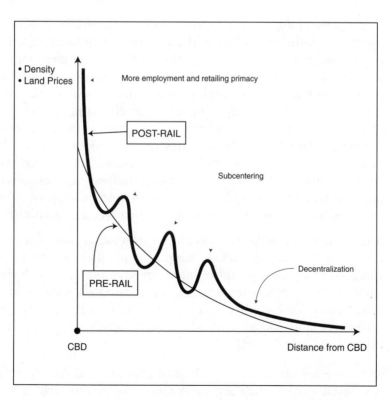

FIGURE 3.3. LIKELY OUTCOMES WHEN TRANSIT INVESTMENTS ARE PRO-ACTIVELY LEVERAGED.

public-resource commitments, transit can not only strengthen the core, but also induce selected subcentering. While transit contributes to outward growth, it can help to more efficiently organize whatever development occurs within traditional built-up areas. Under the best of conditions, then, transit can be counted on to produce more primacy, subcentering, and fringe-area growth.

- *Transit can spur central-city redevelopment under the right conditions.* When public entities are willing to absorb some of the risks inherent in redeveloping depressed neighborhoods, transit investments can help attract private capital and breathe new life into struggling areas. There must be an unwavering commitment to underwrite redevelopment costs and provide needed financial incentives. The quid pro quo is that sharing in upstream risks can mean the public sector eventually shares in the downstream rewards of urban renewal. Experiences suggest that even with such incentives, it is an uphill struggle in turning around severely depressed districts, regardless of transit's presence. More realistically, transit can reinvigorate once vibrant older commercial centers and accelerate the pace of land-use conversion in marginal, working-class districts suffering from slow commercial encroachment.

- *Other pro-development measures must accompany transit investments.* In addition to financial incentives, a number of other preconditions must usually exist if transit is to exert meaningful land-use impacts. Foremost among these are: permissive and incentive zoning, such as density bonuses; the availability of nearby vacant or easy-to-assemble and developable parcels; support for land-use changes among local residents; a hospitable physical setting (in terms of aesthetics, ease of pedestrian circulation, and a healthy neighborhood image); complementary public improvements (such as upgrading sidewalks and burying utilities); and an absence of physical constraints (e.g., preemption of land development by park-and-ride lots or the siting of a station in a freeway median).

- *Auto equalizers help in inducing station-area land-use changes.* Reducing mandatory parking supplies and eliminating free parking can further encourage station-area development, particularly in the suburbs. Such measures are more appropriately viewed as "equalizers" than "disincentives" since they seek to remove the built-in incentives and hidden subsidies that encourage people to drive rather than take transit.

While these lessons are drawn from Canadian and American experiences, as noted earlier, they are even more poignantly driven home by experiences in Europe, Asia, and other parts of the world. Indeed, great

transit metropolises are places where the "fit" between transit and settlements is like a hand in a glove. Many of this book's cases are places where
compact, mixed-use development has been the lifeblood of high-quality
transit. As also noted, however, some cases represent the polar opposite of
Toronto-style compact growth. These are the places where the
transit–land use "fit" has been a product of designing flexible forms of
transit well suited to spread-out suburban landscapes. In our quest to
understand what it takes to create a successful transit metropolis, let us
turn to the lessons of the following twelve case-study chapters, in Parts
Two through Five of this book.

NOTES

1. D. Shoup, An Opportunity to Reduce Minimum Parking Requirements,
    Journal of the American Planning Association, vol. 61, no. 1, 1995, pp. 14–28.

2. M. Wachs, Learning from Los Angeles: Transport, Urban Form, and Air
    Quality, *Transportation*, vol. 20, no. 14, 1993, pp. 329–359.

3. D. Shoup, The High Cost of Free Parking, *Access*, no. 10, 1997, pp. 2–9.

4. *Ibid.*

5. P. Newman, Reducing Automobile Dependence, *Environment and Urbaniza-
    tion*, vol. 8, no. 1, 1996, pp. 67–92.

6. R. Hartley, Is Oxygen Enough? *Access*, no. 7, 1995, pp. 27–31.

7. Urban Mobility Corporation, High Occupancy Toll (HOT) Lanes Revisited.
    Innovation Briefs, vol. 8, no. 3, 1997, pp. 1–2; L. Howe, Orange County's 91
    Express Lanes, *Tech Transfer*, no. 59, 1997, pp. 1–3.

8. Quoted in D. Van Hattum, Lane Fee Could Fund Better Public Transit, *Star
    Tribune*, Minneapolis, November 29, 1997, Section B, p. 1.

9. E. Von Weisäcker, A. Lovins, and L. Lovins, *Factor Four: Doubling Wealth,
    Halving Resource Use* (London: Earthscan Publications, 1997).

10. P. Mokhtarian and I. Salomon, Modeling the Desire to Telecommute: The
    Importance of Attitudinal Factors in Behavioral Models, *Transportation
    Research A*, vol. 31, no. 1, 1997, pp. 35–50.

11. R. Mitchell and C. Rapkin, *Urban Traffic: A Function of Land Use* (New York:
    Columbia University Press, 1954); H. Levinson and F. Wynne, Effects of Den-
    sity on Urban Transportation Requirements, *Highway Research Record*, vol.
    2, 1963, pp. 38–64; B. Pushkarev and J. Zupan, *Public Transportation and
    Land Use Policy* (Bloomington: Indiana University Press, 1977); Parsons
    Brinckerhoff Quade & Douglas, Inc., R. Cervero, Howard/Stein-Hudson
    Associations, and J. Zupan, *Regional Transit Corridors: The Land Use Con-
    nection* (Washington, DC: National Research Council, Transportation
    Research Board, 1996).

12. J. Holtzclaw, *Residential Patterns and Transit, Auto Dependence, and Costs*
    (San Francisco: Natural Resources Defense Council, 1994); L. Frank and G.
    Pivo, The Impacts of Mixed Use and Density on the Utilization of Three

Modes of Travel: The Single Occupant Vehicle, Transit, and Walking, *Transportation Research Record* vol. 1466, 1994, pp. 44–52; R. Cervero, *Ridership Impacts of Transit-Focused Development in California*, monograph 45 (Berkeley: Institute of Urban and Regional Development, University of California, 1993).

13.   W. Smith, Mass Transit for High-Rise, High-Density Living, *Journal of Transportation Engineering*, vol. 110, no. 6, 1984, pp. 521–535.

14.   J. Pucher, Urban Travel Behavior As the Outcome of Public Policy, *Journal of the American Planning Association*, vol. 54, no. 3, 1988, pp. 509–520.

15.   These data were drawn from the study: J. Kenworthy, F. Laube, P. Newman, and P. Barter. *Indicators of Transport Efficiency in 37 Global Cities*, report for the World Bank (Perth: Institute for Science and Technology Policy, Murdoch University, 1997). The sample of thirty-seven global cities includes the following: United States—Houston, Phoenix, Detroit, Denver, Los Angeles, San Francisco, Boston, Washington, D.C., Chicago, New York, Portland, Sacramento, and San Diego; Australia—Perth, Brisbane, Melbourne, Adelaide, Sydney, and Canberra; Canada—metropolitan Toronto; Europe—Hamburg, Frankfurt, Zurich, Stockholm, Brussels, Paris, London, Munich, Copenhagen, Vienna, and Amsterdam; Asia—Singapore, Tokyo, and Hong Kong. The statistics presented in Figure 3.1 exclude the following cases in the calculations: road length per capita excludes data from Denver, Washington, D.C., New York, Portland, Sacramento, Melbourne, Stockholm, Copenhagen, and Amsterdam; cars per capita excludes data from Washington, D.C., and Amsterdam.

16.   P. Newman and J. Kenworthy, *Cities and Automobile Dependence: An International Sourcebook* (Aldershot, England: Gower, 1989).

17.   P. Gordon and H. Richardson, Gasoline Consumption and Cities: A Reply, *Journal of the American Planning Association*, vol. 55, no. 3, 1989, pp. 342–345; J. Gomez-Ibañez, A Global View of Automobile Dependence, *Journal of the American Planning Association*, vol. 57, no. 3, 1991, pp. 376–379.

18.   Gordon and Richardson, *ibid.*, p. 345.

19.   While this debate has been waged largely among American academics, similar debates have surfaced elsewhere. From a simulation of different development scenarios in Great Britain, Michael Breheny concluded that compact growth would reduce travel and energy consumption by a mere 2.5 percent relative to spread-out development. See: M. Breheny, *Sustainable Development and Urban Form* (London: Pion, 1992); M. Breheny, Centrists, Decentrists and Compromisers: Views on the Future of Urban Form, *The Compact City: A Sustainable Urban Form?* M. Jenks, E. Burton, and K. Williams, eds. (London: E & FN Spon, 1996, pp. 13–35).

20.   Conflicting evidence on travel trends in American cities can be found in: P. Gordon, H. Richardson, and M. Jun, The Commuting Paradox: Evidence from the Top Twenty, *Journal of the American Planning Association*, vol. 57, no. 4, 1991, pp. 416–420; M. Rosetti and B. Eversole, *Journey to Work Trends in the United States and Its Major Metropolitan Areas* (Cambridge, MA: John A. Volpe National Transportation Systems Center, 1993). The debate over the

broader social costs of auto-oriented development has evolved from the original *Costs of Sprawl* study, conducted by the Real Estate Research Corporation in 1974. See: Real Estate Research Corporation, *The Costs of Sprawl, Detailed Cost Analysis* (Washington, DC: U.S. Government Printing Office, 1974). Using simulations, this study concluded that a well-designed, high-density community would require up to 44 percent less energy, generate 45 percent less air pollution, and cost 44 percent less for public and private capital infrastructure than a typical suburban community. Parallel studies faulted sprawl for excessively consuming farmland and forestry resources, imposing hardships on the poor and others without access to an automobile, and accentuating racial, ethnic, and class segregation. See: U.S. Department of Agriculture, *Urbanization of Land in the Northeastern United States*, Economic Research Service Publication 485 (Washington, DC: U.S. Department of Agriculture, 1971); Regional Plan Association and Resources for the Future, *Regional Energy Consumption* (New York: Regional Plan Association, 1974); and J. Kain, Housing Segregation, Negro Employment, and Metropolitan Decentralization, *Quarterly Journal of Economics*, vol. 82, 1972, pp. 175–197. Soon after the release of *The Costs of Sprawl*, a cadre of critics who, for the most part, embrace market-dominated patterns of development, began attacking the study and its conclusions. Critics charged the study's methods for measuring energy impacts were flawed (e.g., for failing to control for differences in housing sizes between compact and low-density communities), that compact development posed more serious health problems associated with stress and greater human exposure to pollutants, and that services can be more costly in denser settings because of higher per capita outlays for fire and police protection, mass transit, underground utilities, and grade-separated freeways. See: T. Muller, *Fiscal Impacts of Land Development* (Washington, DC: The Urban Institute, 1975); A. Altshuler, *The Urban Transportation System* (Cambridge, MA: MIT Press, 1980); G. Peterson and H. Yampolsky, *Urban Development and the Protection of Metropolitan Farmland* (Washington, DC: The Urban Land Institute, 1975). For more recent debates on sprawl and its costs, see: P. Gordon and H. Richardson, Are Compact Cities a Desirable Planning Goal? *Journal of the American Planning Association*, vol. 63, no. 1, 1997, pp. 95–106; R. Ewing, Is Los Angeles–Style Sprawl Desirable? *Journal of the American Planning Association*, vol. 63, no. 1, 1997, pp. 107–126; and articles in the special issue of *The Urban Lawyer*, vol. 29, no. 2, 1997.

21. National Trust Enters Fray on Sprawl Issue, *The Edge City News*, vol. 3, no. 1: 1995, p. 4.

22. Rutgers University Center for Urban Policy Research, *Impact Assessment of the New Jersey Interim State Development and Redevelopment Plan* (New Brunswick: Center for Urban Policy Research, 1992).

23. The 1995 report, co-authored by the Bank of America, California Resources Agency (a state government conservation agency), and the Greenbelt Alliance (a Bay Area citizen conservation and public-interest planning organization), called *Beyond Sprawl: New Patterns of Growth to Fit the New California*, questions the sustainability of, in the words of the report, continued "scattershot" development. It encourages infill over speculative, leapfrog

development, full marginal cost pricing of new development, and new political alliances among local officials, business leaders, developers, and environmentalists to support orderly growth. Because of the Bank of America's preeminent position in the mortgage field and its close ties to the home-building industry, its ringing condemnation of current development patterns could not easily be ignored by land developers. See: Bank of America, California Resources Agency, and Greenbelt Alliance, *Beyond Sprawl: New Patterns of Growth to Fit the New California* (San Francisco: Bank of America, 1995).

24. A. Rappaport, Toward a Redefinition of Density, *Environment and Behavior*, vol. 7, no. 2, 1975, pp. 25–36. 1975; J. Bergdall and R. Williams, Perception of Density, *Berkeley Planning Journal*, vol. 5, 1990, pp. 15–38; and L. Bookout and J. Wentling, Density by Design, *Urban Land*, vol. 47, 1988, pp. 10–15.

25. R. Cervero, *America's Suburban Centers: The Land Use–Transportation Link* (Boston: Unwin-Hyman, 1989).

26. R. Cervero, Mixed Land Uses and Commuting: Evidence from the American Housing Survey, *Transportation Research*, vol. 30, no. 5, 1996, pp. 361–377.

27. J. Jacobs, *The Death and Life of Great American Cities* (New York: Vintage Books, 1961).

28. P. Katz, *The New Urbanism: Toward an Architecture of Community* (New York: McGraw-Hill, 1994).

29. R. Cervero, *Transit Supportive Development in the United States: Experiences and Prospects* (Washington, DC: Federal Transit Administration, U.S. Department of Transportation, 1993); R. Cervero, Traditional Neighborhoods and Commuting in the San Francisco Bay Area, *Transportation*, vol. 23, 1996, pp. 373–394.

30. J. Roberts and C. Wood, Land Use and Travel Demand, *Proceedings of the Transport Research Council: Twentieth Summer Annual Meeting* (London: PTRC Education and Research Services, 1992); European Council for Ministers of Transport and the Organization for Economic Cooperation and Development, *Urban Travel and Sustainable Development* (Paris: European Council for Ministers of Transport, 1995).

31. G. Giuliano, The Weakening Transportation–Land Use Connection, *Access*, vol. 6, 1995, pp. 3–11; A. Downs, *Stuck in Traffic: Coping with Peak-Hour Traffic Congestion* (Washington, DC: The Brookings Institution, 1992).

32. M. Dasgupta and F. Webster, Land Use/Transport Interaction: Policy Relevance of the ISGLUTI Study, *Proceedings of the Sixth World Conference on Transport Research* (Lyon, France: World Congress on Transport Research, 1992).

33. Cambridge Systematics, Inc., *The Effects of Land Use and Travel Demand Strategies on Commuting Behavior* (Washington, DC: Federal Highway Administration, U.S. Department of Transportation, 1994).

34. D. Hensher, Selective but Important Challenges Facing the Transport Sector, *Designing Transport & Urban Forms for the Australia of the 21st Century*, J.

Richmond, ed. (Sydney: Institute of Transport Studies, University of New South Wales, 1996).

35. Much of the credit for this idea goes to John Holtzclaw, a San Francisco–based sociologist who has chaired the transportation division of the Sierra Club. Holtzclaw's seminal study of twenty-seven communities in the San Francisco, Los Angeles, Sacramento, and San Diego metropolitan areas found that the number of automobiles and vehicle kilometers traveled (VKT) per household fell by one-quarter as densities doubled, and by about 8 percent with a doubling of transit service intensities, controlling for factors such as household income. See: J. Holtzclaw, *op. cit.*.

36. K. Hoeveler, Accessibility vs. Mobility: The Location Efficient Mortgage, *Public Investment*, September 1997, pp. 1–2.

37. The program has been legally challenged by land developers who fear that forbidding car possession through restrictive covenants could significantly reduce the market value of affected housing. It is likely that the housing will be marketed to a balance of families, some that own cars and some that do not. See: Von Weisäcker, Lovins, and Lovins, 1997, *op. cit.*, p. 131.

38. Members of *Stattauto* who wish to use a car simply phone a reservation center. Schedulers try to consolidate car usage to the best extent possible. In Berlin, where the first German car co-op was formed in 1988, a variety of automobiles are distributed around fourteen neighborhood parking lots. Car keys and travel logs are kept at lots in safe-deposit boxes, to which members have magnetic card-keys. Members fill out travel reports for record keeping and accounting. *Stattauto* bills monthly for kilometers traveled, hours of use, and any taxi rides that are charged to members' cards. Becoming a *Stattauto* member requires a US$600 to US$1,000 one-time subscription fee, modest monthly dues, and on-time payment of monthly car-lease expenses. For discussions on the travel and car-ownership impacts of the *Stattauto* program, see: Von Weisäcker, Lovins, and Lovins, *op. cit.*, pp. 128–130.

39. S. B. Warner, *Streetcar Suburbs* (Cambridge: Harvard University Press, 1962); J. Vance, *Geography and Urban Evolution in the San Francisco Bay Area* (Berkeley: Institute of Governmental Studies, University of California, 1964); R. Fogelson, *The Fragmented Metropolis: Los Angeles from 1850 to 1930* (Cambridge: Harvard University Press, 1967).

40 K. Schaeffer and E. Sclar, *Access for All: Transportation and Urban Growth* (New York: Columbia University Press, 1980); W. Middleton, *The Time of the Trolley* (Milwaukee: Kalmbach Publishing, 1967).

41. D. Boyce, Impact of Rapid Transit on Residential Property Sales Prices, *Space Location and Regional Development*, M. Chatterjee, ed. (London: Pion, 1976), pp. 145–53; D. Damm and A. Lerman, Response of Urban Real Estate Values in Anticipation of the Washington Metro, *Journal of Transport Economics and Policy*, vol. 1, no. 3, 1980, pp. 315–335; P. Donnelly, *Rail Transit Impact Studies: Atlanta, Washington, and San Diego* (Washington, DC: Urban Mass Transportation Administration, U.S. Department of Transportation, 1982); M. Dear, Rapid Transit and Suburban Residential Land Uses, *Traffic Quarterly*, vol. 29, no. 2, 1975, pp. 223–242; D. Dingemans, Rapid Transit and Suburban Residential Land Use, *Traffic Quarterly*, vol. 32, no. 2, 1978, pp.

289–306; D. Dornbush, *BART-Induced Changes in Property Values and Rents: Land Use and Urban Development Projects, Phase I, BART Impact Study* (Washington, DC: U.S. Department of Transportation and U.S. Department of Housing and Urban Development, 1975); C. Gannon and M. Dean, Rapid Transit and Office Development, *Traffic Quarterly*, vol. 29, no. 2, 1972, pp. 223–242; R. Green and O. James, *Rail Transit Station Area Development: Small Area Modeling in Washington, D.C.* (Armonk, NY: M. E. Sharpe Publishers, 1993); Rice Center for Urban Mobility Research, *Assessment of Changes in Property Values in Transit Areas* (Houston: Rice Center for Urban Mobility Research, 1987); M. Webber, The BART Experience: What Have We Learned? *Public Interest*, vol. 12, no. 3, 1976, pp. 79–108.

42. W. Heenan, The Economic Effect of Rapid Transit on Real Estate Development, *The Appraisal Journal*, vol. 36, 1968, pp. 212–224.

43. *Ibid.*

44. R. Dunphy, Toronto: A Pioneering Transit Model in a Suburbanizing Future, *Moving beyond Gridlock: Traffic and Development* (Washington, DC: The Urban Land Institute, 1997, pp. 109-124).

45. R. Cervero, *Suburban Gridlock* (New Brunswick, NJ: Center for Urban Policy Research, 1986, pp. 86–88).

46. *Ibid.*; N. Irwin, Initiatives for Sustainable Transportation in the Greater Toronto Area, paper presented at the 1995 Annual Meeting of the American Planning Association, Toronto, April 1995.

47. J. Pill, *Planning and Politics: The Metropolitan Toronto Transportation Plan Review* (Cambridge, MA: MIT Press, 1979).

48. P. Newman and J. Kenworthy, The Land Use–Transport Connection, *Land Use Policy*, vol. 13, no. 1, 1996, pp. 1–22.

49. Sources: R. Knight and L. Trygg, Evidence of Land Use Impacts of Rapid Transit Systems, *Transportation*, vol. 6, 1977, pp. 231–247; R. Cervero, Urban Transit in Canada: Integration and Innovation at Its Best, *Transportation Quarterly*, vol. 40, no. 3, 1986, pp. 293–316.

50. M. Stringham, Travel Behavior Associated with Land Uses Adjacent to Rapid Transit Stations, *ITE Journal*, vol. 52, no. 4, 1982, pp. 18–22.

51. Recent steps have been taken in the United States, however, to allow transit agencies to be more entrepreneurial in leveraging land development. In early 1997, the Federal Transit Administration introduced a Joint Development Policy that permits U.S. transit agencies to lease or sell land previously acquired with the help of federal grants to private developers if it can be demonstrated that the resulting development will be transit-supportive, generating enough additional riders and fare box receipts to make up for the value of foregone property.

52. J. Pill, Metro's Future: Vienna Surrounded by Phoenix? *Toronto Star*, February 15, 1990, p. B-1.

53. J. Kenworthy, The Land-Use/Transit Connection in Toronto, *Australian Planner*, vol. 29, no. 3, 1991, pp. 149–154; R. Brindle, Toronto—Paradigm Lost? Toronto As a Paradigm for Australian Cities, *Australian Planner*, vol. 30, no.

3, 1992, pp. 123–130; J. Kenworthy and P. Newman, Toronto—Paradigm Regained, *Australian Planner*, vol. 31, no. 3, 1994, pp. 137–147.

54. The Greater Toronto Area consists of the newly expanded city of Toronto plus the regions of Peel, York, Durham, and Halton (which are comparable in size and composition to many suburban counties in the United States). Today, roughly half of the Greater Toronto Area's 4.63 million inhabitants live in the city of Toronto and half reside in the outlying suburbs.

55. Several times during the 1990s, the Ontario government withdrew financial support for rail extensions, including a line to Etobicoke, which was added in the 1994 master plan update as the region's third subcenter. Mounting problems wrought by market-driven suburban and exurban growth have prompted the Ontario government to seriously consider different forms of sprawl taxes and concurrency laws that will force new suburban development to pay its full economic and environmental costs.

56. Accelerated downtown housing construction has been credited with averting serious traffic problems in Toronto's central core despite an office-building boom in the 1970s and 1980s. Research shows that most new core-area housing has been occupied by downtown workers, many of whom walk or ride mass transit to their jobs. *Source*: D. Nowlan and G. Stewart, Downtown Population Growth and Commuting Trips, *Journal of the American Planning Association*, vol. 57, no. 2, 1991, pp. 165–182.

57. Parsons, Brinckerhoff, Hall, and MacDonald, Inc., *Regional Rapid Transit: A Report to the San Francisco Bay Area Rapid Transit Commission* (New York: Parsons, Brinckerhoff, Hall, and MacDonald, Inc., 1956), p. 10.

58. For details on this study, see: R. Cervero, *BART @ 20: Land Use and Development Impacts*, monograph 49 (Berkeley: Institute of Urban and Regional Development, University of California, 1995); R. Cervero and J. Landis, Twenty Years of the Bay Area Rapid Transit System: Land Use and Development Impacts, *Transportation Research*, vol. 31A, no. 4, 1997, pp. 309–333.

59. Superdistricts represent aggregations of census tracts, defined by the Metropolitan Transportation Commission (the region's transportation planning authority) to examine travel patterns at the subregional level.

60. Knight and Trygg, *op. cit.*; R. Cervero, Light Rail Transit and Urban Development, *Journal of the American Planning Association*, vol. 50, no. 2, 1984, pp. 133–147; E. Kelley, The Transportation–Land Use Link, *Journal of Planning Literature*, vol. 9, no. 2, 1994, pp. 128–145; R. Cervero and S. Seskin, The Relationship Between Transit and Urban Form, *Research Results Digest No. 7* (Washington, DC: Transit Cooperative Research Program, Transportation Research Board, National Research Council, 1995); H. Huang, The Land-Use Impacts of Urban Rail Transit Systems, *Journal of Planning Literature*, vol. 11, no. 1, 1996, pp. 17–30.

61. H. Hoyt, *The Structure of Growth of Residential Neighborhoods in American Cities* (Washington, DC: U.S. Government Printing Office, 1939).

ADAPTIVE CITIES: CREATING A TRANSIT-ORIENTED BUILT FORM

The distinguishing feature of adaptive cities is their transit-supportive set-tlement patterns. All four cases reviewed in Part Two—Stockholm, Copen-hagen, Singapore, and Tokyo—feature cityscapes that have been designed and contoured, largely as a result of farsighted and pro-active land-use planning, to support very intensive rail transit services. In these places, mixes of shops, offices, restaurants, apartments, and community facilities huddle around rail stops. Adjacent to many stations are public squares, outdoor markets, and works of civic art, which together help make tran-sit nodes the very foci of local communities.

These are not outcomes of happenstance or good fortune. Rather, they are the result of a clear, well-articulated vision of the future and dedicat-ed individuals who see the vision through to implementation, without compromise. In Singapore and Tokyo, the move toward a transit-oriented metropolis was prompted, in part, by land scarcity. Also important have been economic beliefs—namely, that transit-oriented growth is inherently efficient and socially optimal. These two Asian economic powerhouses, however, have adopted different approaches—in Singapore's case, effi-cient growth has been achieved through the heavy hand of centralized planning, whereas in greater Tokyo, it is largely the product of private entrepreneurial forces. More similar is their approach to pricing the auto-mobile—hefty ownership and motoring fees are passed on in both places. In Stockholm and Copenhagen, the motivation for transit-oriented growth has had more to do with preserving quality of life, attending to social needs, and ensuring a sustainable future. Both Scandinavian cities have radially expanded rail lines to tie together master-planned new towns while strengthening the positions of their respective central cities. In all four case-study areas, a payoff of creating a transit-oriented regional form has been healthy transit ridership gains matched by sustainable levels of private automobile usage.

Chapter 4

Orbiting the City with Rail-Served Satellites: Stockholm, Sweden

Stockholm teaches us the benefits of coordinating new town development and rail transit services within a farsighted, regional planning framework. More than a half-century ago, the region adopted a vision of concentrating spillover growth from the city center into rail-served satellites. Early new towns were meant to be partly self-contained; however, with time the focus shifted to integrating satellite communities through superior-quality regional rail services. In most new towns, high-density housing flanks stations to maximize the share of residents with convenient rail access. Footpaths and cycle ways link lower-density housing to rail stops. Many suburban rail stops are also surrounded by car-free civic squares that function as town centers. Transit-supportive designs—both at the community and corridor levels— have yielded huge mobility dividends: today, more than one-half of Stockholm's new town residents and workers reach their jobs by train or bus. Importantly, the formation of linear axes of transit-oriented communities— some housing mainly residents, some housing mainly workers, and many housing a balance of both—has produced efficient, bidirectional traffic flows. Complementing land-use initiatives have been policies that restrict parking, provide significant price advantages to transit travel, and mildly restrain the passage of cars. Stockholm demonstrates that highly successful and sustainable transit services can be mounted in an affluent region with a very high quality of life. In Stockholm's case, the key has been a workable transit–land use nexus.

Stockholm is arguably the best example anywhere of coordinated planning of rail transit and urban development. Stockholm, Sweden's capital and largest city, has some 720,000 residents, about half of whom live in the central city. About half of the remaining inhabitants live in planned satellite communities that orbit central Stockholm and are radially linked

109

to the core by a regional rail system, Tunnelbana (Map 4.1). The region's star-shaped, multicentered built form is the direct outcome of a comprehensive planning campaign that targeted overspill growth after World War II to master-planned, rail-served suburbs.

Nearly a century ago, Ebenezer Howard first advanced the idea of building satellite new towns separated by greenbelts and connected by intermunicipal railways.[1] As noted in Chapter 1, Howard's vision was to build socially and economically self-sustaining communities that would relieve London from overcrowding and accommodate some of its poor, and at the same time apply value-capture principles to finance infrastructure and services.[2] The physical elements of Howard's plans featured

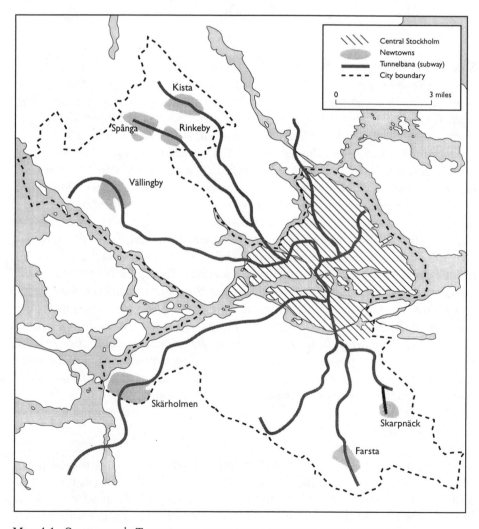

MAP 4.1. STOCKHOLM'S TUNNELBANA METRO AND MAJOR SATELLITE NEW TOWNS.

mixed though physically separated land uses, naturalistic landscaping, and curvilinear, grade-separated passageways.

Many of Howard's followers borrowed from and extended the notion of building safe, peaceful satellite communities surrounded by greenbelts, such as embodied in plans for Radburn, New Jersey, by Henry Wright and Clarence Stein, and Great Britain's early garden suburbs, Letchworth, Hampstead, and Welwyn, designed by Raymond Unwin and Barry Parker. Most of these places were designed on a superblock scale, with clustered housing grouped around communal greens and connected by pedestrian ways (ped-ways). Unlike Howard's garden cities, however, they were not planned as self-contained towns; they were more like dormitory villages, with the source of employment for residents usually in nearby cities. Nor was transit a prominent feature of early British or American new towns. It was only when Stockholm began building, after World War II, what were to be self-contained satellite communities surrounded by protective, open spaces and served by rail transit that Howard's vision of "cities of tomorrow" began to take form.

Building a Transit Metropolis

Over the past fifty years, Stockholm has been transformed from a prewar monocentric city to a postwar polycentric metropolis. The backbone of the multicentered Stockholm region is the Tunnelbana metro. Over time, Stockholm's settlement pattern and rail network have become intimately connected and, indeed, inseparable. They are also the product of perhaps the most comprehensive and ambitious regional planning efforts yet in the free, industrialized world.

What makes the Stockholm story so remarkable is that the rapid transformation to a transit metropolis occurred in a well-to-do nation during a period of economic boom. Today, Sweden is one of the world's most affluent countries, with a 1995 GDP per capita of US$18,200. It also has one of the highest automobile ownership rates (420 cars per 1,000 inhabitants) in Europe.[3] Much of the nation's wealth is concentrated in greater Stockholm—among Sweden's fifty-two companies with more than 5,000 employees, forty have their main offices in the Stockholm region.

Because Sweden was among the last countries in Europe to industrialize, it grew at a rapid pace following World War II, particularly in urban areas. Given that Swedish cities lie in a large, flat, forested country, many could easily have followed a highway-oriented development pattern. Yet Scandinavia's most prosperous country and its capital city took off on a radically different suburbanization path than did America and much of Europe. Why?

Stockholm's progressive-minded city council deserves much of the credit for orchestrating and coordinating land-use and transportation development over the postwar period. Such planning would not have been possible, however, were it not for two other factors. First, beginning in 1904, the Stockholm city council began purchasing land for future expansion decades in advance of need. By 1980, it owned 70 percent of the 188 square kilometers of land within its boundaries and 600 square kilometers of land beyond the city limits. As the city grew, so did its boundaries. Second, Sweden's socialization of public services extended not only to public transport but the housing realm as well. From 1934 to 1965, Sweden was governed by Social Democrats, committed to serving the country's many social needs, including better housing. During the post–World War II period of industrial expansion, Sweden suffered a serious housing shortfall and was unable to provide adequate shelter for new immigrants and factory workers. Quarters were cramped, with few kitchens and washing facilities.[4] In the postwar period, the Swedish government began constructing multistory apartments on the outskirts of metropolises. More than 90 percent of dwelling units built between 1946 and 1970—virtually all built on the city's land—enjoyed some form of state subsidy. Most were built by municipally owned housing corporations and tenant-owned cooperatives.[5] Today, about two-thirds of all Stockholm households live in multi-unit complexes. As in Toronto, a pro-active government became involved in housing production at a time of rapid growth and the extension of regional rail services.

The blueprint for building Stockholm's transit metropolis was Sven Markelius's General Plan of 1945–52. Markelius, an architect by training, believed that, while suburbanization was inevitable and needed to be accommodated, Stockholm's vitality and preeminence as the region's commercial and cultural hub had to be preserved, at all cost. This was to be accomplished by building satellite new towns connected to Stockholm by rail—that is, by putting Howard's garden city concepts into practice.[6] Despite surveys that showed Swedes preferred low- to mid-rise suburban homes, Markelius set about building fairly dense satellite centers so that most residents could be within walking distance of a rail stop. He hoped that by doing so, many households would feel it unnecessary to own or use a car to reach downtown Stockholm.

In designing Stockholm's first generation of new towns—Vällingby (1950–54), Farsta (1953–61), and Skärholmen (1961–68)—city planners sought to avoid a "dormitory town environment." An overriding principle was to distribute industry and offices to satellites roughly in proportion to residential population—that is, to achieve a jobs-housing balance. Public control of land allowed this. Tax incentives were used to lure industries to new towns and promote company-provided employee housing. New towns were also planned for a mix of housing types (single-family and multitenant residences) as well as land uses, with offices, civic buildings, and shops intermingled.

Markelius's plan did not intend to make them complete towns, however. Residents were still to think of themselves as Stockholmers. Accordingly, Markelius devised the rule of halves: half the working inhabitants would commute out of new towns and half of the work force were to be drawn in from elsewhere. Thus, in contrast to other postwar new towns, notably the Mark I new towns designed by Sir Patrick Abercrombie to handle London's overspill growth,[7] Stockholm's satellites were not intended to be fully self-contained—more like "half contained"—even though they were planned for a balance of jobs and housing units.

Building a World-Class Transit System

The regional rail system, Tunnelbana, became the principal device to achieve Markelius's vision of half-containment. (Although mainly an underground system, in outer areas it runs mostly above ground.) Radial in form, the 110-kilometer, 100-station Tunnelbana system was designed to focus on Stockholm's redeveloped core.[8] Under the regional plan, satellite subcenters would function as countermagnets to central Stockholm, inducing efficient, bidirectional traffic flows. This meant building Tunnelbana in advance of demand and incurring huge operating deficits at the outset, but with the expectation that the investment would begin to pay off as the new settlement pattern took form (Map 4.2).

The co-development of rail-served new towns and the Tunnelbana system from the late 1940s to the early 1960s—the region's fastest period of growth—set the stage for a powerful transit–land use nexus. In this sense, Stockholm's experiences closely parallel those of Toronto. Stockholm's experiences differ, however, in the ongoing coordination of transit and fringe-area development in ensuing years—aided by a protective greenbelt and a workable planning framework made possible by public ownership of land.

Regional transit offerings go well beyond mainline rail services. Stockholm was one of the first Western European cities to create a fully integrated public transit system. Since 1967, bus, tramway, and metro services have been planned and coordinated through an instrument of the Stockholm County Council, Storstockholms Lokaltrafik. Service timetables and fares are fully integrated among carriers. Because of both service and land-use integration, Stockholm today has one of the highest work-trip modal splits by transit in Europe. About half of all workers commute by train or bus, nearly twice the share found in bigger rail-served European metropolises such as Berlin and even higher than inner London's market share.[9] Perhaps most impressive, Stockholm is one of the few places where automobility appears to be receding. Between 1980 and 1990, it was the only city in a sample of thirty-seven global cities across four continents that registered a per capita decline in car use—a drop-off

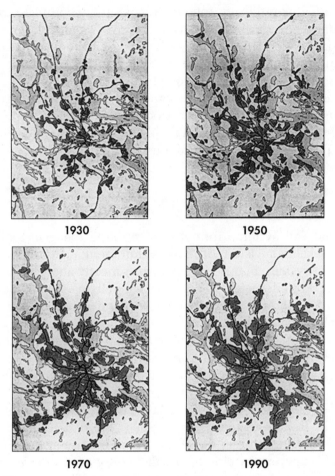

1930   1950

1970   1990

MAP 4.2. EVOLUTION OF A TRANSIT METROPOLIS: REGIONAL GROWTH GUIDED BY RAIL, 1930–1990. *Source*: City of Stockholm, *The Development of Stockholm*, 1990.

of 229 annual kilometers of travel per person.[10] Per capita transit ridership, on the other hand, rose by 15 percent during the 1980s. It has continued to rise during the 1990s, standing today at 325 annual transit boardings per inhabitant. Although many factors have had a hand in transit's success, none have been more important than the emergence of Stockholm's rail-served satellite new towns.

Stockholm's Rail-Served Satellites

Few suburban environments are as conducive to transit riding as Stockholm's rail-served new towns. This section first describes the unusual blending of community and transit-facility design in metropolitan Stockholm, followed by a review of several distinct phases of new town development over the past fifty years.

Transit and Community

In greater Stockholm, the relationship between transit and the surrounding community is quite unique. Rail stations are physically and symbolically the hub of the community. In most master-planned new towns, the rail stop sits squarely in the town center. Upon exiting the station, one steps into a car-free public square surrounded by shops, restaurants, schools, and community facilities. The civic square, often adorned with benches, water fountains, and greenery, is the community's central gathering spot—a place to relax and socialize, and a setting for special events, whether national holidays, public celebrations, parades, or social demonstrations (Photo 4.1). It is the agora of modern-day suburban life. Often the square does double duty as a place for farmers to sell their produce or street artists to perform, changing chameleonlike from an open-air market one day to a concert venue the next. The assortment of flower stalls, sidewalk cafes, newsstands, and outdoor vendors dotting the

PHOTO 4.1. NEW TOWN CIVIC SQUARE. A pedestrian-friendly, car-free civic square functions as Vällingby's town center. The accent on livability is showcased by benches, flower plantings, water fountains, public art, cobblestone walkways, and an assortment of surrounding ground-level retail shops. The Tunnelbana subway entrance is to the left (identified by the T sign).

square, combined with the musings and conversations of folks sitting in the square and everyday encounters among friends, adds color and breathes life into the community.

Just as suburban residents associate the civic square as the focus of the community, they also associate the rail stop as the gateway to the region at large. Transit is the window to the rest of the region, the glue that binds one's own place of residence or work to the greater metropolis. The blending of Tunnelbana stops into the town center, in both a design and a symbolic sense, makes rail transit an integral component of community living.

Stockholm's rail-served new towns have evolved over several distinct stages of community design, reflecting a succession of ideologies about what constitutes a viable and functional community. What is common in each phase, however, is an unwavering commitment to transit as an essential feature of community life. As called for in Markelius's regional master plan, transit became the instrument for linking city and suburb as well as for preserving green space and the surrounding countryside.

First-Generation New Towns

During 1945–57, the first three Tunnelbana lines were built, which allowed the first satellite towns to be built in parallel. Stockholm's first generation of new towns, called ABC towns (A=housing, B=jobs, and C=services), were designed using a common formula:

- Balanced communities of 80,000–100,000 people, with more than 60 percent multifamily housing (at 30 to 80 people per acre).

- A hierarchy of centers, with a main commercial and civic center near the rail station, bordered by neighborhood centers that include schools and community facilities (within 600 meters of the main center).

- Tapering of densities, with the densest residential development surrounding the rail station, flanked by mid-rise apartments, and lower-density housing farther from the center; this arrangement places the majority of residents within an easy walk or bike ride of rail stops.

- Separation of pedestrian and bicycle paths from automobile traffic, including grade separation at intersections.

Built on a monumental Le Corbusier–style scale, with buildings set on vast superblocks in the center of the community, first-generation new towns were roundly criticized by Swedish architects and sociologists as being too institutional and sterile. Critics charged the lack of human scale failed to impart a sense of community attachment. Regardless, surveys showed that residents of first-generation new towns were quite pleased with their surroundings, despite what experts thought.[11]

Vällingby, a community of 25,000 residents located 13 kilometers west of downtown, was Stockholm's first new town, completed in 1954. Ringing Vällingby's Tunnelbana station are high-rise "tower in the park" apartments. Farther from the station is a wider variety of units, including detached single-family homes (Photo 4.2). The central Tunnelbana station rests below a large, open, cobblestone plaza, reflecting pools, and a civic complex. The rail stop also shares space with a large supermarket, allowing returning commuters to do their daily shopping on the way home in the evening. Also nearby are child-care centers, conveniently sited so moms and dads can walk to the town center with their kids each morning, drop them off, and catch the train to work.

Vällingby's road network consists of loops encircling neighborhoods, with a secondary grade-separated pedestrian and bike path system. All paths radially link to the town center. Since Vällingby was conceived before widespread automobile ownership, it was planned with relatively little parking at its core. In most neighborhoods, cars are grouped into small, clustered parking lots.

PHOTO 4.2. MIXED LAND USES AND HOUSING TYPES IN VÄLLINGBY. The foreground shows commercial buildings and "tower in the park" housing that abuts the Tunnelbana line. A train approaches the station, and buses await transferring passengers. The background shows lower-density housing and tree-scaped surrounding neighborhoods.

The second satellite to be built, Farsta (current population 42,000), lies 22 kilometers from downtown Stockholm at the terminus of the southernmost Tunnelbana route. The farm at Farsta was purchased by the city in 1912, "banked" as virgin land, and opened to development in 1956. Because Farsta was built by private developers, industrialized building methods and prefabricated concrete materials were used to construct most apartments. High-rises surround Farsta's central open pedestrian mall, which has three times the car parking built in Vällingby's core.[12] Residential neighborhoods are grouped into clusters of 5,000 to 7,000 dwelling units. Compared to other new towns, Farsta has a large number of light industries, most located on its periphery.

In the early 1960s, the third large new town, Skärholmen (current population 29,000), was built 14 kilometers west of downtown Stockholm. Skärholmen was planned as a subregional center. It features the largest commercial core of all Swedish new towns, with an enclosed pedestrian mall and various commercial attractions. A vast, multistory parking garage for 4,100 cars was also built, the biggest in Scandinavia. Unlike its two predecessors, Skärholmen has no high-rises; most apartments are two to four stories, though blended densities are high. Residential neighborhoods run east-west in parallel rows, descending down the hillside. Skärholmen's civic square, fronting on the Tunnelbana station, contains two large pools and shade trees, providing an inviting place to sit on sunny days.

Later-Generation New Towns

Stockholm's later new towns—notably, Spånga, Kista, and Skärpnack— broke with tradition. Compared to their predecessors, each was designed or evolved as a more specialized community. Accordingly, recent new towns provide a contrast for studying the interrelationship of planning styles, land-use patterns, and commuting (Table 4.1).

Built on former military grounds, Spånga has two primary cores— Tensta and Rinkeby. Spånga's development during the late 1960s coincided with the influx of many non-European immigrants to Sweden, and thus more out of timing than design it attracted a large number of low-income, industrial workers. Most apartments in Tensta and Rinkeby are three to six stories, and buildings are tightly huddled. Spånga introduced Sweden's first residential parking structures, which allowed higher densities while preserving open space. Breaking from Markelius's half-containment formula, Spånga was planned as a residential community (1990 jobs-to-housing ratio of only 0.31). It also has the lowest median income of Swedish new towns. Spånga's two Tunnelbana stations front onto bustling farmer's markets, where village residents buy and sell fruit, vegetables, and wares (Photo 4.3).

Table 4.1 POPULATION AND DEVELOPMENT CHARACTERISTICS
OF STOCKHOLM'S SATELLITE NEW TOWNS

	New Towns				Control Communities	
	First Generation[1]	Spånga[2]	Kista	Skarpnäck[3]	Täby	Central Stockholm
Population						
1980	102,500	42,225	29,081	26,237	47,105	226,405
1990	96,124	44,105	36,415	25,785	56,714	240,098
Employment						
1980	56,298	21,260	15,185	13,516	24,916	114,433
1990	50,548	21,363	18,545	13,676	32,791	324,026
Density (dwelling units/gross acre, 1991)	8.2	14.6	4.7	5.0	1.2	8.0
Percent D.U. Multifamily (1988)	86.1	99.5	91.4	90.8	48.3	99.9
Jobs-to-housing Ratio (1990)	1.02	0.31	3.84	0.58	0.64	1.98
Median Household Disposable Income ($, 1988)	12,400	8,580	10,020	10,350	11,600	11,930
Percent Population Non-Swedish Origin (1988)	28.3	51.3	16.9	24.0	10.8	12.1

[1] These are statistics for Vällingby, Farsta, and Skärholmen combined.
[2] Consists of Tensta and Rinkeby.
[3] Statistics shown are for the Skarpnäck district. The planned new town is a small portion of this district and is planned for up to 3,000 dwelling units at build-out.
Source: Stockholms Läns Landsting, data files.

Located 16 kilometers northwest of downtown Stockholm, Kista has emerged as Sweden's premier technopolis (Photo 4.4). A handful of multinational electronics companies located there in the early 1980s, taking advantage of Kista's proximity to Arlanda international airport (Europe's third-busiest) and its location on the main auto route to the university town of Uppsala. Today, some 240 companies and more than 24,000 employees have moved to Kista. With a jobs-to-housing ratio of 3.84, Kista is hardly self-contained. Most companies are within walking distance of the Tunnelbana, interconnected by a vast grade-separated pathway system. Kista's centerpiece is the Electrum Complex, an indoor shopping and business mall that includes training and conference facilities. Compared to earlier new towns, Kista has a variety of housing, including some high-rise apartments, terrace garden apartments, duplexes, and single-family detached units.

PHOTO 4.3. FARMER'S MARKET OUTSIDE THE RINKEBY STATION. A hallmark of many Tunnelbana stations is that passengers can pick up fruit, vegetables, and fresh flowers when arriving home from work in the evening.

The newest new town, Skarpnäck, is just 10 kilometers south of central Stockholm. Designed as a neotraditional community, Skarpnäck is radically different from its predecessors. Its designers, reacting to the massive scale and institutional feel of earlier new towns, sought to create an urban milieu that is human-scale—two-to-three-story structures, a gridiron street pattern, a fine-grained integration of land uses, and ground-level retail stores and sidewalk cafes on the main street (Photo 4.5). All street crossings are at grade. A variety of housing—more than 3,000 units in all—is available. Apartments are concentrated in the center, with row houses and single-family structures farther away. Most residential and office parking is in rear-lot garages. While Skarpnäck is laid out on a grid, every other street ends in a cul-de-sac to preserve enclosed courtyards. Everyone in the community is within a ten-minute walk of Skarpnäck's recently opened Tunnelbana station.

Stockholm's new generation of rail-served satellites clearly stand out from their predecessors. Yes, they are more specialized—Spånga is an ethnically mixed bedroom community; Kirsta is a vibrant technopolis; and Skarpnäck is Sweden's response to the New Urbanism. However, they also represent a new logic in regional planning. With the post-1960 new towns, a jobs-housing balance was no longer viewed as essential within the confines of a single community; more important was balance across communities that are interconnected by efficient rail services. Thus the principle

PHOTO 4.4. THE HIGH-TECH CENTER OF KISTA. Compact office development is separated from compact housing development by the Tunnelbana line. A protective greenbelt surrounds Kista.

PHOTO 4.5. STREETSCAPE IN THE NEOTRADITIONAL TOWN OF SKARPNÄCK. A sheltered bus stop encroaches on Skarpnäck's narrow main street. The wide sidewalk path allows ample sunlight to pass over the four to five-story flats lining the street.

of in-community balance gave way to one of subregional balance. Rather than stressing the internalization of trips within satellite communities, the new focus was on encouraging balanced flows of travel among communities via electric trains. In a way, a jobs-housing balance was supplanted by a transit-flow balance as normative planning doctrine.

Balance and Self-Containment

Differences in levels of jobs-housing balance among Stockholm's new towns are shown in Table 4.1. As was planned, Stockholm's first-generation new towns (Vällingby, Farsta, and Skärholmen) have comparable counts of workers and housing units. Later new towns differ markedly. Spånga is largely a bedroom community, with three times as many houses as jobs. The newest planned community, Skarpnäck, is also predominantly residential, though in contrast to Spånga, it was designed along traditional lines. Kista, the region's technopolis, stands out as a corporate enclave, with nearly four workers for every dwelling unit.

Table 4.1 also presents data for a "control" suburban community, Täby, which lies roughly the same distance from downtown Stockholm as the new towns. Täby, however, is not a master-planned community, but rather evolved as one of the region's first market-shaped suburbs, originally housing upper-income families in search of single-family living. Täby is a suitable comparison community because, besides lying a similar distance from Stockholm, it has comparable average household incomes to rail-served satellites, other than low-income Spånga. Its share of single-family dwellings is much higher than any of the new towns, however, producing a low average population density.[13] Täby is not on a Tunnelbana line, though it is served by a passenger railroad line, and, like most Swedish communities, has excellent bus service. (The Stockholm city council proposed extending a Tunnelbana line to Täby; however, local officials refused the offer, purportedly because of concerns over other population classes riding transit to their community.) With a jobs-to-housing ratio of 0.64, Täby is predominantly a bedroom community. The other comparison area shown in Table 4.1, central Stockholm, has roughly two jobs for every dwelling unit.

Have the different jobs-housing balance formulas among Stockholm's new towns had any influence on how self-contained, or half-contained, they are? According to Figure 4.1, apparently not. Regardless of how balanced a community is, small shares of workers live in Stockholm's new towns and even smaller shares of residents work where they live. For all new towns, fewer than one out of three workers live within the community, and in the case of Kista, the share is below 15 percent. Far more workers live in Stockholm and reverse-commute, and even more are imported from elsewhere in Stockholm county. The non-master-planned

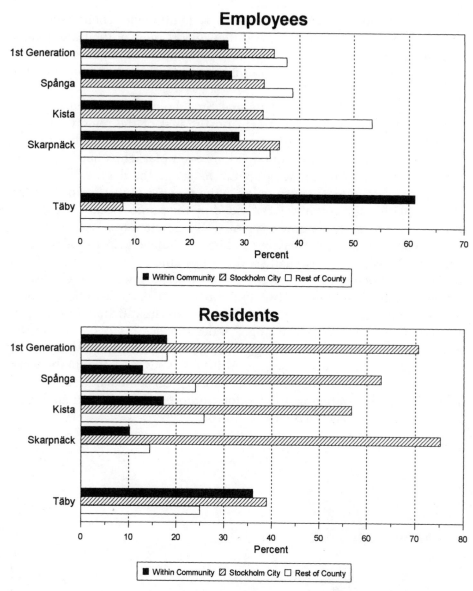

FIGURE 4.1. NEW TOWN SELF-CONTAINMENT. The top graph shows the percentage of workers residing locally, in Stockholm City, and the rest of the county. The bottom graph shows the percentage of employed residents working locally, in Stockholm City, and the rest of the county. All data are for 1990.

comparison community, Täby, has a much larger share of locally residing workers, though part of this is explained by Täby's larger land area.

In all cases, fewer than one out of five new town wage-earners have local jobs. The overwhelming majority work in Stockholm. Even larger shares of new town residents commute to destinations outside central Stockholm than within their own communities. Thus, although the new towns are balanced, they are far from self-sufficient. Their businesses import the majority of workers, and they export most of their adult labor force to jobs elsewhere. The commuting pattern that emerges is a tremendous amount of cross-haul commuting throughout the Stockholm region each workday.

Extensive cross-hauling means that Stockholm's satellites are closely tied to and economically dependent on the rest of the region, for both labor and wages. Even the first-generation new towns are far from being self-contained, or even half-contained, as Sven Markelius had hoped for. A measure used by urban geographers to gauge the degree of self-containment is the "independence index"—the number of work trips that are internal (within the community) divided by the number that are external (into and out from the community). All of Stockholm's new towns, regardless of generation, have very low indices of independence—below 0.15 (Figure 4.2). That is, more than six times as many work trips are external as internal. Independence indices of new towns are well below those of the less-planned suburb, Täby, and Stockholm city. Stockholm's new towns are also far less self-contained than any of Great Britain's two dozen new towns, which together averaged independence indices of 1.2 in the early 1980s.[14] Whereas the majority of wage earners in postwar British auto-oriented new towns, such as Milton Keynes and Redditch, work locally and commute internally, Stockholm's rail-served new towns are polar opposites, averaging tremendous amounts of inbound and outbound commuting each day.

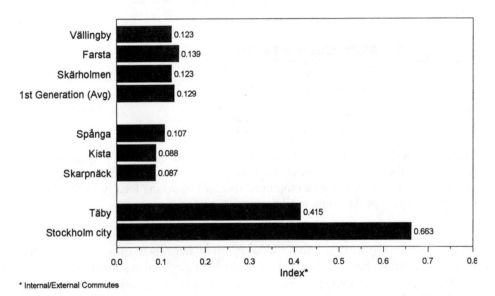

FIGURE 4.2. LEVELS OF SELF-CONTAINMENT. Indices of independence (internal/external commutes) for Stockholm's new towns and control communities, 1990.

Commuting to and from Stockholm's New Towns

With high levels of external commuting and large concentrations of housing and workplaces near rail stations, Stockholm's new towns are natural habitats for rail commuting. Figure 4.3 shows that for all new towns, more than half of all workers and more than a third of residents commute via transit each day. These shares are considerably higher than those of

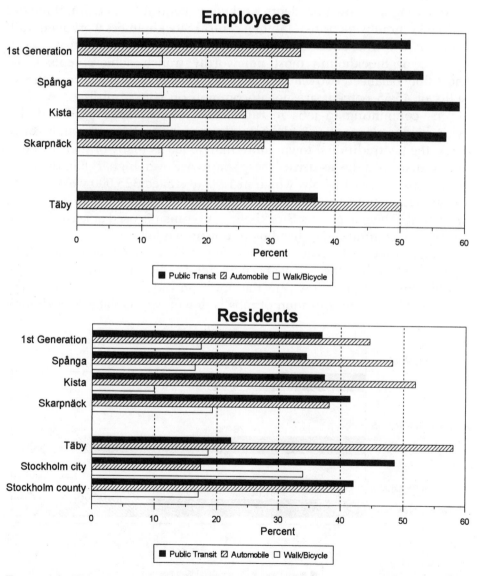

FIGURE 4.3. WORK TRIP MODAL SPLITS. Share of commute trips by modes for workers (top) and employed residents (bottom) of Stockholm's rail-oriented new towns.

the comparison suburb, Täby. Stockholm's new towns have actually come far closer to achieving "half transit commuting" than "half containment." In combination, the built form of rail-fed suburbs and economic dependency on the hinterland has led to transit's extraordinary market share of journeys-to-work in greater Stockholm.

Job location has a strong bearing on how Stockholm area residents get to work. Figure 4.4 shows that more than half of new town residents with local jobs reach work on foot or bicycle. Nearly one out of four rides buses to work; in high-tech Kista, more than a third of internal work trips are by bus. Among new town residents working in central Stockholm, three out of four commute via transit. Among central Stockholmers working in rail-served new towns, about 60 percent reverse-commuted on transit.

One of Stockholm's most noteworthy transit achievements is its incredibly balanced two-way traffic flows. During peak hours, directional splits of 45:55 percent are not uncommon on some rail lines. Workers reverse-commuting to jobs in rail-served suburbs have produced this remarkable balance. For both Kista, the region's technopolis, and Skarpnäck, the neotraditional town, more than twice as many of their workers take transit each day as drive. These shares are even higher than those for Stockholm city as a whole, which in 1992 averaged 325,000 workers who commuted by public transit and roughly 290,000 who drove to work each weekday.[15] Thus, in greater Stockholm, rail transit is used at least as much for reverse-commuting as heading to downtown jobs.

Tidal patterns of rail commuting—full trains in one direction and half-empty ones in the other—have been an Achilles heel in many parts of the world. Unidirectional flows are the norm on radial networks where the only significant concentration of jobs is downtown. Greater Stockholm's

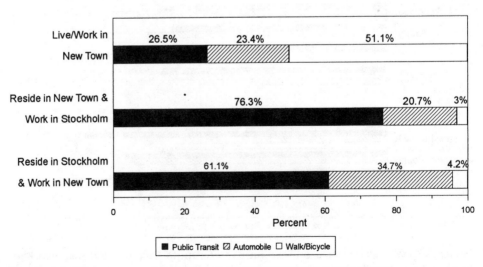

FIGURE 4.4. MODAL SPLITS FOR DIFFERENT SPATIAL PATTERNS OF COMMUTING.

bidirectional balance is a product of well-thought-out regional planning—notably, the channeling of population and employment growth into compact, mixed-use communities sited along rail-served suburban corridors. Each workday, thousands of new town residents walk five or so minutes from their homes to rail stops, take a train three or four stations down the line, disembark, and walk several blocks to their places of work. From a mobility standpoint, Stockholm shows us that a within-community balance of jobs and housing is less important than good-quality transit connections between communities. Having urban activities linearly aligned along radial corridors and well connected by transit leads to highly efficient travel, a lesson that surfaces later in this book in the experiences of Curitiba, Brazil.

Greater Stockholm's transit achievements are impressive given that it is a prosperous region where most households own cars. Stockholmers enjoy high levels of automobility. Many simply choose to leave their cars at home for the daily routine of traveling to and from work, preferring transit instead. Cars have a more specialized role. They are used for hauling groceries, going out in the evening, or taking weekend excursions to the countryside, where many Swedes own second homes.

Supportive Policies and Programs

The physical integration of suburban development and rail transit is not the sole factor behind transit's popularity in greater Stockholm. Various supportive public policies have been important as well. Stockholm officials have opted to reward environmentally sustainable transport by keeping transit fares low. With adult cash fares of US$1 to US$1.50 per trip (depending on distance traveled) and deeply discounted multitrip strips available, passenger revenues cover only a third of operating costs. In an effort to contain costs (so as to be able to keep fares low), all bus and rail services in the region are being competitively tendered. In 1991, the transit authority, Storstockholms Lokaltrafik, was split into two divisions: Planning, which sets service and fare policies, and Operations, which competitively contracts out services for Tunnelbana lines and the region's 400-plus bus routes. By 1995, more than 60 percent of bus and rail services were competitively contracted. Studies show competitively tendered bus services are 37 percent less costly than noncompetitive services, on a per route kilometer basis.[16]

While transit fares are kept low, parking and taxi fares can be expensive, especially in central Stockholm. Curbside parking is generally prohibited except at metered spaces, where charges are graduated outward from the city center. Near Tunnelbana stations, parking standards have been significantly reduced, to as few as one space per ten office workers.

Sweden also has among the highest value-added taxes on motor vehicles and vehicle registration fee structures anywhere.[17] In 1992, vehicle acquisition taxes and registration fees added about 58 percent to the purchase cost of a new car versus only 9 percent in the United States. Motor fuel is taxed at about 80 percent of base price (versus 25 percent in the United States.)[18]

Stockholm officials have, over the years, performed a balancing act between restraining use of the car while also appeasing the desires of an affluent population to drive safely and efficiently. Stockholm was one of the first Scandinavian cities to calm neighborhood traffic on a citywide basis, primarily using low-cost measures such as intersection neck-downs and midblock pedestrian crossings. American-style beltways have been shunned. Earlier plans to build two outer beltways have been replaced by the opening of a much shorter west-side highway link. The region continues to add major roads, however. Plans for an underground expressway that will enable through motorists to bypass the central city are moving forward. The only way backers could win approval for the project was to support the introduction of road pricing in the city center. Building on the experiences in the neighboring Norwegian cities of Oslo and Bergen, electronically collected tolls will vary by time of day, with revenues going to finance both road and transit improvements. Planners hope that higher motoring fees will reduce the number of cars entering the city center by 25 percent.

Not content to rest on its past achievements, Stockholm officials have made renewed commitments to transit in recent years. Under an agreement forged between pro-growth forces and environmentalists, called the Dennis Agreement, the city and surrounding region have pledged more than US$2.1 billion to public transit projects to the year 2006. Plans call for extending Tunnelbana lines farther out and partially ringing the central city with a 14-kilometer express tramway (called *snabbsparvag*). The tramway would continue the tradition of integrated rail and urban development, with the focus on "new towns/in town" versus "new towns/out-of-town." Rolling stock is also being upgraded. All diesel buses are being replaced by clean-fuel buses. Along some routes, buses are given reserved lanes and priority crossing at traffic signals. Also, Tunnelbana's rail cars are gradually being replaced by three-section units that allow passengers to circulate freely from car to car.

Learning from Stockholm

Stockholm's first-generation new towns were consciously planned to promote rail commuting into central Stockholm as well as to be somewhat self-contained. Statistics reveal that they have certainly achieved the former objective but have been far off the mark on the second. Stockholm's new towns import large shares of their work force and send off even larger shares of residents to jobs elsewhere. Commuting to and from new towns, however, is often by transit—and perhaps most importantly, balanced in both directions. What internal commuting does take place tends to be by foot and bicycle. Stockholm's new towns are regional mobility "success stories" not because of balanced land uses or self-containment, but rather because premium-quality train services efficiently connect suburbs together.

Experiences in greater Stockholm demonstrate that transit-oriented communities need not be isolated islands within the larger metropolis. In addition to sharing a regional identity, Stockholm's new towns share labor resources as well. Experiences also show that a jobs–housing balance and self-containment are not essential in reducing automobile dependence. In fact, when compared to British new towns, there appears to be an inverse relationship between self-containment and transit/nonauto commuting. While British new towns are far more balanced and self-contained than their Swedish counterparts, they are also more auto-dependent. For instance, the overwhelming majority of working residents from Milton Keynes (a master-planned new town about 80 kilometers north of London) have jobs there, but about three-quarters drive their cars to work and only 7 percent commute by transit, resulting in one of the highest levels of vehicle kilometers traveled per capita in Europe.[19]

A more recent comparison sheds further light on the sustainability of the Stockholm approach. This study compared travel characteristics among residents of greater Stockholm and the San Francisco Bay Area, both of which have comparable-size regional rail systems.[20] As noted in the previous chapter, relatively little suburban growth has clustered around Bay Area rail stops. The typical Bay Area resident was found to log 2.4 times more vehicle kilometers per weekday as his or her counterpart from greater Stockholm—44.3 versus 18.4. Stockholm's highly functional transit–land use nexus, a product of regional planning, is far more resource-conserving than the Bay Area's auto-directed patterns of market-driven growth. "Market intervention" (i.e., rail-oriented development) has not been at the expense of Stockholmers spending more time getting to and fro. On average, Bay Area residents travel 60 percent farther, in terms of distance, for convenience shopping and 40 percent farther to eat, yet the amount of time devoted to both trip purposes is about the same in the two regions. The average Bay Area resident ends up traveling considerably farther, consuming more finite resources, but without reaping any time-savings benefits.

In closing, Stockholm's built form—a strong, preeminent regional core orbited by transit villages—deserves much of the credit for low automobile dependence. For cities in the United States that are embarking on regional rail-building campaigns, Stockholm's experiences suggest a handful of transit villages in a landscape of sprawling development will not yield significant mobility or environmental benefits. Only when community-based planning and design add up to a coherent whole—something that requires a regional framework—can a sustainable transit metropolis begin to take form.

Notes

1. E. Howard, *To-morrow: A Peaceful Path to Real Reform* (London: Swan Sonnenschein, 1898).

2. P. Hall, *Cities of Tomorrow: An Intellectual History of Urban Planning and Design in the Twentieth Century* (New York: Basil Blackwell, 1988).

3. K. Westin, Sweden: Moving Towards a Safer Environment, *A Billion Trips a Day*, I. Salomon et al., eds. (Dordrecht, Netherlands: Kluwer 1993); Statistics Sweden, *Statistika Centralbyrån* (Stockholm: Statistics Sweden, 1997; available at web site: www.scb.se/indexeng.htm).

4. At the end World War II, 52 percent of Stockholm's housing stock consisted of no more than one room and a kitchen. Living space standards have increased markedly over the last two decades. Today, the region's dwellings have an average of almost three rooms plus kitchen, even though 40 percent are single households.

5. City of Stockholm, *The Development of Stockholm* (Stockholm: City of Stockholm, 1991); Stockholm Stadsbyggandskontor, *Stockholm Urban Environment* (Uppsala, Sweden: Almquist and Wiksells, 1972).

6. Lewis Mumford's writings also had a strong influence on Swedish planning doctrine at the time. Mumford's book *The Culture of Cities* (New York: Harcourt, Brace, and Company, 1938), which had been translated into Swedish, was widely read by Swedish planners. Mumford's exhortations on how the urban environment and social culture could elevate and transform individuals into responsible citizens resonated with Swedish planners of the time. For a further account of Mumford's influences, see: G. Sidenbladh, Planning Problems in Stockholm, *Regional and City Planning: Seven Articles on Planning Problems in Greater Stockholm* (Stockholm: Planning Commission of the City of Stockholm, 1964).

7. A. Watson, New Towns in Perspective in England, *New Towns in Perspective: From Garden City to Urban Reconstruction*, P. Merlin and M. Sudarskis, eds. (Paris: International New Town Association Press, 1991); and C. Ward, *New Town, Home Town* (London: Calouste Gulbenkian Foundation, 1993).

8. Tunnelbana's radial orientation was partly dictated by the region's fragmented landscape of rivers and inlets, which have created wedge-shaped land masses.

9. T. Pharoah and D. Apel, *Transport Concepts in European Cities* (Aldershot, England: Avebury, 1995).

10. J. Kenworthy, F. Laube, P. Newman, and P. Barter, *Indicators of Transport*

Efficiency in 37 Global Cities, a report for the World Bank (Perth: Institute for Science and Technology Policy, Murdoch University, 1997).

11. D. Popenoe, *The Suburban Environment: Sweden and the United States* (Chicago: University of Chicago Press, 1977).

12. While not initially included, Farsta's plan was modified to provide 2,000 mostly surface parking spaces near the core. Parking was not only for visitors and workers, but also to attract large Swedish chain stores, something the private developers felt was essential if the development was to be financially successful.

13. Täby, as is true of much of north and northeast Stockholm, is also home to a much higher share of native Swedes.

14. M. Breheny, Strategic Planning and Urban Sustainability, *Proceedings of the Town and Country Planning Association Conference on Planning for Sustainable Development* (London: Town and Country Planning Association, 1990); R. Cervero, Planned Communities, Self-Containment and Commuting: A Cross-National Perspective. *Urban Studies,* vol. 32, no. 7, 1995, pp. 1135–1161.

15. AB Storstockholms Lokaltrafik, *Stratgisk Utveckling Och Planering* (Stockholm: AB Storstockholms Lokaltrafik, 1993).

16. W. Cox, J. Love, and N. Newton, Competition in Public Transport: International State of the Art (Paper presented at the Fifth International Conference on Competition and Ownership in Passenger Transport, Leeds, England, May 28, 1997).

17. P. Bovy, J. Orfeuil, and D. Zumkeller, Europe: A Heterogenous Single Market, *A Billion Trips a Day,* I. Salomon et al., eds. (Dordrecht, Netherlands: Kluwer, 1993); J. Pucher, Urban Travel Behavior As the Outcome of Public Policy: The Example of Modal-Split in Western Europe and North America, *Journal of the American Planning Association,* vol. 54, no. 4, 1988, pp. 509–520.

18. R. Gorham, *Regional Planning and Travel Behavior: A Comparative Study of the San Francisco and Stockholm Metropolitan Regions* (Master's thesis, Department of City and Regional Planning, University of California, Berkeley, 1996); J. Pucher, Urban Passenger Transport in the United States and Europe: A Comparative Analysis of Public Policies, Part 1, *Transport Reviews,* vol. 15, no. 2, 1995, pp. 99–117.

19. J. Roberts and C. Wood, Land Use and Travel Demand, *Proceedings of Transport Research Council: Twentieth Annual Meeting* (London: Transport Research Council Education and Research Services, 1992); S. Potter, *Transport and New Towns* (Milton Keynes, England: The Open University, New Towns Study Unit, 1984).

20. Gorham, *op. cit.*

Chapter 5

The Hand-Shaped Metropolis: Copenhagen, Denmark

The story of Copenhagen is the story of rail transit's role as an instrument for creating a desired built form—a hand-shaped region with radial corridors, or fingers, that emanate from central Copenhagen, separated by green wedges of woodlands, farmlands, and open recreational space. In 1947, Copenhagen planners introduced the Finger Plan, adopting the image of a hand with five fingers that radiate from central Copenhagen to the north, west, and south, with each finger aligned in the direction of a historical Danish market town. The Finger Plan has taken on an almost religious quality over the years. Foremost, it has proven to be an incredibly effective marketing tool for spatial planning. Danes understand and respect it. With relatively little regional oversight, the Finger Plan has been implemented, step-by-step, through a series of local zoning and land-use decisions that honor it as a guiding principle. Radial rail services, along with the reassignment of streets to pedestrians and cyclists, have strengthened the historic center. Today, the majority of new town residents heading to central city jobs take transit to work.

Copenhagen must be understood in the context of a relatively large city in a relatively small country. Greater Copenhagen, situated in eastern Denmark on the island of Zealand, has a population of about 1.7 million in a nation of only some 5 million. Within its 2,800-square-kilometer land area are five jurisdictions: two central municipalities—the city of Copenhagen and the city of Frederiksborg—which together have about 500,000 residents; Copenhagen county, which rings the central city, with 600,000 inhabitants; and two outer counties, Frederiksborg and Roskilde, also with 600,000 residents (Map 5.1). The city of Copenhagen is the nation's capital as well as its commercial, industrial, and cultural center.

To ensure that greater Copenhagen's development supports broader national interests, the Danish government has spearheaded much of the regional planning that has taken place during the post–World War II era. Rail-served new towns built to the south and southwest, for example, were

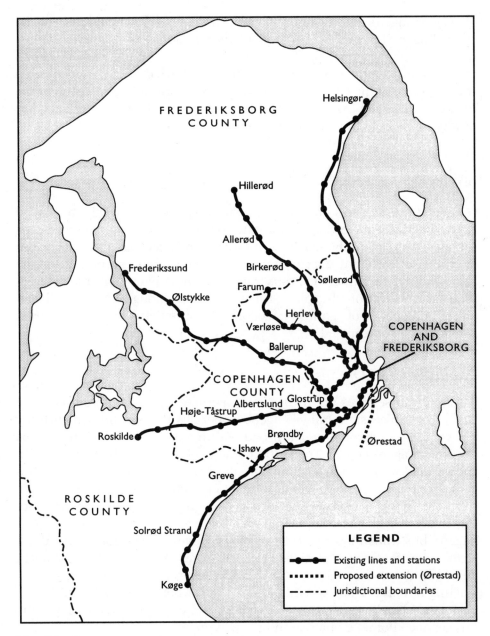

MAP 5.1. COUNTIES, MUNICIPALITIES, AND REGIONAL RAIL LINES OF GREATER COPENHAGEN.

conceived, planned, and developed by national ministries. Over the years, metropolitan authorities have come and gone, as Danish leaders have weighed the pros and cons of regional governance. But national directives have been a steady influence in bringing about coordinated growth.

Copenhagen's guiding light for coordinating development has been the 1947 Finger Plan and its subsequent incarnations. As in greater Stockholm, a strong regional land-use vision has given rise to a radial rail system that efficiently links master-planned suburbs. Today, Copenhagen stands as one of the best examples anywhere of how a cogent vision of the future—buttressed by an extensive rail network and feeder services—has produced a viable transit–land use nexus.

Institutional Landscape

Greater Copenhagen's institutional landscape could hardly be called streamlined. Over the years, both land-use planning and public transport services have been shaped by a multitude of agencies and authorities operating at different tiers of government and often competing for the same limited resources. Land-use and transport planning and development are institutionally split. Still, there exist enough checks and balances, and politics of gentle persuasion, to ensure that development is reasonably well coordinated.

Public Transit: Organizations and Services

Regional rail services are owned and operated by two different entities. DSB, the Danish state railway agency, operates the S-Train, which functions mainly as a commuter railroad within a 30- to 40-kilometer radius of Copenhagen's core. The 170-kilometer, 79-station S-Train system, shown in Map 5.1, radiates along greater Copenhagen's outstretched fingers. Urban rail services, which to most customers are indistinguishable from the S-Train, concentrate on the core region and are operated by Copenhagen Transport. Supplementing these are private railways. Copenhagen's bus transit system, HT (short for Hovedstadsområdets Trafikselskab), coordinates and operates the 1,100 buses that presently serve north Zealand.[1] As in Stockholm, plans call for eventually competitively contracting out all HT bus services. Since 1989, when competitive tendering began, to 1996, bus operating costs fell by 18.5 percent in real terms, while bus service kilometers increased by 5 percent.[2]

Denmark's Hierarchy of Land-Use Planning

In Denmark, physical land use planning is conducted hierarchically, with the national government perched firmly at the top. National directives shape Regional Plans, which in turn shape Municipal Plans, which in turn shape Local (neighborhood) Plans.

National Directives and Policies

Since World War II, the national government has issued policy guidelines every four years aimed at shaping the country's physical development. A cornerstone of Denmark's urbanization policy has been the channeling of growth to the south and west of Copenhagen proper, leading to the emergence of master-planned new towns along radial corridors.[3] The central government has also sought to more uniformly spread development throughout the country while preserving farmlands and open space through strict national zoning laws.[4]

Over the past decade, a series of national directives have called for targeting greater Copenhagen's future growth around rail transit stations. The directives stipulate that all future urban development should occur within 1-kilometer catchments of established or planned rail stops. While they do not exactly carry the force of law, national directives clearly imply that localities are to make good faith efforts in encouraging transit-oriented development. If the national Ministry of Environment feels otherwise, it has veto power over proposed local development projects. These veto powers have so far been exercised sparingly, in large part because most localities strongly support sustainable patterns of development.

National tax laws have also played a vital role in promoting coordinated regional development. Denmark taxes people, not corporations or land. Thus, almost all public revenues come from personal income and excise taxes. This has effectively reduced fiscal competition for tax base, in sharp contrast to the United States, where the competition for high property tax–yielding land uses has been blamed for fractured settlement patterns and sprawl. In Denmark, municipalities are less inclined to zone in commercial land uses and zone out apartments.

Lower Level Plans

Every four years, the three counties and two municipalities of greater Copenhagen jointly prepare a Regional Plan in accordance with national directives. By law, the Plan must be capable of accommodating the next twelve years of forecasted regional growth. From 1974 to 1989, the Greater Copenhagen Council prepared this plan; however, regional governance was abolished in 1989 under pressure from local politicians.[5] National law also requires each of the forty-eight independent municipalities within greater Copenhagen to prepare a Master Plan every four years that is coordinated and consistent with the Regional Plan. A Municipal Plan is reviewed by the county that a municipality lies within and by the Ministry of Environment. Higher levels of government can reject Municipal Plans for being inconsistent with regional policies and national directives and can also stop local development projects for similar reasons.

Below the Municipal Plan are Local Plans, which specify zoning and permitted uses for each parcel of land within a neighborhood. By national directive, then, every parcel within a kilometer of a rail stop is to be zoned for urban activities. While this plan-making process is unabashedly top-down, at each step there is bottom-up participation. Regional planning revisions, for example, must be preceded by a public debate lasting eight weeks, sponsored by county councils.

Evolution of Copenhagen's Land Use-Transport Plans

A steady stream of Regional Plans has evolved over the past half-century that unequivocally embrace principles of coordinated land use and transport planning. With one notable exception, all have sought to extend and refine what has become the beacon of all physical planning within the region, the Finger Plan.

The Finger Plan

The capital region's population surpassed 1 million during World War II. With all signs pointed toward steady future growth and a progressive government in place, the stage was set for the adoption of a bold, inventive, and forward-looking regional plan. Influenced by postwar British town-planning principles, the end product, the 1947 Finger Plan, called for focusing growth along narrow fingers that point in the direction of five historical market towns in north Zealand (Map 5.2). Yet unlike Abercrombie's strategy for greater London, which featured new towns sited on the outer edges of a wide greenbelt, the Finger Plan directed Copenhagen's expansion to contiguous townships strung along well-defined corridors carved out by train lines, with open green wedges preserved between the developing fingers.[6] Strict urban rural zoning was subsequently enacted to enforce the plan.

As in the case of Stockholm, a central premise of the Finger Plan was that by aligning development along well-defined corridors, a large share of the region's work force could reach jobs via rail transit. Fingers, interspersed with green wedges, would allow efficient, radial rail commutes into the core, and in so doing, help to maintain a viable central city. The resulting settlement pattern would also preserve natural habitats and contain infrastructure development costs.

Many of the stated objectives of the Finger Plan and subsequent updates have been framed around principles of regional accessibility and sustainability—principles that are today widely accepted, but which in the early postwar years were not that common or well articulated. Among the stated objectives were: reduce daily travel distances and times; minimize traffic congestion in the central city; provide commerce and industries

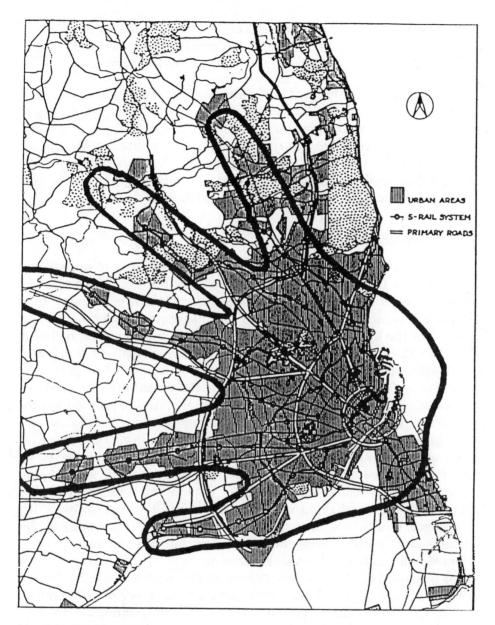

Map 5.2. The Finger Plan.

with suitable locations in relation to labor supplies; and preserve the balance between built-up areas and open landscape. As stated in the 1961 Plan update, these aims were to be realized:

> by means of consistently concentrating all new development along suburban railways. . . . It should be one of the

essential aims of planning not only to increase the speed of
the transport services, but also to restrict the actual length
of the journey to work. . . . to no more than 45 minutes.[7]

Over the years, the Finger Plan has become the region's icon, taking on
a sanctity of its own. The imagery of a hand with five fingers proved to
have tremendous marketing and public relations value. The common citizen could easily visualize and relate to a hand as a template for guiding
future urban growth. To the layperson, its logic seemed simple yet eloquent and compelling. This is in large part why public support for the plan
has remained bedrock solid over the past half-century.

A Multicenter Metropolis?

By the early 1970s, earlier postwar planning efforts began to appear way
too ambitious and out of synch to some factions. Planners had forecasted
far more growth than actually took place. Automobile ownership and travel were exploding, and there was a rising tide of pro-development sentiments. For the first time, the Finger Plan came under serious challenge.
The 1973 Regional Plan update proposed shelving many of the Finger
Plan's principles in favor of creating large nodal centers throughout the
region, interconnected by ring roads and radial transit lines in a cobweb
fashion. Each node was to become a supercenter. And of greatest significance, the region was to change from a single-center to a multicenter
metropolis. A cadre of progressive planners and architects rallied against
this paradigm shift, charging that the region was surrendering to an
American-style pattern of car-dominated sprawl. Nor did the general populace concede to abandoning the Finger Plan. Many were apprehensive
about the prospect of rapid suburbanization and the loss of dwindling
open space. It only took the confluence of two events—the worldwide oil
embargo and ecology movements—to seal the fate of Copenhagen's auto-
oriented multicentered planning movement.

As discussed later, subsequent Regional Plan updates have reaffirmed
principles of the original Finger Plan and the importance of viable public
transit. The most notable commitment has been the continuing development of rail-oriented new towns, predominantly in the thumb (southernmost corridor) and the forefinger (southwest corridor) of the Finger Plan.

New Town Development

As in Stockholm, it has been the successful coupling of rail transit investments and new town development—under the guidance of the Finger
Plan—that has earned Copenhagen's place as a great transit metropolis.

Today, new towns are dotted along the region's five fingers, which extend south (to Køge), southwest (to Roskilde), west (to Frederikssund), northwest (to Hillerød and the park district), and north (to the coastal town of Helsingør) (Map 5.1). Most new town development has been concentrated in the south and southwest, designed, financed, and implemented by the Danish government under the auspices of the Ministry of Environment.

Compared to Stockholm, far less consideration has been given to making greater Copenhagen's new towns balanced and self-contained. As shown in Table 5.1, new towns such as Glostrup and Albertslund in the

Table 5.1 BALANCE AND COMMUTING STATISTICS AMONG NEW TOWNS AND COMPARISON AREAS, GREATER COPENHAGEN, 1991

	Employed		Ratio:	Morning Commutes		
	Residents	Workers	W/ER	Out of:	In to:	I/O[2]
Central City[1]	260,688	362,976	1.39	115,546	213,829	1.92
Suburban ring						
Rail-served new towns						
South and Southwest						
Fingers						
Ishøj	10,763	8,075	0.75	8,019	5,331	0.66
Glostrup	10,864	34,245	3.15	7,547	17,246	2.28
Albertslund	6,170	22,279	3.61	11,360	17,466	1.54
Høje Taastrup	25,336	28,066	1.11	15,934	18,664	1.17
Other Fingers						
Herlev	14,350	18,414	1.28	9,922	13,986	1.41
Ballerup	25,508	32,425	1.27	16,275	23,192	1.42
Værløse	10,480	7,700	0.73	7,827	5,047	0.65
Copenhagen County	328,661	345,532	1.05	227,686	244,557	1.07
Outer suburbs						
Rail-served new towns						
Greve	27,540	14,122	0.51	20,020	6,602	0.33
Solrød Strand	11,833	4,927	0.42	9,180	2,274	0.25
Farum	9,986	8,209	0.82	6,989	5,212	0.75
Birkerød	11,690	13,729	1.17	7,670	9,709	1.27
Rail-served market towns						
Køge	20,448	18,495	0.91	9,368	7,415	0.79
Roskilde	27,029	30,354	1.12	11,893	15,221	1.28
Frederikssund	9,771	7,933	0.81	5,268	9,709	1.84
Hillerød	18,929	20,894	1.10	9,454	11,419	1.21
Roskilde County	127,389	88,440	0.69	78,823	39,874	0.51
Frederiksborg County	192,951	148,444	0.77	114,087	69,580	0.61
Region	909,689	945,392	1.04	532,142	567,845	1.07

[1] Includes cities of Copenhagen and Frederiksberg.
[2] In-commutes divided by out-commutes.
Source: Hovedstadsregionens Statistikkontor, Statistical Yearbook for the Copenhagen Region—Statisktisk Årbog 1993 for Hovedstadsregionen (Stockholm: Hovedstadsregionens Statistikkontor, 1993).

inner suburban ring (and mainly along the southwest finger) have become employment enclaves, featuring large retail centers and industrial complexes huddled around rail stations. In contrast, most rail-served new towns in the outer suburbs (e.g., Greve and Solrød Strand along the southern finger) have evolved into bedroom communities. When compared to Copenhagen city, the older market towns at the terminuses of regional rail lines (e.g., Roskilde), and the three suburban counties as a whole, the region's rail-served new towns tended to be far less balanced in 1991 (as revealed in Table 5.1 by ratios of worker/employed resident that are far below or above the value). Jobs–housing imbalances have resulted in far more external (out-of-community) commuting among residents and workers of rail-served new towns. The independence indexes in Table 5.2 show a particularly high degree of external commuting among rail-served new towns ringing Copenhagen city. In contrast, Copenhagen city and the historical market towns average significantly higher rates of within-city

Table 5.2 PATTERNS OF COMMUTING: INDEPENDENCE INDEXES AMONG NEW TOWNS AND COMPARISON AREAS, GREATER COPENHAGEN, 1991

| | Type of Commute Trip | | | Independence Index |
| | | External | | |
	Internal	In-Commute	Out-Commute	
Central City	181,779	181,197	78,909	0.699
Suburban ring				
Rail-served new towns				
South and Southwest Fingers				
Ishøj	2,744	5,331	8,019	0.206
Glostrup	3,317	17,246	7,547	0.134
Albertslund	4,810	17,466	11,360	0.167
Høje Taastrup	9,402	18,664	16,044	0.271
Other Fingers				
Herlev	4,428	9,922	13,986	0.185
Ballerup	9,233	23,192	16,275	0.234
Vaerløse	2,653	7,827	5,047	0.206
Outer suburbs				
Rail-served new towns				
Greve	7,520	20,020	6,602	0.282
Solrød Strand	2,653	2,271	9,180	0.232
Farum	2,997	6,989	5,212	0.246
Birkerød	4,020	8,693	10,732	0.207
Rail-served market towns				
Køge	11,080	7,415	9,368	0.660
Roskilde	15,133	11,893	15,221	0.558
Frederikssund	4,503	5,268	3,430	0.518
Hillerød	9,475	9,454	11,419	0.454

Note: Independence Index = Internal/External Commutes
Source: Danmarks Statistik, ABBA:Arbejdsmarkedsstatistikkens Bruger-Bank (Copenhagen: Danmarks Statistik, 1994).

commuting. Thus, even more so than in the case of Stockholm, greater Copenhagen's new town residents and workers have become heavily dependent upon mechanized modes of commuting.

This set the stage for what was to become a radial, tidal pattern of commuting, which, because of the integration of transit and new town development, has been predominantly by rail. About a third of those working in the city of Copenhagen today commute by public transport (with most others walking and cycling to work). Among those living in a suburban new town and heading to a central city job, transit captures an estimated 70 percent of all commute trips. A consequence of being a large-ly single-centered metropolis, however, has been directional imbalances. In 1981, 80 percent of S-Train patronage from 7:00 A.M. to 9 A.M. was in the inbound direction. By 1992 this share had fallen to 72 percent as employ-ment decentralized. Still, rail transit usage in Copenhagen remains direc-tionally one-sided during peak hours, especially in comparison to Copen-hagen's Scandinavian peer, Stockholm.

Three notable phases of new town evolution in greater Copenhagen have been the early development of the south finger, the opening of the region's flagship new town, Høje Taastrup, and most recently, the creation of a sixth finger to the planned new town of Ørestad. These are elaborat-ed upon below.

South Finger: The Thumb

The south finger, or thumb of the hand, today extends to the charming medieval town of Køge, hugging the bay shore for some 30 kilometers in length. Developed in the late 1960s under special national legislation, the south corridor was targeted for much of the overspill growth of the region's working class. Under a partnership agreement, municipalities prepared specific local plans while the national government provided funding for major infrastructure and housing development along the cor-ridor. While eminently successful from a transportation point of view, with some two-thirds of employed residents from new towns along the south finger commuting by transit, the south finger's new towns were harshly criticized by local architects for their high-rise social housing and sterile, institutional qualities.[8] Danish architectural critic Peter Olesen laments that suburbs along the south finger have been "disfigured by uninteresting high rise blocks, multi-storey flats and other third rate buildings" and proclaims the rail served new town of Ishøj to be "the num-ber one producer of high rise horrors" (Photo 5.1).[9] Still, it is important that the south finger's new towns are affordable and desirable locations for many lower income and start up households. Also, considerable progress has been made in adding commerce, industries, and retail shops to many new towns and in enhancing the designs and aesthetic character of their rail-served town centers.

PHOTO 5.1. DORMITORY HOUSING IN ISHØJ, ALONG THE SOUTH FINGER. A classic clash of "form versus function." While architects criticize the prefabricated, mass-produced, and standardized form of these mid-rise new towns, their function as accessible, rail-oriented communities has been a success. The bicycle icons on the sides of S-Train cars indicate cyclists are welcome on board.

Høje Taastrup

Partly in reaction to the shortcomings of the south finger's new towns, beginning in the mid-1960s, regional planners embarked on an effort to create a more human-scale and balanced new town that would serve as a model for future generations. Their choice was Høje Taastrup, midway along the southwest finger. Billed as a self-contained community and designed expressly around rail transit, Høje Taastrup closely followed the design traditions of British and Swedish new towns (Figure 5.1). Planned for an eventual population of 400,000, Høje Taastrup was configured as a series of cellular neighborhoods, each accommodating the equivalent of 1,000 flats and interconnected by pathway systems. In part to establish momentum and make a symbolic national commitment, the town-center retail area was built in the early 1980s even before housing was put in (Photo 5.2). With a 1993 population of only one-tenth its ultimate target, the jury is still out on whether Høje Taastrup will ever live up to its expectations. To date, however, it has proven to be a popular place of residence among middle-class households, and a growing number of high-technology firms have chosen to locate there. And from a mobility standpoint, Høje Tasstrup has been an unqualified success, with nearly half of all

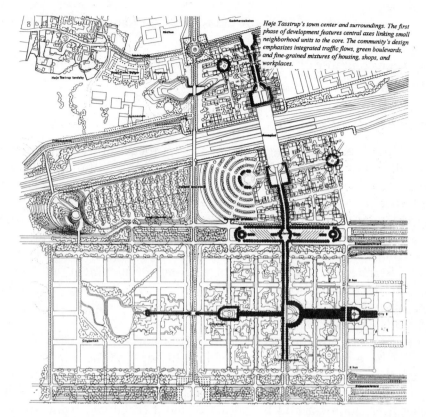

Høje Tasstrup's town center and surroundings. The first phase of development features central axes linking small neighborhood units to the core. The community's design emphasizes integrated traffic flows, green boulevards, and fine-grained mixtures of housing, shops, and workplaces.

FIGURE 5.1. THE HØJE TAASTRUP MASTER PLAN. The plan features two commercial axes emanating from the S-Train transit station. *Source:* Høje-Taastrup kommune, DSB, Hovedstadsrådet, *Høje-Taastrup i 25 år—fra omegn til centerkommune,* 1986.

PHOTO 5.2. CAR-FREE TOWN CENTER OF HØJE TAASTRUP. Conventional buses operate alongside pedestrians and cyclists in the commerical core.

intrafinger commutes by the community's employed residents made via mass transit.

Ørestad Redevelopment

A sixth finger is now taking form to the southeast, toward the international airport and a planned bridge that will connect Denmark with Sweden. In 1992, a national act set aside a 310-hectare area, know as Ørestad, as a future new-town/in-town oriented around a modern new rail transit line. The hope is to create a linear employment zone with some 70,000 jobs and 10,000 to 15,000 residents. Emphasis will be placed on attracting research-based and high-technology businesses, supported by a university, civic functions, and a diversity of housing. Development will be organized around an advanced light rail transit line, called City Line, that is being modeled after Toronto's and Vancouver's SkyTrains and London's Docklands light rail system.

To implement the project, a development corporation, Orestadsselskabet, has been formed, with ownership split between the municipality of Copenhagen and the national government. The corporation plans to finance bank loans through capturing the value added from adjoining property development and by selling off land reclaimed from the sea a half-century ago. The proceeds from the sale of fully served sites will be used to repay the investment loans secured to finance the City Line and the township's main infrastructure.

Copenhagen's emerging sixth finger has not escaped criticism. Some opponents charge that the Ørestad redevelopment represents a bias among public officials toward grand projects in the French Haussman tradition. Money could be better spent, critics argue, by redeveloping existing rail station areas. Some even fear that Copenhagen's almost sacred five-finger hand—the guide to physical growth over the postwar era—will be irrevocably transformed into a deformed appendage, maybe one day replaced by sinuous arms snaking in all directions. With potential job growth resting on the project and unwavering government support, such criticism has so far failed to slow Ørestad's progress.

Development and Transit Ridership Trends

Decentralization has posed a serious threat to Copenhagen's Finger Plan over the past four decades (Table 5.3). Starting in the late 1970s, industrial growth began to intrude into the green wedges of the five fingers. Facing a slowdown in regional growth, many municipalities welcomed the arrival of new industries and businesses, even those wanting to locate in the green wedges, in hopes of attracting workers to local residences (thus

Table 5.3 Population and Employment Growth Rates, Central Copenhagen and the Inner Suburban Ring, 1955 to 1993

	Population			Employment		
	1955	1993	% Change	1955	1993	% Change
Copenhagen, municipality	760,000	460,000	–39.5	460,000	310,000	–32.6
Copenhagen, county (inner suburban ring)	310,000	605,000	+95.2	135,000	330,000	+144.4

Source: Hovedstadsregionens Statistikkontor, *Statistisk Årbog 1993 for Hovedstadsregionen*, 1993.

increasing local income tax yields).[10] Thus, despite the absence of property or corporate taxes that might prompt fiscal zoning, some municipalities willingly accepted new commerce and industries even if it meant compromising the Finger Plan's cherished principles.

Despite the very best intentions of integrating urban development and rail transit, Copenhagen's Finger Plan and radial rail investments have failed to strengthen the central city as a base of employment. Indeed, the S-Train has quite likely helped to spur decentralization. The shift of jobs to the suburbs is reflected in commuting statistics. From 1980 to 1990, the number of suburb-to-suburb work trips within the region rose by 47 percent, whereas radial commutes fell by 3 percent and commutes within fingers fell by 5 percent. With trip origins and destinations increasingly scattered in all directions, transit's ridership has suffered, as in virtually all of Europe. The annual number of public transit trips in greater Copenhagen fell from 310 million in 1982 to 242 million in 1992. The S-Train's market share of all motorized trips dipped from 11.5 percent in 1981 to 10 percent in 1990. Still, transit remains a vital component of greater Copenhagen's transportation system, capturing about one-third of all person-kilometers of motorized travel.[11] Its relatively high share of total motorized trip kilometers reflects the heavy dependence on rail transit for longer, intrafinger trips. And as noted, rail transit continues to carry the lion's share of work trips from outer suburbs to the central city.

The trend toward more spread out patterns of development has not undermined all forms of mass transit. Today, bus ridership is increasing 2 percent per year. During the 1990s, ridership on the S-Bus system—a premium-quality crosstown service (e.g., skip-stop services and over-the-road coaches)—has been rising by 6 to 7 percent annually, versus the 2 to 3 percent drop along other bus routes. In general, greater complexity in travel patterns has lead to greater segmentation in travel mode choice. Rail transit continues to handle mainly radial trips, which constitute a declining share of the market. Bus transit caters mainly to cross-town travel—

currently comprising 15 percent of all mass transit trips and growing. Buses also increasingly serve radial trips within fingers whose origins and destinations are too far from rail stops.

It would be wrong to blame faltering ridership solely on decentralization and nonadherence to the Finger Plan. Mass transit's diminishing role in greater Copenhagen can be attributed to at least two other factors as well: rapid increases in private vehicle ownership (despite a punitive vehicle tax system) and declining real motoring costs. Adjusted for inflation, the price of motor fuel fell by 50 percent in Denmark between 1980 and 1994, while mass transit fares rose by 85 percent over the same period.[12] These price differentials have inevitably encouraged motoring since it is well known that travelers heavily weigh conspicuous, out-of-pocket expenditures, as for transit fares, when making mode choice decisions.

Shoring Up the Finger Plan

Post-1980 patterns of regional development and their implications for future sustainability have not gone unnoticed. In response to spread-out development and eroding transit ridership, regional planners have begun a process of shoring up and indeed reaffirming many of the principles of the original Finger Plan, especially those related to transit-oriented development. The importance of public transit, in both a narrow passenger-carrying sense and a broader environmental context, has been stressed at all planning levels in recent years.[13]

The 1987 regional plan update mandated that all regionally important functions be sited within a 1-kilometer walking distance of rail stations. The follow up 1993 plan update went even further. Under "Limitation Directives" set by the national Ministry of Environment, municipalities with rail services were asked to channel future urban growth within the immediate planning horizon to within 1 kilometer of rail stations. Presently, there is enough buildable land around stations to accommodate greater Copenhagen's growth over the next thirty years across all categories of urban land uses. With some 3,000 new housing units now being built annually in the region, the most recent plan update calls for concentrating all of this growth around transit stations. Consequently, permissible densities have been substantially increased around rail stations during the past five years. Commercial development has similarly been leveraged through density bonuses. At stations such as Ballerup, located along the northwest finger, enclosed shopping centers have been built in the air rights above the rail line (Photo 5.3).

At the subregional level, the city of Copenhagen has done more than any municipality in promoting transit-oriented development. Copenhagen's current municipal plan stipulates that: "sites for industrial

PHOTO 5.3. AIR RIGHTS DEVELOPMENT AND INTERMODAL INTEGRATION AT THE BALLERUP STATION. The top photo shows an enclosed shopping center and pedestrian bridge built in the air space over the station. Physically attached to the station–retail complex is a large office complex, aligned along one side of the rail line, shown in the bottom photo. The station and office-retail complexes enjoy good connections to a large bus interchange and bicycle path network.

purposes will be located in relation to the City's primary transit networks. Service industries and similar operations will be located within one kilometer, and preferably within a half kilometer, of stations on the regional railway system, especially the existing stations outside the historic city."

Nonmotorized Transport

The city of Copenhagen's commitment to transit-oriented development has been tied to a larger agenda of containing central city automobile travel. In this regard, nonmotorized modes—namely, walking and bicycling—are being called upon, not only as travel alternatives but also as viable means of accessing S-Train stations.

The Pedestrian City

As in many European cities, Copenhagen's core retains its medieval street pattern and stock of older walk-up buildings. The medieval city proved to be a natural habitat for creating what today is one of the largest and most successful pedestrian networks anywhere. Copenhagen's first pedestrian street, Strøget, opened in 1962 and quickly became the city's main shopping spine and promenade—indeed the city's main street. Today, it is the longest car-free street in Europe, accommodating some 55,000 pedestrians, often shoulder-to-shoulder, during busy summer days.[14]

Hoping to emulate Strøget's success, other central city streets were converted to pedestrian-only traffic in quick succession at the insistence of local merchants. Many of these converted streets, such as Strœdet, allow both cars and people, but give priority to pedestrians and bicycles. Today, Copenhagen has six times as many car free and pedestrian oriented areas as in 1962, when Strøget was created. Sidewalk vendors, roving musicians, open air markets, and street festivals have taken to downtown pedestrian streets. The head of traffic and planning for Copenhagen remarked, "the city center has changed noticeably over only three decades from a car-oriented to a people-oriented city center."[15]

In Copenhagen, it is important to note, urban designers view street life not only in terms of foot traffic throughputs, but also with regard to stationary activities. Copenhagen is blessed with large public squares (e.g., Gammeltorv and Nytorv) as well as small, remote ones (e.g., Gråbrødretorv). Of the nearly 100,000 square meters of people-oriented spaces in central Copenhagen, public squares make up two-thirds of the total. In contrast to pedestrian streets, squares beckon people to sit, watch, and take in city life. Great public spaces accommodate not only busy pedestrians and city celebrations but also casual sitting and relaxation. In a fascinating study of pedestrian life in Copenhagen, urban designers Jan Gehl and Lars Gemzøer found that the average number of people sitting and mulling around civic squares and pedestrian streets during daylight hours rose from 1,750 in 1968 to 5,900 in 1995.[16] To them, these often overlooked occurrences are part of the heart and soul of a city.

The Bicycle City

Complementing Copenhagen's bountiful pedestrian offerings has been an expanding network of bicycle facilities and amenities. In recent years, the city has made impressive headway in promoting intracity bicycle travel as well as enlisting bikes as means of feeder connections to rail stops.

Since the mid-1980s, the city of Copenhagen has been expropriating car lanes and curbside parking spaces for exclusive use by bicyclists. Between 1970 and 1995, bike lanes increased from 210 to more than 300 kilometers in length. During the same period, the number of bike trips rose 65 percent. When the weather is nice, more Copenhagen residents get to work by bike (34 percent) than by car or mass transit (31 percent each).[17] Even on rainy days, 60 percent of cyclists remain loyal to their preferred means of travel. A dedicated 30 percent of cyclists brave sleet, frost, and snow to get to work.[18]

To further promote cycling, Copenhagen introduced a short term bike lease program, called City Bike, in 1995. The basic idea is to populate the city with enough "spare" bikes to serve trips that are too long to walk but too short to justify waiting for a train or bus. The system operates like stacked shopping carts at supermarkets. More than 2,000 white bikes, stripped down to the essentials and easily distinguished from ordinary bikes, have been placed at some 125 bike stands throughout the city. Inserting 20 krone (about US$3.70) into a coin slot provides one with a bike; borrowers get their money back upon returning the bike. The program is being partly financed through advertisements on the bikes themselves. Besides improving rail access, transit officials hope the City Bikes will reduce on-vehicle carriage of bikes, thus freeing up more train capacity for passengers.

So far, there have not been enough bikes to go around. As might be expected, part of the shortfall is due to people keeping bikes at home, despite the threat of a 1,000 krone (US$185) fine for such infractions. Sponsors have also responded through design modifications: altering components so that no part of the bike will fit on an ordinary bike; gearing them to make distance cycling taxing; and equipping them with small microchip locating devices.

Nonmotorized Access to Train Stations

The value of creating a pedestrian and bicycle city is underscored by Copenhagen's incredibly high shares of access trips to transit stops via nonmotorized modes. A 1994 survey of access trips to fifteen suburban stations found that walking dominated for distances up to 1 kilometer from stations, capturing 38 to 100 percent of access trips. For 1 to 1.5 kilometers away, cycling was the dominant access mode, accounting for about 40 percent of access trips. Only for access distances beyond 1.5 kilometers did motorized modes dominant, with buses carrying 40 to 50 percent of these access trips. Even at 2.5 kilometers away from stations, cycling access exceeded automobile access—30 percent versus 19 percent.[19] These figures stand in marked contrast to rail access modal splits found in North America. In the case of the San Francisco Bay Area, for example, walking and cycling make up less than 4 percent of access trips 2.5 kilometers from rail transit stations, whereas private cars are used two-thirds of the time.[20] Urban designers such as Richard Untermann have demonstrated that acceptable walking distances can be stretched considerably (perhaps as much as doubled) by creating pleasant, interesting urban spaces and corridors.[21] The distaste for walking in unappealing environs is shown in the irony that many Americans will go to great lengths to find a parking spot close to the entrance of a shopping mall, but think nothing of walking 1 or 2 miles once inside the mall. Experiences in Copenhagen clearly underscore the importance of both urban design and basic provisions for pedestrians and cyclists in swaying people to leave their cars at home when accessing transit stops.

Other Constraints on Auto Use

The city of Copenhagen has taken further steps over the years to contain automobile traffic in the core. An offshoot of giving priorities to pedestrians and cyclists has been a policy of "managed congestion." By design, city traffic engineers have sought to temper car use by holding the total capacity of the central city road network constant since 1970. Partly as a result, traffic volumes, measured in terms of kilometers driven per year, have fallen by some 10 percent below the 1970 level.[22] Besides expanding the city's cycling and pedestrian network, Copenhagen's traffic management policies have emphasized preferential signalization and reserved lanes for buses, relocation of on-street parking to the periphery, and the expansion and diversification of transit offerings (including electric minibus circulators and new tram lines). The aim of traffic management has not so much been to remove cars from the city, but rather to ensure that any growth in travel does not translate into increased car traffic.

The management of parking supplies and prices has also been critical to containing central city automobile traffic. Over the past few decades, the city of Copenhagen has been reducing parking supplies by 2 to 3 percent per year. Today, Copenhagen's core has only one-third the amount of parking as Stockholm's. Moreover, parking fees fluctuate to ensure prices are high enough to induce rapid turnover. Today, curbside parking in the central city costs as much as US$4 per hour. Parking rates are highest in areas well served by mass transit.

Lastly, Denmark's tax system has also been used to restrain automobile ownership and consumption. Presently, taxes and fees roughly triple the cost of purchasing a private automobile. To discourage the purchase of large, fuel-inefficient vehicles, taxes increase with vehicle weight and engine sizes. Presently, Danes average 330 cars per 1,000 inhabitants—below that of ten other European countries (including poorer nations like Spain) and even less than Japan's rate. The combination of hefty motoring fees, pro-transit development, pedestrian amenities, and constraints on auto travel have suppressed vehicle ownership rates within Copenhagen proper to one of the lowest among First World cities. In 1994, there were just 185 cars per 1,000 residents, even less than Bangkok's ownership rate.

Learning from Copenhagen

Copenhagen's hand-shaped cityscape is the product of carefully integrated rail transit and urban development, orchestrated under the 1947 Finger Plan and its subsequent updates. Most urban growth has occurred along the five fingers, and until recently, green wedges have not been intensively encroached upon. Central Copenhagen remains easily accessible by train along all five fingers. Many suburbanites live within a convenient walk or bus ride of a rail station. When heading to the central city, the combination of efficient train services and constraints on parking and motoring make transit riding a sensible choice. However, Copenhagen is not just a story of building rail-oriented new towns along fingers. The municipality has strengthened the integration of transit and urban development by enhancing the viability and aesthetic qualities of the traditional city core. Streets and curbsides have been dedicated to pedestrians and bicycles. Most transit users today reach central city train stations by bike and foot. While transit's market shares have been eroding in recent decades, as in the case of nearly all European cities, recent initiatives to target future urban growth around rail transit stations holds considerable promise for reversing this trend.

Copenhagen can hardly be held as a paragon of institutional efficiency. Multiple layers of government are involved in physical planning, largely in a top-down, hierarchical fashion. Levels of commitment to regional planning have vacillated over the years with swings in political mood. In many instances, such instability would be a formula for planning disasters. Greater Copenhagen's saving grace, however, has been its Finger Plan, an almost universally accepted norm for organizing the region's physical growth. It is difficult to overstate the symbolic significance of the Finger Plan. There can be little doubt that if it were not for this normative vision of a hand-shaped future urban form, the nexus of transit and cityscape currently found throughout greater Copenhagen would be far weaker than exists today. Current plans to target future growth to within a kilometer of existing and planned rail stations can only be expected to strengthen this nexus in years to come.

Notes

1.   In 1992, the region's inventory of rolling stock stood at 1,122 HT buses, 302 private buses, 598 S-Trains, and 80 private trains.

2.   W. Cox, J. Love, and N. Newton, Competition in Public Transport: International State of the Art (Paper presented at the Fifth International Conference on Competition and Ownership in Passenger Transport, Leeds, England, May 28, 1997).

3.   Copenhagen's early wave of suburban growth was to the north. Upper-middle-class families were drawn to this area because of its natural beauty—hills, lakes, and open space. The national policy to promote growth to the south was partly aimed at achieving regional spatial balance.

4.   All of Denmark is made up of urban and rural zones. This has served to demarcate urban from rural areas, much like an urban limit boundary. Actual zoning is controlled at the local level.

5.   Established in 1974 in reaction to uncoordinated suburban growth, the Council's main responsibility was public transport and physical planning. The Council was empowered to implement regional plans and was provided with funds to buy land needed for development and new infrastructure. By the time the entity was formed, however, regional growth had virtually stopped, weakening its political imperative. The Council proved unpopular with left-wing mayors, who hoped for major urban changes, and conservative mayors, who viewed it as interfering with local affairs and private interests.

6.   The Finger Plan was prepared by a committee of young town and transportation planners, partly in reaction to the galloping urban sprawl that was occurring in America and parts of Europe. The Finger Plan was heavily influenced by Ebenezer Howard's new town theories and Lewis Mumford's ideas about neighborhoods functioning as the building blocks of regional development.

7.   Copenhagen Regional Planning Office, *Preliminary Outline Plan for the Copenhagen Metropolitan Region: Translation of the Text of the Report, Com-*

prising a Discussion of the Principles on Which Urban Development in the Region Should Be Based in the Period Up to 1980 (Copenhagen: Copenhagen Regional Planning Office, 1961).

8. Critics charged that new towns along the south fingers became repositories for central city slum clearance. In the minds of many middle-class Danes, rail-served new towns to the south are equated with social housing and low-skilled immigrant households. They stand in marked contrast to Copenhagen's hilly northern suburbs, which are inhabited mainly by native Danes and upper-income households.

9. P. Olesen, *Copenhagen: For Better, for Worse* (Copenhagen: NordGraf, 1996), pp. 88.

10. Municipalities sometimes zone for growth in the wedges, in part because it is cheaper and easier to build in these areas and because large commercial investors often prefer these settings. This was especially so in the early 1990s, when the region was beset with a lingering recession, prompting many suburban communities to accept the locational choices of commercial builders.

11. In 1990, the modal distributions for person kilometers of travel by mechanized modes (including bicycle) was: S-Train, 10.0 percent; other train, 8.1 percent; bus, 6.5 percent; car, 67.1 percent; bicycle, 8.3 percent. Netting out bicycles, and thus measuring person kilometer distributions for motorized (versus mechanized) trips, gives mass transit about a 33 percent market share. Source: HT og DSB, Kollektive Trafikplan, Copenhagen, 1993.

12. Source: *Ibid.*

13. H. T. Andersen and J. Jørgensen, Copenhagen: City Profile, *Cities*, vol. 12, no. 1, 1995, pp. 13–22.

14. During the more limited daylight hours of winter months, Strøget handles some 25,000 pedestrians per day. The daily throughputs for all seasons have stayed remarkably constant over the past three decades. Source: J. Gehl and L. Gemzøe, *Public Spaces—Public Life, Copenhagen 1996* (Copenhagen: Danish Architectural Press, 1996), p. 12.

15. Quoted in: Gehl and Gemzøe, *op. cit.*, p. 6.

16. *Ibid.*, p. 62.

17. *Ibid.*, p. 43.

18. B. Eir, A Health Traffic Plan for the City (Copenhagen): Changing the Mode of Transport (Proceedings of the Conference on "Car-Free Cities?" Amsterdam, Netherlands, May 1994).

19. *Source*: DSB S-togy, *Planlægningstemaer for S-Tog* (Copenhagen: DSB, February 1995).

20. R. Cervero, *Rail Access Modes and Catchment Areas for the BART System*, BART @ 20 project, monograph (Berkeley: Institute of Urban and Regional Development, 1995).

21. Richard Untermann, *Accommodating the Pedestrian: Adapting Towns and*

Neighborhoods for Walking and Bicycling (New York: Van Nostrand Reinhold, 1984).

22. Reduced central city automobile traffic has also been a product of the city's
declining population and employment base, limits placed on parking, and
the shift of auto trips to outer ring roads.

Chapter 6

The Master Planned Transit Metropolis: Singapore

Singapore today boasts an internationally acclaimed rail transit system that is the backbone of the island-state's multicentered settlement pattern. Through the heavy hand of centralized planning, combined with an odd blend of free-market economic policies, growth outside the core has been organized into concentrated, mixed-use centers that are efficiently linked by high-capacity transit services—notably rail, but also an assortment of conventional and double-deck buses that are privately owned and operated. Planners have consciously sited high-rise housing and office buildings near transit stops to maximize accessibility and minimize automobility. Singapore's long-range constellation plan calls for a hierarchical pattern of some fifty rail-served town centers in an all-out campaign to increase transit modal splits to among the highest in the world. In Singapore, pro-transit "carrots" have been matched by auto-restraint "sticks." Today, the island-state is at the forefront of managing automobile traffic at levels that are viewed as socially optimal. Singapore was the first to introduce area-wide licensing, a scheme that has been credited with moving travelers into trains and buses and evenly distributing traffic flows throughout the day. Singapore has also pioneered a vehicle quota system that requires prospective car buyers to bid for the right to register and own a new car, with the allowable vehicle stock index for any one year tied to island-wide traffic conditions. Vehicle quotas, along with an assortment of extra fees and surtaxes, have reduce the island's vehicle population growth from 6 percent to 3 percent annually, a remarkable achievement for a city where per capita incomes have risen faster than almost anywhere in the world over the past decade.

Over the past three decades, the city-state of Singapore has progressed from Third World poverty to become one of Asia's most dynamic and modern industrialized economies. Between 1970 and 1980, Singapore's gross domestic product rose 9 percent annually, and manufacturing jobs soared from 25,000 to 287,000, resulting in full employment.[1] With little

155

land or natural resources, Singapore has relied on its strategic location, low-cost labor, infrastructure expansion, and an unprecedented level of physical master planning to catapult itself into the ranks of a modern, industrialized country, with living standards that now match those of Japan and Western Europe. Pivotal to Singapore's economic transformation has been the creation of a comprehensive and efficient transportation system. Today, Singapore boasts the world's second-busiest containerized port, a major international airport, a top-ranked airline, a sizable national shipping line, a network of superhighways, and a new, modern mass rapid transit system (MRT). This massive build-up of transportation infrastructure occurred within the framework of a highly centralized physical and economic planning system that has carefully guided the country's development over the past three decades. Another product of centralized planning has been some twenty satellite master-planned new towns, linked together by the new MRT like pearls on a necklace. Not unlike the suburbs of Stockholm and Copenhagen, most new towns are centered around an MRT station, with housing, retail shops, community facilities, and open space neatly juxtaposed in relation to the transit hub. Complementing this integration of rail and new towns has been a series of draconian measures taken to restrain automobile ownership and usage, diverting the majority of motorized trips into trains and buses.

A review of Singapore's experiences shows what is achievable under extremes—near-complete centralized control over urban development and community design, punitive pricing of the automobile, and a socially minded, pro-transit government. Singapore can claim one of the most efficient transit–land use connections anywhere today though some might say at the expense of excessive government interventions and limits on lifestyle choices. Still, most Singaporeans strongly back their government and the heavy hand of centralized planning, viewing a degree of authoritarianism as a small price to pay for living in a modern, prosperous metropolis with generous public services, including a world-class rail system, matched by few other places.

From Rickshaw to Rapid Transit

Situated just north of the equator, Singapore is made up of several small islands, the largest of which is the diamond-shaped main island of Singapore (42 kilometers from east to west and 23 kilometers from north to south) (Map 6.1). The entire island-nation is 648 square kilometers in size and is home to some 3.4 million residents. Seventy-eight percent of Singaporeans are of Chinese descent.

Following a century and a half of mainly British rule, in 1965 Singapore became an independent republic with a single-tier parliamentary sys-

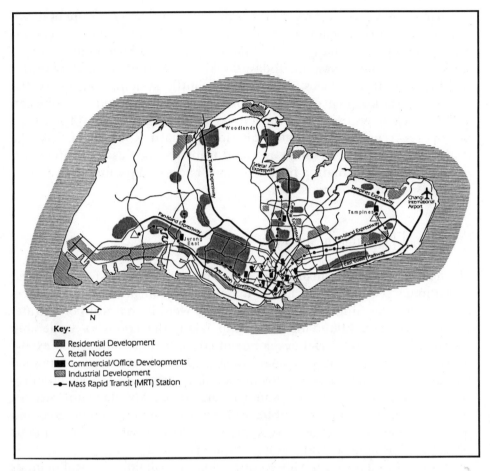

MAP 6.1. DEVELOPMENT OF SINGAPORE ISLAND, 1997. *Source:* Adapted from Richard Ellis (Singapore) Pte., Ltd., *ULI Market Profiles* (Washington, DC: The Urban Land Institute, 1995).

tem of government. Lee Kuan Yew was elected the country's first prime minister, a post he held until his resignation in 1990. It was under Yew's leadership and firm control that Singapore's dramatic economic and physical transformation into a modern, industrialized state took place.

In the early 1900s, Singapore was a poor island-outpost. Its aging port and retail core were ringed by slums and squalor. Most Singaporeans relied on either primitive means of transportation, notably rickshaws and horse carriages, or the several hundred tiny Chinese-run buses, known as "mosquitoes," to get around. As Singapore prospered, the conflict among human- and horse-drawn modes, mosquito buses, and other motorized traffic prompted authorities to consolidate bus services and all but ban slow-moving vehicles.[2] By the mid-1970s, the eleven Chinese-owned bus

companies that had long served the island were, under government directive, merged into three and eventually into a single state-controlled enterprise.[3] And by 1990, many cross-island bus routes had been replaced by a
sleek, modern metro system. Today, the MRT is complemented by feeder
and mainline bus services, a downtown shuttle system, and one of the
world's largest taxi fleets. Though long gone from most quarters, one can
still find rickshaws in older parts of town and plying the tourist trade near
Singapore's renowned shopping district, Orchard Road. In a way, the
transformation from rickshaw to rapid transit stands as a metaphor for
Singapore's transformation from a remote, backward port town to a modern, prosperous metropolis.[4]

Centralized Planning in Singapore

Singapore's physical transformation has first and foremost been shaped
by national economic development policies. Soon after independence,
recognizing that Singapore's primary assets were its natural port, strategic location, and abundance of cheap labor, the country's leadership
embarked on an industrial development strategy that emphasized export
manufacturing and multinational investments. Tax concessions attracted
foreign capital, and industrial towns were built using prefabricated infrastructure, allowing foreign manufacturers to quickly start up low-cost
branch plants. The mix of public sector involvement in commerce and
industry under a free-enterprise system gave rise to what today remains
Singapore's peculiar brand of social capitalism.

Singapore's leadership viewed upgrading the island's physical plant as
absolutely essential in jump-starting foreign investments and triggering
economic growth. During the 1960s, Singapore's surface area was expanded by more than 10 percent through reclamation: hills were leveled,
decaying neighborhoods were flattened and redeveloped, industrial parks
and housing estates were built, Changi International Airport was opened,
and the southern shore was developed into one of the world's busiest
ports. Sewage provisions rose from 650 to 2,145 kilometers of line, and
from serving less than a third to 96.8 percent of the population.[5]

Singapore's one-party rule provided the political unity and stability
necessary for a highly centralized strategic planning process to emerge.
And its land and natural resource constraints meant that the newly independent government could justify to its citizens that a strong guiding
hand was needed to launch Singapore onto a path of sustained economic
growth.[6] One of the first steps taken to win popular support for centralized planning was the relocation of most residents from crowded, poorly
serviced slum housing and semirural compounds into modern, high-rise
housing units. Over the years retail, cultural, and service facilities were
gradually added to high-rise residential nodes, and a network of feeder

roads and expressways was laid to connect residents to the urban core and
newly built industrial estates. From 1970 to 1990, while Singapore's population increased by nearly 50 percent (2.07 to 3.01 million), the number
of dwelling units almost quadrupled (180,600 to 735,900), and commercial floor increased more than 7.5 times (0.31 to 2.45 million square feet).
During the same period, Singapore's urbanized area went from covering
32 to 51 percent of the island. Average densities, on the other hand, fell
from 11,000 to 8,800 persons per square km.[7]

Singapore's physical development during the 1960s was guided in
large part by town planning principles carried over from British colonial-
ism. Rapid growth underscored the need for comprehensive planning.
This led to the approval of a Concept Plan in 1971 that provided a blueprint for the country's physical development for the next twenty years.[8]
Known as the Ring Plan, it called for configuring high-density housing,
industrial sites, and urban centers in a ring around the urban core, linked
together by a high-capacity and efficient transportation network (Map
6.2). This plan formed the basis for the construction of new towns and the

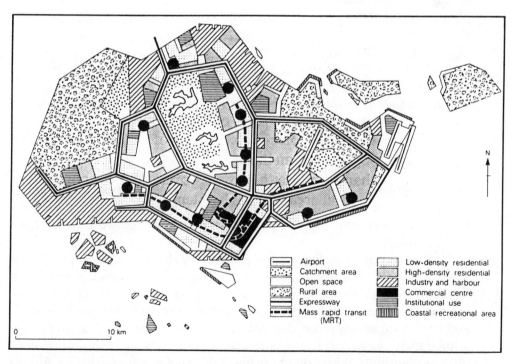

MAP 6.2. SINGAPORE'S RING PLAN. The plan aimed to provide an orderly path for decen-
tralization while maintaining a strong-centered development pattern. The desire for
efficient commuting patterns strongly shaped the resulting plan. *Source:* L. Wang,
Residential New Town Development in Singapore: Background, Planning, and Design,
New Towns in East and South-east Asia: Planning and Development, D. Phillips and A.
Yeh, eds. (Hong Kong: Oxford University Press, 1987).

MRT that would interconnect them. The restructuring of the island's star-shaped transport network into a series of rings, planners reasoned, would allow cross-island traffic to bypass the crowded city center.

Implementing the Plan

In Singapore, as in Stockholm and Copenhagen, one finds one of the most efficient connections between transport technology and settlement pattern anywhere. As with all good planning, land-use visions guided transport investments. Specifically, it was the Ring Plan's vision of a multinodal settlement pattern, featuring satellite new towns, that gave rise to Singapore's highly acclaimed fixed-guideway rail network and supporting bus system.

In Singapore, uninterrupted, top-down decision making has expedited the process of plan execution. Singaporeans are generally highly respectful of and compliant to government. There is no discernible outcry over the lack of grassroots input into urban development decisions. As in Stockholm, an equally important factor in plan implementation has been public ownership of land. The Land Acquisition Act of 1966 empowered the state to take land for any public purpose, including the development of new towns. State land holdings increased from 31 percent of total land area in 1949 to 76 percent in 1985.[9] The Land Acquisition Act in effect greatly reduced the cost and streamlined the process of building new towns, setting up industrial estates, providing public housing, and investing in transportation infrastructure.

New Town Design

Most of Singapore's new towns predate the MRT, though rail transit's eventual arrival was anticipated and planned for. All are compact, with mixed-use cores and extensive pedestrian-cycling networks—in short, transit-oriented.

A hierarchical pattern of development was chosen for Singapore's first wave of satellite new towns. Each is made up of five to seven interlocking residential neighborhoods that orbit a higher-order town center. Most span about 40 hectares in size, contain some 4,000 to 6,000 dwelling units, and have a small neighborhood center of retail shops, schools, and recreational facilities within five minutes of all units. The basic building block of the community is the neighborhood precinct, each of which contains some 600 to 1,000 dwelling units that surround a landscaped village square, playgrounds, several small shops, and one or two eateries.[10] A system of walkways links precincts with neighborhood centers, which in turn are tied to the town center. Major pedestrian streams are separated from busy roads by gently sloped under- and over-passes.

One of Singapore's more successful rail-served new towns is Tampines. From its humble beginnings as a wasteland, Tampines has over the past two decades emerged as Singapore's principal regional hub for the eastern side of the island (Photo 6.1). The centrally located town center contains an MRT station, a bus interchange, and the DBS (Development Bank of Singapore) Tampines Center and Pavilion Cineplex, both built through the tried and trusted government land sale program. Surrounding the town center are eight neighborhoods, each with between 5,000 and 6,000 mid- and high-rise flats. Each neighborhood has its own commercial center serving everyday needs, such as dry-cleaning and convenience shopping. All flats are within a ten-minute walk of neighborhood centers, while schools, parks, and recreational centers are usually a short bus ride away. Tampines was the first Singapore new town to feature "green connectors," a series of interlinked walkways and open spaces through the housing precincts that bring play areas and landscaped green strips almost to residents' doorsteps. In recognition of its exemplary built form and strong transit orientation, Tampines received the coveted World Habitat Award in 1992.

New town centers were Singapore's first real attempt to create commercial districts outside of downtown. They uniquely combine American-style shopping malls and traditional shop-houses found throughout

PHOTO 6.1. TAMPINES CENTER. The privately built shopping complex lies west of the MRT station, flanked by mid-rise and high-rise residential towers.

Southeast Asia. Besides retail shops, town centers provide a full array of community services, including theaters, banks, medical clinics, and telecommunications centers. What is missing from most, however, are offices and other major employment sites. Thus, while the 1971 Ring Plan called for some degree of self-containment, few satellite new towns can claim this. In 1990, 79.3 percent of employed residents worked outside of their new town of residence.[11] Thus like Stockholm and Copenhagen, a considerable amount of cross-haul commuting occurs between Singapore's new towns and the urban core as well as among the new towns themselves.

New Town Housing

The prototype building chosen for Singapore's new towns was a high-rise slab structure, ranging from ten to twenty stories in height and averaging 200 units per hectare. The standardization of housing substantially reduced the time and cost of construction, though at the expense of creating a somewhat monotonous built environment. Egalitarian ideals strongly influenced building designs. Singapore's housing planners deliberately provided for flats of all sizes (one-room to five-room units) to avoid the geographic separation of income groups. In allocating flats, planners sought to strike a balance in terms of racial and ethnic mixes, a policy that continues today. In light of earlier slum conditions and the nation's land constraints, Singaporeans quickly adapted to—and, surveys suggest, have a high degree of satisfaction with—housing conditions, even in high-rise settings.[12]

By 1995, Singapore's chief home builder, the Housing and Development Board (HDB), had housed 87 percent of the population in some 700,000 flats, most located in the island's twenty new towns. Ownership of publicly built flats increased from 25.4 percent in 1970 to 84 percent in 1995. Including private housing, Singapore's home ownership rate today stands at 86 percent of all households, significantly higher than in most developed countries.[13] This has been achieved both through government subsidies and the provision of a basic housing shell, which keeps prices low and allows residents to embellish their homes as they choose.

Singapore's housing planners hope to diversify the island's housing stock by promoting more low-rise, private home construction. From 1991 to 1995, the HDB released more than 200 hectares of land for private housing development. Some parcels are near MRT stations, including Bishan, Simei, and Yishun, in hopes of giving some stations a spacious, open character. At these stations, feeder buses connect outlying high-rise housing to the MRT (Photo 6.2).

Photo 6.2. Bus-rail interface. Bus connections between the Yishun MRT station and outlying high-rise residences.

Industrial and Employment Growth

Since Singapore's independence, the decentralization of employment has been largely orchestrated by the state through the development of planned industrial estates. The Jurong Town Corporation (JTC) was established as a separate statutory body to take over the management and development of industrial estates. By 1968, some 950 hectares of industrial land had been developed in the Jurong Industrial Estate on the western part of the island, with another 285 acres of industrial land spread out over eleven other planned estates, including Toa Payoh, Ang Mo Kio, Bedok, and Kambing Uli. By 1990, the island's twenty-four industrial estates were home to 4,160 companies that employed 254,000 workers, or one-fifth of Singapore's labor force. While many firms continue to leave the urban core in search of cheaper and more plentiful space, as in much of the industrialized world, they have tended to concentrate in planned estates under the direction of government planners, further strengthening the island's multicentered settlement pattern.

Retail Development

Singapore has not only experienced multicentered housing and industrial development, but a fair amount of retail subcentering as well. The MRT has proven to be a particularly strong magnet for retail construction. In all, fifteen of Singapore's twenty-three largest mixed-use shopping complexes lie within 400 meters of an MRT station. In addition, shops near the MRT, notably the City Hall, Orchard, Outram Park, and Bugis stations, earn appreciable rent premiums. A recent study found that commercial property values fell by about US$4 per square meter for every meter a parcel lies from an MRT station, and that otherwise comparable retail space rents for 30 percent more if near a station.[14] Even satellite retail centers have clung to the MRT alignment. By siting next to MRT stations, private shopping centers such as Northpoint (Yishun), Junction 8 (Bishan), Ginza Plaza (Clementi), and DBS Tampines Center tap into the growing and increasingly affluent public-housing populations. Not content to lose out on an opportunity to both integrate rail and land development and share in real estate profits, Singapore authorities have recently embarked on an aggressive effort to develop high-rise sites above and adjacent to MRT stations when constructing new lines.

Urban Transport in Singapore

By Southeast Asian standards, Singapore boasts an impressive roadway system—some 2,900 kilometers of paved roads and 132 kilometers of grade-separated expressways. The city-state averages three times as much road space per capita as Southeast Asia's other large capital cities: Bangkok, Jakarta, and Manila.[15] Consequently, its roads are relatively congestion-free, with peak hour travel speeds on central-area surface streets averaging 30 kilometers per hour.[16]

It is Singapore's public transportation, however, that is the workhorse of the urban transportation system, serving two-thirds of motorized trips. The combination of MRT trunkline services and motor bus feeders, all privately operated, has produced one of the most efficient and integrated transit networks anywhere.

Singapore's Transit Services

Singapore's 1971 Concept Plan called upon a new mass rapid transit system to serve as the island-nation's lifeline, linking residents of new housing estates to jobs, shopping centers, and recreational offerings throughout the island. In late 1983, MRT construction began with the main east-west line opening in 1987, followed by the opening of two north-south spurs in 1990, forming a 67-kilometer, forty-two-station system that was completed two years ahead of schedule and under budget (US$2.2 billion). An additional 16 kilometers and six stations were added in 1996, linking the two north-south lines via a new northern loop.[17] The MRT network is eventually slated to more than triple its current size upon build-out. The timing of the MRT investment is fortuitous, for it is occurring at a time when Singapore's pace of urban development is among the fastest in the world. This means the MRT is in an extraordinarily good position to steer and reinforce where and when growth occurs.

The MRT's performance is impressive by any standard. Trains average speeds of 40 kilometers per hour, 25 percent faster than the average car moves during rush hours. Peak period headways (i.e., time intervals between trains) are just three to four minutes, while off-peak headways are about twice as long. Trains arrive within a minute of schedule more than 99.7 percent of the time. And the MRT goes where its customers are—about half of Singapore's population resides within a kilometer of a rail station.

Complementing the MRT are privately owned, profit-making bus services under license to the Singapore government. The largest company is the Singapore Bus Service (SBS), which provides feeder runs to the MRT stations and crosstown links that both parallel and operate in areas unserved by MRT. Buses on SBS's 200 routes operate on three- to five-minute peak headways. SBS also operates the world's largest triple-axle double-deck buses, the Superbus. In 1983, the Trans-Island Bus Services (TIBS) was formed and given 10 percent of island-wide bus services, mainly in northern districts, to promote greater competition in the local bus sector. Also, there are five shuttle bus routes that connect peripheral parking lots to urban centers operated by the Singapore Shuttle Bus. In most new towns, buses handle about a third of access trips to MRT stations.[18] Nearly all new town residents live within a five-minute walk of a bus stop. Collectively, Singapore's bus services—all of which generate healthy profits—carry more than 3 million passengers a day, more than three times as many as the more celebrated MRT. While the MRT continues to win international praise for its efficiency and smart appearance, it is Singapore's highly functional yet less glamorous buses that are the true workhorses of the island's transit network.

In 1990, TransitLink Pte. Ltd. was formed to integrate the fares, timetables, and passenger information for Singapore's rail and bus services. This has led to the world's first stored-value fare card that can be used interchangeably for bus and rail travel. In 1995, some 2.2 million daily trips were made using the TransLink card.

Transit Ridership

Ridership on the MRT has increased steadily since its opening, rising from about 370,000 riders daily in 1990, to 676,000 in 1992, to about a million in 1997. Part of the explanation for patronage gains is system expansion; however, even in relative terms, MRT ridership has increased—from 24.4

passengers per train km in 1992 to 29.2 passengers per train kilometer in 1996.[19] Despite the MRT's growing popularity, buses continue to capture the lion's share of transit patrons, carrying more than 3 million passengers a day in 1996, with a good share of those trips being feeder connections to the MRT.

In 1994, the typical Singapore resident made 427 transit trips, up from 304 transit trips per capita a decade earlier. In Asia, only Hong Kong could claim as much transit usage per capita. A combination of factors—efficient services, high-density development (more than 10,000 persons per square kilometer), socioeconomics, and auto-restraint policies—account for transit's phenomenal popularity among Singaporeans. Table 6.1 suggests a strong correlation between transit ridership and two of these factors: housing density and occupation. In 1990, two-thirds of Singapore's workers commuted via mass transit—12 percent by the MRT and 54.4 percent by bus transit. Among those living in high-rise public housing, 72.3 percent commuted via public transit. By comparison, only around 37 percent of those living in lower-density, private homes commuted by rail or bus; more than half traveled by car. These modal split differences reflect a combination of land-use and income effects—those living in public housing typically are closer to and better served by transit, and also are less able to afford automobile travel. They also tend to reside in master-planned new towns that were designed around and consciously integrated with the MRT—in 1990, 74 percent of new town residents got to work via transit. Workers residing in high-rise housing also averaged shorter-distance commutes, suggesting they consciously sought out residential locations that minimized commuting time and monetary outlays.

Modal split differences along socioeconomic lines are further revealed by cross-tabulating commuting statistics by occupation. Over 75 percent of clerical and sales workers commuted via mass transit versus 50 percent of professional and production workers and just 20 percent of administrators and managers. The relatively high share of rail commuting among professionals and clerical–sales workers reflects the fact that many work downtown and in urban centers well served by the MRT.[20] Transit is the preferred mode of commuting even to satellite job centers—at Jurong, Singapore's showcase industrial estate, 67.9 percent of the 157,600 workers reached their jobs via MRT or bus in 1990.[21] It should be noted that the MRT was in its infancy when these 1990 commuting statistics were compiled; rail transit is thought to capture higher shares of the commuter market today and even higher shares of shopping trips.[22]

It is noteworthy that while Hong Kong is more than three times as dense as Singapore (and has fairly comparable income and transit service levels), its transit ridership per capita is nearly identical to Singapore's. Singapore's far-reaching set of government strictures that restrain automobile travel largely explain why.

Table 6.1 MODAL SPLITS FOR WORK TRIPS BY SINGAPORE'S WORK FORCE, 1990[1]

	All Workers	Type of Housing			Occupation			
		Public High-Rise	Private Single-Family	Private Flats/ Condominiums	Professional & Technical	Administrative & Managerial	Clerical, Sales, & Services	Production & Other
Bus Transit	54.4	59.0	30.3	28.8	38.6	14.3	57.6	66.4
MRT[2]	12.0	12.2	7.9	7.9	18.3	6.2	18.7	6.9
Automobile	18.5	13.9	50.1	52.1	33.8	68.5	11.9	6.6
Motorcycle/ scooter	5.6	6.5	1.5	1.3	3.2	1.2	4.8	7.9
Other[3]	9.5	8.4	10.2	9.9	6.1	9.8	7.0	12.2
Total	100.0	100.0	100.0	100.0	100.0	100.0	100.0	100.0

[1] For work trips made to job sites away from workers' residences (e.g., excludes those working at home, such as domestic workers who live in private houses).
[2] Includes work trips by both MRT and bus transit (i.e., use of bus as feeder).
[3] Includes trips by ferry, taxi, bicycle, walking, and other means.

Source: Singapore Census of Population Office, Department of Statistics, Singapore Census of Population 1990: Transport and Geographic Distribution (Singapore: Singapore National Press, 1994).

Restraints on Automobiles

Vital to the vision of creating a transit-oriented metropolis have been government initiatives that limit automobile ownership and usage. Since 1972, Singapore officials have increasingly tightened the noose on the island's car population through a steady stream of automobile surtaxes, road-use surcharges, and even a vehicle quota system in recognition of the nation's land constraints and to avoid the traffic gridlock that plagues many world cities, especially those in Southeast Asia. All motor vehicle tax proceeds go into a Consolidated Fund; thus, transportation-related revenues, which have steadily gained importance as a source of government income, are not earmarked for transport projects per se but rather are available for housing construction or any other public purpose.[23] Despite high fees for vehicle ownership and usage, motorized trips continue to grow at a rate of 7 percent annually.[24] Singapore officials are committed to setting motoring prices as high as necessary to shave several percentage points off this figure.

Restraints on Vehicle Ownership

Since its introduction in 1948, an annual road tax has been collected that reaches as high as US$3,500 for vehicles with large engines. In the late 1960s, Singapore instituted a surtax on automobile imports (all cars are imported), which over the years has risen to 45 percent of a car's market value. In 1980, a one-time registration fee of about US$670 (in 1996 currency) was tacked on. But as disposable incomes steadily rose, these surtaxes proved incapable of dampening car ownership. Thus, an additional registration fee was introduced, reaching 175 percent of a car's open market value during the 1980s and standing at 150 percent today, with hefty penalties for registration of vehicles more than ten years old (to keep more polluting vehicles off the road). Together, these surcharges have made new car purchases in Singapore as expensive as anywhere. Despite having one of the highest per capita incomes in Asia, fewer than 30 percent of Singaporean households own cars.[25]

In addition to fiscal deterrents to car ownership, Singapore also directly regulates the supply of motor vehicles. In 1990, a vehicle quota system was introduced, requiring all new vehicles to have a certificate of entitlement (COE), which is obtained through monthly sealed-bid tenders and is valid for ten years. Transportation planners set the maximum allowable vehicle stock each month based on prevailing traffic conditions, with new certificates apportioned among eight vehicle categories based primarily on engine size. For each category (including an "off-peak car" category) interested Singaporeans will bid on a COE.[26] In 1997, about half of the bids were successful. Since introduction of the quota system, prices of COEs have increased geometrically. In 1990, the premium for luxury cars (engine capacities of 2,000 cc and above) was US$330. Two years later, the premium had jumped to US$11,400. By 1995, it had surpassed US$70,000. Besides moderating automobile ownership, the COE has been a cash boon, generating US$1.23 billion in 1996, up from around US$100 million in 1991.[27] During its first five years, Singapore's vehicle quota system was blamed for causing rampant speculation and for creating an elitist system in which only the wealthy and large car distributors could afford to buy new cars.[28] Recent steps to limit bidding to consumers rather than retailers have dampened speculation and profiteering.[29]

Restraints on Vehicle Usage

Import surtaxes, registration fees, and vehicle quotas act as subscription fees—initial buy-in charges motorists must pay for the luxury of owning a car and to cover part of the fixed costs associated with scaling basic road infrastructure. In an effort to further refine automobile pricing, Singapore officials have also introduced a series of use-related charges, beginning with the introduction of the world's first area licensing scheme (ALS) in 1975. That year, government officials designated a 6-square-kilometer core area as a "Restricted Zone," which required a special license displayed prominently on one's car windshield for entry from 7:30 A.M. to 10:15 A.M. at a cost of US$2.00 per day. Motorists without special licenses face stiff fines if caught by patrol officers stationed at zone entrances (Photo 6.3). During the ALS's first year, there was a 76 percent reduction in cars operating within the zone during peak hours; 9 percent of motorists formerly driving through the zone had switched over to bus travel.[30] In early 1994, the ALS was extended to a full day, resulting in an immediate 9.3 percent drop in traffic entering and leaving the restricted zone. And between 1995 and 1997, road pricing was introduced along inner-city stretches of three major expressways. Before entering these expressway segments during the 7:30 A.M. to 9:30 A.M. period, each motorist must purchase and display a license costing US$1.40 (or US$28 per month).[31] The impacts on traffic conditions were immediate. Along the Central Expressway, average peak-hour speeds shot up from 31 kilometers per hour before to 67 kilometers per hour after the introduction of road pricing.

After more than twenty years of only minor changes, Singapore has begun phasing out the ALS, replacing it with a full-blown electronic road pricing (ERP) system. The system—which promises to ratchet the road pricing burden up one more notch—applies a highly sophisticated combination of radio frequency, optical detection, imaging, and smart card technologies. With ERP, a fee is automatically deducted from a stored-value smart card (inserted into an in-vehicle reader unit) when a vehicle cross-

PHOTO 6.3. AUTO-RESTRICTED ZONE. The overhead gantry signifies an entry point to Singapore's Restricted Zone.

es a sensor installed on overhead gantries at the entrances of potentially congested zones. The amount debited varies by time and place according to congestion levels. Cameras mounted on gantries snap pictures of violating vehicles to enforce the scheme. The system has been extensively tested prior to field implementation and demonstrated itself capable of communicating with in-vehicle units, identifying the type of vehicle, accurately deducting charges, and freezing the rear images of violating vehicles in free-flowing, multilane traffic situations with speeds of more than 120 kilometers per hour. Although long touted by transportation economists as the only fail-proof means of eliminating traffic congestion, road pricing proposals have always been stonewalled by political opposition. If all goes according to plan, Singapore's electronic pricing scheme will be the world's first true attempt to pass on real-time congestion charges to motorists.

The first phase of electronic road pricing was introduced along the East Coast Parkway in March 1998, and by mid-1999 the system is to be in place along all expressways and throughout the CBD. Within a month of initiating electronic road pricing, traffic along the East Coast Parkway fell by about 15 percent, from 16,200 to 13,900 vehicles per day. Volumes on parallel free routes rose by about the same amount, suggesting that road pricing has largely redistributed traffic over space versus across modes. Moreover, rush-hour speeds have risen from the 36 to 58 kilometers per hour range to a range of 50 to 60 kilometers per hour. Planners are now concentrating on fine-tuning the toll system to sharpen price differentials between the currently heavily subscribed peak hour (8 A.M. to 9 A.M.) and the more lightly utilized shoulders of the peak (7:30 A.M. to 8 A.M., and 9 A.M. to 9:30 A.M.). Charging peak-hour motorists twice as much as those traveling on the shoulders of the peak failed to shift traffic as much as was hoped. With electronic road pricing, Singapore has entered uncharted waters, thus figuring out the optimal pricing scheme will rely on a certain degree of trial and error.

In addition to road pricing, Singapore motorists face other use-related charges. Fuel taxes are set at 50 percent of pump prices, comparable to most European countries. An additional per liter surcharge is levied on leaded fuels. Moreover, regulations require all Singapore vehicles leaving the country to have at least three-quarters of a tank of gasoline to deter cross-border fuel purchases in Malaysia (where fuel taxes are much lower). Also, while there are private parking garages in Singapore, most off-street parking is government-owned and costly. Currently, a surcharge of US$45 per month is charged for downtown-area parking.

Despite this punitive pricing, Singapore's automobile population continues to grow—from 162,000 in 1980 to 381,000 in 1997, or from one car per 15.8 persons to one per 8.8 persons. Even in Singapore, officials are resigned to the reality that as disposable incomes continue to rise, increased motorization is inevitable. In Singapore, a great deal of prestige is attached to owning a good car. Singaporeans have, over the years, shown themselves to be extremely resilient to rising motoring charges, in part because of their high savings rates and comparatively modest outlays for housing.[32] (In 1991, a four-room public flat cost 2.29 years of an average Singaporean's income; a Toyota Corona would have cost 3.65 years of income.[33]) While future plans call for more freeways and lower-density residential construction, the tight controls over vehicle supplies and motoring charges, combined with the island's efficient transit–land use nexus, almost guarantee that traffic congestion will never get out of hand. While the island's vehicle population continues to grow in absolute terms, the combination of hefty ownership and usage fees has dramatically slowed the growth rate—from more than 6 percent annually in the late 1980s to about 3 percent annually today. No other city, or country for that matter, has come close to matching this.

Looking to the Future: The Constellation Plan

Having succeeded in building a healthy and prosperous export-based manufacturing economy, Singapore has now set its sights on becoming "the Switzerland of Asia," exporting not only goods but also information and services. With continued infrastructure investments, a highly educated work force, and a pro-business government, Singapore hopes to attract the regional headquarters of large multinational corporations and to globalize its service industries, providing everything from banking to construction services for other industrializing countries in the region. Singapore appears well on its way to becoming a global Information Age city—in 1993, three times as many people worked in the financial and business services sector as in 1970.[34]

To meet the demands of an affluent populace in what the government has called the "next lap" of national development, the physical planning component of Singapore's new national development strategy is set forth in the revised 1991 Concept Plan. The plan is structured in three stages: to the year 2000, to the year 2010, and to the year X (some fifty to seventy years in the future when the city-state is expected to reach its "ultimate" population of about 4 million and enlarge in area by another 17 percent). Most notably, it replaces the "ring" concept with a "constellation" scheme. A tidy hierarchical pattern of urban centers, interconnected by the MRT, is envisaged. The Central Area will remain the island's premier commercial and financial hub. A vastly expanded downtown and the addition of in-town housing will ensure that the core continues to be the focal point of the island's economy and culture. Inner-city housing is viewed as particularly important in creating a twenty-four-hour downtown street life.

Singapore's CBD of the twenty-first century, to be sited on land reclaimed from Marina Bay, seeks to become one of the world's most pedestrian-friendly environs.[35] Nearly all moving vehicles, including buses, will be restricted to the downtown periphery. Interceptor parking structures on the fringes will "catch" vehicles at the first point of entry to the CBD. An extensive network of second-story moving sidewalks, or travelators, will link the periphery and interior residences to the commercial core. Plans call for private developers to finance the travelator network as a precondition to receiving building permits. What could emerge is an all-electric hierarchy of mass transportation connections into and within the CBD—MRT mainline services, LRT feeders, and travelator circulators. A lavishly landscaped network of pathways, punctuated by public plazas, tree-lined promenades, and outdoor refreshment areas, is to complement the travelators in forming an attractive walking milieu that, urban designers hope, will help overcome, in the minds of pedestrians, Singapore's ever-present tropical heat and humidity.

Under the Constellation Plan, Regional Centers—Jurong East, Tampines, Woodlands, and Seletar—will orbit the newly expanded CBD. Each Regional Center is slated for some 800,000 residents and will, in turn, be orbited by smaller centers. The plan calls for the eventual build-out of some fifty new towns of various sizes. Some are to be neotraditional communities with road space kept to a minimum. In yet another twist, the new town of Punggol in northeast Singapore, which opened in early 1998, will feature a communal system of car ownership. Punggol residents will lease, rather than own, cars on an as-needed basis. And instead of neighborhoods of 5,000 to 6,000 units, Punggol will be developed in smaller estates of 1,200 to 2,800 units to, in the words of town planners, "create a sense of intimacy amongst residents and to encourage community bonding."[36] Overall, Singapore's long-range Constellation Plan strives to achieve an orderly pattern of "concentrated decentralization"—decentralized to relieve the core of overcrowding, but concentrated into dense, mixed-use nodes to allow for efficient rail services.[37]

The Constellation Plan also distinguishes itself from the previous Ring Plan by calling for a more equal distribution of jobs and housing throughout the island. By creating more self-sufficient communities, the plan seeks to contain trans-island commuting. It also places a great deal of emphasis on more varied housing (calling for more single-family and mid-rise structures),[38] open space, and public access to shorelines—necessary amenities for attracting the highly-paid executives and professionals who will staff a global service-oriented economy. Moreover, the plan affirms and strengthens the role of the MRT in future trans-island movement. New MRT extensions will link the island's primary residential and employment centers, radiating from the core area along three primary axes and providing circumferential connections among outlying centers. The "half cobweb" rail network envisaged for the future is shown in Map 6.3. Buses and new light rail lines will link MRT stations with nearby residences, jobs, shops, and districts unserved by the MRT. Light rail will be the favored form of feeder connection to MRT stations in the future. Around the turn-of-the-century, Singapore's first light rail lines will open—one to the already built community of Bukit Panjang (8 kilometers, thirteen stations), followed by one to the newly emerging community of Sengkang. Like the MRT, light rail services will be fully automated and grade-separated, though trains will have far less capacity and stations will be spaced far closer together. In the case of Sengkang, stations will be an average of 0.6 kilometers apart, ensuring that at least 70 percent of households are within 400 meters of a station. Since Sengkang is an entirely new estate, the design and development of LRT and the new town will be intimately linked to maximize accessibility. Proclaims a government brochure, *Sengkang Light Rail Transit: Integration in Motion:* "Sengkang New Town will enjoy a level of integration unprecedented in Singapore and set a new standard for transport planning for future New Towns."[39]

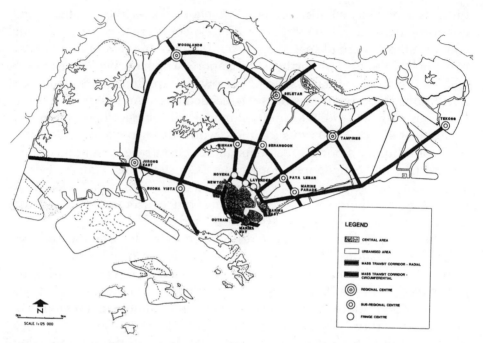

MAP 6.3. LONG-RANGE RAIL TRANSIT PLAN. The Constellation Plan envisages five long MRT lines ultimately radiating from the central area, together with three circumferential routes—a core area "circle line," a middle "semicircle," and an outer, sweeping semicircle. The current 48 MRT stations will increase to about 130.

Singapore's Future Centers

Subcentering will continue to be the primary means of sustaining Singapore as a transit-oriented metropolis. Under the Constellation Plan, the four Regional Centers will function as mini-CBDs, taking Singapore commerce and industry to the already decentralized work force. Each Regional Center will have up to 1.5 million square meters of commercial floor space and will head a new hierarchy of commercial centers, including five smaller Subregional Centers to be created around MRT stations and seven even smaller Fringe Centers formed around the edge of the core area (and also served by the MRT). Plans call for centers to have varying degrees of self-sufficiency so that jobs and amenities are distributed as close to homes as possible (Table 6.2).

Each Regional Center is to have its own industrial and economic base and a distinct identity. Woodlands, close to Johor, Malaysia, will be the Golden Triangle business hub (for the tri-national area of Singapore, south Malaysia, and the Riau Islands of Indonesia). Tampines, close to Changi International Airport, will become a corporate headquarters with an information technology park. Jurong East, already at the heart of manufacturing activities, will add a business park. And Seletar, already a region-

Table 6.2 NONRESIDENTIAL LAND DEVELOPMENT AMONG THE
CONSTELLATION PLAN'S HIERARCHY OF URBAN CENTERS

	Nonresidential Area (sq. meters)	Share of Nonresidential Floor Space			Average Distance to Downtown (kms)
		Office	Retail & Eating	Hotels & Entertainment	
Regional Centers	1.5 million	50%	35%	15%	13.0
Subregional Centers	0.5 million	40%	40%	20%	6.0
Fringe Centers	0.2 million	35%	45%	20%	2.5
Town Centers	0.1 million	40%	60%	0%	—[1]

[1] Varies by location of new town.
Source: Singapore Urban Redevelopment Authority, *Living the Next Lap: Towards a Tropical City of Excellence* (Singapore: Urban Redevelopment Authority, 1991).

al airport and not slated for MRT services until the year 2010, will house an aviation business park to serve the aerospace and oil-related industries.

Presently, Singapore's four Regional Centers are surrounded by vast expanses of open fields (Photo 6.4). Singapore officials hope to capitalize on this by recapturing the value added by public investments, including MRT extensions, through tax supplements. However, most open space surrounding Regional Centers will remain just that—open—as part of a system of protective greenbelts that helps retain natural ecologies and establishes clear edges between city and countryside.

PHOTO 6.4. OPEN SPACE, DISSECTED BY THE ELEVATED MRT LINE, NORTH OF THE TAMPINES TOWN CENTER. The vacant fields separating Tampines from the eastern terminus of the MRT, the new town of Pasir Ris, provide opportunities for value capture as well as the preservation of greenbelts.

Development Phasing

The Constellation Plan is to unfold over three distinct stages. The year 2000 stage calls for the accelerated development of new towns (e.g., Woodlands, Sembawang, Simpang) along the new MRT northern loop. By the year 2010, a new light rail line is to link the Yishun new town with Tampines via the new Seletar Regional Center. By this stage, all four new Regional Centers should be substantially developed. In the build-up to year X, development will shift to new landfills along the southern and eastern shores. By then, one of the world's great transit metropolises should become even greater.

Learning from Singapore

Farsighted and judicious planning has transformed Singapore into a multicentered metropolis whose major urban centers are superbly served by a world-class transit system. Like Stockholm and Copenhagen, Singapore's standard of living is high, as is its per capita transit usage. Also like these places, everyone enjoys high and equal levels of accessibility—young and old, rich and poor, and the physically abled and disabled alike can conveniently and inexpensively travel from anywhere to everywhere. As constraints on the automobile continue to tighten, Singapore officials well recognize that mass transportation options will have to expand and improve continually. Besides extending the MRT, transportation planners are aggressively seeking to upgrade feeder connections by building new LRT lines and adding tertiary systems such as travelators and grade-separated sidewalk networks.

It is important to remember that Singapore's intimate transit–land use nexus is the outcome of deliberate and carefully thought-out government decisions—decisions to restrain ownership and usage of the car; to build compact, transit-oriented communities; and to ensure equality of access to housing, education, and medical care. It is also important to recognize that what is called centralized planning in Singapore is spatially comparable to the scale of regional planning carried out by many medium-size jurisdictions around the world. Of course, Singapore's government wields considerably more power than any regional planning body in North America or Europe. And the absence of multiple levels of government, made possible by Singapore being a tiny island-state, has allowed for efficient and streamlined decision-making. Also unlike other places, authorities in Singapore are widely respected and rarely challenged. Part of the reason is that they deliver on their promises. Another is that they are careful to delineate the responsibilities of the public sector from those of private businesses. Still another reason is the government's vast talent pool. Each year, some of the best and brightest high school students are recruited into the ranks of civil servants. They are sent off to top Ivy League and British universities and upon their return are given compensation packages pegged to the best-paying private sector jobs.

Singapore's transformation into a great transit metropolis cannot be easily repeated elsewhere, of course. Unique confluences of history and geopolitics partly account for what has been achieved. And being a master-planned metropolis has its costs. Residents have had to make do with standardized housing, fairly compact living conditions, and a semi-autocratic government whose presence creeps into virtually all facets of everyday life. The real value of Singapore's experiences is that they show the kinds of efficient and sustainable patterns of urban development that can be achieved in a prosperous economy as well as the kinds of lifestyle sacrifices that people must make to achieve these results.

NOTES

1. GDP per capita rose from about US$1,100 in 1965 to US$16,275 in 1992. All monetary figures in this chapter are in (non-inflation-adjusted) U.S. dollars based on international exchange rates. *Source*: G. H. Chor, Only One Change, *Beyond 2000: A Challenge for a City* (Perth: City of Perth, 1992), pp. 39–43.

2. A. Spencer, Modernisation and Incorporation: The Development of Singapore's Bus Services, 1945–1974, *Environment and Planning A*, vol. 20, 1988, pp. 1027–1046; R. Cervero, Paratransit in Southeast Asia: A Market Response to Poor Roads? *Review of Urban and Regional Development Studies*, vol. 3, 1991, pp. 31–39.

3. P. Rimmer and H. Dick, Improving Urban Public Transport in Southeast Asian Cities: Some Reflections on the Conventional and Unconventional Wisdom, *Transport Policy and Decision-Making*, vol. 1, 1980, pp. 97–120.

4. For an in-depth account of Singapore's political economy and modernized transportation system, see: P. Rimmer, Rikisha to Rapid Transit (Sydney: Pergamon Press, 1986).

5. Richard Ellis (Singapore) Pte., Ltd., Republic of Singapore, *ULI Market Profiles: 1994* (Washington, DC: the Urban Land Institute, 1995).

6. Several statutory agencies have been particularly instrumental in spearheading Singapore's physical transformation. The Housing and Development Board (HDB) cleared slums and built low-cost public housing, the Urban Redevelopment Authority (URA) led physical land-use and infrastructure planning, and the Jurong Town Corporation (JTC) constructed industrial estates and business parks. Important instruments that empowered these organizations were the Planning Act and the Land Acquisition Act, essential to purchasing, controlling, and safeguarding land, and the Central Provident Fund, used to finance and guide the pace and direction of property development and investments.

7. Richard Ellis, *op. cit.*

8. Singapore's initial master plan was approved in 1955. This plan proposed a greenbelt to limit the expansion of the central area and called for urban growth to take place in new towns and new urban areas beyond the existing city. Since 1955, Singapore's master plans have been reviewed and updated every five years.

9. P. S. Young, *Housing Markets and Urban Transportation: Economic Theory, Econometrics and Policy Analysis for Singapore* (Singapore: McGraw-Hill, 1992).

10. L. Wang, Land Use Policy in a City-State: The Singapore Case, *Land Use Policy*, vol. 3, 1986, pp. 180–92.

11. Statistics measure the percent of employed residents working outside their development guide plan (DGP) area, a designated subarea within the five planning regions of Singapore that corresponds closely to new towns. Singapore has fifty-five DGPs—eleven in the core area and forty-four in outlying areas. Source of statistics: Singapore Census of Population Office, Department of Statistics, *Singapore Census of Population, 1990: Transport and Geographic Distribution* (Singapore: Singapore National Press, Pte. Ltd., 1994).

12. L. Wang, Residential New Town Development in Singapore: Background, Planning, and Design, *New Towns in East and South-east Asia: Planning and Development*, D. Phillips and A. Yeh, eds. (Hong Kong: Oxford University Press, 1987).

13. Under the Home Ownership Scheme, the HDB leases public flats to "owners/lessees" for ninety-nine years.

14. A. Chin and A. Suan, Treatment of Land Values and Development Benefits from Land Transport Infrastructure: Impact of the MRT on Commercial and Office Property Values (Paper presented at the Centre for Transport Research Seminar on Infrastructure Management, National University of Singapore, March 1995).

15. Cervero, *op. cit.*

16. J. Kenworthy, P. Barter, P. Newman, and C. Poboon, Resisting Automobile Dependence in Booming Economies: A Case Study of Singapore, Tokyo and Hong Kong within a Global Sample of Cities (Paper presented at the Asian Studies Association of Australia Biennial Conference, Murdoch University, Perth, Australia, July 1994).

17. Two separate entities are responsible for the MRT's construction and operation. The Mass Rapid Transit Corporation (MRTC) was formed in 1983 to build the MRT and plan for future extensions. The Singapore Mass Rapid Transit, Ltd. (SMRT) operates and maintains rail services under license from the MRTC. Both companies sell shares on the Singapore stock exchange. In fiscal year 1995–96, the MRT's passenger revenues exceeded operating costs by 34 percent, and SMRT's net profit topped US$90 million; US$67 million was automatically transferred to an assets replacement reserve to finance future extensions, leaving a net profit of US$33 million.

18. Most remaining access trips to MRT stations are by foot. Source: Kenworthy, et al., *op. cit.*

19. Singapore MRT, Ltd., *Annual Report 1992/93*, *Annual Report 1995/96* (Singapore: Singapore MRT, Ltd., 1996).

20. Historically, there has been a stigma attached to riding mass transit in Singapore, which is widely viewed as being very class conscious. With the MRT, however, white-collar workers have steadily joined the ranks of commuters who leave their cars at home and patronize public transportation.

21. A large share of Jurong's work force has historically resided on the eastern side of the island and endured long commutes to get to work. In 1981, it was estimated that 65 percent of Jurong workers had transit commute times of one hour or more. Of course, with today's efficient east-west MRT connections, hour-long commutes are pretty much a thing of the past.

22. A complete regional travel survey of all trip purposes has not been conducted since the early 1980s (as part of the planning for the MRT), but several nonpublished surveys indicate that mass transit probably captures about three-quarters of nonwalk shopping trips, according to transportation planners in Singapore's Urban Redevelopment Authority.

23. A. Spencer and C. Sien, National Policy Towards Cars: Singapore, *Transport Reviews*, vol., 5, no. 4, 1985, pp. 301–324.

24. Land Transport Authority, *White Paper: A World Class Land Transport System* (Singapore: Land Transport Authority, Republic of Singapore, 1996).

25. Singapore Census of Population Office, *op. cit.*

26. One of the categories is "off-peak car," which gives rebates against COEs (of up to about US$11,400) and annual road taxes (of about US$510) in return for vehicles being driven only during off-peak hours (7:00 P.M. to 7:00 A.M. on weekdays, all public holidays, and on weekends from 3:00 P.M. on Saturday until 7:00 A.M. Monday morning). Weekend cars are identified by a red-number plate, which must be welded onto the vehicle and sealed by an authorized inspection center.

27. N. Chia and S. Phang, Motor Vehicle Taxes: Their Role in the Singapore Revenue System and Implications for the Environment (Paper presented at the Third Biannual Workshop of the Economy and Environment Program for Southeast Asia, National University of Singapore, November 1994).

28. W. Koh and D. Lee, The Vehicle Quota System in Singapore: An Assessment, *Transportation Research*, vol. 28A, no. 1, 1994, pp. 31–47.

29. The prospect of windfalls attracted various profit seekers to the quota system, inflating the price of COEs in the early years. Automobile retailers and speculators sought to outbid each other for vehicle entitlements, sending bid prices skyward. In recent years, steps have been taken to remove the speculative element from the process. Automobile retailers can now bid for a COE only if a vehicle has a confirmed qualified buyer. Double transfers, wherein third parties acquire a COE and later sell it to a prospective auto owner or retailer at a markup, were also banned. As a result of these measures, COE prices have fallen by about 10 to 15 percent in recent years. In 1997, for example, successful bids for luxury cars (200 cc and above) were in the US$50,000 to US$55,000 range.

30. C. Seah, Mass Mobility and Accessibility: Transport Planning and Traffic Management in Singapore, *Transport Policy and Decision-Making* vol. 1, 1980, pp. 55–71; Spencer and Sien, *op. cit.*

31. Rates for motorcycles are about a third below those for automobiles. Proceeds of the road pricing system are partly used to provide rebates (US$14 for motorcycles and US$42 for other motor vehicles) on annual vehicle registration fees. See: S. Phang and M. Asher, Recent Developments in Singapore's Motor Vehicle Policy, *Journal of Transport Economics and Policy*, vol. 31, no. 2, 1997, pp. 211–220.

32. On average, Singaporeans save about 40 percent of earnings under a government-controlled social security program that attaches payment directly to individuals. Many use their savings to directly pay off their relatively inexpensive home loans, and after a few years many have no monthly housing outlays, freeing disposable income for private automobile ownership.

33. S. Phang, Singapore's Motor Vehicle Policy: Review of Recent Changes and a Suggested Alternative, *Transportation Research*, vol. 27A, no. 4, 1993, pp. 329–336.

34. Richard Ellis, *op. cit.*

35. Urban Redevelopment Authority, *New Downtown: Ideas for the City of Tomorrow* (Singapore: Urban Redevelopment Authority, 1996).

36. Urban Redevelopment Authority, Punggol 21: Where Gracious Living Is Defined, *Skyline*, vol. 43, 1996, p. 5.

37. The broad objectives set in the Constellation Plan are being translated into specific actions in fifty-five development guide plans (DGPs), being prepared for each of fifty-five communities, or DGP areas. As each DGP is approved, it modifies and updates the overall master plan.

38. The aim is to increase the share of privately built single-family dwellings and low- and medium-rise apartments. Low- and medium-density housing is to triple to about 450,000 units and high-density housing will double to 1.1 million units. The share of households residing in high-rise public units is expected to fall from the current 83 percent of inventory to about 70 percent.

39. Urban Redevelopment Authority, *Sengkang Light Rail Transit: Integration in Motion* (Singapore: Urban Redevelopment Authority, 1997).

Chapter 7

The Entrepreneurial Transit Metropolis: Tokyo, Japan

Crisscrossing the Tokyo region are some 2,000 kilometers of rail lines, most of which were built by giant conglomerates that are not only in the business of operating trains but selling consumer goods, services, and real estate as well. Tokyo's railway conglomerates have built entire new towns, complete with a full array of community services, from scratch. Rail and bus operations produce modest profits. The windfalls come from the land appreciation induced by the railway investments. In greater Tokyo, the practice of value capture is alive and well. While private interests have gotten fabulously wealthy in the process, the public at large has benefited from the efficient transit–land use nexus that has evolved. Tokyo's unique entrepreneurial approach to linking transit and urban development has produced win-win outcomes: both the private and public sectors have prospered—so much so that local and national governments have begun emulating past practices of private railway syndicates, having recently embarked on their own versions of rail-linked new town development. Tokyo's model of privately led rail and land development of suburbia should not go unnoticed elsewhere. The discordance between public transit investments and private land development in the suburbs of other parts of the world is a clear signal that different models of co-development, such as Tokyo's, deserve serious consideration.

Like Scandinavia and Singapore, Tokyo is an illustrious example of how rail transit and satellite new town development can be successfully linked. Unlike experiences in Scandinavia and Singapore, however, it has been the private sector, driven by profit motives, that has orchestrated the co-development of rail and new communities in greater Tokyo. The co-development of transit and suburbia finds its genesis not in Japan, but in America. A century ago, America's vast urban railway networks were built by entrepreneurs who packaged transit investments with real estate projects. Wealthy industrialists and oil barons gladly ventured into the risky business of building interurban rail lines in hopes of turning handsome profits from land sales. Early streetcar suburbs such as Shaker Heights, outside of Cleveland, and Scarsdale, north of Manhattan, owe their existence to these entrepreneurial motives. In Japan, and especially the Tokyo metropolitan area, co-investment in railways and new towns is still commonly practiced today. The majority of suburban rail lines in greater Tokyo have been privately built, typically by large consortiums that bundle together transit and new town development. In the United States and much of the developed world, the model of publicly led transit and privately led land development has become the norm since the end of World War II, with generally disappointing ridership results. Publicly built rail lines in suburban corridors where office parks, shopping malls, and tract housing can be easily reached only by car are frequent reminders that transit and real estate development have all too often been out of synch. Co-development might be an area where it is advisable to borrow from the past, encouraging entrepreneurs to link transit and real estate projects, just as they did in America a century ago, and just as they currently do in Tokyo.

Railway Development in Greater Tokyo

Tokyo is a huge metropolis with a dense and extensive rail transit network—totaling more than 2,000 kilometers in length, and with private lines today making up 52 percent of metropolitan trackage. The busiest rail-building period was between 1915 and 1935, when 580 kilometers of tracks were laid. As a land-scarce country with a rapidly industrializing economy and urbanizing population, housing development went wherever the rail lines did. New towns blossomed around the suburban rail stations because transit was virtually the only means of reaching central Tokyo, which then and still accounts for more than a third of all regional employment—one of the highest levels of employment primacy in the world.

While the suburbanization of Tokyo along railway lines began in the early 1900s, it was really during the post–World War II era of reconstruction and industrialization that new town building proliferated. Whereas publicly financed freeways paved the way for suburbanization in the United States, privately built rail lines became the channelways for suburbanization in greater Tokyo and other regions of Japan.

The Tokyo Region

Technically, there is no such entity as the city of Tokyo. The core area within a 20-kilometer radius of the historical center, Edo, is known as the Tokyo 23 Ward, home to 8 million residents (Map 7.1). The administrative area managed by the Tokyo Metropolitan Government, responsible for much of the region's public-sector new town planning, is the Tokyo Metropolitan Area (11.9 million population). The entire Tokyo conurbation is called the Tokyo Metropolitan Region, an area measuring some 15,000 square kilometers with a population exceeding 34 million that includes the surrounding prefectures of Saitama, Chiba, Kanagawa (which contains the city of Yokohama), and the southern part of Ibaraki.[1] Map 7.2 shows the geography of the Metropolitan Region, along with the sites of recent large-scale residential and commercial developments outside of the 23 Ward Area. The western part of the region, where much of the rail-oriented, new town activity has been concentrated, is known as the Tama District. Tama, named after a large district of hills, extends west some 50 kilometers from downtown to an area that is mountainous and lightly settled. The region's two largest rail-oriented new towns—the privately developed Tama Denen Toshi and the publicly sponsored Tama New Town—lie in the Tama District, as suggested by their names.

Central Tokyo's primacy as an urban agglomeration is reflected in statistics. While the 23 Ward Area contains 10 percent of the nation's population (on 0.6 percent of its land), it boasts 58 percent of Japan's largest company headquarters, 47 percent of bank deposits, and 84 percent of foreign companies.[2] Of the 8.3 million jobs in the Tokyo Metropolitan Region in 1990, 6.7 million, or 81 percent, were in the 23 Ward Area. Along with primacy, however, has come overcrowding, enormously high land costs, jam-packed subways, chronic traffic congestion, pollution, and difficulties of supplying a huge metropolis with water, energy, and other necessities. For the past few decades, the central government has embraced new town development as an instrument for deconcentrating inner Tokyo. This is

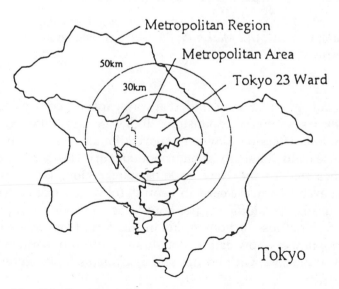

MAP 7.1. THE TOKYO METROPOLITAN REGION AND ITS SUBAREAS.

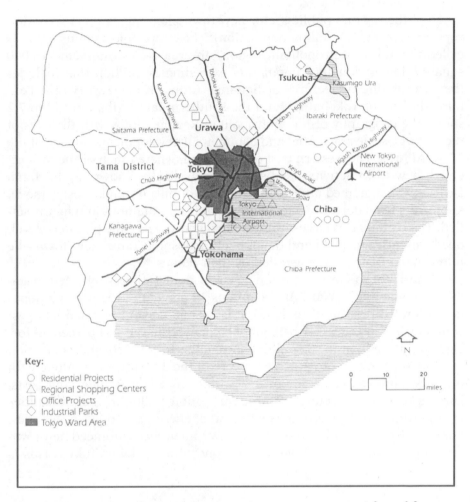

MAP 7.2. METROPOLITAN TOKYO AND RECENT REGIONAL DEVELOPMENT. Adapted from Nomura Research Institute, *ULI Market Profiles: 1994* (Washington, DC: The Urban Land Institute, 1995).

partly out of concern that land and roadway capacity constraints will undermine Tokyo's economic expansion.[3] Today, greater Tokyo averages 14,200 vehicle kilometers per day per square kilometer of land area, 1.9 times the vehicle traffic intensity of metropolitan Paris (Ile de France) and about 1.4 times that of the New York tri-state region. Between 1980 and 1990, the average travel speed in central Tokyo fell from 22.2 kilometers per hour to 15.8 kilometers per hour.[4] Recent exoduses of population (leading to a net loss of households in the core) have created what Japanese demographers now call a "doughnut" pattern of settlement—a hollowing out of the core, with houses and apartments replaced by office buildings.

Regional Railway Network and Ridership

Greater Tokyo's rail transit network and ridership performance are impressive by any standard. This section briefly describes current rail services in the region and their utilization.

Railway System

In 1990, a rail network of some 2,100 directional kilometers of track served a commutershed that expanded more than 50 kilometers from "ground zero"—the Tokyo station just east of the Imperial Palace and where the original Edo castle once stood (Map 7.3). Tokyo's metropolitan rail network—counting both publicly and privately owned railways—is, by far, the world's largest.[5] The system breaks down into the municipally operated subway, streetcars, monorail, and other modes serving mainly the core, the private suburban railways and subways, and the now-privatized Japan Railway interurban system (Table 7.1). Since 1970, aging streetcar lines have been steadily replaced by subways.

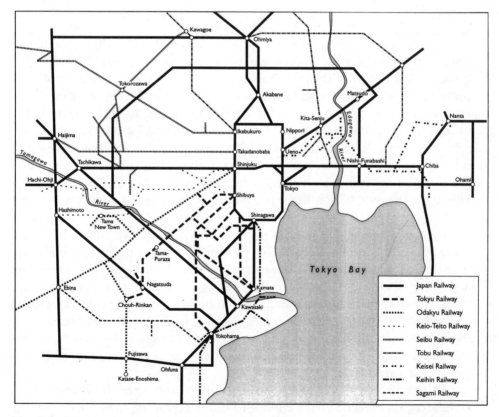

MAP 7.3. PRIVATE SUBURBAN RAIL LINES AND JAPAN RAILWAY LINES IN METROPOLITAN TOKYO.

TABLE 7.1   LENGTH OF URBAN RAILWAYS IN TOKYO METROPOLITAN AREA, 1970–1990

System	1970		1990		Change 1970–1990	
	Directional Kilometers	Percent	Directional Kilometers	Percent	Kilometers	Percent[1]
Japan Railway	713.6	38.9	876.4	42.0	162.8	+3.1
Private suburban railway	805.7	43.9	902.9	43.3	97.2	−0.6
Subway[2]	131.4	7.2	241.0	11.5	109.6	+4.3
Streetcar/light rail	171.3	9.3	17.3	0.8	−154.0	−8.5
Monorail, people-mover, other rail	13.0	0.7	49.8	2.4	36.8	+1.7
Total	1,835.0	100.0	2,087.4	100.0	252.4	—

[1] Percentage point change.
[2] Operated by the Teito Rapid Transit Authority (Eidan Lines) and the Municipal Subway Authority (Toei Lines).
Sources: Annual reports; K. Ohta, Transportation Problems and Policies of the Tokyo Metropolitan Region, Contemporary Studies in Urban Planning and Environmental Management in Japan, Department of Urban Engineering, University of Tokyo, ed. (Tokyo: Kajima Institute Publishing, 1993).

Encircling Tokyo's core area is the Yamanote line,[6] with major terminals (and high-rise office development) at Tokyo, Shibuya, Shinjuku, Ikebukuro, and Ueno. Within the Yamanote loop is a dense network of both public and private subways (Eidan and Toei) that crisscross central Tokyo and several lines of the now-privatized Japan Railway (JR), formerly the publicly owned Japan National Railway (JNR).[7] Radiating outward from JR's Yamanote loop is a thicket of privately built rail lines, plus JR's interurban lines. By national law, private lines are prohibited from passing through central Tokyo; it is at the terminuses on the Yamanote loop, where passengers switch from private lines to subways, that stations are the busiest.

With more than 4,500 daily runs on the subway system alone, headways between trains in central Tokyo average two minutes and waits are usually under a minute. (With average platform lengths of 200 meters and a walking speed of 4 kilometers per hour, even if a passenger misses a train, the next train will normally arrive before he or she can move from one end of the platform to the other.) Most suburban railways average six-to-eight-minute headways during peak hours. Overall, Tokyo's train system is extremely punctual and reliable and enjoys a safety record that is envied the world over.

Although Tokyo's train headways are incredibly short by international standards, this has not translated into quick commute times. In 1990, the average one-way commute within the region took sixty-six minutes. About 21 percent of commuters, or 1.85 million people, spent more than ninety minutes, one way, getting to work.[8] Thus, despite the existence of an efficient, world-class rail network, the sheer size of the Tokyo megalopolis has spread out development so much that commuters spend more time getting to work than in most parts of the world. Tokyo's monocentrism, with most jobs in the core area, has also inflated commuting times.

Transit Ridership

A dominant center and an extensive radial rail network have proven to be an effective combination in luring workers to public transit. Each morning, hundreds of thousands of neatly dressed Tokyo commuters pack into immaculately clean trains to begin their working day. In 1990, 3.5 million commuters took rail or some other form of public transportation to reach central Tokyo, 2.5 times as many that took transit into Manhattan or central Paris (despite Tokyo's central rail network being less extensive than that of either of the other two cities). About half traveled during peak hours under extreme crowding, when loads on some lines exceed seating capacities by a 2.5 factor, requiring white-gloved station attendants to be on hand to push passengers into trains in order to minimize platform dwell times. Trains are so crammed that it is said sardinelike conditions are noticeably worse in winter months, when passengers wear thicker clothing.

On a percentage basis, rail transit serves a quarter of all nonwalk trips in greater Tokyo and 40 percent of those made within the central area. Rail is even more popular for commuting, handling 46 percent of all work trips in the region and 67 percent of commutes into central Tokyo. Overall, the Tokyo metropolitan area averages about 460 annual transit trips per capita, one of the highest rates in the world, higher than in Mexico City, Paris, London, and New York.[9]

Supportive Public Policies

A combination of transportation and land-use policies enacted by national and local governments has paved the way for greater Tokyo's rail-oriented urban development. Because of Japan's land constraints (two-thirds of the country is mountainous) and total reliance on imported oil, the national government has historically imposed stiff controls on automobile ownership through various motor vehicle taxes: a commodity tax on manufacturers and three taxes on purchasers—a vehicle acquisition (excise) tax, an annual automobile (registration) tax, and a surcharge based on vehicle weight. Japan's gasoline taxes, moreover, are three to four times higher than in the United States. In addition, all Japanese intra-urban and interurban expressways are tolled. Overall, Japan has not pursued national road building to the degree of other modern, industrialized nations, concentrating on railway construction instead.[10]

At least as important in constraining the motor vehicle population has been Japan's onerous garaging requirements. Anyone wishing to register a car must present evidence verifying the existence of an off-street parking space at their residence. The narrowness of roads provides little space for on-street parking—in the early 1980s, only 13,500 on-street parking meters existed in all of Japan.[11] Supplies in downtown Tokyo fell from a mere 66 spaces per 1,000 jobs in 1980 to just 43 spaces per 1,000 jobs in 1990. In central Tokyo, a permanent off-street parking space today can cost as much as a small condominium. Government's preference for small, space-conserving cars is reflected by the exemption of vehicles with engine capacities of 550 cc or less from registration and garaging requirements. Despite being a country whose automobile-manufacturing sector generates tremendous economic wealth, the combination of auto-restraint policies and world-class transit services has effectively limited vehicle ownership in large urban centers. In 1990, metropolitan Tokyo averaged 275 automobiles per 1,000 inhabitants, compared to a rate of 350 in greater London and more than 600 in most U.S. cities.

Besides directly sponsoring transit services,[12] Japan's central government further promotes transit riding through tax incentives. All Japanese workers receive a tax-free commuting allowance as high as US$500 per month from their employers (that is fully deductible against corporate income taxes). While full transit commuting costs up to this ceiling are covered, automobile commuters get only 15 percent of this amount, based on distance traveled. This contrasts with U.S. policy, where historically workers have received the tax-free benefit of free parking, yet employer-paid allowances for transit riding have been treated as taxable income.

In more recent years, national policies have promoted integrated rail and urban development by seeking to redirect growth away from urban centers into planned satellite communities. In 1988, the National Law for a Multipolar Land Arrangement was enacted to provide tax incentives and financial support to encourage the development of "business core cities" on Tokyo's periphery. The hope is to create more self-contained communities outside Tokyo that offer both employment and housing opportunities, thus reducing commuting and relieving the strain on railways and roadways. Employer-paid commuting subsidies have further encouraged suburban residency, eliminating the financial burden of long-haul commuting. In fact, growing numbers of Tokyo workers are taking up residence near stations on the Skinkansen "bullet train" line, 100 kilometers or more from downtown Tokyo.

Private Suburban Railways and New Towns

West of central Tokyo, where many of the region's newest and most up-market suburbs are located, entire communities are today the domains of powerful conglomerates that are known best for their department store chains—Tokyu, Odakyu, Keio, and Seibu—but that first and foremost are in the business of railway and real estate development. All started as private railway companies in the early part of this century and branched, over time, into businesses closely related to the railway industry, including real estate development, retailing, bus operations, and electrical power generation.[13] This was purely for financial reasons. Placing shopping malls, apartments, and entertainment complexes near stations generated rail traffic; in turn, railways brought customers to these establishments.[14]

Government policies have had a direct hand in encouraging these side businesses. Because all rail fares in Japan are regulated by the Ministry of Transportation and kept at affordable levels, railway companies found it necessary to expand into other businesses in order to increase their profit margins. In greater Tokyo, moreover, private rail companies have been granted exclusive franchises for specific territories over the years. This has eliminated direct competition and enhanced profitability. Within the same territory, buses are usually operated by the same company or its subsidiary. As a result, the subregional bus-rail network is coordinated both physically and institutionally.

Private Railway Operators

Presently, eight private railway companies own and operate suburban rail services in greater Tokyo (see Map 7.3). The Tobu Corporation operates the most extensive private network, with lines covering the northern part of the region (Table 7.2). From 1955 to 1993, private suburban railway patronage increased by more than two-and-a-half times.

Among railway companies, the Tokyu Corporation has been the most successful at integrating rail and real estate development. Tokyu bought vast stretches of land in the early part of this century in advance of rail construction. Its first major project was Denen Chofu, one of the best known and most prestigious residential areas in Japan, built along Tokyu's rail line between the Shibuya station and Sakuragicho, the downtown of Yokohama. Tokyu anchored these two terminal stations with high-rise commercial centers (featuring Tokyu's own department stores) and attracted several prominent university campuses to intermediate stations. These commercial centers, along with the universities, have produced a steady bidirectional flow of passengers, ensuring efficient train opera-

Table 7.2 SERVICE AND RIDERSHIP CHARACTERISTICS OF
SUBURBAN RAILWAY COMPANIES IN GREATER TOKYO

| Company | 1993 Directional Rail Kilometers | Annual Passengers (in millions) | | % Increase in Ridership 1955–93 | 1993 Passengers per Rail Kilometer |
		1955	1993		
Tokyu	100.7	415.1	961.1	131.5	9,544,100
Odakyu	120.5	113.8	720.6	533.2	5,898,900
Keio-Teito	84.4	159.7	564.9	253.7	6,930,300
Seibu	175.6	149.5	667.3	346.4	3,799,900
Tobu	464.1	181.1	950.3	424.7	2,047,600
Keisei	91.6	97.7	281.4	188.0	3,071,500
Keihin	83.6	177.5	437.8	146.7	5,237,300
Sagami	35.0	26.9	247.9	821.6	7,084,500
Total	1,155.5	1,321.3	4,831.3	265.7	4,181,100

Sources: Japan Ministry of Transportation, *Tetsudo Yoran* (Tokyo: Japan Ministry of Transportation, 1994); Japan Ministry of Transportation, *Mintetsu Toukei Nenpo* (Tokyo: Japan Ministry of Transportation, 1994).

tions. Today, railway operations account for about 35 percent of the Tokyu Corporation's revenues and real estate accounts for about 25 percent; however, the company's real estate operations generate nearly two-thirds of the firm's net profits.

The Tokyu Corporation has become Japan's largest rail-based conglomerate.[15] It operates seven main lines and one streetcar line, together totaling about 100 directional kilometers of track. In 1993, the Tokyu railway network served 961 million passengers, more than any private railway in Japan. Most lines are relatively short (the longest is less than 30 kilometers long). Consequently, rail trips tend to be relatively short, producing the highest patronage and fare-box returns per kilometer of track of all private railways (Table 7.2). Except for several JR lines that diagonally cross its corridor, Tokyu's rail network is largely free from competition with other private lines.

Like the Tokyu Corporation, most private railway companies in Japan have pursued other commercial ventures, including bus operations in addition to the construction and operation of hotels, department stores, sports stadia, amusement parks, and other ancillary businesses (Table 7.3). Tokyo Disneyland, for example, was co-developed by the Keisei Corporation, a railway company. While real estate, retail, and tourism ventures have sought to create trip generators around rail stations, activities such as construction, design, and engineering have sought to capitalize on and expand the domain of the railroad companies' labor forces.

Table 7.3 TYPES OF BUSINESSES OPERATED BY JAPANESE RAILWAY
CONSORTIA AND THEIR AFFILIATED COMPANIES

Business	Range of Activities
Transportation	Railway operations; bus services; taxi services; car rentals; trucking; aviation; shipping; freight forwarding; package delivery; manufacturing of rolling stock
Real Estate	Construction, sale, and leasing of housing, office space, hotels; architectural and engineering services; landscaping
Retailing	Construction and operation of department stores, supermarket chains, station kiosks, catering services, and specialty stores
Leisure and Recreation	Construction and operation of resorts and spas, amusement parks, baseball stadia, multiplex movie theaters, fitness clubs, golf courses; operation of travel agencies

The Economics of Japan's Private Railway Initiatives

Although rail operations have historically been the main business of railway consortia, they have hardly been the most profitable ventures. From 1980 to 1993, Tokyo's private railway sector averaged financial rates of return on railway businesses of 1.16 to 1.21 (Table 7.4). Profit margins increased slightly during the 1980s, though these were considered modest returns during this period of rapid economic expansion. Still, every private railway made a profit, something that few passenger carriers worldwide can claim. This is despite governmental regulation of what private railway companies can charge.

The major sideline business of most Japanese railway companies has been real estate. Table 7.5 shows that all companies earned at least a 30 percent return on real estate investments in 1993, though profits have recently fallen somewhat with the crash in Tokyo's land markets in the early 1990s. Still, in 1993, real estate generated more than half of all profits for the Tokyu, Seibu, and Sagami railway corporations. Figure 7.1 shows the net profits in 1990 (prior to the real estate downturn) across four business sectors—rail, bus, real estate, and others—for the eight private railway companies. All except Keisei and Tobu earned more from real estate transactions than any other business activity (excluding Keio-Teito, for which real estate financial data were unavailable). Interestingly, the two companies with the least successful real estate ventures, Keisei and Tobu, also have among the least intensively used suburban railway ser-

Table 7.4 FINANCIAL PERFORMANCE OF RAILWAY BUSINESSES AMONG EIGHT PRIVATE RAILWAYS, GREATER TOKYO, 1980–1993

	Net Income (US$, millions)[1]			Total Revenue/ Total Costs			Net Profit per Passenger (US cents)[1]		
	1980	1993	% Increase	1980	1993	% Change	1980	1993	% Increase
Tokyu	36.4	184.3	406.3	1.18	1.22	+3.4	4.9	19.2	291.8
Odakyu	32.6	154.7	374.5	1.19	1.22	+2.5	6.1	21.8	257.4
Keio-Teito	29.6	93.3	215.2	1.24	1.18	–4.8	6.4	15.9	148.4
Seibu	11.8	153.3	1,199.2	1.06	1.24	+17.0	2.1	23.0	995.2
Tobu	36.4	187.3	414.6	1.12	1.17	+4.5	4.9	19.7	302.0
Keisei	16.5	88.5	436.4	1.16	1.24	+6.9	7.0	31.5	350.0
Keihin	24.6	101.4	312.2	1.18	1.22	+3.4	6.5	23.2	256.9
Sagami	13.3	38.6	190.2	1.27	1.18	–7.1	7.0	15.6	122.9
Total	201.2	1,001.4	397.7	1.16	1.21	+4.3	6.3	23.9	279.4

[1] Actual (unadjusted for inflation) U.S. dollars; conversion from Japanese yen to U.S. dollars:
1980, 1 US$ = 203 yen; 1993, 1 US$ = 111.1 yen.
Source: Japan Ministry of Transportation, *Tetsudo Toukei Nenpo* (Tokyo: Japan Ministry of Transportation, 1994).

Table 7.5 FINANCIAL PERFORMANCE OF REAL ESTATE BUSINESSES AMONG SEVEN PRIVATE RAILWAYS, GREATER TOKYO, 1980–1993[1]

	Net Income (US$, millions)[2]			Total Revenue/ Total Costs			% of Total Company Profits		
	1980	1993	% Increase	1980	1993	% Change	1980	1993	% Change[3]
Tokyu	99.9	202.6	102.8	1.97	1.46	–25.9	73	61	–12
Odakyu	50.3	99.5	97.8	2.22	1.49	–32.9	56	39	–17
Seibu	50.4	135.5	168.9	1.63	1.77	+8.6	77	58	–19
Tobu	58.0	158.8	173.8	1.83	1.61	–12.0	65	46	–19
Keisei	11.9	19.9	67.2	1.20	1.35	+12.5	45	19	–26
Keihin	2.9	72.5	2400.0	1.65	1.44	–12.7	7	43	+35
Sagami	45.0	123.4	174.2	1.53	1.30	–15.0	83	81	–2
Total	318.4	812.2	155.1	1.72	1.66	–3.5	69	50	–19

[1] Data were not available for the Keio-Teito Railway Company.
[2] Actual (unadjusted for inflation) U.S. dollars; conversion from Japanese yen to U.S. dollars:
1980, 1 US$ = 203 yen; 1993, 1 US$ = 111.1 yen.
[3] Percentage point change
Source: Japan Ministry of Transportation, *Tetsudo Toukei Nenpo* (Tokyo: Japan Ministry of Transportation, 1994).

vices, as reflected in the low annual patronage per track kilometer shown earlier in Table 7.2. This lends support to the proposition that integrated rail and property development are vital to attaining efficient rail passenger services.

Looking at all business activities for all private railway companies combined, Figure 7.1 shows that real estate has historically provided the

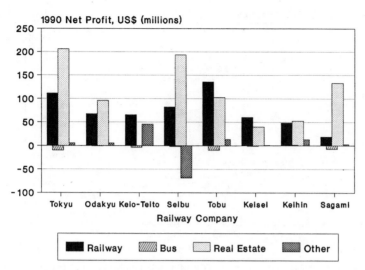

FIGURE 7.1. NET PROFITS EARNED BY RAILWAY CORPORATIONS IN METROPOLITAN TOKYO FROM MAJOR BUSINESS VENTURES, 1990, IN MILLIONS OF U.S. DOLLARS.

greatest investment returns. On the other hand, feeder bus services have generally incurred slight deficits, returning 96 to 98 percent of total costs (including capital depreciation and debt service) through the fare-box— not bad by global standards, but clearly the least remunerative side business. Private railway companies accept losing money operating feeder buses as long as their railway and real estate operations benefit.[16] Buses are what link most residents of private railway companies' housing estates to the companies' rail stations. In recent years, "other" ancillary businesses of the railway companies, such as operating travel agencies and providing engineering consulting services, have barely been profitable, mirroring the slowdown in Japan's economy during the 1990s.

These statistics make clear that Tokyo's railway companies practice a form of internal cross-subsidization—they compensate for the low profitability of their railway and bus enterprises with profits from real estate development.[17] Because rail and bus fares are regulated, property development has become the chief means of increasing profit margins above those possible through rail operations. It has also increased the liquidity and creditworthiness of rail companies to the point that loans they need to finance rail expansion are usually available at very favorable terms (and often from within the consortia themselves, if necessary).

Approach to Property Development

In Japan, the concept of integrated rail and new town development was pioneered by the Hankyu Railway Company following the opening of the

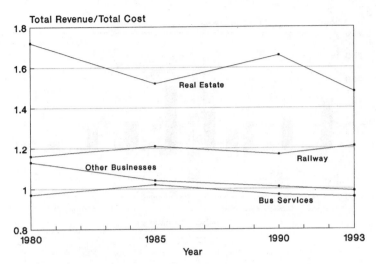

FIGURE 7.2. RETURN ON INVESTMENTS FOR DIFFERENT BUSINESS VENTURES OF RAILWAY CORPORATIONS IN METROPOLITAN TOKYO, 1980–1993.

Takarazuka line in Osaka in 1910. Hankyu soon discovered that passenger rail services, in and of themselves, were barely profitable, and that attracting customers was even harder than raising construction funds. The company thus began building housing estates around several stations, followed over the years by the development of very profitable office towers, shopping plazas, hotels, and entertainment complexes along railways in the Osaka-Kyoto area.[18]

Word of Hankyu's successes quickly spread, and in a short time railway companies in Tokyo and other parts of Japan embraced Hankyu's business practices. In 1934, the Tokyu Corporation opened the first department store at a terminal station (Shibuya) where private and public rail lines met. During Japan's economic expansion following World War II, the transformation of railway companies into multibusiness enterprises became popularly known as *tarminaru*, loosely translated as "terminal culture," a reference to the new genre of high-rise, fast-paced urban existence found around terminal rail stations.

The chief financial reason why Japanese railway companies have aggressively pursued real estate development, of course, has been to exploit "value capture" opportunities—i.e., the appreciation in land values that accrues from increasing the accessibility of properties near rail stations. Japanese railway companies have historically acquired low-priced agricultural land prior to rail construction. Because of land constraints and Japan's economic prowess over the past half-century, land values have skyrocketed during the postwar era, enriching those fortunate enough to own vast suburban land holdings, including railway companies, with huge windfalls. Figure 7.3 shows the tremendous premiums associated with being near suburban rail stations. Following the initiation of rail services,

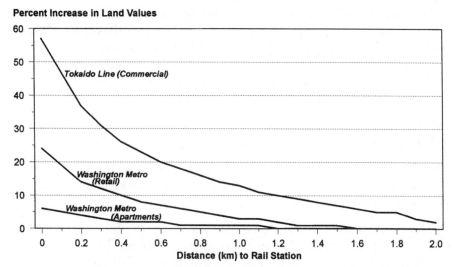

Percent Increase in Land Values

FIGURE 7.3. LAND VALUE PREMIUMS BY DISTANCES FROM STATIONS: COMPARISON OF SUBURBAN TOKYO AND WASHINGTON, D.C. *Sources of data:* T. Yai, Institutions and Finance Systems for Urban Railway Construction, paper presented at the *Seminar on Urban Transportation in Indonesia* (Japan: Ministry of Construction, Government of Indonesia, March 1991); Padeco, Inc., *The Review of Integrated Urban Rail and Land Development in Japan* (Tokyo: Padeco, Inc., 1991); S. Lerman, S. Damm, E. Lerner-Lam, and J. Young, *The Effect of the Washington Metro on Urban Property Values* (Cambridge: Massachusetts Institute of Technology, report prepared for the U.S. Department of Transportation, 1978).

the value of commercial parcels within 50 meters of stations on the Tokaido line (50 kilometers southwest of downtown Tokyo) increased by 57 percent. Premiums tapered quickly with distance from stations, disappearing at about 2 kilometers away. These capitalized accessibility gains were far greater than those recorded, in another study, for retail and residential properties near suburban Washington, D.C., metrorail stations.[19] Japanese railway companies have learned that while the direct benefit of value capture is to generate funds for retiring capital bonds for rail investments, over the long run, an important secondary benefit has been to generate ridership that helps sustain day-to-day rail operations.

The chief mechanism used to by railway companies to assemble the land needed both to accommodate railways and to build real estate projects has been "land readjustment." With this approach, landowners form a cooperative that consolidates (often irregularly shaped) properties and returns smaller but fully serviced (and usually rectangular) parcels to landowners. Roads, drainage, sewerage, parks, and other infrastructure are funded through the sale of the "extra" reserved land contributed by cooperative members. Land readjustment has relieved railway companies of the tremendous upfront burden and cost of acquiring land and funding infrastructure.[20]

There have been cases where railway builders and new town developers have been separate business entities, but even in these cases, the respective investments are usually closely coordinated. This is partly because the central government has promulgated rules for apportioning costs between rail builders/operators and real estate developers for situations in which the two are not one and the same.[21] The rules are as follows.

- The developer pays to the operator half of the construction costs of ground-level urban rail infrastructure.

- Within the new town area, the developer sells the land for rail right-of-ways to the operator at a market price that reflects its undeveloped value.

- Outside the new town, the developer pays the operator the difference in price for land at its historic undeveloped value and its actual value (which will have risen due to the proximity of the new town development).

- On the basis of the above contributions by the developer, central and local governments will each provide grant funding up to 18 percent of the construction cost of the rail system.

New rail lines to Chiba (northeast of central Tokyo) and in the suburbs of Kobe have been constructed based on rules similar to these.

The Tama Denen Toshi New Town

The growth spurred by the Denen Toshi line in Tokyo's Tama area is the largest and widely viewed as the most successful land development initiative ever undertaken by a private railway company in Japan. From 1960 to 1984, the Tokyu Corporation used a 22-kilometer rail line to transform a vast, hilly, and scarcely inhabited area into a planned community of 5,000 hectares and nearly half a million residents. Called Tama Denen Toshi (Tama Garden City), this amalgam of interconnected new towns stretches along a 15-to-35-kilometer band southwest of Tokyo that traverses four cities (Map 7.4).[22] Tama Denen Toshi proceeded from the initial master plan in 1956, to the commencement of land development in 1959, to the opening of the first rail segments in 1966, and to accelerated land and rail development in the 1970s and 1980s.

Development Approach to Tama Denen Toshi

The concept for Tama Denen Toshi dates back to 1918, when Shibusawa Eiichi, one of the most successful entrepreneurs of the Meiji era (1868–

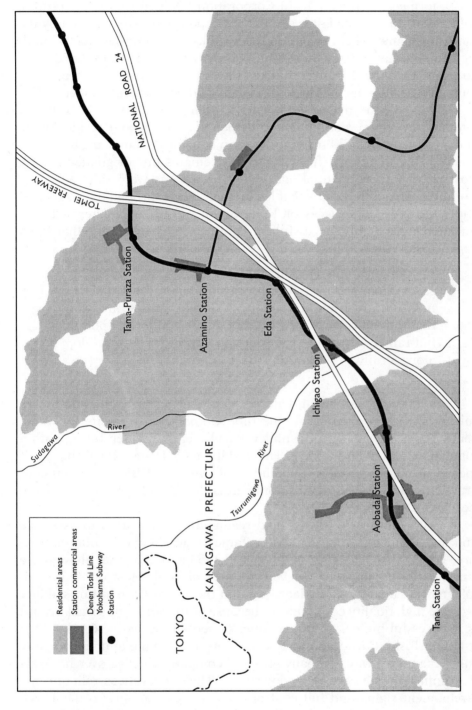

MAP 7.4. CENTRAL PORTION OF TAMA DENEN TOSHI.

1912), formed the Denen Toshi Corporation (Garden City Corporation), predecessor to what today is the Tokyu Corporation. As suggested by the company's name, Eiichi sought to relieve Tokyo of overcrowding by building communities in pastoral settings, borrowing heavily from the ideas of Ebenezer Howard. However, unlike Howard, who sought to create self-contained new towns that were physically and economically independent of London, Eiichi envisioned Japan's garden cities as mainly bedroom communities where commuters and their families would reside. While Eiichi managed to build several suburban housing enclaves, the most successful being Denen Chofu, which today remains one of greater Tokyo's most prestigious residential addresses, his dreams were sidetracked by World War II and the events that led up to it. It was through the vision and leadership of Eiichi's successor, Keita Gotoh, a former Minister of Transportation and a highly successful entrepreneur in his own right, that Tama Denen Toshi began to take form.[23] A Japanese historian writes:

> the philanthropic garden city visions advocated by Shibu-sawa Eiichi had been transformed into a profiteering business venture by Keita Gotoh . . . Gotoh had a conviction that the railway business was not about 'connecting points' but rather about the real estate opportunities that develop along a railway's corridor.[24]

With Tama Denen Toshi, land development occurred slightly before rail services came on line. At the time Gotoh chose the site for Tama Denen Toshi, it was the most undeveloped area in greater Tokyo, with a population of 31,000 in 1955. The 22-kilometer Denen Toshi line itself opened in stages between 1966 and 1984, with the US$160 million construction cost financed half by commercial loans and half by loans from the Japan Development Bank.[25]

As with other new towns, land readjustment was used to assemble land and finance infrastructure for Tama Denen Toshi. A total of fifty-three cooperatives were formed between 1953 and 1966 that allowed the consolidation of more than 4,900 hectares of land. Most original landholders were farmers who placed trust in the Tokyu Corporation's ability to create high-quality communities because of the company's track record as a successful builder of garden cities (when known as the Garden City, or Denen Toshi, Corporation). Tokyu's roots as a town planning company rather than a railway company gave the company an edge over its rivals in winning the support of landowners.[26] The cooperatives relinquished development rights and full control over project planning to the Tokyu Corporation. Among Japanese city planners, this unprecedented approach to new town development became known as the "Tokyu Method."

Under Tokyu's land readjustment system, landowners gave up 45 percent of their land in return for fully serviced parcels. About half of the "land pool" went for public use and half was held in reserve and for eventual sale to cover development costs. Reserve land sold for US$0.43 per square meter during the first phase of development in 1953 and for more than US$1.50 per square meter in the mid-1960s.[27] These were considered extremely expensive prices at the time, but speculators willingly paid these amounts in anticipation of the high-quality, rail-served communities that would eventually be built. Tokyu's coordinated approach to land assemblage and project financing allowed a continuous urban area with uniform and high-quality roads, sewerage, drainage, and other urban infrastructure to take form. Moreover, because of Tokyu's leadership, financial prowess, and position as the largest landowner in the cooperatives, it was able to "replot" the landscape and lay necessary infrastructure in a relatively short period of time.[28] Table 7.6 details how land readjustment was applied for a particular project, Akada, on the Tama Denen Toshi line.

It is with regard to value capture approaches, then, that Tama Denen

Table 7.6 THE AKADA LAND READJUSTMENT PROJECT IN TAMA DENEN TOSHI

Background: The Akada land readjustment project is located between the Eda and Azamino stations (see Map 7.4). Developed between January 1985 and March 1992, the Akada project encompassed an area of 685.7 hectares made up of 1,078 original irregularly plotted lots. Of this total area, 175.2 hectares (25.5 percent) were held in reserve, later sold for a total of US$166 million (based on currency exchange rates from 1985 to 1992) to defray development costs. The city of Yokohama also contributed nearly a million U.S. dollars toward development. By 1992, the Akada neighborhood had the following land-use composition.

Land Activity	Area (hectares)	Percent of Total Area	Population
Reserve Land			
Road development	134.7	19.7	
Park development	35.5	5.2	
Water courses, drainage, sanitation	5.9	0.9	
Land for Public Facilities			
(schools, shrines, etc.)	49.7	7.3	
Housing Development			
Detached housing			
(200 m²/lot; 1,488 lots)	297.7	43.3	5,952
Farmsteads			
(300 m²/lot; 250 lots)	75.0	10.9	1,000
Low-rise group housing			
(85 m²/lot; 267 lots)	22.7	3.3	668
Mid-rise group housing			
(85 m²/lot; 759 lots)	64.5	9.4	2,656
Total	685.7	100.0	10,276

Source: Tokyu Corporation, internal memorandum, 1994.

Toshi also distinguished itself from Howard's English garden cities (in addition to being a bedroom, rather than a self-contained, community). Howard sought to direct profits from capital gains and appreciation in land values to residents themselves, partly as a reward for leaving the security of inner-city living for the unknowns of suburbia. In Tama Denen Toshi, the motives for value capture were rooted in capitalism—to reap speculative real estate profits for the corporation's benefit and to underwrite the cost of railway expansion.

Design of Tama Denen Toshi

Tama Denen Toshi was designed with town centers and housing estates sited around most of the nineteen stations along Tokyu's Denen Toshi rail line. To jump-start housing construction, Tokyu sold land to public housing corporations, companies (for employee dormitories and corporate housing), and private home builders. The Tokyu Real Estate Company, a subsidiary of the Tokyu Corporation, also built homes. While proceeds from land readjustment defrayed the costs of basic infrastructure, Tokyu supplemented this by building swimming pools, tennis courts, museums, and sports facilities, and installing regional cable television services, throughout Tama Denen Toshi. By providing high-quality neighborhood amenities, Tokyu was able to sell housing at premium prices. Well over two-thirds of housing development within Tama Denen Toshi has concentrated within 2 kilometers of the rail corridor in recent years.

Tokyu was particularly committed to attracting institutional land uses, including several universities and prestigious private schools, in addition to medical centers, post offices, libraries, fire and police stations, and government branch offices. Land was either donated or sold below market value to attract these activities. In 1975, Tokyu gave away 36 hectares of land to Keio University to establish a campus south of the Tana station. Besides increasing the marketability of the Tama Denen Toshi project, universities and other institutional uses have generated much-welcomed off-peak and reverse-direction rail traffic. Figure 7.4 shows that while Tama Denen Toshi's population steadily rose during its first thirty-five years, ridership on the railway serving the corridor rose even faster, owing largely to the diversification of the new town's land uses. In 1994, the Denen Toshi line carried 729,000 riders per day, while private buses handled about 83,000 daily passengers.[29]

The greatest concentration of commercial development has been around the Tama-Puraza and Aobadai stations (Photos 7.1 and 7.2). Each station is flanked by a compact, mixed-use urban center featuring a shopping plaza anchored by a Tokyu department store, a large supermarket, mid-rise offices, a hotel, banks, post offices, and recreational offerings, including sports clubs. Walkways radiate from the centers to nearby resi-

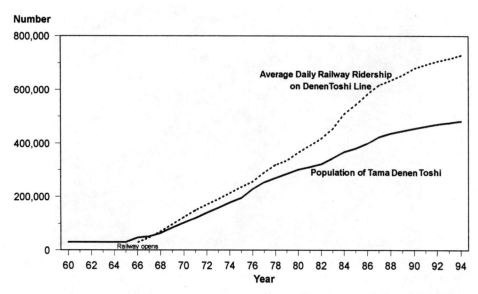

FIGURE 7.4. PARALLEL TRENDS IN POPULATION GROWTH OF TAMA DENEN TOSHI AND RIDERSHIP
GROWTH OF THE DENEN TOSHI RAIL LINE, 1960–1994.

dential neighborhoods whose densities taper off with distance from the
stations. Equally noticeable around most stations is the absence of park-
and-ride lots. This, combined with good bus connections and landscaped
pathways, has marginalized the automobile as a serious station access
mode. In 1988, for example, automobiles accounted for only 6.1 percent
of all access trips to stations in Tama Denen Toshi. By comparison, the
share of access trips by bus was 24.7 percent and by walking/cycling was
67.8 percent.[30]

In 1988, thirty-five years after Tama Denen Toshi was first conceived,
the Tokyu Corporation received awards from the Architectural Institute of
Japan and from Japan's Minister of Construction in recognition of its
excellence in new town planning, the first-ever award given to a private
railway developer. Tokyu is not content to rest on its laurels, however. The
lack of employment opportunities and certain community facilities,
notably hospitals, is widely viewed as a shortcoming of Tama Denen Toshi
and other rail-oriented new towns. In response, the Tokyu Corporation
has recently drawn plans to add a research and educational complex and
several business-industrial parks, all laced with fiber optic cable and
smart buildings. Over time, Tokyu hopes to transform Tama Denen Toshi
from a predominantly bedroom community, albeit a transit-oriented one,
into what its brochures claim will be "a diverse and dynamic multifunc-
tional urban community" with an efficient and balanced flow of traffic
and information.

Pedestrian plaza

Tama Plaza shopping mall

Tama-Puraza station

Park-and-ride lot

PHOTO 7.1. TAMA-PURAZA STATION AREA. Clustered development can be seen around Tama-Puraza, located 23 kilometers southwest of the Tokyo station. Tama-Puraza, which means "Tama Plaza" in Japanese, was designed as the focal point of Tama Denen Toshi. The Tokyu Corporation, which owns 80 percent of the 118 hectares of land comprising the Tama-Puraza community, concentrated high-end retailing around the station. Residential densities taper with distance from the station. The Tama-Puraza station averaged around 70,000 daily passenger boardings in 1994.

Licre shopping mall

Train entering station on elevated tracks

Bus transfer area

PHOTO 7.2. CONCENTRATED DEVELOPMENT AT THE AOBADAI STATION ON THE DENEN TOSHI LINE. Buses owned and operated by a subsidiary of the Tokyu Corporation provide direct transfer connections to the station portal. The Licre, a large commercial building, sits atop the Aobadai station. The complex features some sixty specialty stores and restaurants, complemented by the nearby Tokyu department store and concert hall. A train, as shown in the picture on the elevated tracks above the street, directly enters the Licre building complex. The Aobadai station is one of the busiest on the Denen Toshi line, handling 102,000 turnstile entries per day in 1994.

Recent Publicly Sponsored Rail-Oriented New Towns

Borrowing a chapter from private industry, Japan's public sector has recently gotten into the business of building rail-oriented new towns. This is partly because of the near-prohibitive cost of building new towns in contemporary Japan in the wake of meteoric increases in land values and a stronger Japanese yen (up to the mid-1990s, at least). Today, only a partnership of local and national authorities, in concert with private real estate developers, can muster the resources necessary to mount a venture of coordinated rail and new town development. In greater Tokyo, the two largest publicly backed efforts to create new transit-oriented communities have been the Tama New Town in western Tokyo and the Tsukuba Science City on the northern New Joban line (Map 7.2). Other notable publicly sponsored new towns in the region include Ryugasaki (671 hectares), Chiba (1,933 hectares), and Kohoku (1,317 hectares).

All recent-generation planned suburban communities have been developed under what is called the New Town Rail Construction Scheme. These are co-partnerships of Jutaku Toshi Seibi Kodan, or the nation's Housing Urban Development Corporation (HUDC), local (prefectural or municipal) governments, and railway companies. Under the program, both the local and national levels of government cover up to 18 percent of rail construction cost for a total subsidy of 36 percent, with remaining costs apportioned among major beneficiaries (including transit riders, railway companies, and private developers). The HUDC has emerged as one of the largest landlords in the world, having built more than 1.2 million housing units and developed more than 45,000 hectares of land since 1960.

Tama New Town

Tama New Town is a joint venture of the Tokyo Metropolitan Government, the HUDC, and private sector partners. The Tama New Town Development Program was initiated in 1965, the first stages of residential occupancy began in 1971, and housing development accelerated during the ensuing decade, with the population reaching 100,000 in 1985. While master-planned by the public sector, rail and property development has been a public-private co-venture. The two major rail lines serving Tama New Town—Keio Sagamihara and Odakyu Tama—did not open until 1990. Both lines were built by a public railway corporation and later turned over to a private operator, with construction costs to be repaid over a fifteen-year period. The investment's 10 percent annual interest payments are being split between the private railway company and public-private property developers.

The physical development of Tama New Town has been divided geographically among public authorities (Table 7.7). Of the twenty-one "residential areas," eight in the western and northern sections of the new town are being developed by the Tokyo Metropolitan Government and twelve in the southern and eastern parts are being developed by the HUDC. One centrally located neighborhood is the development responsibility of the Tokyo Metropolitan Housing Supply Corporation. As with other Japanese new towns, most upfront infrastructure in Tama New Town was financed through land readjustment schemes.

Today, Tama New Town boasts 170,000 inhabitants and 35,000 jobs within a 3,000-hectare area, with the target population and labor force set at 360,000 residents and 130,000 workers, respectively. Thus, unlike other new towns in greater Tokyo, Tama New Town is slated to be a balanced community. The Tokyo Metropolitan Government has aggressively recruited companies to locate in the new town, offering tax incentives and below-market-rate land purchases. So far, a modest degree of self-containment has been achieved. A 1991 survey found that 20 percent of employed residents had jobs within Tama New Town.[31] Of the remaining 80 percent leaving the new town for jobs, two-thirds commuted to Tokyo 23 Ward and 70 percent commuted via rail transit. Two factors generally working against self-containment in all Japanese new towns are the commuting subsidies received by all Japanese workers and the culture of life-long employment, meaning even if companies are lured to Tama New Town, employed residents working elsewhere are unlikely to seek jobs with these firms to economize on commuting.

Tama New Town is being physically designed along the lines of an American-style planned unit development (PUD), with the notable exception that rail stops anchor town centers and shopping plazas. The organizing principle of each planned enclave is a junior high school. All

Table 7.7 TAMA NEW TOWN PROJECT AREA AND TARGET POPULATIONS, 1994

Development Responsibility	Development Area (hectares)	Number of Residential Areas	Projected Target Population
Tokyo Metropolitan Government	738.4	7	96,500
Housing and Urban Development Corporation	1,437.5	13	174,700
Tokyo Metropolitan Housing Supply Corporation	49.7	1	10,500
Privately Developed/Pending[1]	758.1	—	80,100
Total	2,983.7	21	361,800

[1]Developed or sold by original landholders under land readjustment scheme, or pending development approval.
Source: Tokyo Metropolitan Government, Housing and Urban Development Corporation, and Tokyo Metropolitan Housing Supply Corporation, Tama New Town (Tokyo: Tokyo Metropolitan Government, 1994).

PHOTO 7.3. HORINOUCHI STATION AREA. Developed by the national Housing Urban Development Corporation, travelators connect residents living in apartments and condominiums on a nearby hillside to the station on the Neiko Sagamihara line and the surrounding retail complex. As suggested by the photo's foreground, the chief architect of the Horinouchi town center is said to have been influenced by Barcelona's Gaudi in his choice of public art.

twenty-one "residential areas" contain a centrally located junior high school as well as two primary schools, are connected by distributor roads, and are interlaced by greenbelts. Tama New Town has won accolades for the variety of housing being offered, a novelty in urban Japan. Public housing built by local and national authorities consists of mid-rise and high-rise apartments sited near rail stops and targeted at low- and middle-income households. These are surrounded by privately built, single-family detached units sold at market rate. About 55 percent of all units are owner-occupied and 45 percent are rented. By regional standards, Tama New Town's housing is considered spacious and attractive, and the wooded surroundings are highly prized by residents.

Four of Tama New Town's rail stations are flanked by urban centers featuring retail plazas, offices, banks, and institutional buildings (Photo 7.3). These urban centers are also notable for their conspicuous absence of park-and-ride lots, even though most new town households have a car and a garage. Tama's residents bus-and-ride, walk-and-ride, or bike-and-ride instead.

New Joban Line/Tsukuba Science City

While most new town development has occurred along greater Tokyo's southwest axis in the Tama district, regional planners have also sought to channel new development along a northern axis, using the New Joban line railway to lead the way. Since the recently opened 60-kilometer New Joban line traverses twelve local governments, and in light of rapidly escalating land and construction costs, a fresh, coordinated approach to new town development was needed. Accordingly, the national government passed the Integrated Development Act, which mandates coordinated master planning, discourages land speculation, and sets the terms of development cost sharing. The act also established an implementing body—a third government sector called Shutoken Shin Toshi Tetsudo Seibi Kaisha (Metropolitan New Town Rail Construction Company)—to orchestrate property development along the New Joban Line and other future rail corridors in the country.

Midway along the New Joban line is the new "Science City" of Tsukuba, chosen as a national center for advanced research and higher education. First planned in the early 1960s, Tsukuba's population has grown to more than 180,000 inhabitants and is planned to reach 220,000 at build-out. Directed by the HUDC (in concert with the Ibaraki Prefecture and city of Tsukuba), one-tenth of Tsukuba's total 28,500-hectare land area is devoted to research and educational activities. The New Joban railway skirts the eastern edge of Tsukuba, but is linked to the town center by frequent bus services and a network of grade-separated pathways (stretching 48 kilometers in length) built exclusively for pedestrians and cyclists.

Learning from Tokyo

Tokyo's experiences underscore the potential rewards of a more entrepreneurial approach to integrated rail and community development. Throughout greater Tokyo, suburban railway services have formed a strategic base from which a whole range of other business activities have been developed. Foremost has been new town development. Driven by profit motives, large conglomerates have successfully packaged together new town and railway investments. While they have fabulously profited as a result, so has the public sector—in the form of efficient and convenient regional rail services, well-designed suburban communities, and, arguably, the most sustainable pattern of regional development among any of the world's megacities. The private sector's successes have spawned recent public sector imitators, such as the Tama New Town co-venture between the metropolitan and national government.

It is interesting that private companies are presently building tollways in the suburbs and exurbs of several large U.S. metropolitan areas, partly to capitalize on the willingness of commuters to pay top dollar to avoid traffic congestion, but also, though not always explicitly stated, to develop land parcels near tollway interchanges. The Dulles Greenway, a 22-kilometer tollway in the booming corridor between Leesburg and Dulles International Airport in northern Virginia, was recently opened by a consortium of roadway builders, toll operators, and landholders. While investors hope to reap profits from the $2-plus tolls motorists are paying to bypass traffic congestion, they also hope to profit from leasing and selling land around major interchanges—that is, they hope to capture the value added by transport investments, just as Japanese railway companies have done over the years and America's earlier generation of private-sector rail builders did a century or more ago. A likely outcome is that integrated tollway-land development will lead to even greater auto-oriented suburban and exurban development in suburban Washington, D.C., and other U.S. metropolises in years to come. America's transit industry might be well advised to borrow from the experiences of Japan's private rail builders and emulate the practices of contemporary U.S. tollway profiteers. Japan teaches us that the combination of profit-seeking entrepreneurs and community-minded government offers the best hope for creating the kinds of built environments that enable mass transportation to compete successfully with the private automobile.

NOTES

1. Prefectures roughly correspond to county government units in the United States and the United Kingdom.

2. R. Cybriwsky, Tokyo, *Cities*, vol. 10, no. 1, 1993, pp. 2–10.

3. In 1993, the 23 Ward Area averaged 12,945 persons per square kilometer. This exceeded the persons per square kilometer of New York City (1990: 8,843), Mexico City (1988: 6,925), and Los Angeles (1990: 2,880). Source: Tokyo Metropolitan Government, *Statistics of Large World Cities* (Tokyo: Tokyo Metropolitan Government, 1993).

4. K. Ohta, Transportation Problems and Policies of the Tokyo Metropolitan Region, *Contemporary Studies in Urban Planning and Environmental Management in Japan*, Department of Urban Engineering, University of Tokyo, eds. (Tokyo: Kajima Institute Publishing, 1993).

5. London, Paris, and Moscow have larger publicly owned and operated metros; however, no other metropolitan area has close to the number of private railways operating as greater Tokyo.

6. Historically, Yamanote has represented the area on higher ground west and southwest of Tokyo's historical center where feudal lords once had their mansions and was known as one of the most prestigious sections of Tokyo. Today, the Yamanote area is packed mostly with mid- and high-rise apartments, international hotels, university campuses, and foreign embassies. Many residents living near the Yamanote rail loop are office workers who work in central Tokyo and who value greatly the nearness of their homes to work and urban amenities. For this, however, they pay a huge rent premium.

7. In 1987, the JNR was broken into twelve private corporations after it had accumulated a debt totaling some US$285 billion and is now called the Japanese Railway, or JR. The privatization initiative was undertaken in hopes of emulating the financial success of suburban rail companies.

8. Ohta, *op. cit.*

9. Excluding former and existing socialist and communist countries, only Zurich, Switzerland, averages more transit trips per capita than metropolitan Tokyo. With 10.8 million annual passengers per kilometer of rail line, moreover, metropolitan Tokyo has one of the most intensively used systems anywhere (e.g., versus comparable statistics of 9.1 million in greater Mexico City, 6.0 million in greater Paris, 2.4 million in greater New York City, and 1.9 million in greater London). Source: Jane, Inc. *Jane's Urban Transport System, 1994–1995* (New York: Jane, Inc., 1994).

10. As late as 1978, more than half of Japan's roads were under 3.5 meters in width—less than a single standard 4-meter lane. Source: M. McShane, M. Koshi, and O. Lundin, Public Policy Toward the Automobile: A Comparative Look at Japan and Sweden, *Transportation Research*, vol. 18A, no. 2, 1984, pp. 97–109.

11. McShane, Koshi, and Lundin, *op. cit.*

12. Under the Underground Rail Construction Scheme, the national government subsidizes the construction of subways by the private-sector Teito Rapid Transit (Eidan) system in Tokyo and by municipal governments in Tokyo (Toei) and other Japanese cities (Sapporo, Sendai, Yokohama, Nagoya, Kyoto, Osaka, Kobe, and Fukuoka). Established in 1978, the program subsidizes about 60 percent of total construction costs for new subway lines and 30 percent of costs for upgrading existing lines. Usually, localities rely on bonds to cover remaining construction costs while private railways borrow from commercial banks, the Japan Railway Construction Corporation, and the Japan Development Bank, and also draw funds from their own reserves. Also, under another national program, the Japan Railway Construction Corporation will construct a railway and transfer it to a private company after completion, with repayment made over a fifteen-to-twenty-four-year period at below-market interest rates.

13. The first private railway was built in the Tokyo region in 1907. The majority of suburban rail lines were built between 1925 and 1940. Source: E. Aoki, *History and Culture of Private Railway Management* (Tokyo: Koin-Shoin, 1992).

14. When expanding their markets, private companies first concentrated on tourist traffic, extending lines to holy temples, beach resorts, and recreational spots. After World War I, several railway companies built and operated amusement parks. In between World Wars I and II, most private railroad companies also began selling electricity, used to power their rail trains, to homeowners and other businesses. Several railway companies—Tamagawa-Denki-Tetsudo (later absorbed by Tokyu Railway), Keise-Denki-Kido, and Keioh-Denki-Kido—made huge profits from electricity side businesses. With the arrival of World War II, however, the central government took control of the nation's electrical power sector. Source: E. Aoki, *op. cit.*

15. The Tokyu Corporation is the nucleus of the Tokyu Group, one of the largest conglomerates in Japan. In all, the Tokyu Group owns 389 subsidiary businesses and 10 foundations divided into 5 major groups: (1) transportation (66 companies, including the Tokyu Corporation); (2) property development (75 companies); (3) retailing and distribution (94 companies and 1 foundation); (4) recreation and leisure (146 companies and one foundation); and (5) culture and education (7 companies and 8 foundations). In 1992, the Tokyu Group earned revenues exceeding US$35 billion, owned capital assets worth more than US$4 billion, and had a work force of 113,000. The Tokyu Corporation itself claimed capital assets of more than US$1 billion, operating profits of US$2.7 billion, and a work force of 5,400.

16. Although three companies (Keihin, Keio-Teito, and Odakyu) made profits operating buses in 1980, none of these private bus services produced profits by 1993. All private railway companies combined lost $41.2 million operating buses in 1993, up from $13.1 million in 1990.

17. Technically, businesses are not cross-subsidized in the sense that rail construction and operation costs are fully recovered through the fare box. Legally, income from property development cannot be earmarked to recover rail construction and operating costs. The purpose of this requirement is to prevent unfair fare increases that might occur if the accounts of rail and real estate businesses were commingled.

18. As with private street car development in the United States a century ago, the ownership of electricity supplies for train services was vital in enabling the Hankyu Corporation and later other railway companies to branch into the housing development business. By 1989, the Hankyu Railway Company had developed some 1,300 hectares of property, sold 2,145 housing units, and opened large department stores along the Takarazuka, Kobe, and Kyoto lines in the Osaka-Kyoto region. Source: Hankyu Corporation, Ltd., *Handbook of Hankyu* (Osaka: Hankyu Corporation, Ltd., 1989).

19. These were recorded changes in land values in anticipation of (i.e., prior to) metrorail's opening. Past studies of rail systems show that, due to land speculation, the greatest property value impacts often occur a year or so before, as opposed to following, the opening of a rail system. See: R. Knight and L. Trygg, Evidence of Land Use Impacts of Rapid Transit Systems, *Transportation*, vol. 6, no. 3, 1977, pp. 231–247.

20. For detailed discussions about land readjustment schemes in greater Tokyo, see: M. Hebbert and N. Nakai, *How Tokyo Grows: Land Development and Planning on the Metropolitan Fringe* (London: Suntory-Toyota International Centre for Economics and Related Disciplines, London School of Economics and Political Science, 1988).

21. P. Midgeley, *Urban Transport in Asia: An Operational Agenda for the 1990s*, Technical Paper No. 224 (Washington, D.C.: The World Bank, 1993); Padeco, Inc., *The Review of Integrated Urban Rail and Land Development in Japan* (Tokyo: Padeco, Inc., 1991).

22. Tama Denen Toshi lies within the city limits of Yokohama, Kawasaki, Machida, and Yamato, all of which are within the Kanagawa Prefecture.

23. Keita Gotoh entered the railway business at an early age; in 1922 he became

the director of Meguro-Kamata-Dentetsu, Inc., the branch company of the Denen Toshi Corporation that first built suburban railway lines in Tokyo's southwest suburbs. Because of the tremendous profitability of the railway business, Meguro-Kamata-Dentetsu eventually took over the Denen Toshi Corporation and, through various hostile takeovers, several rival railway companies as well. In 1928, Gotoh became president of Meguro-Kamata-Dentetsu, which aggressively built rail-oriented projects during the 1930s and, through various mergers, eventually became the Tokyu Dentetsu Railway Corporation. In 1944, Gotoh resigned his post as president to become Japan's Minister of Transportation, but soon after World War II, he was removed from office as part of a national purge of civil servants. When the purge was rescinded in 1951 and his reputation was restored, Gotoh returned to become president of the Tokyu Corporation. The life and history of Keita Gotoh as a great railway builder and power broker is chronicled in the book *The Myth of Land,* by Naoki Inose (Tokyo: Shogakukan, 1990).

24. Inose, *op. cit.,* pp. 154 and 162.

25. The Shin Tamagawa line, which connects the Denen Toshi line with central Tokyo (at the Shibuya station on the Yamanote loop line), was opened in 1977. This line, also owned and operated by the Tokyu Railway Corporation, was fully funded through loans provided by Japan's Railway Construction Public Corporation.

26. To coordinate the activities of the many cooperatives, the Tokyu Railway Corporation formed various "development committees" comprising company employees, local residents, and municipal officials. Six of the thirteen members of development committees consisted of Tokyu Corporation employees.

27. Tokyu Corporation, *35-Year History of Tama Denen Toshi* (Tokyo: Tokyu Railway Corporation, 1989).

28. The Tokyu Corporation undertook all surveying, design, preliminary engineering, and construction work for the new town "free of charge" with the agreement that Tokyu would obtain all reserved land from the cooperatives after the rail line was completed.

29. The Tokyu Corporation operates seventeen bus companies that provide mainly feeder connections to rail stops, but that also operate crosstown services and provide nationwide charter services for tourists. Tokyu bus services are viewed as highly innovative in Japan, with some providing stop-on-request services anywhere along a route.

30. Source: Tokyo Metropolitan Government, *Person Trip Survey for Tokyo Metropolis, 1988* (Tokyo: Tokyo Metropolitan Government, 1990).

31. Tokyo Metropolitan Government, *Tama New Town: Commuting by Residents* (Tokyo: Tokyo Metropolitan Government, 1992).

PART THREE

THE HYBRIDS: ADAPTIVE CITIES AND ADAPTIVE TRANSIT

Places that have struck a workable balance between concentrating development along trunkline transit corridors and adapting transit to serve spread-out suburbs efficiently are the hybrids—partly adaptive cities, partly adaptive transit. In many ways, they enjoy the best of both worlds.

Munich is a metropolis where, in contrast to other German cities, mass transit continues to gain market share. Its highly integrated transit network—both in terms of service and fares—deserves most of the credit. The region's U-Bahn and S-Bahn rail lines are complemented by tramways that circulate throughout central Munich and private buses and minibuses that feed into suburban stations. New towns—both in the city and outside—have sprouted along some rail lines. The traditional core is enjoying a renaissance courtesy of both superb transit services and a pro-active traffic-calming campaign.

In contrast to Munich, two cities at different poles of the Americas— Ottawa, Canada, and Curitiba, Brazil—have opted for bus-based transit to both guide growth and serve suburbia. Busways are the centerpiece of regionally integrated transit services in both places. In addition to being far cheaper than rail investments, busways provide potential service advantages. In Ottawa, the same vehicle that functions as a mainline carrier also operates as an in-neighborhood feeder, thus eliminating the need to transfer. Curitiba uses its busway solely for high-capacity conveyance, akin to a metro except that vehicles operate above ground. An ingenious system of frequent-stop mainline routes, direct-line high-speed services, crosstown connectors, and transfer stations have produced one of the most efficient, well-patronized transit services anywhere. Both Ottawa and Curitiba also demonstrate that good-quality services—regardless of whether by rail or rubber-tire vehicles—will spawn compact development.

Chapter 8

Making Transit Work in the Land of the Autobahn: Munich, Germany

Greater Munich has pursued a balanced approach to linking transit and urban development. The city of Munich itself is preponderantly transit-oriented in its layout and design, while at the same time its periphery is well served by buses and park-and-ride provisions as a concession to the spread-out nature of development. Overall, the region is blessed with a richly embroidered network of rail and bus services that nicely fit with the pattern of settlement. The urban subway, U-Bahn, serves the built-up area. The suburban railway, S-Bahn, takes people beyond the city. Trams and buses function mainly as feeders. A regional authority has been formed to make sure the schedules of rapid transit and feeder services are fully coordinated. Unified ticketing has allowed for a fully integrated fare system. In recent years, local and regional planning authorities have aggressively targeted new and infill growth in and around rail station catchments. Complementing these steps have been an assortment of traffic management strategies, such as parking controls, aimed at "pushing" motorists out of cars, matched by pedestrian enhancements and bikeway investments, aimed at "pulling" residents into alternative, "green" forms of travel.

Any book on great transit metropolises is incomplete without a case from Germany. Just as Germany lays claim to some of the world's best-engineered automobiles, it similarly boasts among the most innovative and efficient transit services and technologies. In Germany, rail is the favored form of public transit since it alone provides the speedy, grade-separated, high-quality services demanded by Germany's traveling public. All large German cities feature extensive rail networks, but none are better designed, coordinated, and adapted to the cityscape than Munich's.

213

Whereas nearly all German, and indeed European, cities have seen transit's market share of urban travel steadily erode with the automobile's ever-growing popularity, Munich is one of the few to buck this trend. It has done so by greatly expanding rail services and upgrading their quality. Vital to transit's turnaround has been the formation of a regional authority for coordinating fares, routes, and timetables across greater Munich's many rail and bus operators. Focused efforts to "push" people out of cars and "pull" them into alternative modes—such as the creation of car-free, pedestrian zones and the relocation of parking to the periphery of the core—have also worked in transit's favor. Not to be overlooked, Munich's commitment to compact, infill development has spawned a number of transit-oriented neighborhoods around rail stops. Cumulatively, these steps have produced Germany's second-highest rate of transit usage—230 transit trips per resident per year, just behind Berlin and well above the per capita rates of larger rail-served metropolises such as Hamburg (183 trips), Frankfurt (160 trips), and the Rhein-Ruhr conurbation (144 trips). In a recent poll of transit managers from Germany's thirteen biggest metropolitan areas, Munich's transit system was rated first in overall performance and service quality.[1]

Along the spectrum of transit-oriented metropolises (e.g., Stockholm) to suburb-adapted transit (e.g., Adelaide) reviewed in this book, Munich is very much a hybrid. The central city is very transit-oriented, as are some outlying station areas. Yet the extensive network of suburban rail and feeder services, plus park-and-ride provisions, reflect an adaptation of transit to spread-out development. While the majority of motorized trips in Munich's traditional core (*Altstadt*, or "old city") are by transit, significant shares—as many as a third—of motorized trips by suburbanites are also by rail or bus.

Munich's transit achievements are all the more noteworthy because Germany is such an auto-oriented society. Prior to reunification in 1990, West Germany had the highest rate of car ownership in Europe, and second-highest in the world, exceeded only by the United States.[2] The former East Germany's higher incidence of auto-less households has deflated the current figure, but even today Germany trails only the United States and Scandinavian countries in per capita car ownership. Despite being one of Europe's densest cities, Munich's 1995 auto ownership rate of 530 cars per 1,000 inhabitants well exceeded the national average. That same year, the typical Munich resident spent US$141 per month on automobiles versus US$16 on transit.[3] Further stacking the odds against transit are Germany's extensive system of limited-access superhighways, or Autobahns, the only highway system in the world without speed limits. In a recent commentary on what they call the country's "virtual obsession with car travel," John Pucher and Christian Lefèvre note that for most Germans, the car is equated with political freedom, postwar prosperity, and socioeconomic status. Any suggestion to impose speed limits on Autobahns invariably invokes the rallying cry "Freie Fahrt für freie Bürger," German for "unlimited car travel for free citizen." Bankrolling the pro-car movement is Germany's politically active and powerful automotive industry and its lobbyists. Curiously, however, Germany is also home to one of the most active anti-car/pro-environmental movements anywhere, spearheaded by the Green Party. The Greens have aggressively championed the cause of promoting "green modes" of transport—that is, everything but the car. Increasingly similar sentiments are being echoed across the general population as traffic congestion worsens, air quality deteriorates, and the unique historical heritages of town centers whose origins date back to medieval times become threatened. Pucher and Lefèvre comment that "the love-hate relationship with the car is probably more passionate in Germany than anywhere else in the world."[4]

Conflicts about the car and its role in society have yielded one side benefit: a near universal agreement among Germans—liberals and conservatives alike—that, regardless of what the car's future might be, public transit is good for cities and should accordingly be expanded and upgraded. Thus, while new road construction has slowed to a trickle in Munich and many other German cities, capital support for transit continues to flow. Today, an overt public policy of the Munich region is to shift travel from private to public transport to the maximum degree possible.

It is worth noting that unlike some of the other transit metropolises covered in this book, Munich's accomplishments are less tied to a particular innovation, an overarching planning philosophy, or a grand theme or idea. Rather, Munich's experiences show what can be achieved when the goal of transit-led sustainable development is pursued on multiple fronts.

Transit and the City

On the surface, Munich has the physical make-up needed to support successful transit services. In their seminal work on *Public Transportation and Land Use Policy*, Boris Pushkarev and Jeffrey Zupan identified three land-use prerequisites for cost-effective and sustainable rail transit services: (1) a large, dominant center; (2) dense residential development; and (3) long, radial corridors of development.[5] Munich has all three. Situated in a largely rural region without a competing urban center, greater Munich is classically monocentric. Today, about 70 percent of regional jobs are within Munich's inner ring—roughly a 4-kilometer radius from Munich's town hall (Marienplatz) that corresponds to the pre–World War II city. The old city, partly encircled by a medieval wall, contains just 0.5 percent of the region's land area, but claims more than 25 percent of its retail shops and 12 percent of its workplaces. Munich also has the residential densities necessary for rail transit. With a gross average density of 43 inhabitants per hectare, Munich is Germany's third-densest city; Germany itself is Europe's third-densest country, surpassed only by Belgium and the Netherlands. With regard to radial development, greater Munich also passes the test. Development outside the city has generally followed the axial corridors of suburban and intercity railways. While the city of Munich itself encompasses 310 square kilometers, supporting a current population of 1.3 million, its laborshed extends some 50 kilometers from the center, an area with about twice as many inhabitants. Decentralization has translated into relatively long trips. From 1970 to 1990, journeys of more than 35 kilometers in length increased by 180 percent, about three times faster than regional population did. In sum, the combination of a dominant commercial center, dense urban neighborhoods, and long, radial axes of suburban growth has made rail transit a natural choice for the region.

Greater Munich's settlement pattern has produced trip patterns that generally square well with transit riding. The 290,000 daily commutes to the city from the outside tend to be tidal (80 percent are in one direction) and radial. Half of these journeys are by transit. Another 565,000 Munich workers live in the city. Among them, transit captures 75 percent of motorized commutes. Although radial trip-making still predominates, as with the rest of the world, the trend in Munich is toward more crosstown travel. Only twenty years ago, 90 percent of commutes were to Munich. Now, half of employed residents living outside the city commute to a non-Munich destination. Still, by global standards, the Munich region is spatially concentrated and self-contained. In 1992, 62 percent more people commuted internally (i.e., within the city of Munich) than externally (i.e., in-commutes plus out-commutes).

Despite transit's strong standing in the region, the aggregate growth in automobile travel in a radially oriented, strong-centered metropolis has predictably caused problems. The daily rhythm of mainly unidirectional car commutes from the outskirts to the city and convergence near the core has produced serious tie-ups along Munich's major thoroughfares. Since road networks can be only marginally expanded due to environmental restrictions, the region has opted for a combination of greatly enhanced transit services and compact, mixed-use development to cope with future growth.

The city of Munich has compiled unusually rich data to support the contention that compact, mixed-use development is consonant with high transit ridership and sustainable growth. Table 8.1 reveals that for all trip purposes, transit modal shares are strongly and positively associated with densities and proximity to the center. Excluding walk trips, transit's role is far greater. In 1995, transit accounted for 45 percent of all motorized trips within the city of Munich and more than 75 percent of shop trips to the

Table 8.1 LAND USE AND TRAVEL CHARACTERISTICS FOR THE CITY OF MUNICH, 1992

| | City of Munich[1] | | | | Outside City |
	Old City	Inner City	Outer City	Total City	Outside City
Gross residential density (persons per hectare)	72	76	34	43	22
One-way trips per day (millions)	0.21	1.19	1.73	3.13	0.33
Percent of trips by:					
Private vehicle	16	31	46	40	78
Transit	55	34	23	27	15
Bicycle	5	8	9	8	3
Foot	24	27	22	25	4
Total	100	100	100	100	100

[1] The old city (Altstadt) represents an area of roughly a half-km radius from city hall in the heart of the city, at Marienplatz; the inner city represents an area encompassing between roughly a half-km and 4 km from Marienplatz, more or less the city's extent prior to World War II; the outer city represents the postwar city, from about 4 km from Marienplatz to the municipal boundary, some 10 to 15 km from the core.

Sources: Landeshauptstadt München, Planungsreferat: KontiMuch (Munich: Landeshauptstadt München Landeshauptstadt München, 1991); Landeshauptstadt München, Verkehr in München—eine Bestandsaufnahme (Munich: Landeshauptstadt München, 1995).

old city.[6] Compact development is even more important in promoting nonmotorized travel. For trips within the city of up to 3 kilometers in length, walking captures 48 percent and cycling 10 percent. For distances up to 5 kilometers, 37 percent are by foot and 11 percent by bicycle. Car travel dominates when journeys exceed 10 kilometers.

Transit and Institutional Coordination

An important contributor to greater Munich's transit success has been an unusually high degree of institutional coordination, on both the land-use and the transit side. From a land-use perspective, a pro-active city government committed to high-quality urban living and a powerful regional association that sets broad development policies have provided clear visions for guiding future urbanization. On the transit side, a regional transit authority, the Münchener Verkehrs–und Tarif-Verbund, or the MVV, has ensured that rail and bus services and fares are closely integrated. An efficient and purposeful regional institutional structure has been absolutely pivotal in creating a harmonious fit between transit and the built environment.

This section reviews the evolution of the MVV and the crucial role it has played in planning, designing, and implementing coordinated and integrated regional transit services. Attention is given to greater Munich's rich variety of transit modes and how services and tariffs have been closely aligned.

The MVV

The MVV was established in 1972 as an umbrella organization for planning regional transit development and coordinating the timetables and tariffs of the area's many rail and bus service offerings. The MVV was modeled after a successful coordinating body set up five years earlier in greater Hamburg, Germany's first *Verkehrsverbund* (transportation federation). The MVV's jurisdiction more or less matches the region's commutershed, encompassing a 5,500-square-kilometer region of some 2.5 million inhabitants that captures virtually all work-trip interchanges. Its executive board—with representatives from the state of Bavaria, the city of Munich, and mayors from suburban townships—sets regional service and fare policies (e.g., maximum headways between trains and interzonal tariffs), in addition to approving budgets for capital investments and operating assistance.[7] A particularly important role of the board is to provide and allocate sufficient operating assistance across operators to ensure that efficient and socially equitable fares can be charged while also rewarding individual operators for being productive and cost-effective. Day-to-day matters—making sure timetables of trains and buses are synchronized, setting boundaries for zonal tariffs, designing multimodal tariff programs, establishing uniform work rules, crafting standard contract terms for services, sharing marketing approaches, and so on—are left to the management board, whose members are mainly bosses and department heads of the rail and bus companies that deliver services. This group, which prides itself on being politically neutral, meets regularly to "tweak" and fine-tune the regional system so that, to the greatest degree possible, timetables and tariffs are well coordinated.

The Verkehrsverbund, now found in large metropolitan areas throughout Germany and central Europe, has proven to be an ideal organizational approach for designing and providing integrated transit services for suburban corridors where growth and change occur quickly and transit services have traditionally been the weakest.[8] In terms of ridership trends and cost containment, Munich's has been one of the most successful. Much of its success lies in having mastered the "3 Ps" of any successful venture, be it running trains or making widgets: "product," designing goods and services that consumers very much want, which in transit's case includes coordinated timetables; "pricing," setting the prices right to achieve corporate goals, which in the MVV's case is to expand ridership and integrate tariffs; and "promotion," aggressively targeting and marketing the product, which in transit's case includes convincing car-owning suburbanites to change over to trains, trams, and buses.

The MVV Network

With three different railway systems and multiple bus operators, the coordination challenges facing the MVV are greater than those of most Verkehrsverbunds.[9] The region's transit network is big and diverse. The MVV inherited a large part of the system. Still, since the early 1970s, the MVV has proceeded to expand the system step-by-step so as to best match the region's settlement pattern while at the same time shaping growth as it occurs.

The MVV's transit network takes the form of a richly layered, four-tier hierarchical network. The top two tiers are devoted principally to providing mainline services, and the two lower ones function as feeders and distributors.

Mainline Services

At the top of the MVV's hierarchical network are the two heavy rail services—the U-Bahn (metro) and the S-Bahn (suburban railway)—that in tandem provide almost all long-distance and a good share of intermediate-distance travel along high-volume corridors. While both are mainline carriers, there are subtle and important differences between the two. The U-Bahn functions principally as an underground central-city circulator with relatively short station spacings and frequent intervals between trains (two-and-a-half to five minutes during peak hours). In contrast, the S-Bahn's role is mainly to radially connect suburbanites to the central city; in the suburbs, it operates mostly at or above ground and averages long station spacings, whereas in the core, like the U-Bahn, it generally operates below surface with stations relatively close together. Its peak headways along suburban stretches are twenty minutes. The S-Bahn effectively augments metro services in the suburbs, while in the central city it functions more as a complement than a competitor since it often traverses districts without U-Bahn services. Map 8.1, which conveys in schematic how dense greater Munich's *Schnellbahn*, or "fast train," network is, shows that the U-Bahn's principally north-south alignment is complemented by the S-Bahn's strong east-west orientation. Institutionally and operationally, the two services are also quite distinct. The U-Bahn is owned and operated by the city of Munich. The S-Bahn, which for decades belonged to the German national railway (Deutsche Bundesbahn), is today the responsibility of the state of Bavaria following 1994 federal legislation that transferred the ownership of suburban railways to states. In keeping with the European Community's policy of introducing

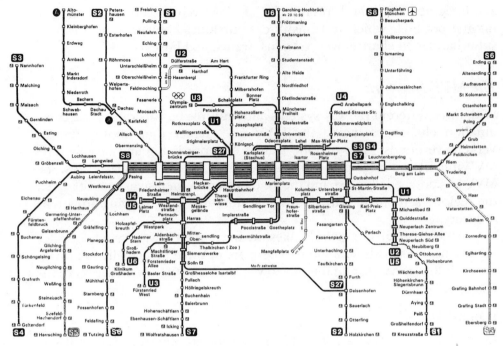

MAP 8.1. MUNICH'S "FAST TRAIN" S-BAHN AND U-BAHN NETWORK, 1995.

greater competition in the public transit sector, this legislation also took the important step of separating the functions of rail track ownership and maintenance, which remained in the public domain, from service delivery, which was opened to public and private providers through competitive tendering.[10]

Both the U-Bahn and the S-Bahn began operations in the early 1970s, in time for the 1972 Olympic Games. The S-Bahn was built mainly along preexisting freight and passenger rail lines to expedite construction. With more than 500 directional kilometers of track and extending as far as 45 kilometers from the city center, the S-Bahn is more than five times longer than the U-Bahn. Eight S-Bahn lines converge along a 4.1-kilometer tunnel that connects the main station (Hauptbahnhof) on the western side of the old city with the Ostbahnhof station on the east side. Bottleneck problems, which have restricted S-Bahn headways, have prompted interest in building a southern route S-Bahn bypass, albeit at a princely sum. For the most part, Munich's S-Bahn is built out, with no major expansion plans in the works. In contrast, the U-Bahn, which has steadily expanded since first opening in 1971, continues to grow, with trackage more than doubling from 36 kilometers in 1983 to 77.5 kilometers in 1995. The U-Bahn network will eventually reach 108 kilometers in length, though with tunneling costs exceeding US$80 million per kilometer, the system's built-out date remains uncertain.

Feeders and Distributors

The third and fourth tiers of greater Munich's transit network are the distributor and feeder services—trams and conventional buses—but even these two supplemental systems are functionally quite different. Trams, which go by the name of *Strassenbahnen,* or "streetcars," in Munich, play more of an intermediate role, with their functions varying to the degree tramways have exclusive right-of-ways. In most instances, tramways are separated from street traffic, providing a finer grain of inner-city circulation than the U-Bahn and more directly penetrating neighborhood districts, though at considerably slower speeds. In the old city, trams are ever-present, sharing many car-free corridors with pedestrians and providing a constant visual reminder that Munich is a very transit-oriented city (Photo 8.1). Compared to the U-Bahn, moreover, tramways tend to be less radially oriented; several newer lines, in fact, provide tangential connections in the northern half of the city. Most tramways, which are entirely owned

PHOTO 8.1. TRAMS IN MUNICH'S ALDSTADT. Trams are an integral part of Munich's overall urban fabric, co-existing with pedestrians in most car-free corridors. Because of their slower speeds and Old World charm, trams blend in nicely with Munich's pedestrian districts and the traditional, human scale of its retail core.

and operated by the city of Munich, predate the U-Bahn and S-Bahn by decades. As with most German cities, many streetcar lines were dismantled during the post–World War II era. In Munich, the tramways that were retained fill in for corridors unserved by the U-Bahn or S-Bahn. Partly in reaction to the exorbitant costs of new U-Bahn construction, the city of Munich has recently adopted a new outlook on tramways, embarking on an ambitious expansion program.[11] Newer lines are more akin to light rail services, with modern, low-floor trains operating on dedicated tracks on street medians. A growing consensus that trams are vital to the life of a compact, human-scale city is also behind the newfound support for trams. Surveys by Munich planners show trams offer certain advantages over other forms of transit: the ability to see outside and take in urban life; easier at-grade access; and, because of their smaller vehicle sizes and above-ground operations, a greater feeling of safety, especially among the elderly.[12]

Complementing greater Munich's three levels of rail services are conventional buses. Those operated by the city of Munich function mainly as feeders to the city's outer U-Bahn stations. Outside the city, buses are mainly privately owned and operated, with routes functioning as either short-haul feeders to S-Bahn stations or long-haul, cross-regional connectors. Some S-Bahn stations are also served by smart paratransit. At the Erding station on the S6 line, 30 kilometers northeast of Munich, privately operated Ruf-Bus (German for "call-a-bus") ply flexible routes, linking the S-Bahn and the hinterland. At the station, arriving customers punch in a ride request on a console and information is automatically relayed to a central computer. Dispatchers assign the closest vehicle to the ride request using radio communication. Since first introduced in 1995, this flexible, one-to-many service has attracted several hundred additional weekday trips to the Erding S-Bahn station.[13]

Supply, Demand, and Performance

The complementarity of greater Munich's transit offerings is revealed by summary statistics on service inputs and consumption outputs. Table 8.2 shows significant variation across transit modes in terms of service provisions, station spacings, and passenger capacities. Within the MVV region, suburban train and bus services are geographically the most extensive and average the longest distances between stops. City tram stops, for instance, are 6.5 times closer together than S-Bahn stops and 2.4 times closer than U-Bahn stops, on average. Munich's buses log the most kilometers each year; however, because carriages are so much larger, the region's mainline rail services offer the bulk of system capacity, when measured in person space kilometers. S-Bahn trains alone account for more than half of total floor space capacity. Such statistics fail to reflect

Table 8.2 SUPPLY AND CAPACITY CHARACTERISTICS OF MVV TRANSIT SERVICES, 1994

| | Lines | | Stations or Stops | | Vehicles[2] | | Capacity[3]: |
	No.	Length (kms)[1]	No.	Avg.Spacing (kms)	No.	Annual Vehicle Kms (millions)	Annual Person Space Kms (millions)
S-Bahn	9	510	137	3.72	549	17.12	13,406
U-Bahn	6	92	68	1.35	420	9.34	6,652
Tramway	9	85	148	0.57	188	6.52	1,145
City Buses	75	703	816	0.86	508	31.54	2,449
Suburban Buses	170	3,541	2,220	1.59	394	13.65	970
Total	269	4,931	3,389	1.46	2,059	78.17	24,422

[1] Single-direction kms

[2] S-Bahn trains operate as 3-vehicle (i.e., car) units, and U-Bahn trains and trams operate as 2-vehicle units.

[3] Capacities are calculated using MVV's service design standard of 4 persons per square meter of floor space. S-Bahn cars seat, on average, 194 passengers and accommodate 254 standees. With 3-car train units, a typical S-Bahn train can handle up to 1,344 passengers. A typical U-Bahn train seats 98 and handles 192 standees. U-Bahn trains usually operate as 2 units, with capacities up to 580 passengers, though on some lines during peak periods, 3-car trains operate (holding as many as 870 passengers). Newer trams seat 82 and accommodate up to 97 standees and thus have 2-car train capacities of 358 passengers.
Sources: MVV GmbH, Report Geschäftsbericht 1994 (Munich: MVV GmbH, 1995); data provided by MVV.

the connection of service provisions to the region's settlement pattern. In terms of access of people to transit stops, the city of Munich is extremely well served. Presently, about 80 percent of all residents and 95 percent of city workers are within 400 meters of a streetcar stop or 600 meters of a U-Bahn or S-Bahn station. The old city is 100 percent rail-served—everyone is within 400 meters of a rail stop of one kind or another. Clearly, the mesh between transit provisions and the central cityscape is a tight one.

The comparative ridership roles and service performance of MVV's transit options are revealed in Table 8.3. Mainline rail services carry 62 percent of all (unlinked) trips in the region, led by the U-Bahn's 284 million annual boardings in 1994. Because of the lengthier trips made by suburbanites, the S-Bahn accounts for 57 percent of total passenger kilometers traveled. Complementarity is perhaps best revealed by the service effectiveness indicators in Table 8.3. The U-Bahn is by far most productive in terms of passengers carried per vehicle kilometer, performing three times above the regional average in 1994. Adjusting for trip length, however, S-Bahn trains are the top performers. And in terms of average loads, trams rank the highest.

Table 8.3 DEMAND AND PERFORMANCE CHARACTERISTICS OF MVV TRANSIT
SERVICES, 1994

| | Annual Ridership (millions)[1] | | Service Effectiveness | | |
	No.	Passenger Kms	Passenger[2]/ Vehicle Km	Passenger[2] Kms/ Vehicle Km	Load Factor (%)[3]
S-Bahn	225	3,014	13.1	176.1	22.5
U-Bahn	284	1,209	30.4	129.4	18.2
Tramway	88	276	13.5	39.3	24.1
City Buses	183	534	5.8	16.9	21.8
Suburban Buses	30	230	2.2	16.8	23.7
Total/Average[4]	810	5,263	10.3	67.3	21.6

[1] Unlinked trips (i.e., including transfers).
[2] For rail (S-Bahn, U-Bahn, and tramway) services, vehicles represent cars (i.e., units of trains).
[3] Annual passenger kms divided by annual person km capacity.
[4] Ridership figures (first two columns) are totals. Service effectiveness figures (last three columns) are weighted averages.
Sources: MVV GmbH, *Report Geschäftsbericht 1994* (Munich: MVV GmbH, 1995); data provided by MVV.

Trends under the MVV

Perhaps the best indicator that the MVV has made a difference is transit's expanding mobility role. Since the MVV's formation, transit's share of regional motorized trips has steadily increased—from 30 percent in 1975, to 36 percent in 1980, to 38 percent in 1990, to 42 percent in 1994. In contrast, Germany's other two large Verkehrsverbunds—Hamburg and Rhein-Ruhr—saw transit's market share slip over the same period.[14] Transit's expanding role in greater Munich is all the more impressive in light of the fact that it occurred despite steep fare increases. To keep its fiscal house in order, the MVV has routinely pegged fares to inflation rates and shifts in operating costs. Over the past two decades, greater Munich's transit fares have increased more than anywhere else in Germany. As a result, MVV's operating cost recovery rate has remained steady in the 45 to 50 percent range, and its real, inflation-adjusted subsidy per passenger trip has been held in check. Based on a comparison of financial performance among Germany's Verkehrsverbunds, John Pucher and Stefan Kurth remarked that "Munich has been the most successful of the German systems at holding down per-unit costs and subsidy needs."[15]

Rising ridership and market shares can be attributed to many factors, but foremost have been increases in the frequency and quality of service. From 1972, when the MVV was established, to 1992, transit services—measured in person space kilometers of service—rose by 62 percent, mainly due to the extension of U-Bahn and S-Bahn lines.[16] The average time devoted to transferring is thought to have fallen at a similar level over this twenty-year period, thanks to MVV's synchronization of timetables.

Munich's experiences lend credence to the conventional wisdom that customers are far more sensitive to changes in service quality than to changes in price—people respond better to high-quality services at high prices than low-quality services at low prices.[17]

Service Enhancements

Besides increasing the amount and quality of train and bus services, the MVV has introduced other enhancements. As a marketing strategy, it provides individualized schedule, route, and fare information—either over the counter, over the phone, via an Internet web site, or through CD-ROM timetables. Given any desired origin and destination, a computer program will recommend an optimal route and schedule.

MVV's fare system gets high marks for unified ticketing and efficiency. Customers can choose between prepaid monthly passes, cash fares, and strip tickets, available from 400 sales offices and 1,500 vending machines scattered throughout the region. Fare payment occurs under the honor system; fewer than 1 out of 200 boardings, it is estimated, involves a fare violation.[18] The highly refined zonal system—there are 134 different zonal fare combinations—has produced a tariff system that pegs charges reasonably closely to distances traveled. There are even short-haul adjustments: while a trip within a single zone normally requires two ticket strips, those of less than five stops require only a single strip. The down side of such efficient pricing, however, is that it is, in the words of Pucher and Kurth, "excruciatingly complicated," adding that "nowhere else in the world have the authors encountered such a baffling fare system," though conceding that "the superb quality of Munich's public transport system . . . (has) more than offset this problematic fare structure."[19] Fare complexity is really a problem for visitors and tourists since most MVV customers are making routine trips for which they readily know the required payment. Also, the majority of MVV passengers use monthly passes that provide unlimited access to the system; for them, zonal fare differentials are inconsequential.[20] To help get around the complexity of distance-based pricing, the MVV has introduced a three-day limitless ride ticket for tourists.

Munich's outstanding transit service quality and integration are also revealed in the details of physical design. Along the main pedestrian axis in central Munich—from Karlsplatz to Marienplatz—U-Bahn, S-Bahn, and intercity train tracks converge as multilevel tunnels, allowing for easy connections between short-, intermediate-, and long-haul services. With three levels of mid-platform boarding at key stations along the main pedestrian spine, transfers are effortless, involving little more than a vertical escalator ride. There are even efficiencies in escalator operations. At some stations, a single escalator is used, with the direction of movement determined according to demand. During periods of slack demand, esca-

lators sit idle for minutes at a time. Such designs save on both construction and electricity costs. Additionally, the needs of bus users have not
gone unnoticed. In recent years, the MVV has modernized and redesigned
hundreds of bus stops to provide comfortable seating, lighted safety, and
protection from the elements. Since bus transit is often viewed by Germans as a second-class service meant for students and transit-dependents,
MVV officials feel they must go the extra distance in providing amenities
if many middle-income suburbanites are to be coaxed out of their cars.

Park-and-Ride Programs

Another contributor to rising transit usage in the Munich region has been
MVV's aggressive campaign to expand park-and-ride facilities. Currently,
there are more than 25,000 free park-and-ride spaces near rail stations,
with plans to add another 18,000 spaces in coming years. Park-and-ride is
a clear example of adapting transit provisions to the spread-out lay of the
land. In ways, it is a dual-edged sword. On the one hand, park-and-ride is
vital toward winning over suburbanites to transit, especially in a strong-
centered, radially oriented metropolis like Munich where commuting by
rail can be faster than by car as long as one can conveniently park near
stations. On the other hand, driving, parking, and riding transit contributes little to improving air quality and reducing energy consumption
due to the inefficiencies of the internal combustion engine for relatively
short car trips (which park-and-ride journeys tend to be), especially when
the engine is cold. Critics also complain that park-and-ride spaces contribute to sprawl by making car travel all the more convenient. On balance, MVV officials view the benefits of park-and-ride as outweighing the
costs. And more and more urban planners are coming around to accepting that park-and-ride lots can contribute toward maintaining a strong,
viable central city in multiple ways: by keeping cars on the periphery
rather than in the core of the region, by indirectly keeping businesses and
shops downtown by helping to sustain high service levels (as a result of
increasing ridership), and by reducing central-area parking supplies.

The MVV's showcase park-and-ride facility is a four-level structure
adjacent to the Fröttmaning U-Bahn station and alongside the A9 Autobahn (linking Munich and Nuremberg) that caters to 1,270 cars and 80
coaches. With U-Bahn trains passing by every five to ten minutes during
peak hours, suburbanites can get to Marienplatz within fifteen minutes.
Three freely programmable large matrix screens have been installed on
the A9 motorway to display real-time park-and-ride information. They
indicate the number of free parking spaces as well as the expected depar-
ture time for the next U-Bahn train to the city. If necessary, information
on downstream traffic conditions and incidents, such as traffic accidents,
can be displayed. Once they arrive at the park-and-ride entrance,
motorists are guided to the nearest free parking space by a dynamic, real-

time surveillance and control system. Information on availability is provided by laser scan detectors mounted beside all entrance and exit lanes
and ultrasound detectors fitted to each parking space. Surveys show that
park-and-ride displays are frequently mentioned by transit riders at
Fröttmaning as the main reason they switched from driving to catching a
train to work.[21]

Coordinating Transit and Urban Development

Munich's successes are not just a product of smartly configuring transit
services to match origin-destination patterns. They are also tied to
decades of efforts to alter origin-destination patterns themselves through
strategic land-use planning that targets urban growth to rail station catchments. Important inroads in coordinating transit and urban development
have been made at both the regional and the municipal levels.

Regional Planning Initiatives

For decades, greater Munich has had a strategic and visionary long-range
regional planning process in place. Leading the effort is the Regional
Association Munich, made up of 145 elected officials from the city of
Munich and its surrounding communities. By federal and Bavarian law,
the association can set only broad regional development policies, with
zoning and land-use controls still the prerogatives of local governments.
However, the association has been granted consummate veto powers to
ensure that land-use decisions made by individual communities are fully
compatible with regional development policies. The principal charge of
the association's professional planners is to make sure that the more than
600 local plans that pass through review each year are wholly consistent
with agreed-upon objectives and directives on how greater Munich is sup-
posed to grow.

  Since the first regional plan in 1963, the physical planning of greater
Munich has been cast firmly in terms of transit and urban form relationships. The original plan embraced the concept of a radial metropolis,
prompting the decisions to invest in S-Bahn and U-Bahn systems. The follow-up 1975 plan envisaged a polycentric future, spawning the construction of several tangential rail lines and proposals to encircle the region
with railways eventually. More recent plan updates have refined the notion
of polycentrism as not just multiple centers on a map but rather inter-con-
nected and purposeful places with mixtures of land uses and urban
designs that help promote broader objectives related to livability and sustainability. With region-wide political agreement that future growth in
travel must be entirely accommodated through public transit, current

PHOTO 8.2. ZAMILA PARK. This 19-hectare mixed-use development includes 1,300 dwellings, a neighborhood center with retail services, 50,0000 square meters of office space, and a lake, all within walking distance of the Berg am Laim S-Bahn station (lines 5 and 6). The same development company that built the successful new-town/in-town of Arabella Park built the new-town/out-of-town Zamila Park. Plans call for eventually moving the S-Bahn station to Zamila Park's neighborhood center.

regional policies call for channeling overspill development into mixed-use town centers aligned along S-Bahn corridors. Zamila Park, shown in Photo 8.2, is a case in point. The regional association has stipulated that from now on, all large-scale housing, commercial, and industrial development must be concentrated around railway stations. Based on land price differentials, it would appear that transit-oriented suburban development is also what the marketplace wants. Currently, land parcels near suburban rail stations are commanding price premiums as high as 130 percent relative to otherwise comparable parcels away from stations.[22]

Regional growth management has also entered the scene as of late. In order to promote a jobs-housing balance in fast-growing areas, particularly around Munich's international airport, where many high-technology firms have concentrated in recent years, regional directives now hold that every hectare of commercial or industrial development must be accompanied by two hectares of housing development.[23] With surveys showing that the majority of workers in the airport district live in nearby housing, managed growth efforts appear to be having their intended consequences.

A Compact, Urban, and Green Munich

Interest in transit-supportive development has also gained momentum within the city of Munich itself. Since the mid-1980s, Munich planners have aggressively sought to revitalize the central city as a mixed-use living and working community. The adopted slogan for twenty-first-century Munich is "Compact, urban, and green." Current plans call for infill development focused around rail stops, with plot ratios (floor area divided by land area) in the range of 0.9 to 2.5 within the catchments of all U-Bahn and S-Bahn stations. Within the 600-meter catchments (roughly equivalent to a ten-minute walking distance), permissible densities taper in 150-meter rings, akin to a wedding cake. For the inner-most ring (150 meters out), plot ratios of 1.2 to 1.6 are allowed for station areas designated as secondary urban centers. A number of secondary centers lie along existing and planned tangential U-Bahn lines, where significant amounts of future infill development is being targeted. For most other outlying stations, commercial and housing development concentrated around stations is being built at plot ratios of 0.9 to 1.2.

One of Munich's most successful planned communities that serves as a model for future transit-linked development is Arabella Park, situated on the U4 subway line 4 kilometers northeast of Marienplatz. Arabella Park is a vibrant and colorful community that has the feel of being a place unto itself in a sea of urbanization that spreads out from the old city (Photo 8.3). Built in the mid-1960s as a large-scale redevelopment project, Arabella Park today features a rich blend of housing, offices, shops, and community facilities, all within easy walking distance of the centrally located subway station. A balanced community, Arabella Park has 10,000 full-time residents and 18,000 daytime workers. Thus, people are around all the time. The Scandinavian model of transit-oriented design was adopted for Arabella Park's first phase, producing a landscape dominated by functional though rather imposing four-to-seventeen-story structures. For its second phase, completed in the early 1980s, a more human-scale design was chosen, with structures three to six stories high that are more varied and distinct in their architecture. The newer phase is actually denser than the earlier one (with an average plot ratio of 1.2 versus 1.0) but involves a more intimate design of interior open space and landscaping. With automobile access limited to the periphery of the community and a generous supply of attractively landscaped pathways in the interior, Arabella Park is an

PHOTO 8.3. ARABELLA PARK. An attractive, mixed-use, planned community is concentrated around an underground U-Bahn station. The pleasantly landscaped car-free center has made walking and cycling the modes of choice for circulating within the community. The second phase of development, consisting mostly of the low-rise, slanted-roof housing structures in the center of the photo, actually averages higher blended densities than the initial phase of high-rise apartments to the north (left of this photo), but has the feel of a more human-scale environment because of the intimate use of interior courtyard space.

especially pleasant place to take a stroll or ride a bike. Its car-free village square, dotted with flower stalls, fruit stands, and outdoor cafes and adorned with urban art and water fountains, has become the heart and soul of the community. Arabella Park's accent on amenities and livability has without question reaped transportation benefits: among residents, about half of all trips for shopping are exclusively by foot or bicycle, and 65 percent of trips to work or school are by some form of public transit.[24]

Promoting Green Forms of Transport

Complementing the planning for transit-oriented communities has been a series of steps taken by the city to "push" people out of cars and "pull" them onto trains, trams, buses, and pathways. The city has adopted what is officially called a "push-pull" program of traffic management.[25] The chief device being used to discourage car travel is parking restraints. Supplies of on-street parking have been greatly reduced, particularly around train stations and in the core in recent times. Concurrently, the zone for metered parking in and around the old city has been substantially enlarged. Between 1990 and 1995, moreover, rates for curbside parking doubled, and meters were changed to allow no more than an hour of payment to deter long-term parking. New off-street parking garages are now officially taboo in central Munich, and neighborhood permits have become universal throughout the city.[26]

Besides substantially upgrading transit facilities and services, a number of steps have been aggressively taken to "pull" residents and workers into green modes, especially nonmotorized ones. Environmentalists are quick to point out that although the lion's share of municipal transportation expenditures have historically gone to motorized modes, walking and cycling today make up 47 percent of the ninety-two minutes spent each day by the typical Munich resident getting around.[27] Among the recent investments made to "level the playing field" have been: the extension and widening of pathway networks; the construction of pedestrian-cyclist overpasses and underpasses at busy crossings; the closing of some streets to cars; the addition of separate signal phases and turning priorities for cyclists; the redesign of intersections and use of chokers, neck-downs, street trees, and speed bumps to slow through traffic within neighborhoods; and the provision of bicycle parking lots and even garages, located mainly around rail stations. Much of the core has been pedestrianized, with some streets banning all but foot traffic, others allowing only bicycles, trams, and buses to accompany walkers, and still others exempting only certain groups of motorists, such as residents and delivery trucks (Photo 8.4).

Today, Munich is one of the world's most bicycle-friendly cities, boasting 644 kilometers of bike lanes (456 kilometers as separate lane markings along streets, 51 kilometers as sequestered urban pathways, and 137 kilometers as freestanding lanes in public parks and green areas). More than 35,000 weather-protected and secure spaces for bicycles are provided at and near the city's rail stations. Such improvements appear to be paying off: today, bicycles account for 24 percent of movements within the old city and along outer corridors where cycle paths skirt the scenic Isar River, and 14 percent of trips made in other urban settings with dedicated cycling lanes.[28] At the insistence of the Greens, even public policies have become kinder to cyclists and pedestrians. German and Bavarian tax codes now allow families to deduct from personal income taxes 7 pfennigs (about 4 U.S. cents) per kilometer for riding a bicycle or walking to work.[29]

PHOTO 8.4. A SEMI-EXCLUSIVE PEDESTRIAN ZONE IN THE OLD CITY. Along this street, trams and cyclists share space with pedestrians, and vehicles with special permits are allowed to enter only during certain hours of the day. The use of flower oases and brick-textured road surfaces helps to calm traffic.

Learning from Munich

Munich's transit achievements are truly remarkable for a land known for its well-engineered cars and expressways with no speed limits. Whereas most other German regions have seen transit's mobility role steadily slip, in greater Munich public transit continues to gain in stature and importance. Transit's prominence in a land of the Autobahn certainly hasn't deterred growth or backfired economically. Munich is widely viewed as one of Germany's most attractive and livable cities, and it leads the nation in tourists visiting from abroad. Over the past decade, the region has become one of Europe's major high-technology centers, with more than 4,000 companies now actively involved in developing and manufacturing microelectronic devices, precision instruments, and computer-related software. Munich reminds us that good-quality transit is wholly consonant with a high quality of living as well as environmental and economic sustainability.

There is a duality to much of the story about Munich as a transit metropolis. Of course, duality pervades much of Germany's political life, with conservatives on one hand aggressively promoting the interests of motorists and the Greens on the other just as aggressively championing the cause of nonmotorists. However, duality is found more fundamentally in the region's transit–urban form relationship. The city of Munich is very transit-oriented while most of its suburbs, like most other places, are anything but transit-oriented. Yet transit services have been smartly designed and configured to competitively serve spread-out development. Good bus and tram connections, combined with a continually expanding supply of high-tech park-and-ride facilities, have made rail services viable mobility options for many suburbanites. Thus, part of Munich's duality lies in being a metropolis that is both transit-oriented and transit-adapted. It also lies in the complementarity of mainline and distributor services, the latter being dually provided by the public and private sectors. There is also duality and complementarity in how transit services and urban development are organized and coordinated. The MVV has devoted itself principally to coordinating both timetables and tariffs and has done so with outstanding success. Its two-tiered institutional structure has ensured that decisions get made efficiently and appropriately: the executive board sets service and tariff policies, and its board of transit managers tends to day-to-day operational matters. On the land-use side, MVV's equivalent is the Regional Association Munich, responsible for coordinating urban growth across multiple jurisdictions. Land-use policies themselves tend to be two-pronged. Station-area catchments are designated for future regional trip generators and large-scale developments, whereas outside station zones, market-driven development pretty much runs its own course. Complementing land-use planning have been various traffic management strategies, and here again duality exists—namely, Munich's "push-pull" approach to inducing modal shifts. Stringent parking controls have pushed people out of cars. The creation of well-designed bike paths, pedestrian-only districts, and traffic-calmed streets have pulled them into alternative modes.

Overall, the lessons of Munich are multiple and are not easily summarized in a single message or statement. Perhaps one of the most valuable lessons is that a sustainable transit metropolis need not be the product of an overarching planning philosophy or a dominant paradigm. Rather, the road to becoming a successful transit metropolis can be pursued along multiple fronts, with each step contributing in some small but meaningful way to what is ultimately achieved. While there has been no dominant vision of how the region should grow in the future, at least not to the degree found in Stockholm, Copenhagen, and Singapore, there has nevertheless been a strong sense and widespread political agreement that building and maintaining a world-class transit system is in the region's best long-term interest. Based on recent experiences, there is every indication that the right institutions and approaches have been put into place to bring this about, even in the land of the Autobahn.

NOTES

1. Landeshauptstadt München, *Verkehr in München—eine Bestandsufnahme 1995* (Munich: Referat für Stadtplanung und Bauordnung, 1995).

2. J. Pucher and C. Lefèvre, *The Urban Transport Crisis in Europe and North America* (Basingstoke, England: Macmillan, 1996), Ch. 3.

3. Landeshauptstadt München, *Münchener Perspektiven einer stadtverträglichen Mobilität* (Munich: Landeshauptstadt München, Referat für Stadtplanung und Bauordnung 1995).

4. Pucher and Lefèvre, *op. cit.,* p. 44.

5. B. Pushkarev and J. Zupan, *Public Transportation and Land Use Policy* (Bloomington: Indiana University Press, 1977).

6. Rich modal split data are also available for radially oriented travel across districts of the city and outside the city (which accounted for 46 percent of trips by Munich residents in 1992). For the 0.49 million trips per weekday between the old city and inner city (across the old-city ring), transit captured 76 percent of the total. For the 1.59 million daily trips between the inner city and the outer city (across the middle ring), transit carried 45 percent of the total. And for the 1 million daily trips between the outer city and outside the city; (across the city boundary), transit carried 31 percent of the total. Source: Landeshauptstadt München, *Münchener Perspektiven einer stadtverträglichen Mobilität,* table 2.

7. The MVV's current peak-period service standards are: three-minute headways for U-Bahn trains; ten-minute headways for S-Bahn trains inside the city and twenty minutes when operating outside the city.

8. J. Pucher and S. Kurth, Verkehrsverbund: The Success of Regional Public Transport in Germany, Austria, and Switzerland, *Transport Policy,* vol. 2, no. 4, 1996, pp. 279–291.

9. In German, the plural is spelled *Verkehrsverbünde.* In this book, the plural forms of foreign nouns are Anglicized.

10. Germany's legislation sought to transform the Deutsche Bundesbahn, or DB, from a protected monopoly to a more efficient, less bureaucratic organization that is more responsive to consumer needs. Introducing greater competition was seized as the best means of accomplishing this. DB was turned into a semiprivate corporation and renamed Deutsche Bahn. In Bavaria, the Bayerishe Eisenbahngessellschaft (BEG) was established as a quasi-public corporation to manage and maintain infrastructure assets (rail lines and stations) and to competitively contract out for all services provided on S-Bahn and intercity tracks. Interestingly, DB won the concession for operating S-Bahn services under competitive tendering. Within the first several years, competitive contracting has lowered S-Bahn operating costs (relative to former monopolized services) by nearly 25 percent, mainly due to the less generous compensation packages provided by private railway companies.

11. The prognosis for trams when the first U-Bahn lines opened in 1971 was that they would be gone from the scene within a decade. With the cost of

tramway expansion put at one-tenth the cost of U-Bahn expansion, however, Munich's trams received a new lease on life. Twenty kilometers of tramway were built in the mid-1990s, and many more are on the drawing boards.

12.   H. König and B. Hüttl, Eine Renaissance der Strassenbahn in München, *Der Nahverkehr,* June 1995, pp. 43–47.

13.   One-to-many represents a single origin (i.e., the S-Bahn station) connected to multiple potential destinations.

14.   Pucher and Kurth, *op. cit.*

15.   *Ibid.,* p. 288.

16.   *Ibid.,* p. 283, table 5.

17.   R. Cervero, Transit Pricing Research: A Review and Synthesis, *Transport Reviews,* vol. 13, no. 1, 1993, pp. 61–81.

18.   In 1994, there were 2.4 million cases of fraud out of a total of 530 million passenger boardings in the region.

19.   Pucher and Kurth, *op. cit.,* p. 286.

20.   Most prepaid passes are purchased by private companies at bulk discounts (with a twelve-month pass costing the same as ten monthly pass payments) and made available to their employees. These are treated by German tax authorities as fully deductible business expenses.

21.   Ministry of Interior, State of Bavaria, Munich COMFORT: Cooperative Transport Management for Munich and Its Surrounding Area (Munich: Ministry of Interior, 1996).

22.   Outside Munich, land within 500 meters of S-Bahn stations was commanding an average price of US$420 per square meter in 1993. In otherwise comparable settings without nearby S-Bahn services, land was going for about US$180 per square meter. Source: Bayerisches Staatsministerium für Wirtschaft, Verkehr und Technologie München, *Gesamtverkehrsplan Bayern* (Munich: Bayerisches Staatsministerium für Wirtschaft, Verkehr und Technologie München, 1994).

23.   Regional planners have become increasingly concerned about the imbalances produced by market-driven growth. Over the past decade, employment growth has concentrated north and east of Munich, whereas most new housing has been built south and west of the city.

24.   Landeshauptstadt München—Planungsreferat, *Die Landeshauptstandt München auf dem Weg zu einem stadtverträglichen Verkehr* (Munich: Landeshauptstadt München, 1992).

25.   For details on Munich's "push-pull" traffic management program, see: N. Bieling, G. Skoupil, and H. Topp, The Munich Car Traffic Reduction Concept, *IATSS Research,* vol. 19, no. 2, 1995, pp. 20–25.

26.   While such management strategies seek to regulate traffic in the city, Munich has not fully abandoned new road construction as a congestion mitigation strategy. As in Stockholm, voters recently approved a proposal to build at least one tunnel (Mittlerer Ring) under the city center. Various tran-

sit improvements were also approved as part of the funding package. Because new roads are to be underground, and thus will not directly impinge on the central city once opened, they have been accepted by the populace.

27. Landeshauptstadt München, *Verkehr in München—eine Bestandsufnahme 1995.*

28. *Ibid.*

29. This was mainly in reaction to what was for decades a built-in incentive to drive to work—the ability to deduct per kilometer expenses for commuting by automobile from one's personal income taxes, without similar provisions for nonmotoring commuters.

Chapter 9

Busways and the Hybrid Metropolis: Ottawa, Canada

Thanks to farsighted planning, metropolitan Ottawa boasts a highly functional bus-based transit system well suited to the region's mixed settlement pattern—a compact center and spread-out suburbs. Using a dedicated busway, Ottawa has achieved many of the advantages of a rail-based rapid transit system, with an added bonus: vehicles can leave and return to the guideway, thus reducing the need to transfer. A bus-based rapid transit system also provides flexibility advantages, such as the ability to open the system in stages. Today, Ottawa's bus-only guideway connects more than 200,000 daily passengers to the region's urban centers. Nearly three-quarters of all peak-hour trips headed to downtown Ottawa are by transit. Transit's share of trips to suburban shopping and employment centers is as high as that to the downtowns of many similar-size North American cities. The most important service feature of the busway has been its ability to accommodate express bus and limited-stop routes that provide passengers with a direct, no-transfer ride between their homes and places of work. Today, virtually all major employment centers in the region can be reached with no more than one transfer between express routes, whether they are on the busway or not. And contrary to conventional wisdom, greater Ottawa shows that busways can attract high-rise development, including condominium towers. Regardless of technology, be it rail or bus, good-quality transit will spawn growth.

Greater Ottawa, Canada, is a hybrid metropolis in the purest sense. Its core area is quite compact for a metropolis of 720,000 residents, but outside the core, its landscape is classic suburbia, not unlike many medium-size Canadian and U.S. metropolises. A notable difference, however, is the presence of a greenbelt that collars the city of Ottawa and its early post–World War II suburbs. The greenbelt was created in 1959 by an act of Canada's Parliament to contain sprawl and preserve open space. As in Stockholm, a protective greenbelt has proven its value over time as an instrument for creating a built form conducive to transit riding—in Ottawa's case, aboard buses that are well adapted to the mixed high-rise/low-rise lay of the land. As development has leapfrogged across the greenbelt in recent times—concentrating mostly around two outlying town centers—a flexible bus-based transit system has demonstrated itself to be the appropriate technology for the region.

The centerpiece of the region's transit system is a grade-separated right-of-way reserved just for buses—what locals call the Transitway. Map 9.1 shows the region's 31-kilometer Transitway, the largest bus-only guideway in North America, in addition to the greenbelt that rings the city of Ottawa and its postwar suburbs. The Transitway plays a dual role: it both funnels buses into the built-up core and, since buses can leave the guideway, provides an efficient conduit for transfer-free connections to the spread-out suburbs. In greater Ottawa, transit's relationship with the cityscape likewise engenders duality. On the one hand, transit has adapted to low-density patterns of development; yet on the other, it has spurred high-rise development around many Transitway stations. Transit has adapted to the city, and the city has adapted to transit. This is not the result of happenstance but, as in the case of Stockholm and Copenhagen, a well-articulated vision of the future, backed by effective regional planning and governance.

The Ottawa-Carleton Region

Ottawa, Canada's capital, with a population of 325,000 residents, is one of eleven municipalities that make up the Regional Municipality of Ottawa-Carleton (RMOC).[1] Situated south of the Ottawa River in northeastern Ontario, the RMOC's jurisdiction extends far into the rural countryside. More than 90 percent of the region's 730,000 inhabitants, however, live inside the greenbelt.

Growth and the Economy

During the 1980s, the RMOC's population grew at an annual rate of 2.1 percent, faster than any urban area in Canada. Much of this growth occurred in and around newly designated urban centers outside the greenbelt, principally Kanata to the west and Orléans to the east (Map 9.1).[2] While regional growth has slowed during the 1990s, as elsewhere in Canada due to a prolonged recession, Ottawa-Carleton retains one of the

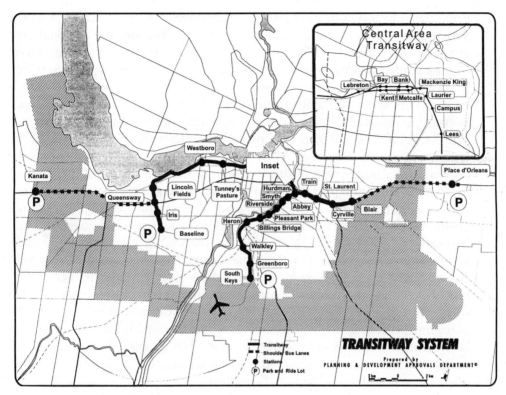

MAP 9.1. METROPOLITAN OTTAWA'S TRANSITWAY AND GREENBELT. *Source:* Regional Municipality of Ottawa-Carleton, Planning and Development Approvals Department, 1997.

nation's healthiest economies. In 1992, per capita disposable income was 33 percent above the national average, 18 percent higher than in Ontario, and 12 percent higher than in metropolitan Toronto.

Unlike many federal districts, Ottawa-Carleton is not a one-industry town. While the federal government remains the region's number-one employer, the share of workers in the public sector fell from 33 percent in 1981 to 20 percent in 1996. Today, the region is home to Canada's largest concentration of high-technology companies and continues to attract jobs in business services and health-related industries.

Downtown Ottawa (represented by the inset in Map 9.1) contains one-quarter of the region's labor force and about half of all federal jobs. As throughout North America, jobs are rapidly suburbanizing, however—a fact that has not gone unnoticed by the RMOC in its long-range planning.

Institutional Structure

Regional planning and governance have been essential to successfully linking transportation and land use in Ottawa-Carleton. The RMOC is the upper level of a two-tier municipal government structure. Created by the Province of Ontario and modeled after Metro Toronto, the regional government was formed in 1969 to carry out comprehensive planning, invest in major infrastructure, and provide regional services within a geographic spread almost four times the size of Metro Toronto.[3] The RMOC's elected members serve on the Regional Council, whose responsibilities include overseeing regional transit services and planning for future development.[4] The Regional Council appoints members within their own ranks to the Ottawa Carleton Regional Transit Commission, or OC Transpo, the region's transit-operating authority.[5] A standing committee of the Regional Council, the Transportation Committee, manages the Transitway.

Local governments, which make up the second tier of the regional structure, perform primarily local functions, such as waste collection and fire services. They also regulate land use through zoning laws and subdivision approvals. While the Regional Council wields approval and veto powers over municipal zoning and subdivision actions, in practice it rarely overrules the wishes of a municipality, barring any egregious conflicts with the region's Official Plan. Other important players in the planning process are the Province of Ontario (which subsidizes transit services and empowers the RMOC with enabling legislation) and the federal government, in particular the National Capital Commission, which owns large amounts of land in the region.

Creating a Transit Metropolis

Ottawa-Carelton offers a textbook example of how to successfully coordinate transportation and urban development. A cogent vision of a preferred settlement pattern set the stage for the eventual development of a world-class busway system.

The Official Plan

Crucial to creating a metropolis with viable transit services has been the Official Plan. This document sets overall regional development policies, determines the types and locations of major permitted land uses, and identifies regional infrastructure investments that are necessary to support land-use objectives. Plan development and approval is a shared responsibility of the RMOC and the eleven local municipalities.[6]

Regional Development Strategy

As with all good plans, the Regional Council first established a vision for the future. In the early 1970s, within a few years of its formation, the

Regional Council embarked on a year-long campaign to elicit broad-based citizen input into defining the region's preferred future settlement pattern—referred to in the plan as a Regional Development Strategy. In 1974, the Council endorsed a multicentered urban structure: downtown Ottawa would retain its position as the dominant commercial, employment, and cultural center of the region and would be orbited by a hierarchy of primary and secondary urban centers. Outside these centers, market-driven patterns of development—including low-density spread—would be largely permitted.

The chief instrument for achieving this physical form would be the Transitway. The 1974 plan made mention of the Transitway only in concept, calling for growth to be channeled along high-capacity transportation axes (Map 9.2). Later plan updates were more specific, identifying designated mixed-use town centers and their spatial relationship to a well-defined Transitway system (Map 9.3).

With a vision in place and the agreement to build a busway to bring the vision to fruition, the Regional Council turned its attention to land-use management. This led to the adoption of transit-oriented development policies that called for substantial increases in the share of regional jobs located near Transitway stations. The long-term goal is for 40 percent of the region's jobs to be within walking distance (400 meters) of the Transitway. (In 1996, the figure was about 32 percent.) This means that over the next two decades, more than half of all new jobs created in the region are to be near Transitway stations.

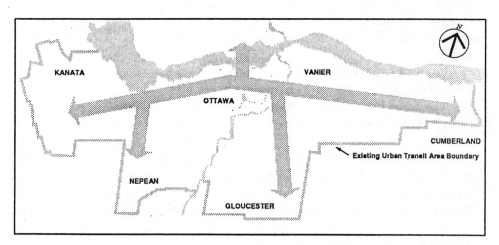

MAP 9.2. RAPID TRANSIT CONCEPT IN THE 1974 OFFICIAL PLAN. The Transitway was described in conceptual form in the original Official Plan only as a five-corridor system extending ultimately to new urban growth areas outside the greenbelt. *Source:* Regional Municipality of Ottawa-Carleton, *Rapid Transit Appraisal Study* (Ottawa: RMOC, 1976).

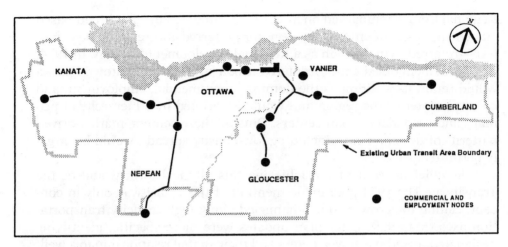

MAP 9.3. REGIONAL GROWTH CENTERS AND TRANSITWAY STRATEGY. Later plan refinements defined the Transitway as a 31-kilometer system connecting multiple urban centers both inside and outside the greenbelt.

The Official Plan gives precise definition to what a transit-supportive, multicentered metropolis is. Immediately below downtown Ottawa in the urban hierarchy are nine Primary Employment Centers (PEC), each with 5,000 or more jobs located within 400 meters of existing or future Transitway stations. The two principal suburban catchments for job growth, the Orléans and Kanata urban centers, are slated for more than 10,000 new jobs.[7] The PECs are targeted for a rich mix of offices, shops, hotels, community facilities, and civic buildings that are architecturally integrated. Provided they meet employment targets, PECs can also include residential units.

Lower in the hierarchy are Secondary Employment Centers (SEC), each slated for 2,000 to 5,000 jobs. The SECs are allowed off the Transitway but must have access to frequent and efficient all-day transit services.

The Official Plan gives attention to other land uses and their relationship to transit services as well. It requires regional shopping centers with more than 34,840 square meters of gross leasable space to be sited near the Transitway or future extensions.[8] Most new residential development is to occur contiguous to PECs and SECs to avoid pockets of isolated, disjointed growth that are inefficient to serve, including by mass transit.

Transportation Strategy

Complementing the Official Plan's Regional Development Strategy is a Transportation Strategy that sets targets for transportation investments and gives specificity to the Transitway concept.

Transit-First Policy

Over the past two decades, an overriding objective of the Official Plan has been to rely on public transit to provide much of the additional transportation capacity needed to accommodate future growth. The 1974 Official Plan embraced a "transit first" philosophy: improvements to the existing transit system and the development of rapid transit should take precedence over all forms of road construction and widening. The regional plan specifically called for creating rapid transit services. No commitments were made on preferred routing or transit technologies.

The region's transit-first policy has paid off handsomely. From 1975 to 1986, approximately one-third of the growth in total trips and virtually all of the increase in trips to downtown Ottawa were absorbed by the transit system.[9] During the same time, few improvements were made to the road network serving the central area. In fact, in 1986, fewer automobiles left the central area in the evening peak hour than in 1975.

The Transitway

The Transitway has been the cornerstone of the Regional Council's strategy to promote transit riding and multicentered growth. The idea of a Transitway surfaced in the early 1970s as both a tool to guide growth and a response to the mobility needs of a rapidly growing population. Ottawa-Carleton opted for a busway at a time when every other medium-size North American metropolis investing in new transit systems selected the eminently more popular light rail transit (LRT) technology. Similar in size to Ottawa-Carleton, Calgary and Edmonton both constructed regional light rail systems in the 1970s and 1980s, while Vancouver, the nation's third-largest metropolis, built an elevated "advanced" light rail system, called SkyTrain. The decision to go with busways made the Ottawa-Carleton region a maverick of sorts, but in dollars and cents made perfectly good sense. Relative to the light rail alternative, busways were shown to be 30 percent cheaper to build and 20 percent cheaper to operate.[10] Because of the busway's relatively high operating speeds, the region has been able to get by with 150 fewer buses than would have otherwise been needed to carry the same number of passengers on surface streets. These savings exceeded the $275 million capital outlay for the first 20 kilometers of the busway.[11] Busways also made the most sense given the region's preferred settlement pattern—concentrated employment and spread-out residences. The resulting "few-to-many" pattern of commuting proved to be tailor-made for a flexible, bus-based system.

Today, Ottawa Carleton averages more riders per capita than any similar-size transit system in North America, including those with rail. In 1991, its 133 unlinked transit trips per capita was nearly double the 69 transit trips per capita recorded in Calgary and Edmonton, the two rail-served Canadian cities of similar size.[12] Ottawa Carleton has spent less than half as much as these two cities on rapid transit, yet enjoys almost double the ridership.[13] In 1994, about 200,000 people used Ottawa Carleton's Transitway each day compared to the approximately 100,000 daily riders on the Calgary and Vancouver rail systems, and even fewer on Edmonton's. And while peak-period transit ridership decreased across Canada in the 1980s, it grew by 10 percent in Ottawa-Carleton. On a passenger per guideway mile basis, Ottawa's busway outperforms Pittsburgh's busway by nearly four to one and North American light rail systems built over the past two decades by as much as thirty-five to one (Figure 9.1).

An important advantage of the region's busways has been their staging flexibility; sections can be immediately put into service when completed, regardless if they are connected to the rest of the system. This has allowed the busway to provide prompt relief to congestion hot spots and to exploit land development opportunities as they avail themselves. Also, the region chose a novel "outside-in" approach in building the system. Rather than constructing the more expensive downtown sections first, the Regional Council instead concentrated on first getting some of the outlying segments of the busway installed. This allowed more kilometers of exclusive busway to be built faster with available funding, which proved valuable in

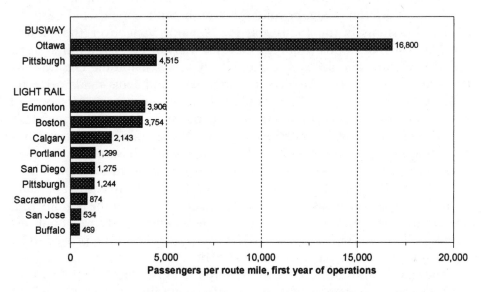

FIGURE 9.1. COMPARISON OF PASSENGERS PER GUIDEWAY MILE AMONG NORTH AMERICAN BUSWAY AND LIGHT RAIL SYSTEMS, 1991–1993. *Sources:* American Public Transit Association (APTA), *Transit Fact Book* (Washington, DC: APTA, 1991, 1992, and 1993); data provided by the Canadian Urban Transit Association (CUTA).

establishing momentum and gaining political credibility. It also allowed completed sections to be put into operation while other sections were being built. Moreover, it meant that transit could influence the development of the region to a much greater extent than if the inner lines serving the already built-out urban core had been constructed first. It was fortuitous that Ottawa-Carleton was the fastest-growing urban area in Canada during the height of busway construction; as a result, outlying busway segments were in a position to channel the growth that was under way. Today, per capita peak period transit usage in Ottawa-Carleton is as high in suburban areas, where the Transitway first opened, as in the older, established parts of the city.[14]

Future Expansions

In 1988, the Regional Council updated its Official Plan to extend the Transitway to the inner edge of the greenbelt. As growth leapfrogs over the greenbelt, the Regional Council is looking to the Transitway to ensure that it occurs in a concentrated form. Presently, dedicated freeway shoulder lanes are used along the busway to connect to the emerging urban centers of Orléans and Kanata; because the freeway section along the greenbelt has no on/off ramps, buses can operate along the shoulder lanes without interruption. Plans call for eventually extending the Transitway itself to the Orléans and Kanata urban centers and possibly beyond, creating a strong east-west growth axis and extending its reach to some 70 kilometers total.

Subdivision Reviews and Design Guidelines

While much of the Official Plan is oriented toward guiding development on a macroscale, microscale design considerations have not been overlooked. Specifically, the plan recognizes the need to design individual projects and subdivisions so that they are transit- and pedestrian-friendly. In Ottawa-Carleton, transit is viewed as an essential service, along with streets, water lines, and sewers. It is a central focus of community design, not a token addition or afterthought.

Working together, planners from the RMOC and OC Transpo have prepared transit-supportive design guidelines. At the concept plan stage, developers must work with transit planners to ensure that proposed collector roads allow efficient on-site transit circulation and that bus stops and shelters are conveniently located. Guidelines call for placing the densest land uses, retail centers, and senior citizens' residences closest to transit lines, and siting single-family homes and recreational parks farthest away. They also encourage mixed-use development at Secondary Employment Centers (SECs) so that office workers are less inclined to drive in order to access off-site restaurants, banks, and other consumer services.[15]

Supportive Parking Policies

Policies aimed at restraining parking have complemented transit-supportive design initiatives. When the Transitway opened in 1983, the federal government began eliminating free parking for its employees and reducing downtown parking supplies. By 1984, downtown parking was 15 percent below the 1975 inventory, despite a near doubling of office space. The federal government also introduced flexible working schedules for its employees, producing a more even distribution of transit usage over the course of the day.

Supportive parking policies have also been introduced at Transitway stations themselves. As shown in Map 9.1, OC Transpo has restricted park-and-ride facilities to the Transitway's terminuses to encourage the use of feeder and express buses as well as to maximize the development potential of selected stations.[16] Additionally, several municipalities have introduced transit-supportive parking policies of their own. The city of Ottawa, for example, allows a reduction of twenty-five parking stalls for every bus stall provided at retail centers (whether in the form of an on-site bus stop or a stall outside a Transitway station that is physically integrated with the retail center.)

OC Transpo: Fitting Transit and the Cityscape

The "proof in the pudding" that coordinated transit and urban development matters is found in the world-class bus system that today serves the Ottawa-Carleton region and its impressive ridership statistics. This section examines how bus services have been adapted to the region's settlement pattern, and the resulting payoff. It is followed by a section that investigates how urban development in turn has adapted to the presence of a fixed guideway system.

Today, the regional transit carrier, OC Transpo, schedules a peak fleet of 800 buses that provide some 2.1 million hours of annual service. This fleet moves more passengers per day than any comparable-size system in North America—on average, about 320,000 riders, including some 200,000 on the Transitway.

Today's Transitway

In 1996, the 31 kilometers of dedicated Transitway first called for in the Official Plan were completed at a cost of about US$400 million. The system consists of three components: 25.8 kilometers of exclusive busway lanes, set in an open cut, grade-separated from the surrounding road system, with ramp access provided at key locations (Photo 9.1); 2 kilometers of downtown bus-only lanes; and 3.3 kilometers of mixed-traffic operations along the Ottawa River Parkway. Supplementing this system are the 10.6 kilometers of reserved freeway shoulder lanes within the greenbelt that serve the Orléans and Kanata urban centers. Presently, the Transitway can be accessed at any one of thirty-four stations or six downtown bus stops. The two beyond-the-greenbelt stations—Orléans and Kanata—have been sited in the heart of the planned urban centers in advance of extending the Transitway itself.[17]

Today, the Transitway functions as the backbone of regional transit services. On a per kilometer basis, it carries ten times as many person trips as the regional road system.[18] About 60 percent of all transit rides in the region include a significant component of Transitway service. At peak load points, nearly 10,000 passengers per hour are carried on the Transitway. To carry this many trips by automobile would require five freeway lanes per direction.

Ottawa's Transitway operates just like a metrorail system. Buses stop at all stations (which are spaced about a half-kilometer apart in the central area and several kilometers apart elsewhere). The two-lane (13-meter-wide) Transitway has passing lanes at stations so that buses can overtake each other. Platforms are up to 55 meters long to accommodate as many as three buses. Stations look and function like those of a subway system;

PHOTO 9.1. OC TRANSPO'S EXCLUSIVE BUSWAY. A bus heads westbound from the Smyth station, which features high-rise housing and office development on one side. In the background is the Abbey station, where additional high-rise housing has clustered.

all are equipped with elevators, are weather-protected, and have seats and schedule information. Some are connected to surrounding areas by pedestrian skywalks. The geometries and overhead clearances of the Transitway were designed to allow an eventual conversion to fixed-rail transit if and when demand warrants such a change.

When passing through downtown Ottawa, buses operate on a one-way couplet along Albert and Slater Streets. The second lane, rather than the curb lane, is dedicated to buses. This avoids conflicts with stopped and turning vehicles. Also at downtown stops, sidewalks have been widened into the curb lane to provide more waiting space for passengers (Photo 9.2). Presently, downtown stops accommodate more than thirty different bus routes during peak hours and handle up to 25,000 boardings and alightings each day. More than 60 percent of regional transit traffic passes through the Albert-Slater Street couplet. Because of these high loads and with passenger throughput approaching the capacity of a surface transit system, OC Transpo is studying the feasibility of operating downtown segments in a subway alignment.[19]

PHOTO 9.2. SIDEWALK EXTENDS OUT AT DOWNTOWN BUS STOP TO SERVE PASSENGERS.
OC Transpo planners recognize other legitimate uses for downtown curb space, such as loading lanes, taxi drop-offs, right turns, and parking. Mixing bus movements with these other activities only increases delays and accidents. Thus, designers gave the right-side curb lanes along the Albert-Slater couplet to these other activities, reserving the second lane out for buses. To protect boarding and alighting passengers, the curbside is extended to the second lane at bus stops, as shown in the photo.

Configuring Bus Services

What has proven to be the right "match" to Ottawa-Carleton's lay of the land is a hub-and-spoke transit network. However, unlike a rail-based hub-and-spoke system, the Transitway allows an integration of mainline and feeder services in a single vehicle. The same vehicle that whisks along the dedicated right-of-way can leave the facility and filter into the region's spread-out neighborhoods, thus eliminating the need to transfer.

In all, three complementary types of services operate along or feed into the Transitway (Figure 9.2). The "rapid" lines (three routes numbered in the 90 series) operate solely along the exclusive guideway, with buses coming by every three minutes and stopping at each station. True to their billing, they are swift, averaging speeds of 45 to 60 kilometers per hour, even taking into account stops and peak bus loads that are 15 to 20 percent higher than those of regular surface-street buses. High average speeds are possible because of the better schedule adherence afforded by busway operations and barrier-free (honor) fare collection, along with the use of multiple-door loadings at stations.[20] Signal prioritization at key traffic lights expedites bus movements along downtown streets.

Supplementing the rapid lines are "Express" routes that connect residential neighborhoods and employment centers during peak hours. Express buses run on eight-to-twenty minute headways, sometimes in a skip-stop mode.[21] To serve outlying employment centers, OC Transpo also operates counter-peak, or reverse-commute, services. It is the Express and reverse-commute bus runs that largely eliminate transfers. The same bus that picks people up near their residence also delivers them near their des-

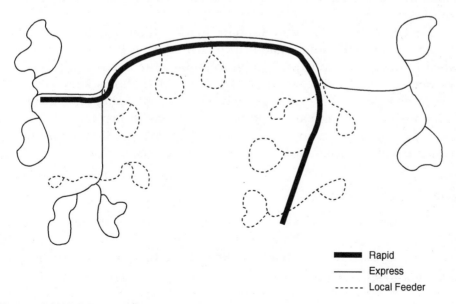

Rapid
Express
Local Feeder

FIGURE 9.2. OC Transpo's three types of transit routes.

tinations via the Transitway. The elimination of transfers has made Express services hugely popular—presently they account for the majority of OC Transpo patronage. Express services are an adaption of transit to settlement pattern par excellence. In Ottawa-Carleton, it is accepted that low-density living environments are preferred by most residents and that transit programs should in no way seek to alter this settlement pattern, but rather to serve it. While high-rise commercial development is actively sought around Transitway stations, it is totally left to the marketplace to dictate where and at what densities housing gets built.

During off-peak hours, services convert to timed-transfer operations. Under this arrangement, the Transitway functions exclusively as a trunk-line—the three rapid routes continue running, though on slightly longer, five-minute headways. Local feeder bus routes—the third type of service—fan into surrounding neighborhoods, connected to Transitway stations, in synch, on thirty-minute pulse schedules. Park-and-ride lots at terminal stations function as intercept points for rural catchments, serving passengers living beyond the region's urban areas.

An important part of OC Transpo's infrastructure is its fully automated telephone passenger information system. All stations and stops in OC Transpo's service area have been assigned a telephone number with a 560 prefix. Customers can dial and find out, for a particular stop, when the next two buses are scheduled to arrive as well as route status information, such as unexpected delays—a valuable service in a place where subfreezing winter temperatures are the norm.[22] Similar information is also displayed on large video screens at major transit terminals and shopping malls—a real convenience for those who would rather spend five or so minutes before a bus arrives window-shopping than idly waiting.

Each month, OC Transpo responds to more than 850,000 inquiries on the automated telephone system, primarily during the off-peak period, when headways are longest. The information system enjoys high visibility—one survey found 82 percent of regional households knew about it, and 26 percent used it on a regular basis. Also, the system has increased OC Transpo's off-peak patronage by an estimated 8 percent, based on a controlled statistical comparison of ridership changes in neighborhoods with and without access to the information service.[23]

The Ridership Payoff

The superb adaptation of OC Transpo services to the settlement pattern is reflected by ridership statistics. This section reviews the evidence. OC Transpo currently serves about 35 percent of all peak-hour vehicle trips originating in the urbanized area.

Modal Splits

Moreover, it handles around 70 percent of peak-period work trips to downtown (coming mostly from low-density suburbs) and nearly 30 percent of trips generated by suburban employment sites near the busway. Even regional shopping centers designed for the automobile, but on the busway, enjoy all-day transit modal splits for shopping trips in the 25 to 30 percent range.[24] At suburban job centers and retail plazas off the Transitway, transit modal splits fall in the 5 to 10 percent range. The region's high suburban transit modal splits are a testament to the fast, efficient, minimal-transfer features of the busway.[25]

Ridership Impacts of Transit-Oriented Development

The best evidence on the ridership impacts of development proximate to Transitway stations comes from a 1986 regional travel survey.[26] Table 9.1 compares transit modal splits for two mixed-use neighborhoods and three local universities that year. Among two nearby neighborhoods with similar land-use mixes, household incomes, and bus service levels, the one with a Transitway station, Tunney's Pasture, averaged nearly a 20 percentage point higher share of trip destinations by transit than the Confederation Heights neighborhood, which is off the Transitway.

Among the three university campuses, Algonquin College, located adjacent to the Baseline station, had higher transit modal shares than Carleton University, which is more centrally located but farther from the Transitway. More than two-thirds of those headed to the University of Ottawa, situated next to the Campus station, arrived by transit, a modal split that is in line with other core-area locations.

Table 9.1 COMPARISON OF TRANSIT MODAL SPLITS AMONG NEIGHBORHOODS AND UNIVERSITY CAMPUSES BY TRANSITWAY LOCATION, 1986

	Percent of All Vehicular Trips[1] in the Urbanized Area[2] of Ottawa-Carleton	
	As a Destination, 6–9 A.M.	As an Origin, 3–6 P.M.
Mixed-Use Neighborhoods		
Tunney's Pasture*	47	49
Confederation Heights	29	31
Universities		
University of Ottawa*	68	50
Algonquin College (Woodroffe Campus)*	51	44
Carleton University	38	40

* Directly served by a Transitway station.
[1] For all trip purposes. Includes only trips made by mass transit, automobiles, or other motorized vehicles. Walking, bicycling, ice-skating, and other nonmotorized means of travel are excluded.
[2] Includes OC Transpo's service area within the RMOC and the central part of Hull, Quebec.
Source: Regional Municipality of Ottawa-Carleton, National Capital Area Origin-Destination Survey (Ottawa: RMOC, Transportation Department, 1986).

Development Impacts

The Ottawa-Carleton region has seen considerable land-use changes around Transitway stations. In keeping with the Official Plan, several hundred thousand square meters of office and commercial floor space have been added within a five-minute walk of suburban stations, with Blair and Place d'Orléans as notable standouts. Regional shopping malls, such as St. Laurent and Gloucester Centre, have also been physically linked to the Transitway. And while not called for in the Official Plan, stations such as Westboro, Tunney's Pasture, and Hurdman have seen nearby mid-rise apartment and condominium development in recent years.

During the boom years of 1988 to 1991, local officials estimate that a billion Canadian dollars of development was added or at various stages of completion within a five-minute walk of the Transitway. This was nearly four times the 275 million Canadian dollars spent on the 20 kilometers of Transitway that were in place at the time. While the Transitway itself did not induce anywhere near this amount of investment (in the sense that growth would have occurred even without the Transitway), it unquestionably had a strong bearing on where new office, retail, and residential construction took place within the region.

It should be noted that it was never intended that land around all stations be intensified. Western sections of the Transitway were built on open parkland owned by the National Capital Commission with no potential for development. Other stations, such as Iris and Lincoln Fields, were placed in locations where physical site constraints and the presence of established single-family neighborhoods preclude any significant new development from ever occurring.

This section summarizes the most significant development activities to date near Ottawa-Carleton's Transitway. Summaries are presented for co-developed projects, office-commercial development, retail activities, and residential housing.

Co-development

There have been two notable examples of co-development, wherein the transit authority and private developers worked hand in hand to physically link their respective projects, to the benefit of all: one at the St. Laurent station, and the other at the Riverside station.

St. Laurent Shopping Center

Concurrent with the opening of the St. Laurent Transitway station in 1987, the St. Laurent shopping mall was expanded to include eighty new retail outlets. The coincidental timing allowed the shopping mall to be physically integrated with the station. The St. Laurent station has three levels: local bus routes use the top level; the mezzanine connects directly to the shopping center; and downstairs are the Transitway platforms. The station cost US$13 million to build, by far the most expensive on the system. Part of the cost, however, was absorbed by the shopping center developer, who donated all of the land for the station and built connecting passageways. The developer also expanded the mall to put stores near the station portal, creating an enclosed pedestrian environment similar to that found at metro stations in downtown Toronto and Montreal. Owners felt that integrated development would not only attract more shoppers but would also save on parking costs. The city of Ottawa allowed them to reduce on-site parking by twenty-five spaces for each transit bay in the station.

Riverside Medical Complex

Perhaps the best example anywhere of a medical facility linked to a transit line can be found on the southeast Transitway at the Riverside station. In the conceptual plan, the Transitway traversed the grounds of this hospital, though no station was planned. Fortuitously, Riverside Hospital was planning an expansion at the same time Transitway planning was under way. An agreement was reached that allowed the Transitway to penetrate the hospital site in return for adding a station that connected directly to the expanded hospital. In 1991, Riverside Hospital opened a new 4,200-square-meter administrative wing over the Riverside station, providing patients, visitors, and medical staff with direct transit access (Photo 9.3). A four-story medical office building was also recently built beside Riverside Hospital and includes an enclosed pedestrian skybridge linked to the hospital and station.

Office-Commercial Development

In keeping with the Official Plan's directives, a significant share of office and commercial growth has concentrated near Transitway stations. From 1986 to 1991, prior to the economic downturn, 35 percent of regional job growth occurred in the vicinity of Transitway stations. In 1990 and 1991, 73 percent of commercial-office development outside the CBD was within a five-minute walk of a Transitway station, up from 53 percent in 1988–1989.[27] Most new commercial growth has occurred around the six designated Primary Employment Center (PEC) stations: Baseline, Tunney's Pasture, St. Laurent, Cyrville, Blair, and Place d'Orléans. Experiences around the Blair and Tunney's Pasture stations are summarized below.

Photo 9.3. Air rights development of medical complex at the Riverside station. Architectural integration of the busway stop with the larger hospital complex.

Blair Station

By far, the largest inventory of transit-oriented office and commercial floor space to date outside the CBD has been added near the Blair station, currently the eastern terminus of the exclusive busway. Built within a five-minute walk of the station are four mid-rise office towers owned by the Glenview Park of Commerce, Telesat Canada headquarters, the Sport Canada complex, and the first phases of the Queensway Corporate Centre. A massive pedestrian skybridge links offices south of the Queensway Freeway to the Transitway. The skybridge was funded by the municipality of Gloucester to promote economic development. Local officials believe that having good access to the Transitway could be a critical factor in luring several projects to the area. Within five years of the Blair station's 1989 opening, some US$75 million in commercial-office development had been built nearby.

One of OC Transpo's site-design success stories was securing the redesign of the Gloucester Centre shopping mall, directly north of the station. Original plans called for the Gloucester Centre to face away from the Transitway station, which would have forced transit customers to wade through a sea of parking to reach the mall's entrances. OC Transpo planners convinced the developers to revise the site plan to reorient Gloucester Centre toward the Blair station. The developers were sold on the idea when it was pointed out that more people pass through the Blair station on buses than on the adjacent Queensway Freeway during some shopping hours. Since three-quarters of OC Transpo passengers use monthly passes, most can stop and shop on the way home to the eastern suburbs without having to pay an additional fare.

Tunney's Pasture Station

Following the opening of the Tunney's Pasture station, a large mixed-use project, Holland Cross, was built in a nearby redevelopment zone (Photo 9.4). The project features 18,200 square meters of ground-floor retail and upper-level offices, and nearby residential towers with 638 units. By building near the Transitway, Holland Cross's developers received density bonuses and approval to lower the project's parking requirements. Without the Transitway, some believe, Holland Cross would probably not have been built.[28] Public sponsorship of below-market-rate housing, in combination with special financing of other infrastructure improvements within the redevelopment zone, also helped leverage the Holland Cross project.

Retail Development and Sales

In keeping with the Official Plan, all large-scale shopping centers in the region have clustered near Transitway stops. Presently, four regional shop-

PHOTO 9.4. TUNNEY'S PASTURE STATION AND HOLLAND CROSS PROJECT. With ground-floor retail, a food court, upper-level offices, and nearby apartments and condominiums, Holland Cross—shown in the upper right side of the photo—is the region's largest mixed-use project built near the Transitway.

ping centers with more than 34,840 square meters of gross floor space are sited near the Transitway: St. Laurent, Rideau Centre, Gloucester Centre, and Place d'Orléans.[29] On the northeast edge of downtown, the attractively restored Rideau Centre is by all accounts the region's most successful transit-oriented shopping complex. About 60 percent of shoppers reach Rideau Centre by transit, a market share in line with the rest of downtown.[30] Several smaller, older shopping centers are also served by the Transitway, including Billings Bridge Plaza, which is directly connected by an enclosed passageway to the Billings Bridge station (Photo 9.5).

Being situated near a Transitway station has clearly benefited retailers. A 1986 survey conducted by the Ottawa-Carleton Board of Trade found that nearly two-thirds of all bus passengers felt that public transit was important to them for shopping, and more than a third said bus routes influenced where they shopped.[31] Nearly one-third mentioned they

PHOTO 9.5. BILLINGS BRIDGE PLAZA AND STATION. The plaza, to the left, has historically been one of the region's most heavily transit-patronized shopping centers.
Currently, an estimated 20,000 shoppers reach the plaza via transit each day.
The station, which is physically connected to the plaza, is a major timed-transfer point along the south line.

included shopping as part of their bus rides, with their purchases totaling
more than US$420 million each year. While these impacts are redistribu-
tive in that purchases would have taken place elsewhere in the absence of
the busway, much of this shopping would likely have been by automobile.
The region, not just merchants, benefited from the substitution of transit
trips for car trips.

Residential Development

OC Transpo's extensive network of express buses and timed-transfer
connections has effectively brought rapid transit services to the front
doors of many suburban residents. In so doing, it has reinforced the
region's fairly low-density residential settlement pattern. The Regional
Council has refrained from promoting high-rise residential development,
such as found in metropolitan Toronto, near Transitway stations. This

has freed up prime real estate around stations for more intensive (and from a transit ridership standpoint, more potentially productive) commercial and office development.[32] In Ottawa-Carleton, carefully configured and integrated transit services have largely eliminated the need for transit-based housing. Nearly everyone, including those living in the lowest-density suburbs, enjoys good-quality service—an estimated 95 percent of residents served by OC Transpo live within 400 meters of a bus stop.

While the Transitway was never explicitly called upon in the Official Plan to attract residential development, the market nonetheless produced more than 2,300 housing units within 800 meters of Transitway stations between 1988 and 1993. Most of these additions were in the form of mid- and high-rise apartment and condominium towers near the Westboro station (290 townhouses and apartments), Tunney's Pasture station (in addition to Holland Cross, 393 mid- and high-rise units), and Lees station (more than 450 nonprofit residential units).[33] Since the opening of the Hurdman station, the upscale three-tower Riviera complex has added 387 condominium units to the immediate area. The Riviera's developers have publicly stated that the presence of the Transitway was a major factor in securing financing for the project. Also nearby is the Classics high-rise tower, which has added another 195 units, with 313 more planned in future phases.[34] Transit-based living also appears to have had a bearing on vehicle ownership rates, which are slightly lower in Ottawa-Carleton than in other Canadian regions of similar affluence.[35]

Collectively, high-rise housing development along the Transitway debunks the myth that people eschew living near bus-transit nodes (e.g., to avoid fumes, noise, or pedestrian traffic) and that densification occurs only around heavy rail stations. It is not the transit technology—rail or bus—that attracts development, but rather good-quality service, which in Ottawa's case is very high.

There is also evidence that the region's transit-friendly site design guidelines have paid off. An example is River Ridge, a new town planned for 30,000 residents located south of the airport. At River Ridge, transit needs are being addressed at the design stage rather than as an afterthought. OC Transpo planners have worked closely with the city of Gloucester and a developer to create a concept plan featuring a future Transitway station as the new community's centerpiece. This has meant protecting corridor right-of-way, dedicating land for the future station, and distributing land uses to take advantage of transit's proximity. Collector streets have also been laid out to allow efficient transit circulation, and the road network has been platted to enable easy access to bus-served collectors. The objective is for all River Ridge residents to be within a five-minute walk (400 meters) of a bus stop.

Learning from Ottawa

Ottawa-Carleton demonstrates the rewards of a well-planned hybrid transit metropolis. While its busway is well suited to serving low-density development, at the same time, thanks to conscientious regional planning, it has been a powerful lever in guiding employment and commercial growth. In Ottawa-Carleton, policy makers have understood and taken advantage of the two-way interaction between urban form and transportation investments.

Today, there is near universal agreement that a bus-based Transitway system was the right technological choice for Ottawa-Carleton. It provides a high level of service to the predominantly low-density residences of the region, while also providing a focus for channeling future employment and commercial growth. Remarks Colin Leech, head of OC Transpo's long-range planning section:

> One of the major advantages of a busway compared to an LRT system is that it gives the benefits of a fixed infrastructure without the drawbacks of a fixed guideway. The presence of a fixed rapid transit infrastructure gives developers and the public the confidence that a high level of service will always be provided to the stations, so that stations can act as a catalyst for promoting transit-friendly patterns of development. The lack of a fixed guideway allows incredible flexibility of operations. The new Transitway station at Place d'Orléans is a prime example of how a busway station will be able to influence growth decades before a separate right-of-way is built to it.[36]

The foundation for Ottawa-Carleton's world-class bus network was established during the 1970s with the passage of the Official Plan and strengthened in subsequent updates. The Transitway was enlisted as the chief instrument for achieving a multicentered built form. As a result of farsighted public policies, today Ottawa-Carleton boasts numerous examples of mid-rise office, commercial, and residential development near Transitway stations. This tradition continues. In coming years, the Transitway will be used as a magnet for concentrating beyond-the-greenbelt development.

It is important to note that the Regional Council first established a regional land-use vision and then developed a transportation strategy to achieve that vision. The Official Plan accepts that most residents prefer to live in low-density residential settings and does not attempt to alter these preferences. The transportation "means" to support this land-use "end" was the introduction of a highly flexible, integrated bus transit network. Buses fan into surrounding neighborhoods and provide either direct express services or feed into nearby Transitway stations on a timed-transfer basis. In contrast to most U.S. rapid transit systems, park-and-ride has been discouraged as an access means to Transitway stations. This not only reduces parking lot expenses and frees land for commercial-office uses, but also yields environmental benefits by eliminating short-hop (high-polluting) automobile access trips to stations.

Currently, the region is engaged in a debate over whether to continue emphasizing a radial transit system focused on downtown—specifically, whether scarce dollars should go to improve downtown busway circulation by constructing tunnels or instead be used to extend the Transitway to new town centers. This debate turns on the question of whether downtown Ottawa will retain its dominance as the region's employment hub, or whether the pace of decentralization will accelerate. True to Ottawa-Carleton's tradition, land-use objectives can be expected to guide which of these two transit investment strategies the region pursues over the next decade.

NOTES

1.   The region encompasses the cities of Ottawa, Gloucester, Kanata, Nepean, and Vanier; the townships of Cumberland, Goulbourn, Osgoode, Rideau, and West Carleton; and the village of Rockcliffe Park.

2.   These areas have captured about 80 percent of new construction of single-family homes and townhouses built in the region. Between 1986 and 1994, more than twice as many people were added to urban centers outside the greenbelt as inside it, almost doubling their populations.

3.   The RMOC was created, through an act of the Ontario government, in direct response to rapid suburbanization and growth overspilling the boundaries of the city of Ottawa. Comprehensive planning within an area large enough to encompass the region's commutershed was considered essential. While there was some local support for regional planning, it occurred only because it was a legislatively imposed requirement of the Provincial government.

4.   Other responsibilities of the regional government include: water distribution, wastewater treatment, solid waste disposal, regional roads, social and health services, and maintaining homes for the aged.

5.   OC Transpo is a separate corporate body run by a nine-member commission that reports to the Regional Council. OC Transpo serves a designated Urban Transit Area, which in 1990 had a population of 586,000 and included the cities of Ottawa, Gloucester, Kanata, Nepean, and Vanier, the township of Cumberland, and the village of Rockcliffe Park.

6. All development within the region takes place within the framework of the Official Plan, but amendments to the plan are made from time to time based on requests from developers or local municipalities. Implications of proposed changes are examined thoroughly before they are approved.

7. The seven other designated PECs are Baseline, Tunney's Pasture, Vanier, St. Laurent, Cyrville, Blair, and South Keys.

8. The only exception is the Carlingwood shopping complex, which for historical and geographic reasons is being accepted as a retail destination that will be reached predominantly by private automobile.

9. Regional Municipality of Ottawa Carleton, *Community Profile*, Report 6-12 (Ottawa: RMOC, Planning and Property Department, 1994).

10. Part of the operating cost savings is attributable to the region's ambitious interlining of buses—40 percent of all vehicles make a trip on one route and then deadhead to the start of a revenue collecting section of another route rather than returning to the original route's start. This scheduling practice, which shaved Ottawa-Carleton's peak fleet requirement by 12 percent in the mid-1980s, could not be exploited with a rail system.

11. J. Bonsall, *Rapid Transit for the Automobile Age* (Ottawa: OC Transpo, 1993).

12. Hit by recession, ridership has fallen to about 110 annual transit trips per resident. Ottawa-Carleton, however, has weathered the recession as well as any Canadian urbanized area, and its relative loss of transit customers has been less than in other areas except for Vancouver. See: OC Transpo, *Operating Statistics* (Ottawa: OC Transpo, 1996); and J. Pucher, Public Transport Developments: Canada vs. the United States, *Transportation Quarterly*, vol. 48, no. 1, 1994, pp. 65–78.

13. J. Bonsall, and R. Stacey, *A Rapid Transit Strategy into the Next Century* (Ottawa: OC Transpo, 1994).

14. *Ibid.*

15. Design guidelines focus mainly on ensuring that traditionally low density, residential subdivisions are suitable to transit services. It is commonly understood that commercial centers and central-area developments should be designed for convenient transit access, such as siting off-street parking in the rear of buildings and orienting building façades to transit-served corridors. Other site design strategies that are pursued in residential settings in Ottawa-Carleton include: orienting corner houses toward side streets to avoid having front yards facing bus stops that are sited on collector streets; creating supplemental, internal sidewalk networks where poor street connectivity imposes long walking distances; and siting bus shelters and pads (paved waiting areas at stops) in strategic locations.

16. There are currently 1,550 parking spaces: 515 at the Place d'Orléans station (eastern terminus); 460 at Kanata; 300 at Greenboro (one station in from the South Keys terminus station on the recently opened south line); and 275 at Baseline (terminus of the southwest line).

17.   The Regional Council hopes these stations will act as magnets for concentrated, mixed-use development. The Place d'Orléans station, serving the surrounding bedroom residential community of Orléans (approximately 50,000 inhabitants), lies in the heart of an evolving urban center that includes an indoor shopping mall and the Cumberland township's new civic center. A similar process of transit-led development is presently under way in Kanata and is being considered for a possible third beyond-the-greenbelt urban center to the south, Barrhaven.

18.   Bonsall and Stacey, *op cit.*

19.   The downtown couplet can theoretically handle up to 200 buses per lane per hour under ideal operating conditions. Scheduled bus volumes are today approaching that figure. Incidents of total system failure—with downtown travel times of forty-five minutes or more on cross streets—now occur once every two to three months.

20.   J. Bonsall, *op cit..*

21.   Under skip-stop operations, buses skip certain stations and stop only when there is a waiting customer at one of these stops who hails the vehicle for a ride.

22.   Electronic signposts strategically placed throughout the region monitor bus movements, relaying real-time information to a centralized computer, which in turn passes schedule adherence information, through digital voice transmissions, to customers who phone in.

23.   Sources: R. Cervero, Urban Transit in Canada: Integration and Innovation at Its Best, *Transportation Quarterly*, vol. 40, no. 2, 1986, pp. 293–316; J. Bonsall and M. Whelan, Better Information Equals More Riders (paper presented at the annual meeting of the Canadian Urban Transit Association, Quebec City, Quebec, June 1981).

24.   The main sources for these estimates are the 1986 Retail Survey and the 1986 National Capital Area Origin Destination Survey, both conducted by the RMOC. The 1986 Retail Survey found the following transit modal splits for shopping centers that are currently served by the Transitway (or dedicated freeway lanes connected to the busway): Rideau Centre, 61 percent; Billings Bridge, 22 percent; Carlingwood, 21 percent; St. Laurent, 16 percent; Bayshore, 13 percent; and Place D'Orléans, 9 percent. At the time of the survey, however, the Transitway did not extend to Billings Bridge, St. Laurent, or Place D'Orléans. Transit modal splits to all of these shopping centers have significantly increased over the past decade. For instance, 1993 figures released by the management of the St. Laurent shopping center showed a transit modal split of 32 percent.

25.   These modal split achievements are also partly attributable to stringent standards set in the Official Plan. The plan sets targets for peak-hour transit modal shares at screenlines (i.e., checkpoints for recording traffic) along all major travel corridors. Targets are used in setting priorities among competing road and transit projects along each corridor. In 1997, targets called for transit to attain a market share of 70 percent of trips to downtown,

40 to 45 percent for destinations near Transitway stations in the central area, and 30 to 35 percent for trips generated by development near suburban stations and on the outer limits of the system. Downtown targets have been reached and considerable headway is being made in achieving the others.

26. In 1986, the Transitway stretched from the Baseline station to the Hurdman station, a distance of 16.4 kilometers (including the 2-kilometer downtown mixed traffic bus lane section).

27. These figures have since fallen, a product of sluggish regional growth. From 1994 to 1996, just 24 percent of office and commercial floor space built outside the CBD was near Transitway stations. Of course, nearly all office and retail additions in the CBD over these years were near bus transit services. Sources: Regional Municipality of Ottawa-Carleton, *Land Development Activity in the Vicinity of Transitway Stations: 1990–1991 Update, 1992–1993 Update, 1994–1996 Update* (Ottawa: RMOC, Planning and Development Approvals Department, 1992, 1994, and 1997); Regional Municipality of Ottawa-Carleton, *1991 Ottawa-Carleton Employment Survey* (Ottawa: RMOC, 1992).

28. Personal correspondence from Colin Leech, head of long-range planning for OC Transpo, dated June 23, 1992.

29. A fifth large regional shopping mall, Bayshore, is located off the planned western extension of the Transitway.

30. By convention, the Rideau Centre (which opened in 1983, the same year Transitway service commenced) should have been laid out east-west along its major access street, Rideau Street, with an anchor tenant on each end. Instead, its principal axis is north-south, perpendicular to Rideau Street and bus lines serving downtown. As a result, Rideau Centre enjoys access to every bus route downtown. Each day, thousands of passengers use the Rideau Centre to transfer between buses.

31. RMOC, 1986 Retail Survey, *op. cit.*

32. Although single-family detached homes are common throughout the region's suburbs, most housing in the central area consists of attached walk-up units, garden apartments, and mid-rise towers. This has produced relatively high average residential densities by North American standards. Today, Ottawa-Carleton has a smaller share of single-detached houses, 42 percent of total units, than most Canadian cities. Source: Regional Municipality of Ottawa-Carleton, *Official Plan of the Regional Municipality of Ottawa-Carleton: Volumes 1 and 2* (Ottawa: RMOC, 1994).

33. Tightly packed, mid-rise housing development around several stations, notably Smyth, Abbey, and Baseline, predated the Transitway. The Transitway, however, has been credited with maintaining healthy residential real estate markets in these areas.

34. While developers of the Riviera and Classics projects note that having a Transitway station nearby was an added bonus to developing these sites, at least equally important was the site's excellent river vistas.

35. Regional Municipality of Ottawa-Carleton, *Land Development Activity in the Vicinity of Transitway Stations: 1992–1993 Update* (Ottawa: RMOC, Planning and Development Approvals Department, 1994).

36. Personal correspondence, April 24, 1995.

Chapter 10

Creating a Linear City with a Surface Metro: Curitiba, Brazil

One of the best, most sustainable transit systems anywhere today flourishes in Curitiba, a medium-size metropolis in southern Brazil. A remarkably efficient all-bus network has evolved that blends the very best features of a metro and conventional transit using surface streets—a veritable "surface metro." The system is very much a hybrid—on the one hand channeling growth along desired corridors and on the other adapting to spread-out development beyond these axes. The road to becoming a greater transit metropolis was not always smooth. Curitiba's world-class bus system is a product of many ad hoc, incremental decisions—most aimed at doing things quickly, pragmatically, and at an affordable price. Guiding these decisions, however, was an overarching vision of the future—one of a linear city with well-defined structural axes that could accommodate much of the city's future growth and physically integrate transit services, roadways, and complementary land uses. Creating exclusive busways in the center of trinary roads, eventually supplemented by circular routes, transfer stations, and direct-line services with boarding tubes, has brought this vision to fruition. Thus, while important decisions were made piecemeal, a clear vision of the future ensured that they added up to something meaningful. Combine this with the political adroitness and dedication of activists such as Jaime Lerner, as well as fortuitous events—including the availability of right-of-ways to accommodate the trinary system—and the ingredients are in place for creating a linear, transit-oriented city.

Curitiba, Brazil, is widely known as a medium-size city in a developing country that, through visionary planning and inspired leadership, has applied highly inventive yet low-cost strategies to cope with rapid growth. Curitiba was one of the first cities anywhere to close off downtown streets to cars and return this space to pedestrians; recycle refuse citywide and exchange surplus food for garbage collected by the poor; and preserve important historical buildings and sites in its core. Nevertheless, it has

265

been the careful, methodical development of a world-class all-bus transit network, in close coordination with physical land-use planning, that most sets Curitiba apart from others. For First and Third World cities alike, the lessons of Curitiba are important and insightful.

As a transit metropolis, Curitiba is very much a hybrid—a "hand in glove" fit between transit and cityscape. More so than in Ottawa, suburban growth—including housing—has been aligned along dedicated busways. But similar to Ottawa, complementary and superbly integrated feeder buses serve low-density areas off guideway axes. Curitiba's cobweb pattern of transit routes stands as a paragon of how transit services and settlement patterns can be harmoniously integrated.

The Curitiba Approach to Growth

Curitiba is the capital of Paraná, a mainly agricultural state in southern of Brazil. Situated near the coastal mountain range, Curitiba grew rapidly during the second half of the nineteenth century, propelled by the arrival of mostly European immigrants and the opening of new economic frontiers. It has been during the past three decades, however, that the city's population has mushroomed, transforming Curitiba into a vibrant industrial and commercial center. In 1965, Curitiba had 400,000 inhabitants; by 1995, its population surpassed 1.6 million, all within a 431-square-kilometer area. Today, Greater Curitiba's population exceeds 2.3 million, spread over a land area nearly twice the size of Curitiba proper. During the 1970s and early 1980s, Curitiba grew faster than any Brazilian city, eclipsing 4 percent annually. The influx of migrants from rural areas and small towns in search of economic opportunities fueled much of this growth. Presently, about 35 percent of Curitiba's work force is employed in retail-commercial and services industries, and 19 percent works in the manufacturing sector. The 1990 national census classified 9 percent of the economically active population of Curitiba as unemployed, quite low by Brazilian standards.

It was because of rapid population growth and the fear by many that Curitiba was poised to become an uncontrollable, sprawling metropolis, like São Paulo to the north, that comprehensive urban planning—and specifically, integrated transportation and land-use planning—found a receptive home in Curitiba. Early on, a number of important guiding principles were established that have, over the years, been religiously observed. Among these are: a realization that Curitiba's downtown had reached saturation and that future growth should be channeled along well-defined linear corridors; the belief that transportation investments and land-use management, in coordination, are the most powerful tools for directing growth; and a decision to plan for the mobility of people rather than cars, giving both pedestrians and mass transit movement priority in highly congested locations.

One of the most visible products of these planning principles is Curitiba's highly integrated bus network. Today, a rich mix of services exists, including high-capacity buses operating on dedicated passageways, limited-stop high-speed buses paralleling busways along one-way couplets, orbital routes that interconnect the busways, and more than 100 feeder lines that run between low-density neighborhoods and trunkline services. The system is built for speed and simplicity. Twenty intermodal stations along Curitiba's five busway corridors allow efficient and convenient transfers. A single fare enables one to go from anywhere to nearly everywhere in the greater Curitiba region at a bargain rate. All ten private companies that operate Curitiba's bus services earn profits. Presently, Curitiba averages about 350 unlinked transit trips per capita each year, the highest rate in Brazil.[1] This approaches the per capita ridership figures of North America's largest urban centers—New York City and Mexico City—both of which have extensive underground metros. Curitiba's all-bus system is used by some 1.2 million passengers each weekday, or about 75 percent of all commuters, a modal split that is much higher than in other Brazilian cities. Transit's work trip market share is 57 percent in Rio de Janeiro and 45 percent in São Paulo.[2] What makes these differences all the more remarkable is that Curitiba has among the highest median household incomes (US$5,150 versus a national average of US$3,160) and the second-highest automobile ownership rate (267 cars per 1,000 inhabitants, just behind Brasília) in Brazil. Incredibly, Curitiba boasts Brazil's most successful transit system even though it is one of the country's most affluent cities with among the highest automobile ownership rates.

Evolution of Integrated Planning in Curitiba

To understand how Curitiba became a great transit metropolis, one must trace the evolution of joint transportation and land-use planning over the past half-century. There were three key periods. The first involved forging a comprehensive future vision of Curitiba, leading to the establishment of bedrock planning principles that guided development decisions during formative years (1943–1970). This was followed by an active period (1972–1988) of plan execution, culminating in the implementation of an Integrated Transit Network (ITN). The most recent period (1989–present) has witnessed the refinement and differentiation of regional transit services, the most significant action being the introduction of high-speed express services (locally referred to as "direct line" services) and high-capacity tube stations.

Curitiba's present settlement pattern and transportation system are not the result of a one-shot visionary plan or a string of lucky events. Early master plans set out broad visions for the future. Actual implementation occurred in small steps, often in fits and starts and on a trial-and-error basis. Mistakes were made, providing lessons that were later put to good use. By keeping the urban development process simple and transparent, as well as emphasizing low-cost, fast-turnaround solutions to problems, Curitiba has been able to get things done quickly, thus building momentum and political credibility. Notes Jaime Lerner, the popular three-time mayor of Curitiba and current governor of Paraná province, who is widely credited with introducing many of Curitiba's innovations, "Simplicity is our system."[3]

Forming Planning Visions and Principles

Curitiba's vision of the future found its roots in what at the time were revolutionary planning ideas, especially for a developing country—in the form of the pre–World War II Agache Plan that promoted full motorization, and what was to eventually supersede it, the highly progressive 1965 Master Plan that gave preference to people over cars.

The Agache Plan

In anticipation of the post–World War II building boom, Curitiba's first comprehensive plan was crafted in 1943 by a French urban planner, Alfred Agache. A central premise of this plan was that automobile traffic would grow exponentially and that grand boulevards radiating from the central core were needed to accommodate traffic increases. In the French Haussman tradition of monumental public works projects, the Agache Plan called for massive infrastructure investments, including a large overpass that would span across two squares in the downtown core while leveling some of Curitiba's oldest, most treasured buildings. A proposed widening of the city's main thoroughfare to 60 meters would have required that virtually all buildings along the corridor, including some of the largest and oldest homes in the city, be razed. The Agache Plan sought to strengthen Curitiba's core by building radial avenues that linked downtown with the rest of the city as well as concentric ring roads, creating a hub-and-spoke road system. The plan's assumption that Curitiba would be besieged by automobiles seemed well founded. This was a period of extremely cheap oil when Brazil was seeking to become a world leader in automobile manufacturing. The city was prospering and, many believed, was on an urban development pathway similar to São Paulo's, the nearest of Brazil's emerging megalopolises.

The 1965 Master Plan

In reality, the city never had the money to implement the Agache Plan. The plan did, however, increase public awareness about the need to orchestrate future growth in the wake of rapid post–World War II expansion. With the financial support of the state's Development Bank, civic leaders organized a plan competition among local architects and planners that led to the adoption in 1965 of the Curitiba Master Plan. The new Master Plan broke away radically from the circularly conceived city of 1943. Curitiba would no longer grow in all directions but rather along designated axes—it was to become a linear city. The city's downtown and historic sector would be partly closed to vehicular traffic and given back to pedestrians. Unlike the earlier radial plan, which required most crosstown trips to go through the city center, the new plan treated the downtown as a hub and terminus. The focus was on preserving and enhancing the core and the linear axes that stretched out from it, as opposed to expediting the passage of cars through the center. Mass transit, versus the private automobile, was to become the primary means of conveyance within the city.

It was this notion that Curitiba would meet the mobility needs of people rather than automobiles that set its Master Plan apart from others. At the time, most Brazilian cities were being planned for cars, epitomized by the spaciousness and extensive highway grid of the nation's master-planned capital, Brasilia. By the 1960s, central Curitiba was showing signs of overcrowding and serious traffic congestion. In an attempt to avoid replicating the sprawling landscapes of São Paulo and other megacities, the Master Plan sought to channel overspill growth along what was initially two and would eventually become five "structural axes." These were integral elements of the plan that stood in marked contrast to the radial avenues of the previous plan. The radial links of the earlier Agache Plan were to have been principally road infrastructure connecting low-density outskirts to the downtown core; this would have produced a unidirectional, tidal pattern of commuting. Under the new plan, the linear corridors, or structural axes, would become the main catchments for new development vis-à-vis the core. These corridors would function as high-density pathways for new growth. This would lead to more balanced, bidirectional traffic patterns and thus help sustain a municipal transit system (by keeping buses full in all directions). The core itself would be preserved primarily for pedestrians and transferring transit passengers, with automobiles relegated to a second-tier status.

The goal of creating a linear city spawned the guiding principle that urban development, mass transit services, and hierarchical road networks must be closely integrated and harmoniously planned. The primary tool for creating structural axes would be exclusive busways. Main transit lines would form the backbone of the new metropolis. Also within the structural axes would be a hierarchy of high-capacity lanes for automobile traffic (and eventually express, direct-line bus services) as well as auxiliary lanes for adjoining land uses. Little new development would occur downtown; instead, mixed-use development would be channeled along the transit-served structural axes, with densities tapering with distance from the busway.

It is important to note that, in Curitiba, larger land-use objectives drove transportation decisions, and not vice-versa. Planners and civic leaders first reached agreement on what physical form the city would take—a linear one that would achieve more balanced growth and preserve the social and cultural heritage of the central city. Transportation decisions were then made to reinforce land-use objectives—namely, building axial transitways that would both guide and serve the linear growth. Thus, while land-use and transportation planning were carefully coordinated, it was this collective vision of Curitiba's ideal future settlement pattern that took precedence and led to the eventual decision to build busways.

Besides the principle of co-developing transportation and land uses, the Curitiba Master Plan and subsequent revisions also called for a cultural, social, and economic transformation of the city. Changes that were achieved over time included: a revival of the city center as a cultural center and meeting place; preservation of historical buildings; creation of public squares and parks throughout the city; solid waste recycling; and the formation of the Curitiba Industrial City on the western outskirts (an area of 40 square kilometers currently with over 400 clean industries, including electronic firms and automotive assembly plants).[4]

Implementing the Master Plan

The first important step toward implementing the Curitiba Master Plan occurred in 1971 with the election of Jaime Lerner as mayor. Prior to this, Lerner served as president of the Curitiba Research and Urban Planning Institute (IPPUC—Instituto de Pesquisa e Planejamento Urbano de Curitiba), the organization created in 1965 to implement the Master Plan. Only after Lerner's election was the IPPUC given the power, resources, and political mandate to put the plan into practice. Lerner quickly proved himself a visionary, willing to challenge conventional wisdom, take risks, and try new experiments in urban planning.

The importance of Jaime Lerner's strong and decisive leadership in seeing Curitiba's plan through to implementation cannot be overstated. From 1964 to 1979, Brazil was under a military dictatorship. National policies favored large infrastructure projects financed through foreign loans, which at the time meant most Brazilian cities were building motor-ways and viaducts to accommodate cars and trucks. The "bigger is better" philosophy prevailed. Proposals to restrain the automobile were viewed as leftist politics. Press censorship left but one outlet for criticism and creative expression: local administrations. To gain credibility and establish momentum, Lerner's philosophy was to do things simply and quickly, which meant at a low cost. Brazil's tenuous political situation demanded this.

Reclaiming Downtown

Once Lerner took office in 1971, the fastest, simplest thing that could be done in implementing the Master Plan was to convert downtown streets to pedestrian ways. As Lerner tells it:

> On a cold, icy night in the winter of 1972, from Friday to Saturday, an army of strange-looking silhouettes surrounded the accesses to the main street in downtown Curitiba. The first ones to arrive were armed with wooden horses bearing the inscriptions "Traffic Not Allowed," and signs indicating alternative routes. Those who came next . . . started to methodically destroy the asphalt pavement of the main street with picks, electric power-drills and mechanical shovels.[5]

This "surprise attack" to transform Curitiba's main thoroughfare, XV of November Avenue, into a pedestrian-only street had been carefully planned for more than a year. Soon after lodging protests and threatening to file lawsuits, shop owners noticed sharp increases in retail sales and quickly became allies; merchants in other sections of downtown began demanding that their streets, too, be turned over to pedestrians. The theater continued. A band of automobile supporters planned a motorized invasion of the pedestrian streets that would retake them by force. The city administration, drawing from the teachings of Gandhi, reacted through passive resistance: when the cars arrived, the street had become a promenade, crowded with children drawing and painting an immense ecological mural that stretched nearly the entire length of the street. Over the past twenty years, it has become a tradition that on Saturday mornings, children take over the XV of November promenade.

From these beginnings, Curitiba's pedestrian street system has since expanded to forty-nine downtown blocks, clogged on any given day with shoppers and strollers (Photo 10.1). Other steps taken to improve the downtown environment during Lerner's first years in office included

Photo 10.1. Curitiba's main pedestrian-only street. The XV of November promenade is the hub of street life in downtown Curitiba. Following its successful debut in 1972, the pedestrian street system was soon extended outward in all directions.

refurbishing historical buildings, expanding programs in support of local arts and culture, and upgrading parks and public squares.

Trinary Road System Concept

A pivotal step toward creating Curitiba's structural axes was the development of the trinary road concept. This uniquely Curitiban innovation embodies the very essence of integrated mass transit, roadways, and land uses. Figure 10.1 provides an overhead perspective of the trinary concept. In the center are two restricted lanes dedicated to high-capacity buses. Buses feed into transfer points, called "terminals" in Curitiba (even though most are not at the end of a line), where convenient connections to feeder and crosstown buses can be made. The central busway is flanked by two one-way roads that function as auxiliary lanes, providing direct access to buildings fronting the busway. Running parallel to the central axis, a block away, are high-capacity one-way streets heading in opposite directions: one for traffic flowing to, the other for traffic flowing from, the central city. These one-way couplets would eventually be enlisted by Curitiba's transit planners to accommodate limited-stop, "direct line" (normally called "express") bus services. One-way streets also define the perimeter boundaries of the structural axes. As envisaged, trinary roads would stretch the entire length of most structural axes, which in the Master Plan was eventually to be a distance of some 10 to 15 kilometers from the core.

Figure 10.1 reveals how mass transit services and hierarchical roadways have been physically integrated. Also important to the trinary concept is land-use integration, portrayed by the cross-section shown in Figure 10.2. Directly fronting the main transit corridor are high-rise buildings, with retail-commercial uses on the ground and second floors, and either housing or offices (or sometimes both) on remaining floors. These buildings typically cover the entire block sandwiched between the busway and one-way streets, and thus wholly make up the land uses within the structural axes. The two most important features of the trinary system's built environment are density and mixed activities. High densities pack enough trip origins and destinations along the dedicated transitway to sustain frequent, high-capacity mainline bus services. And mixed land

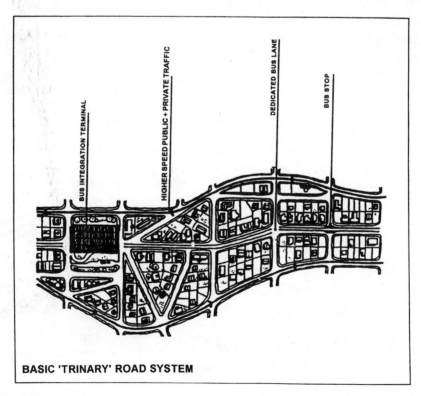

BASIC 'TRINARY' ROAD SYSTEM

FIGURE 10.1. THE TRINARY ROAD SYSTEM. An overhead perspective. *Source:* Instituto de Peisquisa e Planejamento Urbano de Curitiba (IPPUC).

uses guarantee that buildings *both* produce and attract transit trips—that is, there are balanced, two-way flows. Having comparable directional splits was viewed early on as essential toward maintaining a financially viable transit system, and mixed land uses were considered the best way to achieve this. The trinary scheme is arguably the purest example of integrating transit and land use anywhere (Photo 10.2).

Outside the structural axes, but within easy walking distance of the main transit lines, would be a "housing zone." Residential densities would fall off sharply with distance from the busway. On the other sides of the one-way trinary couplets would be mid-rise (eight-to-twelve-story) condominium and apartment towers (ZR 4 [residential zone 4], wherein building area can be up to twice the plot area). The next roads out from one-way couplets would be local streets, with low-rise garden apartments and condominiums (three to five stories). Under ZR 3 zoning, building floor space of up to 1.3 times the size of a parcel would be permitted. And farther out, most residences would consist of zero lot-line structures (e.g., row houses, duplexes) as well as single-family detached units (ZR 1 restricts floor area to the size of the plot). While predominantly residential, the ZR zones would allow some neighborhood retail uses (e.g., small groceries and drugstores).

The trinary concept is careful to ensure that land uses and roadways are also compatible. Land uses that benefit from exposure and busy traffic—namely, retail shops and consumer services—occupy the ground and first floors of the auxiliary lanes and one-way couplets. High-volume roads are buffered from low-density residential neighborhoods by higher-

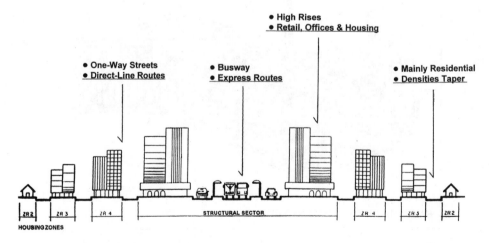

FIGURE 10.2. LAND USES AND DENSITIES ALONG TRINARY ROADS. A cross-sectional perspective. *Source:* Adapted from Instituto de Peisquisa e Planejamento Urbano de Curitiba (IPPUC).

PHOTO 10.2. EXCLUSIVE BUSWAY, THE CORE OF THE TRINARY SYSTEM. Auxiliary lanes for regular traffic abut the busway along the north structural axis to the Barreirinha terminus. High-rise housing, complemented by ground-floor retail, hugs the busway axis.

rise buildings. Low-volume local streets help preserve a sense of place and attachment to neighborhood.

In his manuscript *Curitiba: The Ecological Evolution*, Jaime Lerner pays tribute to the trinary road concept:

> First, it preserved the scale and memory of the city— instead of a highway within the city, (there are) three streets of normal size and width, each with its own functions, its specific "philosophy." Secondly, the greatest obstacle to the implementation of the express-bus system was precisely the lack of space for the construction of exclusive lanes. . . . Finally, it was possible to implement, within a year's time and at perfectly acceptable costs, practically 20 kilometers of the trinary system.[6]

Lerner also maintains that, given Curitiba's phenomenal rate of growth at the time, by guiding urban development as opposed to leaving it up to the whims of the private real estate market, the trinary system has kept land speculation in check. Developers know precisely where they can build high-rise office towers and where they can not. Reducing land speculation not only helps keep the price of housing in line with the budgets of the middle class, but also economizes on the cost of extending new infrastructure and community services.

Ironically, the trinary concept owes its existence, in part, to the 1943 Agache Plan that called for 60-meter-wide radiating boulevards. The city had acquired the necessary right-of-ways along a number of corridors in anticipation of one day building superwide roads. There was no money to do so, however. Fortuitously, public ownership of land along main thoroughfares gave birth to the idea of creating an integrated corridor of transit, roadways, and compatible land uses within the 60-meter right-of-ways, as opposed to 60 meters of continuous pavement. Thus, quite by accident, the Agache Plan served the useful purpose of encouraging land banking. Without the initial plan to build grand boulevards, the right-of-ways necessary to accommodate the trinary system and create a linear city would not have been available.[7]

It is also noteworthy that the trinary concept embraces the idea of hierarchical roads, something that the New Urbanism movement and proponents of neotraditional neighborhood designs steadfastly reject.[8] New urbanists consider uniform grid street networks to be more pedestrian-friendly because they require cars to stop frequently and shorten walking distances. They also, however, usually require more road space per square foot of land area than hierarchical networks.[9] In Curitiba, hierarchical roads were viewed as being compatible with the hierarchy of land uses, urban densities, and transit services that co-exist along trinary corridors. With the trinary scheme, all roads and transit lines would operate at grade, meaning there would be no huge overpasses and flyovers that dwarf pedestrians or splinter the trinary corridor and its adjoining neighborhoods.

Integrated Transit Network

With its land-use strategy in place, the second phase toward implementing Curitiba's long-range vision was to implement what became known as the Integrated Transit Network (ITN). The ITN ensured a workable fit between transit and neighborhoods off the structural axes.

By 1974, Curitiba had opened the first 20 kilometers of exclusive bus lanes. The trinary road system was beginning to take form and steps were being taken to consolidate transit service. Prior to this, there was a loose confederation of competing private bus companies operating in Curitiba. Most competed for lucrative markets, running buses along the busiest streets to downtown. The confluence of buses in the city center was choking downtown streets.

Early on, the Lerner administration wrestled with the choice of continuing with a surface-bus system or constructing a capital-intensive rail network. It opted for bus transit, with exclusive-lane mainline services, on the grounds that rubber-tire services were more appropriate for a medium-size Third World city—they were far cheaper and more adaptable. This was consistent with Lerner's philosophy of doing things quickly and at a low cost. A surface-bus system was also viewed as organic—it could be built incrementally in pace with Curitiba's rapid growth. It could also operate on preexisting roads.

Figure 10.3 sketches the evolution of transit services from 1974 to 1982. The initial 20-kilometer busway formed the first spine of the linear city, a north-south axis. What locals called "express bus" services operated on the busway (even though express bus stops are only a half-kilometer apart; regardless, the term is still used to describe these services.) Some 45 kilometers of feeder buses tied into the two busway termini. Average weekday ridership on the entire system was about 45,000 passen-

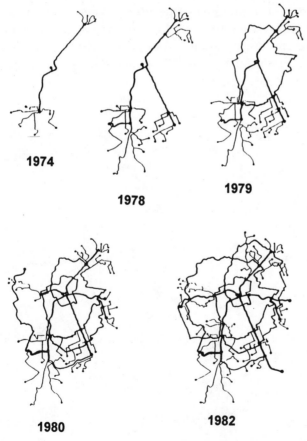

1974

1978

1979

1980

1982

FIGURE 10.3. EVOLUTION OF CURITIBA'S INTEGRATED TRANSIT NETWORK, 1974–1982. *Source:* Urbanização de Curitiba (URBS), *Integrated Transit Network* (Curitiba: URBS, 1993).

gers. By 1978, a third busway was opened to the southeast, forming a new linear growth axis.

In 1979, the concept of an Integrated Transit Network (ITN) was formally born. At the time, Curitiba's bus network poorly served crosstown trips. In response, "interdistrict" services were put into place. The initial route, a 44-kilometer circuit, intersected the three exclusive busways at intermediate stations. By 1980, the ITN had nine intermediate and terminal stations where customers could transfer between feeder, express, and interdistrict routes. Daily ridership had surpassed 200,000. By 1982, four concentric interdistrict routes served the city: one close to the center, the second a little farther out, the third even farther, and the fourth reaching almost to the municipal boundaries. The 167 kilometers of interdistrict services were complemented by 294 kilometers of local routes and 54 kilometers of express bus services. Daily ridership had eclipsed the half-million mark, more than twenty times what it had been eight years earlier.

By the early 1980s, Curitiba's Integrated Transit Network had taken on a distinct cobweb appearance (Figure 10.4). Functionally, it was a trunk and branch system. Buses operating along exclusive lanes in the center of the trinary system formed the system's backbone. Concentric bus loops connected the lower-density wedges of the city to the trunklines at transfer points. Essential to the ITN concept was ensuring passengers

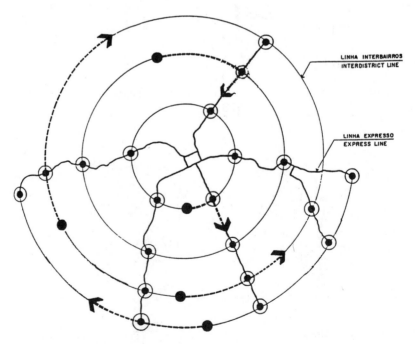

FIGURE 10.4. CURITIBA'S COBWEB SERVICE STRUCTURE. *Source:* Urbanização de Curitiba (URBS), *Integrated Transit Network* (Curitiba: URBS, 1993).

could transfer from interdistrict lines to express buses and then on to feeder buses with ease and a single fare. Transfer stations enabled this. As Curitiba's bus system evolved, it required incremental improvements in fare payment, scheduling, and facility design to ensure that the transferring process was nearly effortless. An important step in this direction was to design transfer enclosures that function like subway stations. Besides boarding platforms, most transfer stations today have benches, shelters, schedule information, and newsstands. The end stations (*terminal de ponta*) are larger than intermediate ones (*terminal de meio*) since they serve a larger ridership catchment as well as intermunicipal services (i.e., private buses that arrive from outside Curitiba). End stations also have a wider assortment of retail concessions and passenger amenities. Inside stations, passengers are free to shop, chat, make phone calls, read newspapers, and switch buses without having to pay another fare.

Service Refinement and Differentiation

By the mid-1980s, Curitiba's bus system had become a victim of its own success. Ridership was steadily rising and express buses were oversubscribed. Schedule delays became common. An initial response was to operate articulated buses, though this proved to be only a stopgap. New capacity unleashed new waves of demand. Along the inaugural north-south busway, convoys of articulated buses were hauling close to 10,000 passengers per lane per hour, volumes that begin to match the loads of many fixed-guideway rail systems.

In Curitiba's case, necessity proved to be the mother of invention. Unable to afford an underground metro system, Curitiba's transit planners came up with a new concept in bus service delivery that exploited the available capacity of the trinary road system and provided the passenger throughput of a rail system. The idea was to operate high-capacity buses on the one-way couplets paralleling exclusive bus lanes. Vehicles would stop only at transfer stations, meaning from the terminus of a structural axis to downtown Curitiba, there would be, at most, two to three intermediate stops. A key component of the system was the use of raised boarding tubes that would allow same-level boarding and alighting, and fare payment to occur prior to the arrival of a bus.

This new transit service was called Linha Direta, Portuguese for Direct Line service. The popular name, however, is Ligeirinho, or "Speedy." Direct-line buses (with 110-passenger capacities) served by boarding tubes can carry 3.2 times as many passengers per hour as a standard bus route, and nearly 70 percent more than articulated buses operating on Curitiba's busways. The theoretical capacity of direct-line services approaches 9,000 passengers per direction per hour, a figure that begins to match the loads of some of the world's busiest light rail systems. True

to Curitiban tradition, the direct-line service with boarding tubes was conceived and designed because it was far cheaper, faster, and less disruptive
to build—about US$200,000 per kilometer, compared to an estimated
US$80 to US$90 million per kilometer for an underground metro and
US$20 million per kilometer for a combined exclusive-lane/shared right-
of-way light rail system.

Direct-line services were started in 1991 with four routes that paral-
leled busways; within the first year, these routes were carrying some
100,000 passengers per day. Because of the express, limited-stop service
feature, transit officials estimate that the direct-line services provide an
average of fifteen minutes' travel time savings for each segment of a work
trip.[10] In 1995, Curitiba boasted twelve direct-line routes serving more
than 225,000 daily trips, most siphoned away from exclusive (frequent-
stop) busway lines (Map 10.1). "Speedy" has become so popular that

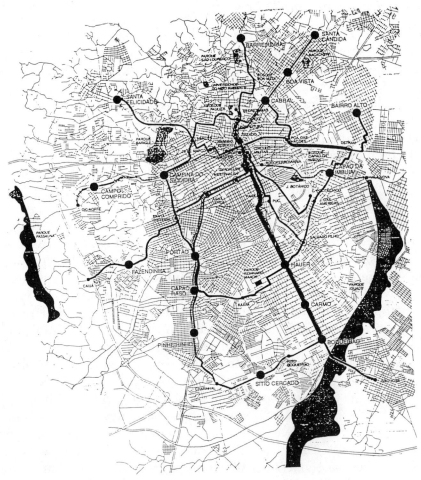

MAP 10.1. DIRECT-LINE ROUTES, PARALLELING BUSWAYS ALONG STRUCTURAL AXES.

many bus lines are filled to capacity at most hours of the day. Learning from past experiences, Curitiba's transit officials refrained from expanding direct-line services because they feared even more customers would switch from the busway lines. This would result in the underutilization of one of the ITN's most expensive pieces of infrastructure, the exclusive busway. Instead, local officials have begun to expand the capacity of express (frequent-stop) services by operating bi-articulated buses (with capacities of 270 passengers), the first of their kind (Photo 10.3). By 1996, more than 100 bi-articulated buses were in operation. Curitiba officials are also currently studying the possibility of perhaps one day converting exclusive busway operations to a rail system.

Direct-line services are arguably Curitiba's most important transit innovation to date. Besides providing bus passenger-carrying capacities that were previously thought to be impossible, the direct-line runs have further refined and differentiated Curitiba's transit service offerings. Importantly, along structural axes, those traveling longer distances, such as from the outskirts to downtown, usually opt for limited-stop, direct-line services. Those traveling shorter distances (e.g., from their residence to a shopping plaza along a structural axis) are more likely to ride exclusive (frequent-stop) busway services. Few rail cities can match Curitiba's

PHOTO 10.3. CURITIBA'S BI-ARTICULATED BUS. Locally manufactured by a subsidiary of Volvo, Inc., bi-articulated buses hold up to 270 passengers and feature turbo engines, five wide doors, low floors, and modern interiors. Other Brazilian cities have begun purchasing and operating Curitiban-manufactured bi-articulated buses as well, hoping to emulate Curitiba's successes.

wealth of choices along major travel corridors. In a way, the variety of transit offerings along structural axes complement the variety of land uses and trip purposes. Short, midday shop trips as well as long, peak-period work trips are conveniently served by buses plying along or parallel to the transitway.

It is noteworthy that the transit planners who created Curitiba's direct-line services, as well as other system innovations, were trained as architects. The city's chief transit planner and head of the municipal transit organization, Carlos Ceneviva, was previously a vice-director with the IPPUC, Curitiba's comprehensive planning organization. Having architect-planners run municipal transit operations has resulted in the careful co-configuration of service strategies and urban development and given birth to many clever, design-oriented solutions, such as boarding tubes and trinaries.

Land-Use Regulations and Supportive Policies

While integrated planning, politics, and personalities account for much of Curitiba's successes, specific public policy initiatives taken over the years also deserve some credit. Among these have been incentive zoning, housing development programs, parking policies, and employer-paid transit subsidies.

Zoning Regulations and Incentives

Curitiba's creative use of zoning within and along the trinary structural axes has produced "wedding cake" density patterns, as shown earlier in Figure 10.2. Various bonuses are also granted that promote land use mixing in addition to higher densities immediate to the transitway.

Nearly all parcels within Curitiba's structural axes (consisting mainly of the two blocks within the trinary road system) have been zoned for mixed commercial-residential uses. Office building areas of five times the plot size are permitted. Residential towers can have up to four times as much floor space as land area. Office buildings can be taller because experience shows that they generate more transit trips per square meter than residential uses.

For structures that directly face exclusive busways and auxiliary lanes, zoning laws allow the first two floors to extend to property lines. This leaves 1.5 meters between buildings and street curbs for sidewalks. Zoning rules require that at least 50 percent of the ground and second floors be devoted to retail-commercial uses such as shops and restaurants. Whatever floor space is applied to retail-commercial use, moreover, does not count against permissible plot ratios. Thus, in practice, nearly all of the first two floors of buildings that front transitways are devoted to retail shops and eateries. This typically means that buildings can go two stories above plot ratio maximums. Zoning regulations also require that, above the second floor, buildings be set back at least 5 meters from property lines. This allows more sunlight to reach the busway, auxiliary lanes, and sidewalks. Curitiba's zoning practices deserve much of the credit for creating the rich mixes of storefronts and high-profile development lining transitways.[11]

Transferable Development Rights

Within the Curitiba Historic Area, owners of historical buildings are allowed to sell and transfer their development rights to property owners elsewhere in the city. This has both served to protect heritage buildings and to transfer densities to locations where they are most beneficial, such as structural axes. Because mixed-use development along structural axes receive bonuses, many of the density transfers have gone to parcels abutting the transitway.

Transit-Supportive Housing Policies

Through land acquired along or close to structural axes, the city of Curitiba has been able to direct new community-assisted housing to transportation corridors. In all, housing for some 20,000 low-income families has been built near transportation corridors over the past twenty-five years. Another transit-supportive housing initiative has been the "buy up" program. Through the state's Municipal Housing Fund Act, developers can "buy up" to two extra floors of residential buildings by contributing to a low-income housing fund. Contributions go to the municipal housing authority, COHAB (Companhia de Habitação Popular Curitiba), which channels the money as housing assistance for poor families. Contributions are set at 75 percent of the market value of the extra building area provided. To date, these density bonuses have been granted only to residential parcels in the ZR 4, ZR 3, and ZR 2 zones that lie within walking distance of the transitway—that is, areas where existing infrastructure can support the higher residential densities.[12]

Siting of Shopping Centers

The location of any proposed shopping center in Curitiba must first be approved by the IPPUC, the municipal planning authority. Since 1970, the only large-scale shopping centers permitted have been those built within structural axes. Plans to build several large American-style shopping malls on the city's periphery have been rejected. This policy has not only strengthened structural axes by channeling new retail growth to transit-served corridors, but has also helped retain the vitality of downtown Curitiba by limiting auto-oriented retail development.

Impacts on Urban Development Patterns

The cumulative effect of Curitiba's integrated planning of transit, land uses, and road space on the city's built form is best appreciated from a bird's-eye view. From the State Telephone Company observation tower, four distinct high-rise corridors are prominent. As envisaged in the 1965 Master Plan, Curitiba is today the archetype of a linear city (Photo 10.4). High-rise mixed-use towers hug the transitway, surrounded by low-density residential neighborhoods. The edges between neighborhoods are clearly defined, commercial centers stand out, and protected green areas dot the landscape. The most built-up areas of the structural axes lie just beyond downtown: on the southern axis, some 5 kilometers in length (between the Guadalupe and Agua Verde transitway stations); on the northern axis, about 2 kilometers in length (up to the Cabral station); on the western axis, stretching more than 4 kilometers (from the 29 de Marco to the Campina do Siqueira stations); and on the eastern axis, about 1 kilometer in length (just beyond the Rodoferroviaria, or main intercity bus station).

Population densities (net of undeveloped land) for Curitiba's structural axes and adjoining residential zones, as of 1992, are presented in

PHOTO 10.4. CURITIBA'S WESTERN STRUCTURAL AXIS. From the observation tower of the State Telephone Company, Curitiba's bus-served western structural axis dwarfs surrounding neighborhoods.

Table 10.1.[13] Average gross residential densities along structural axes are very high, approaching 100 dwelling units per hectare (38 dwelling units per acre). Net densities are often at least twice as high. Closer to downtown, along the northern, western, and southern axes, gross densities of nearly 170 dwelling units per hectare are found along some city blocks. Residential densities have increased about tenfold since 1970, when average net densities were about 9 dwelling units per hectare. The number of dwelling units within the structural axes increased by 855 percent between 1970 and 1992.[14] In 1992, nearly 9 percent of Curitiba's population resided within one of the four high-density structural axes.

Adjacent to the structural axes, residential densities range from around 17 to 40 dwelling units per gross hectare. The medium-to-high-density zones (ZR 4) that immediately flank the structural axes constituted about 14 percent of Curitiba's 1992 population. The medium-density zones, which lie some two to three blocks from the structural axes, made up an additional 16 percent of the 1992 population. Thus, nearly one-third of Curitibanos live within an easy walk of the busway, a testament to bus transit's city-shaping abilities.

Many of the households living in the condominiums along Curitiba's structural axes have upper-middle incomes. Generally, household incomes rise along the structural axes with proximity to downtown. The high premium placed on being close to commercial and cultural amenities in the core have driven up housing prices close to downtown. Given their incomes, it is no surprise that households along the structural axes have the city's highest vehicle ownership rates and generate relatively few transit work trips. Although no formal survey data are available to confirm this, the low boarding counts at bus stops along some of the denser residential portions of the transitway suggest ridership rates among affluent

Table 10.1 RESIDENTIAL DENSITIES IN CURITIBA'S STRUCTURAL AXES AND ADJOINING NEIGHBORHOODS, 1992

Zone	Population	Residential Population		Dwelling Units	
		Per Hectare	Per Acre	Per Hectare	Per Acre
Mixed High-Rise Residential	130,700	294	119.0	93	37.6
Medium-to-High-Density Residential (ZR 4)	217,300	164	66.4	40	16.2
Medium-Density Residential (ZR 3)	240,800	76	30.8	22	8.5
Low-Density Residential (ZR 2)	416,506	63	25.5	17	6.9

Source: Instituto de Pesquisa e Planejamento Urbano de Curitiba (IPPUC), Advanced Planning Section, data files.

households are relatively low. Besides having automobiles available to get to work, low transit usage could also reflect the fact that most express and direct-line buses are generally full once they reach closer-in areas and that flat fares penalize short trips.[15]

Other Transit-Supportive Policies

Land-use regulations are not the only factor to have influenced travel choices in Curitiba. Parking policies have also been important. There is little curbside parking downtown, and cars can only park for short periods. Off-street parking spaces are privately owned and expensive. The supply of on- and off-street spaces has steadily increased over the past decade, though nowhere near as quickly as vehicle ownership. In 1995, there were more than a half-million registered cars in Curitiba, up an astonishing 20 percent from one year earlier. This surge in vehicle ownership was mainly due to the revaluation of the Brazilian currency, the real, which fueled consumer spending starting in mid-1994. While Brazilian officials have discussed levying higher registration fees and import duties as ways to curb the growth in vehicle population, auto disincentives are highly unpopular and politically risky. Most observers agree that carrots, like Curitiba's integrated transit system, are preferable to sticks in encouraging transit usage.[16]

A national policy that has benefited public transit mandates that employers subsidize a portion of their workers' transportation costs, as in Japan (see Chapter 7). Brazilian law establishes that, as a norm, 20 percent of personal income should go toward covering transportation expenses. This law also stipulates that no more than 6 percent of what a wage earner brings home should be spent on transportation. Any amount above this, up to the 20 percent ceiling, must be paid by employers. As a result, transportation allowances have become a standard practice in Brazil, particularly among low-skilled, low-paid jobholders. (Most professionals and skilled workers spend less than 6 percent of gross earnings on monthly transit fares and thus receive no employer subsidies.) In Curitiba, employers are the primary purchasers of bus tokens. At the time workers pick up their paychecks, many also receive a packet of tokens to last the month.

World-Class Transit at a Low Cost: Transit Today in Curitiba

From humble beginnings of operating 65 kilometers of bus routes and carrying 45,000 daily passengers in 1974, Curitiba's transit network had, by 1995, stretched over 1,200 route kilometers, featured some 1,300 buses of all sizes, and served more than 1.6 million daily trip segments. Today, Curitibanos enjoy as rich an assortment of transit offerings as anywhere—

from mainline express buses that operate on two-minute peak headways to crosstown circular routes that interconnect transfer stations.

All buses operating on the Integrated Transit Network (ITN) currently tie into one of the twenty enclosed transfer stations and thus allow free transfers. The four types of integrated services operating today, distinguished by their color schemes, are: 18 express (red bus, frequent stops) busway routes; 115 feeder (orange bus) routes; 7 interdistrict (green bus) routes; and 11 direct-line (gray bus, limited stops) routes.[17]

Surface Metro

With integrated, trunk-and-branch services, Curitiba's ITN functions just like a regional subway system, only above ground. Accordingly, local transit planners have taken to calling the system a "surface metro."

Express Services

At the core of Curitiba's "surface metro" are the regular coach, articulated, and bi-articulated buses running up and down busways, with carrying capacities of 105, 170, and 270 passengers per vehicle, respectively.[18] With 270 passengers per vehicle on seventy-two-second peak-hour headways, operating almost like an elephant train, bi-articulated vehicles have a theoretical throughput of 13,500 passengers per lane per hour, higher than any light rail transit service.[19]

Presently, express "red" buses running along the transitway provide Curitiba's most intensive and frequent transit services. They account for about 18 percent of daily bus kilometers and carry about a third of all passengers. Along some corridors during peak hours, express buses come by roughly every ninety seconds. The mix of regular, articulated, and bi-articulated buses operating along transitways allows transit managers to tailor service levels to demand. As a result, express buses operate with minimum excess capacities. Fares are paid on board express buses (and all other vehicles except direct-line buses connected to boarding tubes). Each bus has a driver and a fare collector.

Direct-Line Services

The "speedy" direct-line services introduced in 1991 largely parallel express bus services on the trinary one-way couplets, providing a faster, limited-stop alternative for traversing transitway corridors (see Map 10.1). Direct-line buses average speeds of about 32 kilometers per hour, compared to 20 kilometers per hour for express buses and 16 kilometers per hour for conventional services. About 40 percent of direct-line services, in terms of route kilometers, operate in sectors of the city without trinaries; two of the eleven direct-line routes are circumferentials. Since "speedy" buses provide the highest level of service to those living on the outskirts (where one can usually find a seat), low-income residents make up much of their ridership. The gray "speedy" buses, which in 1995 numbered 198, stop only at one of the eighty-nine color-coordinated gray-tinted tube stations.

Curitiba's patented boarding tubes and high-capacity buses are one of a kind. Made of tinted plexiglass and aluminum, boarding tubes parallel roadways and feature raised platforms (Photo 10.5). They function as mini-stations, allowing passengers to pay fares before buses arrive and board without having to step up. Embarking passengers pass a turnstile and pay an attendant in charge of the boarding tube. Customers can then rest against a padded bar, protected from the elements. When a bus arrives, the driver lines up the doors of the bus with the sliding, pneumatic doors of the tube stations; a folding ramp automatically drops onto the fixed platform of the tube, allowing same-level boarding and alighting. (Since "speedy" buses operate on one-way streets, typically parallel to express bus lines, doors are on the left side, thus allowing free-body transfers to be made onto express buses with conventional right-hand side doors.) Disembarking passengers exit one set of doors, which are as wide as those on a subway car, and embarking passengers enter immediately afterward, just as if on a metro system. Without stairs to negotiate or on-board fares to pay, boarding and alighting is swift, usually under thirty

PHOTO 10.5. CURITIBA'S BOARDING TUBES. Top left, a folding ramp allows same-level boarding and alighting; top right, interconnected tubes allow transfers across bus lines operating on different streets; bottom left, downtown tubes support five-door boardings on bi-articulated bus; bottom right, the interior of downtown multibus tubes look and function almost like a metro station.

seconds (about one-quarter the dwell time of conventional buses handling comparable loads).[20] The throughputs of "speedy" services are further increased by the absence of fare collectors aboard buses, freeing space for passengers.[21] With capacities of 110 passengers per vehicle and assuming peak headways of forty-five seconds, as previously noted, the theoretical throughput of speedy buses is nearly 9,000 passengers per lane direction per hour. Along trinaries, where "speedy" and express buses operate side by side, passenger flows in one direction currently exceed 15,000 per hour, comparable to the busiest lines on Rio de Janeiro's subway.

Complementary Services

Feeding into express and direct-line routes at transfer stations are Curitiba's 7 interdistrict "green" bus lines and 115 feeder "orange" routes. Because of efficient branch connections to low-density areas, nearly 70 percent of Curitiba's residents live within a half-kilometer of a bus route.[22] It is because of the wide net of services cast by interdistrict and feeder runs that Curitiba is a hybrid transit metropolis. Vital to the integration of low-capacity and high-capacity services are the transfer stations.

Transfer Stations

What makes Curitiba's Integrated Transit Network function like clockwork are the twenty enclosed transfer stations. Figure 10.5 shows a typical station configuration. In the center is the main transitway. Express buses enter the gated station directly from the transitway and dock at a side platform. Feeder and interdistrict buses enter the station from the parallel side streets and park at the opposite end of the platform from express buses. There are two side platforms, one for each direction. Passengers either transfer on the same platform or cross to the opposite platform, usually via a tunnel. Most platforms, or "integrated areas," have newsstands, benches, route maps, and posted schedules. Terminal stations at the end of lines are the largest; several feature small grocery stores, eateries, flower shops, and drugstores. These businesses generate lease revenues that go to the city's general fund.

Direct-line buses approach transfer stations from the one-way streets paralleling the transitway, enter onto auxiliary lanes on the sides of the gated stations, and stop at boarding tubes (which have no attendants). Disembarking passengers exit the left-side doors into the tubes, through a passageway, and onto the platforms, barrier-free.[23]

Management and Organization

Day-to-day operations of Curitiba's bus system are overseen by a municipal agency, Urbanização de Curitiba (URBS). The URBS's responsibilities

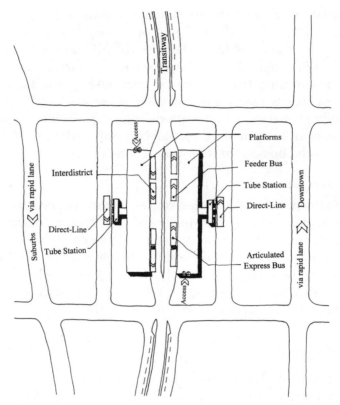

FIGURE 10.5. PROTOTYPICAL TRANSFER STATION ON CURITIBA'S INTEGRATED TRANSIT NET-
WORK. *Source:* Adapted from Urbanização de Curitiba (URBS), *Integrated Transit
Network* (Curitiba: URBS, 1993).

include: setting timetables and performance standards; negotiating contracts with private bus companies; monitoring private operations for compliance with service standards; planning new routes and services; collecting and distributing revenues; and maintaining transfer stations.
Responsibility for long-range planning of the Integrated Transit Network
lies with the municipal planning agency, the IPPUC. The two agencies
work closely together to ensure that long-term planning and near-term
operations are coordinated.

Currently, ten private companies operate all urban and suburban bus
routes in Curitiba. To customers, company buses and personnel are indistinguishable. Companies are reimbursed based on kilometers operated
rather than number of passengers. This ensures that services are fully
deployed and curbs interfirm competition for customers. Companies also
receive 1 percent of their total capital expenditures on buses.[24] This
arrangement provides a rate of return that is 12 percent of annual capital
expenditures. Companies therefore have a financial incentive to renovate
their rolling stock. This largely explains why Curitiba's bus fleet, with an

average age of just three years, is the newest in Brazil if not the entire world.[25]

In 1987, Curitiba replaced competitively bid territorial concessions with a system of "permissions." Under Brazilian law, permissions are simpler to execute and terminate. A simple two-page document sets out the basic legal framework of all permissions. There is no fixed contract period, and contracts can be canceled at any time, provided there is justified cause.

Fares

During the 1990s, adult fares have ranged between 30 and 40 U.S. cents. Fares change frequently due to Brazil's currency inflation, which in mid-1993 exceeded 30 percent per month. Fares are based on the costs (e.g., fuel, parts, consumer goods) incurred by the URBS and private firms. The URBS monitors these costs by surveying prices among retail outlets in the city and periodically recalculates fares to ensure full cost-recovery.

The most popular fare medium is prepaid tokens, used by an estimated 60 percent of passengers each day. Tokens can be purchased at shops, newsstands, and transfer stations. Companies buy, in bulk, most of the tokens, distributing them to workers as a monthly travel allowance. Tokens are not discounted. Their primary advantage is the convenience to both employers and users. A second advantage is that they are resistant to inflation, no small matter in a country with a history of galloping inflation.

The Payoff

The ultimate measure of the success of Curitiba's impressive transit system is ridership, and in particular the number of passengers who switched over from driving cars. Traffic relief and environmental improvements depend on luring motorists to transit, ideally at a reasonable cost.

From 1974 to 1994, system-wide ridership grew by an average annual rate of 15 percent, three to four times faster than population growth. Transit's market share of commute trips rose from 8 percent to more than 70 percent over this same period. Accounting for most of the growth were express buses in the 1970s, feeder and interdistrict services in the 1980s, and direct-line services in the 1990s. About two out of every three Curitibanos currently patronize the transit system each day.

The best evidence of the impact of Curitiba's transit network on traffic and environmental conditions comes from a survey of those patronizing direct-line services. The survey, conducted by the Bonilha Institute in 1991, found that within a month of initiating services, 28 percent of those commuting on "speedy" bus runs previously drove a car to work. From this, analysts estimate that the Integrated Transit Network has reduced automobile usage by some 27 million trips per year and per capita fuel consumption by 25 percent compared to similar-size Brazilian cities.[26] Today, Curitiba purportedly has the cleanest air of any Brazilian city. Another benefit of high ridership has been low per capita transportation expenditures. Currently, Curitibanos spend only about 10 percent of their income on transportation, well below the national norm of 20 percent.[27]

An important ridership benefit of mixed-use development, particularly along structural axes, has been balanced directional splits. In 1970, when conventional buses serving downtown dominated Curitiba's transit services, 90 percent of buses operated in the peak direction. Today, directional splits are 60:40. With trip origins and destinations aligned along structural axes, near-empty buses have become a thing of the past.

Learning from Curitiba

Curitibanos enjoy world-class transit services thanks to careful planning, smart decision making, and inspired leadership. Among all-bus cities, Curitiba has one of the highest per capita ridership levels anywhere. Civic leaders created a vision, built community support, and proceeded to implement, step by step, a highly innovative and integrated transit network that is today the envy of many. Importantly, the city's caretakers started out with a vision of an ideal future settlement pattern—a predominantly linear one—and proceeded to grow an integrated, trunk-and-branch transit network that complemented this vision. Thus, land-use and community development objectives, coupled with a desire to hold costs down, determined the types of transit technologies selected and kinds of services delivered.

Early on, the goal was to transport people rather than move cars. Instead of starting with some preconceived idea of a transportation "solution," city leaders instead asked what would be the most cost-effective transport investments consonant with building a linear city as well as the goals of preserving the inner core, improving environmental quality, and keeping costs reasonable. This led to conceptualizing transportation as part of an integrated system—one linked to housing, land uses, road networks, mixed-use commercial districts, historic preservation, and public spaces. More concretely, it led to the designation of structural axes, the creation of trinary road systems, the construction of dedicated busways, the building of mixed residential-commercial towers along busways, and the eventual implementation of an integrated transit network that efficiently serves low-density areas.

A willingness to experiment and take risks, tempered by a desire to get things done quickly and cheaply, led to many successes—the creation of trinary roads, introduction of zoning bonuses, and initiation of direct-line services that tie into boarding tubes. Luck also played a role. Having a generous supply of preserved right-of-ways, acquired under the original 1943 plan calling for Parisian-style radiating boulevards, for example, gave birth to the trinary road system. Nevertheless, it was a bold and utopian vision matched by sheer determination and cleverly designed programs, more than anything, that brought Curitiba's integrated transportation and land-use system to life.

More generally, Curitiba offers important lessons in urban management. One lesson, preached often by former Curitiba mayor and now state governor, Jaime Lerner, is to keep things simple. Curitiba set off with a small set of realistic long-range goals. These goals then served as guides to three decades of incremental, pragmatic change.

Experiences with creating a highly successful transit system have been put to good use in other areas of urban policy—such as solid waste disposal, refuse recycling, housing refurbishing, open space preservation, and urban greening. In these areas, too, the approach has been pragmatic in that it begins with real problems and practical solutions. For Curitibanos, what matters most is that these small, incremental steps have added up to dramatic improvements in quality of life and put the city on a path to a sustainable future.

Curitibanos are not wedded to bus transit per se. What matters is high-quality, cost-effective transit services that support travel desires. Historically, this has meant bus transit. But as the city has grown and the trinary axes have densified, there is growing pressure to convert busway corridors to electrified trains. A referendum to do so was turned down by voters in 1997, largely for fiscal reasons. However, most observers agree that it is just a matter of time until such a changeover occurs. In Curitiba, an effective transport–land use connection matters most. Whichever transit technology can best provide this will ultimately prevail.

NOTES

1. These consist of unlinked transit trips (i.e., treating each segment of a multileg transit trip as a single trip). On a single-fare, linked transit trip basis, there were 205 trips per capita in 1995. This is still among the highest in Brazil.

2. J. Rabinovitch and J. Leitman, *Environmental Innovation and Management in Curitiba, Brazil*, Working Paper Series 1 (Washington, DC: UNDP/UNCHS (Habitat)/World Bank, Urban Management Programme, 1993).

3. J. Brooke, The Secret of a Livable City? It's Simplicity Itself, *The New York Times*, May 28, 1992, p. A4.

4. For in-depth discussions on Curitiba's evolution as an "ecological city," see: J. Rabinovich, Curitiba: Towards Sustainable Urban Development, *Environment and Urbanization*, vol. 4, no. 2, 1992, pp. 62–73; J. Rabinovitch and J.

Leitman, *op cit.*, 1993; and J. Rabinovitch and J. Leitman, Urban Planning in Curitiba, *Scientific American*, vol. 274, no. 3, 1996, pp. 46–51.

5. J. Lerner, Curitiba: The Ecological Revolution, unpublished manuscript, 1992, p. 14.

6. *Ibid.*, p. 16.

7. By the early 1970s, many main routes emanating from downtown Curitiba already had three parallel roads that, together, constituted 60 meters of right-of-way. During the post–World War II era, the city proceeded to extend and improve roads as Curitiba expanded outward, and the public right-of-ways established under the Agache Plan allowed these road improvements to be made, albeit at a much more modest scale than envisaged in the initial plan.

8. P. Katz, *The New Urbanism* (New York: McGraw-Hill, 1994).

9. A. Moudon, and R. Untermann, Grids Revisited. *Public Streets for Public Use*, A. Moudon, ed. (New York: Columbia University Press, 1991).

10. Curitiba's transit officials estimate that workers patronizing direct-line services save an average of one hour per day. This consists of four segments of a trip: from home to work in the morning; from work to home in the mid-day (for lunch); from home back to work in the early afternoon; and from work back to home in the evening. Thus, the average time savings per work trip segment is fifteen minutes.

11. Beyond the structural axes, residential densities taper with distance from transitways as shown previously in Figure 10.2. Mixed-use development is encouraged through density bonuses—up to 10 percent of ground-floor building space can go to shops and consumer services without being included in allowable densities. Through these zoning practices, small retail outlets dot the residential neighborhoods that flank Curitiba's structural axes.

12. This has normally meant developers can add two more floors to structures in ZR 4 zones and one more floor in ZR 3 and ZR 2 zones. During its first four years, the program generated about US$2 million in funds, most of which went to site and services improvements on parcels owned by poor households, some near the transitway, though most on the outskirts, where Curitiba's poorest neighborhoods are located.

13. Net residential densities were estimated by eliminating vacant parcels from the total land area of each zoning classification. All data were obtained from the Advanced Planning Department of the IPPUC.

14. C. Taniguchi, Transport Integration Strategy in Urban Planning: The Experience of Curitiba, *Urban Transport in Developing Countries, Full Text, CODATU VI* (Paris: CODATU, Proceedings of the Sixth Conference on Urban Transport in Developing Countries, pp. iii–11 to iii–16; Instituto de Pesuisae Planejamento e Urbano be Curitiba (IPPUC), *Compartimentos Territorials do Municipio Definidos Pela Legislação de Zoneamento e Uso do Solo* (Curitiba: IPPUC, 1992).

15. It is odd that Curitiba's structural axes have attracted the very households that patronize transit the least, at least to get to work. Although no survey

data have been compiled to date, local transit officials believe the ridership rates of those working in office buildings along the structural axes are substantially higher, perhaps accounting for as many as half of all work trips made to these corridors. It is partly for this reason that Curitiba planners have sought to attract more office development along the structural axes in recent years by establishing a density differential (i.e., permissible plot ratios of 5 for mixed-office uses versus 4 for mixed-residential uses). Curitiba officials believe that the transitway attracts higher shares of nonwork bus trips among those living in the structural axes, such as trips to downtown shops and cultural events. It is hoped that by expanding capacity along the transitway (e.g., using bi-articulated buses) and restraining parking downtown, that the transit modal splits of those residing within the structural axes will increase with time.

16. Outside downtown Curitiba, on-street parking is generally prohibited on all but local streets. Within structural axes, the city imposed no parking requirements until the early 1980s. Developers could build thirty-story skyscrapers with no parking. In practice, off-street parking was supplied, though at far lower levels than found elsewhere in the city. Since higher-income households owned most of the condominiums that lined the transitway, parking demands quickly outstripped supplies, and parked cars began spilling over into surrounding neighborhoods. In the early 1980s, the city imposed the same parking standards as elsewhere in the city. For residences, this meant at least one parking space per dwelling unit. Even retail shops within the structural axes today face the same parking standards as retail plazas on the periphery of the city. In fact, retail parking demands in outlying areas tend to be less than along transitways since poor households without cars generally reside on the outskirts and shop nearby. Curitiba planners struggle with the paradox that, outside downtown, the highest parking demands per unit of land area are in the high-density, transitway corridors. Incomes rather than urban densities are clearly the stronger determinant of parking demand in Curitiba.

17. In addition, there are 84 conventional (yellow) bus routes that do not feed into transfer stations. Most conventional bus routes predate Curitiba's initiation of integrated services and operate between suburban neighborhoods and the central core. There are also specialized services—including bus runs for disabled children, downtown (white bus) circulators, neighborhood (white bus) circulators, and late-night routes—that are not integrated (i.e., in the sense that they do not tie into transfer stations).

18. Bi-articulated buses run only along the southeast corridor to the Boqueirão station and the north-south axes between the Santa Cândida and Pinheirinho stations.

19. Vehicle design has been an important factor in increasing the throughput of bus services. In the early 1970s, municipal engineers designed a prototype vehicle with lower floors and wider doors than usual that could handle heavy loads and provide the comfort of a touring bus. In 1974, Curitiba began replacing old-style buses (mounted on truck chassis), the kinds of buses still used in most Brazilian cities, with modern buses featuring lowered platforms, greater power, wider doors, and a suspension designed for

transporting people versus hauling goods. These designs expedite passenger boarding and alighting, thus reducing dwell times, in addition to providing a smooth, more comfortable ride.

20. Tube stations allow the loading of up to eight passengers per second. At conventional stops, buses with stairs and on-board fare collection can handle two passengers per second, at most.

21. In addition, by equipping each boarding tube with a hydraulic wheelchair lift and providing same-level boarding and alighting, specialized lifts (e.g., kneeling floors) are not necessary on buses. This saves money, reduces mechanical weight, and shortens dwell times (since the lifting of disabled passengers has occurred prior to the arrival of buses).

22. Taniguchi, *op. cit.*

23. To handle walk-on traffic, each platform has a turnstile and a fare collector. Also, at road entrances to the transfer stations are kiosks manned by guards. In all, four full-time station attendants oversee station operations—two fare collectors and two guards.

24. For a US$450,000 bi-articulated bus, a company will receive US$4,500 each month over a ten-year, or 120-month, service life. This totals a US$540,000 profit over this ten-year period, not adjusting for inflation.

25. J. Rabinovitch and J. Hoehn, *A Sustainable Urban Transportation System: The "Surface Metro" System in Curitiba, Brazil*, Working Paper No. 19 (New York: Environmental and Natural Resources Policy and Planning Project, 1995); M. Major, Brazil's Busways: A "Subway" That Runs Above the Ground, *Mass Transit*, vol. 23, no. 3, 1997, pp. 26–34.

26. These estimates assume that 20 percent of ITN's ridership would have otherwise traveled by private automobile, with an average vehicle occupancy level of two, an average trip length of 7.5 kilometers, and an average fuel consumption of 1 liter per 7.5 kilometers. Source: Rabinovitch and Hoehn, op cit., 1995.

27. Rabinovitch, op cit., 1992; Major, *op. cit.*

PART FOUR

Strong-Core Cities: Transit and Central City Revitalization

An offshoot of hybrid metropolises are places that have effectively tied rail transit improvements to central city revitalization. The two cases presented in Part Four—Zurich and Melbourne—have become strong-core cities by virtue of having invested in radial rail systems and retained their traditional, richly embroidered tram networks. Both cities have adaptive transit services—trams that circulate efficiently throughout urbanized districts. They also have the character of adaptive cities—compact, mixed-use built forms conducive to transit riding—but unlike such adaptive cities as Stockholm and Tokyo, their transit-supportive environments are confined mainly to the central city.

In both Zurich and Melbourne, trams have been particularly valuable in maintaining a human-scale city, safely co-habitating downtown streets with pedestrians and cyclists while also adding character and charm to life on the street. In both Zurich and Melbourne, trams, and trams alone, are allowed into several otherwise pedestrian-only zones. Both cities' primacies—the high shares of regional jobs and retail sales in their respective cores—and healthy levels of transit usage testify to the value of linking the renewal of both central city districts and traditional tram services. In Zurich's case, various traffic engineering and design solutions have been introduced that give trams and buses priority treatment along most city streets. The combination of minimum-delay surface-street transit connections and fast suburban railway services has won over most Zurich residents to mass transit, producing one of the highest per capita rider-

ship levels anywhere. Melbourne has relied more on redevelopment planning and a gentrification movement to provide the customer base to sustain intensive core-area transit services. Melbourne's renowned green-
and-gold trams, the very icon of the city, have in turn spurred
reinvestment along tram-served commercial streets.

Chapter 11

Creating First-Class Transit with Transit-First Policies: Zurich, Switzerland

Zurich has pioneered one of the most efficient surface transportation systems in Europe by expropriating a significant share of road space for trams, buses, and bicycles, supplemented by numerous incentives to use these modes. The city responded to worsening traffic congestion not by expanding capacity but rather by redistributing road space to public transit. This was followed by the introduction of an imaginative traffic management program based on modern information technology and dynamic traffic signalization approaches. The additions of a regional transit authority and various fare incentives have further strengthened public transit's market position in recent years. Generous provisions for pedestrians and cyclists have produced a cityscape where green modes of travel are often more convenient and economical than car motoring.

Zurich, Switzerland, boasts one of the highest rates of transit usage anywhere today—about 560 transit trips per resident per year. This is almost twice as many transit trips per capita as in Europe's largest cities—London, Paris, and Berlin—made all the more remarkable in that Zurich is one of Europe's wealthiest cities and, unlike these places, has no downtown metro circulator. Zurich's success lies largely in the execution of numerous carefully conceived measures—from efficient management of road space to neighborhood traffic calming to deeply discounted fares that reward customer loyalty—that together give clear priority and preference to trams, buses, bicyclists, and pedestrians.

Transit and the City

The city of Zurich, with more than a third of a million inhabitants, lies in a conurbation of some 1.2 million residents and 171 communities within the canton of Zurich, situated in north-central Switzerland. In this compact city of only 92 square kilometers, electric trams have become the mainstay of the public transit network. Comprising 117 kilometers of the city's 265-kilometer transit network, trams account for two-thirds of vehicle kilometers and a similar share of passenger kilometers. Trolley and diesel buses make up the city's remaining transit services, filling in gaps as necessary. Overseeing and operating the city's tram and bus network (in addition to a hillside funicular) is a quasi-independent municipal corporation, the Verkehrsbetriebe Zürich (VBZ).

Zurich's population has fallen in recent decades, owing to both suburbanization and declining average household sizes. Yet because Zurich is a major international financial center, office and commercial employment has continued to grow at a healthy pace. Since 1970, the city's inventory of office space has more than doubled. Consequently, the amount of external commuting from the suburbs to the city has grown markedly: in 1970, 34.2 percent of Zurich's workers arrived each workday from outside the city; by 1990, this share was up to 47.6 percent. In 1990, in response to increased external commuting, the canton opened a regional train service, the S-Train, that connects the outreaches of the region to the city. In addition, a regional transit authority similar to Munich's, the Züricher Verkehrsverbund (ZVV), was formed at the same time to plan and coordinate all public and private transit services within the region.

The combination of central city tram and regional rail services, both supplemented by trolley buses and motor coaches, has produced an incredibly rich and dynamic set of transit service offerings. Felix Laube, a transit planner from Zurich, has characterized the physical configuration of transit services in his home town as an integrated network of three components: (1) a primary net, a radially oriented line-haul system (S-Train) that connects the central city with major urban centers and outlying municipalities, forming the backbone of the network; overlaid by (2) a secondary net, a timed-transfer network, in which line-haul buses and intercity rail connect to major stations on pulse schedules, producing short-wait transfers; supplemented in the core by (3) a fine-grained grid of mainly tram lines that circulate within dense, built-up areas, providing nearly ubiquitous access and short-haul services within the city (Figure 11.1). This combination represents adaptive transit in the truest sense— an integrated configuration of networks and services that mesh with the cityscape and mimic its origin-destination patterns.

The city of Zurich's transit network, run by the VBZ, is today so dense and services are so frequent that one never has to walk more than a hun-

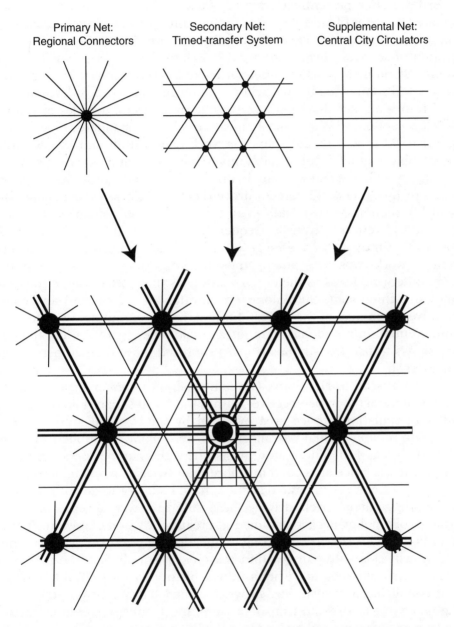

Primary Net:
Regional Connectors

Secondary Net:
Timed-transfer System

Supplemental Net:
Central City Circulators

FIGURE 11.1. REGIONAL CONFIGURATION OF PUBLIC TRANSIT SERVICES IN GREATER ZURICH: INTEGRATING THREE LEVELS OF NETWORKS. *Source:* Adapted from F. Laube, *Fully Integrated Transport Networks: An International Perspective on Applied Solutions* (Perth: Murdoch University, Institute for Science and Technology Policy, 1995).

dred meters or wait more than five minutes to catch a ride. On a typical weekday, Zurich presently averages 2,400 kilometers of transit service per square kilometer of land area. By comparison, Essen, Germany, a similar-size city, averages 600. Transit's ubiquity, combined with the careful integration of services, means one need not think too much about its availability. Standing at a major street corner, one can rest assured that a tram or bus will soon come by that will promptly get one to one's destination.

From a market share perspective, the past several decades of transit development have been a smashing success by any standard. Figure 11.2 shows 1992 transit modal splits for work trips within and across three geographic markets: Zurich city, inner-ring areas, and outer-ring areas. Among those living and working in Zurich, 76 percent got to their jobs on trams or buses. Only 12 percent drove their cars. These modal splits also held for shopping trips. Additionally, more than 40 percent of reverse-commutes were via transit, frequently aboard S-Trains. Figure 11.2 reveals that transit's second-biggest market share, capturing some 55 percent of work trips, was among those making long-distance commutes from outer-ring areas to the city. This reflects the extensiveness (thirteen lines stretching some 900 kilometers throughout the canton) and comparative advantages of the S-Train for long-haul commuting. Even for circumferential, intraregional commutes outside the city of Zurich, the figure shows transit (mostly bus transit) captured more than 20 percent of the market.

Comparisons to Hamburg, Germany, help put greater Zurich's ridership achievements in perspective. Within the 1,730-square-kilometer, 1.2-million-population service area overseen by the regional authority, the ZVV, 644 million annual passenger trips were made by public transit in 1993. This was 170 million more transit trips than in metropolitan Hamburg, whose service area contains more than twice as many inhabitants.

While extensive, integrated services have had a lot to do with transit's success in greater Zurich, driving these initiatives were a series of deliberate public policy decisions aimed at creating a world-class transit system. Figure 11.3 suggests a strong connection between key policy events and transit ridership gains within the city of Zurich over the past two decades. A watershed in Zurich's transit history was a 1973 referendum that established a "transit first" program aimed at dramatically enhancing the quality of traditional transit services, most notably speeding up the movements of trams and buses. Once the full program was in place a good decade later, patronage began to rise markedly. More recent ridership gains can be attributed to improved service and fare coordination (through the ZVV), deeply discounted fare offerings, and a continuation of auto-restraint measures. Today, Zurichers enjoy extensive, frequent, comfortable, and relatively cheap transit services that are envied the world over.

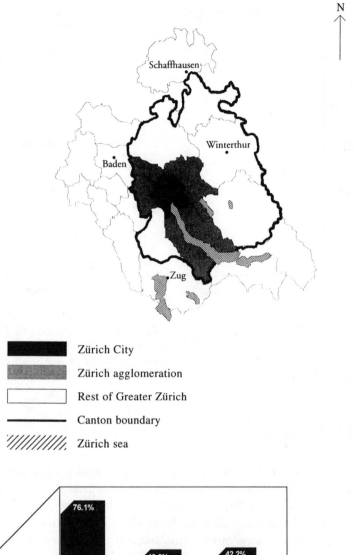

Zürich City

Zürich agglomeration

Rest of Greater Zürich

Canton boundary

Zürich sea

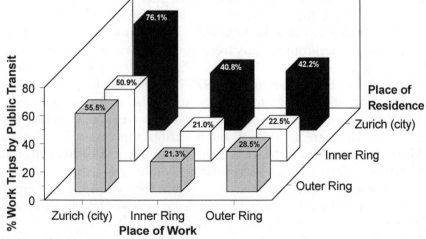

FIGURE 11.2. TRANSIT WORK TRIP MODAL SPLITS IN METROPOLITAN ZURICH, BY GEOGRAPHIC SUBMARKETS, 1992. *Source:* Stadtplanungsamt Zürich, *Siedlungsentwicklung und Pendlerverkehr* (Zurich: Stadtplanungsamt Zürich, informiert 18, 1994).

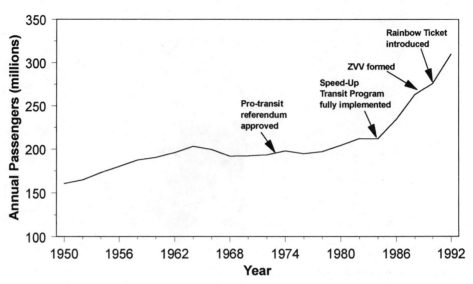

FIGURE 11.3. TRAM AND BUS TRANSIT RIDERSHIP TRENDS IN THE CITY OF ZURICH AND
SIGNIFICANT POLICY EVENTS, 1950–1992. *Sources of ridership figures:* Verkehrsbetreibe
Zürich, data files; Stadt Zürich, *Statistisches Jahrbuch der Stadt Zürich* (Zurich:
Stadt Zürich, 1993).

Zurich's Transit-First Policy

In 1973, Zurich found itself at a crossroads. Traffic congestion was mounting and air pollution was worsening. Consequently, the quality of inner-
city living was suffering. Something needed to be done, and quickly. To
some, the solution was simple: follow the lead of many German cities by
putting trains underground, thus freeing up surface streets for cars and
trucks. When an initiative to build an urban metro, or U-Bahn, was put
before the voters in the summer of 1973 (see the accompanying box), it
had been resoundingly defeated, just as it had been eleven years earlier.
Instead, Zurichers passed a measure that would give priority to trams and
buses on existing streets and, through various operational techniques,
would ensure that mass transit vehicles moved smoothly, with minimal
delays and interference from car traffic.

This was seen as a clear mandate to retain the qualities and character
of the core city by favoring more human-scale forms of transit—trams and
trolley buses—that mesh with the fabric of the city.

Part of the explanation for transit's ascendancy in an affluent city like
Zurich lies in Switzerland's unique form of local democracy. In Zurich, citizens make policies, not politicians. By law, any public investment of more
than $10 million Swiss francs (US$7 million in 1998) has to be approved
through a referendum. Over maybe ten weekends of the year, citizens vote

PUBLIC CAMPAIGN OF 18 JUNE 1973 FOR THE PROMOTION OF PUBLIC TRANSIT

At the expense of the investment fund, a credit of 200 million francs will be approved to permit, in the course of the ten years following the referendum, at a rate of 15 to at most 25 million francs per year, the financing of structural additions and improvements to the network of the transport company of the City of Zurich, which will serve exclusively and substantially to eliminate all interference by private traffic and internal problems within the companies, so that the vehicles of the VBZ (Zurich transit corporation) can travel along their lanes or tracks virtually as fast is technically possible. . . . Such directives cover the provision of separate tram and bus lanes, the construction and conversion of traffic light operating systems remotely controlled by public transit, and the conversion of the important traffic intersections entirely to meet the requirements of the VBZ and pedestrians.

The municipal parliament advises the voters to reject the proposal.

on anywhere between one and ten referenda pertaining to local, canton, or federation policies. Local democratization has buffered Zurich from the usual pork-barrel politics. In the case of the urban metro proposal, this meant the decision to go forward with improved tram and bus services was less encumbered by pressures from road lobbyists and subway builders to do otherwise.

With each referendum comes public dialogue. The level of knowledge about and involvement in public affairs among Zurich's citizenry is extraordinarily high. The transit-first policy approved in 1973 was very much a grassroots initiative. With support from both the left and right, citizens joined ranks in collecting enough signatures to get the referendum on the ballot. "Why not modernize and improve what has been in place for a century?" residents were asked when signatures were solicited for the ballot initiative. Upgrading existing services proved to be a policy with broad ideological and political appeal, one that all sides could embrace. Liberals and environmentalists feared that an urban metro, with long station spacing, would destroy Zurich's unique urban fabric by expanding the city's scale. On the other hand, trams, which have been around for more than a century, helped to create the pedestrian-friendly city that Zurichers have long cherished. (Switzerland's past has also played a part; without a ruling monarchy in its history, Swiss cities have avoided the imperial designs and enlarged streetscapes found in such places as Paris and Vienna. Swiss cities also escaped the widespread physical damage suffered by German cities during the war.) To conservatives, expanding tram services in lieu of building a pricey new metro meant taxes could be held in check. Without any federal financial support for transit, as is common in Germany and other parts of Europe, Swiss voters have become especially sensitive to the cost implications of new capital investments for transit. Thus, the pro-tram/anti-metro stance made for strange yet effective bedfellows.

One cannot overlook the fact that the ability to forge a popular consensus on transit policies was abetted, to a significant degree, by Zurich being a fairly socially and culturally homogeneous city. The pro-transit leanings of its citizenry were underscored in a recent survey by German scholars that showed a substantially higher share of "anti-car types" (47 percent of those polled) in Zurich than in comparable-size German cities.[1] It is equally noteworthy that a clear, unified vision of the kind of city people wanted was the driving force behind the decision to go with expanded tram and trolley bus services. Some criticize Zurich's referendum approach to policy making on the grounds that it thwarts strategic long-range planning since each large-scale project has to be voted upon independently. Others see it as the only way to ensure fair and carefully reasoned policy making. Ernst Joos, deputy director of the VBZ, contends that the referendum process has been absolutely essential in neutralizing the patriarchy of transit decision making, noting that Zurich's elected officials are generally men between thirty and sixty years of age who, compared to the average citizen, drive their cars the most and patronize transit the least.[2]

Solidifying the move to embrace transit fully were several decrees passed by the Swiss Confederation in the late 1980s that set stringent air pollution limits for the two main smog precursors: nitrogen oxides and hydrocarbons. Studies showed that car traffic was responsible for two-thirds of nitrogen oxide and one-quarter of hydrocarbon emissions in the city.[3] Along several busy streets, pollution levels were two to three times above standards. In response, Zurich's city council adopted an air quality strategy that further committed the city to public transit as an environmentally friendly and preferred means of motorized travel.

Speed-up Transit Program

A major reason for proposing massive underground metro systems in the 1960s and 1970s was that surface-street transit services were deteriorating rapidly. Trams and buses were competing for road space against more and more private cars, bringing speeds to a crawl during rush hours. Disabled vehicles, cars forced onto tram tracks by parking maneuvers, and left-turning traffic meant trams and buses were constantly stopping and going.

In response to the earlier voter mandate to substantially upgrade sur-face-street transit within a decade, Zurich's city council issued a directive in 1979 aimed at speeding up green modes of transportation—trams, buses, and bicycles. The directive specified three objectives: (1) build sep-arate bus lanes and more dedicated tracks so as to transform trams into more of a modern LRT type of service; (2) give priority to transit vehicles at intersections, regulated by traffic signals that are directly actuated by trams and buses by means of a dynamic traffic control system; and (3) install information technologies that identify vehicle location and devia-tions from scheduled timetables, allowing for corrective actions.

A corollary to these directives was the understanding that promoting "ecological transport," in and of itself, was not enough. The odds still would be stacked in favor of car travel; trams and buses, for example, could never match the door-to-door service qualities of the private auto-mobile. Thus, complementary auto-restraint initiatives were also intro-duced, including traffic calming in residential neighborhoods and parking management. Most important was the decision to maintain citywide road-way capacity at a constant level. When a northern bypass and new tunnel passage were built in the mid-1980s, the city reduced the capacity of exist-ing roads to keep overall system capacity more or less constant. By remov-ing through lanes, shortening green signal phases, and restraining traffic flows through channelization, overall regional traffic throughput remained about the same. A later referendum to build an underground thoroughfare was rejected by 70 percent of voters; exit polls revealed many felt they would have to give up too much (of existing road space) in return for speedier below-surface motoring.

Repartitioning Road Space

Much of Zurich's success with transit is found in the details of system design. Roads have been partitioned and facilities microdesigned to give clear priority and preference to transit vehicles and customers. The idea is to reward efficiency: Zurich's planners estimate a single tram line han-dles the same throughput, 8,000 persons per hour, as ten lanes of car traf-fic; in addition, trams and buses do not require inner-city parking.

Today, Zurich's trams and buses occupy as much space as automobile travelways. Dozens of bus stops have been painted yellow within curbside traffic lanes, requiring cars to stop (Photo 11.1). Some forty raised islands have been installed at tram and bus stops. Dedicated bicycle lanes and fre-quent pedestrian crosswalks have further shrunk available right-of-way to cars (Photo 11.2). To allow trams and buses to overtake slow-moving and queued cars and avoid having to stop behind left-turning cars, other measures have been introduced, including: prohibition of parking and stopping along seventeen road sections; forty-one bans on left turns;

PHOTO 11.1. CARS LINED UP AT A BUS STOP. In adjusting traffic signals, buses and trams are treated as if they move alone along a street. They thus tend to operate at the front of a pack. With only a single passage lane, cars often have to stop behind buses and trams.

installation of seventy-two "give way" to trams and buses signs at key intersections; outright banning of cars in certain zones; and the opening of 21 kilometers of dedicated bus lanes (out of a city bus network of 90 kilometers).

Dynamic Traffic Signalization

An equally important part of Zurich's program to speed up trams and buses has been the implementation of a highly sophisticated traffic signalization system. There is not a system like it anywhere. In Zurich, traffic signals are continuously adjusted to create a "green wave," allowing transit vehicles to pass through intersections in succession and unobstructed. This "zero waiting time" policy recognizes that trams and buses do not require traffic signals to remain green for very long, but rather only for a few seconds when they approach an intersection.

The system works as follows. More than 3,000 induction loop sensors have been implanted throughout the city's road system. Sensors can detect the location of trams and buses, all equipped with individual signal transmitters, within an accuracy of 10 meters. When a tram or bus approaches a signalized intersection, it activates a short green signal phase that allows for continuous movement. For car motorists, signal preemption results in frequent stopping (Photo 11.3). Complementing this prioritiza-

PHOTO 11.2. PRIORITIES FOR CYCLISTS. The top photo shows curb lanes reserved for cyclists. These lanes, called "veloroutes" locally, now total more than 300 kilometers of the city's 800-kilometer road network. The bottom photos show a separate traffic signal phase for cyclists, forcing all motorized traffic to a standstill while the cyclist crosses a busy intersection.

tion scheme is a dynamic signal switching-system that affects the rate at which cars and trucks are discharged from one part of the city to another. The system functions like a citywide ramp-metering program. Zurich traffic engineers have divided the city into sectors, each consisting of three to twelve sets of traffic signals (Figure 11.4). Through real-time monitoring, traffic signals in each sector are adjusted to keep traffic volumes and queues evenly spread throughout the city. If a sector near the core is congested in the morning, green time in outlying sectors will be shortened to reduce the discharge rate of inflowing traffic. In all, more than 400 traffic signals placed throughout the city are interlinked through a centrally controlled computer system that directs flows toward underutilized signal groups and restricts flows to saturated ones. Since the full introduction of the system in 1985, waiting times for trams and buses at signalized intersections during the evening rush hour have fallen, on average, by 38 percent.[4] Moreover, average tram speeds during peak and off-peak hours are today virtually equivalent (Figure 11.5).

PHOTO 11.3. SIGNAL PRIORITIZATION FOR TRAMS. Approaching trams trip a switch that forces all other traffic to yield the right-of-way, not unlike how a freight train halts surface traffic in many cities.

Automated vehicle location technologies have also allowed for improved schedule adherence. Central computers continuously compare actual versus scheduled positions of trams and buses, relaying information to traffic managers, drivers, and waiting customers. By adjusting speeds and layovers, drivers are able to stay pretty much on schedule.

It is noteworthy that Zurich's dynamic traffic control and vehicle location system was designed not by traffic engineers but rather electrical engineers schooled in operations research. Their task was to invent ways of restricting rather than optimizing car traffic flows. A single agency within the city, staffed with six full-time programmers, runs the central system of sixteen data-processing computers and twin servers. The overall system requires five times more hardware and software than traffic signal systems installed in similar-size European cities.[5]

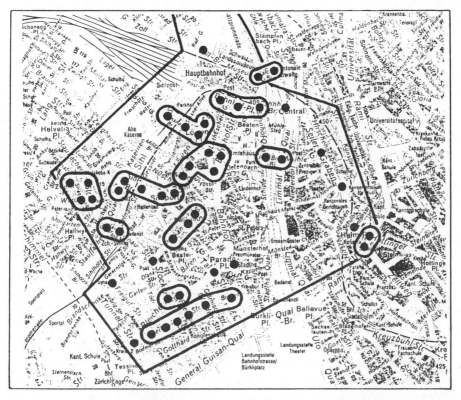

FIGURE 11.4. CELLS OF INTERCONNECTED TRAFFIC SIGNALS IN THE CENTRAL CITY SECTOR OF ZURICH. Cellular units are dynamically coordinated to control ambient traffic flows so as to optimize the movement of trams and buses while also spreading traffic congestion more uniformly throughout the city. *Source:* E. Joos, *Three Messages from Zurich Concerning the New Transport Policy: Economy and Ecology Are No Contradictions* (Zurich: Verkehrsbetriebe Zürich, 1994).

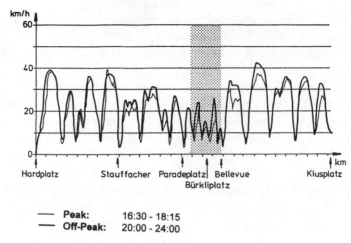

FIGURE 11.5. COMPARISON OF AVERAGE SPEEDS ALONG TRAM LINE 8 DURING PEAK AND OFF-PEAK EVENING HOURS. For the 5.6-kilometer distance from Hardplatz to Klusplatz, tram line 8 maintains similar speeds during the peak as during the late-night hours, even in the densest stretch with frequent stopping, between Paradeplatz and Bellevue. *Source:* Verkehrsbetriebe Zürich, *Beschleunigungsprogramm 2000* (Zurich: Verkehrsbetriebe Zürich, 1991).

Restraints on Automobiles

Complementing "transit incentives" have been a host of "automobile disincentives." In the past decade, Zurich has embraced traffic calming with a passion. Today, most residential streets are dotted with raised berms, intersection chockers and neck-downs, zebra stripes, and other devices that slow down moving traffic. Diverters and channelization further deflect traffic out of neighborhoods. Collectively, traffic restraint measures have reduced vehicle kilometers logged within some neighborhoods by as much as 25 percent.[6]

Limits on parking have also constrained automobility in the city. On-street parking is fairly scarce and off-street parking can be prohibitively expensive.[7] The city's supply of curbside parking has fallen from 61,200 spaces in 1970 to under 50,000 today. The overall supply of commercial off-street spaces has been halved. Most center city parking is reserved, with a license number assigned to each stall. Parking violators are promptly towed. To park along the street of a residential neighborhood requires a special permit. The prospect of building future parking garages is pretty slim. Any proposal to construct a new municipal parking facility must first be approved through a voter referendum. New, private, multistory parking has been effectively banned through zoning restrictions.

Zurich planners have also "incentivized" transit-oriented development by relaxing parking requirements near rail stops. The better the access to public transit, the less the amount of parking required. For new apartments near a tram or S-Train station, for example, minimum parking is only 30 to 40 percent of the normal requirement.

Regional Service and Fare Incentives

With the transit priority schemes largely in place, transit customers in Zurich and surrounding communities were rewarded in the early 1990s with a series of service and fare incentives that made transit riding all the more attractive. Tram and trolley bus services operated by Zurich's transit corporation (the VBZ) increased 10 percent between 1990 and 1993 (from 9.9 to 10.9 billion seat kilometers). Outside Zurich, service offerings have grown even faster, thanks to a cantonal regulation requiring a bus or tram stop within 400 meters of all households of settlements with 300 or more inhabitants.[8] Through the introduction of various deeply discounted multiride pass programs, the real price of average fares in the region fell by nearly 50 percent from 1985 to 1990. Orchestrating these improvements was a newly formed regional transit coordinating body, the ZVV, charged with planning new services and integrating schedules and fares throughout the canton.

The creation of a single, integrated fare—pegged to the distance traveled within a forty-five-zone system—has been a boon to transit ridership, especially for trips requiring a transfer. Between 1990 (when the single-fare system was introduced) and 1992, ridership on feeder buses within the region rose by 53 percent. Also important was the introduction of a new environmental ticket program, Regenbogenkarte (rainbow ticket), that allows multiple rides at under half the cost per ride of a regular single-trip fare. Another innovation, the Combi-ticket, includes transit fares (usually all-day or multiday passes) in the entrance fees for concerts, sports events, conventions, and festivals. For some events, transit operators are actually co-sponsors. Several central city hotels now even include transit tickets in their room prices. Also offered are heavily discounted youth fares (valid for people up to twenty-five instead of the usual sixteen years of age), which, according to Felix Laube, aim "to get young people in the habit of buying periodical fares before they consider buying a car."[9] Collectively, these programs have had a huge impact on fare payment habits. More than half of transit customers within the region today use some kind of multiride monthly or annual ticket.[10]

Another important feature of greater Zurich's fare system is that it operates entirely on a self-service basis. Fares are collected and tickets issued at more than 800 automated ticket machines spread throughout the region instead of aboard trains, buses, and trams. This has significantly reduced average dwell times (by expediting passenger boardings), which in turn has contributed to more punctual services.

Zurich's Verkehrsverbund

As in Munich, a regional transit federation, or Verkehrsverbund, has been absolutely indispensable in coordinating tariffs and services in recent times. The Züricher Verkehrsverbund (ZVV) was created in 1990 by the canton of Zurich specifically to plan and coordinate schedules and networks, set and integrate fares, market services, provide capital assistance, and administer operating grants for more than 270 transit lines within a 2,300-square-kilometer service area. The ZVV presently oversees and coordinates the transit service offerings of forty-three independent transit companies and agencies: two federal operators (SBB and PTT), two private intercantonal railroads, two municipal transit authorities (Zurich and Winterthur), two older intracantonal railroads, twenty-nine public and private bus companies, and six specialized operators (of ferries, funiculars, and gondolas).

The organization's overall philosophy is to produce transit services as efficiently as possible while meeting minimum service standards set by a nine-member Transport Council. This has given rise to a highly competitive transportation marketplace. The Transport Council sets a maximum budget deemed sufficient to meet a minimum set of service standards over a six-year period. The ZVV must then design services and set fares with the resources available. Through a competitive bid process, the ZVV enters into agreements with concessionaires to serve specific areas for two-year contract periods. The ZVV sets schedule timetables and route connectivity requirements within defined areas, collects revenues, and pays operators based on a mutually agreed upon reimbursement system indexed to the amount of service rendered and performance criteria. The ZVV views itself as having a watchdog role, encouraging and at times pestering operators to restrain costs where possible. In recent years, the agency has introduced a cost-control program, called *Zuri-Schalankline* (loosely translated as "ZVV on a diet"), that judiciously redeploys services to the more productive districts of the region within the constraint of meeting minimum service standards.

The Payoff

The payoff from the last several decades of transit-friendly policies is seen in Zurich's incredibly high market shares and rates of transit usage—presently about 62 percent of all motorized trips made by residents of Zurich city are aboard trams, trains, and buses. The city continues to boast one of the highest per capita ridership levels anywhere. The flip side of high transit usage has been below-average automobile ownership. Despite being one of the world's wealthiest cities, Zurich has only about

380 registered cars per 1,000 inhabitants, considerably below the average of German, Swiss, or Austrian cities of comparable size. Roughly a third of Zurich households own no cars at all. Car-sharing has gained tremendous popularity in recent times—currently, more than 9,000 residents of greater Zurich participate in a nationwide car co-op that gives them access, on an as-needed basis, to more than 800 automobiles spread across some 500 locations throughout Switzerland.

The city has also been able to add jobs without increasing car traffic, as was hoped. From 1989 to 1992, S-Train services were introduced, and the city was a good decade into the "transit first" program. Over this three-year period, the number of daily motorized trips to the city center increased by 50,000, rising above 1.35 million. However, the number of car trips remained unchanged.[11] Thus, the entire growth in traffic was absorbed by trams, trains, and buses.

Improved rail access has also stimulated development along transit corridors, notably S-Train lines. While the outer portions of the S-Train network operate like commuter railways, within the city, the S-Train functions more like an advanced light rail system. Zurich has twenty-four tightly packed S-Train stations, compared to Munich, which is more than three times as large in area and counts forty S-Bahn stations. The mix of closely spaced central city stops and widely spaced suburban stops has made parcels near S-Train stops attractive development sites. The mixed-use project Tiergarten—which contains a car-free urban center and underground parking on the edges—along S-Train line 10 is a good example (Photo 11.4).

The harmonious relationship between public transit and the city has clearly had a bearing on real estate prices. Partly because the interior of the city is so accessible and well served by transit, and the milieu for walking, strolling, and sightseeing is so pleasant, land values in the central city are staggeringly high. The price of land along Bahnhofstrasse, Zurich's main commercial avenue, is purportedly among the highest in the world—selling for about 250,000 Swiss francs (US $170,000) per square meter. From 1988 to 1990, prior to and just after S-Train services opened, office rents rose sharply for sites within two blocks of central city rail stations.[12] Of course, the relationship between land prices and transit provisions is circular. High land prices have deterred parking and roadway expansion, which in turn have further strengthened the hand of public transit and promoted a more pedestrian-friendly downtown.

Learning from Zurich

Zurich shows the prominent mobility role that public transit can play when first-rate services are offered. Thanks to the city's unwavering com-

Photo 11.4. Tiergarten mixed-use project. A few kilometers southwest of the central city on the number 10 S-Train line to Uetliberg, Tiergarten (shown in the middle of the top photo) was built on an old quarry site. It boasts a variety of housing, from five-story apartments to low-rise flats (lower photo). Mid-rise offices and a retail complex occupy the project's car-free center. Tiergarten is also an ecological project: on-site management of stormwater is used aesthetically as a design element; restoration of creeks disrupted by sewer pipes improved water runoff and enhanced soil percolation; and the restoration of local vegetation has helped colonize native flora and fauna.

mitment to upgrading traditional transit services and keeping fares low, it is generally much faster, more convenient, and far cheaper getting around by trams, trains, and buses than by private automobile.

Zurich also shows what is possible, even in medium-size cities, when transit-first policies are aggressively pursued. Reassigning road space to high-occupancy transit vehicles has been a cornerstone of the city's transportation policy. Complementing this have been advanced technologies that not only give preference to trams and buses at signalized intersections, but also provide a continuous flow of information to drivers, control centers, and customers about schedule adherence. And in Zurich, transit improvements have been matched by constraints on auto-motoring. Driving in Zurich often means stopping at most intersections, waiting behind buses, stopping for trams, detouring around established neighborhoods, and paying appreciable amounts to park in a commercial district.

While culture, history, geography, and happenstance have had a hand in creating the world-class transit services that Zurichers now enjoy, for the most part this outcome is the consequence of deliberate and calculated public policy choices. Moreover, Zurich's successes are not really the product of a few grand-scale projects or quick fixes. Rather, they are the cumulative sum of numerous carefully reasoned policy decisions, each guided by a common goal—to put transit first in an all-out campaign to create a livable, enjoyable, and sustainable city and metropolis.

NOTES

1. See: R. Ott, Conurbation Transport Policy in Zurich, Switzerland, *Proceedings of the Institution of Civil Engineers in Transportation*, vol. 111, 1995, pp. 225–233.

2. E. Joos, *Three Messages from Zürich Concerning the New Transport Policy: Economy and Ecology Are No Contradictions* (Zurich: Verkehrsbetriebe Zürich, 1994).

3. Kanton Zürich, *Luftprogramm für den Kanton Zürich* (Zurich: Kanton Zürich, Massnahmenplan Lufthygiene, 1990); T. Pharoah and D. Apel, *Transport Concepts in European Cities* (Aldershot, England: Avebury, 1995).

4. F. FitzRoy and I. Smith, Priority over Pricing: Lessons from Zürich on the Redundancy of Road Pricing, *Journal of Transport Economics and Policy*, vol. 27, no. 2, 1993, pp. 209–214.

5. Stadt Zürich, *Verkehrspolitik der Stadt Zürich* (Zurich: Stadt Zürich, 1994); Stadtplanungsamt Zürich, *Case Study of Zurich for OECD* (Zurich: Stadtplanungsamt Zürich, 1992).

6. Ott, *op. cit.*

7. In the core, on-street parking starts at about US$1 per hour and is generally limited to one to two hours. Off-street parking is far more expensive, with hourly rates increasing with the duration of parking.

8. The Canton Public Transport Act of 1988 set a minimum service standard for the region: for settlements with at least 300 inhabitants or workers, a bus or tram stop has to lie within a catchment of 400 meters of all households, or a train stop within a distance of 750 meters, with at least one transit vehicle coming by each hour during normal operating periods.

9. F. Laube, *Fully Integrated Transport Networks: An International Perspective on Applied Solutions* (Perth: Murdoch University, Institute for Science and Technology Policy, 1995), p. 10.

10. Two-thirds of all revenues collected by the ZVV come from deeply discounted passes and multiride tickets. The resulting drop in revenues has reduced overall cost recovery rates from 78 percent in 1985 to 42 percent in 1993. To regional policy makers, the benefits of additional patronage (from 479 million annual trips in 1985 to 644 million in 1993 within the ZVV service area) has more than justified the increased subsidy outlays. Source: J. Pucher and S. Kurth, Verkehrsverbund: The Success of Regional Public Transport in Germany, Austria and Switzerland, *Transport Policy*, vol. 2, no. 4, 1996, pp. 279–291.

11. Stadtplanungsamt Zürich, *S-Bahn-Eröffnung und Verkehrsaufkommen* (Zurich: Stadtplanungsamt Zürich, 1993).

12. Pharoah and Apel, *op. cit.*, 1995.

Chapter 12

Trams, Trains, and Central City Revitalization: Melbourne, Australia

Melbourne has experienced rapid rates of auto-fed decentralization in recent decades, as have all Australian metropolises. Yet the core area has not been gutted of urban vitality and, in fact, is currently staging a comeback. A principal reason is that city leaders have retained and indeed enhanced the century-old tram network, an important contributor to both aesthetic quality and surface-street mobility within the central city. Along with strategic planning initiatives, trams have played a vital role in attracting new investments and dwellers back to the core area. Along many tramway streets, storefronts are being refurbished, sidewalk cafes are opening, and street life is abuzz. For residents of gentrified neighborhoods, trams are a valued means for circulating in and around the core area as well as a sensible option for short-haul commuting. A proposed beltway around the central city, however, could undo much of what the tramway and other transit improvements have accomplished. Continuing to strengthen public transit so as to match improvements in central city automobility might very well be the best response.

Melbourne is a bit of an enigma. While much of the modernizing world was dismantling streetcar lines following World War II, Australia's second-largest city opted to retain its extensive, fine-grained tram network. Indeed, civic leaders extended tram lines in the early postwar period in anticipation of the 1956 Olympic games, and to this day the city continues to upgrade streetcar services. Complementing trams is an extensive radial train system connecting the far reaches of the metropolitan area to the central city. Today, Melbourne proudly holds claim to the largest urban rail network outside Europe and Japan.

Yet as elsewhere, Melbourne's rail transit system has struggled to maintain its market shares in recent times as jobs, housing, and retailing decentralize. Unlike Stockholm or Singapore, much of Melbourne's suburban growth has turned its back on rail corridors, taking the form of auto-oriented shopping centers, business parks, and residential subdivisions. Indeed, most of Melbourne's outer suburbs are not terribly distinguishable from those of many American cities. Today, Melbourne has among the lowest suburban residential densities anywhere, outside the United States, for a metropolis its size. The region today finds itself in the throes of a heated debate over whether to plan for, and in so doing further encourage, decentralized, auto-oriented growth, or to strengthen the central city and its fine rail transit services. A proposed inner-city beltway that would allow traffic to bypass the region's core has become a lightning rod for this debate. Recent progress in revitalizing the central city and its rail services, and a commitment to preserving open spaces on the fringes, bode well for the future of central Melbourne. The story of Melbourne, then, is much the story of aggressive, preemptive efforts to revitalize the central city in the face of mounting decentralization pressures, in part by building upon its rich public transit heritage.

The City and Public Transit

Melbourne is home to some 3.2 million residents, some of the finest Victorian-era architecture anywhere, and the world-renowned, locally built, green-and-gold trams, the city's icon. Greater Melbourne actually consists of several hundred independent municipalities spread throughout a massive 1,700-square-kilometer area—50 kilometers from east to west and more than 70 kilometers from north to south—on the shores of Port Phillip Bay. The city of Melbourne itself occupies an area of 36 square kilometers in the center of the region. Thus, while technically speaking, "Melbourne" refers to a single jurisdiction of some 48,000 people, as used here, the name is customarily applied to the metropolitan area as a whole.

It was the gold boom of the 1880s that ushered in a period of spectacular growth, unprecedented prosperity, and architectural grandeur. At the time, Melbourne was reputedly the world's richest city. And it showed. The city was and continues to this day to be graced with stately civic buildings, ornate and colorful terrace houses, charming inner-city neighborhoods, bustling retail districts, magnificent tree-lined boulevards, and bountiful public parks and gardens. It is in part because of Melbourne's beautifully preserved nineteenth-century architectural heritage that it has been rated one of the world's most livable cities.[1]

It was also during the 1880s that Melbourne's first tram lines were laid.[2] As elsewhere, Melbourne's rail lines were a product not so much of enlightened city planning as a drive to reap windfall profits through land speculation. At the time, a syndicate, including some members of Victoria's parliament, bought up extensive holdings of land very cheaply on the city's fringes. With the city awash in gold-rush fortunes and a growing merchantile class seeking home ownership, the stage was set for coupling rail lines and real estate ventures. It was through these profiteering motives that Melbourne evolved over the years into a highly centralized city with a decidedly radial transportation sytem. The city and its railway system were, and many argue still are, compatible and mutually reinforcing. In 1919, the city's numerous small tramway syndicates were consolidated into the Melbourne and Metropolitan Tramway Board. Under public ownership, critics argue, Melbourne's rail network began to falter, failing to modernize and "keep up with the times," leaving the city with a largely antiquated technology, a relic of a bygone era. By one account, today's "stations are archaic, ticketing systems primitive, running speeds unchanged over 50 years, rolling stock old fashioned."[3] Others see the situation entirely differently, viewing the "old fashioned" trains and trams as an asset and a key to revitalizing the central core. To them, the suburban rail and tram network is an "invaluable resource," "enormous by world standards,"[4] and "plays an essential role supporting major initiatives aimed at making the central city more vibrant."[5]

How is it that Melbourne managed to keep its tram network intact over the years when most other cities—certainly in the developed world—were systematically dismantling theirs? Much of the credit, local historians agree, goes to one person, Major General Robert Risson. Risson was a former military officer who, old-timers will tell you, ran Melbourne's tram system like an army brigade. By sheer force of personality, and aided by a boom-box voice, he managed to intimidate his opponents and fend off efforts to curb tram services. When speaking at public gatherings and before the Tramway Board, a fiercely independent body loyal to its executive, Risson would steadfastly defend public transit, insisting that it was essential to the city's lifeblood. His tactical training in military defense, some maintain, proved the difference in Melbourne's trams avoiding the fate of aging trolley systems in other parts of the world.[6]

The Lay of the Land

Today, Melbourne is in many ways a region of two faces. The central area, including the core and the first-generation postwar suburbs, is compact and transit-oriented in its design and layout. In large part because of its railway legacy, Melbourne has retained a strong focus on the central city, even as growth spread to the outskirts. Until the late 1960s, the core and its immediate surroundings were the only major concentration of white-collar employment to speak of. Today, central Melbourne still claims a healthy share—about a third—of metropolitan jobs. By international standards, net employment densities in the core are quite high—about 65,000 workers per square kilometer, compared to per square kilometer averages of 50,000 workers in the United States and 36,000 workers in Europe for comparable-size regions.[7] Residential densities are also quite high in the many neighborhoods that ring the core, what Melburnians call the "inner suburbs" (representing the first generation of railway-led suburbanization). Inner-ring neighborhoods such as Fitzroy, Prahran, and St. Kilda average gross densities of 45 to 60 persons per hectare, similar to those found in European cities.

Beyond Melbourne's inner suburbs, densities plummet markedly. Few tram lines reach this far, and most railway stations are surrounded by park-and-ride lots instead of commercial centers. Single-family housing, open fields, and an occasional retail or industrial center dot the landscape. Except when heading to the core region, the car becomes the only practical way of traveling for many living and working in the outskirts.

While railways have unquestionably contributed to the maintenance of relatively high central city densities, equally important has been Melbourne's reluctance to build high-capacity freeway links to the core. In 1969, the Metropolitan Transportation Plan predicted that a 500-kilometer freeway network would be required by 1985 to avoid citywide gridlock. An ensuing campaign to build American-style beltways and freeways met with stiff resistance. The Committee for Urban Action mobilized against the freeway proposal, maintaining that the unique fabric of the inner city as a "high density, mixed and narrow-fronted area" had to be preserved at all costs against "the destructiveness of imposing freeway structures." The anti-freeway revolt not only protected many established inner-city neighborhoods from bulldozers and looming overpasses, but also created a ready-made market of railway and tram users. Yet as the automobile population continues to grow, Melbourne's arterials are being increasingly called upon to carry far more peak-period traffic than they were designed for. While congestion on radial links has forced many into trains and trams, this has been at a cost—pegged by one recent study at about US$400 in lost time per capita each year.[8] Such costs, whether real or perceived, are behind current efforts to build a massive inner-city bypass, called the City Link.

In many ways, Melbourne's city-suburb dichotomy is emblematic of its two dominant eras of transportation: the central region and immediate surroundings remain a testament to the powers of rail transit to concentrate and focus development, while the middle and outer suburbs are largely a product of postwar automobile-led expansion. The two have managed to co-exist, though somewhat tenuously as time moves on. Peter Newman of Murdoch University in Perth, who was raised in one of Melbourne's rail-served outer suburbs and remains one of Australia's staunchest transit advocates, cautions that "Melbourne is caught between the competing directions of car-based dispersal and transit-based concentration."[9]

Transit Today

Today, Melbourne boasts one of the ten largest rail networks in the world (Map 12.1). The suburban railway, called Met Train, extends some 4,900 route kilometers along fifteen lines, served by 206 stations. More than 100 electric trains, operating in six-car carriages, carry some 380,000 passengers on a typical weekday. The railway functions predominantly as a commuter service, ferrying suburbanites to central city jobs. All trains encircle the central business district (CBD) along a one-way underground loop that enables them to backtrack without having to reverse out of a terminal station. The loop, opened in stages from 1981 and served by five stations, has put some 85 percent of CBD workers within a five-minute walk of a station.

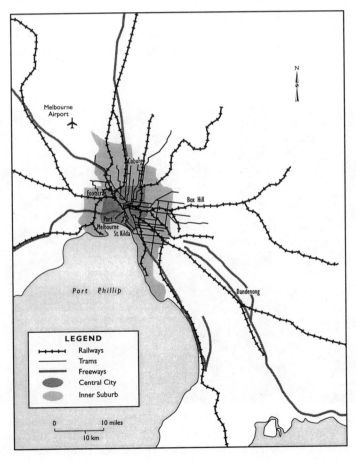

MAP 12.1. MELBOURNE METROPOLITAN AREA AND MAJOR TRANSPORTATION LINKS.

As one of the few cities outside Europe that retained and indeed expanded upon its original streetcar network, Melbourne is today blessed with a 230-kilometer tram system that functions as both a distributor, feeding into central-area train stations, and a circulator in its own right, interconnecting the core and inner-ring suburbs. Some 550 tram cars, of differing vintages, designs, and passenger capacities, carry about 370,000 customers per weekday along forty-two routes.[10] Virtually all tram routes pass through the CBD, and all major retail, tourist, and entertainment destinations in the central city are served by them. For locals, trams are cheap, fairly reliable, and often entertaining ways to travel. For many visitors, they're a novel yet functional means of getting to places of interest. Indeed, Melbourne's older-style W-class wooden trams, built in local shops mainly in the 1920s and 1930s, have become tourist attractions in and of themselves (Photo 12.1). It was only a decade or so ago that anyone could become the proud owner of a decommissioned W-class tram for a few hundred dollars. That changed in 1992 when the National Trust classified them as historic relics, effectively removing them from the auction block.

In the core, Melbourne's trams are seemingly ubiquitous, sharing road space with cars, cyclists, and pedestrians. Outside the core, they operate mostly on surface streets and occasionally along dedicated median strips. In 1987, two former heavy rail routes to the south of the CBD were refur-

PHOTO 12.1. LOCALLY BUILT, OLD-STYLE W-CLASS MELBOURNE TRAM. Popular with tourists, the city circle tram loops the central business district, passing ornate Victorian structures, such as the Windsor Hotel, that flank modern forty-story office towers.

bished and converted to exclusive right-of-way tram services, qualifying them, technically speaking, as light rail services.

Buses have become Melbourne's gap-fillers. Today, some 1,100 conventional coaches, most privately owned and contracted, circulate throughout the outer suburbs, concentrating on corridors unserved by rail transit. To users, privately owned buses are indistinguishable, each sporting the Met Bus logo. In total, buses carry some 360,000 passenger trips on an average weekday. Contracts to private bus operators are performance-based. With subsidies tied to patronage (rather than bus kilometers), contractors are rewarded for luring in paying customers as opposed to logging kilometers.

While the extensiveness of Melbourne's transit system is impressive by any standard, the quality of service leaves much to be desired in the minds of critics. Train and tram services can be slow and not always reliable. Average tram speeds have declined progressively to about 16 kilometers per hour, victims of increasing surface street congestion in the city core. While rail trains move along considerably faster, averaging 39 kilometers per hour, their speeds only compete favorably with cars in inner areas during peak periods. Many suburban train stations are poorly sheltered from the elements and show signs of age and neglect. On-board conductors collect fares on some trams, raising operating costs. With zonal fares and an assortment of multiride ticketing, fare payment can be confusing. These shortcomings, however, have not gone unnoticed. During the 1990s, the Public Transport Corporation, the region's public transit operator (under contract to state Department of Transportation), embarked on an aggressive campaign to upgrade services.[11] Rolling stock has been modernized, routes expanded, rail stations refurbished, and information technologies introduced.

After nearly constant ridership levels of about 300 million paid trips annually between 1980 and the early 1990s, patronage has started to rise noticeably in recent years, the product of both service improvements as well as an upturn in the region's economy. During 1995, train patronage grew by 4.4 percent, more than any time during the previous twenty years. Ridership on trams and buses increased comparably. Since 1980, per capita patronage has risen from 90 to 108 trips per year.[12] Services have become more punctual and reliable as well. In 1995, 99.6 percent of scheduled tram service was delivered, compared to 95.4 percent the previous year.[13]

Decentralization and the Future of the Metropolis

With jobs, housing, and retailing continuing to spread throughout the region, concern over the future well-being of Melbourne's vibrant and attractive central city and the trams and trains that serve it has heightened. Some argue that decentralization, spawned by the transformation to an information-based economy, has on balance been positive. Others view it, and in particular the growing reliance on the private automobile, as a looming threat to the region's cherished quality of life.

Table 12.1 shows that the share of regional employment in the central city (whose boundaries are shown in Map 12.1) fell sharply in the early post–World War II period, with the dropoff having slowed some over the past several decades. In 1991, the tram-served central city, representing Melbourne's spatial extent a century or so ago, made up 31 percent of the regional work force. Paul Mees, a planning instructor from Melbourne University, argues that these statistics mask the fact that the CBD's employment role has remained pretty steady since 1951. If one adjusts the CBD's boundaries to reflect its enlarged contiguous area of development (just as the regional boundaries of contiguous development themselves have expanded), one finds that CBD employment has generally kept pace with the increase in total work force. Employment growth in the inner suburbs, an area also generally well served by rail, likewise seemed to mirror regional patterns during the 1980s. Table 12.1 suggests that the greatest shifts in regional employment shares appear to be occurring between older inner-city districts, such as Prahran and Fitzroy, and the outer suburbs.

One positive benefit of decentralization, some argue, has been a greater jobs-housing balance. This view, championed by Kevin O'Connor of Monash University and John Brotchie of CSIRO, a Melbourne-based think tank, holds that decentralization has allowed jobs and households to

Table 12.1 PERCENT OF REGIONAL EMPLOYMENT, BY YEAR AND LOCATION

Subregion	Percent of Regional Employment			
	1951[1]	1976[1]	1981[1]	1991[2]
Central City	65.0	36.7	35.2	31.1
CBD	24.9	—	—	23.3
Remainder of Central City	40.1	—	—	7.8
Inner Suburbs	—	18.5	16.7	17.0
Middle and Outer Suburbs	—	44.8	48.1	51.9
Total Region	100.0	100.0	100.0	100.0

Sources:
[1]J. Brotchie, The Changing Structure of Cities, *Urban Futures* special issue no. 5, 1992, pp. 13–26; K. O'Connor, Getting to Work: Thirty Years of Travel in Melbourne, *Australian Transport Policy '94* (Melbourne: Monash University, 1994); P. Mees, Dispersal or Growth? The Decentralisation Debate Revisited, *Urban Futures* no. 18, 1995, pp. 35–41; and Melbourne and Metropolitan Board of Works, *The Future Growth of Melbourne* (Melbourne: Melbourne and Metropolitan Board of Works, 1967).
[2]Estimates for central city and inner suburbs are based on calculations by Mees, defining CBD boundaries as the central activities district (CAD). See: P. Mees, Dispersal or Growth? The Decentralisation Debate Revisited, *Urban Futures*, no. 18, 1995, pp. 35–41. Estimates for Middle and Outer Suburbs are based on: K. O'Connor, Getting to Work: Thirty Years of Travel in Melbourne, *Australian Transport Policy '94* (Melbourne: Monash University, 1994).

co-locate so as to maintain constant average commute distances and shorter average travel times, even as the region grows. They point out that the share of employed residents working locally in the "subregion of residence" increased from 31 percent in 1961 to 44 percent in 1991. They also show that Melbourne's inner areas are the least self-contained, requiring substantial in-commuting, while the outer suburbs are the most balanced. Paul Mees claims that O'Connor's and Brotchie's calculations are faulty due to the undercounting of some 50,000 central city workers; correcting for this omission, he maintains that average regional commute times actually increased from 32.5 minutes in 1981 to 33.2 minutes in 1986. Regardless, in part because the research findings of O'Connor and Brotchie suggest that spread-out regions such as Melbourne are "self-regulating and environmentally sustainable," the powers that be in Canberra have opted to back off from the federally sponsored urban consolidation strategy, aimed at encouraging central-city infill development, in recent years. For now at least, leaders at both the national and the provincial levels seem to accept auto-oriented spread-out growth as an outcome of marketplace preferences.

What all sides agree on is that as more and more urban activities and functions pour into suburbs and exurbs, travel becomes better suited to the private automobile and less suited to public transit. The share of commute trips within the region that both begin and end in the suburbs rose from 45 percent in 1961 to 67 percent in 1991.[14] The trend toward crosstown travel has unquestionably hurt public transit. Table 12.2 shows that while in 1951 transit handled a healthy majority of all trips within the region, its current market share has dipped below 10 percent. Transit's

Table 12.2 PERCENT OF TRIPS BY TRANSIT VERSUS AUTOMOBILE, STRATIFIED BY PURPOSE AND CBD DESTINATION

	Percent of Regional Trips			Percent of Trips to CBD			
	1951[1]	1991[2]	1994[3]	1951[1]	1964[1]	1991[2]	1994[3]
All Trips							
Public Transit	56.9	15.0	8.9	—	66.0	—	73.4
Automobile	18.1	75.2	75.3	—	11.5	—	20.2
Work Trips							
Public Transit	—	15.5	—	84.0	83.0	61.7	61.0
Automobile	—	75.2	—	12.2	16.8	35.0	32.0

Sources:
[1]Melbourne and Metropolitan Board of Works (MMBW), *The Future Growth of Melbourne* (Melbourne: MMBW, 1967), p. 8.
[2]Australian Bureau of Statistics, *Melbourne: A Social Atlas* (Canberra: AGPS, 1991 Census); P. Mees, Dispersal or Growth? The Decentralisation Debate Revisited, *Urban Futures*, no. 18, 1995, p. 38.
[3]The Transport Research Centre, *Melbourne on the Move: A Sampling of Results from the 1994 Victorian Activity & Travel Survey* (Melbourne: RMIT University, 1996); D.Yencken, Moving Pictures: Transport Research, Policies and Assumptions, *Urban Futures*, no. 32, 1996, p. 34.

market share of work trips is substantially higher, and it continues to dominate all forms of travel to the CBD.[15] For districts surrounding the CBD, transit today carries about a quarter of peak-hour work trips.

Outside the central city, transit's lackluster ridership performance is a consequence of several factors, including low densities, transit-unfriendly designs, and the prevalence of free or cheap parking. Using 1986 work trip data, Rob Ellison found a strong positive correlation between the densities of Melbourne's neighborhoods and transit market shares, summarized in Figure 12.1. The graph shows that at 10 persons per hectare, representing many outer suburban neighborhoods, transit captures 5 to 10 percent of work trips. In Melbourne's tram-served inner suburbs, such as St. Kilda and Prahran, where densities exceed 40 persons per hectare, public transit carries about a third of work trips headed there.[16]

Box Hill, Melbourne's largest suburban employment center with some 15,000 workers, demonstrates that compactness and convenient services alone will not lure suburban workers into trains and buses. Despite the presence of mid-rise office and commercial towers and a railway station in the middle of the district center, only 7 percent of Box Hill's workers commuted by transit in 1991.[17] This is despite the fact that many workers there are making radial trips suited to transit—about 45 percent live near a rail corridor.

These statistics underscore the vital importance of coordinating transit and urban development in years to come. Transit's ability to hold its

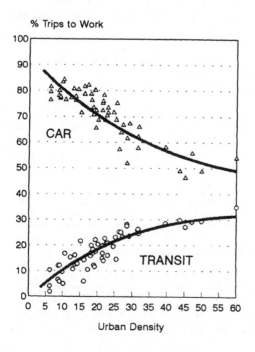

FIGURE 12.1. PLOT OF URBAN DENSITIES AND COMMUTE MODAL SHARES IN MEL-BOURNE, 1986. *Source:* R. Ellison, Melbourne's Public Transport Service, *Urban Futures*, no. 20, 1995, p. 41, figure 11.

own against the car for CBD-destined trips is in part a consequence of concerted planning efforts in recent times to channel decentralized growth along radial corridors and to maintain a viable and functional central city.

Planning Responses to Decentralized Growth

The first concerted planning response to decentralization was in the late 1960s, when the region adopted a "Green Wedges Plan." As in the case of Copenhagen, the plan called for Melbourne to develop along defined fingers so as to create a radial metropolis with a strong city center, while also preserving open space and natural habitats. According to the plan, growth would be channeled along six corridors emanating to the north, west, and east of the CBD. In the early 1970s, at the height of the environmental movement, the number of fingers was reduced from six to four in an effort to preserve the eastern foothills and southern peninsula. With a change in political power in the late 1970s came an abrupt shift in planning philosophy. Under conservative leadership, the Green Wedges Plan was set aside in favor of the 1980 Metropolitan Strategy Plan, which embraced the concept of "District Centres."[18] The plan designated fourteen historical centers spread throughout the region as future growth catchments, each slated to serve a district with a targeted population of about 150,000 persons. With the region poised for a multicenter settlement pattern, Michael Thomson, in his book *Great Cities and Their Traffic*, warned that "Melbourne is gradually being transformed from a strong-center to a weak-center structure."[19] While calling for "a balanced transportation approach," it was clear that the District Centres plan forebode a future of massive roadway expansion and quite likely a significant curtailment in transit services.

The early to mid-1980s brought still another abrupt shift in planning philosophy. During this period, important zoning and land-use controls were devolved from the state to the region's 210 local councils. Given more freedom to control their own destiny, the city of Melbourne and other close-in municipalities joined forces in adopting the "Central City Plan," by all accounts a watershed in Melbourne's planning history. With an overriding goal of strengthening the region's core, the plan put the region back on the pathway of a strong-centered metropolis. The Central City Plan was buttressed by passage of the 1987 Strategy Plan, spearheaded by Victoria's state planning office, which recommitted the region to the "Green Wedges" concept. The plan also embraced the principle of "urban consolidation," Australia's version of what American planners call "infill development," aimed at "achieving a greater proportion of future urban growth within established areas."[20] Subsequent updates have further solidified the region's commitment to developing along radial, rail-served corridors "interspersed by green wedges that delineate city from countryside." However, as Australia's body politic continues to favor market-driven growth and a retrenchment in government, much in the Reagan/Thatcher tradition, the jury is still out as to whether concentrated radial growth will be the region's destiny. For many, the greatest hope lies in further strengthening the region's core and its transit services.

Central City Transformation

In 1980, Melbourne's central district was showing signs of strain and neglect. Swanston Street, the main north-south connector into the CBD, was plagued by through truck and car traffic. Freight lines cut off the city center from the river to the south and from the docklands to the west. The riverfront had become an eyesore, dotted with semi-industrial activities. Links to the bay and its beaches were poor. Few people wanted to live in the central city and growing numbers of businesses were pulling out.

The mid-1980s are considered by many to be Melbourne's golden age of planning, a period when politicians, merchants, business interests, environmentalists, grassroots supporters, and many others collaborated in an all-out effort to reverse the falling fortunes of Melbourne's CBD. Leading the charge was Evan Walker, at that time head of Victoria's planning office and today a professor of planning at the University of Melbourne. Having worked as an architect in Toronto, Walker fell back on his experiences there to build a vision, articulated in very clear ways, of how central Melbourne might be transformed. It was essential, Walker reasoned, to build upon central Melbourne's many assets: a grid-iron street pattern; grand boulevards leading into the core, accented by quaint back streets, lanes, and arcades; the nearby Yarra River and its pleasant, undulating riverscape; colorful and ornate architecture; a functional, world-renowned tram network, designed around architecturally distinct, multi-modal train stations; close proximity to an active maritime waterfront, the docklands; and good tram connections to the southern bay and its beaches (Map 12.2).

Walker's first task was to remove unwanted car traffic—those driving into the city without an origin or destination there, or cruising the streets for parking. Swanston Street was closed to cars and transformed into the city's main ceremonial axis (Photo 12.2). This was followed by the opening of the Bourke Street Mall, a nicely landscaped outdoor stretch of several blocks fronted by major retailers, where slow-moving trams commingle with pedestrians (Photo 12.3). The Swanston-Bourke ped-ways formed an elegant †-shaped axis, giving Melbourne's CBD an identifiable "core," where people began to congregate. The ped-way pair also formed the

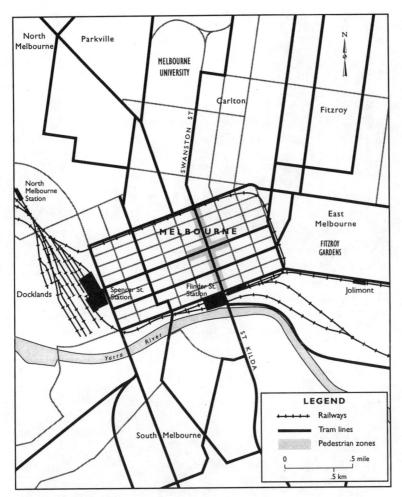

MAP 12.2. CENTRAL CITY MELBOURNE.

backbone of an integrated network of connecting walkways, plazas, and arcades. By giving over road space to pedestrians, a number of major shopping, cultural, and entertainment attractions in central Melbourne likewise became easily accessible by foot. This maneuver also proved effective in deflecting traffic away from the city center. In 1964, 52 percent of traffic entering the CBD was passing through; by 1986, the share had plummeted to about 8 percent. Also important to the task of returning the core to pedestrians was the opening of peripheral parking garages. Restrictions on parking supplies were also introduced.[21]

Besides reclaiming the core for pedestrians, other urban design initiatives were introduced in an effort to make the core a more attractive place. Many ideas came from Jan Gehl, an urban designer from Copenhagen (Chapter 5), who was brought in to advance some of the same ideas he

PHOTO 12.2. TRAMS INTERMIX WITH PEDESTRIANS ALONG SWANSTON STREET, MELBOURNE'S CEREMONIAL THOROUGHFARE. By operating within roadbeds at moderate speeds, trams are perceived as human-scale and compatible with a pedestrian-oriented environment.

PHOTO 12.3. BOURKE STREET MALL. This tree-lined east-west mall lies in the core of Melbourne's largest retail district.

had so effectively applied in his home town. Height limits were placed on the retail and entertainment core to ensure that sunlight hit the streets. Historic façade controls were introduced to maintain the charm and integrity of heritage buildings. Roads on the southern edge of the Yarra River were closed and turned into walkways. Great care was given to landscaping. Skywalks were extended over railroad tracks to connect to the riverfront, and a striking new pedestrian bridge was erected across the Yarra. Step by step, an urban milieu that imparted a sense of community, enjoyment, and civic pride began to take form.

A key premise of the central city's metamorphosis was that public amenities and good urban design would in turn lure private investment and new land uses. This formula for jump-starting redevelopment proved highly successful. In the late 1980s, a massive multi-use complex, called Southbank, transformed what was once an industrial wasteland on the southern edge of the Yarra into a popular weekend and evening destination (Photo 12.4). Southbank today features two office towers, a large convention hotel, condominiums, an aquarium, an international food hall, riverside cafes and restaurants, and an up-scale shopping galleria.

Two urban activities that were considered absolutely essential in rejuvenating the central city were housing and retailing. The addition of full-time residents and contemporary shops in and around the core, many believed, would do more than anything to perpetuate the central city's economic recovery.

PHOTO 12.4. SOUTHBANK WATERFRONT DEVELOPMENT. Featuring outdoor cafes, upscale shops, and a promenade along the Yarra River, Southbank has become one of Melbourne's most popular weekend destinations.

Living in the City

Throughout the 1980s, planners worked in earnest to attract new house-holds in and around the central city. The aim was to provide a wide array of housing offerings that would appeal to increasingly diverse lifestyles and residential preferences.

As with mixed-use projects like Southbank, the many public amenities added to the central city proved to be an effective formula in attracting new residents. In recent years, there has been a remarkable upswing in residential activity throughout the central city. From 1992 to 1994, 2,589 housing units had either been built in the central area or were in the development pipeline. This was fully one-third of all housing activities in the region for the same period.[22]

Many inner-city neighborhoods, such as Fitzroy and Prahran, are being gentrified, staking claim as the most popular and expensive places to live among young professionals and small households. In 1996 alone, more than a thousand people moved into the central city, compared to annual losses in population for as far back as records go. With relatively high discretionary incomes, new residents have in turn attracted many new services and businesses back to the city. Studies show Melbourne's inner-city residents own fewer cars and use them less often. With the CBD nearby and tramways so prevalent, more than 40 percent of those with jobs walk or catch transit to work.[23] One study found that inner Melbur-nians average just 41 percent of the per capita fuel consumption of their counterparts living in the outer suburbs.[24] Another found that in-town residents were much more satisfied with their neighborhoods than those living on the outskirts.[25]

Retailing in the City

The gentrification of Melbourne's inner-city neighborhoods has borne out Hotelling's Law of Retail Gravitational Pull—wherever reasonably affluent people reside, retailers will soon follow. In the 1980s, obituaries were being written about central Melbourne's retail sector. The CBD's share of retail sales fell from about 50 percent at the end World War II to 11 per-cent in 1986. Since 1986, however, a number of large retail developments have opened in the core, attracted by the many other changes under way. According to Paul Mees, "CBD retailing has expanded substantially in Melbourne in recent years and probably increased its share of metropoli-tan sales for the first time in four decades."[26] The core dominates higher-order retailing and in the last twenty years has actually increased its edge over suburban rivals in the variety of top department stores it offers. The CBD's retail sector now claims more than three times the turnover of Mel-bourne's largest suburban shopping mall, and, by one estimate, its share of regional retail sales today hovers around the 15 percent mark.[27] No American metropolis comes close to matching Melbourne's share of regional retail sales in the core; by comparison, the CBDs of Boston, Chicago, and Los Angeles account for only 1.6 percent to 2.8 percent of regional retail sales.[28]

Central Melbourne's fine-grained tram network and buoyant retailing and housing markets have proven to be a perfect match. With a flat, free-transfer fare and heavily discounted all-day tickets, trams have emerged as the preferred mode for many short-haul shopping trips within the central city. A 1994 intercept survey of 2,300 pedestrians in Melbourne's CBD found that about 70 percent of those shopping had arrived by public transport, a higher transit share than that found for work trips.[29] Until the arrival of megamalls adorned with parking, Melbourne's history has always been one of retail outlets aligning themselves along tram and train lines. A 1961 study found the vast majority of suburban shops to be within a five-minute walk of a transit stop, producing transit modal splits of 39 to 43 percent, even for shopping trips to out-of-city destinations.[30] Today, fewer than one of ten shoppers at suburban malls arrives by transit. Without question, the retail renaissance currently taking place in inner-city Melbourne has been a boon to both public transit and central city revitalization.

The City Link

Nothing has polarized greater Melbourne more in recent years than the proposed City Link project. To backers, it is a sorely needed infrastructure addition that will relieve central city congestion and strengthen the economy by allowing for more efficient freight movement in between docks, railheads, and other depots. To opponents, it is an American-style supply-side response to traffic gridlock, that would provide only ephemeral relief, spawn sprawl, and threaten the very lifeblood of the central city.

The 22-kilometer project, slated to open around the year 2000, is to skirt the western and southern parts of Melbourne's core, connecting the airport, the docklands, Port Melbourne, and several freeways that now terminate east and west of the CBD. Priced at more than US$1 billion, it will be the largest infrastructure project ever built in Australia by private interests—a joint Australian-Japanese consortium under a build-own-operate-transfer (BOOT) arrangement. Most costly will be two tunnels on the Southern Link and a new bridge spanning the Yarra River. To finance the project, tolls as high as US$2.50 will be collected using automated technologies. The facility is forecasted to carry some 300,000 vehicles per day.

In many ways, the City Link symbolizes, in one project, the deep divide among the populace about how Melbourne should grow in years to come. The division relates not only to what is the preferred settlement pattern of the future, but also to what kind of place, physically, economically, and socially, Melbourne will be. Today, Melbourne's identity is intrinsically tied to its role as a strategic national and international transport hub. Melbourne's port is the nation's largest, handling 42 percent of Australia's container traffic. Facilitating freight movement on city streets through projects such as City Link, proponents argue, is in the national economic interest. Additional ring roads will also cater to growing demands for crosstown travel. Echoing this sentiment is John Brotchie: "The development of circumferential urban links (e.g., a ring road) would provide further focus for development of future productive industries at the periphery, and further relieve congestion resulting from cross-town trips and freight movement."[31] A much different take on this comes from Peter Newman. He views the campaign to promote Melbourne as a global freight hub through massive road building as woefully out of step with the times. "If this were to occur, the city would become an economic dinosaur as it attempted to take on the mantle of Los Angeles and other such cities which are now realizing that high capacity roads are not the answer to economic health in a post industrial world."[32]

Learning from Melbourne

In 1924, Le Corbusier, the French architect enamored by megascale cities, proclaimed that "the tramway has no right to exist in the heart of a modern city." Le Corbusier might feel differently were he to visit modern-day Melbourne. Trams and trains have played an integral part in revitalizing Melbourne's central city. The core's prospering retail sector and expanding housing market owe much to the green-and-gold trolleys that lace the city streets and the aging yet dependable trains that tie suburbia to the city proper. As in other cities profiled in this book, notably Zurich and Munich, much of the credit for central city revitalization has to go to proactive and strategic planning. Redevelopment planning and tramway services have effectively worked together in leveraging the downtown turnaround.

Past investments in tramways and other transit armature are valuable assets that should not be lightly discarded. Fortunately for Melbourne, they had a guardian—in the person of Major General Risson—to make sure this did not occur. Melbourne's experiences demonstrate that by smartly capitalizing upon longstanding public transit assets, in combination with other pro-active steps, downtowns can be restored to their former glory.

As the new millennium approaches, Melbourne finds itself at a critical juncture in terms of deciding how it will best grow. Its rich heritage of tramways and train lines, coupled with recent inroads in rejuvenating the CBD, suggest that it will retain a viable central city for years to come. Decentralization is inevitable and, all sides agree, must be planned for. The commitment to the Green Wedges Plan would suggest that future suburban growth will be oriented to radial, transit-served corridors. Yet commitments to projects like City Link suggest otherwise. Mediating between opposing factions as to what course Melbourne should take is a difficult challenge, but one that responsible leaders must rise to. Melbourne's standing as one of the world's most livable cities hangs in the balance.

NOTES

1. Chamber of commerce brochures proudly publicize Melbourne's first-place rating, along with Montreal and Seattle-Tacoma, as the world's most livable city, based on an international study carried out by the Population Crisis Committee.

2. For a colorful history of Melbourne's trams and suburban railroads, see: M. Cannon, *The Land Boomers* (Melbourne: Sun Books, 1966).

3. B. Russell, Funding Better Urban Public Transport: Change and Reinvention, *Urban Futures*, no. 20, 1995, p. 31.

4. K. W. Ogden, Technological and Social Change: Their Relationship to Urban Transport—a Melbourne Scenario, *Urban Futures*, no. 20, 1995, p. 25.

5. R. Ellison, Melbourne's Public Transport Service, *Urban Futures*, no. 20, 1995, p. 29.

6. For an interesting account of Risson, see: M. Venn, A Fair Go for the Streetcar, *The New Electric Railway Journal*, Winter 1995–1996, pp. 25–29.

7. J. Kenworthy and P. Newman, *Moving Melbourne: A Public Transport Strategy for Inner Melbourne* (Perth: Institute for Science and Technology Policy, Murdoch University, prepared for the Inner Metropolitan Regional Association, Inc., 1991).

8. Australian Department of Housing and Regional Development, *Timetabling for Tomorrow: An Agenda for Public Transport in Australia, Strategies Paper 2* (Canberra: Australian Urban and Regional Development Review, 1995), p. 39.

9. Kenworthy and Newman, *op. cit.*, p. 12.

10. Oldest are the W-class trams, 15-meter-long wooden vehicles built from 1923 to 1956 that seat 48 and can carry as many as 150. Currently, about 100 W-class trams are in service and another 100 are in storage. Transit officials hope to refurbish and redeploy the mothballed W-class fleet over time. W-class trams are generally used on shorter inner-city routes, including the free city circle route that circumnavigates the CBD. Three W-class trams are also used as moving restaurants. The vast majority of Melbourne's trams consists of the modern A, B, and Z classes, featuring automatic doors and more spacious interiors. There are some 230 Swedish-made Z-class trams with seat-

ed conductors, each seating 45 passengers and carrying up to 125. The modern A-class tram, built in the mid-1980s, seats 42 passengers and carries as many as 120; some 70 are in use today. Introduced in 1984 and still being built, the B-class modern articulated tram, or light rail vehicle, seats 76 and has a capacity of 182; about 90 operate today.

11. Established in 1989 and called the Met, the Public Transport Corporation (PTC) is one of Australia's 100 largest enterprises in terms of asset value and turnover. The PTC is structured along business lines. Separate entities are responsible for passenger train, freight train, tram, metropolitan bus, and intercity bus services. Each provides its own infrastructure, rolling stock, management, and other services.

12. This figure is for linked trips, representing a single fare payment. Since Melburnians pay a single fare for all public transport modes, regardless of the number of transfers, within the same fare zone, enumerating unlinked (single-leg) trips is problematic. Per capita levels of unlinked trip making are considerably higher than 108 per year.

13. Public Transport Corporation. *Public Transport Corporation: 1995 Annual Report* (Melbourne: PTC, 1996).

14. K. O'Connor, Getting to Work: Thirty Years of Travel in Melbourne, *Australian Transport Policy '94* (Melbourne: Monash University, 1994), Table 2 (unpaginated).

15. The CBD represents the core area bounded by Flinders, Spring, Victoria, and Spencer Streets.

16. Kenworthy and Newman, *op. cit.*, p. 11.

17. P. Mees, Dispersal or Growth? The Decentralisation Debate Revisited, *Urban Futures*, no. 18, 1995, pp. 38–40.

18. Melbourne and Metropolitan Board of Works, Metropolitan Strategy (Melbourne: MMBW, 1980). At this time, the Board of Works, under the auspices of Victoria's State Cabinet, was responsible for planning growth at the regional level.

19. M. Thomson., *Great Cities and Their Traffic* (London: Victor Gollancz Ltd., 1977).

20. Victoria Ministry for Planning and Environment, *Shaping Melbourne's Future* (Melbourne: Ministry for Planning and Environment, 1987), p. 1.

21. Melbourne adopted a policy of limiting off-street parking to no more than 500 spaces per city block. According to Jeff Kenworthy and Peter Newman, central Melbourne still has too much parking, averaging 283 spaces per 1,000 CBD jobs in 1990, compared to rates of 211 spaces per 1,000 CBD jobs in Europe and just 67 spaces per 1,000 CBD jobs in Asia. Melbourne's CBD parking supplies, however, are still relatively low compared to those in the United States and other Australian cities. See: Kenworthy and Newman, *op. cit.*, p. 10.

22. D. Yencken, City Centres in Australia (Mimeo, College of Architecture and Planning, University of Melbourne, 1995).

23. P. Newman and G. Zhukov, *Toward a Just, Sustainable and Participatory*

Transport Policy, (Perth: Institute for Science and Technology, Murdoch University, A Federal Election Manifesto, 1996).

24. Kenworthy and Newman, *op. cit.*, p. 9.

25. The study compared ratings of neighborhood quality among residents of Albert Park, a traditional in-town community served by trams, and Blackburn, an auto-oriented outer suburb with comparable average income and educational levels. Besides rating their neighborhoods more positively, residents of Albert Park also expressed much stronger support for policies aimed at improving services for transit users, pedestrians, and cyclists as opposed to motorists. See: Yencken, *op. cit.*, p. 32.

26. P. Mees, "The Report of My Death is an Exaggeration": Central City Retailing in Melbourne Since 1900, *Urban Policy and Research*, vol. 11, no. 1, 1993, p. 28.

27. Government of Victoria and Melbourne City Council, *Creating Prosperity: Victoria's Capital City Policy* (Melbourne: Government of Victoria and Melbourne City Council, 1994), p. 31.

28. Mees, 1993, p. 26.

29. Yencken, *op. cit.*, p. 24.

30. R. Johnston and P. Rimmer, *Retailing in Melbourne, Publication HG/3* (Canberra: Research School of Pacific Studies, Australian National University, 1969).

31 J. Brotchie, The Changing Structure of Cities, *Urban Futures*, no. 5, 1992, p. 23.

32 P. Newman, Roads, Cargo Cults and the Post-Industrial City, *Urban Futures*, no. 20, 1995, p. 17.

Adaptive Transit: Tailoring Transit to Serve Cities and Suburbs

Instead of reshaping cities and suburbs to support intensive rail services, some areas have instead reshaped transit to serve spread-out patterns of development. These are places where the private real estate market has been largely left to its own dictates and transit's role has been one of best serving the scattered trip origins and destinations that have evolved. In the realm of transit metropolises, these are the polar opposites of Stockholm and Singapore.

The three cities profiled in Part Five have chosen markedly different pathways in adapting transit services to the lay of the land. In Germany, Karlsruhe's adaptive transit has taken the form of light rail vehicles that share regional and national rail tracks with high-speed trains. The same vehicles that amble along downtown ped-ways transform into fast, minimal-stop mainline carriers once they leave city streets. In the suburbs, they often make slight detours from the mainline tracks to directly serve residents of the many towns and villages that surround Karlsruhe. Owing to the superb-quality, almost door-to-door rail services, greater Karlsruhe's transit ridership has risen sharply at a time when most German cities are losing rail customers.

Adelaide, Australia, has adopted a German technology, the track-guided busway (O-Bahn), for serving its northeast corridor. Same-vehicle, smooth-ride connections between outlying suburbs and central Adelaide have won over many former motorists to bus commuting. Competitive tendering has further introduced efficiencies into Adelaide's bus system.

In Mexico City, the melding of public metrorail and private minibus services has created a well-integrated, hierarchical transit network that is the mobility lifeline of this sprawling megalopolis of more than 20 million inhabitants. Driven by profit motives, private minibus operators have introduced a mix of community-based and subregional services—coordinated through route associations—that fill in the mobility gaps left unserved by the heavy rail system.

Chapter 13

Adaptive Light Rail Transit: Karlsruhe, Germany

Karlsruhe has pioneered a system of track sharing that allows an intimate integration of inner-city tram and intercity heavy rail services. By tying into German Railway tracks, Karlsruhe has managed to extend the reach of light rail services at a fraction of the cost of constructing a new suburban railway. Most importantly, by running dual-voltage light rail vehicles on central city tramways and regional rail tracks, Karlsruhe has engineered a versatile form of light rail service that virtually eliminates the transfer. The payoff has been a healthy rise in transit patronage over the past decade, despite a downward ridership trend in the rest of Germany. While well tailored to the region's spread-out settlement pattern, Karlsruhe's dual-mode form of light rail transit has also blended nicely with pedestrian-only commercial districts, both in the city itself and in numerous small towns aligned along suburban rail corridors. In greater Karlsruhe, one finds a harmonious fit between transit technology and cityscape that is one of a kind.

Light rail transit has become the technology of choice in most cities seeking to join the modern rail transit age. Yet light rail transit often struggles to compete with the private automobile outside central cities, in large part because suburban patrons must make "the dreaded transfer" when connecting to a light rail station. Karlsruhe, a medium-size city in southwest Germany, has made tremendous strides in eliminating transfers by pioneering an incredibly versatile form of light rail service, one in which LRT vehicles run on both citywide tram tracks and intercity high-speed rail tracks. In Karlsruhe, the same vehicles that crawl along the main pedestrian street, Kaiserstrasse, at 4 to 5 kilometers per hour, transform into efficient line-haul carriers when they exit the city, blazing along tracks owned by the federal railway authority at close to 100 kilometers per hour, shoulder to shoulder with high-speed trains heading to Bavaria and beyond. This adaptation of transit technology to the region's spread-out lay of the land has meant the same vehicles providing point-to-point line-haul services also function as inner-city circulators, not unlike a busway system. While fortuitous circumstances, such as the presence of an extensive federal railway network in its hinterland, played a big role in the formation of Karlsruhe's unique hybrid services, the lessons Karlsruhe offers on creatively adapting light rail services to low-density environs have relevance for many places with or contemplating light rail services.

Inventing a New Form of Light Rail Transit

Why Karlsruhe, one might ask? Karlsruhe's foray into the enterprise of creating new transit technologies is a product of history, public choices, and personalities. Founded in 1715, Karlsruhe was master-planned as the capital of Germany's newly formed state of Baden-Württemberg. Its extensive network of wide streets—twenty-three radiate from the city's imposing castle, and are overlaid by an elongated grid connecting the castle to the Rhein River to the west—stands in marked contrast to the medieval cores of many German cities. Wide streets eventually proved to be a blessing, allowing Karlsruhe to expand and upgrade its tram network, in existence since the late 1800s, at a time when many German cities were paring back theirs.

Karlsruhe grew rapidly, both in people and in cars, during Germany's post–World War II reconstruction period. By the early 1970s, a time when downtown Karlsruhe had free and plentiful parking and no pedestrian precinct, urban trams were losing customers to the car in droves. One by one, tram lines were being replaced by buses. As elsewhere, Karlsruhe's public transit system was caught in a vicious circle of declining transit ridership and service cuts. It was during this period that an important decision was made by city leaders: to become an active player in the suburban travel market by becoming a regional transit service provider. By forming a regional transit agency, the AVG (Albtalverkehrsgesellschaft), as a counterpart to the city transit operator, the VBK (Verkehrsbetriebe Karlsruhe), the institutional apparatus was in place to expand public transit's territory of operation. Both the AVG and VBK are owned by the city of Karlsruhe. Through the AVG, the city has negotiated contracts with local communities in the region to help pay for services provided.

The region's acquiescence to market-driven growth during the postwar period further set the stage for transit innovations. While the city of Karlsruhe itself is fairly compact, with some 280,000 residents in an area of 173 square kilometers (much of it parkland), many of the remaining 800,000-plus inhabitants of metropolitan Karlsruhe (2,100 square kilometers) live in villages and small towns surrounded by rolling countryside and forests. There has been little regional effort to orchestrate where growth occurs, largely in deference to consumer preference for detached housing. To the credit of Karlsruhe's civic leaders, it was recognized early on that city-sponsored transit services operating outside the city boundaries needed to effectively respond to and serve spread-out development. Metropolitan form, it was understood, defined the parameters around which good-quality public transit services had to be designed.

The only kind of transit service that would effectively compete with the car in suburbia, it was reasoned, would be one that emulates the car—providing seamless, door-to-door connections that eliminate the physical act of transferring as well as the added penalty of having to pay extra fares. In medium-size cities such as Karlsruhe where virtually all households have a car (500 per 1,000 residents in 1996), frequent transferring, it was concluded, would be transit's death knell.[1] Yet until dual-mode transit services were introduced in the early 1990s, transferring was a way of life for suburban transit patrons headed to Karlsruhe city and its main shopping precinct, Kaiserstrasse. This was largely because the main station (Hauptbahnhof) of the German railway in Karlsruhe is situated on the city's edge, and over the years heavy rail tracks and services have been oriented to this peripheral location. Thus, intercity and regional rail services into Karlsruhe, operated by both the city (AVG) and the German national railway (Deutsche Bahn, or DB), historically have terminated at a station far removed from the destination of most passengers, requiring a connecting tram ride and extra fare.[2]

The adopted policy of eliminating time-consuming transfers lead to the creation of Karlsruhe's own unique breed of transit service, the Stadtbahn, or S-Train. Not to be confused with the S-Bahn, the single-mode suburban rail services of large German cities such as Munich, the S-Train was conceived as a blending of modes (urban tram and intercity heavy rail) and operating environments (city and countryside). The basic idea was to integrate mainline and feeder services using a single vehicle. This required a highly versatile type of train, one capable of operating slowly and in harmony with pedestrians while in the core and quickly and in harmony with heavy freight trains along mainline stretches outside the city. It also required an extensive network of suburban rail trackage, something that the region already had, being crisscrossed by heavy rail DB passenger and freight lines linking Stuttgart and Frankfurt. Since the regional operator, the AVG, had already successfully run trams along disused DB freight tracks, a logical next step was to do likewise along the extensive network of active DB tracks.[3] For the AVG's general manager, Dieter Ludwig, who provided much of the vision and leadership in pioneering Karlsruhe's hybrid transit services, the region's extensive DB network was an asset that had to be fully exploited if integrated and seamless regional transit services were to become a reality. Ludwig saw an opportunity to provide an S-Bahn type of service, as in Munich and Frankfurt, without the expense of conventional S-Bahn construction. However, as he saw it, Karlsruhe's S-Trains would actually outperform the train services of Germany's larger cities by tying together suburban and inner-city services with one vehicle.

With local support and the eventual buy-in of the DB, starting in the mid-1970s, at a time when many cities were dismantling their tram networks, Karlsruhe began upgrading its transit offerings from a standard urban tram operation to a hybrid light rail/heavy rail regional system. This was done largely through innovation—designing and building a dual-mode LRT vehicle and adapting it to the heavy rail tracks of the German National Railway. Also important were various supportive measures: formation of a regional coordinating entity, the Karlsruhe Verkehrsverbund (KVV), devoted to integrating network timetables and fares; construction of new and reshaping of existing tracks; and refurbishment of old, disused railway tracks.

In the quest for transfer-free services, why, one might ask, did Karlsruhe not opt for a more conventional, "off the shelf" technology—namely, buses operating on dedicated right-of-ways similar to Ottawa? Part of the answer lies in Germany's tradition of first-rate rail services and a cultural predilection for speed, comfort, and convenience. In a land of Mercedes and BMWs, high-speed trains, and hyperspeed Autobahns, Germany's urban transit systems must provide a very high quality of service if they are to compete. The choice to go with dual-mode rail rather than busways stemmed from the belief that, in Germany at least, rail travel is preferable. Karlsruhe transit officials maintain that even if a bus journey takes the same time and is as comfortable, people still overwhelmingly prefer rail. Recent ridership surveys bear this out: most of the region's bus riders are captives (only 3 percent had cars available in 1994) while much higher shares of rail passengers are choice riders (20 percent of Karlsruhe residents riding trams and 40 percent of dual-track, S-Train customers had cars available in 1994).[4]

The attention given to quality and image carries over to the details of service design. The interiors of all trains serving greater Karlsruhe, for example, are free of advertising so as to make them more visually appealing to middle-class riders. As a matter of policy, all graffiti is immediately removed, even if it means taking a train out of service. Low-floor trains that allow convenient and expeditious boarding and alighting have also become the norm. Most recently, the city has begun operating four rail cars with small center-section cafes. In Karlsruhe, the mindset of providing extraordinarily high quality urban transit services pervades the entire transit operation.

Principles of Adaptive Light Rail Transit

The precepts of what was to become Karlsruhe's S-Train services were defined in a 1984 feasibility study conducted by the regional operator, the AVG, and funded by the federal government. The study advanced three design principles:

1. *Dual-system vehicles:* a new form of light rail transit was to be created, capable of operating on the regional DB heavy rail tracks as well as the city's tram tracks.

2. *Junctions:* tracks would be inserted at strategic locations to connect DB heavy rail line and Karlsruhe's inner-city tram system.

3. *Improved access:* new stops would be added along existing railway lines and branch lines to town centers and constructed so as to shorten rail access distances.

These principles, shown in schematic in Figure 13.1, formed the foundation for building integrated suburban transit services. While the

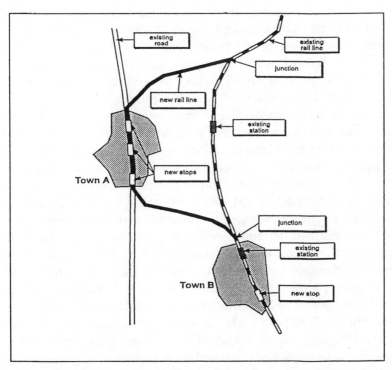

FIGURE 13.1. DESIGN SCHEMA FOR INTEGRATED LIGHT RAIL TRANSIT. *Source:* C. Jefferson and A. Kühn, Multimodal LRT Vehicles: A Development for the Future? *Urban Transport and the Environment II,* J. Recio and L. Sucharov, eds. (Barcelona: Urban Transport 96, 1996).

through-running of trains would eliminate transfers, the addition of stations and spur lines to town centers would bring people closer to stops, allowing for more door-to-door service possibilities.

It was the ability to share tracks that crystallized Karlsruhe's commitment to a new form of light rail technology. Some changes to business as usual were needed. While conventional trams could match the gauge of DB heavy rail tracks, they would be too slow in providing mainline services. And intercity trains would be far too heavy to operate on city streets, exceeding the weight limitations of bridges and underground water and sewerage lines.[5] Shared-track services would necessitate the design of a new type of light rail vehicle, one that blended the physical and operating features of a city tram and a heavy rail train.

Creating a Hybrid Vehicle

The first hurdle that had to be overcome in designing a new breed of light rail transit was the need to operate on different power supply systems. Shared-track vehicles had to be designed that could operate at 750 volts DC on city tramways and 15,000 volts AC on heavy rail DB tracks. Vehicles also had to be nimble enough to safely operate as conventional trams on regular streets, alongside pedestrians and cyclists, yet sturdy and robust enough to mix with heavy rail passenger and freight trains on mainline tracks. Specifically, they had to be able to near instantly stop when encountering pedestrians, yet withstand a collision with a freight train. Given these charges and supported by a grant from the Federal Ministry of Technology, a small team of AVG engineers, lead by Dieter Ludwig, in concert with several German rail manufacturers, proceeded to design a hybrid light rail vehicle that would fit the bill.[6] After carefully reviewing statistics on all train accidents that had occurred on Germany's rail network over a thirty-year period, the team opted for an eight-axle bidirectional articulated unit developed on modular principles. While dual-mode locomotives adapted to multiple-voltage systems have been used in Europe since the 1960s, adapting the technology to light rail vehicles was far more challenging because of the need to conserve space and avoid overly weighing down the vehicle.[7] Electrical hardware that converts 15,000-volt AC power to 750 volts DC was installed in a center section that has an extra bogey (Photo 13.1). Transformers and rectifiers were placed below the floor, and special high-voltage switchgear was placed on the roof, leaving interior space to passengers. Technically speaking, the dual-system vehicle is an alternating-current (AC voltage) vehicle with its own rectifier substation on board.

The greatest challenges in bringing a hybrid light rail vehicle on line were institutional, not technical. Notably, DB officials were skeptical as to whether a light rail vehicle could ever meet Germany's stringent crash-worthy standards. Upon numerous computer simulations of potential collision incidences and several months of field-testing a prototype dual-voltage light rail vehicle, Karlsruhe's designers demonstrated to the satisfaction of all that hybrid vehicles and DB trains could safely co-exist. Soon thereafter, federal authorities gave a green light to proceed with implementing shared-track services. Two factors, in particular, helped to allay fears about safety. One, the vehicle's light, modular, flexible frame, which evenly transfers kinetic energy throughout the chassis, proved far better at absorbing a train crash than was thought possible. Second, the vehicle's highly responsive disk braking system, installed to provide quiet, soft, but quick stoppage in pedestrian zones, provided superior acceleration and deceleration capabilities relative to heavy rail trains. While the hybrid light rail technology scored lower than heavy rail trains in passive safety (i.e., crashworthiness), it rated much higher in active safety (i.e., ability to avoid accidents). Because of the vehicle's fleetfootedness, DB officials admitted that a hybrid light rail train sharing tracks might actually be safer to travel in than their own heavy rail trains. The field-test runs of

PHOTO 13.1. DUAL-VOLTAGE S-TRAINS IN THE CORE OF KARLSRUHE. S-Trains line up for customers at Marktplatz in the heart of the city. The center section of the bidirectional articulated vehicles accommodates the dual-voltage electrical hardware. Speeding up S-Trains within the city limits is a system of induction loops imbedded in surface streets that allow signal preemption. S-Trains are permitted to travel as fast as 50 kilometers per hour while in the city.

prototype vehicles along DB tracks between Karlsruhe and Pforheim also showed that, because of swifter acceleration and deceleration as well as lighter weight, LRT vehicles were seven minutes faster than DB trains operating on the same route. This finding convinced DB authorities that stations could be added along shared-track corridors without increasing overall terminal-to-terminal travel times.

In late 1988, a full agreement was reached to implement the first segment of shared-track passenger services, between Karlsruhe and Bretten, some 28 kilometers to the east.[8] (See Map 13.1 for Karlsruhe's rail transit network.) Besides making electrification improvements, new branch lines, junctions, stations, and double-track sections were added to the corridor (Photo 13.2). Completed and opened to service in 1992, the price tag of 45 million deutschemarks (US$30 million) was about a tenth of what an underground S-Bahn–type rail system would have cost.[9]

Karlsruhe Network

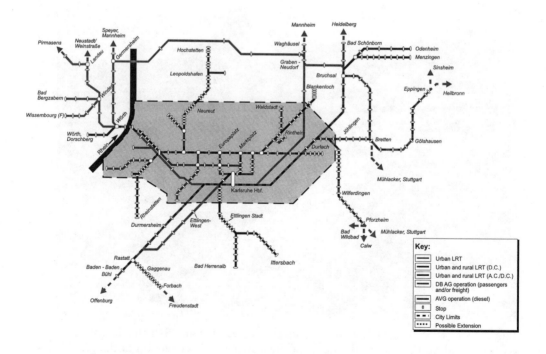

MAP 13.1. METROPOLITAN KARLSRUHE'S RAIL TRANSIT NETWORK. *Source:* Courtesy of Transport Technologie-Consult Karlsruhe (TTK), GmbH.

PHOTO 13.2. SWITCHING FROM CITY TRAM TRACKS TO DB HEAVY RAIL TRACKS. An S-Train enters a junction connecting the city tram tracks and the DB heavy rail tracks along the eastern line to Bretten and Eppingen. The actual conversion of power source occurs along a neutral straightaway section of the junction that allows vehicles to coast at zero voltage for some 180 meters. On-board equipment recognizes the neutral section and automatically opens the main circuit breaker. (If the circuit breaker fails to open within three seconds after reaching the neutral section, the pantograph [i.e., extendible arm] is automatically lowered and can be raised again only if the circuit breaker is open.) As soon as the new voltage is detected, the appropriate circuit is selected, without any action required by the driver, and the main circuit breaker closes again.

Institutional and regulatory reforms, it should be noted, were absolutely essential in moving Karlsruhe shared-track, hybrid light rail service from concept to reality. The German government's decision to functionally separate track ownership (a public sector responsibility) from train operations (open to the private sector) provided a receptive institutional environment for track sharing. In years past, the DB would have viewed light rail trains running on its tracks as unwanted competition and a potential nuisance. To the now privatized DB, track sharing was viewed as a potential source of revenue. Local observers also note that a close professional relationship between Karlruhe's transit chief, Dieter Ludwig, and the head of the DB's local office for short-distance train services was instrumental in successfully negotiating a track-sharing agreement.

Metro Light

Following the initial extension to Bretten, nearly 300 kilometers of shared-track rail services had been introduced in metropolitan Karlsruhe by 1997. Through careful planning and execution, what was only two decades earlier a conventional tram and commuter rail network has today evolved into a metropolitan-wide, transfer-free light rail service—"metro light"—superbly adapted to the region's spread-out settlement pattern. Karlsruhe's rail network successfully combines the best features of conventional trams and heavy rail metros. By this is meant:

- *Cost-effectiveness:* expands the reach of transit services beyond central cities at a fraction of the cost that would have been incurred in laying new tracks.

- *Line-haul efficiencies:* delivers fast, point-to-point services in the suburbs, making light rail time-competitive with the private automobile.

- *Central-city circulation:* provides fine-grained circulation along city streets and malleability in aligning routes (i.e., the ability to negotiate the tight curves of a grid network).

- *Pedestrian compatibility:* slow speeds and responsive vehicle braking make light rail vehicles hospitable additions to Karlsruhe's downtown pedestrian streets.

- *Close station spacing:* lighter vehicles and exceptional braking allow for faster acceleration and deceleration, enabling stations to be placed closer together, thus shortening the access distances of suburban trip makers.

- *Service penetration:* branch lines enable light rail to penetrate the cores of suburban communities, further reducing access distances.

While Karlsruhe is best known for its dual-mode track sharing, seven distinct types of adaptive transit services are actually offered in the region, each involving some degree of resource sharing and service integration. Table 13.1 reveals the rich variety of adaptive transit services that serve the region as of 1997. The sharing of DB and city tram tracks using dual-voltage vehicles constitutes the lion's share of new, integrated services, with S-Train services extending to all quadrants of the region. These services are complemented by single-voltage light rail trains and trams that share active DB freight tracks. All but one S-Train line ties into Kaiserstrasse, Karlsruhe's main pedestrian-tram corridor and retail center (Photo 13.3). Spur lines also penetrate the cores of small towns and

Table 13.1 Seven Types of Adaptive Rail Transit Services
in Metropolitan Karlsruhe, as of 1997

Type of Service	Lines (one-way kilometers, 1997)
1. Track sharing of DB lines with DB trains and city tram lines, with junctions connecting tram and heavy rail networks	Karlsruhe-Bretten-Eppingen (54 km) Karlsruhe-Rastatt-Baden Baden (30 km) Karlsruhe-Bruchsal (16 km) Karlsruhe-Pforzheim (22 km) Karlsruhe-Wörth (9 km) Ittersbach-Reichenbach (31 km)
2. Use of active DB freight track for non-dual-voltage (15,000-volt AC only) LRT operations	Bruchsal-Bretten (11 km)
3. Use of active DB freight track for non-dual-voltage (750-volt DC only) LRT operations	Bad Herrenalb-Hochstetten (43 km)
4. Addition of a third track parallel to existing DB lines	Grötzingen-Söllingen (4 km)
5. New LRT line through town center running parallel to existing DB line	Durmersheim (3 km) Stutensee (2 km) Linkenheim (3 km)
6. Use of former DB lines by LRT with new tracks through town center	Neureut (1 km) Eggenstein-Leopoldshafen (2 km)
7. Conversion of non-DB freight lines to LRT	Karlsruhe Hauptbahnhof (1 km) Bruchsal-Menzingen/Odenheim (29 km)

villages, such as Linkenheim and Wörth (Photo 13.4). In all, more than forty dual-voltage S-Train vehicles combine with some eighty trams, ninety buses, and about a dozen intercity DB-operated heavy rail trains to provide highly integrated regional services, serving towns as far as 40 kilometers from downtown Karlsruhe. And since S-Train services tie directly to rail lines to the east connecting into Heilbronn, itself a hub of regional rail services, the spatial reach of Karlsruhe's light rail services is effectively doubled along the north-east axis.

Functionally, Karlsruhe's local and regional services involve a blend of three transit modes: trams (operating solely within the city on single voltage, thus not sharing heavy rail tracks); light rail (operating on dual voltage and sharing tram tracks in the city and heavy rail tracks outside the city); and heavy rail (operating solely outside the city on single voltage, thus not sharing tram tracks). And in terms of the joint running

PHOTO 13.3. RAIL SERVICES ALONG KAISERSTRASSE, KARLSRUHE'S MAIN PEDESTRIAN SPINE.
All trams and virtually all S-Trains operate along Kaiserstrasse, one of the
longest and busiest pedestrian-transit precincts in Europe, at speeds of up to 25
kilometers per hour. A 2-kilometer stretch of Kaiserstrasse is reserved solely for
pedestrians, cyclists, and trams; even buses and taxis are banned from this no-
car zone. People, trams, and LRT vehicles have proven to be good neighbors
over the years. Despite a virtual elephant train of trams and S-Trains—some seventy-two vehicle units per hour in each direction, providing a theoretical
throughput of some 15,000 passengers—there have been few problems, even at
rush hours. Rail operators and pedestrians are used to sharing the street, and as
a result there are few accidents—fewer than at signalized street crossings. Sub-
minute headways are possible because of visual train control and ultrarespon-
sive vehicle braking. Still, as Karlsruhe's S-Train services continue to expand,
authorities are considering placing regional light rail vehicles operating along
Kaiserstrasse underground, leaving the road surface for city trams.

PHOTO 13.4. RUNNING LIGHT RAIL INTO LINKENHEIM. Linkenheim's main street before (top photo) and after (bottom photo) S-Train services. S-Train tracks branch from the edge into the heart of the village center of Linkenheim, located 20 kilometers north of Karlsruhe. The village of 8,000 inhabitants has seven stations, putting most residents within an easy five-minute walk of rail services. A pedestrian zone was also created in the heart of Linkenheim using a former national highway.

of services, two forms exist: light rail and heavy rail on suburban tracks; and light rail and trams on city street tracks. It is Karlsruhe's light rail vehicles, then, that are the common and critical link in track sharing and the provision of integrated services.

Complementary Measures

Technology cannot claim sole credit for Karlsruhe's achievements. It was necessary to supplement hardware innovations with software support— namely, the formation of a regional transit coordinating body and the introduction of downtown parking constraints.

As in Munich and Zurich, a Verkehrsverbund (transportation federation) was formed to coordinate schedules and fares among transit operators in the region. The Karlsruher Verkehrsverbund (KVV), established about the same time dual-mode services began, does not itself provide services but rather contracts with the region's operating entities—the city tram operator (VBK), the regional S-Train and bus operator (AVG), the provider of inter-city heavy rail services (DB), and several private bus companies. A unique feature of the KVV is that it oversees a rotating pool of qualified drivers, drawn from both the AVG and DB, to operate S-Trains. S-Trains require specially trained drivers who can operate trains both at high speeds and in very slow-moving, unpredictable pedestrian settings. Versatile trains require versatile drivers. Driver pooling has proven particularly effective at reducing the amount of extraboard labor— that is, fewer back-up drivers are needed to cover unexpected absences. The KVV also plays an important marketing role, symbolizing the integration of transit services within the region. All transit vehicles in greater Karlsruhe carry the KVV logo, even though different entities own and operate the vehicles. So far as the customer is concerned, there is but one regional transit network, and the particular mode operating between point A and point B, be it tram, dual-mode LRT, or heavy-rail train, is of little relevance.

Karlsruhe's integrated fare system is vital to providing integrated services. S-Trains, DB trains, bus services, and inner-city trams can be patronized using a single ticket. Environmental passes, educational passes, and one-day limitless ride tickets are the most popular forms of tariff payment, accounting for more than 80 percent of all fare transactions. Combi-tickets are also used to tie fare payments to admission tickets of most major sports and entertainment events. And respectable transit services evidently succeed in getting passengers to respect the fare payment honor system—fare evasion rates are very low, under 1.5 percent.

Parking policies have also lured customers to transit. Downtown parking is expensive and limited. There are no curbside spaces in the CBD. Off-street parking garages, located on the edges of Karlsruhe's pedestrian zone, cost about US$3 per hour. Several parking garages have been torn down since the mid-1980s and replaced mostly by open spaces. Ludwig Square, a popular pedestrian zone with outdoor restaurants and cafes in downtown Karlsruhe, was previously a 250-vehicle parking structure. Problems related to parking spilling over into residential neighborhoods have been avoided by requiring residential parking permits.

While official policy frowns on downtown parking, Karlsruhe's traffic engineers have made sure that whatever parking takes place does so in an efficient manner. An electronic parking management system guides motorists to the nearest vacant facility by the most direct route. Signposts show, in real time, the current number of vacant spaces in each parking structure. (Studies have shown that up to 15 percent of total downtown automobile traffic in German cities without such guidance systems consists of motorists searching for parking.[10]) By reducing the amount of cruising for parking, Karlsruhe's signpost system further contributes to creating a pedestrian- and cyclist-friendly downtown.

A totally different philosophy toward parking applies outside the central city. At suburban S-Train stations, park-and-ride lots are normally provided. Park-and-ride is viewed as an effective means of keeping cars out of the city and coaxing suburbanites into trains. It represents another example of adapting service provisions to the region's settlement pattern. While station-area parking is often viewed as a deterrent to transit-oriented development, since there is little direct policy interest in attracting growth to parcels surrounding suburban stations, in Karlsruhe, park-and-ride lots are viewed as assets, not liabilities.

The Payoff

Recent transit ridership trends provide the best evidence that Karlsruhe's adaptive light rail services have made a difference. While transit patronage has fallen sharply in most medium-size German cities since the mid-1980s,[11] in greater Karlsruhe it has been on a steady upward ascent. Between 1985, when the idea of dual-mode transit and track sharing was just taking form, and 1996, four years into the program, annual transit ridership more than doubled from 62.2 million trips to more than 130 million trips. Presently, some 40 million annual trips, or about 30 percent of the regional total, are made on the S-Train. Surveys show that 38 percent of S-Train commuters are former drive-alone motorists and 22 percent previously carpooled to work.[12] Transit riding has particularly caught on within Karlsruhe city itself. In 1995, 263 transit trips were taken per resident—more than any medium-size German city. Transit's growing popularity has helped put transit's fiscal house in order. In fiscal year 1995–96, the KVV was able to recover 86 percent of operating costs through fare box receipts, one of the highest rates of return in Europe.

It was the initial experience of jointly running LRT and heavy-rail trains along the Karlsruhe-Bretten corridor that yielded the most impressive ridership results to date. The S-Train to Bretten, a quaint town of 13,000 inhabitants that dates back to medieval times and today is home to several thousand Karlsruhe workers, began service in September 1992. It replaced a short-haul DB heavy-rail service that required a transfer at Karlsruhe's main station, and because of more frequent service and faster average speeds, it reduced average commute times to the city by twenty minutes. Within the first week of the Bretten service, transit patronage along the corridor jumped by 600 percent, from 2,000 to 12,000 trips per day.[13] Transit went from 5.7 percent of all trips made by Bretten residents in 1991 (one year before) to 10.2 percent in 1993 (one year after).[14] For those working in Bretten, transit shares of work trips rose from 4.6 percent to 9.8 percent within the first six months of S-Train services.[15] A panel survey of 2,000 Bretten residents, conducted one year before and after S-Train services were introduced, found that more than 80 percent felt transit services to Karlsruhe had substantially improved over this period.

Most of the credit for these stellar results goes to the superior service features of S-Trains. While the previous DB intercity train tied into the peripherally located central station, requiring most customers to transfer to and pay an extra fare for trams, with the S-Train Bretten residents could go directly to the city center. Services were also intensified, operating at twenty minute headways, more frequently than the short-haul DB trains that were replaced. DB responded in kind by transferring resources, initiating a new semifast train service to Heilbronn using the same track. This further expanded transit options available to Bretten residents, to three regular-stop S-Trains per hour plus one to two skip-stop semifast trains per hour. Also important was the fact that S-Trains ran and continue to run more hours of the day, well past midnight, whereas the previous DB heavy rail trains stopped service at 7:00 p.m. Other factors contributing to transit's success were the restructuring of feeder bus services to provide timed-transfer connections, the elimination of transfer fare penalties, the addition of more stations in Bretten itself (from one on the edge of town to seven spaced 300 to 400 meters apart), and a successful local campaign to create a more pedestrian- and cyclist-friendly village center. With the aid of a pro-active mayor and town council, Bretten phased in a series of measures that removed car traffic from the village center: some parking was eliminated; an internal bike path system was built; and streets were closed off to all but pedestrians. Today, Bretten lays claim to being one of the smallest communities in Europe with a multistreet pedestrian zone, one that spans more than a kilometer in length. As a result of improvements in the walking environment, coupled with the addition of six new stations, three-quarters of Bretten's current train customers reach a train station by foot.[16]

The impacts of innovative new rail services have been just as impressive in Karlsruhe city. Transit patronage among Karlsruhe residents tripled from 1988 to 1994, while the share of trips by private car drivers fell to just 14 percent over the same period.[17] Surveys show that 75 percent of Karlsruhe's citizens are "very satisfied" with their public transit services.[18] When headed to the city center, 40 percent of residents go by train. When making a shopping trip, the share is closer to 60 percent.

The benefits of seamless rail services have been expressed in other ways as well. Since the early 1990s, commercial rents along Karlsruhe's Kaiserstrasse have skyrocketed, attracting mainly big retailers and high-end restaurants and consumer services. Downtown shopping well surpasses sales volumes of suburban retail centers. Communities such as Bretten have seen commercial rents near train stops approach those of the city of Karlsruhe since the start of S-train services. The replacement of cars in the inner-city core with trams, S-Trains, pedestrians, and cyclists has also yielded important air quality benefits. Before the downtown pedestrian zone was introduced in 1972, Karlsruhe's CBD frequently violated national ozone and carbon monoxide air quality standards. There were also few trees. Today, the downtown air is much cleaner, and deciduous trees and vegetation thrive.

Learning from Karlsruhe

Greater Karlsruhe has been exemplary in adapting transit technology to the regional landscape. Throughout the region, transit seeks to follow and serve development rather than shape it. Trains and buses connect the places where people want to go rather than trying to recontour the places themselves.

In Karlsruhe, public transportation is taken seriously. Through visionary leadership and an entrepreneurial-like willingness to innovate and take risks, this medium-size region with high automobile ownership has managed to create a world-class transit system. Track sharing has allowed the reach of transit services to expand at a fraction of the cost that would have been incurred laying new track. In greater Karlsruhe, one finds villages of 5,000 inhabitants surrounded by rolling countryside yet served by multiple stations and S-Trains that come by every twenty minutes. Speedy, seamless, and reliable light rail services that minimize tedious changes of mode have paid off. Patronage is steadily rising. The commercial centers of Karlsruhe and its suburbs are teeming with life. Transit has become the mobility choice of many city-dwellers as well as suburbanites and villagers.

The Karlsruhe approach cannot be cloned, carbon-copy-like, nor is it suited for everywhere. Its experiences are probably most transferable to

small-to-medium-size areas where standard-gauge and electrified commuter passenger and freight tracks exist in the suburbs and exurbs that
are not heavily used. If tracks are busy, there may not be the capacity to
add light rail services. However, since many intercity city rail lines cater
to commuter markets or operate limited numbers of passenger runs per
day, in many cases there is likely untapped track capacity, as in greater
Karlsruhe.

The lessons from Karlsruhe are not limited to technology and hardware. Karlsruhe's experiences underscore the importance of strategic
planning: setting clear objectives; formulating and articulating a vision;
advancing untested yet imaginative ideas; marketing these ideas to gain
broad-based support; and perhaps most importantly, always keeping the
target in view—that is, being responsive to customer needs and preferences. Karlsruhe also shows the value of conserving resources and exploit-
ing opportunities when and where they avail themselves. The very
premise of track sharing was that it represented a way of providing high-
quality and expanded transit services by making efficient use of available
yet underutilized resources—in Karlsruhe's case, DB tracks. While federal
officials remained leary about the safety of this venture, sufficient care
and attention was given to the design of dual-system light rail vehicles to
eventually overcome these concerns. To date, there have been no serious
encounters or collisions between S-Trains and heavy rail DB trains. Karlsruhe's exemplary track record demonstrates that the safety barriers to
shared-track transit services are not insurmountable.

If imitation is the highest form of flattery, then Karlsruhe is certainly
the envy of many medium-size cities of the world. Adopting the Karlsruhe
model, shared-track light rail services have recently been introduced in
Saarbrücken and Kassel, Germany, and are seriously being considered
in some thirty cities across Europe and as far away as New Zealand. Interest has been so great that a private company, TransportTechnologie-Con-
sult Karlsruhe (TTK), has been formed to manage and market the knowledge transfer from Karlsruhe. If other places can successfully follow in
Karlsruhe's footsteps, the future of adaptive light rail transit should be a
bright one.

NOTES

1. Source: Stadt Karlsruhe, *Verkehr in Karlsruhe: Daten zur Verkehrsentwick-
    lung* (Karlsruhe: Stadt Karlsruhe, 1996).

2. For most medium-size German cities without metros, rail transit services
    are provided via two separate systems: urban tram or LRT services, provid-
    ed by municipalities, and the intercity, regional railway services of the Ger-
    man Railway (DB). As a rule, DB passengers who want to reach the city cen-
    ter have to transfer to a tramway.

3. As far back as the 1960s, trams were run on unelectrified freight lines and

abandoned railroad tracks in the region. The adoption of standard-gauge tram vehicles allowed for this early track sharing. These were not dual-propulsion services, however, since vehicles operated under a single-voltage electrical system.

4. Source: Karlsruher Verkehrsverbund (KVV), data files.

5. The maximum weight most urban roads can handle is eleven tons per axle.

6. Joining in partnership with the AVG to design and eventually build the hybrid rail cars was ABB (now Adtranz, Inc.) and Düwag (now merged into Siemens, Inc.).

7. For example, international trains must convert from 15,000 volts AC while in Germany to 25,000 volts AC when entering France and 3,000 volts DC when crossing Italy's borders. Designing such systems for locomotives in the vehicle was relatively easy because space was readily available. With light rail trains, where space is at a premium and weight is an important consideration, the design challenges were much greater.

8. The signatories of the agreement were the city of Karlsruhe, DB, the town of Bretten, and the administrative subregion (Landkreis).

9. Capital costs were apportioned among three tiers of government. Federal and state (Baden-Württemberg) grants covered 85 percent of capital facility costs. The city of Karlsruhe and communities along the shared-track corridors picked up the remaining 15 percent of costs. Rolling stock expenses were also borne by local governments.

10. Source: C. K. Orski, Livable Communities: Lessons from Abroad, *Innovation Briefs*, vol. 6, no. 4, 1995, p. 2.

11. J. Pucher and C. Lefèvre, *The Urban Transport Crisis in Europe and North America* (Houndsmill, England: Macmillan Press, 1996).

12. Source: Verkehrsbetriebe Karlsruhe and Albatal-Verkehrs-Gesellschaft mbH *Report '95* (Karlsruhe: VBK and ABG, 1996).

13. D. Ludwig, Light Rail on DB AG Tracks, *RTR*, vol. 36, 1994, pp. 3–6.

14. Rail transit market shares rose from 4.2 percent to 7.2 percent over this two-year period.

15. Kommunalentwicklung, Baden-Württemberg, *Modellvorhaben Bretten* (Stuttgart: Kommunalentwicklung, 1995).

16. *Ibid.*

17. Karlsruhe, Amt für Stadtentwicklung, *Daten Kakten Informationen, 1995, Karlsruher Statistik* (Karlsruhe: Amt für Stadtentwicklung, 1996).

18. W. Wyse, Light Rail through the Valleys: Karlsruhe's "Product of the Year," *Light Rail and Modern Tramway*, vol. 57, no. 683, 1994, pp. 283–293.

Chapter 14

Guided Busways: Adelaide, Australia

Some 600 kilometers northwest of Melbourne, in South Australia's capital city of Adelaide, a new form of suburban transit service, the track-guided busway, has been in operation for the past decade. Called O-Bahn, the service is perfectly suited to greater Adelaide's low-density, auto-oriented landscape. Along the 12-kilometer O-Bahn busway, guide rollers steer vehicles along a concrete track at speeds of up to 100 kilometers per hour, providing safe, efficient, and fast services, partly because drivers can concentrate on optimizing speeds rather than on maneuvering the wheels. Once buses reach the city center, drivers take the helm and operate the vehicles like regular buses. By combining feeder and line-haul functions in a single vehicle, O-Bahn services virtually eliminate the need to transfer. Providing door-to-door services from one's home to the CBD has been key in winning over customers to the O-Bahn. Ridership on the O-Bahn system has steadily increased despite a downturn in the local economy and eroding transit patronage outside the O-Bahn's service area. Complementing the O-Bahn technology have been environmentally friendly initiatives, most notably the integration of the busway with a linear parkway and the introduction of Australia's largest fleet of buses propelled by compressed natural gas. Also important have been moves to inject greater competition into Adelaide's public transport sector. The institutional separation of responsibilities for planning and overseeing transit services from the actual running of buses has also led to full fare integration, similar to what is currently found in Germany.

It is perhaps stretching things to include Adelaide, Australia, in the company of Stockholm, Karlsruhe, and even Melbourne as a transit-friendly metropolis. After all, public transit carries just 6 to 7 percent of all trips in the region. Yet as a comparatively small metropolis that is striving to introduce innovative and cost-effective transit services, Adelaide deserves attention. As an example of a spread-out area that is earnestly trying to adapt transit technologies and services to handle dispersed travel, few

362

places can match Adelaide. And in the spirit of addressing the challenges of making transit work in a small, remote region absent any serious traffic congestion, Adelaide makes an interesting case study.

Transit in an Auto-Oriented Metropolis

Much of the credit for Adelaide's free-flowing traffic goes to its illustrious history of town planning. The core city is laid out as a square-mile grid ringed by a greenbelt according to the specifications of William Light's 1839 plan, well known internationally, not the least because of its inclusion in Ebenezer Howard's celebrated work on "garden cities." The center city, home today to some 16,000 residents (down from 50,000 in the early part of the century), is very distinctive, with stately Edwardian buildings and quaint Victorian homes laced with gracious ironwork abutting modern office towers. Outside the inner greenbelt, the landscape takes on a contemporary, post–World War II appearance, with large-lot, detached development predominating. Hemmed in by the sea to the west and hills to the east, urbanization has occurred along a north-south axis some 80 kilometers in length and 30 kilometers in width, forming a linear metropolis that is home to about a million inhabitants. Prominent is the region's neatly platted supergrid network of wide arterial streets. The combination of spread-out, low-density development and generous road capacity has dispersed trips and virtually eliminated traffic congestion, save for a few arteries entering the core during peak hours. Today, Adelaide prides itself as the "twenty-minute city"—one can seemingly go from anywhere to everywhere by car within twenty minutes. With some 500 cars per 1,000 residents and market-driven patterns of suburbanization, the region as a whole is unabashedly automobile-oriented. Against such odds, how does such a place win over motorists to transit? The answer is to offer a very attractive public transit option that, at least in part, mimics some of the door-to-door service features of the car.

Greater Adelaide's well-developed public transit network features a balance of train and bus services, augmented by a single aging tram line connecting the core to a beachside suburb. Four heavy rail lines link outlying areas to the central city and function mainly as commuter railways. It is buses, however, that are the real workhorses of the public transport system, today carrying 82 percent of regional transit trips. Operated by three different transit companies under competitively awarded contracts, bus routes have been configured to provide a mix of local feeder runs, intermediate-haul connections, and long-distance, mainline services. The region's most distinctive, and certainly most internationally renowned, mainline bus service is its track-guided busway (Photo 14.1). The guided busway and connecting feeders are superbly adapted to the area's subur-

PHOTO 14.1. ADELAIDE'S TRACK-GUIDED BUSWAY. A conventional coach equipped with roller guides is steered along a tree-lined busway corridor.

ban landscape, evidenced by their superior ridership performance relative to all transit services in the region.

Adelaide's Track-Guided Busway: The O-Bahn

Track guidance is a simple yet cost-effective way of blending the features of bus and rail service in one vehicle. Rollers directly connected to the steering knuckle of a bus guide the vehicle along a raised concrete track. The interaction of the guide rollers and track steers the bus (Figure 14.1). Designed by Daimler Benz AG and Ed Zublin AG and first introduced in Essen, Germany, the patented technology carries the name of O-Bahn. Track guidance allows buses to reach high speeds safely along mainline corridors, comparable to railway services. However, unlike rail cars, buses can leave the guideway, filtering into residential neighborhoods. This allows the same bus to function as a feeder and mainline carrier. And, of course, same-vehicle services virtually eliminate transfers, the scourge of suburban transit services worldwide. Today, Adelaide boasts the world's fastest and longest guided busway.

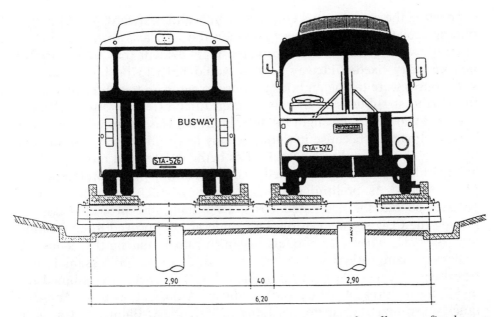

FIGURE 14.1. TYPICAL TRACK-GUIDED BUSWAY CROSS-SECTION. Guide rollers are fixed to rigid arms that are in turn connected to the front axle of the bus. The rollers, functioning as horizontal stabilizers, interact with a raised concrete lip to automatically guide the vehicle, freeing the bus driver of steering duties. In Adelaide, the track consists of precast concrete elements assembled like a railroad track. Concrete crossbeams are supported on bored piles to provide long-term stability. L-shaped concrete slabs atop the crossbeams form the guidance surfaces. To handle Adelaide's high-speed bus services and provide a comfortable ride, a continuous and precisely fitted concrete surface was needed. Prefabrication was a prerequisite to achieve the required accuracy. Adelaide's busway tracks were constructed to tolerances of plus or minus 2 millimeters. To achieve such precision required the introduction of rigid quality-control procedures both at the manufacturing plant and during track assembly. *Source:* Passenger Transport Board, Adelaide.

Why O-Bahn?

Why is it that a medium-size metropolis in a fairly remote part of Australia has taken on the mantle of O-Bahn as the future of suburban transit services? The answer lies largely in a confluence of events that made O-Bahn a natural choice for meeting the mobility needs of the region's comparatively fast-growing northeast corridor. During the 1960s, when the region was most rapidly suburbanizing, studies called for major freeway development to handle the growth in traffic, and public officials dutifully began preserving right-of-ways. However, by the 1970s, growing concerns over environmental quality and energy consumption led to a public backlash against the freeways, and none were built except for an interstate connecting the central city's edge to the hills and eastward. Yet with continuing growth in the northeast corridor, the only axis from the central city unserved by rail, it became increasingly evident that some form of high-capacity fixed-guideway service would have to be built. Surface-street buses were taking an hour or more to get from the outer reaches of the northeast suburbs to the city center. After extensive study, officials decided to go with a new light rail line. Light rail was preferred over a conventional busway because it would occupy less right-of-way, would emit less air pollution, and was perceived as being quieter and more comfortable to ride. Also, surveys revealed an overwhelming public preference for LRT services. As preliminary design work on LRT construction progressed, so did the estimated costs. Eventually, the projected cost of putting the CBD segment of the LRT underground proved to be prohibitive. By 1981, when city officials began to rather reluctantly reconsider building a conventional busway, a few local transit professionals had heard about a new German innovation, the O-Bahn, that combined the operating features of a bus and a railway. A delegation from Adelaide quickly organized a trip to Germany to visit the O-Bahn test tracks in Stuttgart and witness the first field application in Essen. The group was immediately impressed by what it saw and reached a quick consensus that the O-Bahn was the right technology for Adelaide's northeast corridor. After a follow-up economic analysis confirmed this, the decision was made to move forward with the O-Bahn technology.

The commitment to O-Bahn was a courageous choice, considering that no area, not even in Germany, had built anything comparable to what was planned for Adelaide.[1] However, among Adelaide's transit leaders, the choice was a prudent one. At a substantially lower capital cost than LRT, yet with a similar carrying capacity, it would incorporate the best features of LRT—safe, comfortable, and speedy mainline services—with the best features of a busway, notably the flexibility to leave the guideway and provide transfer-free connections between suburbia and the central city. Much of the capital cost savings would come from not having to build a CBD tunnel since buses could operate on Adelaide's spacious grid of downtown streets. Besides providing faster point-to-point services, track guidance was viewed as preferable to a conventional busway because considerably less right-of-way would be needed along the northeast corridor's river valley alignment. Minimizing intrusion on the River Torrens and its sensitive surroundings was viewed as a high priority by all.

Adelaide's O-Bahn Services Today

The first stage of Adelaide's O-Bahn opened in 1986, and the full 12-kilometer northeast corridor was in place by 1989 (Map 14.1). Today, buses from eighteen different routes wind through residential streets in the

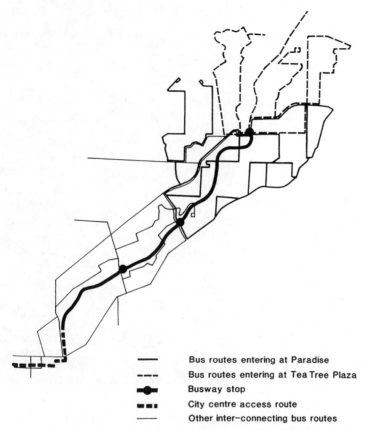

——	Bus routes entering at Paradise
- - -	Bus routes entering at Tea Tree Plaza
●—●—	Busway stop
■ ■ ■	City centre access route
——	Other inter-connecting bus routes

MAP 14.1. ADELAIDE'S NORTHEAST O-BAHN CORRIDOR. Eighteen bus routes feed into the mainline guided busway. On average, 55 percent of the distance traversed is on normal suburban streets, 30 percent is on the guideway, and 15 percent is on city streets. *Source:* Passenger Transport Board, Adelaide.

northeast suburbs before entering the guideway at one of two access stations, what locals call "interchanges": the terminus at Tea Tree Gully (15 kilometers from the CBD) or the Paradise interchange (9 kilometers out) (Photos 14.2 and 14.3). With steering completely controlled by the guideway, buses reach speeds of up to 100 kilometers per hour on the fully grade-separated facility, stopping at a third station, Klemzig (5 kilometers out) if there is customer demand.[2] Unlike the other two stations, Klemzig has no direct bus ingress-egress or park-and-ride facilities; all of its passengers are either walk-ons or arrive by bike or bus transfers. Upon reaching the outer edge of the CBD, vehicles leave the guideway and travel the remaining 3 kilometers to the core on city streets, just like regular buses.

Having just three interchanges along the guideway has been crucial to instituting high-speed mainline services. It was possible to get by with fewer stops than would be required with light rail since bus transit can be

PHOTO 14.2. O-BAHN GUIDEWAY ALONG THE LOW-DENSITY NORTHEAST CORRIDOR. The Paradise interchange has 500 park-and-ride spaces that fill up by 7:00 A.M. on weekdays. The provision of park-and-ride around stations such as Paradise, as opposed to efforts to concentrate transit-oriented development, reflects Adelaide's acceptance of low-density, suburban development as a market preference.

PHOTO 14.3. PARADISE INTERCHANGE, O-BAHN'S INTERMEDIATE STOP. An articulated bus, on the right, leaves the guideway as it converts from its line-haul to its feeder role. A bike path, at the lower right of the photo, winds alongside the guideway and its tree-shrub parkland.

a circulator-distributor as well as a line-haul carrier. That is, fewer stations were possible since, with buses, direct access does not depend solely on stations. Currently, 81 percent of O-Bahn patrons board buses at street stops, and the remaining 19 percent board at station interchanges.

A total of 110 O-Bahn buses, fitted with guide rollers, currently operate along the guideway, out of a total regional bus fleet of more than 700. Most are articulated diesel buses.[3] During peak periods, individual buses operate on ten- to fifteen-minute intervals, resulting in an O-Bahn bus coming by, on average, every fifty-three seconds. Local officials maintain that O-Bahn buses can operate at intervals as short as twenty seconds apart, without expensive signaling equipment, because of the superior traction of rubber-tired vehicles, horizontal stabilization from guide wheels, and the advanced antilock braking systems and independent front suspensions on all O-Bahn buses. Extensive field tests show that from a speed of 100 kilometers per hour, O-Bahn buses can stop—quickly, smoothly, and in a straight line—within two vehicle lengths. With such vehicle responsiveness and fleetfootedness, the O-Bahn can theoretically handle 18,000 passengers per hour in one direction.[4] This is in the ballpark of what most advanced LRTs can handle and begins to approach the lower-bound capacities of older heavy rail systems. Currently, the O-Bahn averages 4,500 passengers per direction per peak hour, or just a quarter of theoretical throughput. With some 27,000 passengers presently traveling along the busway each weekday, local transit officials feel the current guideway could handle well over 150,000 daily trips, a volume that is many decades away given the region's fairly slow economic and population growth.

Environmental Mitigation

Adelaide's O-Bahn planners have gone the extra distance to make the O-Bahn an environmentally friendly addition to the local transit scene. Through the care taken in designing and integrating the busway into the surroundings, they overcame environmental concerns about impinging on the delicate Torrens River Valley. The O-Bahn alignment traverses along a riverbed made up of unsteady alluvial deposits. The extreme plasticity of soils required extraordinary engineering and design. The O-Bahn's unique track system, with its precast track elements and sleepers resting on piers, proved to be highly adaptable to the unstable soil conditions.[5] Moreover, its relatively light weight put far less load on the river valley than the originally planned LRT alignment would have.

Prior to the arrival of the O-Bahn, the Torrens riverbed had become a neglected urban drain, littered with rubbish and inaccessible to the public. With the O-Bahn, landscape architects and planners saw an opportunity to transform the corridor into a healthy linear park. The corridor was attractively landscaped with berms, and the guideway itself was mostly depressed below ground level to minimize noise impacts on surrounding residents. Walking paths and bikeways were aligned along the entire 12-kilometer stretch. Trees planted along the busway formed part of an "oxygen bank" in a novel "trees for transit" scheme, part of Adelaide's continuing commitment to reduce the emission of greenhouse gases into the atmosphere. Because plants take in carbon dioxide as they grow and give out oxygen, a campaign has been under way to plant some 300,000 trees and large shrubs along the O-Bahn corridor to neutralize emissions from buses.

Another significant effort to become an environmentally friendly transit system has been the push to introduce CNG (compressed natural gas) buses. Currently, Adelaide has the largest CNG bus fleet in Australia—110 of the region's more than 700 buses are currently CNG vehicles, with plans to replace some 100 existing diesel buses with CNG by the year 2000. Because natural gas burns much more cleanly than liquid fossil fuels, does not emit diesel particulates, and generates much lower levels of nitrogen oxides and sulfur oxides, local environmentalists have actively lobbied for these conversions. Use of CNG also makes good economic sense. Because of Australia's significant reserves of natural gas and its exemption of CNG from federal excise taxes, the cost of natural gas is significantly less than that of diesel. In that CBG involves additional capital costs, notably for pressurized on-vehicle tanks, special fuel discharging systems, and off-site compressor stations, fuel prices had to be significantly lower to justify the investment. In 1997, a liter of CNG cost about half as much as a liter of diesel fuel. Taking into account the slightly lower fuel efficiency of CNG, studies show that it still provides an estimated savings of about US$8,200 per year per bus over diesel fuels (in 1997 dollars).[6] Experiences so far show CNG buses to be as reliable as the diesel fleet, with the added advantage of being more cost-efficient and environmentally friendly.

The O-Bahn Advantage

Adelaide's ten-year foray into the uncharted waters of mounting and sustaining O-Bahn services reveals a number of clear advantages over alternative systems, notably light rail transit and conventional busways. These include:

- *Adaptability:* The O-Bahn's chief advantage is that is well suited to the suburban milieu. Same-vehicle services virtually eliminate transfers. Adaptability also means that if a vehicle breaks down and blocks the track, buses can leave the guideway upstream, using regular surface streets to bypass the disabled vehicle.

- *Right-of-way savings:* Because the O-Bahn's 6.2-meter-wide tracks are only a little (100 millimeters) wider than a bus, considerably less right-of-way is needed than for a busway, where vehicles are manually steered. This provided significant savings in Adelaide, particularly in tunnels, on bridges, and along areas requiring substantial earthwork and landscaping.

- *Cost savings:* The avoidance of new capital expenses for depressing the CBD alignment and for advanced signaling systems resulted in a capital cost that was about half what a light rail system would have cost for the 12-kilometer corridor. At US$6 million per kilometer (in 1985 dollars), the guided busway cost only 12 percent more than a busway would have, in part because it required less right-of-way acquisition.

- *Lighter weight:* The O-Bahn placed less deadweight load on the corridor's fragile riverbed than an LRT line or a wider conventional busway would have.

- *Faster service:* As an exclusive, grade-separated corridor, the guideway cut in half the time needed to get to the city center from the northeast terminus—from forty-six minutes on previous regular-stop bus services to twenty-three minutes on the O-Bahn.

- *Safer service:* Exclusive segregation from other traffic, guided steering, and the guideway's high-quality running surface have increased passenger safety. Relieving drivers of steering duties and freeing them to concentrate on managing speeds and braking, if necessary, have reduced the chance of driver error in high-speed operations. Safety has also been enhanced by a back-up steel-wheel system that allows vehicles to proceed along the busway at up to 50 kilometers per hour in the event a tire suddenly deflates.

- *Greater comfort:* Because guide rollers act as horizontal stabilizers and the precast concrete track was built to such fine tolerances, buses run very smoothly, providing a ride quality well above that of a normal busway.

- *Quieter ride:* Owing to the smoother running surface and the absorption of tire noise by the L-shaped guideway surface and surrounding berms, the O-Bahn provides a relatively quiet ride. Nearby residences are also spared from loud noise, less than what a busway or steel-on-steel railway would have generated.

- *Staging flexibility:* As with a busway, the O-Bahn provides staging advantages over rail systems. The guideway does not have to be continuous or built and opened in one fell swoop; rather, it can be built incrementally. Whereas railways must run the full length, penetrating the CBD, to become operational, busways can commence services in segments.

Ridership and Development Impacts

That Adelaide's O-Bahn technology is the right "fit" for the northeast corridor's spread-out landscape seems indisputable from ridership evidence. Between 1986–87 and 1995–96, annual patronage on the region's bus, rail, and tram system fell from 82.0 million to 62.9 million boardings, or by about 23 percent (Figure 14.2).[7] During the same period, ridership on the eighteen bus routes using the guideway shot up by 75 percent, from 4.2 million to 7.4 million, an increase well in excess of the 18 percent growth rate in the busway's primary catchment area. Moreover, while the region's transit modal split was just 7 percent of all trips in 1991, for radial journeys along the northeast corridor to the city center, transit captured a 42 percent market share.[8] In real dollar terms, operating costs per boarding fell by 27 percent during the first seven years of O-Bahn operations, while rising 5 percent for all bus transit services operating within the region.[9]

Cross-system comparisons are also revealing. Between 1986 and 1996, ridership on the O-Bahn increased three times faster than ridership on the region's other mainline transit connector—the commuter railways serving the northwest, southwest, and southeast corridors. The O-Bahn's "guideway effectiveness" is also nearly ten times higher than that of the railways,

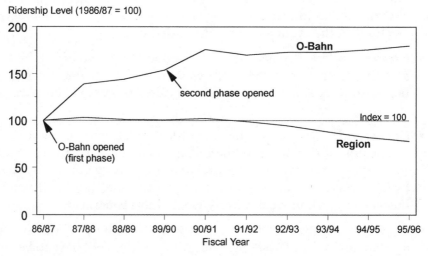

FIGURE 14.2. COMPARISON OF TRANSIT RIDERSHIP TRENDS BETWEEN THE O-BAHN AND THE REGION AT LARGE.

handling about 670,000 versus 69,000 passengers per route kilometer per year. And "vehicle effectiveness" is far higher as well—over the 1984–85 to 1991–92 period, boardings per vehicle kilometer rose 36 percent along the northeast corridor while falling 14 percent along railway lines.[10] These differences underscore the superior match of O-Bahn to the cityscape. Railways rely in good part on concentrated development around stations, which really has not occurred along suburban corridors. O-Bahn, on the other hand, accepts and works with low-density development, providing nearly transfer-free door-to-door services.

Who is patronizing O-Bahn? During peak hours, riders are predominantly workers and students heading to the city center, producing a directionally biased, tidal pattern of patronage. Surveys show that some 40 percent of new passengers during commute hours previously drove their cars to work.[11] During the O-Bahn's first five years of service, the greatest ridership growth actually occurred in discretionary trips headed to the CBD during the midday, mainly for shopping purposes. Besides receiving transfer-free services, surveys reveal midday, discretionary trip makers are attracted by the pleasant views of the corridor's riverscape and the safety of the guided, segregated track. The most frequently cited benefit of the O-Bahn is its convenience.[12]

While the very premise of building an O-Bahn was to adapt to rather than reshape the suburban landscape, it is noteworthy that some degree of clustered, station-area development has occurred, the joint product of regional planning and market forces. For several decades, the busway's terminus, Tea Tree Gully, has been designated as one of five regional town centers. The region's latest *Planning Strategy* continues the commitment to directing future suburban growth along high-capacity transit axes, including the northeast O-Bahn corridor.[13] To date, the O-Bahn appears to have accelerated the conversion of Tea Tree Gully from a somewhat sterile new town designed around a regional shopping mall to an emerging urban village featuring a wide range of land uses. In the early 1990s, the site of a new regional college campus was relocated adjacent to the terminal station to take advantage of the parcel's superb access to the CBD. A medical complex has also sprung up nearby. Tea Tree Gully's shopping mall is presently being expanded atop existing surface parking in the direction of the busway terminus. Around the two other O-Bahn interchanges, local residents want nothing to do with transit-oriented development, however. They remain adamant that the surrounding neighborhood remain exclusively low-density residential. In fact, a recent request to open a small retail kiosk at the Paradise interchange was denied by the local council on the grounds that any commercial use was incompatible with the neighborhood's character. With such a mindset firmly rooted in Adelaide's suburbs, an O-Bahn system geared to serving low-density residences seems all the more appropriate for the northeast corridor.

Competitive Transit

While the O-Bahn remains Adelaide's claim to fame in the transit world, the region has also won kudos for injecting competition into the local transit arena. Triggering the move to a competitive transit marketplace were various institutional reforms introduced in mid-1994. Chief among these was a move to separate the policy and regulatory functions of transit services from the operations function. Borrowing a chapter from Germany, asset ownership and service oversight became the purview of the public sector while service delivery was opened to market competition, with the lowest bidders granted the rights to operate within contract areas, subject to meeting minimum service standards.[14] A new authority, the Passenger Transport Board (PTB), was formed by the South Australian government to oversee all rail and bus services within greater Adelaide. As the region's policy and regulatory body, the PTB plans, regulates, and funds all land-based passenger transport in South Australia, which includes taxi and paratransit services in addition to buses and rail.

In 1995, the PTB began tendering competitive bids for operating bus services within the region. Contracts were introduced in phases over the next two years. TransAdelaide, which formerly operated all bus services as the State Transportation Authority, won the contract for the southern sector of the region, while a private firm, Serco, was awarded the franchise for serving the northern sector. A much smaller concession went to Hills Transit to serve some suburban and rural communities in the far eastern suburbs.

The impact of competitive contracting was immediate. Within the first year, transit ridership increased by 2.5 percent on contract routes, compared to a 1.7 percent decline for the metropolitan area as a whole. Competition also served to contain wage rate increases and spawn staff reductions. Moreover, it resulted in featherbedding clauses being removed from labor agreements, allowing transit managers to assign drivers clerical and minor mechanical duties during slack periods. The combination of ridership gains on contracted routes and cost containment resulted in an increase in the region's cost recovery rate from 26 percent to 29 percent during the 1995–96 fiscal year.

From the user's perspective, perhaps the biggest benefit of institutional reform has been the emergence of an integrated fare system, also akin to that found in Germany. Now the same ticket can be used to hop on a tram or train and transfer to the O-Bahn. Similar to Germany's *Verkehrsverbunds*, Adelaide's PTB pools all fare box receipts and guarantees each operator a certain payment depending on the kilometers of services delivered. Institutional reform has also led to a more efficient fare structure. As an incentive to midday riding, 40 percent discounts are given during the interpeak (9:00 A.M. to 3:00 P.M.). Fares also reflect distance traveled, costing almost twice as much for journeys of more than 3 kilometers versus those of less than 3 kilometers. Customer loyalty is rewarded through price incentives. A one-day, limitless-ride ticket goes for about US$3.60. Most popular is the multiride book, which for about US$12 provides ten tickets, any one of which can be used multiple times within a two-hour time window.

Learning from Adelaide

Adelaide's O-Bahn has proven to be a sensible choice for serving low-density, auto-oriented markets. By blending the speed and safety of light rail transit with the inherent flexibility and efficiencies of bus transit, the O-Bahn system has won over legions of loyal customers. Ridership continues to increase, even though regional transit patronage has fallen.

Despite the success of Adelaide's O-Bahn, guided busways have not been widely adopted. Apart from the slower-speed, shorter-distance O-Bahns now operating in Essen and Mannheim, Germany, there is no other similar system. This is a bit perplexing given some of the inherent advantages of O-Bahn—comparatively low capital outlays, single-vehicle operations that reduce transferring, and a high-quality, smooth ride, among others. Adelaide's transit leaders seem particularly puzzled that no other city has copied the concept so far. City officials had hoped to cash in on Adelaide's pioneering success with the O-Bahn, expecting money was to be made in transferring its operating experiences and technical know-how to other places. A slick, well-produced video, *Adelaide O-Bahn: The Innovative Solution*, warmly offers to build an Adelaide-style O-Bahn under a turnkey arrangement in any city that is interested.[15] Despite a constant parade of transit officials who come from around the world to witness Adelaide's O-Bahn firsthand, so far there have been no takers.

The reluctance to make the huge leap from curious observer to O-Bahn implementer likely reflects, in part, the second-class image problems that continue to plague bus transit. Whether rightly or wrongly, light rail transit is still widely perceived as a more modern, higher class of service more in keeping with the times. Evidently, elected officials see more political capital to be gained from laying rail tracks than paving busways. Of course, some outsiders cast suspicion in the failure of Adelaide itself to expand O-Bahn services beyond the inaugural corridor. While this is mainly due to the region's slow population growth and economic woes, the inability to expand O-Bahn services has no doubt hurt its promotional cause.[16] A new high-capacity service to the south, from Adelaide to Darlington, is currently being studied, with O-Bahn one of several options under consideration. And from time to time there has been talk of replacing existing rail lines with guided busways. In the meantime, Adelaide continues to make headway in fine-tuning bus services and upgrading transit's image. The ambitious campaign to convert the bus fleet from diesel to CNG propulsion has won public praise. Less noticeable but equally important have been ongoing efforts to refine bus services—altering a route here, adding more park-and-ride spaces there—along the northeast corridor.

As a radial line-haul connector to the CBD, O-Bahn's future will hinge, in part, on maintaining a strong, viable center. While the suburbanization of residences is inevitable, local planning officials recognize that a dominant center must be maintained if transit is to compete effectively with the private automobile. Historically, Adelaide's square-mile CBD has been a true hub. In 1991, the latest year for which data are available, 21 percent of regional jobs and 13.5 percent of regional retail sales were in the CBD; the retail share was higher than in any Australian metropolitan area.[17] As elsewhere, these shares have no doubt slipped in recent years. In the case of retail, the recent closing of several large central city department stores has alarmed CBD interests, though this has had more to do with organizational restructuring within Australia's retail industry than with a decline in CBD business. While long-range planning controls guarantee that Adelaide's CBD will continue in its role as the preeminent commercial center for decades to come, the emergence of new second-tier centers has already sparked some discussions of what would become another Adelaide first: the opening of a crosstown O-Bahn corridor linking Tea Tree Gully to Port Adelaide to the east. If such a link is built, it will continue Adelaide's proud tradition of pioneering new forms of adaptive suburban transit services.

NOTES

1. Essen's O-Bahn service, introduced in 1981, operates mainly at the surface in the median strip of a freeway (*Autobahn*), with guideway buses running much slower and stopping more frequently than in Adelaide. The most unique feature of Essen's original O-Bahn service was its dual propulsion. While operating in a CBD tunnel and along the freeway corridor, buses were electrically propelled. The notion was that electricity would be more energy-efficient for mainline services and would avoid the problems of recirculating diesel fumes in the CBD tunnel. Diesel propulsion was considered superior for stop-and-go conditions on regular surface streets when buses left the guideway. However, because of technical problems and excessive cost over-runs, Essen eventually eliminated the electrical component of O-Bahn operations, did away with its underground tunnel, and converted to pure diesel, track-guided bus services outside the CBD.

2. Two of the bus routes serving the farthest reaches of the northeast corridor operate nonstop along the guided busway.

3. While Adelaide's O-Bahn relies on diesel-powered buses, the system was designed for conversion to electrical traction if and when petroleum fuel prices rise high enough to justify it.

4. This assumes an average of 100 passengers per bus and 180 bus runs per direction per hour (e.g., twenty seconds between buses).

5. H. Sack, The O-Bahn Guideway, Adelaide: Technical Constraints and Challenges. *Guided Busway Transit: Proceedings of the International Seminar* (Adelaide: Sagric International, 1989), pp. 11–13.

6. This assumes a price of US$0.51 per liter for diesel versus US$0.22 per liter for CNG. Adjusting for differences in fuel efficiency results in an average diesel cost of US$0.21 per kilometer compared to US$0.11 per kilometer for natural gas, assuming buses travel 60,000 kilometers per year. Source: H. Ng, Adelaide's Clean Public Transport (Staff paper, Adelaide Passenger Transport Board, 1996).

7. Data were compiled from annual reports provided by the Passenger Transport Board, including: Passenger Transport Board, *Annual Report 1995/1996* (Adelaide: Passenger Transport Board, 1996). Also see: J. Brown, Adelaide's Guided Busway: Popular with Passengers, *The Urban Transport Industries Report*, vol. 1 (Hong Kong: Campden Publications, Ltd., 1993), pp. 58–59.

8. Sources: Regional travel surveys and census statistics from: Australian Bureau of Statistics, *1991 Census Journey to Work* (Canberra: Australian Bureau of Statistics, 1992). Surveys show that in the first seven years of O-Bahn service, from 1986 to 1993, transit's modal share of work trips held steady in the 10 to 11 percent range. For 1986 modal split data, see: Pak-Poy & Kneebone Pty., Ltd., *Transport Planning Model Development Study* (Adelaide: Department of Transport, 1990). For 1993 modal split data, see: P. Gardner, *Drivers and Passengers: Travel to Work*, Catalogue No. 9203.4 (Adelaide: Australian Bureau of Statistics, Adelaide Statistical Division, 1993).

9. Cost recovery rates for buses operating in the northeast corridor increased from 24.5 percent in 1985–86, just before O-Bahn services commenced, to 38.3 percent in 1991–92, five years into the project. For all bus services in the region, rates increased only from 29 percent to 29.8 percent over the same period. Source: State Transport Authority, *Performance Indicators Report, 1984/85—1991/92: Eight Year Time Series* (Adelaide: State Transport Authority, Strategic Services Branch, 1992).

10. *Ibid.*

11. P. Chapman, The Adelaide O-Bahn: How Good in Practice? *Australasian Transport Research Forum*, vol. 17, part 1, 1992, pp. 83–100.

12. Denis Johnston and Associates Pty., Ltd., *Northeast Busway Before and After Study; Final Report: Evaluation of the Busway* (Adelaide: State Transport Authority and Department of Transport, 1988).

13. With regional population growth at under 1 percent annually, the plan commits to efficiently managing change as the region gradually transforms from a single-center to a multicentered metropolis. The long-range plan seeks to shift the balance of future urban development to the northern suburbs, away from the vulnerable vineyards to the south and hillscapes to the east. It also strongly commits to urban consolidation and infill development, though it recognizes that single-family housing remains a strong market preference

and attempts to plan for it accordingly. The plan calls for giving development preference to regional town centers that are well served by public transport. This bodes favorably for Tea Tree Gully since it receives more intensive transit services than any outlying center. See: Department of Housing and Urban Development, *Planning Strategy: Metropolitan Adelaide* (Adelaide: Department of Housing and Urban Development, State Government of South Australia, 1997).

14. All assets, including depots, buses, trains, and the O-Bahn system itself, became the property of the state's Department of Transport. Besides asset ownership, the Department of Transport is responsible for planning, building, and maintaining all highways and roads within South Australia.

15. Passenger Transport Board, *Adelaide O-Bahn: The Innovative Solution* (Adelaide: Kensington Studios and Passenger Transport Board, 1996).

16. The reluctance to move forward with additional O-Bahn lines also seems related to the release of a controversial study that found that, upon extending full capital costs and ridership projections over a thirty-year period, the O-Bahn would yield a negative economic rate of return: a net present value of –US$37.45 million or a benefit/cost ratio of 0.77. The projected loss was attributable mainly to the cumulative increase in access time (i.e., walking and waiting) for those converting from automobile to O-Bahn travel as well as the conclusion that the O-Bahn had little effect on traffic volume flows. It is this latter assumption that has drawn the most criticism, especially among environmentalists, who contend that the study grossly underestimated the external benefits, such as reduced energy consumption, produced by the O-Bahn. Clearly, the O-Bahn project has not been immune to criticism or the fairly common disagreements between economists and environmentalists about the net worth of mass transportation systems. See: Department of Transport, *An Economic Evaluation of the Northeast Busway in Adelaide* (Adelaide: Department of Transport, State Government of South Australia, 1991); and Chapman, *op. cit.*

17. R. Bunker and A. Tuttle, *The Role and Function of the Adelaide Central Area: Prospects and Trends*, A core paper prepared for Adelaide 21 (Adelaide: Municipality of Adelaide, 1996); P. Mees, "The Report of My Death Is an Exaggeration": Central City Retailing in Melbourne Since 1900, *Urban Policy and Research*, vol. 11, no. 1, 1993, p. 28.

Chapter 15

Hierarchical Transit: Mexico City, Mexico

Mexico City's free-enterprise paratransit sector provides vital links to the region's mainline rail and bus transit services, producing a public-private transit network that is superbly tailored to the region's spread-out landscape. At the top of the regional transit hierarchy is the 178-kilometer, predominantly underground Metro system. One of the world's most intensively used rail systems, Metro crisscrosses the core of the region, connecting most major activity nodes. Complementing Metro are intermediate carriers, including trolley bus, light rail, and diesel bus services, that both augment mainline services and provide longer-distance feeder connections. It has been the dynamic and wide-ranging network of privately owned and operated sedans, microbuses, and minibuses that accommodates the largest share of regional trips, feeding into Metro stations and filling other market niches, such as serving poor communities on the periphery. Route associations have emerged to self-police service practices as well as advocate the interests of the paratransit sector. Among its many benefits, Mexico City's hierarchical transit system has helped compensate for the poorly developed hierarchy of urban roads in the region. In adapting to the region's settlement pattern, Mexico City's Metro-bus-paratransit combination has unavoidably reinforced spread-out patterns of growth. As long as market-driven development continues to dominate, with few planning incentives to concentrate growth near station nodes, adaptive transit services are the only realistic means of sustaining a metropolis of Mexico City's size and complexity.

As the world's largest metropolis, with an estimated population as high as 22 million, Mexico City poses mobility challenges that are unparalleled. The Federal District (Distrito Federal, or DF), the 1,254-square-kilometer administrative area that makes up the national capital and economic and cultural hub of the country, claims a more manageable 9 million inhabitants. With population having nearly doubled every decade since 1930, however, urban growth has, in recent decades, spilled well beyond the

Federal District into the surrounding states of Mexico and Morelos. It is the Federal District and its adjoining suburbs that make up the megalopolis of Mexico City, with an official 1990 population of 15.1 million and an unofficial one at least 25 percent higher. Today, about one-quarter of Mexico's population resides in greater Mexico City, which covers just 1 percent of the country's surface area.[1] With urban development of such magnitude occurring at such a rapid pace have come strains on public infrastructure and services—from water supply to refuse disposal to transportation—that tax the public treasury as well as natural ecologies.

Presently, more than 37 million motorized trips are made each day within metropolitan Mexico City, 70 percent occurring within the Federal District.[2] Nearly 3 million private automobiles are registered in the metropolis, and vehicle ownership has risen at least twice as fast as the region's 2.5 percent annual population growth rate. Traffic congestion has become nearly pandemic. During peak hours, traffic within the District crawls at an average speed of 9 kilometers per hour. The crush of automobiles has produced some of the worst smog conditions anywhere, exacerbated by mountains that ring the valley and contain pollutants. (By one account, breathing Mexico City's air on a typical weekday is equivalent to smoking two packs of cigarettes a day.) Conditions are further aggravated by the large population of old, poorly running cars that have no catalytic converters and Mexico City's high altitude, which reduces engine efficiency.[3] The Federal District has imposed a "Days Off the Road" (*Hoy No Circula*) scheme that restricts private and government vehicles from operating at least one day a week, on a rotating basis, according to the last digit of license plates. Vehicle travel bans, also introduced in Santiago and Athens, have encouraged people to take mass transit and share rides, but there are often compliance problems. One problem has been the creation of a market for cheap, secondhand vehicles that are generally more polluting and less efficient than newer models. Motorists purchase these vehicles for use on days when they are prohibited from driving their primary vehicle, thus subverting the intent of the ban. In Mexico City, the market for cheap second vehicles is a brisk one.

Mexico City's congestion and pollution would be much worse were it not for the dynamic and wide-ranging transportation system that has evolved over the years in response to explosive growth. Notably, a hierarchy of transportation services—both public and private—has emerged, providing a rich mix of travel options in terms of geographic coverage, vehicle carrying capacities, and levels of integration. At the top of the hierarchy and forming the backbone of the system is Metro, a predominantly rubber-tire, high-speed subway network that crisscrosses the Federal District. With Metro forming the main arteries of the region's transit network, equally vital to the lifeblood of the metropolis have been the network's capillaries: the extensive system of paratransit feeder services known locally as *peseros* and *colectivos*. In the 1950s, taxi drivers operating along the city's busiest boulevards began augmenting income by picking up multiple unrelated passengers, charging them a flat fee—one peso. The mode quickly grew in popularity and became known as a pesero. As peseros increasingly became the public transportation mode of choice, taxi sedans were gradually replaced by Volkswagen vans, also known as combis, and microbuses during the 1960s and 1970s. Combis are rapidly being replaced by twenty-three-seat minibuses that burn unleaded fuel (also called *magna sin*, Spanish for "without lead"). Today, *colectivos* is the term of choice to represent the full spectrum of paratransit services available in the region, from shared-ride taxis to minibuses. Supplementing these modes are intermediate carriers—electric trolley buses, suburban diesel buses, and an advanced light rail service. As hybrids between public mainline and private feeder services, these intermediate carriers represent a mix of both government-sponsored and commercially run distributor services.

Over the years, what has evolved is a hub-and-spoke transport network that closely mimics the predominant travel patterns of the region and facilitates intermodal transfers. Institutionally, the arrangement has clear lines of responsibility: government is the provider of mainline, high-capacity services, and the private sector largely takes care of most branch connections. The resulting transit network very much represents the adaptation of transit to the urban landscape. Unlike in Stockholm or Singapore, rail station nodes have not attracted significant shares of regional growth. Mexico City's adaptive transit, moreover, has relatively little to do with technology. Rather, the lesson of Mexico City has more to do with the power of the marketplace, when left to its own accord, to deliver niche services well suited to the lay of the land and to fill gaps left unfilled by the public sector.

Metro: The Region's Transit Backbone

The Sistema de Transporte Colectivo (STC), or Metro, first opened in 1969 as a single 12-kilometer line with 16 stations and has gradually expanded to what is today a network of ten lines with 154 stations spanning 178 kilometers, the fifth-largest metro system in the world (Map 15.1). Five of the lines are oriented in a predominantly east-west direction and five extend mainly north-south, together forming a supergrid. Originally modeled after the Paris subway and built by a French-Mexican co-venture, trains on nine of the lines run on pneumatic tires, providing relatively smooth, quiet rides (Photo 15.1). Trains can accelerate and decelerate faster with rubber tires, allowing for short station spacing in the dense city core. Moreover, since pneumatic trains can negotiate tighter turns,

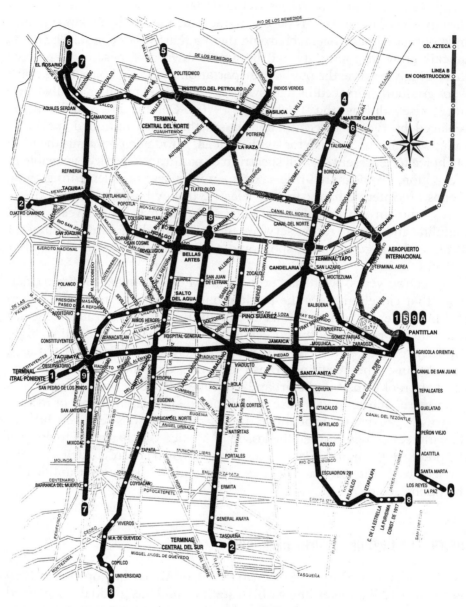

MAP 15.1. MEXICO CITY'S METRO NETWORK, 1997. *Source:* Sistema de Transporte Colectivo, Ciudad de Mexico.

subway tubes could be more easily aligned to connect major activity nodes in the core. Minimal vibrations also made pneumatic services well suited to Mexico City's unstable soils, long a concern in building a subway, and also allowed for extensive air-rights development above tubes and stations. The major drawback of pneumatic services has been higher main-

PHOTO 15.1. MEXICO CITY'S METRO TRAINS. Rubber-tired trains operate at surface within the arterial median strip along Route 2, south of the central city.

tenance expenses and a higher incidence of in-service breakdowns from deflated tires, not a trivial matter for a system with trains that come by every two minutes and passenger queues that back up very quickly on the busiest lines. Partly for this reason, the 17-kilometer Line A, which serves several low-income communities in the State of Mexico and which opened in 1991, is the system's first section of steel-wheel services.

Presently, Mexico City's metro services are the most intensive in the world, with more train cars per rail kilometer than anywhere. In all, 190 nine-car trains make more than 2,400 trips per day. Transit fares have historically been pegged to worker salaries, fluctuating between 1.1 and 3.6 percent of minimum daily wages—a tacit policy to promote social stability in a country where average wages are kept low for the sake of international competitiveness. In 1994, a Metro ride cost about seven U.S. cents.[4] Extensive and frequent services, coupled with cheap fares, has proven a successful formula for attracting patrons. With daily ridership nearing 5 million, Metro is one of the most highly patronized rail transit systems in the world, exceeded only by Moscow and Tokyo. Mexico City's Metro is larger in size and claims more riders than all others metros in Latin America—São Paulo, Rio de Janeiro, Buenos Aires, Santiago, and Caracas—put together. About one in five daily trips made within the District use the Metro for at least one leg.[5] A third of regional work trips are via Metro; the next highest rail commute modal split in Latin America is Santiago, at 16 percent. During rush hours, sardinelike conditions prevail—averaging 1,900 passengers per train, or some 210 passengers per car. Peak-load crunches have prompted the introduction of a "rationing" system that reserves certain train cars for women and children.[6]

Heavy ridership has helped to offset cheap fares in producing a fairly respectable cost recovery rate—in fiscal year 1994–95, Metro covered 38.3 percent of total costs, including annualized debt service on capital expenditures.[7] Cost efficiencies have also helped—at US$0.15 per passenger trip in 1994, Metro recorded the lowest unit cost of any subway system in the world. Still, Metro's financial burden has been substantial and a source of political conflict over the years. Since the late 1960s, Metro has consumed the largest share of the Federal District's budget—in some years, exceeding 30 percent of the total. Metro's heavy debt load, in combination with anti-urban movements, have intermittently stalled the system's expansion, such as between 1972 and 1978 when planned extensions and new lines were put on hold amid political infighting.[8]

To the disappointment of some, there has been little clustering of urban development around Metro stations to date. Except for a few downtown skyscrapers that predate the Metro project, Mexico City's urban density gradient does not noticeably rise near subway portals (Photo 15.2). Only a few outlying stations have spurred new office building construction. Outside the core, employment concentrations have occurred only as a result of pro-active planning, such as around the Zapata station on Line 3, where several large employers, including the largest national newspaper, *Reforma*, several federal offices, and Roche Labs, Inc., an international pharmaceutical interest, have located. It was because supplemental land was purchased and pre-assembled around the Zapata station to accommodate a minibus transfer area and an adjoining commercial zone that large employers were attracted to this location (Photo 15.3). Such leveraging of private development has been rare, however. In part, very little strategic land-use planning has occurred around stations because Mexico City has had neither the institutional capacity nor the luxury of doing advanced master planning—urbanization has occurred so rapidly that government ends up concentrating on immediate needs and exigencies, constantly playing catch-up. Limited land-use regulations and zoning controls have tended to spawn a hodgepodge of commercial activities around stations, comprising an assortment of small restaurants, retail kiosks, repair shops, newsstands, and street vendors. Around some stations to the east and north of downtown, where most of the poor live, numerous small specialized adult training schools have opened in recent years. The existence of marginal mixed-commercial activities, coupled with other perceived nuisances, such as street peddlers and swarms of colectivos, have deterred middle-class housing construction around stations.

Photo 15.2. Central Mexico City's skyline. Uniform urban densities exist in the core. High-rise towers are concentrated around only a few core-area Metro stations.

Metro's greatest impact on urban form has been to further spur decentralization. Rich and poor communities alike have taken form near and beyond Metro's terminal stations over the past several decades. In a largely unregulated regional land market, the combination of relatively cheap peripheral land, proximity to Metro's outer reaches, and less crowded conditions has lead to mammoth new town developments on the fringes. To the south and west, new towns such as San Ángel and Bosque have catered mostly to the region's burgeoning middle and upper-middle classes. To the east and west, often downwind from industrial belts, are large concentrations of unskilled laborers, poor households, and rural inmigrants. Some of the region's densest and poorest municipalities, such as Nezahualcoyotl and Tlalnepantla, border the Federal District in the State of Mexico.[9] Metro's busiest stations—Indios Verdes and Pantitlan, each handling 170,000 to 190,000 customers a day—mostly serve the factories and residents of these poor outlying areas.[10] The high dependency of the peripheral poor on Metro services results in a predominantly captive ridership profile: more than half of Metro's passengers earn below minimum wage, and only one in eight has an automobile available.[11]

Greater Mexico City's spread-out pattern of development is reflected in travel statistics. Regional home-interview travel surveys conducted

PHOTO 15.3. STATION-AREA ACTIVITIES OUTSIDE THE CORE. A minibus transfer zone is surrounded by mid-rise office development outside the Zapata station on Line 3.

in 1983 and 1994 show a strong shift in origin-destination patterns from the center to the periphery of the region.[12] The heaviest and fastest-growing origin-destination flows are radial movements from adjacent, low-income communities in the State of Mexico to the Federal District. In 1994, more than half of all motorized trips from municipalities in the State of Mexico were to the Federal District.[13] Decentralization has resulted in exceedingly long average per trip travel times—in 1994, 46 minutes for the region as a whole and 53.5 minutes for those residing outside the Federal District.[14]

In response to mounting decentralization pressures, the Mexican government has announced plans to significantly extend Metro services. New extensions and lines will add 31 kilometers by the year 2003. And by 2020, if all goes according to plan, twenty-seven Metro lines—a combination of subways and elevated commuter tracks—will weave an elaborate pattern across the metropolitan landscape, more than doubling Metro's current trackage. These announcements have brought on fears that Metro expansions will only fan the flames of galloping sprawl. In a press interview following the release of Metro's master plan, Miguel Valencia Mulkai, president of the Regional Ecology Forum for the Valley of Mexico, cautioned, "Expanding the Metro is the surest way to urban sprawl. The further out the lines run, the broader the secondary transport web."[15] By "secondary transport web" is meant the system of paratransit feeders and bus transit distributors that tie into Metro's terminal stations, effectively extending the travelshed for Metro services by several orders of magnitude. A consequence of spread-out development has been high rates of intermodal transferring—35 percent of regional trips in 1994 involved a change from one mode to another.[16] In the absence of a regional transportation authority, owing mainly to a protracted history of political squabbling and infighting, there has been very little coordination of intermodal services, either within the public sector or among public and private providers.[17] Interestingly, as discussed later, it has been in the private transport sector that one finds the greatest degree of service coordination, mainly in the form of route associations. It has required the natural workings of the marketplace in a loosely regulated paratransit sector to close the coordination gap.

Intermediate Carriers

A patchwork of intermediate-capacity transit services has evolved to largely fill in service gaps left by the Metro. The two publicly supported intermediate carriers—trolley buses (nineteen lines in all) and the 27-kilometer Tren Ligero light railway—largely supplement Metro services by operating parallel to Metro lines, filling in mainline service gaps of the subway. Functioning mainly as intermediate-distance distributors are the District's more than 100 diesel bus routes, called Ruta Cien. Their suburban counterparts, providing longer-haul links between peripheral communities in the surrounding states of Mexico and Morelos and Metro's terminal stations, are privately operated diesel buses. In 1994, some 36 percent of passengers entering Metro's twenty-two major intermodal transfer stations arrived by urban and suburban diesel buses. Hierarchically, then, intermediate surface carriers function both to extend the reach of Metro mainline services as well as to collect and distribute transit customers.

While the government-sponsored and -subsidized intermediate carriers—trolley buses and light rail—serve a small fraction of daily trip segments (under 1 percent), the region's privately operated diesel buses carry more than 10 percent of daily unlinked trips, a share that is steadily growing. Ruta Cien's ridership and service quality, in particular, have risen since services were recently turned over to the private sector under a concessionary arrangement.[18] There are signs of a richer assortment of regular-route bus services—from standard operations to more premium commuter services—now taking form under private ownership.

Where the intermediate carriers falter, especially when compared to privately operated paratransit feeders, is with respect to service and fare coordination. There are no obvious efforts to synchronize timetables, though, since Metro services tend to be so frequent, this is not a serious concern. However, the lack of fare integration is. Though tariffs are relatively cheap, multiple fare payments can be quite burdensome to Mexico City's millions of daily transit-dependent customers. The biggest discrepancies are between Metro fares and the much higher priced suburban bus services, which can cost five times as much as Metro. Also troublesome to surface-street intermediate carriers is the region's ever-worsening traffic congestion, which not only compromises the reliability and security of services, but also increases fuel consumption, person-hours of labor, and vehicle wear and tear. Diesel buses are also criticized for exacerbating the region's air pollution problems, spewing several tons of particulate matter into the air basin each day.

Paratransit Feeders: A Market Adaptation

Mexico City's pesero and minibus sector has grown and adapted over the years in response to Metro's rapid expansion. As a fairly loosely regulated industry, paratransit has evolved to fill service gaps and meet specialized mobility needs—namely, providing short-to-intermediate-distance feeder connections to mainline carriers, as well as serving poor and politically powerless neighborhoods outside the District that have been bypassed by bus operators, in part because of their inaccessibility.

Mexico City's hierarchy of small-to-intermediate-capacity paratransit services has also helped compensate for the region's poor hierarchy of roads and highways. Just as rivers rely on tributaries, there must be a well-functioning network of local streets that interconnect with collectors and arterials for traffic to circulate efficiently. While a limited-access freeway arcs around the northern portion of the Federal District, and several monumental-scale boulevards (the *ejes vigles*) crisscross the built-up core, there is a serious shortage of collector streets to distribute traffic onto the main arteries. A significant portion of collectors are discontinuous, abruptly ending and then picking up again a kilometer or so down the road. Just as crippling is the poorly designed tertiary network of local roads, many of which are too narrow to accommodate oncoming vehicles, have irregular alignments, lack parking, and above all, are invaded by street vendors, peddlers, auto repair shops, and other activities that spill onto the right-of-ways. Mexico City's paratransit sector has thus evolved in number and composition to serve the region's under-capacity, poorly connected, and subhierarchical road network. It functions, in part, as a modal response to the inadequacies of the road system.[19]

Colectivos: The Supply Side

The hierarchy of paratransit services in greater Mexico City is revealed by Table 15.1. A rich spectrum of services is offered in terms of seating capacity, geographic coverage, levels of comfort, and fares. Taxis provide on-call, curb-to-curb services—both exclusive and shared rides—whereas other paratransit modes ply principal routes. Pesero sedans tend to serve the lowest volume corridors and make slight route detours at riders' requests. Combis normally carry two to three times as many riders as sedans and concentrate mainly on intermediate-volume markets in the suburbs. Some combi operators guarantee seats. Minibuses seat up to twenty-five passengers with room for an equal number to stand. Table 15.1 also shows that vehicles have segmented themselves geographically, with smaller vehicles serving shorter-haul customers (more often in the suburban-exurban fringes of the State of Mexico) and larger vehicles traversing longer distances (more often within the Federal District). Overall, market segmentation by vehicle capacity and corridor has helped to rationalize the use of scarce road space and increase the passenger throughput of the District's underdesigned road net.

Presently, there are about 100 paratransit routes in Mexico City, and each route averages about fifteen deviations or branches. Thus, there are some 1,500 variations among the 100 or so main paratransit routes. Central Mexico City is virtually saturated with peseros and minibuses during peak periods. Middle-class suburbs are also well served. Many barrios and slum areas on the periphery receive thinner services, not only because their residents are less able to pay market-rate fares but also because roads leading to these areas are often substandard and steep. Still, paratransit manages to penetrate some of the narrow and poorly maintained roads and alleys that buses can not. The routes of nearly all peseros and minibuses in the surrounding State of Mexico end at a Metro terminal station (Photo 15.4).

Peseros and minibuses normally begin service at about 6:00 A.M. and continue until as late as 10:00 P.M. to 11:00 P.M. Some high-demand routes provide twenty-four-hour service. Headways vary by demand. During peak hours, a steady stream of jam-packed vehicles funnel into and out of Metro stations. During the off-peak, vehicles line up outside stations and normally leave only when they are at least half full.

Table 15.1 MEXICO CITY'S HIERARCHY OF PARATRANSIT SERVICES, 1994

	Seating Capacities (No. of Passengers)	Typical Route Operating Ranges (One-Way Kilometers)	Vehicle Inventory		
			Federal District	State of Mexico	Total
Taxis	2–3	3–6	56,059	8,456	64,515
Peseros: Sedans	5–6	2–4	763	2,626	3,389
Peseros: VW Vans	10–14	5–10	22,690	13,860	36,550
Minibuses	22–25	10–20	20,493	9,527	30,020
Total	—	—	100,005	34,469	134,474

Source: La Coordinación General de Transporte del DDF, data files; field surveys, November 1994.

PHOTO 15.4. MINIBUSES AT MAJOR TRANSFER STATION. Privately owned and operated minibuses tie into the Pantitlan station, one of Metro's busiest stations and the terminus of four rail lines.

Mexico City's paratransit sector has become an important source of urban employment. Most peseros and colectivos are individually owned and operated under the direction of a route association. Many owner-operators drive during an eight-to-nine-hour morning-afternoon shift and lease their vehicles during evening hours.[20] Minibuses cost an estimated US$0.71 per kilometer to operate in November 1994 (just prior to the devaluation of Mexican currency), yielding about US$0.22 in driver earnings per kilometer. Minibus owner-operators averaged about US$50 in net daily income, whereas lease-operators cleared around US$28.[21] On average, minibus drivers earn a salary comparable to public bus drivers, though they receive no benefits and have less job security.

Where Mexico City's paratransit services fall short is in vehicle quality, as they are victims of constant, heavy usage. Fleets are often minimally maintained and toward the end of their service lives. It must always be kept in mind, however, that First World quality transit services equate to First World price levels, something few Mexican transit patrons can afford. Crowded and sometimes tattered vehicles are a necessary evil in the Third World paratransit marketplace in order to keep fares low. Outside oversubscribed peak hours, however, peseros and minibuses usually provide reasonably comfortable rides. Moreover, drivers are generally no more aggressive than other motorists, unlike in most other developing countries with thriving paratransit sectors. This is mainly because Mexico City's paratransit routes are controlled by associations, thus easing some of the competition for customers. In fact, there tends to be a fair amount of camaraderie among paratransit operators belonging to the same route association.

Colectivos: The Demand Side

In terms of demand, paratransit reigns supreme among all forms of travel in greater Mexico City. Table 15.2 shows that minibuses, peseros, and taxis combined to handle about 40 percent of motorized trips in the Federal District and 37 percent of trips in the State of Mexico in 1994. Paratransit was more heavily patronized than all public transit combined in the Federal District and carried loads comparable to motor buses in the State of Mexico.[22] It is noteworthy that all forms of mass transportation serve more than 70 percent of all motorized trips even though they constitute just 15 percent of the total vehicles circulating in the region. Combining demand and supply figures (i.e., from Tables 15.1 and 15.2) reveals that the average daily passenger load of a minibus operating in metropolitan Mexico City is about 280. Average daily peseros ridership is 120 passengers per Volkswagen van and 65 passengers per sedan.

Mexico City's paratransit sector plays a dominant role in getting patrons to and from Metro for trips originating within the Federal District

Table 15.2   DAILY MOTORIZED TRIPS IN GREATER MEXICO CITY, 1994

	Federal District		State of Mexico		Metropolitan Area	
	Total	Percent	Total	Percent	Total	Percent
Public Transportation						
Metro	4,488,000	17.6	0	0.0	4,488,000	12.2
Light rail	15,000	0.1	0	0.0	15,000	0.1
Ruta Cien (surface diesel bus)	3,208,000	12.6	0	0.0	3,208,000	8.7
Electric trolley bus	330,000	1.3	0	0.0	330,000	0.8
Other bus (autobus)s	0	0.0	4,385,000	38.2	4,385,000	11.9
Paratransit						
Minibuses	5,738,000	22.5	2,287,000	19.9	8,025,000	21.7
Peseros (combis and sedans)	2,772,000	10.9	1,831,000	16.0	4,603,000	12.5
Taxis	1,615,000	6.3	102,000	0.9	1,717,000	4.6
Private Automobile	7,316,000	28.7	2,864,000	25.0	10,180,000	27.5
Total	25,482,000	100.0	11,469,000	100.0	36,951,000	100.0

Source: Instituto Nacional de Estadistica Geografia e Informatica (INEGI), Encuesta de Origen y Destino de los Viajes de los Residentes del Area Metropolitana de la Ciudad de México (Mexico City: INEGI, 1994).

and ranks second to buses in connecting residents of outlying suburbs to terminal stations. Region-wide, nearly ten times as many people access the Metro via paratransit as they do by walking.

Together, Metro and its paratransit feeders have dramatically increased accessibility to the urban edge, home to millions of rural in-migrants and squatters. Unsubsidized paratransit fares have generally been far higher than Metro's subsidized ones—about US$0.18 in 1994, or about 5 percent of the average daily wage of an unskilled worker.[23] Because many of the poor living on the periphery make as many as five connections per day, public transport expenses can consume as much as a quarter of a day's minimum salary.

As an adaptive transit system, suited to serving predominant origin-destination patterns, Mexico City's Metro-paratransit combination has indelibly shaped urban form. Prior to 1970, the radial, bus-based transit network served to reinforce the region's monocentric structure. With near-ly all buses running to the core of the metropolis, congestion on radiating boulevards became increasingly intolerable. By increasing regional acces-sibility by several orders of magnitude, the Metro and its feeder network have been a powerful force toward decentralization, redistributing growth outward. Gross densities for the metropolitan area, for instance, stood at 160 inhabitants per hectare in 1994, nearly identical to what they were in 1940, despite the region's population having risen from 1.76 million to some 20 million over this period.[24] Peseros, minibuses, and intermediate carriers have served as the tentacles that allowed those living on the periphery to reach the core, thus adapting to, and in so doing, reinforcing, the region's dispersed settlement pattern. Mexico City's Metro-paratransit combination, then, exemplifies the adaptation of services and technolo-gies to the lay of the land. And in so doing, it has unavoidably reinforced and possibly even helped trigger peripheral growth (e.g., by making it eas-ier for rural in-migrants to continue populating the region's outer edges and still seek job opportunities). The fact that rail transit and paratransit have managed to co-exist in a mutually rewarding way is largely due to public and private oversight.

Public Oversight

As a mostly free-enterprise, unrestricted paratransit sector emerged fol-lowing Metro's 1969 opening, it quickly became clear that laissez-faire transport in such a large, complex metropolis was leading to chaos. Prior to this time, although peseros and combis were technically illegal, they were tolerated by local officials in the absence of suitable alternative public transportation.[25] Over time, government policies that both legit-imize and control peseros and colectivos have evolved, in recognition of paratransit's vital importance, yet potential threat, to mobility within the metropolis.

The regional transportation planning authority, la Coordinación General de Transporte del DDF (CGT), oversees paratransit within the Federal District, and a counterpart authority has jurisdiction over the seven municipalities and unincorporated areas in the outlying suburbs. These organizations control market entry by issuing permits and licenses. They also negotiate permitted routes of operation, set tariffs, and maintain performance standards (e.g., driver and vehicle fitness).[26] Within these limitations, however, private operators are free to operate as they choose, including the hours they work and schedules they maintain. Because of a purported oversupply of minibuses, the Federal District has not issued new paratransit permits for many years. On Route 2, one of the busiest and longest-standing minibus routes in the District, no new permits have been granted since 1968. The presence of a bustling black market for counterfeit colectivo licenses and permits (costing about US$100), however, suggests publicly sanctioned minibus supplies are too low.

In controlling routes, regulators deserve credit for rationalizing services and reducing inefficiencies on the urban transit network. Upon Metro's 1969 opening, the CGT began issuing paratransit licenses only for routes that fed into Metro stations. Crosstown and long-haul radial services were largely eliminated. Most likely, even without government's guiding hand, peseros and minibus operators would have adapted services quite similarly in order to maximize efficiency and profits. Regulators have also prohibited suburban buses and colectivos from the surrounding states of Mexico and Morelos from entering the District core, restricting them to peripheral Metro stations instead.

Other government offices oversee other aspects of paratransit affairs in greater Mexico City. Federal involvement is largely limited to regulating vehicle exhaust, a responsibility of the Secretary of Transport and Communications. More problematic has been enforcement of regulations. Over the years, these responsibilities have vacillated between the city's police department and the Direción General de Autotransporte Urbano, the District authority in charge of public transportation services. Shifting roles have mainly been a result of internal power struggles as different political groups have gone after what is often viewed as a potentially lucrative business: collecting fines for actual and alleged violations of government rules. However, no District authorities have the resources to enforce rules among some 100,000 licensed paratransit operators in the city, much less the tens of thousands of unlicensed ones. Currently, only about 200 officers in the District enforce paratransit regulations. Despite the presence of a thick handbook of rules and regulations for peseros and minibuses, requirements are largely unenforceable.

Private Regulation: Route Associations

In light of the difficulties in enforcing paratransit regulations and given the enormity of Mexico City's paratransit sector, the emergence of pro-active route associations was inevitable. Each of the more than 100 peseros and minibus routes in the Federal District is today represented by a route association.[27] Additionally, there are fifteen umbrella organizations that actively lobby for the interests of the paratransit industry in general and their constituent route associations specifically. Overall, then, a hierarchical organizational structure has evolved to administer, self-police, and promote the city's hierarchy of paratransit services.

Among the functions carried out by route associations have been to secure authorizations for branch routes and organize the allocation of vehicles on those routes; assist owner-members in obtaining vehicle loans from banks and the government; settle claims stemming from accidents; and represent members in dealings with government officials. The city's largest route associations elect full-time presidents and governing boards and maintain administrative offices, central dispatchers (for vehicles equipped with shortwave radios), and service garages. In addition to routine maintenance and repairs, associations' garages stockpile vehicle parts, such as tires and oil filters, which are available to members at discounts.

Over the years, some route associations have evolved more or less into cartels, successfully lobbying to set limits on licensing and route expansions. The amount of power wielded by associations is by all appearances directly proportional to size. For the largest and most established associations, such as the Route 2 association, which oversees 2,500 minibuses and VW vans in central Mexico City, the degree of control is considerable—besides chasing away illegal operators from its members' routes, it hires field attendants to direct passenger boardings at busy terminals, keeps the police at bay, and maintains records of drivers' log-in and log-out times.

Learning from Mexico City

Mexico City's multi-tier, hierarchical network of Metro, intermediate carrier, and paratransit services has been absolutely essential in restraining car travel and serving the mobility needs of a megalopolis as enormous as the Federal District and its suburbs. Minibuses and peseros handle more than a third of motorized trips within the region, more than either the private automobile or all public transit services combined. They provide essential feeder services into rail stops without government subsidies, in addition to delivering badly needed services for and jobs in poor neighborhoods. In terms of seating capacities, operating speeds, and geographic coverage, Mexico City's paratransit sector is well adapted to the physical road plant, serving narrow passageways impenetrable by buses and compensating for inadequate road hierarchy. Overall, the network of radial rail lines and branching paratransit feeder services has allowed a spread-out, polycentric metropolis to take shape, relieving pressure on, yet maintaining the preeminence of, the central core.

Mexico City's transit network is as noteworthy for its institutional configurations as it is for its physical ones. There is a clear division of public and private responsibilities. Public operators provide mainly trunk-line rail and bus services, which are complemented by private paratransit feeders. Straddling this public-private spectrum are route associations. In a lightly regulated (or at least loosely policed) marketplace, Mexico City's route associations have become absolutely indispensable organizations for coordinating and rationalizing paratransit service delivery, while at the same time protecting and promoting the interests of their members.

Mexico City's free-enterprise, open-market approach to providing supplemental transit services has relevance beyond Third World megacities. Many First World cities would also profit from opening up the transportation marketplace to greater competition, allowing profit-seeking entrepreneurs to seek out new market niches and, in so doing, fill service gaps left by the public sector. In the United States, Canada, and much of Europe, commercial paratransit services have been largely regulated out of existence, resulting in a fairly standardized public transit product, one that is less and less capable of seriously competing with the private car in the fastest-growing market, suburbia. Deregulation of paratransit market entry, service practices, and pricing could spawn various forms of shared-ride, door-to-door services, not unlike the airport shuttle vans popular in many U.S. cities. Besides serving airports, however, paratransit vans would likely branch out into other market niches in a deregulated marketplace, such as feeding into mainline rail stations, providing premium crosstown connections, and serving such major destinations as college campuses, shopping malls, sports complexes, theme parks, and suburban downtowns. Technological advances in vehicle location systems, on-board navigational aids, and real-time scheduling-routing optimization software could give rise to a type of "smart paratransit." In a spread-out metropolis, intelligent forms of small-vehicle transit hold some of the best hopes for competing with the on-demand, many-to-many, and front-door delivery service features of the private automobile.

Despite the overwhelming popularity of colectivos and minibuses, there have been rumblings in the central government in recent years to replace vans and minibuses in the District with standard bus coaches. Paratransit would be limited to serving less-traveled suburban markets. Some high-level officials believe bigger vehicles will ultimately reduce congestion and air pollution. Many are clearly uncomfortable with the stigma attached to paratransit as an inferior, obsolete mode unsuited to rapidly modernizing countries, much less their image-conscious capital. Because route associations have become a strong political force in their own right, however, few observers believe that Mexico City's free-enterprise paratransit can be completely done away with as it has been in most other parts of North America. With no end to growth in sight and little policy interest in transit-oriented development, the world's largest metropolis will likely need a healthy, entrepreneurial paratransit sector, well adapted to the region's spread-out cityscape, for many years to come.

NOTES

1. Cushman and Wakefield, Mexico City Metropolitan Area, *ULI Market Profiles: 1994* (Washington, DC: The Urban Land Institute, 1994).

2. La Coordinación General de Transporte del DDF, *Viajes Pasajero en Día Habil en la Ciudad de México y su Area Metropolitana* (Mexico City: Comisión General de Transporte, 1994).

3. A. Amstrong-Wright, *Public Transport in Third World Cities* (London: HMSO Publications, 1993).

4. Fares were substantially raised in 1996 as a fiscal austerity measure and in reaction to the peso's devaluation to over an average of US$0.15 per ride, or around 3 percent of minimum daily wages.

5. N. Benítez and G. Gomez, The Mexican Experience, *Rail Mass Transit for Developing Countries* (London: Thomas Telford, 1990).

6. Rationing takes place on the three busiest and oldest lines—Routes 1, 2, and 3—which together account for two-thirds of all patronage. This share is actually down from the mid-1980s when these three lines carried about 90 percent of rail passengers.

7. Sistema de Transporte Colectivo (STC), *Informe de Actividades 1994* (Mexico City: STC, 1995).

8. Marxist critiques and conspiracy theories hold that Metro's construction was motivated largely by capitalist profit making. Critics charge that a private engineering conglomerate, Inginieros Civiles Asociados (ICA), worked closely with downtown landholders, export-minded French subway builders, and a District governor enamored by monumental public works projects to bring the project to fruition. Backers would argue that Metro's stellar ridership performance over the years, and the traffic paralysis that has been avoided, prove the investment to be an economically sound one. For further discussions, see: D. Davis, *Urban Leviathan: Mexico City in the Twentieth Century* (Philadelphia: Temple University Press, 1994).

9. Nezahualcoyotl, adjoining the Federal District to the east, averages 335 inhabitants per hectare, well above Mexico City's 180 residents per hectare and above national standards for acceptable population densities. See: J. Flores Moreno, El Transporte en la Zona Metropolitana de la Ciudad de

México, *Grandes Problemas de la Ciudad de México*, R. Zenteno and J. More-los, eds. (Mexico City: Plaza y Valdes, 1988), pp. 265–279.

10. Turnstile surveys at the Indios Verdes station reveal that more than 80 percent of entering passengers are low-skilled factory workers drawing minimum wages. S. Lizt Mendoza, Respuestas del Transporte Urbano en las Zonas Marginadas, *Grandes Problemas de la Ciudad de México*, R. Zenteno and J. Morelos, eds. (Mexico City: Plaza y Valdés, 1988), pp. 215–242.

11. B. Benítez, *Ciudad de México: El Metro y Sus Usuarios* (Mexico City: Universidad Autónoma Metropolitana, 1993).

12. G. González, Expectativas del Transporte, *El Transporte Metropolitano Hoy*, L. Becerril et al., eds. (Mexico City: Universidad Nacional Autónoma de México, 1995), pp. 99–105.

13. Moreno, *op. cit.*

14. Mean travel time for residents of the Federal District was 40.6 minutes in 1994. Sources: Instituto Nacional de Estadistica Geografia e Informatica (INEGI), *Encuesta de Origen y Destino de los Viajes de los Residentes del Area Metropolitana de la Ciudad de México* (Mexico City: INEGI, 1994); and M. Cervera Flores, La Encuesta Origen y Destino de Los Viajes de los Residentes del AMCM, 1994, *El Transporte Metropolitano Hoy*, L. Becerril, ed. (Mexico City: Universidad Nacional Autónoma de México, 1995), pp. 73–83.

15. M. Lloyd, First Phase of Transport Expansion Plan Unveiled, *The News*, vol. 66, no. 258, March 27, 1996, p. 5.

16. INEGI, *op. cit.*

17. The region's transportation institutional landscape is very fragmented today. In 1984, the CGT (la Coordinación General de Transporte del DDF) was created for the purpose of planning and managing the operations of public transit and road development in the Federal District. A counterpart authority for the State of Mexico, called COTREM (la Comisión del Transporte del Esado de México) was also created. Both entities are charged with coordinating mass transportation development with COVITUR (la Comisión de Vialdad y Transporte Urbano), the authority formed to manage and oversee the construction of Metro and other large transportation infrastructure projects. Also involved in transportation matters are the seventeen municipalities that make up the Mexico City metropolitan area. In practice, political loyalties, interjurisdictional feuding, and petty jealousies have stood in the way of institutional coordination. For further discussions, see: M. P. Cohen, ed., *La Modernización de las Ciudades en México* (Mexico City: Universidad Nacional Autónoma de México, 1990).

18. Historically, diesel bus services have been chaotic and fractured. In response, all private bus services in the Federal District were brought under a single public authority, Ruta Cien, in 1982. The principal aim was to enhance bus services in parts of the District bypassed by Metro. After acquiring the private concessions, the government rationalized routes, modernized and refurbished buses, and improved maintenance standards. Driver wages, benefits, and working conditions also markedly improved.

However, as in the United States and much of the developed world, the combination of a protected public monopoly and non-performance-based compensation eventually proved to be Ruta Cien's undoing. In 1990, services were suspended outside the Federal District. Falling ridership forced service cuts, setting off a downward spiral. While the District has retained some control over routing and service policies of the former Ruta Cien, the operations themselves were totally privatized in hopes of increasing service productivity.

19.   Studies have similarly shown that paratransit plays a vital role in compensating for poor road systems in Asia. See: R. Cervero, Paratransit in Southeast Asia: A Market Response to Poor Roads? *Review of Urban and Regional Development Studies*, vol. 3, 1991, pp. 3–27; and H. Dimitriou, *A Developmental Approach to Urban Transport Planning: An Indonesian Illustration* (Aldershot, England: Avebury, 1995).

20.   From field surveys, it was found that the typical owner drives his vehicle from 6:00 A.M. to about 2:30 P.M. The driver then washes the vehicle and fills it up with gasoline. The vehicle is then leased for a set fee (an average of US$15 per day in 1994) from 3:00 P.M. until about 10:30 P.M. Upon completing his shift, the lessee washes the vehicle and fills it with gasoline so that the owner can begin his shift promptly the next morning.

21.   These estimates are based on field interviews with minibus owners, drivers, and route association officials for Route 2, one of the busiest and most established routes in the city. They are based on late-1994 cost figures, when the Mexican new peso (NP) was worth approximately one-third of a U.S. dollar and rely on the following input assumptions. Minibuses are assumed to be driven an average of 80,000 kilometers per year. Expressing all monetary figures in 1994 U.S. dollars, a new minibus costs $32,000 and is resold after seven years for 20 percent of the original price (i.e., for $6,400). New equipment purchases are paid over a three-year loan period at a 21 percent interest rate (i.e., $43,300 in total payments). The fixed costs per 100 kilometers of service are: $4.65 for depreciation; $7.70 for interest payment; and $1.10 for license, insurance, and fees. Variable costs per 100 kilometers of service are: $22.00 for fuel and oil; $2.50 for maintenance and tires; and $22.10 for driver wages. Thus, total operating costs are about $60 per 100 kilometers. With an average fare box income of $92 per shift, or $71.50 per 100 kilometers, the profit margin to vehicle owners for the first three years is 19 percent. Once the vehicle is paid off after three years, the rate of return increases to 36 percent (i.e., for years four through seven).

22.   In terms of total trip segments, paratransit's role was even greater than shown in Table 15.2—colectivos accounted for 55.1 percent of unlinked trips in the metropolitan region in 1994.

23.   In late 1994, a distance-based fare structure was in place, with officially regulated fares ranging from 0.55 new pesos (US$0.18) for trips up to 5 kilometers and 1.1 new pesos (US$0.36) for trips over 17 kilometers. In practice, however, colectivo operators collected 1.5 new pesos (US$0.50) for long-haul trips within the metropolitan area.

24.   Moreno, *op. cit.*

25. See: M. Roschlau, Urban Transport in Developing Countries: The Peseros of Mexico City (Master's thesis, University of British Columbia, Centre for Transportation Studies, 1981).

26. Among the performance standards, minibus and van drivers are required to attend a training school, must have four years of driving experience, and must be more than twenty-three years of age. A driver's license can be suspended or revoked in the event of an accident. Regulations also prevent owner-operators from holding permits for more than three vehicles. The only significant vehicle fitness standard is that minibuses and vans must be replaced after seven years of service. Normally, vehicle owners sell their fleets to operators in other states of Mexico after their seventh year of service life.

27. Despite their strong presence in the Federal District, route associations are not found in the surrounding State of Mexico. Instead, the state itself plans, administers, and organizes all local colectivo services.

PART SIX

THE TRANSIT METROPOLIS OF TOMORROW

What have the experiences of this book's twelve international cities taught us? Chapter 16 summarizes fifteen key lessons. While there is no simple formula for charting a path toward becoming a transit metropolis, there are plenty of cross-cutting themes and common experiences that provide helpful signposts. The twelve international case studies also dispel a number of lingering myths about transit and the city. Chapter 16 exposes those as well.

Chapter 17 reviews efforts under way in five North American metropolitan areas—Portland, Oregon; Vancouver, British Columbia; San Diego, California; St. Louis, Missouri; and Houston, Texas—to mount successful transit programs that are in harmony with their respective cityscapes. Borrowing from the lessons of this book's twelve cities, the chapter discusses factors that are working both for and against these metropolitan areas becoming transit metropolises of the twenty-first century. Portland and Vancouver show promising signs of becoming adaptive cities—places whose built forms, as a consequence of farsighted, comprehensive planning, are highly conducive to transit riding. San Diego and St. Louis are more likely to evolve into hybrid transit metropolises—places where rail-served, transit-supportive growth is complemented by flexible bus transit better suited to serving non-transit-supportive growth. And Houston is on the right track to one day becoming a metropolis with world-class adaptive transit services, highlighted by what is evolving into the world's largest network of dedicated high-occupancy vehicle (HOV) lanes. The chapter closes with a discussion of the challenges of nurturing and growing transit metropolises in the twenty-first century.

Chapter 16

Drawing Lessons and Debunking Myths

This book's twelve case studies portray the transit metropolis as a place where mass transportation is a viable, respected mobility alternative to the private automobile. In some cities, this is because urban form and community design are conducive to transit riding. In others it is because transit services are well suited to serving what are largely market-driven patterns of spread-out development. Still other cases—the hybrids—have struck a middle ground between redesigning their cityscapes to support intensive transit services and redesigning their transit offerings to serve their cityscapes efficiently. What matters in all instances is that transit and the city harmoniously co-exist. Successful transit metropolises not only enjoy high levels of regional mobility but support larger policy objectives as well—sustainability, accessibility, livability, social diversity, entrepreneurship, and the broadening of choices in where and how people live and travel.

What have the experiences across this book's twelve transit metropolises taught us? This penultimate chapter summarizes these lessons. It also dispels various myths that have evolved over time about transit and the city. It is followed by a closing chapter that highlights North America's aspiring transit metropolises, and discusses how some of the lessons drawn from international cases might be put to good use by cities such as Portland, Oregon; Vancouver, British Columbia; San Diego, California; St. Louis, Missouri; and Houston, Texas, as they plan for the future.

Drawing Lessons

Fifteen lessons can be drawn from the experiences of the twelve case-study areas. In combination, they speak to the kinds of actions—and sometimes sacrifices—that are required to create a successful transit metropolis. While there is obviously no single, easy-to-use recipe, the ingredients for achieving a workable nexus between transit and metropolitan form show consistency across this book's case experiences.

Visioning

Transit metropolises evolve from well-articulated visions of the future. To achieve a vision, there must be a sense of exactly what the target is, defined well enough to gain public buy-in and build political support. In pluralist societies, striking a common vision can be difficult. Yet the end itself is often less important than the public dialogue that takes place and the contrasting views of the future. Common ground is often found across differences of opinion. Open dialogue can often bridge disparate views.

A vision of what tomorrow's metropolis should ideally look like is one of the hallmarks of adaptive cities. Greater Stockholm's early vision of compact, mixed-use new towns interlinked by regional rail services led to the "pearls on a necklace" built form found today. Copenhagen's Finger Plan provided an eloquent and cogent image of how the metropolis should ideally evolve. By defining an east-west axis for channeling overspill growth, Ottawa's 1974 Official Plan planted the seeds for what eventually would become North America's largest and most successful busway network. In Singapore, the Constellation Plan is widely embraced as the guiding light for the island-state's physical evolution. It defines some fifty subcenters of varying sizes and compositions whose primary lifelines to the region are or will be rail connections. In both Copenhagen and Singapore, metaphors (fingers on a hand, a planetary cluster) have helped enormously in articulating and marketing future visions.

Perhaps most importantly, in all of the cases reviewed, it has been land-use visions that have driven transportation decisions, not vice-versa. What matters most about cities and regions are people and places. Transportation is of secondary importance—a means to connect people and places. If anything, transportation is often something we want to minimize so that we can spend more time at a desired destination—be it working, shopping, socializing, recreating, or being with our families. Successful transit metropolises have gotten the order right—land-use visions lead transportation policies, not the other way around.

Visionaries

Visions need visionaries who can articulate what the future might hold and convince others of a desired course of action. Many transit metropolises have benefited from inspired leadership, including Sven Markelius's stewardship of Stockholm's regional plan, Keita Gotoh's entrepreneurial drive to couple rail and new town development in suburban Tokyo, and Lee Kuan Yew's wish to catapult Singapore into the ranks of a global city

by luring multinational corporations into efficient, transit-served industrial estates. Curitiba's emergence as one of the world's most sustainable
metropolises is in good part a product of Jaime Lerner's tireless commitment to ecology, sustainability, and efficient governance. Markelius,
Gotoh, Yew, and Lerner—all were leaders who had a vision of "place," as
well as the personalities and talents to win others over to this vision. And
then there are those with a vision of transit and its role in the city. Melbourne's Major General Robert Risson almost single-handedly saved the
city's century-old tramway system from expulsion, the fate suffered by
trams in virtually every city outside central and eastern Europe. Melbourne's central city turnaround owes much to Risson's relentless support
of tramways. A modern-day champion of light rail transit is Karlsruhe's
Dieter Ludwig, whose enlightened ideas about track sharing have given
birth to what is almost a many-origin to many-destination form of regional tramway services.

   Where do visionaries come from? People cannot be recruited into
these roles. They must seek them out themselves. Visionaries must have
the passion, commitment, and determination to advance the cause of the
transit metropolis.

Efficient Institutions and Governance

Transit Metropolises such as Stockholm, Ottawa, and Singapore owe
much to their efficient institutional structures and regional forms of governance that promote the close coordination of transportation and land
use. In these areas, decisions affecting built environments and transportation take place within a geographic context that matches regional
commutersheds—roughly the spatial extent of 95-plus percent of the
region's trip origins and destinations. Only then can what is truly a
regional phenomenon—transportation and land-use interactions—be
effectively planned and coordinated.

   A successful institutional approach to coordinating regional transit
services and fares has been the Verkehrsverbund, presently found in Germany, Switzerland, and other parts of central Europe. These umbrella
organizations ensure that problems that commonly plagued regional transit services—such as fare penalties for transferring, conflicting timetables,
and interagency rivalries—are eliminated. With a Verkehrsverbund, transit is designed and operated like a regional service. Parochial interests
take a back seat to regional ones.

   Efficient institutional arrangements also ensure that public and private domains are well delineated. Mexico City's hierarchy of regional transit services benefits from a clear and rational division of institutional
responsibilities between the public and private sectors. In the transit
arena, the public domain is largely one of sponsoring mainline services,

like metro lines, that exhibit economies of scale. The ownership and operations of paratransit feeders—for which economies of scope prevail—falls mostly within the sphere of the private sector.

Pro-active Planning and Urban Management

In adaptive cities, transit-supportive built forms are substantially the result of planning processes that are farsighted, pro-active, and strategic. In Stockholm, Copenhagen, Singapore, Munich, and Curitiba, classic textbook approaches to urban planning and management have been carried out: the setting of clear goals and objectives; the formulation and articulation of land-use visions and comprehensive plans; the careful evaluation of transportation and infrastructure investment alternatives; the programming of capital improvements within realistic budget constraints; plan execution and follow-through; and the leveraging of transit and land-use programs. It bears repeating that, in each case, it has been the land-use "ends" that have determined the transportation "means," including the design and delivery of transit services. Among the tools used for leveraging transit-oriented development have been: the preservation of right-of-ways and control of development through land banking; zoning incentives, such as the issuance of mixed-use density bonuses; the granting of tax concessions for affordable housing; and targeted investments in supplemental infrastructure, such as sidewalk and public-space improvements.

Public ownership and control of land have been pivotal to compact, mixed-use development around transit stops in Singapore and metropolitan Stockholm. Both areas have tight urban growth boundaries—in Stockholm's case, a protective greenbelt, and in Singapore's case, the Straits of Malacca and its tributaries—that have spawned inward-focused growth.

Viable Centers

All transit metropolises maintain strong, vibrant central business districts. In Stockholm, Copenhagen, Munich, Curitiba, and Karlsruhe, downtowns are where the action is. Even Adelaide, whose inclusion in this book admittedly stretches the boundaries of what constitutes a transit metropolis, has one of the largest shares of retail sales and jobs in its urban core among Australian metropolises. In Zurich and Melbourne, public transit—in particular, trams—has been instrumental in rejuvenating central city neighborhoods. The CBDs of Munich and Karlsruhe have also profited immensely from on-street tram circulation. Viable downtowns are not only important as transit hubs and major transfer points; as destinations, they generate the highest shares of transit riders.

All transit metropolises also exhibit some degree of subcentering. Singapore and Ottawa have well-ordered hierarchies of second- and third-tier centers. Subcenters are essential building blocks for mounting and sustaining integrated regional transit networks. It is in large part because of transit's presence that decentralization has taken on a more concentrated form in many transit metropolises.

Balanced Development and Traffic Flows

A strong-centered metropolis can backfire from a mobility standpoint unless complemented by mixed-use subcenters. Unidirectional, radial movements into a dominant center often produce congestion from converging flows and inefficiencies from empty back-hauling of trains and buses. Experiences in Stockholm, Ottawa, and Curitiba demonstrate that intermixing of land uses along linear corridors can produce efficient bidirectional flows. Putting the same activities found throughout a region near transit stops generates high ridership levels in all directions. Stockholm makes it clear that it is less important to have balances of jobs, housing, shops, and community services *within* as opposed to *between* communities. The mobility benefits of concentrated mixed-use development along transit-served corridors easily match those of more aggressive land-use interventions, such as self-contained growth and a jobs-housing balance.

Competition and an Entrepreneurial Ethos

Elements of competition are found in many successful transit metropolises. Competition not only contains costs and rewards efficiency, but also spurs service innovations, something that is badly needed in many suburban travel markets.

The two Scandinavian cases, Stockholm and Copenhagen, contract out bus services on a competitive basis and have begun doing likewise for rail services. Operating costs have plummeted on a per kilometer basis as a result. In Munich, Karlsruhe, Curitiba, and Adelaide, efficiencies have been achieved by separating asset ownership and service delivery. In these places, fixed capital infrastructure belongs to the public sector. Rolling stock belongs to competitively chosen providers, often from the private sector. Within the confines of standards set by government sponsors (e.g., regarding timetables, fares, and routing), the lowest-cost provider delivers the service. Thus, the public sector retains control over how services are configured, leaving it to market forces to determine at what price.

In successful transit metropolises, profiteering is not discouraged as long as the broader public good is promoted. Tokyo's rail-served suburbs are a product of real estate speculation that has enriched many large conglomerates yet also produced a strong, transit-oriented built form. For the past three decades, Japanese railway companies have branched into real estate, retailing, construction, and bus operations. The practice of value capture is alive and well in Tokyo's suburbs, with some companies reaping more than 30 percent returns on investment from joint railway and new town projects. Society as a whole has gained from the efficient co-development of transit services and suburban settlements. A spirit of entrepreneurship also pervades Mexico City's transit sector. Thanks to thousands of independent paratransit owner-operators, efficient minibus services link outlying neighborhoods with Mexico City's regional metro system. Driven by the profit motive, minibus operators fill the market niches left unserved by the region's metro service.

Giving Transit Priority

Many transit metropolises go the extra distance in making transit time-competitive with the private automobile. Ottawa and Zurich give clear preference to high-occupancy vehicles in the use of scarce road space, under their respective "transit first" programs. Signal preemptions allow Zurich's trams and Ottawa's buses to move briskly along surface streets, with stops largely limited to picking up and dropping off customers. Copenhagen and Zurich have reassigned large amounts of downtown streets to trams, buses, and nonmotorized transportation. Over the past decade, both cities have managed to absorb the growth in downtown-destined travel without expanding road capacity.

Small Is Beautiful

A number of this book's cases have shown that large-scale megaprojects are not necessarily the only means of creating a successful transit metropolis. Small, incremental steps matter—provided they are guided by some general vision of where the region is headed. Much of the successes in Curitiba, Karlsruhe, and Zurich are attributable to the cumulative effects of many modest, low-cost, but fast-turnaround actions. Ingenuity and a willingness to experiment and take risks have also played a role. Examples abound across case-study cities: Curitiba's trinary road system and raised boarding tubes; Karlsruhe's dual-mode, track-sharing technologies; Adelaide's adaptation of O-Bahn to a linear parkway with restricted right-of-ways; and Zurich's reappropriation of road space and resignalization of traffic lights, transforming tramways into something akin to grade-separated light rail services. Reasons for "small is beautiful" approaches have varied—from a desire to establish political credibility (Curitiba) to a need to preserve the traditional core city (Zurich) to a spirit of entrepreneurship and innovation (Karlsruhe).

Cities such as Ottawa and Curitiba show that low-cost systems do not

necessarily equate to low-quality services. Nor do large-scale transit projects have to be budget busters. Ottawa, Adelaide, and Curitiba have
designed bus-based guideways that match the service features of many
underground metro systems at a fraction of the cost. The integration of
mainline and feeder services within the same vehicle has virtually eliminated transfers along some corridors. Curitiba's inventive system of
boarding tubes and transfer stations has made transferring between tangential and radial bus lines seemingly effortless.

Urban Design: Cities for People and Places

An overarching design philosophy of most transit metropolises is that
cities are for people, not cars. High-quality transit is viewed as consonant
with this philosophy. In Copenhagen, Munich, and Curitiba, parts of the
historical cores have been given over to pedestrians and cyclists. In all of
the European cases, trams and light rail vehicles blend nicely with auto-
free zones, moving at a pace and operating at a scale that is compatible
with walking and cycling.

Urban design is every bit as important outside central cities. In the
suburbs of Copenhagen and Stockholm, transit stations are treated as
community hubs. Rail stops and the civic spaces that surround them are
often town gathering spots. They are the places where people congregate
during national holidays, community celebrations, and public protests.
Many civic squares do double duty as farmers' markets and venues for
open-air concerts. Nearby retail shops, grocery stores, newsstands, and
movie houses benefit from having transit customers delivered to their
front steps. Street furniture, greenery, urban art, and water fountains add
comfort and visual aesthetics. Through conscious design, transit is both
physically and symbolically at the community's core.

It is tempting to label design features such as pedestrian-ways and
public squares "amenities." Providing functional spaces for pedestrians
and cyclists is, however, no more of an amenity than providing parking
and freeway on-ramps for cars. They are basic provisions, not amenities.

Auto Equalizers

Many transit metropolises have matched provisions for pedestrians,
cyclists, and transit users with restraints on motoring and auto ownership. In Singapore, Tokyo, and Stockholm, this has mainly taken the form
of punitive pricing: steep surcharges on gasoline and automobile purchases, hefty vehicle import duties, and expensive central city parking.
Singapore has done more than any city to pass on true social costs to auto
motoring. It was the first city to introduce road pricing on a large scale—
initially through an area licensing scheme that charged motorists to enter

downtown zones during peak hours, and more recently using a sophisti-cated combination of radio frequency, optical detection, imaging, and smart card technologies to instantaneously pass on variable charges. Sin-gapore's vehicle quota system, which indexes the allowable number of vehicle registrations for any one year to ambient traffic conditions, is also one of a kind.

In other transit metropolises, automobile restraints have been achieved through regulations and physical design strategies. Tokyo's garaging requirements have long held the city's car population in check. Mexico City's alternating ban on car usage, depending on vehicles' license plate numbers, has curbed auto motoring as a pollution reduction strate-gy. Munich, Zurich, and Curitiba have slowed down, redistributed, and sometimes deterred automobile travel, especially in residential neighbor-hoods, by narrowing roads, designing in speed tables, and necking down intersections. Parking management is also crucial to rationalizing the use of central city space. Limited parking encourages transit riding and frees up more central city space for pedestrians, cyclists, and transit vehicles. When heading downtown, most residents of medium-size cities like Zurich and Ottawa either leave their cars in their garages or at peripher-al park-and-ride lots.

Transportation planners often refer to these measures as "auto dis-incentives," though this is a misnomer. More accurately, they are "auto equalizers"—they seek to level the playing field by removing many of the built-in biases that encourage and indeed sometimes reward auto motoring.

Hierarchical and Integrated Transit

Many of this book's successful transit metropolises feature well-designed, hierarchical forms of transit services. By carefully integrating services—high-capacity mainline services, intermediate connectors, and communi-ty-scale feeders—many origin-destination combinations can be efficiently served by transit offerings. Trams are critical intermediate carriers in Zurich, Munich, Karlsruhe, and Melbourne. In Munich, Curitiba, and Ottawa, limited-stop buses provide essential tangential, crosstown con-nections. In many cases, integration also extends to fares. Zurich, Munich, Copenhagen, and Karlsruhe reward frequent travelers through various discount arrangements. Unified tariffs and ticketing allow passengers to transfer across and modes without having to pay an extra fare.

Flexibility

For some of the smaller transit metropolises reviewed in this book, bus-based technologies not only reduce capital outlays but also provide important flexibility advantages. Flexibility is a fundamental trait of adaptive transit cities. As settlement patterns evolve and unfold, rubber-tire services—be they minibuses, conventional buses, or bi-articulated buses—can easily adjust to shifting patterns of travel. Ottawa's cost-effective mix of peak-hour express services and off-peak timed-transfer feeder services epitomizes the inherent malleability of bus-based transit. Curitiba's joint running of limited-stop, direct-line services and frequent-stop, high-capacity services along structural axes is also only possible with a bus-based system. Moreover, experiences in Ottawa, Curitiba, and Adelaide underscore the staging advantages of busways over rail lines. In all three cities, busways have opened in phases, prior to the completion of entire projects, because regular surface streets were available in place of missing links. In Curitiba and Ottawa, busways are also used by fire trucks, ambulances, and emergency vehicles.

Necessity Is the Mother of Invention

The technological advances reviewed in this book were not a result of new gadgetry seeking an application, but rather a real-world need spawning an innovation. Munich's call-a-bus form of "smart paratransit" was launched because of the need to provide flexible and efficient one-to-many connections between S-Bahn stations and their hinterlands. Munich's real-time displays of park-and-ride information at the entrances to multistory garages has similarly filled a market need—to expedite transit commuting by reducing the time spent finding a parking space. Other technologies that have filled a market gap and materially benefited transit users include Ottawa's real-time, signpost-based passenger information system, Zurich's citywide dynamic traffic signalization system, and Karlsruhe's versatile dual-voltage trains that run on both tramway tracks and intercity train tracks.

Serendipity

Of course, not all of the outcomes reviewed in this book are the result of deliberate actions and farsighted planning. Some are beneficiaries of good timing and good fortune. Curitiba's ability to build trinary roads along structural axes stemmed in part from the generous supply of right-of-ways that were preserved following the 1943 Agache Plan. Part of the reason Ottawa and Adelaide were able to build busways at relatively low costs was the availability of linear riverside parkways. Ottawa's heritage of national capital planning and land preservation provided the right-of-ways for western portions of the city's busway as well as natural buffer strips that insulated surrounding neighborhoods. And, in many cases, transit investments occurred during an upswing in a particular region's economy, ensuring a close correspondence between transportation and urban growth.

Debunking Myths

The twelve case studies reviewed in this book also serve to dispel at least six myths about transit and the city.

Myth 1: Except for downtown destinations, only poor people ride transit. Statistics for three cities alone will hopefully bury this myth. In Stockholm, one of the wealthiest cities in one of Europe's wealthiest countries, well over 60 percent of commute trips to downtown and more than a third of commutes to suburban job sites are by public transportation. Zurich averages more transit trips per capita than virtually any city in the world while also holding honors as one of the world's most affluent cities, with purportedly the highest commercial real estate prices anywhere. Curitiba has both the highest per capita income and the highest transit modal split of any Brazilian city.

Transit and affluence are not inherently at odds. To the contrary, prosperous urban environments and good transit are mutually supporting.

Transit's stigma as a means of transport for the underclass and marginalized populations stems in large part from its legacy of poor-quality services. In affluent societies, poor services generally attract poor people. Ramping up the quality of service will polish transit's image faster than anything.

In Melbourne and Zurich, tramways have been partly credited with luring well-to-do households back to central city neighborhoods. There is also ample evidence that middle-class households are willing to give up a second car when living in transit-supportive central city environs.

Myth 2: Public transit is inherently a public sector enterprise. This view is largely rooted in the belief that transit engenders economies of scale and is therefore a natural monopoly.[1] Defenders of the status quo argue against competition under the guise of "cream skimming"—profit-seeking operators will concentrate only on lucrative services, leaving the money-losers to public operators. The reality is that there is often little cream, or profits, to skim from public operators, and in most places where competition is encouraged (such as Stockholm, Copenhagen, and Curitiba), governments still control the supply, quality, and price of services. Once standards are set, the lowest bidder is awarded the service. The customer is blind to the fact that a private interest owns the transit vehicle and a non-government employee is driving it. What matters to the customer is service quality and value for price.

The majority of transit metropolises profiled in this book—Stockholm, Copenhagen, Singapore, Munich, Curitiba, Karlsruhe, and Adelaide—have warmly embraced competition as a means of producing cost-effective services. In all of these places, governments own and control the non-rolling-stock assets—guideways, railway tracks, land, and buildings, like maintenance facilities. Competitive tendering is used primarily to reduce costs. In the case of Tokyo, the private sector's role is far greater—many private intrametropolitan railway companies own all assets outright. Public oversight in Tokyo is largely restricted to ensuring that public safety standards are met.

Too often, "public transit" is literally interpreted to mean publicly owned and operated transit. "Public" simply means the service is available to the general populace, not that there is a public sector provider. As demonstrated by the world's transit metropolises, the business of designing and providing efficient transit services is not inherently a public sector enterprise—it involves private participation as well, to varying degrees.

Myth 3: Transit always loses money. Experiences in Singapore, Tokyo, and Curitiba prove otherwise. In 1995–96, the Singapore Mass Rapid Transit, Limited (MRT)—the owner-operator of the city's metro system and a company whose shares are sold on the Singapore stock exchange—collected passenger revenues that exceeded operating costs and expenses for debt service. All of the city's private bus companies today operate in the black. Most of Tokyo's private railway companies earn modest profits from rail services and more or less break even from operating ancillary bus services. As noted, their windfalls come from real estate development around rail stops. In Curitiba, private bus companies earn enough profit to replace rolling stock, on average, every three years, making the city's bus fleet among the newest in the world.

Transit need not be a deficit-riddled business. The key to attracting riders and generating profits is to provide high-quality service. The key to providing high-quality service is to match transit supply to the cityscape—in short, to become a transit metropolis.

Myth 4: Bus transit is incapable of shaping urban form and attracting high-rise development around stops. Besides buses being stigmatized as a second-class form of conveyance, the conventional wisdom holds that buses repel development because of their negative by-products: diesel toxins that spew from tailpipes. Experiences around busway stops in Ottawa and Curitiba should put this myth to rest. In both cities, some of the priciest condominiums anchor sites adjacent to busway stops. Retail and office developers have also flocked to busway corridors in both cities.

Good-quality service—whether vehicles are propelled by electricity or fossil fuels, or whether they roll on steel wheels or pneumatic tires—will spawn compact development. It is the accessibility premium that attracts real estate development, not the type of transit equipment. In fact, compared to freeways and even railway corridors, busways produce relatively low ambient noise levels. Its inherent flexibility advantages and superior adaptability to spread-out patterns of development make bus transit—especially when combined with dedicated busways—a potentially stronger shaper of growth patterns than rail transit in some settings.

Myth 5: People loathe compact suburban development. Granted, many suburbanites move to the outskirts to escape busy streets and small-lot, urban living. Compact living, however, does not necessarily translate into high-rise dwellings. Recent rail-served new towns in Stockholm, most notably Skarpnäck, show that attractive and very livable communities can be designed with no higher than three-story flats that still generate high rates of transit riding. Munich's Arabella Park and Zamila Park, Zurich's Tiergarten, and Tokyo's Tama Denen Toshi are prime examples of mixed-use communities with moderate densities, healthy absorption rates of new housing and leasable commercial space, and respectable transit modal shares. A general rule in these and other places is that as densities increase, so should amenities, such as attractive landscaping, tree-lined pathways, and on-site recreational facilities. The coupling of good-quality transit and community amenities can go a long way toward lowering perceived densities, especially in the suburbs.

It should be kept in mind that the objective of more compact development is not density for its own sake, but rather to reap the environmental benefits of more efficient patterns of growth and, just as importantly, to expand choices. In countries such as the United States, suburbia cries out for more diversity—a wider array of living, working, shopping, and travel options. Some Americans would jump at the chance to live in a well-designed, transit-friendly community where they could conveniently reach places by train and perhaps save on the cost of having to own a second or third car. Many would no doubt like to live closer to their suburban jobs if only there were decent affordable housing nearby. Expanding choices is not only good for consumers, but ultimately for society as a whole. Transit-supportive development is as much about enriching consumer choices as it is about inducing transit ridership.

Myth 6: In modern societies, the link between transportation and land use is too weak to matter. Perhaps the biggest myth of all, this view, while patently absurd, has nonetheless gained wide acceptance among many transportation academics, especially in the United States.[2] It is a view framed in part by studying experiences in countries like the United States where perverse price signals and other market distortions, such as exclusionary zoning, stack the odds heavily in favor of car travel. This view holds that regions are already so ubiquitous (i.e., one can travel from anywhere to everywhere) and low-density development is so well established that the incremental gains in accessibility wrought by transit investments are negligible, if not meaningless. Tell this to planners and policy makers in Stockholm, Copenhagen, Singapore, Munich, Zurich, and Curitiba.

Of course the transportation–land use connection matters. It matters if it matters—that is, if the public sector is willing to invest the time, effort, and resources necessary to nurture the often delicate relationship between transit and urban form. In the United States, it is no surprise that transportation–land use outcomes have been suboptimal in a world of suboptimal pricing. This is not an indictment of the land use–transportation connection, but rather an indictment of policies that underprice and mismanage transportation and land resources. If the efficient pricing that economists so often tout were introduced into America's urban transportation sector, then transit investments would exert far greater influence on land-use outcomes than is now the case.

Several North American cities still believe that the transit–land use nexus is of immense importance, so much so that they have begun to chart a path in the direction of one day becoming transit metropolises. The challenges of growing transit metropolises in the United States and Canada are explored in this book's closing chapter.

NOTES

1. With a true natural monopoly, such as water utilities, average costs decline with output, meaning that a single firm can provide consumers with the least expensive service, provided, of course, that regulations ban the firm from raising prices to monopoly profit levels. Besides economies of scale, other attributes of natural monopolies are peak-load demands and storable resources. Mass transit has these latter two traits: high diurnal (morning and evening) peak demands and the ability to store idle equipment (buses and trains) in reserve during slack hours and low seasons. Research shows, however, that it generally exhibits, at best, constant returns to scale and, in the case of many larger cities, diminishing economies. Only in the cases of very capital-intensive rail systems do any significant economies accrue from limiting services to a single provider. For further reading, see: A. Kahn, *The Economics of Regulation: Principles and Institutions* (New York: John Wiley and Sons, 1971); N. Lee and I. Steedman, Economies of Scale in Bus Transportation, *Journal of Transport Economics and Policy*, vol. 4, no. 1, 1970, pp. 15–28; and R. Cervero, *Paratransit in America: Redefining Mass Transportation* (Westport, CT: Praeger, 1997).

2. *See*: G. Giuliano, The Weakening Transportation–Land Use Connection, *Access*, no. 6, 1995, pp. 3–11; and A. Downs, *Stuck in Traffic: Coping with Peak-Hour Traffic Congestion* (Washington, DC: The Brookings Institution, 1992).

Chapter 17

North America's Aspiring Transit Metropolises

Nowhere are the challenges of becoming a transit metropolis greater than in the United States and its neighbor to the north, Canada. In a land of affluence with plentiful space, the world's highest vehicle ownership rates, a strong cultural preference for large-lot, detached housing, and, in the case of the United States, a politically powerful automobile manufacturing industry, the obstacles to becoming a transit metropolis are many. Yet against this backdrop a handful of metropolitan areas are committed to one day joining the ranks of successful transit metropolises. Their approaches vary and the obstacles some face are huge. Still, all are charting a slow but methodical course toward eventually making the transit–land use nexus work. While the jury is still out on how successful they will be, all are attempting to mount transit programs—in harmony with their cityscapes—that provide respectable mobility alternatives to car travel. Quite likely their futures will lie in adopting and extending many of the lessons from the twelve transit metropolises discussed in the previous chapter.

This chapter reviews the experiences and efforts under way in four U.S., plus one Canadian, metropolitan areas that are following in the footsteps of the world's great transit metropolises. Portland, Oregon, and Vancouver, British Columbia, show all signs of one day becoming adaptive cities—places whose built forms are highly conducive to transit riding. Two emerging hybrid transit metropolises are San Diego, California, and St. Louis, Missouri. The U.S. city that stands the best chance of mounting world-class adaptive transit services is Houston, Texas. After reviewing past experiences and future plans in these areas, this chapter discusses factors that are working in favor of these places becoming successful transit metropolises as well as barriers that must be overcome. These assessments draw upon this book's international case-study lessons.

Portland, Oregon

If any American region is poised to become a great transit Metropolis during the twenty-first century, it is metropolitan Portland. No other place in the United States has made a stronger commitment to integrating transit and urban development than Oregon's largest city and its surroundings. The region has many factors working in its favor: metropolitan governance; a strong tradition of pro-environmental legislation; a cogent, farsighted comprehensive plan; a pro-active station-area planning process; urban growth boundaries; a prosperous and growing CBD; and broad-based public support for regional planning. In greater Portland, transit is considered the linchpin in creating a livable and sustainable metropolis.

Today, Portland is known the world over as America's city-planning success story. No region has done more over the past two decades to contain sprawl, strengthen public transit, and revitalize its core. Presently, about a million people live in the Tri-Counties of Multnomah, Clackamas, and Washington. With almost a half-million new residents forecast for the region over the next twenty years, light rail transit is at the forefront of a concerted effort—articulated in the Region 2040 Plan—to create a metropolis of compact and interlinked mixed-use centers, all within a protective greenbelt.

MAX

As in other North American cities, it was the threat of a freeway that galvanized public support for upgrading transit. In the early 1970s, the region needed a transit project to absorb federal funds from the withdrawn Mount Hood Freeway project. Light rail was favored over busways because it was widely viewed as providing superior services and a more modern image.[1] This proved to be a monumental decision, for it completely redirected how the region would evolve for decades to come.

The Tri-County Metropolitan Transit District (Tri-Met) plans, manages, and operates the region's rail, bus, and paratransit services. The light rail system, MAX (short for metropolitan area extension), is the backbone of the network. Opened in 1989, the east-side line connects downtown Portland to the suburban community of Gresham, 24 kilometers to the east. Since 1990, regional voters have agreed to tax themselves to fund a fourfold expansion of the original east-side MAX system. A west-side line to the fast-growing, well-to-do community of Hillsboro opened in 1998. By sometime during the first decade of the twenty-first century, light rail backers hope to have a 93-kilometer network in place that serves all quadrants of the region.

Despite the region's strong commitment to transit, the private automobile still reigns supreme. In 1990, 6 percent of employed residents in the Tri-Counties and 11 percent from Portland got to work by transit. In contrast, the automobile captured 73 percent and 65 percent of commute trips, respectively. Critics point out that, during the 1980s, transit lost a larger share of the commuter market in metropolitan Portland than in most regions of the country (from 8 percent to 5 percent, and among Portland's employed residents, from 16 percent to 11 percent).[2] For all trip purposes, transit carried just 3 percent of trips in 1990.

Transit supporters are quick to note that 1990 statistics reflected only four years of operating a single 24-kilometer rail line, and that once the complete network is in place and transit-oriented neighborhoods take form, modal shares should increase dramatically. These statistics, moreover, obscure the vital passenger-carrying role of transit to key destinations. Downtown Portland's transit modal split for work trips exceeded 40 percent in 1990, largely attributable to two decades of targeted efforts aimed at revitalizing the core.[3] In the Lloyd District, just east of downtown across the Willamette River, 8 percent of workers reached jobs by transit. Transit's role in serving nonwork trips to the Lloyd District is far greater, capturing as many as 40 percent of journeys to major sports events.

Development along MAX Corridors

The east-side line has failed to spawn the amount of development that was hoped for. This is mainly because it passes near established single-family neighborhoods and lies partly in a freeway median.[4] A recent study found multifamily housing development is actually occurring at a faster rate near bus stops and arterials along the east-side corridor than around light stops.[5] Still, more than 1,000 multifamily housing units have been built on infill sites near the rail corridor, in no small part due to aggressive efforts to leverage these projects through such steps as fast-tracking the review of building permits for transit-supportive development.

It has been downtown Portland and the Lloyd District where transit's presence has been most felt. Downtown Portland has attracted some $400 million dollars in investments since the early 1970s, when a bus mall was installed.[6] The mall, aligned along a one-way couplet, consolidated downtown bus services and symbolized the city's commitment to rejuvenating the core. All bus rides within the CBD, including along the mall, are free. According to Tri-Met, more than $700 million has been invested in public and private developments in the Lloyd District since MAX's inauguration.[7] The Lloyd District is one of the most successful inner-city redevelopment projects anywhere served by—indeed spurred by—light rail. Since MAX's arrival, the Oregon Convention Center, the Rose Garden Arena, and a large, enclosed shopping complex have opened. MAX's presence—and the savings in parking costs it afforded—was said to have been a decisive factor in locating the arena, home to the Portland Trailblazers, in the Lloyd

District versus off a suburban freeway exit. MAX supporters credit light rail with physically as well as psychologically bridging the river that divides the Lloyd District and downtown.

Factors in Portland's Favor

Today, Portland enjoys the most conducive institutional environment for supporting transit-oriented development in the United States. Portland's progressive form of governance and pro-environmental policies can be expected to promote highly integrated transit and urban development over many years to come.

Regional Governance and Planning

As do Stockholm and Ottawa, greater Portland has a metropolitan form of governance. This, perhaps more than anything, bodes favorably for the prospects of achieving a workable transit–land use nexus. Formed in 1978 to manage regional growth, Metro powers were expanded in 1990 when it was granted a home rule charter, giving the region the nation's first direct-ly elected regional government. Its powers include the ability to override municipal zoning decisions that are inconsistent with regional plans.[8]

Metro has worked closely with local governments, the business community, environmental interests, and citizens to forge a consensus on the region's preferred future settlement pattern, in a process known as Region 2040. A fifty-year planning horizon was chosen to force everyone to think over the long haul.[9] The adopted growth strategy, Framework 2040, calls for concentrating future growth in regional centers that are served by multimodal arteries and high-capacity transit. Nine regional centers are to be interconnected by light rail links. Some of the twenty-five smaller mixed-use centers are also to be rail-served. Up to 85 percent of new growth in the region is to occur within a five-minute walk of a transit stop. With an urban growth strategy now in place, the region has begun to move toward designing specific neighborhood plans for existing and planned rail stops.

State and Regional Policies

Part of the credit for Portland's broad-based commitment to transit goes to a supportive legislative and policy environment. Oregon has a long his-tory of progressive land-use and environmental legislation, going back to the nation's first laws governing bottle recycling and coastal zone man-agement. In the early 1970s, an odd coalition of farmers, timber interests, environmentalists, and politicians pushed through America's first statewide land-use law. The law explicitly called for preserving farm and forest land and containing urban growth, both to conserve resources and reduce public outlays for extending infrastructure and services. A state agency, the Land Conservation and Development Commission (LCDC), was formed to set statewide land-use goals. Localities were required to prepare comprehensive plans that comply with these goals. For metropolitan areas with more than 50,000 inhabitants, an urban growth boundary (UGB) had to be designated.

Another important state initiative has been the Transportation Planning Rule. Passed in 1991, the rule requires urbanized areas to take steps that will reduce per capita vehicle kilometers traveled by 10 percent in twenty years and by 20 percent in thirty years. Failure to do so jeopardizes state infrastructure funding. This rule—which provides much of the clout needed to enforce the 2040 Plan—has set into motion various initiatives to limit parking near rail stops, upgrade walking environments, and build transit-oriented communities. Most recently, Oregon passed a law that exempts affordable rental units sited near transit stops from property taxes.

Urban Growth Boundaries

As in Stockholm, greater Portland has defined UGBs for hemming in growth. In 1997, the boundary's perimeter stretched 320 kilometers and enclosed an area of 950 square kilometers.[10] The principal objectives of Oregon's UGB—not just in Portland, but in greater Eugene, Salem, and Corvallis as well—have been achieved. More than 90 percent of the state's population growth during the 1980s took place inside UGBs. The average size of farms in the state's prime agricultural belt, the Willamette Valley, has increased, as has productivity per hectare. Still, the UGB has come under harsh attack. Critics charge that by artificially restricting land supplies, the UGB has overly inflated housing prices and driven up densities beyond tolerable levels, and, by contributing to gentrification, has displaced longtime working-class residents from in-city neighborhoods.[11] Regardless, Portland-area planners contend that only by strictly honoring the boundary will the goals of the 2040 Plan be achieved.

A Vibrant Downtown

Today, Portland's downtown is full of life and vibrancy, far more than any similar-size U.S. city. A bus mall, civic spaces, bountiful landscaping, caps on parking, a restored riverfront, and the preservation of heritage buildings have combined to create what by all accounts is a very pedestrian-friendly, European-like urban milieu. Downtown Portland is a walker's delight thanks to wide sidewalks, restored century-old buildings, colorful storefronts, urban art, and a generous supply of benches and other street furniture. Much of the credit goes to the 1972 Downtown Plan, a thoughtful document that set the blueprint for the core area's transformation. Since the plan's adoption, downtown employment has grown from 50,000 to more than 105,000 today. Over the same period, downtown's share of

Photo 17.1. MAX's busiest loading point. Tri-Met's busiest stop is downtown where Pioneer Square and Pioneer Place meet.

retail sales shot up from 5 percent to 30 percent.[12] Despite this growth, no new road capacity has been added in the core since the early 1970s.

Downtown Portland's pride and joy is Pioneer Square, a delightful public space with crescent-shaped steps that form a perfect amphitheater. It replaced what was to be a new parking structure. Because the square was designed at the same time as MAX, the two blend together nicely.[13] Adjacent to the square is a very successful in-town shopping center, Pioneer Place, also Tri-Met's busiest stop (Photo 17.1).

Aggressive, Pro-active Planning

Learning from the experiences and perhaps disappointments of the east-side line, the region is committed to making sure outcomes are fundamentally different along the westside corridor. Today, an ambitious, state-of-the-art planning campaign aims to create new transit-oriented communities along the west-side line. The western corridor has received particular attention because of its phenomenal rate of growth—during the 1980s, Washington County (wherein the west-side line extends) accounted for two-thirds of population growth and 95 percent of employment gains in the region. Planning for this corridor has been a joint public-private endeavor. Metro, in close coordination with Tri-Met and local and county governments, has led public sector planning. In parallel, the 1,000 Friends of Oregon, an independent pro-environmental group, carried out its own corridor analysis—called the LUTRAQ (Land Use, Transportation, and Air Quality Connection) study—in reaction to a proposed west-side beltway. The LUTRAQ study concluded that transit-oriented communities could accommodate 65 percent of new homes and 78 percent of new jobs in Washington County.[14]

Public-private master planning of transit-oriented communities, involving some 600 hectares of vacant land, is currently under way along the west-side line. Between 1990 (when the west-side extension got the green light to proceed) and 1996, more than 6,000 dwellings and $230 million of mixed-use development were built, permitted, or proposed within a half-mile of west-side MAX stations.[15] Beaverton Creek, located in the upscale suburb of Beaverton, is billed as the first project built under Portland's transit-oriented design guidelines. The site is being designed and developed by a team of private landowners, the city, and Tri-Met. The west-side alignment was altered to take advantage of Beaverton Creek's prime development potential. At completion, some 1,600 multifamily units at blended densities of twenty-two to thirty-five units per acre (or fifty-four to eighty-six per hectare) and several hundred single-family homes are to be added to the Beaverton Creek site. Planned for Beaverton's central station is a huge civic plaza, modeled after one in Siena, Italy, that is to be ringed by 150 townhouses, four-story office structures, a market hall, and a large hotel.

Interim zoning is being used throughout the west-side corridor to prevent land use conversions during the planning stages that might be incompatible with transit-oriented development. Besides prohibiting auto-oriented uses within a half-mile of stations, interim zoning sets minimum densities, limits parking supplies, and requires buildings to be physically oriented to light rail station entrances.

The last leg of the west-side line—the 10-kilometer extension to Hillsboro—features a noteworthy funding arrangement. The U.S. Federal Transit Administration agreed to fully fund the $75 million extension as long as transit-supportive development called for in the 2040 Plan and the state Transportation Planning Rule, and that supports ridership projections, occurs; otherwise, Tri-Met will have to refund the money.

Parking Policies

As in all good transit metropolises, parking is rationed in Portland's transit-served areas. Portland was one of the first U.S. cities to place a ceiling on downtown parking—tight maximums, but no minimums. Downtown parking is also tied to transit access. Buildings fronting the bus mall are zoned for the lowest ratios (0.7 spaces per 1,000 square feet, or 93 square meters, of floor space) and those farther away have higher ratios (up to

2.0 spaces). Violation of carbon monoxide standards was a key factor in prompting city leaders to cap downtown parking. Since 1984, there have been no recorded carbon monoxide violations in the core.

Among the sixteen stops along the east-side line between the Lloyd District and Gresham, only five have park-and-ride facilities. Tri-Met instead encourages bus-and-ride access to MAX. Some thirty-five bus routes tie into four timed-transfer centers along the east-side line. The downtown bus mall serves as the connection point for the region's remaining forty-five bus routes. Parking is also being restricted along the west-side extension.

Traffic Calming

More so than any other U.S. city, Portland has warmly embraced traffic calming. Its "Reclaim Your Street" program brings residents and city architects together to figure out how best to slow traffic on neighborhood streets. A "Speed Watch" program lends radar guns to citizens so that they can report speed violators. Under the "Skinny Streets" program, some residential streets have been narrowed to 18-foot (5.5-meter) curb-to-curb widths, requiring oncoming cars to make way for each other.

Overcoming Impediments

While the west-side extension has been a very important addition to the region's rail network, a single east-to-west corridor does not make for a transit metropolis. Completing the proposed 40-kilometer south-north line will be vital in creating a true regional network. The proposal suffered a setback when state voters turned down a funding referendum to help pay for the line.[16] Voters in Vancouver, Washington, what was to have been the northern terminus, have also refused to ante up money for the project. Recent citizen signature drives to repeal the UGB and even regional governance have environmentalist interests worried. Developers have so far been hesitant to build untested transit-oriented housing on the prosperous west side. A mixed-use proposal on a strategic parcel in Beaverton was recently abandoned.[17] Yet mounting growth pressures and an unwavering public commitment to transit-supportive zoning almost guarantee that significant shares of future development will occur along MAX corridors. Backers are also counting on one or two successful mixed-use developments to unleash a bandwagon of new rail-oriented projects.

Outlook

On balance, the many pros outweigh the few cons that potentially stand in the way of Portland's quest for sustainable, transit-oriented growth.

Several key factors favor Portland's transformation into a highly functional and livable transit metropolis of the twenty-first century. Foremost is the fact it is a prosperous, growing region. There is a lot of future growth to channel, and the physical and planning apparatuses to do so are in place. Importantly it enjoys a very supportive institutional environment. Add to this a cogent vision for the future and the prognosis for the future is bright.

The region has been able to reach remarkable consensus on how it should grow. There is broad-based support for using light rail as a lever to guide growth. A united front has evolved in spite of the many players and stakeholders: a state that is pro-active in urban affairs; twenty-four municipal governments; three counties; an intermediate level of government, Metro; hundreds of activist neighborhoods; and numerous watchdog organizations, such as 1,000 Friends of Oregon. Also important, the business community is on board, strongly supporting both transit and urban planning.

Many reasons are given for Portland's accomplishments, but as has been the case in all transit metropolises, the results are largely a product of dedication and farsighted planning. Notes one longtime activist: "The explanations people give for why Portland is different are hogwash. It's our attitude toward growth management. And the reason we've accomplished what we've accomplished is that we've been working on it hard for twenty-five years."[18]

Vancouver, British Columbia

Greater Vancouver, home to some 1.8 million residents, has a long history of regional planning dating back to the 1920s. A high mark was the adoption of the 1975 Livable Region Plan, which crystallized a vision of transit-oriented growth, very much in the tradition of Stockholm and Copenhagen. The plan—widely considered a landmark in the annals of city planning—contained wonderful illustrations and maps that sketched out a future of hierarchical town centers interlinked by high-capacity transit services. It also called for an improved jobs-housing balance and a wider range of housing choices. It provided the type of cogent vision that is all-important in charting a path toward becoming a transit metropolis.

The lifeline that would eventually connect the planned town centers was the SkyTrain, opened in time for the 1986 World Expo, whose very theme was futuristic transportation.[19] The 28-kilometer, fully automated, driverless SkyTrain system is complemented today by high-quality bus and catamaran ferry services. The region's transit operator, BC Transit, is a Crown Corporation with considerable clout and purse-string powers. As a quasi public-private entity, BC Transit has taken an entrepreneurial approach to the transit business over the years. Through its joint development office, the company has aggressively leveraged private investment around rail nodes. At all stations with commercial development potential, BC Transit invites developers to propose direct-access connections to stations. Besides generating ridership, the station-connection program produces about US$5 million in revenues per access point.

Greater Vancouver does not enjoy the same degree of regional planning powers found in other Canadian metropolises, such as Ottawa-Carleton or metropolitan Toronto. In 1983, following a power struggle with the province, the regional planning entity, the Greater Vancouver Regional District, was stripped of its land-use and transportation planning authority. By then, however, the Livable Region Plan had already won broad-based support, providing a common vision for the region's future. While the region has no formal UGB, it has successfully contained development through an agricultural reserve policy that takes large portions of peripheral lands out of the speculative market. Mountains and water features have further restricted buildable land, driving up average densities.

Recent events bode more favorably for the future of regionally coordinated development in greater Vancouver. In 1995, the Livable Region Strategic Plan and the Transport 2021 Long-Range Plan were approved, setting the stage for what planners hope will be more coordinated and sustainable patterns of future growth. The Strategic Plan rejects "business-as-usual" approaches to regional growth, calling instead for more compact development that encourages the use of transit and discourages drive-alone motoring. It also promotes the formation of "complete" communities, where the need for travel is reduced by providing work, goods, and service within easy reach of residents. In order to expand transportation choices, the Transport 2021 Plan explicitly supports a "transit-oriented and automobile-restrained transportation system" and boldly calls for assigning "priority for increased roadway capacities first to high occupancy vehicles." To carry out this charge, a regional multimodal transportation entity, the Greater Vancouver Transportation Authority (GVTA), was formed in 1998. GVTA is slated to replace BC Transit as the region's transit operator, in addition to taking on the responsibility for planning, developing, and financing all transportation improvements in the region. While the authority operates independent of the Greater Vancouver Planning District, its programs have to conform to the Livable Region Strategic Plan.

Town Centers

Various zoning mechanisms and design approaches have been used to spur town center development around rail nodes to date. Transferable development rights and density bonuses are actively used to funnel development to station areas.[20] Within most regional town centers, off-street surface parking is not permitted, allowing for more intensive use of land. The high cost of structure and underground parking has prompted some developers to orient their projects to take advantage of transit's proximity. In most town centers, commercial buildings are designed with limited or no setbacks, creating a pedestrian scale.

An example of successful transit-oriented development is the Burnaby Metrotown, one of four designated regional town centers along the Sky-Train corridor. Burnaby, a first-generation suburb of 160,000 inhabitants, is located 10 kilometers south of downtown Vancouver. Its transit-friendly core consists of moderate-density retail, office, and entertainment uses (Photo 17.2). Several large public utilities—BC Hydro and BC Telephone—have relocated their corporate headquarters to Metrotown. The addition of governmental offices has helped prime the development pump by creating a critical mass of daytime workers. As the largest single employer in the region, government offices have considerable sway over local real estate markets.

Metrotown's core is surrounded by parks and a supporting ring of multifamily mid-rise apartments and townhouses. Single-family residences lie beyond the higher-density housing. This tapering of residential densities has put those most likely to ride transit—shoppers, office workers, and apartment dwellers—closest to the SkyTrain station. Ninety

PHOTO 17.2. SKYTRAIN AND METROTOWN. A driverless, computer-controlled Sky-Train departs Burnaby's Metrotown station and the high-rise, office-commercial development that surrounds it.

percent of all commercial parking spaces in Burnaby are in structures or below ground. This has freed up land for parks, passageways, and connecting bike paths.

Other Supportive Measures

Greater Vancouver has other traits of a successful transit metropolis. Downtown Vancouver continues to grow as the region's employment and commercial hub. At most of the twenty SkyTrain stations, little or no parking is available. Instead, BC Transit bus routes have been reconfigured to efficiently feed into stations. Also missing from the local transportation scene is much freeway capacity. Partly because of grassroots freeway revolts in the early 1970s, the region has only 170 kilometers of freeway, less than half of that found in U.S. cities of similar size.[21] Moreover, all freeways terminate before reaching the city proper. Those wishing to get into the city must use public transit, surface arterials, or other means.

Outlook

Perhaps the region's biggest asset is its clear, lucid vision for the future. Thanks in large part to the 1975 Livable Region Plan and subsequent updates, a transit-oriented regional form is beginning to take shape. The limited reach of the SkyTrain corridor, however, could hamper efforts in becoming a full-blown transit metropolis. To date, relatively few land-use changes have occurred around the other two SkyTrain-served town centers outside downtown: New Westminster and Surrey. Beyond the SkyTrain corridor, growth has been decidedly auto-oriented. Presently, transit captures 13 percent of morning peak-hour trips, a respectable market share, but a far cry from that achieved my eastern Canadian cities, including the much smaller Ottawa-Carleton region.[22] Should the region be able to repeat the success at Burnaby Metrotown elsewhere and expand high-quality transit services into traditional suburbs, its prognosis for achieving the long-range goals set in the Livable Region Plan will be much improved.

One factor that could eventually work in Vancouver's favor is sheer growth. The region's population increased by nearly 3 percent annually from 1991 to 1996, by far the fastest rate of metropolitan growth in Canada during this period. Fueled by immigration from Asia and in-migration from other parts of Canada, greater Vancouver is today growing by more than 40,000 residents a year, making it one of the ten fastest growing metropolitan areas in North America. Whether this growth will be transit-supportive will hinge on whether the visions set forth in the original and updated Livable Region Plan are actually implemented. The recent formation of a regional transportation authority whose mandate includes helping to achieve the visions set forth in the Livable Region Plan bode favorably for this prospect.

San Diego, California

As one of America's fastest-growing cities over the past two decades, San Diego has seen traffic congestion steadily worsen and quality of life slip as a consequence. Wishing to avoid becoming an appendage of Los Angeles, citizens of San Diego considered a Portland-style approach to growth management. In 1988, a time when a deep recession was beginning to set in, the voters resoundingly rejected a flurry of citizen ballot initiatives mandating caps on building permits and bans on large-scale development. However, Proposition C, an advisory measure, did pass. Proposition C called on San Diego County and its nineteen cities to prepare a regional plan that would resolve metropolitan-wide problems related to transportation, air quality, solid waste management, and unplanned growth. In a surprise vote of confidence, local governments gave the responsibility for developing the regional plan to what had long been mostly a consensus-building organization, the San Diego Association of Governments (SANDAG).[23]

Based on long-range projections showing that historical growth trends were unsustainable, both economically and environmentally, SANDAG prepared a plan that called for a future of transit-oriented compact growth. Instead of heavy-handed growth controls, however, it was agreed that incentives, such as density bonuses and targeted infrastructure improvements, would work best. The centerpiece of the region's soft approach to growth management would be a light rail transit system, the San Diego Trolley. Increasing residential densities and focusing growth around rail stops would reduce pressures to develop rural land and preserve tens of thousands of hectares of natural habitat.

Transit-Oriented Development

In 1992, the San Diego city council adopted transit-oriented development (TOD) guidelines—one of the first U.S. cities to do so—upon the advice of hired consultant Peter Calthorpe. SANDAG incorporated the city's TOD initiatives into a regionwide "land use distribution" element that encouraged other cities in the county to follow suit. Included in this program was the usual list of TOD approaches: mixed uses; high densities near transit nodes matched by lower densities farther away; pedestrian-friendly neighborhood design; and a balance of housing and jobs near large employment centers.

An important step toward promoting compact, mixed-use development in the city of San Diego has been the replacement of traditional zoning with a performance-based land guidance system. The aim is to mitigate the negative effects of growth while allowing the marketplace to determine the best use of individual properties. The system allows any activity on a piece of property provided it is compatible with neighboring uses and satisfies larger community goals. City planners use a point system to assess each case. Criteria reward infill projects and redevelopment, especially near trolley stations.

The recent attention given to the transit–land use nexus stems in part from the inactivity that followed the opening of the initial 25.4-kilometer trolley line to the Mexican border in 1981 and the 27.7-kilometer east-side extension to El Cajon a decade later.[24] Few land-use changes occurred because the lines went through inhospitable territories. In the case of the south line, the trolley follows an abandoned railroad right-of-way through sagebrush and an aging industrial district. Most of the eastern line either passes through established neighborhoods or skirts a busy freeway. The most visible signs of change have been in downtown San Diego. Two notable standouts are Horton Plaza (a major high-rise retail center flanked by condominiums, hotels, and office space) and the Uptown District (a gentrified, compact, mixed-use area) (Photo 17.3). Both were aided by an active downtown redevelopment campaign, funded mainly through tax increment financing. There have also been a few surprises along the eastern line, most notably the La Mesa Village Plaza, a mid-rise project with ninety-nine condominium units, ground-floor retail, and upper-level offices abutting the Spring Street trolley station. Surveys show that about 8 percent of the project's residents use transit for all trip purposes, six times the rate of usage among all residents of La Mesa.[25] Another notable accomplishment has been the attraction of child-care facilities near suburban stops—currently five lie within 800 meters of a trolley stop, a real convenience to moms and dads who need to drop off their kids prior to catching a train to work.

The city of San Diego and the trolley operator, the Metropolitan Transit Development Board (MTDB), are taking an altogether different approach with the new Mission Valley line. Mission Valley is being looked upon as a model for transit-oriented growth. In contrast to the two earlier lines, the corridor was chosen first and foremost to maximize development potential, with cost savings taking a second seat. Mission Valley's alignment crosses the San Diego River three times in order to site development on the flat valley floors and preserve the sensitive hillsides that define the valley. Since 1982, when the Mission Valley extension was first proposed, the corridor has seen more new growth than any axis in the region—more than 7,000 new housing units and in excess of 1 million square meters of new commercial and office space.[26]

Rio Vista West is the first large-scale project to fall under the city's

Photo 17.3. Transit-oriented development in San Diego. A trolley directly serves a condominium complex near downtown.

TOD guidelines. A large, mixed-use project adjacent to a Mission Valley trolley stop, it is being designed so that all residents, shopping, and jobs are within easy walking distance of transit. Although the region's economic woes have set the project back, project developers are committed to introducing new phases when the economy turns around.

Becoming a Hybrid Transit Metropolis

San Diego's resemblance to a hybrid transit metropolis stems from its acceptance of market-driven suburbanization and its progress in improving feeder bus and paratransit services in response. The region boasts one of America's most extensive minibus dial-a-ride (DAR) services. DAR consists mainly of shuttles that connect residents to mainline rail and bus stops. Two levels of service are provided: DART (direct access to regional transit), which functions as an extension of fixed-route services into low-density areas, and internal community circulators, found in the cities of El Cajon, Spring Valley, and La Mesa. Curb-to-curb DAR has proven to be very costly on a per passenger trip basis, however.[27] The best performer has been the Sorrento Valley Coaster. Sorrento Valley, located near the junction of Interstates 5 and 805, has some 70,000 employees, more than downtown San Diego. Express shuttles operated by a private contractor provide door-to-door connections between a commuter rail station in north San Diego County and Sorrento Valley. Costs per passenger trip are about half those of community-based DAR.[28] Virtually all customers are middle-income choice riders who would otherwise solo-commute to work were it not for the express services.

Another unique form of flexible paratransit found in the region is the jitney. As a result of a 1979 county-wide ordinance that deregulated paratransit, a dozen or so privately owned and operated jitneys ply their trade today, mainly in the San Ysidro area just north of the Mexican border.[29] Serving almost exclusively Spanish-speaking patrons, this novel service has more to do with the region's unique setting (just across the border from a fast-growing Third World city of some 2 million inhabitants) than a commitment to privatized, small-vehicle transit. Still, the presence of jitneys shows a willingness among local officials to allow alternative forms of transit into the marketplace.

Outlook

The San Diego region must learn to balance its strong commitment to transit against an equally strong acquiescence to market-driven patterns of suburbanization. Without a Portland-style growth boundary and a crystal-clear land-use vision, the region faces more of an uphill struggle than either Portland or Vancouver in making the transit–land use connection work. Its enlightened approach to land-use management—a performance-based guidance system in lieu of strict zoning—could be its saving grace. The region also seems willing to put up the money to leverage TOD projects, despite hard economic times. The TOD projects that have moved forward so far have required unusual efforts—primarily by local governments, redevelopment agencies, and transit operators—in assembling land and underwriting costs. These initiatives appear to be paying off, however. During the 1980s, the region was one of only three regions of the country where transit did not lose market share. From 1990 to 1994, transit ridership rose by a healthy 27 percent, despite a lackluster economy.[30] The region's relatively large number of transit-dependents—retirees, enlisted military, and day workers from Mexico—accounts for some of this gain, but a significant portion is also due to integrated transit and urban development.

Also working in the region's favor is the sheer extensiveness of the present and planned rail network. At 74 kilometers, it is already considerably larger than Portland's and Vancouver's networks, and by the year 2010, if all goes according to plans, the region will have a 138 kilometer light rail network, complemented by a 69-kilometer commuter rail line.[31] San Diego has a better chance than Portland in following through with its long-range transit-building program because it has a more secure local funding source.

Also, unlike other areas of the country, San Diego has a budding paratransit sector. Demand-responsive minibuses have materially improved services to low-density areas, though at a high per trip subsidy. Finding ways of operating more cost-effective feeder services remains a challenge. The region's unwillingness to clamp down on car usage, such as by eliminating free parking, will make it difficult for any form of transit to compete with automobile travel in suburbia, however.

One positive sign is a reenergized citizens' movement. A grassroots organization, Citizens Coordinate for Century 3 (C3), is seeking to resurrect a wonderfully illustrated plan, "Temporary Paradise," prepared by urban design luminaries Kevin Lynch and Donald Appleyard in 1974. "Temporary Paradise" called for future development patterns to be more human scale and respectful of natural settings. Its emphasis on sustainability and livability is consonant with principles embraced by TOD and the transit metropolis.

St. Louis, Missouri

St. Louis has become the darling of America's transit industry. MetroLink—a light rail line that stretches from east of the Mississippi River to Lambert International Airport—averaged 40,000 daily riders within two years of its 1993 opening, twice what was projected and even more than the year 2010 forecast of 35,000 daily riders. This is despite the St. Louis region having suffered one of the worst recessions in the country during the early 1990s.

Much of MetroLink's success stems from smart routing. The 29-kilometer line connects downtown to three large professional sports complexes, three universities, two medical centers, an active riverfront and gaming boat port, colorful Union Station, entertainment sites, and the airport—land uses that in combination guarantee traffic throughout the day and week. The line is largely a product of having pieced together abandoned railroad right-of-ways that happened to skirt a lot of big trip generators (Photo 17.4). Notes Robert Dunphy, research director of the Urban Land Institute, "MetroLink created heavy-rail service at light-rail prices."[32] There were other good fortunes, such as the arrival of the Rams football team from Los Angeles, which produced tens of thousands of rail trips on sports days that were never factored in. Transit proponents contend the relationship has worked both ways: downtown reinvestment—notably in new sports facilities—has likewise occurred because of MetroLink.

Like San Diego, the region has the makings of a budding hybrid transit metropolis. Most bus routes in St. Louis have been reconfigured to feed into MetroLink stations. About 43 percent of MetroLink riders currently reach stations by bus. During MetroLink's first four years, bus ridership

PHOTO 17.4. METROLINK CORRIDOR.
Available railroad right-of-ways
and modest station designs helped
contain project construction costs.

rose 40 percent. Many transit patrons are choice riders—surveys reveal
that a third earn more than $45,000 per year and about half live in house-
holds with two or more cars.[33]

Planned MetroLink Extensions

If all goes according to schedule, the region hopes to have 151 kilometers
of light rail lines in place sometime over the next fifteen years, which
would earn it top honors for the largest light rail network in North
America. This would bring the region full circle, for, at the turn of
the twentieth century, St. Louis's interurban streetcar network was the
world's biggest.[34] Local citizens have generally been willing to tax themselves to support rail, having passed sales tax initiatives to finance
improvements and extensions in 1993 and 1994. There is tremendous
civic pride in MetroLink. The work of local artists adorns all stations.
Some of MetroLink's earliest critics are now among its strongest supporters. In MetroLink some see a return to the city's illustrious past, some see
a modern technology that helps the region shed its Rust Belt image, and
most see a convenient form of travel, especially to downtown. The pro-rail
movement suffered a setback in 1996, however, when voters failed to
approve the MetroLink extension into St. Charles County. Proposition M,
which would have extended a line to Clayton, an edge city to the west, was
defeated in 1997.

Still moving forward, however, is the 32-kilometer extension through
the corn fields of St. Clair County, Illinois, to the Mid-America Airport,

slated for a year 2001 opening. While there is tremendous development potential around a number of stations along the St. Clair corridor, the fact that it passes through the heart of one of America's poorest, highest-crime cities, East St. Louis, has dampened developer interest.[35] The prospect of rejuvenating East St. Louis itself has not gone unnoticed, though all sides agree it will take a lot more than a light rail line to solve the city's deep-rooted problems. All nine stations along the St. Clair extension will be enveloped by parking spaces (3,300 in all), which should work in favor of continued low-density development.

Development Deterrents

To date, little new development has occurred around MetroLink stops, to the disappointment of many. All activity centers served by MetroLink pre-date the project. Segments of the line traverse abandoned industrial areas and depressed neighborhoods. Several sites near stations (such as Well-ston and Dellmar) cry out for redevelopment, but despite the best efforts of local authorities, few private investors have shown much interest.[36] The reality is that it is risky to redevelop former industrial land. One is never sure what is in store when unearthing abandoned sites. Ground contami-nants and expensive cleanup bills are always a possibility. The areas also suffer from obsolete public infrastructure, high crime, and urban blight.

Another deterrent to station-area growth has been the vast amounts of developable land in the region. Greater St. Louis has among the lowest residential densities in the country. Most growth has been on the fringes, a trend that has hurt transit. In 1990, one out of five downtown workers who lived within 10 kilometers of downtown took transit to work. In the fastest-growing ring, 19 to 21 kilometers out from the CBD, only 6 percent of workers heading to downtown jobs took transit. During the 1980s, before MetroLink opened, greater St. Louis lost more transit commuters than any U.S. urbanized area—a consequence of what Robert Dunphy calls "sprawl without growth."[37]

Unlike the other transit metropolises reviewed in this book—present or potential—greater St. Louis has no shared vision of the future. Despite the existence of a regional authority—the Bi-State Development Agency (BSDA), which is also the regional transit operator—there is virtually no regional land-use planning. Because of intergovernmental and interstate squabbles and competition, the BSDA uses only a fraction of its autho-rized powers. There is a regional waste management program, a regional zoo, and regional transit, but no regional land-use plan.

Building on Strengths

Despite residential sprawl, the region has seen some degree of employ-ment subcentering. There were fifteen centers with more than 10,000 jobs each in 1990. All are potential hubs of a regional rail network. Currently, however, few are served by MetroLink. Clayton, the largest suburban center with more than 25,000 jobs, lies along a planned route, however, as noted, residents recently voted down a sales tax initiative to finance the extension. Moreover, an alignment that would have directly penetrated Clayton was changed to a more peripheral location because of neighborhood opposition.

One factor working in St. Louis's favor is the presence of a very active advocacy group, Citizens for Modern Transit (CMT), which has become an important behind-the-scenes force in promoting rail investments. The group spent almost a decade building broad-based community support before the first line was opened.[38] Its commitment to seeing the MetroLink project through to its ultimate target of 151 kilometers is unwavering.

Outlook

Despite MetroLink's impressive ridership history, the St. Louis region faces stiff odds in its quest to become a transit metropolis. There are few signs that new growth will be drawn to rail stops. Continued sprawl favors auto travel. In 1990, the region had America's third-highest rate of drive-alone commuting and ranked fourth in freeway capacity per capita.[39] Except at bridge crossings, there is little traffic congestion. One critic charges that MetroLink has played less of a mobility role than boosters claim; he calculates that when adjusting for trip length and regional growth, passenger kilometers of transit travel, expressed on a per capita basis, rose just 1.1 percent from 1990 to 1995.[40]

Perhaps the region's best hope is to improve feeder-to-mainline transit connections. More attention should be given to making transit better serve spread-out development. If transit advocates set their sights on becoming a hybrid transit metropolis instead of the next Stockholm, or even Portland, transit's future will be far brighter. This will most likely happen if regional interests, namely the Bi-State Development Agency, step forward and articulate such a vision.

Houston, Texas

It may be surprising to find Houston, Texas—a sprawling, auto-oriented metropolis if there ever was one—in a book about the transit metropolis. Does freewheeling and dealing Houston—a city that even shuns zoning—even want to be recognized as an aspiring transit metropolis? Since Houston has, by far, the largest high-occupancy vehicle (HOV) network of any U.S. metropolis—one well suited to the spread-out lay of the land—its transit system and relationship to the region at large deserve recognition.

Houston is one of the few U.S. metropolitan areas where public transit's market share of commute trips has been on the rise. From 1980 to 1990, transit's share of work trips rose from 2.0 percent to 3.6 percent, the fastest percentage increase in the country.[41] Granted, it started from a very small base, so there generally was only one direction to go—up. Yet it is also true that greater Houston is implanting a regional transit system, step by step, that is more in harmony with the regional landscape than most American metropolises can lay claim to. Increasing ridership—today two-and-a-half times what it was in 1980—is a direct outcome.

In 1982, Houston was second only to Los Angeles in traffic congestion. Over the past sixteen years, the region has invested about a billion dollars annually on massive road improvements, mostly financed by public bonds backed by toll revenues. Congestion has consequently fallen (despite rising employment and traffic volumes), one of only three U.S. metropolitan areas where this has been the case. Improved traffic conditions are reflected by statistics on travel speeds. From 1980 to 1990, average freeway speeds increased from 38 miles per hour to 46 miles per hour (61 kilometers per hour to 74 kilometers per hour).[42]

The needs of transit riders have not been overlooked, however. During the 1990s, transit has received 21 percent of all monies spent on upgrading transportation, even though it claims but 2 percent of the travel market.[43] A dedicated sales tax generates about $250 million annually for transit.[44] Original plans called for building a massive heavy rail system, but they were rejected by voters in 1973 and 1983. A light rail proposal was gathering steam in the early 1990s when the former chairman of the regional transit agency (METRO), Bob Lanier, decided to run for mayor, largely on the platform of scrapping rail in favor of a more cost-effective, bus-based alternative. Upon winning the mayoral seat, Lanier moved quickly in designing a transit system suited to Houston, instead of the other way around. Under Lanier's leadership, Houston has taken on the mantle of America's premier example of adaptive transit.

Transit in a Polycentric Metropolis

While overall densities in Houston and its surroundings are low, the area is curiously also a land of subcenters. Greater Houston probably has more widely dispersed activity centers—some twenty-two at last count—than anywhere else in the world.[45] The Uptown/Galleria area boasts some 26 million square feet (2.4 million square meters) of office space, more than downtown Denver. Other megacenters include the Texas Medical Center (the world's largest medical complex, with more than 60,000 workers), the Energy corridor along the Katy Freeway, and the Greenway Plaza area.

Subcentering set the stage for designing a transit network suited to serving scattered trip origins and destinations. At the core of Houston's all-bus system is the HOV network, designed mainly to funnel suburbanites to downtown jobs via bus, vanpool, or carpool. There are currently the 108 kilometers of HOV lanes in the medians of five freeway corridors; the system is to expand to 165 kilometers and seven corridors by the year 2000.[46] HOV lanes are reversible, operating in one direction only—downtown-bound in the morning and outbound in the evening (Photo 17.5). Flyover ramps link twenty-four park-and-ride lots to the HOV facilities.

While technically an HOV facility, METRO's planners prefer to think of the facility as a dedicated busway that accepts smaller "transit vehicles"—vans and packed cars—to exploit available capacity. In 1991 dollars, it cost about $4 million per kilometer to build, about half as much as no-frills light rail investments in San Diego, Portland, and San Jose.[47] Economies have partly accrued from adding links in conjunction with freeway expansion projects as opportunities have arisen. Because average speeds more than doubled for buses that use the facility, operating costs have also fallen, by an estimated $5 million annually (in 1991 currency).

Cars with multiple occupants make up 94 percent of the 35,000 vehicles that use the HOV lanes each day.[48] Buses and vans each make up 3 percent. However, buses account for 34 percent of the daily passenger throughput of 80,000. The majority of people traveling on the North

PHOTO 17.5. BUS AND CARPOOLS SHARE HOV LANE. Protected lanes in the freeway median allow HOV traffic to travel at rush-hour speeds of 80 to 90 kilometers per hour, compared to 50 to 55 kilometers per hour on regular freeway lanes.

(Interstate 45) HOV lane are aboard buses. In all, about 5 percent of the region's work force uses the HOV lanes each workday.

Aided by the HOV lanes and often subsidies from employers, vanpools have become an important feature of the local transportation scene—an entrepreneurial, small-vehicle form of mass transportation well adapted to spread-out development. In 1990, some 15 percent of commuters were in vanpools or carpools, one of the highest rates in the country.[49]

Houston's Adaptive Transit

Metropolitan Houston's adaptive transit services fall into three categories: local; express; and specialized. Local buses serve short-hop neighborhood trips. Express routes provide direct, peak-hour connections, mainly along the HOV lanes, to downtown and subcenters. To aid transfers between local and express routes, there are presently fourteen partially enclosed transit centers (complete with seats, telephones, and route information) and plans for five more. More than half of local bus routes stop at a center.

The clienteles of local versus express services differ markedly. Local buses serve mainly transit-dependents (only 28 percent have access to a car) who walk-and-ride (93 percent). Express routes serve mainly choice riders (93 percent have access to a car) who park-and-ride (92 percent).[50] Park-and-ride connections to express runs tend to be fast and efficient. At the Addicks park-and-ride lot off the Katy Freeway HOV lane, articulated buses depart every three minutes during rush hour.

Houston's radial HOV arrangement provides superb services to the CBD, but for other destinations routes tend to be circuitous. To reach the Uptown/Galleria or Greenway Plaza areas by express bus, for example, requires passengers to go downtown first. Presently, 29 percent of downtown workers arrive by bus, compared to just 7 to 8 percent of workers in the Uptown and Greenway areas. The one-way operation of HOV lanes compromises the ability to provide reverse-commute and crosstown express services.

In an all-out campaign to better serve nonradial trips, Houston has introduced a number of unorthodox services in recent years. While many have struggled financially, they represent a willingness to take risks and test uncharted waters. The six specialized services listed below are emblematic of Houston's unique approach toward designing adaptive transit.

1. *Circumferential routes.* Houston has introduced the nation's only true circumferential bus route, the TC Flyer, which circumnavigates the Interstate 610 inner beltway, interconnecting the Texas Medical Center, Uptown/Galleria, and Greenway Plaza. Operating on fifteen-

minute headways throughout the day, the service incurred deficits of $23 per passenger in 1995.[51]

2. *Tangential routes.* METRO has experimented with several crosstown express connections between park-and-ride lots and suburban centers. The most successful routes serve the Texas Medical Center (TMC), where 14 percent of workers commute by bus, by far the highest market share of all subcenters. This stems partly from tangential routes, but also from a more transit-supportive built environment. Compared to other subcenters, parking is expensive at TMC, comparable to what it costs downtown. Moreover, parking garages lie on the periphery, whereas buses provide near-door delivery. Most TMC employers underwrite commuting expenses of employees who take transit or ride-share. TMC also has an integrated pedestrian network, including second-story skywalks.

3. *Subscription services.* A number of private subscription buses supplement METRO express services. Employers at Greenspoint, a small edge city north of downtown, sponsor several subscription services that use HOV lanes. The Woodlands, a master-planned new town 40 kilometers north of downtown Houston, supports subscription services that cater to both employees and residents.

4. *Vanpools.* Some 2,500 vanpools, one of the largest fleets anywhere, operate throughout greater Houston, providing door-to-door services and filling in gaps left unserved by the bus system. Many are sponsored by employers. METRO itself sponsors more than 100 vanpools, focused mainly on suburban centers. Vanpools have proven to be a cost-effective alternative to nonradial bus runs. Their per passenger subsidy of under a dollar is just half that of comparable park-and-ride express bus runs.[52] The sharing of driving duties among vanpool participants accounts for part of the cost savings.

5. *Midday circulators.* A deterrent to riding transit to suburban job sites is the restricted ability to get around in the midday. In response, METRO and employers co-sponsor midday shuttles that circulate within the Uptown/Galleria, TMC, and Greenpoint areas.

6. *Jitneys.* In 1995, Houston's city council opened the marketplace to private jitneys, lifting restrictions on fares and services. (Besides meeting driver and vehicle fitness standards, the only restrictions are that jitneys cannot stop at METRO stops and vehicles can be no older than five years.) This has unleashed competition, something sorely needed in suburban markets. Seeing the handwriting on the wall, METRO decided to get a step up on jitney entrepreneurs by

contracting out supplemental van-size services for an 8-kilometer stretch of the Westheimer Boulevard corridor.[53]

Outlook

In greater Houston, transit aims to serve development rather than shape it. By improving the quality of services to sprawling areas, of course, transit has unavoidably reinforced growth patterns. This is the Houston way, however, and to the credit of civic leaders, an appropriate role has been defined for transit that is in accord with residents' lifestyle preferences.

Although Houston may never truly fit the bill of a transit metropolis, it is nevertheless a region where respectable transit services can be and are being designed. Many things are working in its favor. One is a clear vision for the future. Its long-range plan, Access 2010, calls for a balance of capital-intensive roadway and transit improvements. While it is largely left to the marketplace to determine where and by how much growth occurs, the plan provides a clear statement of where future transportation investments will be targeted. Importantly, it preserves right-of-ways and secures funding for proposed projects. In addition to a vision, Houston has benefited from a visionary, Bob Lanier, whose unbending advocacy and willingness to stake his political future on bus-based transit is what distinguishes Houston from many areas.

Houston's willingness to take risks also bodes favorably for the future. Plans call for continued experimentation with nontraditional services, such as crosstown express runs. METRO has begun retrofitting HOV facilities with new on-off ramps to provide direct connections to subcenters, such as Uptown/Galleria. It is also the only regional transit agency that is actively experimenting with advanced vehicle control systems (AVCS) today. Using machine vision and forward-looking radar sensors, METRO hopes to one day laterally and longitudinally guide buses on and off HOV lanes. Articulated buses that serve transit centers and park-and-ride lots would also operate more efficiently and safely with on-board guidance systems. If new-age technologies are to find useful applications in the transit field, odds are that Houston will be one of the first places to introduce them.

Building Transit Metropolises of Tomorrow

Proposals to build and extend fixed-guideway systems, especially light rail, in the United States have triggered a wrath of criticism. Even cities that show great promise, such as Portland, have come under attack. And with some justification. The track record with new rail systems in the

United States leaves a lot to be desired. Studies show that new-generation rail systems have failed to produce the ridership that was promised and ended up costing far more than was forecast.[54] Critics charge that America's new rail projects have had nothing to do with economics and everything to do with politics: civic boosterism; political monument building; a "make no small plans" mentality, in deference to Daniel Burnham's plea to all city planners; a belief that, like being home to a professional baseball or football team, all "great cities" must have a metro; the prospects of job creation through federally funded capital grants; the self-interests of downtown merchants bent on stemming the tide of retail losses to suburban malls; and what John Kain of Harvard University calls a "Lionel train complex"—"a major part of the appeal of transit is a childish fascination with electric trains" (an argument akin to 'the only difference between men and boys is the price of their toys').[55] Kain and others suggest that a reason taxpayers vote for sales tax referenda in support of rail transit is a naive belief that "the other guy" will now starting riding transit, freeing up more road space so they can drive their cars unimpeded.

Although the reasons for transit's poor showing over the years are many, the gross underpricing of automobile travel—especially along heavily trafficked corridors where transit is most needed—heads the list. An absence of coordinated and comprehensive planning, carried out on a regional scale, is also to blame. Putting a point-to-point rail system in a sea of spread-out, auto-oriented development is hardly a recipe for successful and sustainable transit. Quite simply, too often across America, transit and cityscapes have been way out of synch.

It should be kept in mind that some cities, such as Stockholm and Copenhagen, began investing in high-capacity transit systems a good half-century ago. In these places, too, it took time for the benefits of these investments to accrue. Much of the rationale for large-scale transit programs, especially in countries like the United States, must be viewed intergenerationally. Today's residents of East Coast cities such as Boston and New York owe a considerable debt of gratitude to their forefathers and foremothers for having had the foresight to invest in regional metros. Indeed, intergenerational transfer of benefits captures the very essence of what is meant by sustainability. Faulting today's ambitious transit programs overlooks potentially important societal benefits that will be passed on to our children and their children. Hank Dittmar, executive director of the Surface Transportation Policy Project in Washington, D.C., notes: "Rail is a long-term investment, and evaluating it at three years or even five years of age is like judging a human infant at that age—it's mostly potential."[56]

Of course, transit investments that are out of kilter with how our cities and regions grow do nobody any good. Running trains and buses that fail to draw people out of drive-alone cars does little to relieve traffic congestion, conserve fuel, or reduce pollution. The best prescription for filling trains and buses, and winning over motorists to transit, is to find a harmonious fit between transit systems and the cities and suburbs they serve. This is the core lesson of the transit metropolis.

NOTES

1. S. Edner and G. B. Arrington, Jr., *Urban Decision Making for Transit Investments: Portland's Light Rail Transit Line* (Washington, DC: U.S. Department of Transportation, 1985).

2. W. Eager, Accommodating Land Use and Transportation, *Land Use in Transition: Emerging Forces and Issues Shaping the Real Estate Environment* (Washington, DC: The Urban Land Institute, 1993). For a particularly critical perspective on Portland's experiences, check out the Internet Public Policy Journal at the following web site: http://www.publicpurpose.com.

3. The market share of downtown workers commuting by transit was placed at 43 percent in a case study of Portland prepared by Judith Corbett of the Local Government Commission for the Surface Transportation Policy Project, a nongovernmental organization based in Washington, D.C., that promotes balanced, multimodal transportation. A lower figure of 33 percent is reported by Kenneth Dueker and Martha Bianco based on the analysis of 1990 journey-to-work census data for the Portland metropolitan area. Sources: J. Corbett, *Portland's Livable Downtown: From Auto-Dependence to Pedestrian Independence* (Washington DC: Surface Transportation Policy Project, 1994); K. Dueker and M. Bianco, *Effects of Light Rail Transit in Portland: Implications for Transit-Oriented Development Design Concepts*, Discussion Paper 97-7 (Portland: Center for Urban Studies, Portland State University, 1998).

4. The east-side line was the nation's first joint freeway/light rail project. A total of $107 million went to reconstructing 6.9 kilometers of the Banfield Freeway (Interstate 84) and $244 million was spent on the rail facility itself.

5. K. Deuker and M. Biano, *op. cit.*, 1998.

6. G. B. Arrington, Jr., *Beyond the Field of Dreams: Light Rail and Growth Management in Portland* (Portland: Tri-Met, 1996).

7. *Ibid.*

8. Besides growth management and transportation–land use coordination, Metro provides technical services to local governments and operates and maintains regional parks, greenspaces, and a zoo. Governed by an executive officer who is elected at large and a thirteen-member council elected by districts, Metro is advised on transportation issues by a Joint Policy Advisory Committee on Transportation (JPACT) made up of elected officials and transit agency representatives.

9. D. Porter, A 50-Year Plan for Metropolitan Portland, *Urban Land*, vol. 54, no. 7, 1995, pp. 37–40.

10. The UGB was never intended to be static. From 1979, when the UGB was first formed, to 1998, only 2,800 hectares had been added to the bound-

ary. A reservoir of more than 7,200 additional hectares exists for future expansion.

11. A 1997 *Washington Post* article, "Cracks in Portland's 'Great Wall,'" chronicled this debate. According to the National Association of Home Builders, Portland is second only to San Francisco in the cost of housing relative to local incomes. The average lot size for homes fell from 13,000 square feet (1,200 square meters) in 1979 to 7,400 square feet (690 square meters) in 1997. The back-to-the-city movement has purportedly displaced thousands of minority and low-income households over the past decade. Others counterargue that benefits have more than offset these costs and that reinvestment in the core has caused less hardship on the poor than sprawl and the racial and class segregation it produces. See: W. Claiborne, Cracks in Portland's "Great Wall": A Strict Model of Controlled Growth Begins to Budge, *Washington Post*, September 29, 1997, pp. A-1 and A-12; J. Walljasper, Portland's Green Peace: At Play in the Fields of Urban Planning, *The Nation*, October 13, 1997, pp. 11–15; G. Mildner, K. Dueker, and A. Rufalo, *Impact of the Urban Growth Boundary on Metropolitan Housing Markets* (Portland: Portland State University, Center for Urban Studies, 1996).

12. P. Newman, Reducing Automobile Dependence, *Environment and Urbanization*, vol. 8, no. 1, 1996, pp. 67–92.

13. Project for Public Spaces, Inc., *The Role of Transit in Creating Livable Metropolitan Communities*, Transit Cooperative Research Program Report 22 (Washington, DC: Transportation Research Board, National Research Council, 1997).

14. 1000 Friends of Oregon, *The LUTRAQ Alternatives Analysis* (Portland: 1000 Friends of Oregon, 1992).

15. Washington County, Department of Land Use and Transportation, Eastside Lessons Helping Westside Thrive, *Connections: Westside Light Rail Station Community Planning News*, vol. 7, 1997, p. 2.

16. The 1996 Ballot Measure 32 would have provided $375 million in state lottery funds to construct the bistate light rail line. The rejection has forced planners to go back to the drawing board and consider shorter segments and new possible alignments.

17. R. Dunphy, Transportation and Development in Portland: Challenging the Idea of Laissez-Faire Development, *Moving Beyond Gridlock: Traffic and Development* (Washington, DC: The Urban Land Institute, 1997), pp. 39–56.

18. Walljasper, *op. cit.*, p. 15.

19. R. Cervero, Urban Transit in Canada: Integration and Innovation at Its Best, *Transportation Quarterly*, vol. 40, no. 3, 1986, pp. 293–316.

20. BC Transit, which owned much of the original right-of-ways for the SkyTrain project, sold most of the land underneath aerial tracks to private investors. TDRs allowed landholders to shift development rights to station areas. Under this arrangement, then, BC Transit gained revenues and the region at large benefited from transit-oriented development.

21. R. Willson and J. Anderson, Planning for Transit-Oriented Development in San Diego and Vancouver, British Columbia (Paper presented at the 35th

Annual Meeting of the Association of Collegiate Schools of Planning, Philadelphia, October 28–31, 1993).

22. Parsons Brinckerhoff Quade & Douglas, Inc., *Transit and Urban Form: Six International Case Studies*, Transit Cooperative Research Program Report 16 (Washington, DC: Transportation Research Board, National Research Council, 1996).

23. R. Dunphy, Transportation and Development in San Diego: Protecting Paradise, *Moving Beyond Gridlock: Traffic and Development* (Washington, DC: The Urban Land Institute, 1997), pp. 125–142.

24. The east-side line was further extended by three stops to Santee's central business district in 1996. Also completed was a 5.1-kilometer north-line extension that connected the CBD with Old Town, one of the city's primary tourist destinations and the terminus of a commuter rail service linking the city to the affluent suburbs of north San Diego County.

25. V. Menotti and R. Cervero, *Transit-Based Housing in California: Profiles*, Working Paper 638 (Berkeley: Institute of Urban and Regional Development, University of California, 1995).

26. W. Lorenz, *Designing Light Rail Transit Compatible with Urban Form* (San Diego: San Diego Metropolitan Transit Development Board, 1996).

27. Per trip deficits on San Diego's community-based DAR services ranged from $6.25 to $11.50 in 1995, compared to $0.84 for local fixed-route bus services. The lower average loads of minibus services accounted for much of the difference. DART, which requires at least one-hour advance reservations and assigns priority to transfer trips, incurred deficits in the $3.35 to $7.20 range. Sources: Urbitran Associates, Inc., Multisystems, Inc., SG Associates, Inc., and R. Cervero, *Improving Transit Connections for Enhanced Suburban Mobility* (Washington, DC: Transportation Research Board, National Research Council, Transit Cooperative Research Program, 1997); and R. Cervero, *Paratransit in America: Redefining Mass Transportation* (Westport, CT: Praeger, 1997).

28. The 1996 operating cost per passenger trip was $3.35. Customers ride the shuttle free upon showing an eligibility pass. Employers underwrite most of the costs for operating shuttle connections. Source: Urbitran Associates, Inc., et al., *op. cit.*

29. R. Cervero, 1997, *op. cit.*

30. Dunphy, *op. cit.*

31. In 1987, the region's voters passed Proposition A, which committed the region to build the 138-kilometer network, largely to be paid for by a dedicated local sales tax.

32. R. Dunphy, Transportation and Development in St. Louis: Sprawl Without Growth, *Moving Beyond Gridlock: Traffic and Development* (Washington, DC: The Urban Land Institute, 1997), p. 107.

33. P. Weyrich and W. Lind, *Conservatives and Mass Transit: Is It Time for a New Look?* (Washington, DC: The Free Congress Foundation, 1997).

34. B. Katz, *One Hundred Years of City Transit in St. Louis*, Occasional Paper No. 3 (St. Louis: National Museum of Transport, 1961).

35. The greatest potential is at the next to last station out, where supporters hope the ample amount of open space between the planned station and Belleville Area College will attract a large, mixed-use project.

36. L. Howland and R. Dunphy, Transit Sparks Redevelopment in St. Louis and Chicago, *Urban Land*, vol. 55, no. 7, 1996, pp. 43–89.

37. Dunphy, Transportation and Development in St. Louis, *op. cit.*, pp. 93–108.

38. A. Yong, Lobbying for Light Rail in St. Louis, *The New Electric Railway Journal*, vol. 8, no. 2, 1995–96, p. 16.

39. Dunphy, Transportation and Development in St. Louis, *op. cit.*, pp. 93–108.

40. Wendell Cox Consultancy, St. Louis Public Transport Trend in Passenger Miles: 1990–1995, Analysis to Factor Out Double Counting from Implementation of Light Rail, *The Public Purpose Urban Transport Fact Book*, July 1997; accessible at the web site: http://www.publicpurpose.com.

41. M. Rossetti and B. Eversole, *Journey-to-Work Trends in the United States and Its Major Metropolitan Areas, 1960–1990* (Washington, DC: Federal Highway Administration, U.S. Department of Transportation, 1993).

42. R. Dunphy, Transportation and Development in Houston: Beyond Edge City, *Moving Beyond Gridlock: Traffic and Development* (Washington, DC: The Urban Land Institute, 1997), pp. 143–156.

43. *Ibid.*

44. Significant shares of these monies have been diverted to road improvements in recent times, mainly under the logic that smoother flowing surface roads also benefit buses.

45. R. Cervero, *America's Suburban Centers: The Land Use–Transportation Link* (Boston: Unwin-Hyman, 1989).

46. The five freeway corridors currently served by HOV lanes are: Gulf (Interstate 45); Southwest (U.S. Route 59); North (Interstate 45); Katy (Interstate 10); and Northwest (U.S. Route 290). Carpools of two or more occupants are allowed on all HOV lanes, except the Katy Freeway, which requires three or more occupants during rush hours. During the first decade of HOVs, only buses and vanpools were allowed. Complaints that lanes were underutilized prompted the opening of the lanes to carpools in 1990. HOV lanes are free. A high-occupancy toll (HOT) experiment—which allows one- or two-occupant vehicles on the Katy Freeway facility during rush hours for a fee—is currently under way. See Chapter 3 for more about the HOT concept.

47. D. Christiansen and D. Morris, *An Evaluation of the Houston High Occupancy Vehicle Lane System* (Washington, DC: Federal Highway Administration, U.S. Department of Transportation, 1991).

48. J. Sedlak, *Lessons Learned in the Development of Houston's HOV System* (Houston: Metropolitan Transit Authority of Harris County, 1995).

49. Rossetti and Eversole, *op. cit.*

50. Metropolitan Transit Authority of Harris County, *1990 Origin and Destination Study* (Houston: Metropolitan Transit Authority of Harris County, 1991).

51. Urbitran Associates, Inc., et al., *op. cit.*

52. *Ibid.*

53. R. Cervero, 1997, *op. cit.*

54. D. Pickrell, *Urban Rail Transit Projects: Forecasts Versus Actual Ridership and Costs* (Cambridge, MA: John A. Volpe Transportation Systems Center, U.S. Department of Transportation, 1989).

55. J. Kain, Deception in Dallas: Strategic Misrepresentation in Rail Transit Promotion and Evaluation, *Journal of the American Planning Association*, vol. 56, no. 2, 1990, pp. 184–196; J. Kain, Choosing the Wrong Technology: Or How to Spend Billions and Reduce Transit Use, *Journal of Advanced Transportation*, vol. 21, no. 3, 1988, pp. 197–213. For a lively debate on the pros and cons of rail transit investments in the United States, see *TR News*, vol. 156, pp. 2–19, 1991, including essays by: D. Pickrell, Urban Rail Transit Systems: Are They Fulfilling Their Promise? pp. 3–5; J. Simon, Let's Make Forecasts and Actual Comparisons Fair, pp. 6–9; C. Lave, Playing the Rail Transit Forecasting Game, pp. 10–12; and V. Vuchic, Recognizing the Value of Rail Transit, pp. 13–19.

56. H. Dittmar, Is Rail Transit Right for Your Community? Asking the Right Questions, Measuring the Benefits (Paper presented at the First Annual Railvolution Conference, Portland, September 17, 1995, sponsored by the City of Portland, U.S. Federal Transit Administration, and the Surface Transportation Policy Project).

Selected Bibliography

Banister, D. *Transport and Urban Development*. London: E & FN Spon, 1995.

Bernick, M., and R. Cervero. *Transit Villages in the 21st Century*. New York: McGraw-Hill, 1997.

Calthorpe, P. *The Next American Metropolis: Ecology, Community and the American Dream*. Princeton: Princeton Architectural Press, 1994.

Cervero, R. *Suburban Gridlock*. New Brunswick, NJ: Center for Urban Policy Research, 1986.

Cervero, R. *America's Suburban Centers: The Land Use–Transportation Link*. Boston: Unwin-Hyman, 1989.

Cervero, R. *Paratransit in America: Redefining Mass Transportation*. Westport, CT: Praeger, 1997.

Dimitriou, H. *Transport Planning for Third World Cities*. London: Routledge, 1990.

Downs, A. *New Visions for Metropolitan America*. Washington, DC: The Brookings Institution and Lincoln Institute of Land Policy, 1994.

Downs, A. *Stuck in Traffic: Coping with Peak-Hour Traffic Congestion*. Washington, DC: The Brookings Institution, 1992.

Dunphy, R. *Moving Beyond Gridlock: Traffic and Development*. Washington, DC: The Urban Land Institute, 1997.

Garreau, J. *Edge City: Life on the New Frontier*. New York: Doubleday, 1991.

Gómez-Ibáñez, J., and J. Meyer. *Going Private: The International Experience with Transport Privatization*. Washington, DC: The Brookings Institution, 1993.

Gordon, D. *Steering a New Course: Transportation, Energy, and the Environment*. Washington, DC: Island Press, 1991.

Hall, P. *Cities of Tomorrow: An Intellectual History of Urban Planning and Design in the Twentieth Century*. New York: Basil Blackwell, 1988.

Jacobs, J. *The Death and Life of Great American Cities*. New York: Vintage Books, 1961.

Jones, D. *Urban Transit Policy: An Economic and Political History*. Englewood Cliffs, NJ: Prentice-Hall, 1985.

Katz, P. *The New Urbanism*. New York: McGraw-Hill, 1994.

Lave, C., ed. *Urban Transit: The Private Challenge to Public Transportation*. Cambridge, MA: Ballinger, 1985.

Lynch, K. *Good City Form.* Cambridge, MA: The MIT Press, 1992.

Newman, P., and J. Kenworthy. *Cities and Automobile Dependence: A Sourcebook.* Aldershot, England: Grower, 1989.

Pharoah, T., and D. Apel. *Transport Concepts in European Cities.* Aldershot, England: Avebury, 1995.

Pucher, J., and C. Lefèvre. *The Urban Transport Crisis in Europe and North America.* Basingstoke, England: Macmillan Press, 1996.

Puskarev, B., and J. Zupan. *Public Transit and Land-Use Policy.* Bloomington: Indiana University Press, 1977.

Thomson, M. *Great Cities and Their Traffic.* London: Victor Gollancz Ltd., 1977.

Tolley, R., and B. Turton. *Transport Systems, Policy and Planning: A Geographical Approach.* Essex, England: Longman Scientific & Technical, 1995.

Untermann, R. *Accommodating the Pedestrian: Adapting Towns and Neighborhoods for Walking and Bicycling.* New York: Van Nostrand Reinhold, 1984.

Von Weisäcker, E., A. Lovins, and L. Lovins. *Factor Four: Doubling Wealth, Halving Resource Use.* London: Earthscan Publications, 1997.

Weicher, J., ed. *Private Innovations in Public Transit.* Washington, DC: American Enterprise Institute, 1988.

Whitelegg, J. *Transport for a Sustainable Future: The Case for Europe.* London: Belhaven Press, 1993.

World Bank. *Sustainable Transport: Priorities for Policy Reform.* Washington, DC: The World Bank, 1996.

Wright, C. *Fast Wheels, Slow Traffic: Urban Transport Choices.* Philadelphia: Temple University Press, 1992.

Index